# THE TIMES ON THE ASHES

# THE TIMES
# ON THE ASHES

## COVERING SPORT'S GREATEST RIVALRY FROM 1877 TO THE PRESENT DAY

EDITED BY RICHARD WHITEHEAD

FOREWORD BY MIKE ATHERTON

PHOTOGRAPHS BY MARC ASPLAND AND GRAHAM MORRIS

First published 2015

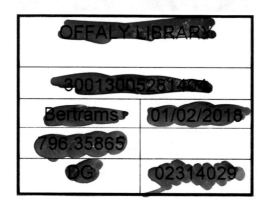

This paperback edition first published in 2017

The History Press
The Mill, Brimscombe Port
Stroud, Gloucestershire, GL5 2QG
www.thehistorypress.co.uk



British Library Cataloguing in Publication Data.
A catalogue record for this book is available from the British Library.

ISBN 978 0 7509 7919 1

Typesetting and origination by The History Press
Printed in Turkey by Imak Offset.

# CONTENTS

*Foreword by Mike Atherton* 7
*Introduction by Richard Whitehead* 9
*Cricket Correspondents of The Times* 13
*Other Writers* 16
*Photographers* 21
*Notes on Style* 22

England's Heroes 25
Australia's Heroes 53
Flashpoints 75
Brickbats 95
Captains 117
Pitches 129
Great Batting: England 139
Great Batting: Australia 185
Great Bowling: England 213
Great Bowling: Australia 241
Great Writing 253
Weather 269
Beyond the Boundary 281
The Fast Men 297
Fielding 313
Selection 327
England's Glory Days 337
Australia's Glory Days 365

*Photographic Credits* 382
*Acknowledgments* 383
*About the Editor* 384

THE
When Ivo
Studds, Steel
The welkin
The great crowd
With Barlow
And the rest
TRION:Z

# FOREWORD

## *by Mike Atherton*

'But now that suddenly a bowler, Larwood, has come into his own, and has dominated the play ... we find that the full force of attack has returned to its proper place in cricket ... and at once Test Match cricket has awakened from the sloth of the last 10 years and is again a glorious game' so wrote 'our cricket correspondent' about the Bodyline series more than 80 years ago.

Cricket has changed immeasurably since then, but in some ways it has not changed at all. Clearly, our correspondent, reflecting on the events in Sydney in December 1932, was worried about many of the same things that our current cricket correspondent frets over; namely, the long-term health of the five-day game and the precarious eco-system that is the balance between bat and ball, upon which the greatness of the game depends.

For all the cricket correspondents of *The Times*, named or unnamed atop their copy, this last would be a central concern. We spend our days watching cricket and we all would prefer to watch decent cricket, no matter the result. If that eco-system is out of kilter, if bat dominates ball excessively, or vice versa, then the game is diminished as a result. Cricket writers are, ultimately, only as good as the deeds they describe.

It is this overriding feature – the competitiveness of the cricket – that has historically set the Ashes apart. Along with its wonderful history and tradition, which gives it prized context, it has more often than not highlighted the best of cricket in all its competitive glory, and occasional goriness.

The practicalities of the job have changed tremendously in the years since Bodyline. John Woodcock, the longest serving and best known, perhaps, of all our correspondents, once told me, with a twinkle in his eye, of his professional commitments on the last tour to Australia that went by boat. A few hundred words at Tilbury Docks, a few hundred more on the stopover in what was then Ceylon, and a few hundred more on arriving in Fremantle. And, of course, a trip to Jermyn Street for a suit on expenses prior to all that.

He played quoits on a daily basis with the England players on the long journey over, he came to know them as friends, socialised with them regularly, so that it was not unusual to find himself in the England changing room from time to time at the invitation of the captain. The players were not paid very much, if at all, and journalists were regarded as their social equals, and probably had much better expense accounts. Very different days, indeed.

The England dressing room is not unknown to me, but I would not dream of entering now without the invitation of captain and coach, which would be unlikely in any event. The dressing room is for players, the press box for cricket writers and very early on in my transition from one to the other, I had to come to terms with the difference. Once you do, it transforms your writing and improves the experience, I would like to think, for our readers. Retain empathy with the players (for the game is immeasurably more difficult to play than to write about), but retain a distance, too, so that you can report and comment without fear or favour.

The distance now between players and reporters, because of the layers of intermediaries such as PR people, agents and press officers, is one of the main disadvantages of modern-day cricket reporting. The daily press conference has actually reduced the power of players' words and introduced a level of stiltedness to relationships between writers and players. The other disadvantage is the all-consuming nature of it: the internet means that cricket writers are never out of contact and always within the frame of a deadline. Cricket doesn't sleep any more.

But with the internet has come the ease of actually getting copy from one end of the world to the other. Forty minutes after a match, a thousand words accompanied by the most elegant pictures from our photographers will arrive instantly, allowing readers to download the latest action from Australia on their iPads on the way to work. Radio and television mean that the words do not carry quite the same impact as before, but what impact there is is, at least, immediate.

Nothing comes close to playing in an Ashes series. It stands to reason, then, that nothing comes close to reporting on it. The 2015 series will be the eighth I have covered as an observer, which now means that I have been a professional observer longer than a player (I played in seven Ashes series). A sobering thought. The magic remains, though.

The best series I have ever watched – and I think of myself as extraordinarily privileged to have done so – was the 2005 Ashes, won by Michael Vaughan's team. With England rising and Australia falling, the protagonists were well-matched, the cricket was superb, a star or two (Andrew Flintoff, Kevin Pietersen) was born, the spirit was competitive and hard but fair, and for three matches in August the narrative turned magically this way and that. It was a truly memorable series and represented the very best of the Ashes.

In this book, you can enjoy a trip down memory lane and relive some of those moments, and many more that *The Times* has brought to you with, we like would to think, accuracy, style and a little flair.

# INTRODUCTION

## *by Richard Whitehead*

What would have caught the eye of readers of *The Times* as they scanned their favourite daily newspaper – then already 92 years old – on the morning of Monday, 14 May 1877? At first glance it looks much like any other edition from that era – dense columns of type, pages (including the front) devoted to small advertisements, few illustrations to lighten the seas of grey and small headlines giving bare, factual signposting to the stories beneath. There is little doubt, however, what the editor, John Thadeus Delane, thought was the most important issue of the day: most of a page was devoted to the Russo-Turkish war, which had begun the previous month, with despatches from *Times* correspondents in Bucharest, Vienna, Berlin and Paris. Clearly the world was an unstable place.

On page 5 of a 20-page edition, however, was a rather gentler item and one with a comforting familiarity to sport-loving 21st-century readers – a report of a cricket match between Australia and England. It is easy to miss – appearing three quarters of the way down a long column headlined simply 'Victoria' and stuck at the end of an account of events in the state parliament. Filed by 'our own correspondent' it tells, in a little over 350 words, the story of the victory, by 45 runs, of a 'Grand Combined Melbourne and Sydney XI' against 'James Lillywhite's professional touring team'. It is datelined 22 March, three days after the match had finished, but, such was the speed of communications from the other side of the world, that no *Times* reader would have thought it odd to be reading news that was nearly two months old.

This was the first Test match, although it would not be accorded that status until the end of the 19th century, and the start of a unique sporting rivalry that continues to thrive and beguile nearly 140 years later. For those who hold the paper dear, it is good to know that *The Times* was there at the start because England v Australia for the Ashes has been one of the great running stories in the history of the newspaper.

To read the accounts of the early skirmishes in international cricket is to marvel at how swiftly the matches acquired a form and pattern that we recognise today. By the mid-1890s there were home and away series, with matches at – among other venues – Lord's, the Melbourne Cricket Ground, Old Trafford and the Ovals of Kennington and Adelaide. There were centuries, both dour and dashing, terrifying pace bowlers, guileful spinners, masters of seam and swing, brilliant fielding and the odd catastrophic dropped catch.

All these elements quickly became fixtures in the cricket reporting of *The Times*, even if the style of writing and presentation can sometimes seem endearingly anachronistic.

In compiling this book there were twin fascinations in making a detailed examination of the newspaper's coverage of contests between England and Australia. Most obviously is the journalist's excitement at discovering how storied moments were reported the next day, fresh on the page before they had acquired a patina of myth and legend. On these pages, for instance, you will find *The Times*' account of W.G. Grace's run out of the Australian tail-ender Sammy Jones at the Oval in 1882, a piece of blatant chicanery that had far-reaching consequences. Grace's action rebounded spectacularly when the enraged fast bowler Frederick Spofforth then bowled England out for 77. Australia's seven-run victory prompted the much-quoted mock obituary in *The Sporting Times* (just for clarity, a different newspaper altogether) and, from there, the creation of the Ashes.

Later there are other occasions that have become milestones in cricket history: Fred Tate's dropped catch at Old Trafford in 1902; Warwick Armstrong's ostentatious reading of a newspaper at the Oval in 1921; the extraordinary impact of Don Bradman in 1930; the sporting and diplomatic cause célèbre that was Bodyline in 1932–33; Jim Laker's 19-wicket tour de force at Old Trafford in 1956; the twin terror of Lillee and Thomson in 1974–75; Shane Warne's 'ball of the century' at Old Trafford in 1993; and the dizzying roller coaster of the epic 2005 series. All these have been witnessed first-hand by the men from *The Times*.

Just as engrossing is to study the development of journalism, the evolution of the coverage and its presentation, and how it has been shaped by changing technology. When the Hon. Ivo Bligh took his team to Australia in 1882–83 he was presented with a tiny terracotta urn by some genteel Melbourne ladies (one of whom became his wife) containing, it was said, the ashes of a charred bail, a jokey reference to the *Sporting Times*' obituary. *The Times* understood that the cricket lovers among its readership would be sufficiently interested to read short accounts of the matches, but communications with Australia were still such that by publication they were hopelessly out of date; the first Test concluded on 2 January, but was not reported until 14 February. And then there was the potential for misinformation and confusion, as a slightly panicky story published three days later confirmed:

> The extraordinary mistake in the telegram which announced that the Australian Eleven had been defeated by Mr Bligh's team – an announcement which the last mail disproved – caused a little uneasiness in the minds of Englishmen interested in the national game as to whether the subsequent telegrams might not also, have been incorrect. We have been given to understand, however that the second and third matches against Mr Murdoch's Eleven ended in victories for the English.

However, by the time A.E. Stoddart's team contested the classic series of 1894–95, the world had moved on at breathtaking pace. Thanks to an expansion of the undersea cable network and an improvement in the equipment and in its reliability, *The Times* was able to carry full reports of each day's play only 24 hours later, establishing a timetable for coverage that remains broadly the same today, at least in print. This development was not, however, followed by other innovations. Photographs from series in Australia, sent by wire, did not begin to appear regularly until England's triumphant tour in 1954–55 and the method of filing copy remained pretty much as it had in the late Victorian era for decades. John Woodcock covered ten tours to Australia as cricket correspondent and switched from telegraph to the more modern telex only in the 1960s.

Latterly, the pace of change has quickened frantically. In 2002–03, for instance, the chief cricket correspondent Christopher Martin-Jenkins filed bite-sized match reports at the close of each day to be sent to readers' mobile phones. Four years later there were videos for the paper's website in which he gave his thoughts on the unfolding Australian whitewash. *The Times* quickly became a leader in keeping pace with the digital world and its unceasing demand for information. The arrival of tablet computers meant that by the time of Mike Atherton's first Ashes tour as chief cricket correspondent, in 2010–11, he and the other *Times* writers were filing their reports soon after the close of play in order to appear in an early morning digital edition as well as on the website.

The language and presentation of the coverage has, of course, evolved dramatically, if at times barely perceptibly. To the modern reader the use of 'Mr' to describe an amateur, where a professional warrants only a surname, appears extraordinarily old-fashioned (the Australians, being amateurs, were all known as Mr). Likewise, immediately after the First World War there was a vogue for using the players' military ranks, so England's first post-war Ashes captain was not Mr Douglas, J.W.H.T Douglas or Johnny Douglas, but Colonel Douglas. Other now seemingly quaint aspects of the reporting language lingered on, notably in referring to the day's first interval as luncheon.

But *The Times* was not shy of innovation. It is now customary to have three or four writers covering one day at a Test, each approaching events from a different angle, but the paper had been quick to appreciate the benefits that this division of labour could bring. Colour writers were often sent to the big days, such as England's long-awaited regaining of the Ashes in 1953 and, from 1954–55, Australian writers have frequently been employed to provide a baggy green perspective.

Fashions in presentation, page layout and typography come and go. Photographs were once a scarce commodity, not least because only news agency photographers were allowed into English Test grounds until 1972, but now reports are illustrated with brilliant colour pictures that can make it appear as if the photographers are out in the middle with the players. Graphics are employed to underline a statistical point, and a great deal of time and trouble is taken to make sure the pages look as enticing as possible. It is a far cry from the days of long, unbroken columns of type that were the standard well into the second half of the 20th century.

The aim of this book is not to provide a definitive, blow-by-blow history of the Ashes as seen through the pages of *The Times*. Rather, the idea is to select a mixture of memorable moments and performances, to recall some of the great players and characters, and to look at how such things as the weather, the pitches and the paying public have been reported. It was also, needless to say, a chance to showcase some great cricket writing and photography.

All the names you would expect are here: Bradman and Botham; Warne and the Waughs; Hobbs, Hammond and Hutton; Larwood and Lillee; McCabe and McGrath; Grace and Gower; Tyson and Thommo; Bailey, Bedser and Boycott; the Freds of Trueman and Flintoff. But there are scores of others too, those who may have only been bit-part players in cricket's equivalent of the Bayeux tapestry, but are part of the great Ashes story nonetheless.

It is hard to think of two more venerable and highly regarded institutions than *The Times* and the Ashes – I hope you will savour their remarkable union.

# CRICKET CORRESPONDENTS OF THE TIMES

## GEORGE WEST: 1880–1895

Although, from 1867, Charles Box was the first person specifically appointed to write about cricket for *The Times*, George West seems to have been the first to have the word 'correspondent' as his job title. He was 29 at the time he took over from Box and was related on his mother's side to Squire Osbaldeston, the renowned single-wicket player. He was also the editor of *Wisden Cricketers' Almanack* for six years from 1880, thus beginning a long and enduring association between the game's bible and *The Times*.

## ERNEST WARD: 1895–1903

There were several Wards on *The Times* staff at the time so Ernest Rootsey Ward was awarded the sobriquet 'Sporting' in the newsroom at Printing House Square. He was certainly the senior cricket writer and covered many important matches of the time without being given the title of cricket correspondent. Despite his seniority, he shared coverage of Test cricket with R.H. Lyttelton and Philip Trevor. Ward left for the *Morning Post* in 1903.

## SYDNEY H. PARDON: 1903–1925

The redoubtable editor of *Wisden* for 35 years, he established the Pardon Cricket Reporting Agency and wrote on music, drama and racing for *The Times* as well as cricket. He was, said his *Times* obituary, 'the greatest living authority on the game'. Pardon was blessed with an extraordinary memory for all his specialist subjects and was particularly good at identifying new talent; Jack Hobbs and Victor Trumper were among those he tipped for greatness. Curiously, however, his cricket reporting for *The Times* was confined to features, previews and notes; coverage of matches was mainly left to R.H. Lyttelton and his eventual successor, A.C.M. Croome.

## A.C.M. CROOME: 1925–1930

Arthur Croome had the joyous task of reporting the regaining of the Ashes in 1926 after England's humblings following the First World War. Croome was a fine all-round sportsman who at Oxford earned cricket and athletics Blues and played cricket for Gloucestershire. It was while fielding on the boundary at Old Trafford in July 1887 that he seriously injured his throat on spiked railings and it was only the prompt action of W.G. Grace – who held the wound together with a rock-steady hand – that saved his life. Croome came to journalism after a spell teaching at Radley and wrote on golf for the *Evening Standard* and *Morning Late Post*, as well as on cricket for *The Times*.

## RICHARD 'BEAU' VINCENT: 1930–1951

'Beau' Vincent – who held the rank of major from his First World War service with the Gordon Highlanders – had been reporting on cricket as a 'special correspondent' for some years when he became cricket correspondent, just in time for Bradman's first tour. He had won a golf Blue at Cambridge and was the first salaried cricket correspondent of *The Times*, although it was still not the practice to cover overseas tours. During the Bodyline series of 1932–33, Vincent provided commentaries on events 12,000 miles away based on the various cabled accounts. He shunned typewriters and sometimes arrived in the press box without even a pencil, although he was known to carry his dentures in his coat pocket. He brought to his work a 'fanatical devotion and lively intelligence'. Vincent had never liked travelling, not even to Trent Bridge or Headingley, so it was optimistic of *The Times* to persuade him to cover the 1950–51 Ashes series. He was photographed with the sports editor on departure from Tilbury, but on arrival, unable to cope, he came straight home. He retired soon afterwards.

## GEOFFREY GREEN: 1951–1954

The most celebrated of all *Times* football writers was for a time also the paper's cricket correspondent. Remarkably, he was also briefly the lawn tennis correspondent. Green's short tenure in the cricket job included England's regaining of the Ashes in the Coronation year of 1953, which he reported in typically colourful terms. In the same extraordinary sporting year he also reported on the Matthews Cup final and Hungary's 6-3 victory over England at Wembley, which inspired one of his most brilliant and famous pieces. It was when he was asked to edit the sports pages as well that he had to give up his cricket duties, even though he had been looking forward to reporting on England's defence of the Ashes in 1954–55.

## JOHN WOODCOCK: 1954–1987

'I wonder if anyone has written better about the game,' Henry Blofeld mused in his autobiography and the answer for generations of *Times* readers would be definitely not. Woodcock was the newspaper's longest-serving cricket correspondent and the most revered, even if his name did not appear in print until January 1967 when the paper reversed its policy on bylines. Blessed with a deep love of the game and a vast knowledge of its lore and history, Woodcock wrote beautifully. He formed lasting friendships with many players without compromising his journalistic objectivity. Following in the footsteps of West and Pardon, he edited *Wisden* for six editions from 1981. He covered 18 Ashes series, plus the short 1979-80 series where the Ashes were not at stake, and was for years reckoned to have seen more days of Test cricket than anyone else in the world. After his retirement he continued to attend Test matches regularly and contributed many more outstanding pieces. In 2014 he had had been contributing to *The Times* for more than 60 consecutive years.

## ALAN LEE: 1988–1999

The task of following John Woodcock might have been overwhelming to some, but Alan Lee had been cricket correspondent for *The Mail on Sunday* from 1982 to 1986 and quickly put his own stamp on the role. As a graduate of the famous Hayter's news agency, he had a keen nose for a story and wrote sharp, punchy prose. It was his misfortune that his period in office coincided with a dreadful era for the England team – especially against Australia – and the aggregate score in the Ashes Tests he covered was 20–5. Nevertheless, the continuing sense of crisis in English cricket was perfectly suited to his talents as a newsman. He went on to be *The Times*' racing correspondent, a job in which he has been a serial winner of awards.

## CHRISTOPHER MARTIN-JENKINS: 1999–2008

Journalists changing jobs rarely attracts interest outside newspaper offices, but when CM-J, as he was known throughout the cricket world, joined *The Times* from *The Daily Telegraph* in 1999 it caused a considerable stir. Thanks to his many years as a commentator on *Test Match Special*, Martin-Jenkins enjoyed a level of recognition which his *Times* predecessors had not. He had edited *The Cricketer* and twice been cricket correspondent of the BBC. The high point of his tenure was undoubtedly the epic 2005 series in which England finally regained the Ashes after five matches of unrelenting drama. He completed a unique collection of cricket appointments by serving as president of MCC in 2010–11. His death, aged 67 on New Year's Day 2013, was mourned by all in the game.

## MIKE ATHERTON: 2008–PRESENT

No previous occupant of the post could bring to his work first-hand experience of the white heat of Test cricket. Mike Atherton – usually referred to as 'Michael' in *The Times* in his playing days – made his Test debut during the Ashes series of 1989, taken over the England captaincy during the 1993 series and led the team in Australia in 1994–95. In an injury crisis, he returned to captain the team again for two matches in the 2001 campaign, his farewell series. In retirement he made an instant mark as a television commentator and Sunday newspaper columnist and he has combined his role at *The Times* with being a leading member of the Sky Sports commentary team. Atherton's second summer at *The Times* saw England regain the Ashes and he formed a formidable partnership with Gideon Haigh. His many journalistic awards include being voted sports journalist of the year at the British Press Awards.

# *Other Writers*

## SIMON BARNES

One of the most distinctive and highly original voices in sports writing, Barnes joined *The Times* in the mid-1980s and was chief sports writer for a number of years. Although he was closely associated with the Olympic Games and Wimbledon, he was a cricket lover who relished attending Test matches, especially the Ashes, and was several times sent to Australia to report on key Tests on tour.

## JEROME CAMINADA

One of two writers from outside the sports desk sent to the Oval in 1953 to record the reaction to England's regaining of the Ashes, Caminada was a foreign correspondent before the Second World War but was captured at Boulogne in 1940 and was a prisoner of war until 1944. He worked overseas again after the war.

## NEVILLE CARDUS

Merely to say the name Cardus is to invoke thoughts of some of the greatest sports and music writing. Cardus was the celebrated cricket and music correspondent of *The Manchester Guardian* and inextricably linked with that newspaper, but in the first post-war Ashes series of 1946–47, *The Times* and its rival shared his reports. Cardus apparently negotiated twice the fee.

## DUDLEY CAREW

No less an authority than John Arlott considered that if it had not been for the giant shadow cast by Cardus, Carew would have been recognised as one of the great cricket writers. He wrote several books on the game and sometimes stood in for Vincent at Test matches. Perhaps his versatility counted against him; in a 33-year *Times* career he wrote on football, the theatre and films, and also contributed fourth leaders and book reviews.

## GEORGE CRAIG

Taking a break from covering events in parliament and writing leaders, George Craig was put on colour-writing duties at the Oval in 1926 as England regained the Ashes for the first time since the First World War.

## ROY CURTHOYS

*The Times*' Australia correspondent for 21 years, between 1936 and 1957, Curthoys had previously been on a retainer for the paper. He covered Tests in Melbourne in 1928–29 and 1932–33.

## TIM DE LISLE

The Saturday sports section of *The Times* was considerably enlivened between 2004 and 2006 by a highly original cricket column by de Lisle. He had been editor of *Wisden Cricket Monthly* and, in 2003, of *Wisden* itself, provoking outrage among traditionalists by putting a photograph on the cover.

## JACK FINGLETON

Like Atherton, Fingleton knew what it was like to open the batting in Test cricket, in his case amid the unsurpassed hostility of the Bodyline series. Fingleton played in 18 matches for Australia, scoring 1,189 runs at an average of around 42. He was already working as a journalist before his career took off and he returned to the press box on retirement. He provided an Australian viewpoint alongside Woodcock on the 1968 and 1972 series in England.

## PAT GIBSON

One of the most respected figures in cricket writing, Pat Gibson was for many years cricket correspondent of *The Sunday Express*. He joined *The Times* in the 1990s and was often used as an additional writer at Tests, providing sharp commentaries and quotes. He was a chairman of the Cricket Writers' Club where the laconic humour of his speeches at the annual lunch was a regular highlight.

## GIDEON HAIGH

After making his name with a string of outstanding cricket books – including an account of the Kerry Packer affair and a biography of Australian spinner Jack Iverson – Haigh established himself among the front rank of cricket writers and historians working in any era. He has written a number of books about Ashes series and first worked for *The Times* during the summer of 2009.

## STEWART HARRIS

When John Woodcock was taken ill before the key Adelaide Test of the 1954–55 series, the sports desk sent for Harris, who had only just rejoined the staff as assistant to Curthoys in Melbourne. He was later the paper's Australia correspondent from 1957 to 1973.

## MICHAEL HENDERSON

A true original and a writer of considerable style and humour, Henderson was a regular, distinctive presence on *The Times*' cricket pages throughout the 1990s. Like his idol, Neville Cardus, he also wrote on classical music and his pieces were sprinkled with a wide mix of cultural references. He moved to *The Daily Telegraph* as cricket correspondent in 2009.

## RICHARD HOBSON

After joining *The Times* in the mid-1990s, Hobson first wrote about cricket in 1997 and became deputy cricket correspondent in 1999, working alongside Martin-Jenkins, who praised his 'independent mind and genuine love of the game'. He has covered eight Ashes series for the paper and on tours is often sent out as the advanced guard, covering early matches and setting the scene before the arrival of the cricket correspondent.

## R.H. LYTTELTON

A member of a famous cricketing family, he was a brother of Alfred Lyttelton who kept wicket in England's first home Test match in 1880. Robert Lyttelton, a passionate advocate of reform of the LBW law, covered many important matches for *The Times* until the First World War, including the nerve-shredding finish at the Oval in 1902.

## ANDREW LONGMORE

A genuine sportswriting all-rounder, Longmore covered a wide variety of sports in a long career at *The Times* and *The Sunday Times*. He acted as No. 2 to Lee in the 1989 series.

## DELAMORE McCAY

A distinguished Australian journalist, McCay held a number of important positions in newspapers and in publishing. He was Australian Correspondent of *The Times* from 1924 to 1928, and then New South Wales correspondent to 1931. He covered the Sydney Tests in the 1932–33 series. McCay is remembered by colleagues as 'an explosive personality', who had at his command 'an inexhaustible fund of quite original expletives'.

## FIRMIN McKINNON

A well-known journalist in Australia before the Second World War, McKinnon was Queensland correspondent of *The Times* from 1925 to 1942 and covered the Brisbane Test of 1928–29.

## A.G. MOYES

'Johnny' Moyes was a familiar voice on ABC cricket commentaries in Australia and the author of several cricket books, including biographies of Don Bradman and Richie Benaud. He provided the Australian perspective for *The Times* during the 1954–55 series.

## E.W. PARISH

He may not have appreciated the distinction, but Ted Parish covered the most explosive Ashes Test in history – the Adelaide match in the Bodyline series in 1932–33 in which serious crowd disturbances often looked likely to break out. He was Adelaide correspondent of *The Times* from 1921 to 1954.

## ALAN ROBBINS

The distinction of being the first film critic of *The Times* fell to Robbins who was appointed in 1913 and wrote a film column after the First World War. It was in his later capacity as special writer that he was sent to the Oval in 1926.

## R.C. ROBERTSON-GLASGOW

A right-arm fast-medium bowler for Oxford University and Somerset, Raymond Robertson-Glasgow, often known as 'Crusoe', became a much-loved cricket writer and journalist. In 1950–51, when Beau Vincent returned home soon after arriving in Australia, Robertson-Glasgow covered the tour for *The Times*.

## ED SMITH

It was while still a highly successful batsman with Kent that Smith first made his name as a writer with a number of excellent books, which included *On and Off the Field*, a diary of the 2003 season during which he made three Test appearances. He later captained Middlesex and on leaving the game wrote for various sections of *The Times*, including a spell as a leader writer.

## SIMON WILDE

Although best known as cricket correspondent of *The Sunday Times* for 15 years, Wilde's career started as a sub-editor on *The Times* in the mid-1980s. The first of several highly regarded books, *Ranji: A Genius Rich and Strange*, was written while on *The Times*. He moved to writing full time in 1994 and covered a number of Ashes Tests as No. 2 writer to Alan Lee.

## F.B. WILSON

A genuine all-rounder, 'Freddie' Wilson covered some twenty sports for *The Times*, including the Headingley Ashes Test of 1921 (A.C.M. Croome was at the university match at Lord's). He was a former captain of Harrow and Cambridge who also won Blues for rackets and real tennis. He was the father of Peter Wilson, the celebrated *Daily Mirror* sports columnist, and grandfather of Julian Wilson, the BBC racing correspondent.

## GILBERT WOOD

The main piece of colour from the Oval in 1953 was provided by Wood, who, at that time, had only recently moved from parliament to home news. He was a correspondent with British forces during the Suez crisis in 1956.

# *Photographers*

## MARC ASPLAND

The chief sports photographer of *The Times* for 25 years has won a string of awards and is recognised as one of the leaders in his field. He is a fellow of the Royal Photographic Society of Great Britain.

## GRAHAM MORRIS

After covering his first Test in the late 1970s, Morris decided to specialise on cricket in the 1980s. He has covered matches at home and abroad for 35 years and has worked for *The Times* for the past 15 years.

# NOTES ON STYLE

Every effort has been made to ensure that the extracts in this book appear as closely as possible to how they were originally published in *The Times.* However, on occasions some small changes have been made.

It was once the custom, for instance, to put a full point after the word 'Mr' and to hypenate 'today' but these have been removed, as have other examples of outdated style. Obvious literals or copytaking errors have been corrected. At Brisbane in 1974-75, for instance, John Woodcock clearly did not write: 'There was snow on the last tour to Australia ...' even if that was what appeared in print. It made sense to correct such mistakes.

Most of the text in the book consists of short extracts from longer pieces, but three dots indicate where the words have been edited or paragraphs removed.

The biggest change is the inclusion of the names of the writers where it has been possible to find these in *The Times*' archive. *The Times* did not give bylines until January 1967, but in an effort to give full credit to the journalists who have written about the Ashes for the paper their names are now revealed. I hope they would not have minded.

*Richard Whitehead, editor* The Times on the Ashes

An indefinite vista of matches, belonging potentially as much to the vanquished as to the victors of today, stretches across the tracts of the future. Perhaps the popularity of this competition in national sport between the different parts of the Empire is worthy of the serious attention of statesmen.
*Leading article, January 7, 1892*

Australia is so far away, its climate and its life are so different from those of Great Britain, that we want some special tie, other than that of common descent, common language, and citizenship of one Empire, to bring the two peoples together. We have fought together, and there is no stronger bond. But happily it is seldom that an Empire is called upon to pass through the ordeal of war; and it is necessary to have links that shall hold perpetually and normally in times of peace. Such a link exists in the common delight which the people of England and the people of Australia find in the national game and in the mutual respect engendered by the prowess of the two sides.
*Leading article, August 17, 1905*

Striking, above all, has been the spirit of the combat. Never less than wholehearted, it has also, largely, been generous spirited. These two teams have produced thrilling human theatre. Whichever ultimately triumphs is, of course, the point. But so is the manner of their moment. It would suit the summer if the victors shared the praise for their triumph. Because in a way, we have all won.
*Leading article, September 8, 2005*

Sporting …

…OW ENGLAND KEPT TH…
ASHES

…WO GREAT HEARTS OVERTHROW AUSTRALIA

England beat Australia by five wickets in the fourth Test match at …delaide yesterday and so, gaining a lead of three matches to one in the …ries, have retained the Ashes. In an interview after the match L. Hutton, …e England captain, paid a tribute to the younger members of the side. Much of the credit, he thought, should go to J. B. Statham, F. H. Tyson, M. C. Cowdrey and P. B. H. May, together with the wicket-keeper, T. G. Evans.

From Our Special Correspondent

ADELAIDE, FEB. 2

Many years from now young Cowdrey will point to his broken nose and tell boys yet unborn that he was at Adelaide on February 2, 1955, when England won the Test match and kept the Ashes. And the boys will think him wondrous lucky. A ma… should dip his pen in blood to write … is day. Let no one talk and … …ket and explain away … …ms more fit for … …l in dull …

the catch. (We asked Hutton afterwards what he thought of Miller's bowling. Hutton thought Miller ought to concentrate much more on batting.) England 10 for 2. In comes the battered Cowdrey. Miller hits him twice running on the pads and appeals, and everybody here who isn't English appeals too. What a man is Miller. He comes in from a shortish run, loose of limb like an African, hair streaming, and as he pulls up the hair goes on and falls about his face.

Meanwhile May has begun driving, and Johnson has gone from mid-off to square-leg. For Cowdrey Miller brings fine-leg up to third slip, and Cowdrey cover drives classically for 4. Miller heaves his shoulders over even faster, and Cowdrey is taken by Archer at first-slip. England 18 for 3. Four Meteor jets fly over at 200ft.; they look …d sound quite tame beside this wild man … His figures now are 3 overs, no … 2 runs, 3 wickets.

Sporting News

ENGLAND HAVE LAST WORD

THREE YEOMEN FOIL AUSTRALIA

GREAT STAND BY WATSON AND BAILEY

FROM OUR CRICKET CORRESPONDENT

Out of darkness, through fire into light. Thus did England yesterday rise like some Phoenix from the ashes of apparent defeat to save the second Test match at Lord's and so gain a … draw against Australia with … seven wickets, … original aim fo…

The age of … yet past, nor c… cany scarce f… dramatic and … a match alrea… But within t… longest and … of a match it… that last spa… back with le… yeomen of … nearly the w…

The yeom… were Watso… greatest of … Yorkshiren… order, was … rearguard … twentieth …

…ngland all too obligin…
…eaches new heights of greatness

One that got away: Gilchrist misses a stumping chance off Warne to give Pietersen an extra life, but it was to make little difference as …

High five: Warne acknowledges the Melbourne crowd after his haul ripped the heart out of England's fragile batting

…nting run out (Flintoff) 66

…8 P Siddle c Flintoff b Harmison 10

5.37 343-9 S Clark c Cook b Harmison 0

…iant leap

for proud S…

THE FIR…

36 TUESDAY AUGUST 1 1989

THE TIMES

First published 1785

England's abject surrender marks new low in series

Inglorious procession at Old Trafford

18-1: Curtis c Boon b Alderman 0

25-2: Robinson lbw b Lawson 12

27-3: Smith c Healy b Alderman 7

28-4: Gooch c Alderman b Lawson 13

38-5: Botham lbw b Alderman 4

59-6: Gower c Marsh b Lawson 15

SCOREBOARD FROM OLD TRAFFORD

Gower unfairly blamed for failings of others

Simon Barnes

Border rewarded for hard labour

Only two men so far decline

SPORT

Cricket

Was this English c…
most desperate d…

# ENGLAND'S HEROES

THE TIMES SATURDAY JUNE 11 1938

CH: A GOOD BEGINNING BY ENGLAND

4

Sporting News

LAKER'S SUPREME PART IN RETAINING THE ASHES

ALL TEN AUSTRALIAN WICKETS AND 19 IN MATCH

From Our Cricket Correspondent

pitch perked up and the ball showed signs of misbehaving.

At luncheon McDonald and Craig were still together. They had then added only 59, but the important thing was that they had each been batting for more than four hours. Ahead of them stretched another four and only 15 minutes of these had ticked away when Laker

TEST MATCH

BRADMAN 309 NOT OUT

ALL RECORDS BROKEN

*The Third Test Match between England and Australia was begun at Leeds yesterday. A. P. F. Chapman, for once, lost the toss and Australia went in to bat on a perfect batsman's wicket. By the end of the day they had scored 458 runs for the*

stumped aiming to hit Mallett over the hill, and the end draws nearer.

dismally surrender Ashes

THE TIMES

HOW THE AUSTRALIANS WERE SKITTLED OUT AT LORD'S

LOCOMEN'S BAN BOUND CAUSE GREATER

Gaullists may get back with clear majority

Inquiry over bank chief's salary

Police alerted by strike ship

Railways must act alone, Marsh says

OF REGRET

# MIKE ATHERTON

## THIRD TEST, SYDNEY, 1990–91

ALAN LEE, CRICKET CORRESPONDENT

*January 8.* Atherton very nearly did not make it to his rehabilitating hundred. He made only a single in the first 50 minutes and then, in trying to scamper another to Marsh at short fine-leg looked very fortunate to escape a run-out verdict. His response, however, was a joy, the next ball from Rackemann being driven majestically through cover to complete the slowest century in Ashes history. Atherton will not mind a bit.

## SECOND TEST, LORD'S, 1993

ALAN LEE, CRICKET CORRESPONDENT

*June 21.* Success is a relative term as far as the present England cricket team is concerned, and it is not saying much to acclaim this as their best day of the Lord's Test match. They batted all day, with great resolve, and lost only four wickets. But defeat, by an undignified margin, is still the probable outcome today.

Nobody deserves this less than Michael Atherton. For more than eight hours over the weekend, he defied and exasperated the Australians. His first-innings 80 was the work of a man making up in determination what he lacked in form.

His second innings was different. On Saturday, he let the Australians bowl to him; yesterday, he drove them back and drove them mad.

Assertive in his shot-making and imperturbable under the verbal onslaught that Merv Hughes, in particular, reserves for him, Atherton richly merited his first century in 14 Tests. It eluded him in as cruel a fashion as this game can provide: run out, 99.

Atherton, called for a third run by Mike Gatting and then sent back, slipped twice as he tried to regain his ground. Hughes's accurate throw from deep mid-wicket found Atherton flat on his stomach, two yards out.

After a day of taut cricketing theatre, this, for England, may turn out to be the equivalent of the moment in which the Whitehall farce hero is caught red-handed with his trousers down.

## THIRD TEST, TRENT BRIDGE, 2001

CHRISTOPHER MARTIN-JENKINS, CHIEF CRICKET CORRESPONDENT

*August 4.* After a morning's cricket dominated by the brilliance of Gilchrist and the promise of Alex Tudor, the game reverted for two hours and more to a theme it knows and loves: Atherton versus the rest. Relishing the challenge of hostile fast bowling as only he does and given determined support by Marcus Trescothick and Ramprakash, he kept the match in the balance and the spectators on the edge of their seats until, for the second time in a thrilling match, he was the victim of an erroneous decision.

**ARTS 27-28**
Hugh Laurie as Bertie Wooster: Toodlepip, chaps

**EDUCATION 31**
How much fun are the best French students allowed?

**BUSINESS 32-36**
Fortress Europe or free trade: the EC choice

# THE TIMES 2

MONDAY JUNE 21 1993

PHOTOGRAPHS: DAVID MUNDEN/SPORTSLINE

In a spin: Hayden, the substitute, takes an acrobatic catch at short leg to remove Smith off the bowling of May at Lord's yesterday. It was the fourth time in as many innings Smith has fallen to spin during the Ashes series

## Atherton's defiance keeps slim hope alive

By Alan Lee, cricket correspondent

*LORD'S (fourth day of five): England, with seven second-innings wickets in hand, are 190 runs behind Australia*

SUCCESS is a relative term as far as the present England cricket team is concerned, and it is not saying much to acclaim this as their best day of the Lord's Test match. They batted all day, with great resolve, and lost only four wickets. But defeat, by an undignified margin, is still the probable outcome today.

Nobody deserves this less than Michael Atherton. For more than eight hours over the weekend, he defied and exasperated the Australians. His first-innings 80 was the work [illegible] different. On Saturday, he let the Australians bowl to him; yesterday, he drove them back and drove them road [illegible] and imperturbable under the verbal onslaught that Merv Hughes, in particular, reserves for him. Atherton richly merited his first century in 14 Tests. It eluded him in as cruel a fashion as this game can provide: run out, 99.

Atherton, called for a third run by Mike Gatting and then sent back, slipped twice as he tried to regain his ground. Hughes's accurate throw from deep mid-wicket found Atherton flat on his stomach, two yards out.

After a day of taut cricketing theatre, this, for England, may turn out to be the equivalent of the moment in which the Whitehall farce hero is caught red-handed with his trousers down.

Gatting remained to the close, by which time he had been in residence all but four hours. For more than three of them, he had struggled desperately to survive, utterly at sea against spin bowling he habitually seeks to dominate. But this was Gatting playing for his future. Fail, and he was almost certainly out of the side; succeed, and he could even be captain by next week. Somehow, he kept the second of these extreme options alive.

The captaincy remains an issue only because Graham Gooch insists it must. Nobody is about to sack him; the summer's lease is his if he wants it. But if England's numbing Saturday surrender, in which unarguably good players batted as if gripped by fatalism, had [illegible] tion speech ready by the end of it.

If it is ingrained on his mind that the team no longer re[illegible] wearing the stripes when the regiment is in retreat. As Atherton and Gatting can now be thought the likeliest candidates to succeed him, there

Gatting: survivor

were paradoxes aplenty in the main passage of play [illegible] It was ushered in by a half-[illegible] wicket pair at the end of a first innings in which the next highest score to Atherton's was 22. Only one run behind [illegible] was warmly applauded for keeping out the first ball of the day and almost raised the roof when he straight-drove May for four to bring up 200.

Australia had to resort to the new ball to remove him and they were to wait another 92 minutes for their next wicket. England, following on 427 behind, reached the seventies without loss as, incongruously, they have done three times out of four in this series. It was in the second over of the afternoon, when many picnickers were still away from their seats, that Shane Warne committed Gooch on off stump, turned the ball sharply and found the edge, Healy taking the catch.

Gooch returned to a muted, almost embarrassed pavilion, as if the members sensed they were intruding on private grief. They were given little cause to change that view as [illegible] bled against Warne and May [illegible] in which it sometimes seemed humane to put him out of his misery.

When Hughes, the only [illegible] turned, Gatting gloved him just short of second slip, a pregnant moment. But if Hughes accepted that one stoically, he was driven to fits of rage whenever Atherton was on the receiving end.

The glowering and cursing not only brought boos from the packed crowd but an unobtrusive caution from the umpire. Mervyn Kitchen was said to have had "a gentle word", a phrase that could probably not be used to describe the other Mervyn's vocabulary.

Atherton just smiled back, in that way the Australians find so irritating, and got on with one of his best innings for England. He swept and pulled especially well and, as Gatting searched vainly for his timing, Atherton's was on vivid display.

The shot that should have taken him to his century was a [illegible] for once undeservingly [illegible]

Three overs later, Robin Smith was out to May for the second time in the game and to spin for the fourth time in the [illegible] atic: an anxious prod, a flurry of bat and body and a catch to short leg. Smith will probably be England's best batsman in the Caribbean this winter; right now, he is wasting a place.

The same is said by some of Graeme Hick and one ridiculous waft against a short, wide ball from Hughes backed them up. But Hick had already treated May with contempt and he now buckled down to his own personal battle against pace.

With Gatting, whose half-century took 219 minutes but whose survival will put doubt in Australian minds, he saw England into a final day of tension, salvation still a distant objective.

Letters, page 15
John Woodcock, page 20

Fatal slip: Atherton, sent back by Gatting, struggles in vain to regain his ground after losing his footing and is run out for 99 as Healy breaks the wicket

### LORD'S SCOREBOARD

AUSTRALIA: First Innings

| | | 6s | 4s | Min | Ball |
|---|---|---|---|---|---|
| M A Taylor st Stewart b Tufnell *jumping down the pitch to drive* | 111 | 1 | 10 | 323 | 245 |
| M J Slater c sub (B F Smith) b Lewis *low drive to mid-wicket* | 152 | - | 18 | 293 | 263 |
| D C Boon not out | 164 | - | 15 | 471 | 378 |
| M E Waugh b Tufnell *deflected off pad playing forcing shot* | 99 | 1 | 8 | 222 | 162 |
| *A R Border b Lewis *inside edge on to middle stump* | 77 | - | 12 | 164 | 121 |
| S R Waugh not out | 13 | - | 1 | 61 | 32 |
| Extras (lb 1, w 1, nb 14) | 16 | | | | |
| Total (4 wkts dec, 768min, 196 overs) | 632 | | | | |

†I A Healy, T B A May, M G Hughes, S K Warne and C J McDermott did not bat.

FALL OF WICKETS: 1-260 (Taylor 100), 2-277 (Boon 2), 3-452 (Boon 77), 4-591 (Boon 137).

BOWLING: Caddick 38-5-120-0 (nb 6) (8-1-23-0, 5-1-15-0, 5-0-22-0, 9-3-18-0, 6-0-30-0, 5-0-12-0); Foster 30-4-94-0 (7-0-27-0, 4-2-12-0, 8-2-18-0, 2-0-2-0, 5-0-21-0, 5-0-14-0); Such 36-6-90-0 (4-1-5-0, 6-3-17-0, 4-0-9-0, 20-5-48-0, 2-0-11-0); Tufnell 39-3-129-2 (nb 6) (4-0-21-0, 7-1-35-0, 4-1-9-1, 8-1-23-0, 16-0-41-1); Lewis 36-5-151-2 (nb 13) (8-1-23-0, 7-0-34-1, 7-2-27-0, 7-1-26-0, 7-1-41-1); Gooch 9-1-26-0 (w 1) (6-1-15-0, 3-0-11-0); Hick 8-3-21-0 (2-2-0-0, 2-1-3-0, 4-0-18-0).

ENGLAND: First Innings

| | | 6s | 4s | Min | Ball |
|---|---|---|---|---|---|
| *G A Gooch c May b Hughes *top-edged hook to fine leg boundary* | 12 | - | 1 | 36 | 41 |
| M A Atherton b Warne *forward defensive, ball spun back* | 80 | - | 9 | 255 | 210 |
| M W Gatting b May *bowled through gate attempting drive* | 5 | - | 1 | 33 | 35 |
| R A Smith st Healy b May *missed pull, failed to ground bat (TV umpire consulted)* | 22 | - | 3 | 42 | 43 |
| G A Hick c Healy b Hughes *fending at straight short-pitched ball* | 20 | - | 3 | 51 | 39 |
| †A J Stewart lbw b Hughes *beaten off pitch* | 3 | - | - | 15 | 14 |
| [illegible] | | | | | |
| N A Foster c Border b Warne *bat-pad catch at silly point* | 16 | - | 3 | 47 | 60 |
| A R Caddick c Healy b Hughes *edged rising ball to keeper* | 21 | - | 1 | 94 | 97 |
| P M Such c Taylor b Warne *edged turning ball to first slip* | 7 | - | 1 | 42 | 37 |
| [illegible] | | | | | |
| Extras (lb 8, nb 9) | 17 | | | | |
| Total (334min, 98 overs) | 205 | | | | |

FALL OF WICKETS: 1-33 (Atherton 11), 2-50 (Atherton 22), 3-84 (Atherton 32), 4-123 (Atherton 49), 5-131 (Atherton 54), 6-132 (Atherton 55), 7-167 (Atherton 73), 8-174 (Caddick 0), 9-180 (Caddick 7).

BOWLING: Hughes 20-5-52-4 (7-2-16-1, 9-2-25-2, 3-1-9-0, 1-0-2-1); M E Waugh 6-1-16-0 (nb 5) (one spell); S R Waugh 4-1-5-0 (nb 1) (one spell); May 31-12-64-2 (19-6-45-2, 2-1-4-0, 6-3-7-0, 4-2-7-0); Warne 35-12-57-4 (nb 3) (12-3-32-0, 7-0-12-1, 19-9-13-3); Border 3-1-3-0 (one spell).

Second Innings

| | | 6s | 4s | Min | Ball |
|---|---|---|---|---|---|
| *G A Gooch c Healy b Warne *edged leg break to keeper going forward* | 29 | - | 4 | 91 | 93 |
| M A Atherton run out (Hughes-Healy) *slipped twice after mix-up over third run* | 99 | - | 13 | 242 | 215 |
| M W Gatting not out | 58 | - | 7 | 234 | 201 |
| R A Smith c sub (M L Hayden) b May *diving catch at short leg off miscue* | 5 | - | 1 | 10 | 14 |
| G A Hick not out | 30 | - | 4 | 71 | 65 |
| Extras (b 9, lb 7) | 16 | | | | |
| Total (3 wkts, 327min, 98 overs) | 237 | | | | |

FALL OF WICKETS: 1-71 (Atherton 38), 2-175 (Gatting 31), 3-180 (Gatting 31).

BOWLING: Hughes 19-5-37-0 (7-0-15-0, 6-3-10-0, 6-2-12-0); M E Waugh 12-1-45-0 (7-1-24-0, 5-0-25-0); May 27-13-48-1 (19-12-19-0, 4-1-13-0, 4-0-16-1); S R Waugh 2-0-13-0 (one spell); Warne 30-9-62-1 (18-6-41-1, 4-1-9-0, 7-1-12-0, 1-1-0-0); Border 8-3-12-0 (4-1-6-0, 4-1-6-0).

Umpires: M J Kitchen and D J Shepherd (replay umpire: J C Balderstone).



*Defiance from Mike Atherton can only delay the inevitable at Lord's in 1993*

## TREVOR BAILEY

### FIFTH TEST, THE OVAL, 1953

GEOFFREY GREEN,
CRICKET CORRESPONDENT

*August 19.* England at the start had their backs to the wall, still needing 40 to draw level with Australia on the first innings and seven wickets gone. Yet Bailey remained, in all for just short of four hours, to steer his side with an unflinching innings of 64 to a precious lead of 31.

Bailey's efforts in this whole series through have been monumental and they will be remembered whatever the final outcome. Wise men use study. Bailey has studied the Australians quite a bit this summer. He possesses patience and patience possesses him.

### FIRST TEST, BRISBANE, 1954–55

JOHN WOODCOCK,
CRICKET CORRESPONDENT

*December 1.* This cricketer of inestimable value played in a way foreign to his nature for he lost no opportunity to attack and, when the day was 40 minutes old, he set up what might be considered a landmark in matches between England and Australia by pulling Johnson high and far for 6. It was a rare moment of humour in a tense day, and he looked so ashamed that the umpire had a word with him, as though assuring him that he was within the law and inquiring whether he required the attention of a doctor.

But that stroke apart, Bailey hit 11 4s and a 5, mostly with hooks and cuts, and not until a few balls before he was bowled, taking a swing at Johnston after batting for four hours 20 minutes, did he give a chance or look like getting out. It was a fine performance, worthy of a century, and one which enhanced his considerable reputation as a stubborn fighter in the hour of need.

## KEN BARRINGTON

### FOURTH TEST, OLD TRAFFORD, 1961

JOHN WOODCOCK,
CRICKET CORRESPONDENT

*July 31.* The highest testimony to Barrington's determination is that he can have a successful season though not properly in form. What his batting lacks is not virtuosity so much as confidence, for as he showed on Saturday he has the strokes when he chooses to use them. In his innings of 78, lasting three hours 40 minutes, he hit 10 fours, mainly from shots which made the rest of his performance seem over-cautious.

## GEOFFREY BOYCOTT

### THIRD TEST, EDGBASTON, 1968

JOHN WOODCOCK,
CRICKET CORRESPONDENT

*July 11.* By the time the England team signed in yesterday afternoon it had stopped raining, though they could do no more than throw a ball about. The exception, needless to say, was Boycott, who soon had the groundstaff bowling to him in the indoor school. To Boycott, batting is not a chore but a hobby. When, on tour, others go off to play golf or to bathe, Boycott prefers to have a net, if he can find a bowler or two. In the West Indies, where even the most humble onlooker can pitch a length, he was in his element.

JOHN WOODCOCK
*June 21, 1993.* On Friday evening, by which time England had only a draw to play for, I ran into Geoff Boycott and said how much I would give to see him batting for us next day. 'I'll tell you this, Uncle John,' he replied, 'it would be over my dead body that they'd get me out.'

---

# IAN BOTHAM

## THIRD TEST, TRENT BRIDGE, 1977

JOHN WOODCOCK,
CRICKET CORRESPONDENT
*July 29.* The honours went to Botham who must have been uncertain when he arrived at the ground soon after breakfast whether he would even play. After a loose first spell Brearley probably brought him on for his second, in the middle of the afternoon, with some misgivings.

**Botham chooses happy time to make his impact in a Test**

By John Woodcock
Cricket Correspondent

*NOTTINGHAM : England, with all their first innings wickets in hand, are 234 runs behind Australia*

Except for the first two in their order and the last three, Australia batted no better when the third Test match began at Trent Bridge yesterday than they did at Old Trafford in the second. After an opening partnership of 79, they were bowled out for 243, Ian Botham, in his first Test match,

While it was disappointing for England that Australia's last two wickets should add 88, it brought home to them just how well they had done to account for the main batting so cheaply. O'Keeffe always sells his wicket dearly, playing straight and attempting few of the strokes that get others out. If he is not quite the batsman one would have chosen to entertain the Queen on her annual visit to Test cricket, she would have recognized his resolution and realized how badly it must have been needed.

What Brearley did know, though, was that with 75 wickets already to his name, Botham has been the most successful bowler of the current season. He is 21 years young and conspicuously strong. He is fit, too, having bowled more first-class overs in the past three months than anyone else. It was a happy time to choose to make the impact he did, having, as he does, no Packer strings attached to him.

## FIFTH TEST, EDGBASTON, 1985

JOHN WOODCOCK,
CRICKET CORRESPONDENT
*August 20.* For obvious reasons Border set purely protective fields, though when Lamb was out, caught at mid-wicket five minutes after tea, and Botham came in even that became difficult. There were four balls left of McDermott's thirtieth over when Botham appeared, cheered to the echo. The first, straight and on a length, he heaved into the pavilion for six. He failed to score off the next, but hit the third to where the first had gone, this time with a stroke of classical purity. On Sunday he had driven the tenth green at The Belfry Golf Club, a carry of over 280 yards only rarely achieved. Greg Norman and Severiano Ballesteros, who have done it, would not, I imagine, fancy their chances of dispatching McDermott into the far yonder.

*The arrival of a new star in Ashes cricket – Ian Botham's debut at Trent Bridge in 1977*

*A wicket for Ian Botham, celebrated with typical gusto, at the Oval in 1985*

## SIXTH TEST, THE OVAL, 1985

JOHN WOODCOCK,
CRICKET CORRESPONDENT

*September 3.* But it was not Taylor who shared the limelight with Ellison yesterday, but the irrepressible Botham, who took his thirty-first wicket of the series, his 343rd for England (only 12 behind Lillee), and, into the bargain, held one breathtaking catch as well as another easier one.

It is wonderful what Botham's winter off has done for him. Gower has never seen him bowl faster than in this match; yet a year ago it looked as though he might have shot his bolt. And after seeing him catch McDermott, diving to his left at second slip, I promise never to say again that he deprives himself of a potentially crucial split second by standing with his hands on his knees.

Quite simply, Botham is a law unto himself. Besides his 343 Test wickets, he has scored 4,409 runs for England and held 91 catches. Hardly a day passes without him doing something which very few others could. Besides having a wonderful eye for a ball and great strength, he is very athletic. Standing at slip he dwarfs those alongside him.

---

# PAUL COLLINGWOOD

## THIRD TEST, PERTH, 2010–11

RICHARD HOBSON

*December 17.* Describing the catch as instinctive does no justice to the hours Collingwood devotes to practice. Instinct, yes, but honed from hard graft. At 34, he is still England's best fielder. In the one-day team he continues to patrol the most important area at backward point. Scabby elbows like the ugly knees of a Gruffalo are war wounds resulting from years of diving around. Those elbows are given no opportunity to heal.

---

# DENIS COMPTON

## FIRST TEST, TRENT BRIDGE, 1938

DUDLEY CAREW

*June 13.* The contrast between Paynter and Compton was marked. Paynter looked utilitarian and post-War; he is a fine man for doing the honest work of getting runs. Compton, on the other hand, looked an artist, and the instincts of the great cricketers who played in the days when the war meant the Boer War moved in his strokes. He cut McCabe for 4 handsomely and showed an off-drive which was technically perfect. When he played his defensive strokes, too, he played them as though he had been reading text-books.

Compton soon went ahead of Paynter, but they were both running neck and neck in the nineties and then O'Reilly came on and Paynter in his first over first cut him square to the boundary and then hooked him for another 4, which gave him his hundred. The over altogether cost O'Reilly 14 runs. Compton was not long in following him – it was that delectable cut of his which brought him safely home – and then was out hitting at Fleetwood-Smith and being caught by C.L. Badcock deep at square-leg. It was a lovely and memorable innings, and it had only taken him two and a quarter hours.

### SECOND TEST, LORD'S, 1938

R.B. VINCENT,
CRICKET CORRESPONDENT

*June 29.* Compton during this time definitely established himself as a Test match player of class. His batting is so compact, the blade so straight both in his forward and defensive play, and his short-armed hook, which he used freely to McCormick, is played with immense power. Some of his off-side strokes came as a delightful relief in a game which had been made up to a great extent of pushes to leg.

### FIRST TEST, BRISBANE, 1946–47

NEVILLE CARDUS

*December 4.* Compton played with a lovely gallantry. He ran out of his ground first ball to Miller and drove defiantly straight, and then he pulled a long hop from Toshack for 4. Bradman then held consultations with Toshack, who now attacked from round the wicket, as Wilfred Rhodes and Blythe did every ball they bowled. Toshack improved a little in direction, but not in power of abstract, and Compton was free to pull him again for 4. Compton eventually fell to a ball that kept low. His little innings shone with a youthful confidence in the good rewards supposed to come from adventure.

### FIFTH TEST, THE OVAL, 1956

JOHN WOODCOCK,
CRICKET CORRESPONDENT

*August 24.* Yet, although these 15 minutes turned the whole match upside down, they did not dim Compton's performance, which came straight out of a story book. He went in when England earlier in the day had also been struggling hard, and Australia were out for his blood. He might have been thinking of those who felt he should not have returned. Certainly no one could have been sure that he would justify his selection, and one wonders if he has ever experienced anything much more nerve racking.

But his eye still seemed wonderfully quick and dependable, and gradually he got the feel of a Test match again. Slowly, too, he realized that with care and discipline he could still do most of the things that once made him the scourge of bowlers. And he proceeded to play an innings which increased considerably in value after he was out. It was a triumph as much of character as skill, and when eventually he fell at 94 everyone must have shed a silent tear.

---

## DENIS COMPTON AND LEN HUTTON

### THIRD TEST, OLD TRAFFORD, 1953

GEOFFREY GREEN,
CRICKET CORRESPONDENT

*July 13.* Two unworthy strokes in 32 runs reduced England to a sombre tone. But in the half-hour before tea there came the first defiant ring as Hutton and Compton, perhaps the best players in the world for an awkward wicket, met the challenge. About this time there came one very fine over from Hill in which Hutton was twice struck on the pads, to bring a particularly explosive appeal, and then edged the ball to slip. Now, too, a passing train gave three encouraging toots on its whistle which curiously eased the tension and saw England in to tea at 50 for two.

The evening brought yet a third change in note. The wicket clearly was easing all the time, and now Hutton, frail but majestic, and Compton, determined and sure, showed their mastery, Compton adding to his worth by the wise judgment of his calling. Each searched the boundary on both sides of the wicket with some fine strokes. One remembers two lovely late cuts by Hutton off Miller and there was one remarkable lazy upward sweep, finely angled just over long leg's head, by Compton that cost Davidson a 6.

So England moved serenely on against a field now set defensively. The clock pointed to a quarter past six. The score was 126 for two, with Hutton 66, Compton 45, and the partnership worth 94. Suddenly Compton played gently forward to Archer and edged Langley a catch standing back.

---

## COLIN COWDREY

### SECOND TEST, PERTH, 1974–75

JOHN WOODCOCK,
CRICKET CORRESPONDENT

*December 11.* Whatever the Australians may say about his age there is none in England, not even Boycott, who would have a better chance of successfully making the change from a Surrey fireside to the sound and fury of an Australian Test match all within a week. If he plays it will be as though he dreamt that he was batting against Australia at Perth and woke up to find he was.

JOHN WOODCOCK,
CRICKET CORRESPONDENT

*December 14.* Cowdrey looked in a different class to anyone else, which, of course, he is.

### THIRD TEST, MELBOURNE, 1974–75

JOHN WOODCOCK,
CRICKET CORRESPONDENT

*December 27.* Edrich initiated two short singles, which cannot be that short with Cowdrey as one of the partners. Between wickets these days Cowdrey is like a ship in full sail. During the luncheon interval there was a mile race between representatives of the local football clubs. I quite expected to see Cowdrey running in it, only because he is asked to do everything at the moment. On Christmas Day he found himself, among other things, addressing 150 people at a golf club luncheon.

---

## BILL EDRICH

### FOURTH TEST, HEADINGLEY, 1948

R.B. VINCENT,
CRICKET CORRESPONDENT

*July 24.* As so often happens after a long stand, another wicket fell almost at once, Edrich being caught at mid-wicket. One can pay Edrich no higher compliment than to say that he resolutely restrained his natural inclination to play that one false stroke somewhere in the direction of long-on which has so often cost him his wicket. For a cricketer who obviously enjoys his game so much it was a dour affair, but this was a Test match, and a five-day business at that, and he did his duty gallantly.

## JOHN EDRICH

### SIXTH TEST, ADELAIDE, 1970–71

JOHN WOODCOCK,
CRICKET CORRESPONDENT

*January 30.* Boycott's partner, Edrich, made another opportune and ruthlessly practical hundred, his sixth against Australia out of his 10 for England. When he was seven he should have been caught in the gully by Mallett, but that was his one chance and only five minutes were left by the time Stackpole eventually caught him in the gully.

Hobbs (12), Hammond (9), Sutcliffe (8) and Leyland (7) are the only Englishmen to have made more hundreds against Australia than Edrich and of these Sutcliffe and Leyland also had their temperament to thank for their success as much as their natural ability.

All Edrich's innings are the same: in all weathers and on all wickets and in all hemispheres, he plays his game, trying nothing beyond a few trusted strokes. In his eight innings in the present series he has made 521 runs at an average of 86.8 which is a record that Hobbs, Hammond, Sutcliffe and Leyland would all have been proud of.

## GODFREY EVANS

### FOURTH TEST, ADELAIDE, 1954–55

STEWART HARRIS

*February 2.* Evans square drove Davidson for 4 and chopped him down to third man for 3. Bailey drove for 2 and Davidson's over had cost nine runs.

Evans reached 20 in 12 minutes, having once hit Davidson back over his head and run 5. He actually set out for a sixth. His innings was more than a cheerful wallop; there was skill and decision in everything he did, not least his running. He scurried, low-slung like a rabbit, up and down between the wickets and Bailey helped him put on 49 in 27 minutes.

## ANDREW FLINTOFF

### SECOND TEST, EDGBASTON, 2005

MICHAEL HENDERSON

*August 8.* If heroism has any place in sport, Freddie Flintoff's performance bordered on the heroic.

The jolly Prestonian twice shaped the match with the bat (nobody who witnessed his thrilling hitting can possibly forget it) and supplied a third shift when Michael Vaughan threw him the ball on Saturday afternoon with a simple request, 'we need a wicket or two'.

Seven balls later, Langer, the roundhead, and Ponting, the cavalier, had been unhorsed. Responding to the noisy enthusiasm of a crowd that responded in turn to his renewed all-round purpose, Flintoff proved unstoppable.

Figures reveal only so much about a player's performance, whatever the sport. What matters most of all is the influence a player has on a game when it lies in the balance and, in company of the highest class, at the crucial moments, Flintoff's brilliance transformed this Test.

Two moments on Saturday will remain imperishable. First, despite the restriction of a sore shoulder and with nine fielders on the ropes, their mouths open like

*A familiar sight in the summer of 2005; the England players congratulate Andrew Flintoff on another wicket*

crocodiles at feeding time, he heaved Lee high into the television gantry at long-on. As the crowd roared at the eighth of his nine sixes in the match, an Ashes record that is worth bragging about, Flintoff laughed at his own impudence.

As if we didn't know, an unfettered enjoyment of the game is one of his most endearing qualities.

Then came that booming leg-cutter to Ponting, who touched it and walked. Any bowler who gets the Australian captain for a duck should be paid his body weight in Burgundy.

SIMON BARNES

*September 19, 2005.* If team spirit was at the heart of England's victory over Australia in the Ashes series, then Flintoff was at the heart of the team spirit. His was the summer, his the glory. Need a few runs? Send for Freddie! Need a wicket? Toss the ball to Freddie! It was the summer when Flintoff ceased to be a large man and became a giant.

## FIRST TEST, BRISBANE, 2006–07

SIMON BARNES

*November 25.* There was a fine moment shortly after Australia had passed 400 with three wickets down when Flintoff broke the decisive partnership by beating Mike Hussey for pace and clean bowling him. The more Australia batted remorselessly on, the more Flintoff didn't droop, the more he didn't falter, the more he didn't surrender. And to have that burst of dynamic energy to shatter Hussey's stumps was a beautiful moment in a very horrid day.

### FIFTH TEST, THE OVAL, 2009

MIKE ATHERTON, CHIEF CRICKET CORRESPONDENT

*August 24.* This, then, was the fairytale ending that Flintoff craved, and his was a scene-stealing effort of which a late version Marlon Brando would have been proud. Moving and swooping like a primed athlete for possibly the last time, he threw down Ponting's stumps and stood, as he had at Lord's, with his arms aloft while he waited for his colleagues to embrace him. There were no runs and wickets for him yesterday, but the gods had granted him, out of recognition for a remarkable career, the day's defining image.

## ANGUS FRASER

### THIRD TEST, EDGBASTON, 1989

ALAN LEE, CRICKET CORRESPONDENT

*July 8.* Play began 5½ hours later and Waugh had managed a mere mortal 43 when he was bowled between bat and pad by the eleventh England bowler to try his luck against him in three Tests.

The triumph, and psychologically it is all of that, belonged to the 23-year-old new cap, Angus Fraser, and he quickly followed up by removing Ian Healy with a similar ball, seaming back from a disciplined line just outside off-stump.

This was overdue reward for Fraser, whose 14 first-day overs had cost only 26 runs and might well have earned a wicket or two. In a series where England have showered favours on the Australians with wasteful bowling and profligate batting, it is heartening to see anyone, let alone a raw newcomer, adhere so skilfully to the essentials […]

The resulting single brought Waugh to face Fraser and brought him to his downfall. It was a ball of perfect length, catching Waugh half-forward and unusually indecisive. The crowd reacted as if they could barely believe what they had seen, but, recovering themselves, they gave Waugh a marvellous ovation as he retired with an enviable average.

If the pitch had sweated under its prolonged covering, Fraser was making the best use of it and Healy, no more positive in footwork than Waugh, fell in similar style with the addition of an inside edge.

## MIKE GATTING

### SECOND TEST, LORD'S, 1981

JOHN WOODCOCK, CRICKET CORRESPONDENT

*July 3.* Gatting played very well for 59. He has the bulldog spirit, much as Ken Barrington did, and the same sturdy, pugnacious, reassuring appearance. His play through the covers, especially off the back foot, was superb. It is easier to think of men of Gatting's build – Edrich, for example, and Leyland as well as Barrington – who have enjoyed the fight against Australia than of those with more willowy contours. Gatting should not, though, have got out when he did – in bright light and on a good wicket with so much to play for.

## GRAHAM GOOCH

### THIRD TEST, TRENT BRIDGE, 1993

ALAN LEE, CRICKET CORRESPONDENT

*July 6.* They came to Trent Bridge for a last, respectful viewing of the body, only to discover that the patient could not yet be pronounced dead. It might have been the day to bid farewell both to an Ashes crusade and an England captain. Instead, it was a day when the captain kept the Ashes alive.

Graham Gooch has played greater innings than the 120 he made in the third Cornhill Test yesterday, though most of his contemporaries have not. Never, though, even in his turbulent years in charge of England, has he batted under such an onerous burden regarding the future of a match, a series and his own career.

That he could rise above it all to play in commanding fashion for all but 70 minutes of the penultimate day, carrying England to virtual safety and to within visions of victory, restated the immense stature of a man who still attracts as much uninformed criticism as respect.

This was Gooch's eleventh century in 27 Tests since he resumed the captaincy in 1990. It was also, incidentally, his first in 12 Tests batting down the order, where a new role has opened up that could yet employ him in home Tests for another couple of years. If so, having become the third Englishman to pass 8,000 runs at this level yesterday, he looks certain to eclipse both Boycott and Gower.

MICHAEL HENDERSON

*July 6.* Greatness should not be a word that comes easily, for so few achieve it and it comes at a price. Alongside Rembrandt, Beethoven and Chekhov, what is a cricketer? Within his limited world, Gooch is indisputably a great player; David Gower, his natural antipode, is brilliant though probably not great [...]

If a batsman's mettle can be judged by his response to adversity, Gooch has made three centuries in successive summers that testify to his. After that unbeaten 154 against West Indies at Headingley, and the 135 he made on the same ground last year against Pakistan, both of which helped win matches that would otherwise have been beyond reach, came his innings yesterday that was no less important for being understated.

Sensation seekers who pine for that most overrated quality, 'charisma', may give up with Gooch. Publicly he may be a sourpuss, a misery guts and a cautious captain but, as a Test batsman, he has had no equal since Geoff Boycott and there may not have been a better player for all seasons since Len Hutton.

## DARREN GOUGH

### THIRD TEST, SYDNEY, 1994–95

ALAN LEE, CRICKET CORRESPONDENT

*January 3.* Although Gough grinned and giggled, this was more than mere knockabout stuff. It spoke of a spirit of defiance and self-belief that had been conspicuously lacking in much of the early order batting.

Some of the most experienced and accomplished players on this tour are at present in the grip of powerful emotions, overpowered by failure to the point where the basic co-ordination of head, hands and feet has seized up. Graham Gooch has managed 94 runs in five Test

20P

# THE TIMES

No. 65,155 WEDNESDAY JANUARY 4 1995

### Plan to cut budget and lawyers' role

## Mackay calls for legal aid fundholders

By Frances Gibb, legal correspondent

THE Lord Chancellor will next week unveil proposals for a legal aid system controlled by a regional network of NHS-style fundholders, working within budgets that strictly limit how much money they can hand out.

The proposals by Lord Mackay of Clashfern, described by officials as a major restructuring of the £1.4 billion legal aid scheme, spell the end of a demand-led approach and the dominant role of lawyers in settling publicly-funded disputes.

At the heart of the proposals is a plan to create a regional network of intermediaries or "fundholders for justice", loosely based on the reforms in the National Health Service.

The intermediaries, who need not be lawyers, would come under the regional offices of the Legal Aid Board. They would deal with all applications and act as a filter, ensuring that aid was reserved for disputes that could not be settled in any other way.

The proposals will be outlined by Lord Mackay in a speech that foreshadows a Green Paper in the spring. The speech, intended to initiate debate by posing questions rather than prescribing solutions, will nonetheless include ideas that mark a fundamental departure from the way legal aid operates. One of those changes would be to move away from lawyers as the first port of call for settling a legal dispute. People would be directed to mediators, ombudsmen, arbitrators

Mackay: "At present the money goes rolling out"

and advice workers in law centres and citizens' advice bureaux.

Lord Mackay's main concern is to direct legal aid to the right people. Before Christmas he outlined proposals to curb aid to the apparently rich: the Green Paper will look at how to improve access to people who need legal help and are denied it.

These measures will include legal expenses insurance; conditional fees (no win, no fee), which are due to come into force shortly; and possibly tackling the absence of legal aid for tribunals.

At present everyone who passes tests on means and merit can obtain aid for payment of lawyers' fees. Under the new proposals, people would be directed to ways of resolving disputes that need not involve lawyers. This year 3.6 million people were helped under one of the various legal aid schemes and that number is expected to reach a record 4.4 million by 1997-98. Lord Mackay's speech will be made at a seminar entitled "Addressing cost-effective access to justice", which is being held in London by the Social Market Foundation. It was the foundation that initially proposed the idea of "fundholders" in a pamphlet drawn up by Tony Holland, a past president of the Law Society, and two academics.

The idea of cash-limiting has already been strongly attacked by the Law Society, which says that justice will become a lottery. Legal aid funds would run out at different rates in different parts of the country.

Legal aid is one of the fastest growing areas of public spending. Costs are rising from £500 million in 1989 to an estimated £1.6 billion by 1996. But much of the increase has been caused by government legislation, such as the Police and Criminal Evidence Act 1984, which gave every accused person the right to a solicitor. Controls on growth have already meant the legal aid budget was underspent last year by £70 million.

In a BBC *Newsnight* programme last month, Lord Mackay first indicated he was attracted to cash-limiting the budget. He said: "Cash limiting has attractions in being able to put priorities on the system. At the moment there is no relative priority between one case and another. Once they qualify they enter into the system and the money goes rolling out to the lawyers involved in the case."

Letters, page 15

REBECCA NADEN/PA

Darren Gough, right, and colleagues after another Australian wicket. At left, Anna Gough and Liam.

## A new hero rises from the Ashes

By Paul Wilkinson and John Young

YORKSHIREMEN have long boasted that they represent the heart and stomach of English cricket, and that in the nation's hour of need a knight of the White Rose will ride to the rescue.

History, alas, has not always supported that theory, but new life has been breathed into a dead Ashes series by the rumbustious figure of Darren Gough, 24, whose performance in the Sydney Test has restored pride to a team racked by ridicule and despair.

Following his half-century by taking six Australian wickets for 49, Gough has become an instant hero. Yesterday his wife Anna declared herself "the proudest wife in all England", and said she would fly out with Liam, the one-month-old son he has not seen.

Joining them will be the hero's father, Trevor, who said "I will give him a good hug." Mrs Gough added: "I thought there was every chance he would rescue England. He always likes to go out there and belt it around the place. That is just the way he plays."

Delight yesterday in Gough's home village of Monk Bretton, near Barnsley, was tempered by a characteristic Yorkshire reluctance to overdo the excitement.

"It's only because there's a Yorkshireman, Ray Illingworth, running the side that he's there at all," said Steve Lockwood over a pint at The Norman. Mr Lockwood knows Gough from his days in the Monk Bretton team. "He was in there at 13, and there's not many who have done that."

Alan Southwell, the landlord, said: "He's done more to put the 'feel-good' factor back into Britain than anything the Government has achieved. He's given us all a lift."

Bold Gough, page 40

### Rosemary West case review

Prosecution and defence lawyers are to make an urgent review of the case against Rosemary West after the suicide of her husband Frederick at Winson Green jail on New Year's Day. She is charged with the murder of nine young women whose bodies were unearthed at the couple's Gloucester home last year.........Pages 5, 15

### Second victim of meningitis

Five-year-old Alexandra Yates, of Rottingdean, East Sussex, last night became the second victim of the meningitis which killed her best friend, Emma Harris, on Boxing Day. Alexandra died in Great Ormond Street Children's Hospital, *London*.........Page 3

### Death threat defied

British envoys are to defy a threat from Islamic extremists that unless all diplomats are withdrawn from Algeria by Saturday, they will be killed "in cold blood".........Page 11

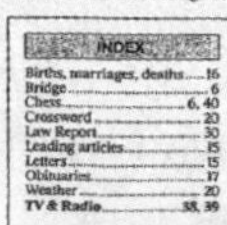

INDEX
Births, marriages, deaths.....16
Bridge.....6
Chess.....6, 40
Crossword.....20
Law Report.....30
Leading articles.....15
Letters.....15
Obituaries.....17
Weather.....20
TV & Radio.....38, 39

## Chechens claim a victory amid ruins of their capital

From Bill Gasperini in Grozny and Richard Beeston in Moscow

BATTERED Russian troops retreated from central Grozny yesterday, leaving hundreds of bodies and destroyed tanks in the ruined streets around the Presidential Palace.

On the fourth day of heavy street fighting, the Chechens consolidated their position after halting the Russian assault, and even counter-attacked in places. The heaviest fighting was around the railway station, about a mile northwest of the palace. Another battle line lies three miles to the north.

A huge Russian artillery bombardment from north-eastern Grozny, where the Russian forces have regrouped, was apparently designed to protect 60 stranded Russian tanks still surrounded by Chechens. The Russian guns pounded the Presidential Palace, and one shell blew the Chechen flag off the roof. Russian aircraft bombed factories in the west of the city.

But the centre remained firmly in Chechen hands. The Chechen fighters showed their elation with victory dances. Near by, dead Russian soldiers lay sprawled beside their burnt-out tanks and armoured personnel carriers.

Buildings facing the central square were gutted by fire and pockmarked with bullet holes. The air was full of the roar and howl of Russian shells. Smoke from the shelling spiralled up into a sky already darkened by oil fires.

Outside the palace, Schamil Besiav, the Chechen military commander, said: "We intend to defend ourselves whatever it takes." The bearded commander was dressed in the favourite uniform of the Chechens: green camouflage fatigues and a black ski cap. As he spoke, a group of fighters erupted: *"Allahu Akbar"* (God is greatest).

Moscow women protest yesterday against the war

Boris Agapov, Vice-President of the neighbouring republic of Ingushetia, which is sympathetic to the Chechens, said: "Many Russian tanks have been withdrawn to the perimeter of the city, and at least 100 Russian soldiers have been captured."

Three Russian prisoners displayed by the Chechens said that they were the only survivors from two infantry companies which led the initial attack on the railway station on New Year's Eve.

Civilians were again caught in crossfire yesterday. In one incident shown on Russian television, jets trying to knock out a bridge hit civilian vehicles, killing at least ten people.

Motley alliance, page 8
Leading article, page 15

## Three dangerous men on run after Parkhurst escape

By Adam Fresco

THREE top-security prisoners escaped from Parkhurst prison on the Isle of Wight last night.

Extra police were immediately sent to the island to set up roadblocks and to begin searches using dogs and a spotter plane. Police gave a warning that the men, two Category A prisoners and a lower security Category B inmate, were dangerous.

A Prison Service spokesman said last night: "At 8 o'clock a dog patrol at Parkhurst discovered a hole in the perimeter fence. A subsequent roll check confirmed that three life-sentence prisoners were missing."

The hunt switched to a farm early today when police received a 999 call from a couple who returned home to discover an outhouse had been forced open. Police went to Chawton Farm at Northwood and began a detailed search of the area. The village is midway between Parkhurst and Cowes.

The escapers have been named as Keith Rose, 45, serving life for murder, and described as 5ft 10in, thin and with a scraggy grey beard; Matthew Williams, 25, serving life for an attempt to kill Christmas shoppers with a nail-bomb, who is 5ft 10in, clean-shaven and with sunken eyes and short black hair; and Andrew Rodger, 44, serving life for murder, who is 5ft 5in, described as "very stocky" and with short hair.

Police said that members of the public should not approach the men but should telephone 0983 528000 if they see them.

Richard Gully, chairman of the board of visitors, confirmed last night that he was launching an investigation.

Builders working on a major contract at the Victorian prison have said that there have been astonishing breaches of security. They claim that they have been given the freedom to smuggle "absolutely anything" into the jail.

Terror trail, page 2
Everthorpe rioting, page 2



## Skydivers leap for lives from 'sabotage' plane

By Michael Horsnell

FIVE skydivers escaped unhurt after baling out of a light aircraft which police believe may have been sabotaged by a firebomb wedged in the engine.

Detectives were yesterday investigating a theory that the incident was a revenge attempt against the pilot over the death of a skydiver in an accident three years ago. Lyn George, 35, the pilot, who was told two weeks ago that he would not be prosecuted, shouted to the skydivers "Bale out, bale out" at 4,000ft after noticing a drop in power and irregular instrument readings. He made an emergency landing, minutes after taking off from the airfield near Whitchurch, Shropshire, on Monday.

When he inspected the Cessna 206 he found a plastic bottle containing aviation fuel inserted in the cowling next to the engine. Mr George said the container was close to melting. "I dread to think what could have happened," he said. "The aviation fuel was just millimetres away from spraying over the red-hot engine block. Not only could it have brought the plane down, killing everyone on board, but there's no knowing how many it could have killed on the ground."

Mr George was charged with the manslaughter of a skydiver because the plane involved was allegedly not authorised to carry parachutists. John Ward, 42, plummeted 12,000ft to his death after hitting the plane tail wing on August 26, 1991. The charge was dropped on December 20 at Shrewsbury Crown Court.

Detective Sergeant Andrew Thomas of West Mercia police said that revenge was being considered as one possible motive. Residents have been protesting about alleged nuisance from increased skydiving at the centre.

*Darren Gough's all-round heroics in Sydney in 1995 make front-page news at home* innings, Mike Gatting a meagre 57. Aside from his splendidly stubborn 80 in the Brisbane rearguard action, Graeme Hick has scored 30 runs in the series.

Michael Atherton, the captain, has been heroic, trailing his Union Jack through 2½ days of unyielding batting already. But it took Gough's untutored style and uncomplicated outlook to show that there is another way of conquering the Australians. Gough, 24, from Yorkshire, is the irrepressibly smiling face of this tour, and, alone among the England party, his cricket can be reported with unreserved enthusiasm.

'I went out to thrash the bowling around the park and that's what I did,' he explained without a trace of vanity. 'It's the way I play, and the captain and manager had told me I should play my natural game.' This, at least, is to be applauded. The chain of command in the England camp is not easy to follow, and it would be a rarity and a relief to find unanimity that Gough must be left alone to do things his way.

JOHN WOODCOCK

*January 4.* I can think of no other English cricketer who has become so instantly popular out here. They loved Patsy Hendren and enjoyed jousting with Fred Trueman and laughed at Johnny Wardle and gasped at Frank Tyson and goggled at Denis Compton and turned somersaults with Derek Randall; but Darren Gough they have adopted. There is something of Ian Botham in him, and he has yet to be broken in.

## FIRST TEST, BRISBANE, 1998–99

ALAN LEE, CRICKET CORRESPONDENT

*November 21.* Gough against Taylor was a duel worthy of all the frothy billing that preceded this series. Taylor believes that he is batting better than he has for years, while Gough has probably never bowled better than he is now. From his first over, which contained a rapid, precise bouncer and an appeal for leg-before that demanded careful thought, he was probing and challenging, examining the mind-set and the reflexes.

---

# DAVID GOWER

## SECOND TEST, MELBOURNE, 1990–91

ALAN LEE, CRICKET CORRESPONDENT

*December 27.* Christmas had found this England party at its lowest ebb and Gower showing his shortest fuse. England could barely perm 11 fully fit men from their swollen party of 18 for the critical second Test against Australia and Gower, unable to shake off his second injury in a month, publicly bared his frustration at a tour slipping away from him.

His outburst during the Christmas morning net practice was not so much about insensitive television crews as a sensitively bruised right wrist which had refused to heal. By the time he dressed up as Biggles for the team's lunch party it seemed unlikely that he would be performing any Boxing Day heroics.

But Gower's sense of self-preservation has served him well before. At Lord's last June, when his captaincy was being undermined by the threat of a heavy defeat and a hotheaded walkout from a press conference, he made a redeeming century. At the Oval in September he took the last available chance to reserve his place on this tour with another hawkish hundred.

Yesterday morning, he played with some discomfort through a gentle net, spent a considerable time in lonely meditation on the Melbourne Cricket Ground outfield and then went into a prolonged, animated conference with Graham Gooch and Allan Lamb which ended in backslaps and handshakes all round.

Gooch had told Gower that the team needed him. Gower had told Gooch that he wanted to play and felt able to do a job. The deal was done, and with the aid of regular painkilling tablets, Gower batted 203 minutes and helped revive this Ashes series as a contest.

## WALTER HAMMOND

### FOURTH TEST, HEADINGLEY, 1938

R.B. VINCENT,
CRICKET CORRESPONDENT

*July 23.* Hammond, for half an hour or more, was the true majestic Hammond, reaching his 50 with two exquisite drives wide of extra cover-point. Fleetwood-Smith kept Paynter quiet, although one short ball was cut square for 4, and Waite was given a short spell to rest O'Reilly before Hammond had become too insolent. The first ball Waite bowled to Hammond came back off the bat so violently that there would have been fears for the umpire's life had he not thrown himself on the ground. In any case there was a spare umpire on the ground.

### FIRST TEST, BRISBANE, 1946–47

NEVILLE CARDUS

*December 4.* Greeted by a royal welcome, Hammond slowly walked to the hazardous middle and there, with Edrich, he remained an interminable 20 minutes before luncheon using his bat like an old Roman centurion's shield, a spectacle of dignity in surroundings of turbulence, though from time to time he was shaken rudely on his pedestal.

## JACK HOBBS AND HERBERT SUTCLIFFE

### FIRST TEST, TRENT BRIDGE, 1926

A.C.M. CROOME,
CRICKET CORRESPONDENT

*June 14.* But Mr Gregory, though his bowling was faster than anything I have seen this year, was in nowise terrific to Hobbs or Sutcliffe. He made two or three balls bounce uncomfortably, but the recipient had plenty of time to drop his hands and let them proceed harmlessly to the wicket-keeper. For the rest, they played forward or back as they pleased, and took frequent singles in the direction of short-leg or third man. Many of their strokes would have been more productive of runs if the fielding had been of merely ordinary quality, but the Australians – in particular Mr Andrews and Mr Bardsley – were consistently brilliant in this department of the game.

### SECOND TEST, LORD'S, 1926

A.C.M. CROOME,
CRICKET CORRESPONDENT

*June 29.* The Australians had made so many runs that a victory for England seemed practically out of the question, but Hobbs and Sutcliffe started as if they considered it possible. Mr Gregory, if his arm was not so high as it used to be, bowled quite fast. But he rarely made either man play a stroke in a hurry, and, a significant fact, they struck the ball or left it alone as they pleased. From the Nursery end Mr Macartney bowled a good length, but Sutcliffe drove him past cover-point to the boundary and Hobbs got four for a patted cut, played very late, a delightful stroke. About five overs sufficed for the taming of Mr Gregory, and when Mr Mailey went on for Mr Macartney both batsmen ran yards out of their ground to drive him. These strokes seldom counted more than one or two because the field was cunningly placed, but they were varied by more productive cuts and hooks when Mr Mailey pitched short. It goes without saying that the short chase, which yields the stolen single, was laid down with consummate skill. The first half hour produced 45 runs, and it was delightful, after our post-war experiences, to see English batsmen really set about Australian bowlers.

## JACK HOBBS

### FOURTH TEST, ADELAIDE, 1928–29

FROM OUR SPECIAL CORRESPONDENT*

*February 2.* Hobbs, who seems now to tire very quickly, played a master's innings, but the strain of running singles obviously tells against a man 46 years of age. His 74 was marked by a wide variety of delightful strokes that would, 20 years ago, have contained at least ten 4's. Today there were only two in it and no fewer than 38 singles. These, with his partner's sharp runs, had their inevitable effect, and a tired stroke ended an innings of which many younger men might well be proud. One stroke revealed his great genius: he set himself to play a ball to the on, but it must obviously have swerved, for without apparent trouble he shifted his feet and made a perfect hit to cover.

* *The Times* archivist has not been able to identify the author of this report.

## LEN HUTTON

### FIRST TEST, TRENT BRIDGE, 1938

DUDLEY CAREW

*June 11.* Hutton played his part perfectly. Something of Sutcliffe's own grace and imperturbability moved through his strokes, and he scored his runs with a diffidence which did not disguise the fact that he had a prim and proper answer to every question the Australian bowlers set him.

## ALAN KNOTT

### FIFTH TEST, ADELAIDE, 1974–75

JOHN WOODCOCK, CRICKET CORRESPONDENT

*January 31.* Knott, of course, is a law unto himself. Batting at number seven in this series – and there is a world of difference between doing that and going in in the first four – he has now scored 339 runs for an average of 40, the highest aggregate and the best average by an Englishman. Only Greg Chappell has scored many more runs in the series than Knott. Today Knott cut and hooked and dabbed and glanced and generally played cat and mouse until he ran out of partners. As an

Englishman he is an exception, being a better cricketer than he usually is when playing against Australia rather than slightly worse. Knott's innings today was a joy in the shadow of sorrow.

### THIRD TEST, TRENT BRIDGE, 1977

JOHN WOODCOCK, CRICKET CORRESPONDENT

*July 30.* Compared with Knott, Boycott looked an ordinary mortal. If Boycott's innings will he remembered as one of his more famous, it was not technically one of his best, not by a long way. Knott, on the other hand, played like a genius. He came in with England in danger of conceding a sizable lead, perhaps a decisive one. He is, though, when in yesterday's form, one of the game's most awkward customers to bowl to. Some of his driving was magnificent. As soon as he arrived he took the pressure off Boycott. Within a few overs he had wrested the initiative. He played with the effrontery of a bandit, happy to have Boycott as his partner again. Boycott knew better than to try to calm him down. Instead he applauded his best strokes and shook his head at the more outrageous ones.

---

## JIM LAKER

### FIRST TEST, TRENT BRIDGE, 1948

R.B. VINCENT, CRICKET CORRESPONDENT

*June 11.* Then came the fun of the day which stirred the Trent Bridge crowd to full-throated cheering. The innings looked to be over when Surrey, represented by Laker and Bedser, came to the rescue. Let there be no mistake about the innings of Laker. Quite truthfully he played strokes of a quality immeasurably superior to any other batsman who had preceded him. His driving through the covers was the perfection of poise and timing and his placing to leg deliberate and certain.

With Bedser stubborn at the other end, Laker welcomed the changes in the bowling and played one stroke after another. This gallant pair had added 89, 15 more than all their previous colleagues had made between them, for the ninth wicket, when Bedser drove a ball into the hands of deepish mid-off. Laker's grand innings, for in the circumstances it was a grand innings played with a straight bat, came to an end when he had one intemperate flash at a ball outside the off stump and was caught at the wicket.

---

## ALLAN LAMB

### FIRST TEST, HEADINGLEY, 1989

ALAN LEE, CRICKET CORRESPONDENT

*June 12.* Allan Lamb, never more resolute than in the direct path of danger, took out a personal insurance policy with his thrilling century on Saturday. Today he should give fully comprehensive cover to England in the first Cornhill Test match.

Four hours of Lamb at his abrasive best have done much to restore the psychological balance of this series after two days of revealing, relentless leather-chasing for the England team. They need a further 118 to avoid the follow-on and, effectively, save the game, whereupon attention can turn to doing certain things rather differently at Lord's next week.

Lamb is one who can be sure of his place, however serious a view the selectors take of the brutally exposed shortcomings in this match. Not since 1984, when he took three centuries off the West Indies attack, has he played with such heroic confidence at this level. This, indeed, was only his second Test century in that five-year period, spanning 30 games and 50 innings. The figures insisted he was playing for his place and Lamb, who can be sensitive under criticism, was this time not blind to the moment of judgement.

It has already been a turbulent season for him. His response to the county captaincy at Northampton was initially invigorating but has had to survive a period in which the team briefly lost form, the club came under fire for its pitches and Lamb himself for the handling of his benefit. His batting form was good but his character wobbled; thankfully the signs are that he has now recovered reason, humour and stature.

His right to bat in England's competitive middle order is certainly re-established, for he reacted courageously to an alien situation. When the need was simply to occupy the crease and accumulate the imposing first target of 402, Lamb properly opted to bat naturally, refusing to be restrained.

As Allan Border persisted, quite rightly, with attacking fields, Lamb kept crashing the ball through the off-side gaps, exposing the Australian seam attack as being no more potent nor precise than England's had been.

He reached his ninth Test century, every one of which has been scored in England, with his nineteenth four and jubilantly saluted his team-mates massed on the balcony, with Ian Botham an animatedly welcome guest.

# HAROLD LARWOOD

## SECOND TEST, LORD'S, 1926

A.C.M. CROOME,
CRICKET CORRESPONDENT

*June 28.* Larwood is, I believe, the youngest professional bowler ever selected to play for England. He completely justified his selection, proving himself to be possessed of confidence and, when wisely used, sufficient stamina. He got an appreciable amount of life out of the true and easy-paced wicket, and for a fast bowler his length was commendably regular.

## FIFTH TEST, SYDNEY, 1932–33

DELAMORE McCAY

*February 27.* Alexander desperately hurled down some bumpers, but Larwood treated them with contempt, and twice in succession he punched the ball to the on boundary. Larwood continued to hit with great power, making a straight drive for 6 and a stroke to the on boundary off successive balls from Lee. The leg-theory squabble was completely forgotten as the spectators, taking Larwood to their hearts, cheered him loudly. There was genuine disappointment when Larwood, with his score at 98, played the ball to the on for his century and was caught by Ironmonger at mid-on. The crowd stood and cheered as Larwood made his way back to the pavilion.

## EDDIE PAYNTER

### THIRD TEST, ADELAIDE, 1932–33

E.W. PARISH

*January 19.* It was evident at the start of play that Jardine wanted every possible run in order to make victory certain. Even when England had set Australia an almost impossible task he sent in Paynter, who was still suffering badly from a sprained ankle. Leyland ran for Paynter, who was seriously handicapped in his footwork and clearly in pain.

### FOURTH TEST, BRISBANE, 1932–33

DELAMORE MCCAY

*February 14.* The surprise of the day was the appearance of Paynter. He left hospital in the morning, not intending to play, but courageously went to the wickets when he saw the play was going against his side.

*February 15.* Paynter and Verity resumed their innings, and their policy from the outset apparently was to tire the bowlers while they added to the score. They achieved the unexpected, and Paynter's exhibition of batsmanship was unusually good. In the Adelaide match Paynter showed himself to be a fine batsman; today he showed himself to be both a fine batsman and a determined player. When the Australian score was passed the spectators gave a generous demonstration of cheering to the batsmen. Both had played on the principle that no game is ever lost till it is won, giving an ample demonstration of the truth of that remark. Paynter was dismissed by a good catch taken by Richardson. He had played a great innings; the partnership for the ninth wicket had added 92 runs. It was a splendid performance, especially in such weather, fierce heat and high humidity.

## WILFRED RHODES

### FIFTH TEST, THE OVAL, 1926

A.C.M. CROOME,
CRICKET CORRESPONDENT

*August 17.* Nine runs later Rhodes began a remarkable little spell of bowling from the Vauxhall end. His first four overs were maidens, and every ball of them had to be played, and was played, with the bat. But the fifth ball of his fourth over came with his arm, and Mr Woodfull barely touched it as it proceeded to hit his stumps.

## WALTER ROBINS

### FIRST TEST, TRENT BRIDGE, 1930

R.B. VINCENT,
CRICKET CORRESPONDENT

*June 16.* […] it as the manner in which R.W.V. Robins then attacked the Australian batsmen rather than Tate's earlier success which was of the greater value. Robins, in fact, has so far had a wonderful match, and if ever a young player has at once been labelled as a true Test match cricketer it is he. His batting, when he flung himself at the bowling to score as quickly as possible to allow the Australian batsmen to have full use of the bad pitch, was really splendid, and later in the day the way in which he took a gruelling from V.Y. Richardson but plugged away to the end, knowing that the taking of wickets was more important than keeping down runs, was equally great.

---

## BRIAN STATHAM

### FIRST TEST, EDGBASTON, 1961

JOHN WOODCOCK,
CRICKET CORRESPONDENT

*June 12.* A captain could ask for no more doughty fighter than Statham. Cowdrey must have known when he summoned him for an effort that nothing would be spared, and he bowled magnificently. If he beat Mackay once he beat him a dozen times and his figures for the day of one for 61 in 19 overs were a travesty of justice.

---

## DAVID STEELE

### SECOND TEST, LORD'S, 1975

JOHN WOODCOCK,
CRICKET CORRESPONDENT

*August 1.* By now the crowd – the gates were closed at 12.45 – was taking Steele to its heart. In his rimless spectacles he looks like some member of the American Academy of Arts and Sciences and at 33 he is at the age when most Australians are ending their Test careers. But he really did play well. Three times when Lillee pitched short he hooked him for four, the third of these being as good a stroke as there was all day.

10

SPORT

Cricket

**England take Steele to their heart on a memorable first day**

By John Woodcock
Cricket Correspondent

*LORD'S : England, with one first innings wicket in hand, have scored 313 against Australia in the second Test match.*

Given three, four or five days as good as the first and the second Test match between England and Australia which started yes-

except at Melbourne, when Thomson was missing and Lillee bowled only six overs before breaking down. Unlike Lillee, Thomson has yet to convince one that he is going to be a great force in England. Walker was steadiness itself, as he always is ; Mallett threatened little to start with, but in successive overs after tea he beat Knott and Woolmer and he fin-

*David Steele makes an immediate impact on his magnificent Test debut at Lord's in 1975*

When drinks were taken Alley, out of the corner of his mouth, looked to offer Steele a word of approval. By lunchtime, when Steele was 36, he was given the reception of a century-maker.

### THIRD TEST, HEADINGLEY, 1975

JOHN WOODCOCK,
CRICKET CORRESPONDENT

*August 15.* Instead we had a long, oppressive slog, with England's batsmen, after quite a promising morning, having a fearful struggle to score as many as they did.

It was the sort of day on which they could almost equally well have been bowled out for 150. But for Steele, who made 73, they probably would have been. Anyone watching Steele yesterday, for the first time, might reasonably have assumed that he had turned grey in long service for England. He played like an old-timer. As that great Yorkshireman, Herbert Sutcliffe, might have done, he put behind him, without the sign of a tremor, every difficulty that he met, and there were more than enough of those.

Steele was never playing well – but as the saying goes: 'It is not how you get them that matters, but how many you get.' Upon his forward defensive stroke he based his resistance. In Australia, playing like that, one would fear for his safety; in England, as Trevor Bailey used to show, it can be the surest method of defence, with the ball bouncing so much less. [...]

After batting for an hour Steele was 35; an hour and a half later he was 45. His resolution never stood him in better stead. The set of his stance, head thrust forward, is that of a determined man. At no time did he look like a batsman of nature, in the same way, if you like, as Hampshire did; but he really does need digging out, and that is why he was chosen.

## ALEC STEWART

### FOURTH TEST, MELBOURNE, 1998–99

ALAN LEE, CRICKET CORRESPONDENT

*December 28.* The conditions failed to daunt Stewart, a fish suddenly back in water. He had needed some persuasion – and the happenstance of a late injury to Alex Tudor – to give up the gauntlets to Warren Hegg, but the relish with which he played the opening role, for the first time since becoming captain, demonstrated once again that it is his best and natural habitat.

That England appear to be incapable of completing a tour without reversing the policy applied to Stewart is an unfortunate side-effect of his status in the side. The latest switch can be interpreted as an admission of failure in his multi-faceted duties, but a more reasonable argument is that the demands could never be met, long-term, and his career can most profitably be extended by sensible streamlining. [...]

The last time that Stewart batted in a Melbourne Test was in an emergency, with a broken finger, and he stood at the non-striker's end while Shane Warne completed a humiliation of England with a hat-trick. This was an altogether more satisfying experience, the shedding of a shadow over his record, an Ashes century at the 45th time of asking.

It came, appropriately enough, with a confident cut off Stuart MacGill, whose predatory effect on him at the start of an innings had helped generate his move back up the order. Stewart saluted all corners of this great ground, relief surely blending with the knowledge that his average when opening – 47 – now compares still more starkly with the 32 that he averages lower down.

## HERBERT SUTCLIFFE

### FIRST TEST, SYDNEY, 1932–33

R.B. VINCENT,
CRICKET CORRESPONDENT

*December 8.* To find fault with Sutcliffe's splendid innings on the pretext that at one time or another he did not make his runs fast enough is to ignore the value of this great batsman, who has had previous experience of what may happen when once he is out. In the end he himself made 30 more runs than the whole of the Australian side could total in their second innings, a feat which is surely worth ungrudging praise.

*Glenn McGrath, on the receiving end for once, as England captain Alec Stewart takes advantage during the 1998–99 series*

## GRAEME SWANN

### FIRST TEST, BRISBANE, 2010–11

SIMON BARNES

*November 27.* Australia have adopted a policy of going after Swann. Destroy Swann and you win the Ashes, that's the idea. So every time Swann has been given the ball, it's been a licence to swing. His first two balls in a single-over spell the previous day went for four. His ritual over before lunch was likewise walloped. In the afternoon he came on for his first proper spell and was clobbered again. He had bowled four overs for 34.

It was the most brutal examination he has faced as an England bowler. It was not so much calculated disrespect as tactical contempt. And Swann was, I suspect, at least partially overawed. Partially and temporarily. His next four overs cost three runs and had a wicket in them. It wasn't victory, but it was damn good stuff.

## DEREK RANDALL

### SECOND TEST, OLD TRAFFORD, 1977

JOHN WOODCOCK,
CRICKET CORRESPONDENT

*July 12.* Marsh, Australia's vice-captain, found time for a longish talk with Chappell before pulling Underwood to Randall, standing deep and fairly wide at mid-on. This was a straightforward catch which Randall held only after several desperate grabs at the ball. Once it was safely apprehended Randall fell flat on his back, legs and arms wide apart, a gesture of relief which delighted crowd and colleagues alike, his colleagues as they converged upon him.

## A.G. STEEL

### SECOND TEST, LORD'S, 1884

*July 23.* Mr A.G. Steel has again shown himself to be a wonderful cricketer. His bowling was excellent, but his batting when he went in third wicket down was simply superb. All the devices of which the visitors were masters did not interfere with his free batting.

## RAMAN SUBBA ROW

### FIRST TEST, EDGBASTON, 1961

JOHN WOODCOCK,
CRICKET CORRESPONDENT

*June 13.* Subba Row found batting much easier than Pullar. His tranquil character is reflected in his play. Nothing ruffles him and he is splendidly unselfish. As a natural striker of a ball he may not be in the top flight and yet when England's second innings started no one was likely to fight harder to keep the flag nailed to the mast. He plays within his limitations and for a Test match batsman that can be an inestimable virtue.

## CHRIS TAVARE

### FIFTH TEST, OLD TRAFFORD, 1981

JOHN WOODCOCK,
CRICKET CORRESPONDENT

*August 17.* Until Botham put them out of their agony on Saturday afternoon, England had had a fearful struggle for runs. Australia, by reducing their hosts from 70 for one to 105 for five, had clawed their way back into contention. Had Botham failed, Australia might have been left with fewer than 250 to make on a sunny Sunday. Besides Botham, England were indebted to Tavare for his tenacity. As against West Indies last year in the first two Tests, he showed an adhesiveness which has been singularly lacking since he was dropped.

The danger is of his overdoing the caution. It has mattered not at all in this match. Indeed, if Botham were not seemingly certain to be made man of the match, Tavare might be. In the 12 hours for which he batted – four and three-quarters in England's first innings and seven and a quarter in the second – he was seldom beaten and gave only the two chances to which he was out.

It was a remarkable exhibition of watchful defence. He has the strokes when he chooses to use them. An innings he played recently against Yorkshire on a Sunday is said to have been a breathtaking affair. Once established as England's number three, more will be expected of him in the way of attack.

## JONATHAN TROTT

### FOURTH TEST, MELBOURNE, 2010–11

MIKE ATHERTON,
CHIEF CRICKET CORRESPONDENT

*December 28.* That apart, Australia maintained their standards and their rewards might have been all the greater but for a very fine hundred from Jonathan Trott, an innings that displayed all the hallmarks of the kind of proper Test-match batting so lacking the day before. [...]

Trott has five Test-match hundreds now, three of them against these opponents, an impressive return given that he has been playing top-level cricket for little more than 12 months. But his game, based on unerring concentration and discipline and no little flair through the on side, is ready-made for the demands of Test cricket. There are more eye-catching players for sure but none that seem as able, day in day out, for every innings played, to be so mentally tuned for what they need to do.

Talent comes in many forms and this readiness for the job at hand is Trott's, despite his many idiosyncrasies at the crease. Say what you like about them, and many do, but they are designed to keep him in a bubble into which no outside influence is allowed. He took his Test average north of 60 yesterday, which is remarkable, and it will be a surprise if it does not end up around the 50 mark, the hallmark of a very, very good player.

## DEREK UNDERWOOD

### SECOND TEST, OLD TRAFFORD, 1977

JOHN WOODCOCK,
CRICKET CORRESPONDENT

*July 12.* Underwood bowled without a break from half an hour after lunch until he ended Australia's innings with 20 minutes left. His figures in that time were, 25.5-11-37-5. Altogether he took six for 66, which gives him 261 Test wickets in his career and brings him to within 38 of Lance Gibbs's world record. This was one of Underwood's best days. He used the air more than he used to and was almost unfailingly accurate, making the batsmen play every ball and finding just enough turn to unsettle them. More than once, Chappell, aiming to mid-on, found the ball going into the covers off the leading edge. The duel between Chappell and Underwood provided a fascinating piece of cricket.

## JOHNNY WARDLE

### FIRST TEST, TRENT BRIDGE, 1953

GEOFFREY GREEN,
CRICKET CORRESPONDENT

*June 15.* Wardle, too, was no less admirable in his unbeaten knock of an hour. It was a characteristic effort, built on a mixture

*With a souvenir stump for his sons, Johnny Wardle is welcomed home by his family after England's 1954–55 triumph in Australia*

of Yorkshire grit and unorthodox attacking strokes of his own left-handed variety. He brought character and humour to the dark picture, too. Bless a man who rubs his chest when hit on the toe by a fast full toss, thus stripping the mask of convention from a Test match, however desperate.

## CYRIL WASHBROOK

### THIRD TEST, OLD TRAFFORD, 1956

JOHN WOODCOCK,
CRICKET CORRESPONDENT

*July 13.* But Washbrook's success was another matter. His Test career seemed to have finished before May's started and he was recalled to the colours amid a storm of criticism.

It was asking a tremendous amount of him to answer that call, and the doubts that he might not be able to throw back the years were understandable. Yet the reserves of stamina and of knowledge that he was able to call upon and the many grillings he has battled through in the past stood him in the best stead. He never seemed ruffled from the moment he went to the wicket. One thought of Graveney and realized that he has never served the side quite as Washbrook did. In a sense Washbrook backed himself to do it for had he not felt the ability within him he would hardly have allowed himself to be chosen, and perhaps he considers this vindication of his selectorial colleagues to be his finest hour.

## BOB WYATT

### FIFTH TEST, THE OVAL, 1930

R.B. VINCENT,
CRICKET CORRESPONDENT

*August 18.* At this point R.E.S. Wyatt had to face a trial as severe as any he is likely to undergo. The situation was critical. The success or failure of his side depended for the moment on his own personal achievement. It can hardly have escaped his notice that his appointment as captain had failed to secure universal approval. Finally his appearance on the ground occasioned a demonstration which must have been startling to him, and in some degree unnerving. Every spectator present in the pavilion and in the ring stood up and applauded until he had reached the batting crease. The spectacle must have been wholly gratifying to the Selection Committee. Wyatt was becomingly nervous for the first few overs; he fidgeted when he was not receiving the ball. But nervousness did not affect his technique. In particular it did not cause him to curtail the free lift of his bat and so omit to get his wrists under his striking implement. In the last two hours or so the score was raised from 199 to 316 without further loss, and the jauntiness disappeared from the demeanour of the fielding side.

Sporting
W ENGLAND KEPT ASHES
O GREAT HEARTS OVERTHROW AUSTRALIA
England beat Australia by five wickets in the fourth Test match at Adelaide yesterday and so, gaining a lead of three matches to one in the series, have retained the Ashes. In an interview after the match L. Hutton, the England captain, paid a tribute to the younger members of the side. Much of the credit, he thought, should go to J. B. Statham, F. H. Tyson, M. C. Cowdrey and P. B. H. May, together with the wicket-keeper, T. G. Evans.
From Our Special Correspondent
ADELAIDE, FEB. 2
Many years from now young Cowdrey will point to his broken nose and tell boys yet unborn that he was at Adelaide on February 2, 1955, when England won the Test match and kept the Ashes. And the boys will think him wondrous lucky.
the catch. (We asked Hutton afterwards what he thought of Miller's bowling. Hutton thought Miller ought to concentrate much more on batting.) England 10 for 2. In comes the battered Cowdrey. Miller hits him twice running on the pads and appeals, and everybody here who isn't English appeals too. What a man is Miller. He comes in from a shortish run, loose of limb like an African, hair streaming, and as he pulls up the hair goes on and falls about his face.
Meanwhile May has begun driving, and Johnson has gone from mid-off to square-leg. For Cowdrey Miller brings fine-leg up to third slip, and Cowdrey cover drives classically for 4. Miller heaves his shoulders over even faster, and Cowdrey is taken by Archer at first-slip. England 18 for 3. Four Meteor jets fly over at 200ft.; they look and sound quite tame beside this wild man
England all too obliging
eaches new heights of greatness
One that got away: Gilchrist misses a stumping chance off Warne to give Pietersen an extra life, but it was to make little difference as E
High five: Warne acknowledges the Melbourne crowd after his haul ripped the heart out of England's fragile batting
Sporting News
ENGLAND HAVE LAST WORD
THREE YEOMEN FOIL AUSTRALIA
GREAT STAND BY WATSON AND BAILEY
FROM OUR CRICKET CORRESPONDENT
Out of darkness, through fire into light. Thus did England yesterday rise like some Phoenix from the ashes of apparent defeat to save the second Test match at Lord's
iant leap
for proud S
36 TUESDAY AUGUST 1 1989
England's abject surrender marks new low in series
THE TIMES
Inglorious procession at Old Trafford
SCOREBOARD FROM OLD TRAFFORD
Gower unfairly blamed for failings of others
Border rewarded for hard labour
Only two men so far decline
Was this English c most desperate o
SPORT
Cricket

# AUSTRALIA'S HEROES

## ASHTON AGAR AND PHILLIP HUGHES

### FIRST TEST, TRENT BRIDGE, 2013

MIKE ATHERTON,
CHIEF CRICKET CORRESPONDENT

*July 12.* When Agar came to the crease, Australia had just lost five wickets for nine runs in 32 balls. Graeme Swann, finding some turn from a dry pitch, and James Anderson, in the middle of a superb spell that had brought him his fourteenth five-wicket haul in Tests, were rampant.

Australia, 117 for nine, looked beaten, undermined again by the soft underbelly of a flimsy batting line-up. England were eyeing a significant lead and a day or two on the golf course.

Two-and-a-quarter hours later, after Agar and Phillip Hughes, reminding everyone of the talent that first came to notice with a debut hundred against South Africa, had shattered just about every record possible for a last-wicket partnership in Test cricket – not just the highest for Australia, but the highest for any country – it was England who looked done for and utterly bereft of ideas. One young man, who had only found out about his selection three days ago, had arrived; another had come again. [...]

This England team have cause to be suspicious of No 11s. Last summer, Tino Best flogged them around Edgbaston for 95, but this was a very different type of innings.

Whereas Best's innings was a fluke scored by a genuine 'jack' who chanced his arm, Agar's innings was punctured with classy strokes: a straight six off Swann, the best of them, a cover drive and deft late cut to the fence off the same bowler almost as good, and numerous other thundering drives and pulls off the seamers.

England, captain and bowlers, had no answer as, tall and willowy, Agar picked up his bat and hit straight and hard and fearlessly through the line of the ball. This was the exuberance of youth laid out before us and was a feather in the cap for the Australia selectors.

Nor could England dislodge Hughes, a batsman whom they had previously held in the lowest regard. But he has worked feverishly on his technique, both against spin and pace, so that he is more confident in his defence against the former, and more able to score through the leg side and down the ground against the latter. Hughes surveyed the carnage of the opening hour, and was good enough to survive, and then to flourish, initially in Agar's shadow, and then of his own accord. Hughes finished unbeaten on 81 but left the stage for Agar to soak up the applause of another packed house when the youngster fell two shy of what would have been a remarkable debut hundred.

Aiming a firm pull to leg off Stuart Broad, who had been left out of the attack for 2hr 20min in the morning because of his shoulder, he picked out mid-wicket and managed a rueful smile for what might have been when Swann took a difficult, tumbling catch. It was a magnificent story nonetheless, missing only the punchline, and you would have needed to possess a stone cold heart not to have wanted him to reach three figures.

NEWSPAPER OF THE YEAR

# THE TIMES

Max 29C
Min 9C

Friday July 12 2013 | thetimes.co.uk | No 70935

Only £1

Blood on the dance floor

Fear and loathing at the Bolshoi Times2

## No more tax rises, Osborne pledges

### Chancellor sets battleground for next election

Michael Savage, Francis Elliott

George Osborne fired the first salvo in one of the next election's key battles yesterday by vowing to avoid further tax rises to plug the deficit.

In a move designed to steal a march on both the Liberal Democrats and Labour, the Chancellor said that he would eliminate the £23 billion hole in the public finances after the election by cutting spending.

"I'm clear that tax increases are not required to achieve this," he told the Treasury Select Committee. "This can be achieved through spending reductions. I don't think we have reached the end-point in reforming welfare."

Mr Osborne immediately threw down the gauntlet to Labour. "I'm not sure whether they would do big tax increases," he said. "I suspect they would, but that is for them to explain."

[illegible] fresh assault on the welfare budget should the Tories win a majority in 2015. It will also force Tory ministers to make even deeper cuts in their departments, which have just lost £11.5 billion in last month's spending review.

The Government's austerity programme is mapped out until 2017. Independent experts have calculated that about £6 billion in tax rises would be needed to maintain the current balance between spending cuts and tax increases. But laying down an election pitch yesterday, Mr Osborne said that he would not need tax rises in 2017 and 2018 to make the Government break even.

Speaking at a Westminster lunch yesterday, he also turned his guns on the Lib Dems, who have promised to introduce a mansion tax on homes worth more than £2 million.

"[Deficit reduction] can be delivered by spending savings in welfare and elsewhere and there is no need for tax rises," he said. "The Liberal Democrats are signed up to the path of fiscal consolidation, but not to the 100 per cent spending mix. It's up to them to explain what taxes they are going to put up."

Mr Osborne cheered Tory MPs by promising that a tax break for married couples, championed on his party's back benches, would be announced in the autumn. He rounded off his bullish address with a hint to householders worried about rising interest rates and mortgages. Mark Carney, the Governor of the Bank of England, is expected to indicate that interest rates will remain low for years to come when he unveils a new set of targets early next month.

Since 2010, 80 per cent of the Government's programme to reduce Britain's budget deficit has been made up of spending cuts. Tax rises, such as the increase in VAT, have accounted for the rest. If no further tax rises were announced, spending cuts would have to account for 85 per cent of the deficit reduction package in 2017 and 2018.

Treasury insiders said that Mr Osborne's resistance to using tax rises was partly informed by the difficulties it had created in the past. They pointed to the 2012 Budget, in which small rises on pasties, caravans and charitable

Continued on page 10, col 5

The Australian teenager Ashton Agar reflects after his dismissal on 98 following a multi-record-breaking innings at Trent Bridge. News, page 5; Sport, pages 66-72

## Alarm over Iran's new underground complex

Roger Boyes Diplomatic Editor

A huge new underground labyrinth uncovered by Iranian dissidents is being scrutinised by British and other Western intelligence agencies to determine whether it could be used for nuclear enrichment.

Intelligence sources in London and Europe confirmed yesterday that they have been monitoring the secret construction work. "The plant has been on our radar for some time," said a British government source. It was unlikely to be innocent, the source added.

German intelligence officials said that the site, 45 miles northeast of Tehran, had been tracked since tunnelling began in the mountains in 2006-07.

The latest information has been gathered by the Paris-based National Council of Resistance of Iran, drawing, it says, on informants inside Iran.

The significance of a possible hidden nuclear complex would be to shield it from attack by Israel or the United

### Tehran digs in 'to expand nuclear project'

World, pages 30, 31

States. "Building a facility underground keeps it not just out of view but also protected from a bombing campaign," said Mark Jansson of the Federation of American Scientists.

So far the complex consists of four tunnels, two of them 550 metres long, six giant halls and four warehouses. Iranian dissidents say that the second [illegible] for 30 tunnels.

The strongest indicator that the plant is intended for nuclear enrichment is the involvement of Mohsen Fakhriuzadeh, perhaps the key figure in the Iranian nuclear programme. He is director general of the lead contractor, the Imran Gostaran Mohit company.

Western experts were, however, open minded about the labyrinth. "It could very well be for a military site, but it is not illegal for Iran to develop underground tunnel for military purposes," said Mr Jansson. "There are many underground facilities around Iran." Not all, he said, served Iran's nuclear energy programme.

### IN THE NEWS

**Tagging inquiry**

The Serious Fraud Office is investigating why the security companies G4S and Serco charged up to £50 million to monitor criminals who had died. News, page 4

**BBC cash questions**

A former Barclays chairman is to be questioned by MPs over his role in approving two payoffs for BBC executives that cost licence fee payers £1.4 million. News, page 6

**Wales, by Jupiter**

Scientists from the European Space Agency are using an MoD firing range at Pendine Sands in Wales to simulate a mission to Jupiter's frozen moon, Europa. News, page 17

**Clegg the kingmaker**

Nick Clegg is open to doing a deal with Ed Miliband and is poised to be the kingmaker again after the 2015 general election, argues John Kampfner. Opinion, page 26

Caitlin Moran's Celebrity Watch

Times2

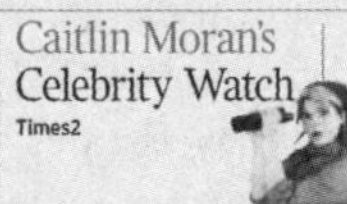

IT MEANS MPS CAN KEEP MORE OF THEIR EXTRA CASH


*Ashton Agar's rueful smile lights up the front page after his heroics at Trent Bridge in 2013*

## RICHIE BENAUD

### FOURTH TEST, OLD TRAFFORD, 1961

JOHN WOODCOCK, CRICKET CORRESPONDENT

*August 1.* How Benaud viewed the prospects of his side as he walked out to inspect the wicket in his blue suede shoes after the crowd had gone I would not care to say. What I do know is that no one relishes a fight like this much more than he.

## ALLAN BORDER

### FOURTH TEST, ADELAIDE, 1990–91

ALAN LEE, CRICKET CORRESPONDENT

*January 29.* Australia's captain is the role model for a team which tolerates only real men with the selfless singlemindedness to play through pain and adversity in search of a common goal. Yesterday, Border batted almost four hours in vivid discomfort to slam the door shut on any fanciful notions of an England win in this fourth Test.

If he erred on the side of caution in extending Australia's lead to 471 before declaring 45 minutes from the close, this was his privilege. Being 2-0 ahead, with one game to play, Border was entitled to believe that bravado was now exclusively England's province.

He had dropped himself down to No.7 in the order to protect the groin strain which might have put lesser mortals out of the game, but at regular stages of his innings he winced, hobbled or doubled up with the pain of the injury. His running, usually such a lively virtue of his batting, was badly impaired.

It must be possible that Border's extraordinary run of 116 consecutive Tests, stretching back 12 years, will end in a prudent rest for the Perth game later this week, if only to ensure his fitness for the upcoming Caribbean tour. But he was positively intent on staying at his post until the present job was completed to his satisfaction and, if he had to do the hard work himself, there were to be no complaints.

### SECOND TEST, LORD'S, 1993

ALAN LEE, CRICKET CORRESPONDENT

*June 19.* Removing Waugh, however, had its drawback for England. Border himself arrived to bat, as ever, in the style his team most needed. He played his shots selflessly, often thrillingly, yet the determination to take a personal memento from his fifth and last Test on this ground was plain. Few in the full-house crowd begrudged him that and, when his vibrant 77 ended in self-destruction just a few minutes from the close, the ground rose to acclaim a fine innings from a great cricketer.

## DON BRADMAN

### THIRD TEST, HEADINGLEY, 1930

R.B. VINCENT,
CRICKET CORRESPONDENT

*July 14.* Bradman while he was batting was wonderful, but the recollection of his innings was a hundred times more wonderful when Hobbs and Sutcliffe were playing definitely inferior bowling. Bradman and Woodfull, and Kippax for that matter, had played ball after ball right on the exact middle of the bat, killing the heart of the pluckiest of bowlers. Hobbs and Sutcliffe, as an opening pair, have never been surpassed, but Bradman has unquestionably set a new standard in batsmanship and when the ball passes Hobbs's bat or hits his pads there is a feeling that even he belongs to a generation which is now learning something quite new. If Bradman had been out to the first ball he received from Tate yesterday, and it was not so very far from hitting his stumps, one would have been quite content with the batting of Hobbs and Sutcliffe today, but as things turned out cold figures and records cannot nearly describe the incalculable superiority of Bradman. Opinion and sympathy may differ as to whether he has made or spoiled this Test match, but he most certainly has controlled it.

**TEST MATCH**

**BRADMAN 309 NOT OUT**

**ALL RECORDS BROKEN**

***The Third Test Match between England and Australia was begun at Leeds yesterday. A. P. F. Chapman, for once, lost the toss and Australia went in to bat on a perfect batsman's wicket. By the end of the day they had scored 458 runs for the loss of three wickets and D. G. Bradman had eclipsed R. E. Foster's record Test Match score, made at Sydney during the 1903-1904 tour, by scoring 309 not out. Bradman has now scored 702 runs in the three Test Matches played during this tour, the most ever made by any Australian batsman in a***

*Bradman's feats in 1930 made the whole of England gasp*

### SECOND TEST, MELBOURNE, 1932–33

ROY CURTHOYS

*January 3.* Bradman was at his best and defied all the bowlers. He gave no chance in scoring another hundred in a Test match. He was never in trouble and dominated the play by the versatility of his strokes. It was remarkable that he hit only seven 4's during his innings, which lasted over three hours and in which he hit all round the wicket. The last five wickets fell for 56 runs, of which Bradman scored 46. When at last he reached his hundred there was one of the greatest demonstrations ever seen on the Melbourne ground and play was suspended for several minutes. He had a great ovation as he returned to the pavilion at the close of the innings.

## FIRST TEST, TRENT BRIDGE, 1938

DUDLEY CAREW

*June 10.* Also they will have Bradman, and the influence Bradman has on the side is not to be assessed by the virtue of his office or of the splendour of his thousand runs. The team seem to take their cue from him as an orchestra takes it from an inspired and trusted conductor.

## FOURTH TEST, HEADINGLEY, 1938

R.B. VINCENT,
CRICKET CORRESPONDENT

*July 25.* It was certain that, if the game were to remain evenly balanced, England's bowlers would have to toil not only manfully but successfully, and that the terrible Bradman would have to be dismissed cheaply. The bowlers did their part magnificently, and they were well supported by the fieldsmen and ably directed by their captain. As to Bradman, I can say no more than that I consider that he was dismissed cheaply. Such prodigious scores are expected of him, and he has given such trouble before on the Headingley ground, in particular, that a mere century can be regarded as a comparative failure. [...]

This brought in Bradman, a Bradman who was not only at first subdued but rather uncomfortable when playing Verity. This period of indecision lasted no more than two overs, and from then onwards Bradman batted with an ease which even for him was almost ridiculous.

## FIFTH TEST, THE OVAL, 1938

R.B. VINCENT,
CRICKET CORRESPONDENT

*August 25.* There was a feeling of unreality when play was begun in the morning, akin to a performance of *Hamlet* without the Prince. Had Bradman been there Australia would still have been struggling against the inevitable, but at least their death agony would have been relieved by a gay and gallant challenge to fate. During that long, and sometimes wearisome period when England were amassing a score which might have run into four figures but for the merciful decision of their captain to declare the innings closed, Bradman's fielding and his continual liveliness of spirit were a reminder that even a time-limitless Test match can provide its measure of enjoyment. His unhappy injury not only denuded the game of all meaning that it had ever possessed, but it robbed us of an opportunity of admiring the greatest of living batsmen in conditions in which he assuredly would have given of his best and most brilliant.

## FIRST TEST, BRISBANE, 1946–47

NEVILLE CARDUS

*November 30.* This time Bradman's opponents are free to wear their rue with a difference, for in the first half-hour of his innings he committed more miscalculations and streakiness than memory holds of all one's experience of him. It was a resurrection innings; even on the doorstep of his hundred he snicked a ball almost fatally through the slips. Australia had lost two wickets for 47, and a quick overthrow of Bradman might well have brought about effects and influence not only decisive in this present engagement but psychologically important in the others to come. By experience and concentration Bradman prevailed; still, the Englishmen have caught another glimpse of a seat of error in him not even conjecturable eight years ago on a good wicket.

## FOURTH TEST, HEADINGLEY, 1948

R.B. VINCENT,
CRICKET CORRESPONDENT

*July 24.* There was a shock when, with the score at only 13, Morris was caught at mid-wicket, supplemented by a greeting which accompanied Bradman all the way to the wicket on the ground on which he had achieved so many a triumph. After an occasional preliminary spar he soon set to work with hooks of perfect certitude, and just for one half-hour one felt that this was indeed Bradman, the Bradman we remembered and not merely a man bearing the same name and wearing the same cap.

## FIFTH TEST, THE OVAL, 1948

R.B. VINCENT,
CRICKET CORRESPONDENT

*August 19.* This then is Bradman's last Test match in this country, suitably recognized yesterday at the Oval by speeches, cheers, and general acknowledgement of a great cricket career. Whether, as was said, he is the greatest cricketer of all time will not be accepted by those who must retain that honour for 'W.G.' Let us say that he is the greatest of the present age, and can rank with Trumper, Ranji, Macartney, and Hobbs. Surely that is in all conscience sufficient praise.

JOHN WOODCOCK

*August 12, 1989* ... Bradman's innings, his wife once told me, used to start as soon as he woke up. It was then that the concentration began. He had business to attend to.

## PETER BURGE

### FIFTH TEST, THE OVAL, 1961

JOHN WOODCOCK,
CRICKET CORRESPONDENT

*August 21.* This was Burge's maiden century in a Test match since he first played for Australia seven years ago. He is a rugged, gum-chewing character, thickset and confident. Harvey may perform like a piece of quicksilver, O'Neill like a natural games player, Benaud like a suave and seasoned all-rounder; Burge could be a light-heavyweight boxer, or a foreman on a Queensland sheep station.

Moreover, he can adapt his game to a situation. When, against West Indies recently, Benaud asked him at a critical time to go in and hit the bowlers off a length, he did so, even though he had been out of favour with the Australian selectors. On Friday he was a perfect foil for O'Neill. On Saturday he showed sound judgment in keeping Australia on the move. His innings lasted for close on seven hours and included 22 fours.

## GREG CHAPPELL

### FIFTH TEST, THE OVAL, 1977

JOHN WOODCOCK,
CRICKET CORRESPONDENT

*August 29.* This meant that the scores at which Greg Chappell, batting at No 3, has come in in the present series have been 27, 5, 4, 0, 79, 18, 8, 31, and 0.

On Saturday he had scarcely time to get his pads on before he was cheered all the way to the wicket as the crowd's farewell to a marvellously gifted player. If a memorial ever has to be raised to those players lost in the great TV hijack of 1977, Chappell's name will stand out with perhaps a dozen others (and that is a high proportion) as having been a player capable of greatness.

His record against England hardly reflects just how good he is. In 45 innings, excluding his present one, he has scored 1,768 runs at an average of 42. At his best he has been as beautifully balanced, as unhurried and as neat a batsman as one will see. Having served a part of his apprenticeship with Somerset, in 1968 and 1969, he was already a player of some experience by the time he scored 108, batting at No 7, in his first Test match, against Ray Illingworth's side at Perth.

Though never one to complain, he may not always since then have been in the best of health. That could be the reason for his averaging 42 rather than 55, for he has been for most of his time in a winning Australian side and there is no questioning his temperament or technique.

As Chappell walked out on Saturday the brief touching of his cap with which he acknowledged the applause (others would have had their bats aloft all the way), the brisk step, the upright carriage, the well-groomed appearance, were all in keeping with the standards he has gone by. In a game of declining manners I have practically never seen him, outwardly at any rate, compromise his character. If this really is the end of his Test career it is not only as a batsman that his example will be missed.

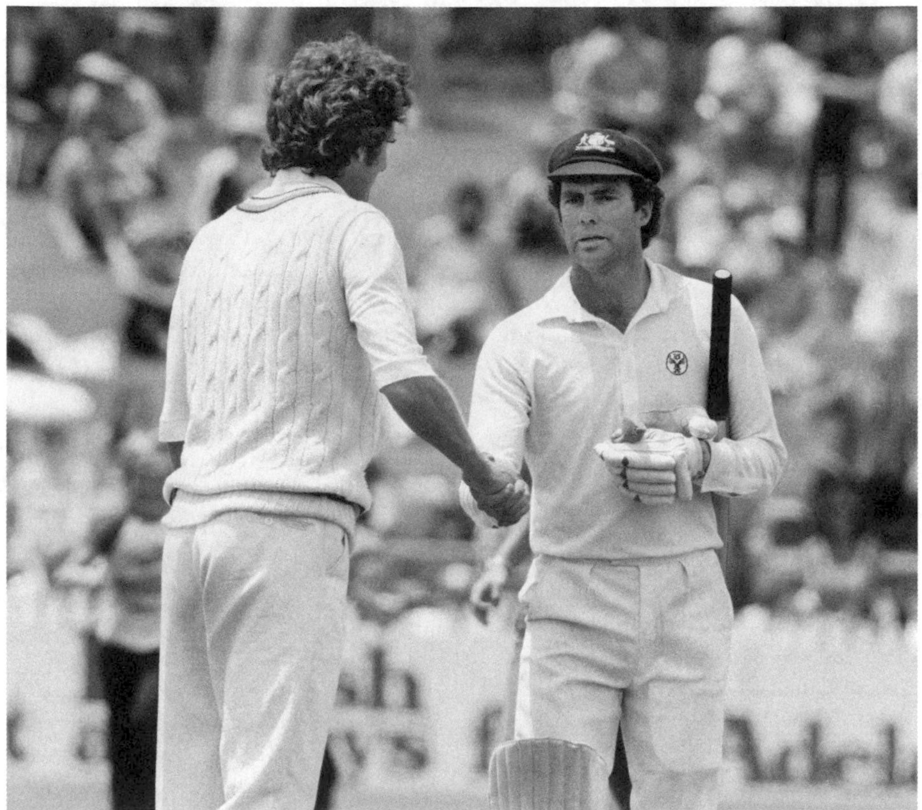

*England captain Bob Willis congratulates Greg Chappell, his opposite number, on his century in the third Test at the Adelaide Oval in 1982–83*

## JOE DARLING

### FOURTH TEST, OLD TRAFFORD, 1905

R.H. LYTTELTON

*July 26.* There was nothing to be said of the Australian batting except a plucky stand by the two last men, Mr Laver in particular playing well, and the hitting of Mr Darling. As an exhibition of plucky and fierce hitting few innings have excelled this effort of Mr Darling's. He was, no doubt, very lucky, being missed four times, but his hitting was splendid. Four mighty drives were sent a long way over the ropes, and he almost savagely went for nearly every ball which was the least over-tossed. His innings fairly roused the crowd to enthusiasm, and all the time his colleagues were giving him very feeble assistance. The boundary was about 90 yards from the wicket, and one hit nearly went into the press-box, and two of the chances he did give were off clean and fairly low drives. He was finally well caught by Tyldesley, who judged a very high hit very well, and the innings was brought to an end at half-past 4 for 197.

## ROSS EDWARDS

### THIRD TEST, TRENT BRIDGE, 1972

JOHN WOODCOCK, CRICKET CORRESPONDENT

*July 18.* This is only Edwards's second Test match. A dapper, pipe-smoking accountant, he is a neat, quick-footed batsman, whose particular joy is the cut. He reminds me rather of Brian Booth, who made so many runs for Australia in the same quiet and efficient way. At 29, Edwards is old for an Australian making his mark in Test cricket, but he can look forward to a regular place for some time now. His 170 not out was chanceless. It took him five hours and three quarters and contained 14 fours.

## BRAD HADDIN

### THIRD TEST, PERTH, 2013–14

MIKE ATHERTON, CHIEF CRICKET CORRESPONDENT

*December 14.* After George Bailey had hooked tamely to deep backward-square leg, Smith was joined by Brad Haddin, who is having almost as much of an impact upon this series as Mitchell Johnson. Australia have been lucky in this department as Adam Gilchrist, fêted at tea-time during his induction into the ICC's Hall of Fame, reminded us. Haddin may not be quite as good a wicketkeeper as Ian Healy, nor as good a batsman as Gilchrist, but he does not bend his knee to either as a doughty competitor.

While Johnson milks the publicity in this series – before the opening day, the local newspaper printed cut-out Johnson moustaches – Haddin's understated influence has been central to Australia's revival. He made vital, match-turning contributions with the bat in Adelaide and Brisbane, and knuckled down here to haul his team out of trouble again, and now he joined Smith in the day's defining partnership of 124.

## LINDSAY HASSETT

### FIFTH TEST, THE OVAL, 1948

R.B. VINCENT, CRICKET CORRESPONDENT

*August 19.* And there has been Hassett, as welcome and popular a cricketer on every ground in this country as ever Australia sent to us. That air of detachment, while in effect taking the fullest share in the conduct of the game, belongs to Hassett, and Hassett alone. In truth a charming cricketer, and let us hope that when Australia visit us again he will captain the side.

## MERV HUGHES

### FIRST TEST, OLD TRAFFORD, 1993

ALAN LEE, CRICKET CORRESPONDENT

*June 8.* With McDermott malfunctioning, the burden fell more onerously than ever on Merv Hughes to provide penetration through pace. He rose to the task and more, taking eight wickets with the familiar unsubtle variety act of which, now, not even the most disapproving should deride. There is quality behind the bluff and bluster and, if his verbal abuse of batsmen remains constantly unattractive, his bowling is a formidable proposition.

## SIXTH TEST, THE OVAL, 1993

ALAN LEE, CRICKET CORRESPONDENT

*August 23.* The innings was wound up by Warne and Hughes. The leg spinner won another leg-before verdict as Such played down the wrong line and Ramprakash, sensing that time was short, made room to carve Hughes head-high to mid off. Hughes, so tired he was beyond celebrating, dragged himself to the pavilion gate, sweater slung over his massive shoulders, then paused to shake the hands of his wicketkeeper and his three fellow bowlers.

*In 1993 it became increasingly obvious that Merv Hughes was more than just a caricature of an Australian fast bowler*

At times, Hughes is a preposterous figure, something between pantomime villain and school bully, but his input to Australia's success in this series has been immense. Robbed of his partner, McDermott, in only the second Test, he has answered Allan Border's every call, although sometimes it has seemed his legs could not support one more delivery. He has finished with 31 wickets, Warne with 34, and they have been the difference between the teams.

# MICHAEL HUSSEY

## SECOND TEST, ADELAIDE, 2010–11

GIDEON HAIGH

*December 4.* Again, the go-to guy Hussey was gone-to. His arms no longer send a tremor down Australian spines, as it did in England last year, and his defensive bat now seems to descend in ample time, and almost to be waiting for the ball. As at his zenith, he is acquiring busily, advancing a few paces with every nudge and nurdle, as though a single is his default setting. Shortly before tea, he worked Finn to leg and set off at such a gallop that he almost lapped his partner in completing three.

## ALAN KIPPAX

### SECOND TEST, LORD'S, 1930

R.B. VINCENT,
CRICKET CORRESPONDENT

*July 1.* But every now and again one got through, and every now and again their threat to run in made White pitch short, and that meant four somewhere between long-on and long-leg. Bradman was the more efficient and frequent hooker of the two batsmen. In every other department Kippax was his equal in efficiency, his superior in grace. Since Hammond lost something of the stylishness which distinguished him in his freshman's year, we have seen no such graceful attitudes as those into which Kippax flows in making his strokes.

## JUSTIN LANGER

### FIFTH TEST, THE OVAL, 2001

CHRISTOPHER MARTIN-JENKINS,
CHIEF CRICKET CORRESPONDENT

*August 24.* Henry Lawson, most revered of the early Australian poets, first suggested a phrase long ago for players such as Justin Langer. The epitome of 'the great little Aussie battler', he responded to his first opportunity of the series by making a century in the fifth Test that sent the clearest of messages to those who had left him out of the side. His opening partnership of 158 with Matthew Hayden, much the largest of the series, put Australia firmly in the box seat again yesterday, setting up fluent innings by Ricky Ponting and Mark Waugh. [...]

In making 102 before retiring hurt, Langer showed both his sterling character and the unyielding vigilance of his batting method. No contemporary batsman smells the leather quite like he does, playing the ball under his feet whether he has rocked back to stop a short one or danced down to the pitch of the ball against a spinner. He it was who was chiefly responsible for taking the initiative away from Phil Tufnell on a white featherbed of a pitch taking spin already.

*The archetypal Aussie battler Justin Langer takes one for the team at Edgbaston in 2005*

# DENNIS LILLEE

## FIRST TEST, OLD TRAFFORD, 1972

JACK FINGLETON

*June 13.* Lillee's six wickets will put a lot of ginger into this series from now on, more so if the Australians scramble out of this one.

I recall seeing Lillee at Nottingham when that game was abandoned. He appeared in a tracksuit and did six circuits of the ground in heavy rain. Those gentlemen who gather early in the morning at the Covent Garden Markets might have recognized Lillee. They used to see him at the end of April padding around London's streets to get fit.

Nobody has worked harder. His original back trouble concerned him so much that one wondered whether some of it wasn't psychological and might disappear when he began to get wickets. Some judged him harshly midway through May, but a fast bowler would be unwise to try to force himself early in the summer when the cold gives rise to slow pitches and pulled muscles.

Lillee has enjoyed the perfect Test triumph here and his success will inspire him to deeds just as bright in the future. He knows now that he is of Test calibre. He doubted himself before, for all that he got five wickets in Adelaide in his first Test against Illingworth's side. He played in two Tests of that series. He is no longer the new boy, although he is not yet 23. He ran in more smoothly yesterday, not striving and straining as he has been doing.

# RAY LINDWALL

## FIFTH TEST, SYDNEY, 1954–55

JOHN WOODCOCK, CRICKET CORRESPONDENT

*March 3* ... and it was when Lindwall bowled Bailey, with the last ball before England's declaration, that the spectators were given what they had been anxiously awaiting.

Lindwall is one of their own, in that he is a New South Wales man only recently exiled in Queensland, and everyone sensed that if he is not picked to visit England next season this would be his last chance of reaching his target. They realized, too, that Hutton would almost certainly declare at tea time, and anyone with superstition in the blood was keeping a couple of fingers crossed when Lindwall began to bowl the last over of the afternoon with only one wicket to get.

The batsmen seemed as keen as anyone that Lindwall should succeed, but off the first ball Davidson dropped a steepling hit at deep mid-on. For four balls then Bailey and Wardle tried unsuccessfully to get out, until the former ensured that he was bowled by the sixth ball of the over. Lindwall, one is certain, would have liked to have got his last wicket the hard way, and without the rain he would probably have needed no help from sentiment. As it was, he did, but the generosity of his reception was not the less for it.

Trumble, Noble, Griffen, Grimmett, O'Reilly, and Turner make up the list of eminent Australian bowlers which Lindwall joins. None approached Lindwall's speed and no one will question his right to a place among such great names. He has taken only five series to climb the ladder – O'Reilly took but four – and through that time he has gradually and subtly built up a mastery of his art. If that mastery is not now quite what it was, he is still the bowler whom Englishmen respect perhaps more than any other.

## KEN MACKAY

### SECOND TEST, LORD'S, 1956

JOHN WOODCOCK,
CRICKET CORRESPONDENT

*June 23.* Mackay now entered, chewing away, his knees occasionally making contact with each other, his toes turned in, his technique equally mystic. His bat hangs loosely in his grasp, his backlift is not detectable, and his first movement is a backward shuffle. It may be a long time before his like is seen, and his purpose now was to attach himself to one end while runs came at the other. He, as it happened, played his cautious part quite adequately, having a fair ration of luck, deflecting occasionally, hooking once, and driving for four twice.

### FIRST TEST, EDGBASTON, 1961

JOHN WOODCOCK,
CRICKET CORRESPONDENT

*June 12.* It was only unfortunate that Saturday's full house should have been committed to grey, dispiriting skies and to a long look, not at Harvey and O'Neill, but at Mackay. Mackay is an economy cricketer. Between him and Harvey is the difference between the parsimonious days of war and the extravagant days of peace. His boundary strokes are made with no backlift and little follow-through. For their power they depend upon timing. He edges the ball so often between slip and gully with an open blade that it is not always accidental.

At the wicket he is full of mannerisms, like a man doing various mimes for a television panel. He chews eagerly, and holds the bat as though taking guard. As a lawn tennis player he might be a tireless baseline retriever; as a golfer his short game would probably drive his opponents to distraction. As an all-round cricketer of considerable character he is having a most effective Test match, and his innings of 64, peculiar though it may have been, was not especially slow.

## ROD MARSH

### FIRST TEST, OLD TRAFFORD, 1972

JACK FINGLETON

*June 14.* Marsh's innings was an epic. Last year against Illingworth's team he made 92 not out in Melbourne and Lawry, who then declared, has never since been in danger of getting the Freedom of the City of Perth. Marsh was on the verge again yesterday of becoming the first Australian wicketkeeper to make a Test century against England. This innings of 91 will never be forgotten by those who saw it. It was a blaze of brilliance over two hours. It yielded rich red blood when not only did the Australian innings need an immediate transfusion but also the spirit of Australian cricket. [...]

Greig yesterday got in Stackpole's way with Marsh, then 12, over half-way down the pitch. Boycott most gallantly held the ball and Marsh scrambled back. What an innings we would have missed had it been otherwise.

Marsh, as he so richly proved yesterday, is worth his place in this side as a top batsman. His first innings was a slather-and-hack affair but yesterday he was full of composure. His bat is always straight, unlike those of a few others and he drives beautifully. He uses top and bottom hand, the top dominating in his power shots. His four sixes were beautifully struck, in the family tradition. His brother Graham is one of Australia's leading golfers, recently topping the Asian circuit. He is coming for the Open.

## KEITH MILLER

### FOURTH TEST, HEADINGLEY, 1953

GEOFFREY GREEN,
CRICKET CORRESPONDENT

*July 24.* At the end Evans, after being missed off Lindwall at nought, was still there with Lock at his side to end a grim day lightened only once when Miller, after being refused an l.b.w. appeal, performed a new form of hat trick as he lifted umpire Chester's homburg from his head in mock retaliation.

### FOURTH TEST, ADELAIDE, 1954–55

STEWART HARRIS

*January 29.* After tea Miller took an over from Tyson that made superb cricket. It was a maiden, and as Tyson ambled back for each ball Miller stood cross-legged in the sunshine, hand on hip, elegant, nonchalant, waiting, and once Tyson flung a full toss at his chest and Miller smote it down and back at Tyson viciously.

## BERT OLDFIELD

### FIFTH TEST, THE OVAL, 1930

R.B. VINCENT,
CRICKET CORRESPONDENT

*August 19.* Wyatt also fell to an even more spectacular catch by W.A.S. Oldfield when he glanced a leg ball from Fairfax and Oldfield anticipated the stroke. This began the end of England's innings, though Larwood batted in capital form for a while. Appropriately enough, Oldfield secured a third victim. His wicket-keeping has been a feature of the play. It has been as efficient as stylish, and he has earned full marks by the courtesy with which he has addressed occasional questions to the umpires and accepted their answers.

## BILL O'REILLY

### SECOND TEST, LORD'S, 1938

R.B. VINCENT,
CRICKET CORRESPONDENT

*June 27.* England had certainly not made as many runs as was expected of them, and heads wagged when their owners said that the total of 494 was by no means big enough. That it was not greater was due to O'Reilly, who bowled like a lion throughout the innings. He was always ready for work and more work, was continually attacking the batsmen, and an analysis of four wickets for 93 does not begin to do him justice.

# RICKY PONTING

## FOURTH TEST, HEADINGLEY, 1997

SIMON WILDE

*July 24.* ... Ponting, 22, is a gifted batsman, the youngest and perhaps potentially the best of Australia's new generation, and it could be argued that, if he takes his chance, he will stay in the side for years to come. In about 100 first-class innings, he has scored 17 centuries, a one-in-six ratio that few players of his age have matched.

He is, then, no stop-gap replacement. Indeed, the surprise is that he was not in the team already, but therein lies the tale, for Ponting has been handed the 'boy wonder' tag that every talented young Australian batsman should dread. For years, such precocious youths were hailed, wholly unreasonably, as 'the next Bradman' and few survived the ordeal. Now, the icons are less forbidding, but the burden remains irksome.

*Ricky Ponting, Australia's greatest batsman since Bradman according to some judges, after a net at Headingley in 1997*

## FIRST TEST, BRISBANE, 2006–07

CHRISTOPHER MARTIN-JENKINS
CHIEF CRICKET CORRESPONDENT

*November 24.* To anyone watching closely as Australia held their last practice session in and around the nets at the Gabba before yesterday's triumphant opening to the Ashes series by the home team, it was obvious that Ricky Ponting was honed to the minute like a thoroughbred for the biggest race of his life.

Just before he faced the media for the umpteenth time in the past two weeks, the home captain spent some 20 minutes, without a second's break, diving and scrabbling with astonishing agility and amazing hand-eye co-ordination as Australia's American fielding coach, Mike Young, hurled a hard rubber cricket ball at a plastic step from which the ball rebounded at all angles. Ponting never fumbled, never looked like missing a catch.

England felt the full impact of his intense preparation, physical sharpness, natural skill and profound determination to gain the earliest possible revenge for last year's defeat as he scored his ninth hundred in Australia's past 12 Tests.

## FIRST TEST, BRISBANE, 2010–11

MIKE ATHERTON,
CHIEF CRICKET CORRESPONDENT

*November 30.* What we did see, though, at the end was just how tough the Australia captain is: despite two horror days in the field, he strode out to bat, shoulders back and jaw jutting out, as confidently as ever. 'To be the benchmark of resilience' is how Steve Waugh once described the job of the Australia captain and Ponting fulfils that role remarkably.

# MICHAEL SLATER

## FIFTH TEST, THE OVAL, 2001

CHRISTOPHER MARTIN-JENKINS
CHIEF CRICKET CORRESPONDENT

*August 23.* Slater's absence will lessen the spectacle. If this is the end of him after 74 Tests in which he has scored 5,312 runs at 42, with seven of his 14 hundreds against England, he will be remembered as one of the great entertainers. Had he scored more than 176 runs in this series (six more than Hayden and 77 of them in his influential first innings at Edgbaston), his individualism within a closely knit team would have been overlooked. Like Butcher he is great company, enjoys himself off the field and plays all the strokes on it.

Slater was admonished after a tantrum on the field in India and fined after missing a bus on this tour, although he has officially been dropped on form. The media awaits him with open arms as it does the estimable Michael Atherton.

# STEVEN SMITH

## THIRD TEST, PERTH, 2013–14

MIKE ATHERTON,
CHIEF CRICKET CORRESPONDENT

*December 14.* Steven Smith felt the final ball of the 77th over on the middle of his bat and let out a yelp of joy. He knew the moment was his; the moment, perhaps, when the public's – and England's – view of him changed. No longer an unreliable rookie, no longer a skittish, inconsistent player of promise, but an established performer who could be relied upon in a crisis.

The ball from Ben Stokes whistled away to the mid-wicket boundary. It was the thirteenth four of Smith's four-hour innings, to go with two sixes he had collected earlier, and he ran to the non-striker's end, jumping and thrashing his arms wildly in a manner not unlike Michael Clarke, almost a decade ago in Bangalore when Australia's present captain had announced his arrival with a debut century.

*Steven Smith just makes it home at Sydney in 2010–11*

## MARK TAYLOR

### FIRST TEST, HEADINGLEY, 1989

ANDREW LONGMORE

*June 9.* Mark Taylor may be a new name to most English spectators, but not to devotees of the Bolton League. Last season, the New South Wales left-hander who was schooled in Wagga Wagga before becoming a surveyor scored 1,300 runs to lead Greenmount to the league title and the experience helped him on his Test debut in England yesterday.

'It taught me to play cricket in freezing cold weather,' he said. 'It also helped me adapt, because, though the wickets in league cricket are obviously much worse than in Tests, they are all slower than I am used to back home.'

Apart from ample concentration and a sweet cover-drive, Taylor's greatest asset was that he did not treat the Headingley pitch as if it were a minefield. He'd only ever seen it on television and so was not tainted by its wicked reputation.

'The pitch is not too bad. There is a little uneven bounce and it's not easy to score runs quickly, but if the batsmen applies himself he will score runs.'

On a day of gambles, Taylor's long bout of self-denial at least bore out the Australians' surprising decision to break up the highly successful opening partnership of David Boon and Geoff Marsh. Since they came together in adversity five years ago, Boon and Marsh have developed into one of the most effective, if not the prettiest, opening partnerships in Test cricket.

### FIRST TEST, EDGBASTON, 1997

JOHN WOODCOCK

*June 9.* Only the most jaundiced of Englishmen could not have been pleased for Mark Taylor at Edgbaston over the weekend. After all that he has been through, and the pressure to which he was subjected, his 129 in Australia's second innings was a heroic effort.

He saved his own neck, if not his side's, and he did it without any show of triumphalism. As captain's innings go it must rank with the very best. Not even Allan Border in his 93 Tests in charge played a better one for Australia.

All the criticism of Taylor in the past month or so has seemed to me to be out of place. That his run of poor form was unsettling the Australia party became fairly clear, but it was the selectors who chose him, not the captain himself, who should have been the target of the critics.

Now theirs and the captain's agony is over. Taylor is good for Test cricket. We shall have to forgive him his gum chewing, manic as it is, for in other ways he has a generosity and level-headedness that it is not easy to maintain at this level, whether under fire from the press or in adversity in the middle. He is not quite a great player, but he is a very good and stubborn one.

## SHANE WARNE

### SIXTH TEST, THE OVAL, 1993

JOHN WOODCOCK

*August 19.* It is hardly conceivable that the modern English game could have spawned Shane Warne. That is partly because he has had the advantage in Australia of learning his trade in a more favourable climate and on faster, bouncier pitches. But there is more to stimulate him in the way the game is played there.

He is a freak, too, which helps. I doubt whether there has ever been another bowler who possessed such prodigious powers of spin, and yet gave so few runs away, as Warne.

Wrist spinners with anything like the same accuracy have mostly been rollers of the ball; those who have really spun it have invariably been more prodigal. After the last Test match, Allan Border said that England's batsmen are being too cautious in the way they play Warne and that they should be going down the pitch to him. That was how Lindsay Hassett came to be such a bane to Bill O'Reilly, more so than anyone else O'Reilly bowled against.

### THIRD TEST, OLD TRAFFORD, 2005

RICHARD HOBSON

*August 12.* For once in the life of Shane Warne there appeared to be no dramas. His Hollywood scriptwriter would have invented something special for a 600th wicket. First ball, certainly. A brilliant caught and bowled, perhaps. Or maybe a first victim of some wicked new ball hatched at morning nets. The pathos emerged only later.

Warne had plugged away for 28 balls before the 29th went into the gloves of Adam Gilchrist, via the back of Marcus Trescothick's bat. The bowler immediately raised his arms and kissed a wristband that he revealed had been given to him by Brooke, his older daughter, before the family left for Australia after the breakdown of his marriage. [...]

There are many remarkable aspects of his career. Not least is the way that he continues to baffle batsmen when so much technology is available to scrutinise his work. Opponents have been flippered, googled and zooted to their downfall. Most of all, they have succumbed to a leg break that can still turn several feet.

### FOURTH TEST, TRENT BRIDGE, 2005

SIMON BARNES

*August 27.* Watch him appealing. Warne has never been diffident when asking the overwhelming question, but as the series has developed he has taken appealing to a new pitch of intensity. He was always a ten for volume (perhaps even a Spinal Tap 11) but he has added an element of length.

He holds the note of interrogation for about 16 bars, like the fat one in The Three Tenors, agonising, beseeching, demanding. He has lost all shame, all embarrassment, nothing matters to him any more except wickets. A man with fewer than 600 Test wickets may have known official reproof, for Warne is taking the players' code to the limit and beyond.

It's vibe that saves him. He is not cheating, he is not trying to get something for nothing, he is not trying to intimidate. He is just mad.

Mad with desperation for a victory that he can increasingly feel slipping from his sandpaper fingers. He is not really addressing the umpire, he is howling to Job's God to cease the torment and return the world to his accustomed order, ie, Australia beating England by a considerable margin.

## FIFTH TEST, THE OVAL, 2005

CHRISTOPHER MARTIN-JENKINS
CHIEF CRICKET CORRESPONDENT

*September 9.* It is often said that geniuses are weak vessels who sow the seeds of their own destruction. Warne the cricketer is as weak as Hercules: his talent is backed by as indomitable a will as any cricketer in the Ashes has ever possessed.

## FOURTH TEST, MELBOURNE, 2006–07

CHRISTOPHER MARTIN-JENKINS
CHIEF CRICKET CORRESPONDENT

*December 27.* Shane Warne must seriously have been wondering last night if he has done the right thing [in retiring]. It is hard to think that he has ever had a much easier five-wicket haul than the 37th of his Boy's Own career or that England, against whom he has prospered from start to finish of his extraordinary journey in Test cricket, have ever been quite such willing accomplices to his peerless act. The audience, at 89,155 some 6,000 fewer than had bought tickets, was smaller than expected, kept at home by the threat of rain and a biting wind from the Antarctic, but the star played his part to perfection.

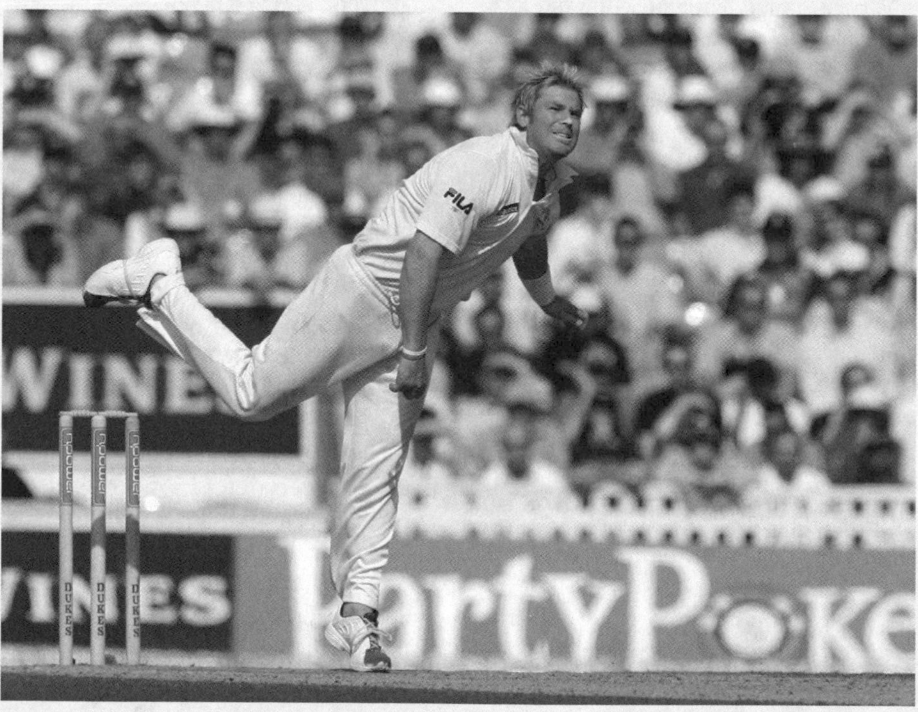


*Shane Warne took an extraordinary 40 wickets in a losing cause in the 2005 series*

## STEVE WAUGH

### FIRST TEST, HEADINGLEY, 1989

ALAN LEE, CRICKET CORRESPONDENT

*June 10.* After the anaesthetist, the surgery. England, numbed to near-impotence on day one, yesterday suffered the surgeon's knife in their exposed wound. Last night's bulletin could give no guarantee that they would recover.

Painfully short of manoeuvrability with their stereotyped attack, they had arguably been batted out of this first Cornhill Test by Mark Taylor's maiden century. But the longer the second day went on, the worse their predicament became.

Steve Waugh illuminated a grey Yorkshire scene with the first of what will surely be many Test hundreds, carrying his country to their highest total on this ground since 1934, when they totalled 584 and a man named Bradman scored 304.

Waugh was majestic, mixing effortlessly timed on-side strokes with savage square drives off either foot. The crowd, twice the size of Thursday's and several times as noisy, warmed to him, and eventually Waugh abandoned his intensely deadpan demeanour. He has waited 27 Tests for this century, which is every bit as strange as the uncomfortable time it took Mike Gatting to score his first for England.

When it came, just before tea, this dapper 24-year-old, probably destined to captain Australia, punched the air and danced down the wicket waving his bat. For him this was the height of demonstrative behaviour.

Waugh has a technique any schoolboy could profitably copy, but correctness has not stifled his flair. His century came from only 124 balls and, in an object lesson of selectivity, hardly a loose ball was allowed to go unpunished.

ANDREW LONGMORE

*June 10.* Half an hour after the close of play, Steve Waugh was signing autographs for a group of delighted youths outside the Headingley pavilion. Nothing surprising about that, except that Waugh was still wearing his whites and baggy green cap. This was a day one young Australian did not want to end. And who can blame him?

Since he made his Test debut at the age of 20 four years ago, Waugh has been saddled with some extravagant comparisons; his delight yesterday was not just for his long-awaited maiden Test century but for the glimpse of fulfilment. With his craggy features, matter-of-fact manner and classical technique, it did not seem such a hard act to follow Jackson, Bradman and McCabe.

Sporting

OW ENGLAND KEPT TH

ASHES

WO GREAT HEARTS OVERTHROW AUSTRALIA

England beat Australia by five wickets in the fourth Test match at delaide yesterday and so, gaining a lead of three matches to one in the eries, have retained the Ashes. In an interview after the match L. Hutton, he England captain, paid a tribute to the younger members of the side. Much of the credit, he thought, should go to J. B. Statham, F. H. Tyson, M. C. Cowdrey and P. B. H. May, together with the wicket-keeper, T. G. Evans.

From Our Special Correspondent

ADELAIDE, FEB. 2

Many years from now young Cowdrey will point to his broken nose and tell boys yet unborn that he was at Adelaide on February 2, 1955, when England won the Test match and kept the Ashes. And the boys will think him wondrous lucky. A ma... should dip his pen in blood to write ... this day. Let no one talk and writ... ...ket and explain away the ... ...ms more fit for ... ...al in dull ...

the catch. (We asked Hutton afterwards what he thought of Miller's bowling. Hutton thought Miller ought to concentrate much more on batting.) England 10 for 2. In comes the battered Cowdrey. Miller hits him twice running on the pads and appeals, and everybody here who isn't English appeals too. What a man is Miller. He comes in from a shortish run, loose of limb like an African, hair streaming, and as he pulls up the hair goes on and falls about his face.

Meanwhile May has begun driving, and Johnson has gone from mid-off to square-leg. For Cowdrey Miller brings fine-leg up to third slip, and Cowdrey cover drives classically for 4. Miller heaves his shoulders over even faster, and Cowdrey is taken by Archer at first-slip. England 18 for 3. Four Meteor jets fly over at 200ft.; they look and sound quite tame beside this wild man ... His figures now are 3 overs, no ...2 runs, 3 wickets.

ngland all too obliging ...
eaches new heights of greatnes

One that got away: Gilchrist misses a stumping chance off Warne to give Pietersen an extra life, but it was to make little difference

...legendary accuracy and a lush outfield, they ran poorly between the wickets, chose the wrong balls to try to hit in the air and failed to justify the decision to bat.

"We didn't expect conditions to change dramatically over the first day and a half," Strauss said, "but it seamed about more than we expected." It did so slowly but Glenn McGrath, Stuart Clark and Brett Lee all got enough past the bat to suggest that the wrong option had been taken.

Australia missed two catches, two clear run-out opportunities and a gaping stumping, but still bowled England out for 159 after they had been 101 for two. Very few Test matches are won after such a start. All of Warne's wickets were taken by flight and dip, as batsmen spied what they believed to be boundary opportunities. Only Kevin Pietersen got anywhere near the boundary as he attempted to drive Warne straight for six, but by now he was, as usual, batting with the tail.

Even he needed 70 balls for 21 runs, having come close to running out Andrew Flintoff for six as, for the third Test in succession, he attempted a ridiculous single in order to get off the mark. He had only made four when he also survived a simple stumping chance offered to Adam Gilchrist after charging Warne and missing.

England, we all know, have too long a tail, but tweaking it made no difference. Matthew Hoggard is back where he started, No 11, pushing Monty Panesar and Stephen Harmison up a place each, which reflects their various abilities with the bat. It is higher up, however, that the balance is wrong. Ed Joyce or Jamie Dalrymple should have played...

six, but Chris Read for Geraint Jones was the only change.

As the best player in the team, Pietersen needs to bat at four. Since Paul Collingwood shared the only partnership of any substance with Strauss — 57 for the third wicket — it may appear that England's strategy, to keep him away from the new ball, had worked again, but to have Pietersen batting with the tail repeatedly is not satisfactory. In any case Collingwood might have been leg-before to Clark for nought, one of four apparently plumb leg-before decisions turned down by Rudi Koertzen.

Panesar was the other, ...ly out to Warne before ... out instead, but it was turned down when ... Hayden was hit on front of the stu... gard, the first w... the other whe... more signif... captain's ... when Ju... ball ... seco...

Australia's recent practice of not using a nightwatchman.

Ponting said that Australia, too, would have chosen to bat first, but it was one of those tosses that either captain would prefer to have lost. Play was delayed by rain for half an hour and only 16 overs were bowled before an early lunch was taken, Alastair Cook ...

High five: Warne acknowledges the Melbourne crowd after his haul ripped the heart out of England's fragile batting

Sporting News

ENGLAND HAVE LAST WORD

THREE YEOMEN FOIL AUSTRALIA

GREAT STAND BY WATSON AND BAILEY

FROM OUR CRICKET CORRESPONDENT

Out of darkness, through fire into light. Thus did England yesterday rise like some Phoenix from the ashes of apparent defeat to save the second Test match at Lord's and so gain a ... draw against Australia with ... seven wickets, ... original aim fo...

The age of ... yet past, nor c... cany scarce fo... dramatic and ... a match alrea... But within t... longest and m... of a match it... that last spa... back with le... yeomen of ... nearly the w...

The yeom... were Watso... greatest of ... Yorkshirem... order, was ... rearguard ... twentieth ...

...iant leap

for proud S...

THE HUNDRED UP.—...

36 TUESDAY AUGUST 1 1989

THE TIMES

England's abject surrender marks new low in series

Inglorious procession at Old Trafford

10-1: Curtis c Boon b Alderman 0

25-2: Robinson lbw b Lawson 12

27-3: Smith c Healy b Alderman 1

38-4: Gatting c Alderman b Lawson 13

SCOREBOARD FROM OLD TRAFFORD

Gower unfairly blamed for failings of others

Simon Barnes

Border rewarded for hard labour

Only two men so far decline

Was this English c... most desperate ...

# FLASHPOINTS

THE TIMES SATURDAY JUNE 11 1938

H: A GOOD BEGINNING BY ENGLAND

4

Sporting News

LAKER'S SUPREME PART IN RETAINING THE ASHES

ALL TEN AUSTRALIAN WICKETS AND 19 IN MATCH

From Our Cricket Correspondent

England won the fourth Test match against Australia at Old ...

pitch perked up and the ball showed signs of misbehaving.

At luncheon McDonald and Craig were still together. They had then added only 59, but the important thing was that they had each been batting for more than four hours. Ahead of them stretched another four and only 15 minutes of these had ticked away when Laker struck ...

THE TIMES

LOCOMEN'S BAN BOUND TO CAUSE GREATER ...

HOW THE AUSTRALIANS WERE SKITTLED OUT AT LORD'S

Gaullists may get back with clear majority

Inquiry over bank chief's salary

Police alerted by strike ship

Railways must act alone, Marsh says

... stumped aiming to hit Mallett over the hill, and the end draws nearer.

... dismally surrender Ashes

TEST MATCH

BRADMAN 309 NOT OUT

ALL RECORDS BROKEN

*The Third Test Match between England and Australia was begun at Leeds yesterday. A. P. F. Chapman, for once, lost the toss and Australia went in to bat on a perfect batsman's wicket. By the end of the day they had scored 458 runs for the loss of three wickets ...*

## ONLY TEST, THE OVAL, 1882

*August 30*. With the score at 113, Mr Murdoch hit a ball to leg, which was fielded by Mr Lyttelton, who threw it at the wicket; the object was missed, and the ball went to Dr Grace, who as Mr Jones was out of his ground, put the wicket down, the batsman being adjudged run out.

LETTER TO THE EDITOR
*August 19, 1926*. Sir, My recollection of the 1882 incident does not agree with that of the late Mr Spofforth. Alfred Lyttelton ran after the ball and threw it in to the wicket-keeper's end, but no one had gone to the wicket, and it was fielded by 'W.G.' at forward point. The batsman having completed the run, left his ground, and went out on to the wicket before the ball was 'dead.' Someone – not Grace – had by then reached the wicket, to whom 'W.G.' tossed the ball. That fieldsman put the wicket down and on appeal the batsman was given out. I have no recollection of ever hearing that Thoms said 'he was sorry' to have to give it out.

The incident aroused much excitement, one party holding it was too sharp practice, the other that the batsman should comply with the rules, or suffer the penalty, and I dare say opinion would be equally divided nowadays if the incident occurred again.
Faithfully yours
Harris
Belmont
P.S. Did it nearly occur again on Monday evening? Did Hobbs leave his ground after the last ball of an over, before the ball was 'dead' and before 'over' had been called.

## THIRD TEST, THE OVAL, 1888

*August 15*. When the last two Englishmen were in an incident of great rarity occurred. Law 14 of the game states that 'The bowler may not change ends more than twice in the same innings, nor bowl more than two overs in succession.' With the figures at 289, Mr Ferris, who had previously crossed over and gone back to the end from which he started, was again put on at the opposite wicket. After he had bowled one ball Dr Grace from the pavilion directed the umpires' attention to this infringement, and for the minute they seemed puzzled how to proceed. After a short discussion the bowler was not allowed to resume the over, and went back to the other end. The ball itself was lost to the match. A somewhat similar case happened in the Rugby v Marlborough match at Lord's two years ago. On that occasion, however, the player had completed an over before the infringement was detected, and the umpires ruled him unable to bowl further at either end.

## FIFTH TEST, THE OVAL, 1902

R. H. LYTTELTON
*August 13*. There is only one other point to which attention ought to be drawn, and that is the inordinate extent to which leg play was indulged in. Some of the English batsmen get very much in front of the wicket, but they play at the ball with the bat. But several of the Australians, notably Mr Armstrong and Mr Gregory, and in a lesser degree Mr Noble and Mr Hopkins, continually got in front of the wicket to Braund's leg-breaks and made no attempt to play the ball.

This is not cricket, and the hope that such play was a thing of the past has been ruthlessly dispelled this season. It may, however, produce a change in the laws, which will be a point gained.

## FIFTH TEST, THE OVAL, 1905

R.H. LYTTELTON

*August 17.* After luncheon the game went altogether in favour of England; but again it most unfortunately happened that Mr Spooner was loudly appealed against for 'l.-b.-w.' when his score was only five, and was given in. The word 'unfortunately' is used not because it was certain that the decision was a wrong one, for this is practically never the case on the question of 'l.-b.w.,' but because it was unfortunate that twice in a day an umpire had to give a difficult decision on an occasion when the match was in a critical position. But, although there is every wish to condole with a young bowler like Mr Cotter on what he felt to be such a disappointment, it was distinctly bad taste on his part to show his feelings so obviously as he did.

## SECOND TEST, MELBOURNE, 1911–12

*January 1.* Runs came steadily, and at 117 Mr Douglas and Barnes resumed bowling. Barnes was applauded on taking the ball, but after Mr Carter had scored a single off his first delivery Barnes took some time to change his field and the crowd grew noisy. He threw down the ball and refused to bowl, and thereupon the crowd made a variety of noises mingled with cheers and hoots. When Barnes continued each run scored off him evoked great enthusiasm, and there was much cheering when Mr Carter glanced him for two.

## THIRD TEST, ADELAIDE, 1911–12

*January 17.* Mr Douglas very quietly raised an objection to Mr Kelleway's and Dr Hordern's use of resin while they were bowling in order to make the ball grip. The umpires were uncertain what to do, and the matter was allowed to stand over.

## FOURTH TEST, MELBOURNE, 1911–12

*February 10.* Owing to the recent heavy rain the pitch was soft; it was solely on this account that Mr Maclaren, the Queensland fast bowler, was omitted from the Australian side, and not because of the threatened boycott of the match by the trade unionists if he played.

## FIRST TEST, TRENT BRIDGE, 1921

A.C.M. CROOME

*May 31.* Mr Gregory bowled very fast, but Mr Knight played him delightfully. He made one magnificent square cut, and scored infallibly on the leg side, however high the ball bumped. Tyldesley was less quick in dealing with a long hop that flew up at his head; he missed it, and received a stunning blow. He was assisted to the Pavilion, and later was informed that the ball had carried on to break his wicket. The batsman was more to blame than the bowler for the accident, and neither the advice tendered by the crowd to

*Michael Clarke argues about the light with umpires Marais Erasmus and Tony Hill at Old Trafford in 2013. Matt Prior offers a helpful word*

Mr Armstrong, nor the cheering when he took it, was justified. After all, he merely substituted Mr Macdonald for Mr Gregory, and the frying-pan is proverbially cooler than the fire.

## FOURTH TEST, OLD TRAFFORD, 1921

A.C.M. CROOME

*July 26.* In 40 minutes 80 runs were put on, and at 6 o'clock Major Tennyson declared the innings closed. Mr Armstrong rightly protested, and went into the pavilion to introduce the rule governing the declaration of the innings in two-day matches to the notice of the rival captain. This wasted some valuable minutes, and, when the Australians came out again, Mr Armstrong, who had bowled the last over before the temporary stoppage of play, started to bowl again. The crowd endeavoured to prevent him from breaking the law, but he was at last allowed to proceed.

## FIFTH TEST, THE OVAL, 1921

R.B. VINCENT

*August 15.* A very heavy shower after luncheon, however, made the ground actually swampy, and with little wind to dry it, even the bright sun which shone at intervals could not possibly have rendered the pitch playable for some time. The crowd, apparently, considered that it only required that the rain should stop for the pitch to recover immediately. And they further considered that it was Mr Armstrong's fault that their false hopes were not gratified. Their manner of protest, when a large number assembled in front of the pavilion, and the studied insults which were hurled in to the Australian dressing-room were unworthy of a cricket crowd, however debased they may have been rendered by watching, and betting on, other games. The scene was particularly regrettable in that the Philadelphian cricketers, who are on a visit to this country, were present in the pavilion, and so, perhaps, obtained a false impression of the spirit in which a Test match is played in England.

A great deal of the trouble undoubtedly arose from the fact that a certain proportion of the cricket-watching public throughout the country have taken an ungenerous view of Mr Armstrong's captaincy. There have been small but noisy bands of hooligans who have laid themselves out to insult Mr Armstrong on the least provocation and the fact that he is much too good a captain to be in the least worried by these discourteous outbursts only spurs the hooligan spirit to fresh enormities. On Saturday many of the spectators considered that they had an opportunity of giving vent to the dissatisfaction which was felt with regard to Mr Armstrong's conduct of the recent match against Kent at Canterbury, when he allowed his team to bat until 5 o'clock on the second day, and so robbed the game of all interest as a cricket match. There is, moreover, a feeling among many that our men were treated rather unkindly last winter by the Australian crowds. For behaviour such as was seen at the Oval on Saturday, however, there is no excuse.

## SECOND TEST, SYDNEY, 1928–29

FROM OUR SPECIAL CORRESPONDENT*

*December 15*. The day did not pass without its incidents. The dismissal of Kippax brought the first, and with it an unseemly demonstration against the Englishmen, and Duckworth in particular, who for long into the afternoon was the butt of unkind remarks. The facts of the case were that Geary bowled a ball well on the leg side. Kippax made a poor stroke, trying to turn it and getting his feet mixed up, and the ball, hitting the inside of his left pad, curled round and knocked off his leg bail. Kippax stood there thinking, possibly, that the ball had rebounded off Duckworth's pads. All the English team saw what happened and gathered in groups, surprised at Kippax not going out. In the meanwhile the bowler's umpire had walked towards square leg, indicating the end of the over. An appeal was therefore made to the square-leg umpire, who was in no doubt and gave Kippax out, bowled off his pad. The crowd resented the Englishmen's appeal and showed this by much booing. The only question arising is whether the square-leg umpire was right in giving the man out without being appealed to by the bowler's umpire. The question of fact scarcely arises. Kippax would probably have been better advised to have appealed himself instead of standing still, thus creating a false impression in everyone's mind.

* *The Times* archivist has not been able to identify the author of this report.

## BODYLINE: 1932–33

*September 19.* All along the line, right to Tilbury, where they embarked on the SS *Orontes*, thousands of people were wishing them good luck. People were assembled at every station, women waved from back gardens, and men stopped working on their allotments to join in the send-off. Many relations and friends of the cricketers accompanied them to the ship. The final message from Mr Warner before he sailed was: 'On behalf of Jardine, the captain, and the whole of the English cricket team, we should like to thank the public for the wonderfully enthusiastic and affectionate send-off which they gave us at St Pancras this morning. We shall do our utmost to maintain the high prestige of English cricket, and the thought of the warm send-off before leaving England will be a great incentive to us on the day of battle.' The players will be able to practise at specially prepared nets, while swimming and other sports will play a big part in their daily routine.

## FIRST TEST, SYDNEY, 1932–33

LEADING ARTICLE

*December 8.* But, fine as was the performance of England's first three wickets, the most satisfactory feature of the match was the evidence that it gave of the renaissance of English bowling. If, as seems probable, Larwood and the rest can keep up to their present high standard, it will mean that the attack has once more returned to its proper place in cricket. No true cricketer will expect our bowlers and their captain to pay any attention to the irresponsible critics who object to their methods. It is puerile, as the *Sydney Morning Herald* observes, to complain about shock bowling as something unfair. 'As for the bumping ball,' it goes on to ask, 'are Jones, Cotter, McDonald, and Gregory so soon forgotten?' No complaints were heard when these great bowlers were gathering a harvest of English wickets, and certainly none was uttered by young McCabe when he was making his big score against the bowling of Larwood and Voce. Australians are always great fighters and cricketers, and their first-flight men would be the last to wish their opponents to modify their bowling or batting tactics in deference to the suggestions volunteered by a handful of fault-finders and grumblers.

## SECOND TEST, MELBOURNE, 1932–33

ROY CURTHOYS

*December 31.* Larwood began with four slips – Hammond, Sutcliffe, Voce and Jardine – with Allen at short-leg and Bowes at mid-on, but later he employed the leg trap and had Allen and Jardine at short-leg, Hammond at deep-square-leg, Sutcliffe at fine-leg, Leyland at long-leg, and Bowes at mid-on. Voce was also bowling with the leg trap, and with both bowlers making the ball bump head high the batsmen were naturally cautious. In one over Fingleton had to duck four times in succession while the ball whizzed over his head. Larwood, the bowler, came in for some mild barracking from the crowd, who renewed it shortly afterwards when he retired to change his boots at 16.

LETTER TO THE EDITOR

*January 3.* Sir, Until recently stumps were erected on the cricket pitch to be defended by the batsman and hit by the bowler. Endeavours were made by the bowler to make the batsman miss the ball so that he could be bowled. If the batsman made a bad stroke, which was his own fault, he could be caught out. These were among the essentials of cricket. In the leg trap theory all these are reversed. The stumps are not bowled at, endeavour is made to make the batsman hit the ball either in order to defend himself (not his wicket) or to make a run. He can be caught off a good stroke. The application of the leg trap theory, therefore, is an artifice, and such a thing, in some opinions, is foreign to 'cricket.'

Although not expressed in the same way, this is probably the basis of Australian criticism, which is not due to ill-feeling, as suggested in some quarters. This method of restricting a batsman to strokes on the leg side does away with the possibility of cutting and driving, strokes which the public has paid much money to see.

Your obedient servant
Horace Hill
Laverstock, Salisbury

LEADING ARTICLE

*January 4.* Before this last match began and while it was in progress so much has been said and written in both countries about the fairness or unfairness of this or that line of tactics, so many outsiders have wasted their time and energy in telling the two captains what they ought and ought not to have done and left undone, that, but for the unruffled common sense with which both have steered their course, the chorus of conflicting advice and criticism might well have put a severe strain on the nerves and judgment both of themselves and of their teams. The less of such talk there is in future the better for all concerned. Each side has now won a match; the lists are set for the remaining three; it is high time to cut the cackle and get on with the game.

## THIRD TEST, ADELAIDE, 1932–33

E.W. PARISH

*January 16.* Larwood began by bumping the ball disconcertingly, and after Fingleton had been dismissed by Allen he switched over to leg theory. At one time he had only two men on the off side. He was successful in trapping McCabe and Bradman, who fell surprisingly easy victims. This did not meet with the approval of the crowd, who made hostile demonstrations when the batsmen ducked. Vehement protests followed when Woodfull was hit over the heart and had to leave the ground in order to receive massage.

*January 17.* There had been mild demonstrations early today when Ponsford was hit on the body, but when Oldfield was struck on the head by a ball from Larwood the crowd of over 35,000 gave vent to their feelings. Larwood was then bowling to an orthodox off field, and Oldfield swung at a rising, ball which seemed to fly off the edge of the bat, on to Oldfield's temple. Oldfield staggered away and collapsed, and after receiving treatment had to retire. The indignant crowd abused Larwood and Jardine, and continued their wild shouting when England opened their innings. Oldfield is suffering from concussion and shock, but is expected to play tomorrow.

*January 19*. The weather was still hot and cloudy when play was continued today. Jardine had the heavy roller used, but it is probable that the very slight rain which fell in the early hours of the morning had not affected the wicket. As play began a dove circled over the wicket. It is to be hoped that it was an omen of a more happy spirit.

*January 20*. But as we have hitherto heard only the Australian point of view, it is permissible to suggest that there has been a form of interference quite as serious as the alleged unfairness of 'leg-theory' bowling. Larwood has had to bowl under the disability that if a batsman as a result of his own negligence were hit the blame would be assumed by the mass of spectators to lie with the bowler. The knowledge of this, had it weighed with Larwood, could only tend to limit the value of a fast bowler, and it is to the credit of Larwood and his captain that they stuck imperturbably to their work in distressing circumstances.

LETTER TO THE EDITOR

Sir [...]

A proportion of the Australian public and some critics seized on the idea that the leg-theory of the M.C.C. bowlers was conceived at the commencement of the tour for the purpose of intimidating the leading Australian batsmen. Its success has stimulated bitterness, and the spectacle of a batsman dodging successfully or otherwise fast bowling aimed at the body has rankled and developed the present contretemps.

Hard knocks must always be occasionally expected in cricket. True enough, 'Home' players took hard knocks when facing the Macdonald-Gregory bowling of the 1921 tour; but the fact remains that truly fast bowlers have not previously bowled leg-theory. Dangerous balls as bowled by Macdonald, Gregory, or other fast bowlers of either country were not premeditatively bowled in succession at a batsman, neither was other than a more or less orthodox offside field set.

All good critics appear to agree that leg-theory reduces the chances of good stroke play to a minimum, and that there is no rule to prevent its being bowled. One cannot conceive the imposition of such a rule possible, but a large proportion of cricket lovers in Australia and here are doubtful if its continuance by 'express' bowlers is in the good interest of the great game. Possibly Australia's viewpoint today may become England's tomorrow. Woodfull, a cricket idealist, sees in it a menace to cricket and a positive danger to batsmen, one that by the good ethics of the game he should not be called upon to face.

Yours faithfully

N.E. Douglas

Lloyd's Building, E.C.3

LEADING ARTICLE

*January 19*. In due time, no doubt, the M.C.C. will send a considered and courteous reply to the cable of protest against what has begun to be called 'body-line bowling' which they received yesterday from the Australian Board of Control. Meanwhile an attempt to give some idea of how the matter strikes the average Englishman may not be amiss. First of all there is nothing new in the kind of bowling to which exception is now taken. Really fast bowlers are as rare as truly great statesmen. But they do every now and then spring up, both here and in the Dominion, and have been known before now to hit the batsman as well as the wicket. English players who some years ago suffered many a shrewd knock from the bowling of Macdonald and

Gregory – not to speak of Jones in still earlier days – have the right to recall their own experiences to those who are now criticizing the tactics of Larwood and his captain. Australians know as well as our men that the game of cricket is not played with a soft ball, and that a fast ball which hits a batsman on the body is bound to hurt. They also know that, so long as a 'shock' bowler is not deliberately bumping down short-pitched balls or purposely aiming at the batsman, his bowling is perfectly fair. It is inconceivable that a cricketer of Jardine's standing, chosen by the M.C.C. to captain an English side, would ever dream of allowing or ordering the bowlers under his command to practise any system, of attack that, in the time-honoured English phrase, is not cricket. To do the Australians justice the grievance at the back of their complaint is probably neither the pace nor the direction of Larwood's deliveries. What they apparently do object to is the array of leg-fielders – corresponding to the closely packed posse in the slips and the gully when the bowler exploits the off-theory – on whom the English captain relies to increase the effectiveness of his fast bowlers. But in that policy there is nothing dishonourable or unsportsmanlike or foreign to the spirit of the game. After all, the object of every fielding side is to get their opponents out for as low a score as possible. If with that aim in view Jardine has made more use of the 'leg-theory' than other captains before him, the development is largely due to the fashion of the two-eyed stance and the modern batsman's habit of covering the stumps with his legs, thereby preventing the bowler from getting a clear view of the wicket, and incidentally making it more likely that he himself will be hit.

In the opinion of the Australian Board of Control bowling of this type has become a menace to the best interests of the game, is causing intensely bitter feelings between players, and unless stopped at once is likely to upset the friendly relations between Australia and England. Their protest, which is at once a warning and an appeal, is the direct outcome of the Adelaide Test match. Apart from the skilful bowling that in the first innings sent back to the pavilion seven such batsmen as Sutcliffe, Jardine, Hammond, Ames, Fingleton, McCabe, and Bradman for an average of fewer than five runs apiece, the game was remarkable for the dogged pluck with which the batsmen of the two teams that followed them retrieved for the time being the fortunes of their side. Those first two innings were a constant succession of ups and downs, brimful of excitement, as English and Australian players in turn, fighting with their backs to the wall, upset all the calculations of the prophets. Under normal conditions these fluctuating changes and chances would have been enough in themselves to win for the Adelaide match a niche of its own in the annals of Test match cricket. Unfortunately it will be remembered rather as a game in which good-humoured barracking degenerated as the play went on into angry booing on the part of the spectators, irritated by the failure of their idols, and to acrimonious comments in the pavilion and elsewhere on the particular style of bowling which was one of its causes. On the other hand let it be remembered that the crowds on the mounds, in spite of their disappointments, showed that they could cheer as well as barrack their English visitors, and that Oldfield and other Australian batsmen who were hurt by our fast bowlers were the first to own that the bowlers were not to blame.

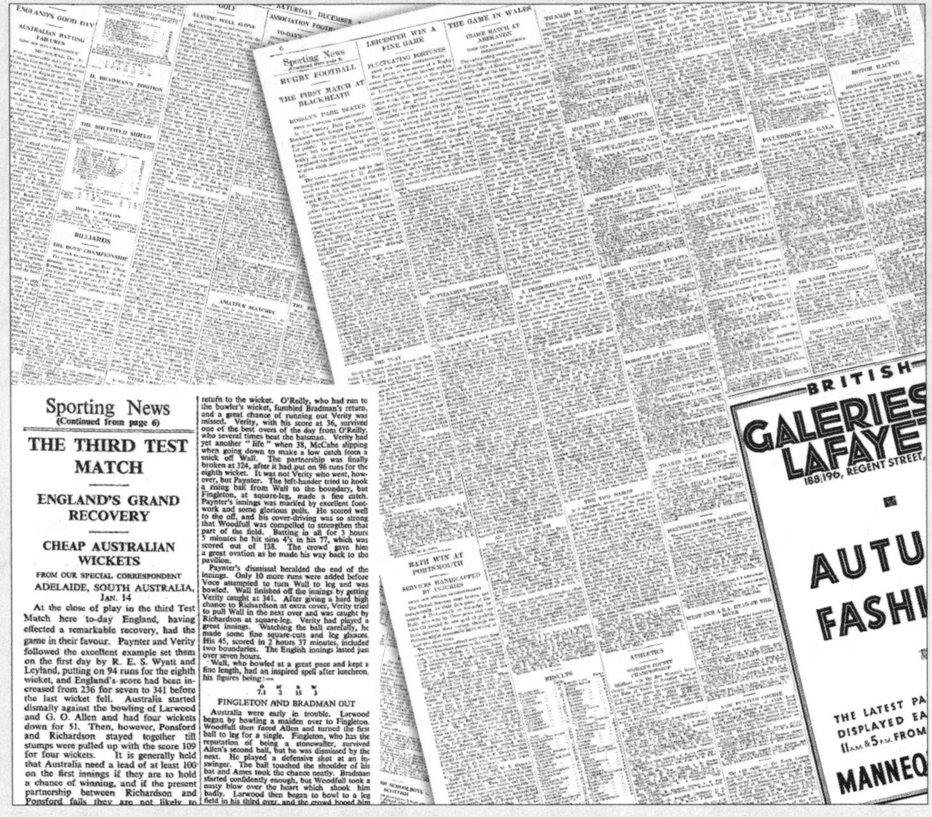

Sporting News
(Continued from page 6)

THE THIRD TEST MATCH

ENGLAND'S GRAND RECOVERY

CHEAP AUSTRALIAN WICKETS

FROM OUR SPECIAL CORRESPONDENT

ADELAIDE, SOUTH AUSTRALIA, JAN. 14

At the close of play in the third Test Match here to-day England, having effected a remarkable recovery, had the game in their favour. Paynter and Verity followed the excellent example set them on the first day by R. E. S. Wyatt and Leyland, putting on 94 runs for the eighth wicket, and England's score had been increased from 236 for seven to 341 before the last wicket fell. Australia started dismally against the bowling of Larwood and G. O. Allen and had four wickets down for 51. Then, however, Ponsford and Richardson stayed together till stumps were pulled up with the score 109 for four wickets. It is generally held that Australia need a lead of at least 100 on the first innings if they are to hold a chance of winning, and if the present partnership between Richardson and Ponsford fails they are not likely to return to the wicket. O'Reilly, who had run to the bowler's wicket, fumbled Bradman's return, and a great chance of running out Verity was missed. Verity, with his score at 36, survived one of the best overs of the day from O'Reilly, who several times beat the batsman. Verity had yet another "life" when 38, McCabe slipping when going down to make a low catch from a snick off Wall. The partnership was finally broken at 324, after it had put on 96 runs for the eighth wicket. It was not Verity who went, however, but Paynter. The left-hander tried to hook a rising ball from Wall to the boundary, but Fingleton, at square-leg, made a fine catch. Paynter's innings was marked by excellent footwork and some glorious pulls. He scored well to the off, and his cover-driving was so strong that Woodfull was compelled to strengthen that part of the field. Batting in all for 3 hours 5 minutes he hit nine 4's in his 77, which was scored out of 138. The crowd gave him a great ovation as he made his way back to the pavilion.

Paynter's dismissal heralded the end of the innings. Only 10 more runs were added before Voce attempted to turn Wall to leg and was bowled. Wall finished off the innings by getting Verity caught at 341. After giving a hard high chance to Richardson at extra cover, Verity tried to pull Wall in the next over and was caught by Richardson at square-leg. Verity had played a great innings. Watching the ball carefully, he made some fine square-cuts and leg glances. His 45, scored in 2 hours 37 minutes, included two boundaries. The English innings lasted just over seven hours.

Wall, who bowled at a great pace and kept a fine length, had an inspired spell after luncheon, his figures being:—

| O | M | R | W |
|---|---|---|---|
| 7.1 | 2 | 15 | 3 |

FINGLETON AND BRADMAN OUT

Australia were early in trouble. Larwood began by bowling a maiden over to Fingleton. Woodfull then faced Allen and turned the first ball to leg for a single. Fingleton, who has the reputation of being a stonewaller, survived Allen's second ball, but he was dismissed by the next. He played a defensive shot at an in-swinger. The ball touched the shoulder of his bat and Ames took the chance neatly. Bradman started confidently enough, but Woodfull took a nasty blow over the heart which shook him badly. Larwood then began to bowl to a leg field in his third over, and the crowd booed him

*Despite the distance, timing and absence of television pictures, the Bodyline controversy still provoked huge interest in England and was covered in depth by The Times*

Any breach in the mutual good will and friendliness between the players of the two countries which have survived the ordeal of many a desperate encounter over a period of more than half a century would be a cricketing disaster of the first magnitude, and the M.C.C. may be trusted to do everything in their power to prevent the dismal forebodings of the Board of Control from coming true. It is difficult to conceive the possibility of their placing a ban on any particular type of bowling or to see by what authority they could instruct the captains of Test teams or any other eleven how to place or not to place their men in the field; but no doubt the common sense of the two great governing bodies of the game will be able between them to hit upon some means of coming to a satisfactory agreement. In all probability the present delicate and difficult position would never have arisen but for the irresponsible chatter of elderly critics in the pavilion and in the press, and the craving in some quarters for sensational news-stories which has magnified words or incidents natural enough in the heat of a hard-fought battle.

LETTER TO THE EDITOR

Sir, Now that it is officially announced that the bitter feeling already aroused by the colour of Mr Jardine's cap has been so intensified by the direction of Mr Larwood's bowling as to impair friendly relations between England and Australia, it is necessary that this new 'leg theory,' as it is called, should be considered, not only without heat, but also, if possible, with whatever of a sense of humour Test matches can leave to a cricketer.

It seems funny, then, to one who did not serve his apprenticeship as a writer by playing for Australia that a few years ago we were all agreed that cricket was being 'killed' by 'mammoth scores' and 'Marathon matches,' and that as soon as a means is devised of keeping scores down to a reasonable size cricket is 'killed' again. It seems comic to such a one that, after years of outcry against over-prepared wickets, a scream of horror should go up when a bowler proves that even such a wicket has no terrors for him. It is definitely the laugh of the year that, season after season, batsmen should break the hearts of bowlers by protecting their wickets with their persons, and that, when at last the bowler accepts the challenge and bowls at their persons, the outraged batsmen and ex-batsmen should shriek in chorus that he is not playing cricket.

These things seem funny: but there is, of course, a serious side to the Australian Board of Control's protest. This says that the English bowling has made 'protection of the body by the batsman the main consideration,' and if this were so there would be legitimate cause of complaint. But let us not forget that Mr McCabe, in his spare moments during the first Test match, managed to collect 180 runs, and Mr Bradman, in the second, 100; each of them scoring (even though scoring was necessarily a minor consideration) four times as quickly as Mr Jardine, whose body (up to the cap) was held as sacred. Let us not forget that, if this new form of bowling is really as startlingly new as is implied, lesser batsmen than these two should at least be given a chance of adapting themselves to it before the white flag is waved. But if modern batsmanship is really so unadventurous and unflexible that after three failures it announces itself beaten and calls for the laws to be altered, why, then, let the laws be altered; let everybody go on making runs, the artisan no less easily than the master; and let us admit frankly that the game is made for the batsmen only, and that it ceases to be cricket as soon as it can no longer be called 'a batsman's paradise.'

Yours, &c
A.A. Milne
Mallord Street, Chelsea, SW3

### LETTER TO THE EDITOR

*January 21.* Sir, Pitches like billiard tables and spectators numbered in thousands make people forget what cricket used to be. Fifty years ago this new danger was a common incident of every match played outside the few places where groundsmen guarded the turf. I remember on one occasion the first ball of a match slung with immense violence straight at the big black beard of W.G. Grace. Did he object? Certainly not; he simply hit it out of the ground and waited for the next.

Buckmaster
Portchester Terrace, WC2

### LEADING ARTICLE

*October 11, 1933.* The quarrel is now over, and, it is to be hoped, will be quickly forgotten. The terms of settlement are such as to leave no sore feeling on either side. There is not complete agreement upon the question of 'body-line' bowling – a term that, since it does not occur in the final Australian message, we may hope is now used for the last time.

## FIFTH TEST, THE OVAL, 1938

R.B. VINCENT, CRICKET CORRESPONDENT

*August 25.* There was an unusual occurrence when Hutton, with the intention perhaps that Fleetwood-Smith should receive the first ball of the next over, helped a stroke by Brown on to the boundary with his foot. The umpire, however, acting according to the instructions issued by the M.C.C., which say that 'the runs which have been arranged for a boundary hit are to be added to the runs already made should a fieldsman wilfully cause the ball to reach the boundary,' signalled five runs, and Brown gained the bowling.

## FIRST TEST, BRISBANE, 1946–47

NEVILLE CARDUS

*November 30.* Bedser bowled really well, with something of Tate's vitality and late swing, and the English out-cricket was antagonistic, so much so that luncheon came as much as a haven and quiet port after stormy seas to Australia as to England. When Bradman was 28 Ikin, at second slip, confidently claimed to hold a catch from a slice at a potential half-volley off Voce. The umpire rejected the appeal.

## FOURTH TEST, HEADINGLEY, 1948

R.B. VINCENT, CRICKET CORRESPONDENT

*July 22.* Whatever the outcome of the match, it is to be fervently hoped that the game will be played in a spirit free from a certain waywardness of humour which greatly spoiled the pleasure at Manchester.

## SIXTH TEST, ADELAIDE, 1970–71

JOHN WOODCOCK, CRICKET CORRESPONDENT

*January 30.* The first day of the sixth Test match between England and Australia will be remembered as much for the scene which occurred with Boycott's dismissal as for the fact that Edrich made another hundred and England, with a score of 276 for two, got away to a splendid start.

On a cool day of small, fast moving clouds Boycott and Edrich, continuing where they left off in Melbourne last Tuesday, had made 107 for the first wicket when Boycott went for a short single to mid-on. Ian Chappell, the fielder, hit the bowler's stumps with an underarm throw and in what to everyone seemed a close finish, Boycott was given out by umpire O'Connell. From the press box, which is side-on, there was no telling with the naked eye whether or not Boycott had got home. Just as there was no mistaking Boycott's anger at the decision.

Having been given out, he threw his bat and set about haranguing all those around him, including the umpire. So far as I could tell, he met his match in the two Chappells. Greg, being the bowler, had joined his brother and with a few well-chosen words they sent Boycott packing, having first picked up his bat and handed it to him. By now the crowd was lending its support, so that Boycott was booed all the way in.

Golfers, who are responsible only to themselves, sometimes throw a club in self-reproach, but to see one of the world's finest batsmen making an exhibition of himself in a Test match against Australia was really rather lamentable.

## FIRST TEST, BRISBANE, 1974–75

JOHN WOODCOCK,
CRICKET CORRESPONDENT

*November 30.* Of bouncers there were enough to be sure that England, when their turn, comes, will not be spared. Not until the penultimate over, though was anyone warned for overdoing them. Lever then had his name taken, as it were, for letting Jenner have three fliers in three balls, as much a waste of a new ball as an ill-tempered piece of cricket.

## THIRD TEST, MELBOURNE, 1974–75

JOHN WOODCOCK,
CRICKET CORRESPONDENT

*December 27.* Greig, having flashed three or four times through or over the slips, was run out going for a third for an edge of Knott's off Mallett which went over Ian Chappell's head at slip. Chappell chased it, threw strongly on the turn and Greig was adjudged not to have beaten the return. Greig stood there, hands on hips, exchanging unparliamentary words with Greg Chappell, before departing. It was a scene which did no one any credit, except the fielder.

*December 31.* Soon Amiss was spreading his powerful wings. Four overthrown from a return by Ross Edwards, in Thomson's second over, helped him on his way. When he edged Lillee just wide of third slip the two of them came face to face in the middle of the pitch, with Lillee snarling at Amiss. I had better not repeat what he said.

*January 3.* At Melbourne yesterday two beauties in their bikinis, both bearing bunches of pink roses, came on to the field and threw themselves into the arms of their adorable Greig. That is all very fine. And the belligerence and spirit with which Greig plays are indomitable. But he lets himself down by making childishly offensive gestures to the batsmen when they are out, such as pointing towards the pavilion. Bill O'Reilly was saying in Melbourne earlier this week, after the umpires there had had a word with Ian Chappell about his side's language, that never during the whole of his career does he remember a cricketer swearing on the field. Or doing what Greig does either, I imagine, when he sends a batsman packing. By means of television bad habits spread too fast not to be curbed.

## FOURTH TEST, SYDNEY, 1974–75

JOHN WOODCOCK,
CRICKET CORRESPONDENT

*January 6.* It was while Walker and Lillee were together that the first of the day's incidents erupted. Greig got a ball to lift at Lillee, from not that short of a length, which hit Lillee on the left elbow. Unable to conceal his delight at seeing the biter bit, Fletcher clapped at this, which was honest but silly. When, after that, he picked up Lillee's bat to return it to him Fletcher got a flea in his ear. Very soon the umpires were in the ring, talking first to Lillee and then to Edrich.

When in his next over Greig got two more balls to rear at Lillee the umpires took Greig as well as Edrich aside, as they did again at the end of the over, to say that they would not tolerate as much short-pitched bowling at the later batsmen as at those better able to defend themselves. Although fair enough this view is not always easily applied.

Where Greig and the umpires disagreed was over what constitutes 'a systematic attempt at intimidation'. It was the same here four years ago, when Illingworth wagged his finger at the umpire while arguing this very point. The umpires, Brooks and Bailache, have resolved to 'cool' the present series when, as they think, it comes too near to boiling point, there being a world of difference between Greig bowling short at a tail-end batsmen (and Lillee is no fool with the bat) and Thomson, Lillee or Willis doing so. I thought the umpires were being rather pedantic this morning, but better that way than to risk the game becoming a rough house.

## FIRST TEST, LORD'S, 1977

JOHN WOODCOCK,
CRICKET CORRESPONDENT

*June 17.* When Thomson, having been hit for seven in an over, gave the time-honoured sign to those on the free seats who suggested he was bust, the balance seemed to be shifting.

## SECOND TEST, LORD'S, 1981

JOHN WOODCOCK,
CRICKET CORRESPONDENT

July 4. Everyone behaved – players and umpires alike – as though they were much less interested than they ought to have been in putting on a show – in playing cricket, in fact.

Altogether four hours' play were lost, the day ending soon after seven o'clock with the sun shining and Messrs Palmer and Oslear, the umpires, deciding, either with alarming insensitivity or ignorance of the playing conditions, that the light was unfit. Whereupon, as an expression of the crowd's disapproval, the ground was showered with cushions.

All day one thing after another had conspired against there being any continuity of play. After a prompt start and a quarter of an hour's cricket, in which Willey and Emburey scored four runs, it rained. It was 2.45 before another ball was bowled, a succession of showers, some heavy, keeping the ground staff busy.

By mid-afternoon there were those who felt sufficiently aggrieved, when the Australians took drinks, to make it known that they considered it cissy. So it was. The same applied just before tea when Willey and Emburey reached the pavilion at the double, though it was not actually raining at the time, and again when the Australians took further drinks in the cool of the evening.

## THIRD TEST, HEADINGLEY, 1981

JOHN WOODCOCK,
CRICKET CORRESPONDENT

*July 16.* He [Brearley] dealt briefly with the Australians who wanted to know what he would do if and when Lillee left the field to change his shirt after each of his spells of bowling. 'Let's wait and see, shall we?' Kim Hughes, Australia's captain, is quoted as saying that he considers it a slur upon a great bowler that Brearley should have questioned the rightness of Lillee's frequent visits to the dressing room.

Secrets of fashion's most powerful women times2

No. 68491 ■ TUESDAY SEPTEMBER 13 2005 ■ www.timesonline.co.uk ■ 60p

# AT LAST...

ENGLAND'S ASHES SOUVENIR EDITION

**Schoolboy friends dead in woods**

Murder squad detectives are trying to piece together the violent last minutes in the lives of two schoolfriends found lying side by side in a Berkshire wood. The boys, 16 and 14, are thought to have been stabbed and left for dead.
**NEWS** page 3

**Belfast ghost town**

Belfast ground to a halt as security alerts, loyalist protests and public fears about resurgent violence combined to plunge the city into chaos and empty it of people.
**NEWS** page 11

**Cancer drug hitch**

Breast cancer sufferers in England are missing out on a leading drug that is available to all patients in Scotland because of disarray in treatment funding.
**NEWS** page 8

**Gaza takeover**

Thousands of Palestinians [illegible] youths set light to synagogues and other symbols of the [illegible]
**WORLD NEWS** page 29

**Net gain for eBay**

Traditional phone companies such as BT were dealt a blow when eBay, the online auction group, bought Skype, the internet phone company, for $4.1 billion (£2.2 billion).
**BUSINESS** page 43

'Read my lips, you fake Christians: no parade route is worth this'
**LIBBY PURVES** page 20

| | | | |
|---|---|---|---|
| COMMENT | 18 | WEATHER | 55 |
| BUSINESS | 36 | TELEVISION & | |
| REGISTER | 51 | RADIO | times2 |

Michael Vaughan and his victorious England cricket team after regaining the Ashes from Australia for the first time in 16 years. **NEWS** page 6 **SPORT** pages 62-72

# Petrol panic begins to spread as oil prices rise

**By Ben Webster, Philip Webster and Gary Duncan**

EMERGENCY powers to reserve fuel for essential users will be reviewed by ministers and oil companies today amid panic buying at petrol stations across the country.

Dozens of filling stations ran dry yesterday after bogus reports of weekend panic proved self-fulfilling when motorists rushed to join queues at the pumps. Hundreds more forecourts are expected to run out of fuel by lunchtime today despite concerted efforts by oil companies to calm the situation by denying that there was a problem.

Doctors, nurses and police officers, among others, will be reserved supplies under plans by a working group involving the oil industry, police and the Department of Trade and Industry. A minimum sale of fuel could also be imposed in an attempt to stop people buying small volumes.

Public fears about fuel supplies and prices are expected to increase today as hauliers prepare to start protests outside oil refineries tomorrow. Overall fuel costs for companies were 39 per cent higher last month than a year before, the sharpest rise since 1991, according to figures released yesterday.

Gordon Brown will table an emergency international plan today to bring down oil prices. He will tell the TUC conference in Brighton today that the Government understands the problems faced by hauliers, farmers and motorists and is taking joint action to tackle the problem. Hauliers are angry that other European countries have introduced rebates for bus and lorry operators. In France companies are given a 1.5p rebate for every litre and in Belgium the figure is 4.5p. The Chancellor will propose the five-point plan, discussed yesterday with representatives from 24 countries, at meetings of the G8, the International Monetary Fund and the World Bank over the next two weeks.

The proposal involves: Opec raising supply to meet increased demand and opening its books to show where the world's reserves are; the profits of oil-producing countries being ploughed back into investment; the World Bank setting up a fund to help developing countries to invest in alternative energy; and the IMF creating a new fund for poor countries hit by oil price shocks.

Mr Brown is unlikely to refer directly to his expected decision to continue the freeze on fuel duty imposed in the Budget. He will announce in the Pre-Budget Report in November that it will be extended for the rest of the financial year.

If oil remains at $65 (£35) a barrel, compared with the Chancellor's Budget forecast of $40 a barrel, Mr Brown will gain an estimated $2.75 billion extra from North Sea revenue in the present financial year. Economists said that the gains for the Treasury would almost certainly be cancelled out by the £1 billion-a-year cost of continuing the freeze on fuel duty.

**Call for calm, page 4**

*After a breathless series in which cricket was rarely off the front page, England finally reclaimed the Ashes in 2005*

I am delighted Brearley has mentioned the matter to the Test and County Cricket Board, though he has heard nothing from them since doing so. What he feels is that if you want a game when the bowlers come and go, then one should be arranged accordingly.

What has, in fact, happened in Brearley's absence is that it has become a not uncommon practice for English and West Indian bowlers, as well as Lillee, to go and have a rub down after bowling, as though they had just run a marathon in the Congo.

## FOURTH TEST, EDGBASTON, 1981

JOHN WOODCOCK,
CRICKET CORRESPONDENT

*August 1.* The message to those watching yesterday's fourth Test match at Edgbaston, sponsored by Cornhill, was to try not to behave as some of the players did or to bat as most of the batsmen did. During an ill-humoured day's play Australia took a first innings lead of 69 and by the close England, batting again, had reached 49 for one wicket.

Hughes, Willis, Lillee, Gooch and Taylor were all carried away by their emotions. Had this been a horse race they would have been up before the stewards; in a game of ice hockey they would have been sent to cool off. Hughes became embroiled with Willis, and Lillee with Gooch and Taylor with Lillee, and finally Hughes with one of the umpires. Except that it showed how much the players care, it was not attractive.

## FIRST TEST, OLD TRAFFORD, 1993

ALAN LEE, CRICKET CORRESPONDENT

*June 8.* It was appropriate that a Test match that had almost everything should turn on an event so rare that decades pass without it occurring. At 2.18pm yesterday, Graham Gooch was dismissed for 133. The man who desires nothing more passionately than an Ashes success as his epitaph now has 'handled the ball' instead. [...]

Hughes, two overs earlier, had been responsible for Gooch's dismissal, though the laws dictate that he will not receive the credit. Defending, on the back foot, Gooch saw the ball bounce backwards, threatening leg-stump. As it fell, he instinctively knocked it away with his free, right hand. Umpire Bird rightly upheld the appeal and Gooch had another first to his name, no Englishman in history having been out this way in Tests.

*Captain Graham Gooch and coach Micky Stewart tried to shape the England side in their own hard-working image in the early 1990s*

## SIXTH TEST, THE OVAL, 1993

JOHN WOODCOCK

*August 21.* Feelings ran high when England were in the field on Thursday evening, and it was not a pleasant sight. If what was said by the players of both sides, much of it from under the cover of a helmet, could have been recorded, few reputations would have remained untarnished.

It all began when the Australians thought Alec Stewart had been caught at slip off Warne. Their reaction when he was given not out by umpire Kitchen was like a parody, it was so exaggerated. Eventually Stewart and Fraser were to be seen answering back while the umpires, true to form, seemed mildly entertained, or, at any rate, unconcerned.

It was impossible to be certain from the television replay whether Stewart had got an outside edge or not, which suggests that Kitchen's decision was a good one. But that is not the point.

It is now the practice for Test cricketers to try and fool the umpires, whether by appealing melodramatically for a catch, say at short leg when they know perfectly well that the ball has not hit the bat, or by not walking even when so palpably caught by slip as Hussain had been shortly before the Stewart incident. The more the players tried to get away with, the harder it becomes for the umpires to get things right.

## THIRD TEST, SYDNEY, 1994–95

ALAN LEE, CRICKET CORRESPONDENT

*December 31.* It had always been the plan to have a free day between these back-to-back Tests and a full-scale practice was

*Mike Atherton and Raymond Illingworth, the chairman of selectors, see things from different angles in Australia in 1994-95*

scheduled for today. Nevertheless, the situation indicated a rethink, a display of intent, and the relaxed regime being run by Atherton and Keith Fletcher seems to be grating on the chairman of selectors, Raymond Illingworth.

Yesterday, he stopped short of openly castigating the decision to rest, but was also careful to distance himself from it. 'It's not my job,' he said pointedly. 'That's Keith's job. They possibly could have rested. It's their jobs on the line, not mine. It's up to them.'

## FIRST TEST, TRENT BRIDGE, 2013

MIKE ATHERTON, CHIEF CRICKET CORRESPONDENT

*July 13.* So Broad should not be condemned for his refusal to walk, even though there would not have been many batsmen with the audacity to stand there after such an enormous deflection, certainly none with the kind of puzzlement to suggest he did not know why the Australians were appealing in the first place.

THE TIMES — 1GM — Monday January 6 2014 | THE TIMES

# Sport

thetimes.co.uk/sport

**Broken United**

**Red card, recriminations and regrets: problems pile up for Moyes as Swansea City inflict FA Cup third-round defeat at Old Trafford**

*the game, inside Times 2*

SPORTS NEWSPAPER OF THE YEAR

# Broken England

## Flower admits to personal agendas within team as criticism rains down

**Richard Hobson**
Deputy Cricket Correspondent

Andy Flower admitted that he should have anticipated the dreadful batting that sent England spinning to only their third 5-0 Ashes whitewash in history.

As former captains and coaches lambasted England with some of the strongest criticism in memory, the team director also hinted yesterday at personal agendas in the dressing room and said that players lost confidence as early as the first Test in Brisbane.

England were accused of raising the white flag after being dismissed for 166 in 31.4 overs to lose the fifth Test in Sydney by 281 runs inside three days. David Lloyd, the former coach, described the performance as "disgraceful" while past captains Michael Vaughan and Geoffrey Boycott used the words "pathetic"

**Inside today**

**Mike Atherton**

'It was not pretty. A defeat was inevitable, but you can still lose with dignity and grace and pride. England gave up'

The Ashes
Pages 59-63

and "humiliation", respectively, by way of variety on a lamentable theme.

England were bowled out for less than 180 six times out of ten during the series and it is 27 innings in all since they last reached 400, a total described before the tour by Alastair Cook, the captain, as the minimum first-innings requirement in Australia.

Flower said: "We have underperformed badly. Perhaps, if I am honest, we could have seen it coming a little earlier than right now. We have underperformed in the first innings for quite a long period. We have not scored many runs … and people lost confidence pretty early on in this tour. The pace rocked the batting order in the first Test and we never quite recovered."

GARETH COPLEY / GETTY IMAGES

**Feeling shattered: Carberry adds an element of farce to the tragicomedy of England's Ashes whitewash on the third and ultimately final day in Sydney yesterday**

Asked by Ian Ward, on Sky Sports, whether players have been pulling in the same direction or pursuing their own interests, Flower said: "There are always some personal agendas in most teams. No team is perfect and our team is no different.

"Team spirit always gets its closest examination under pressure and we have been put under a tremendous amount of pressure by a good side on their home turf. That is one area we will look at."

Flower had said already that the eight-wicket loss in the fourth Test in Melbourne marked the end of an era and an opportunity for renewal.

He repeated his pledge to continue after the latest heavy defeat, and *The Times* understands that Paul Downton, the new managing director of England Cricket, fully supports both Flower and Cook retaining their positions. Cook learnt of what he described as his own vote of confidence via quotes from David Collier, the ECB chief executive, in an article on the ECB website.

The captain admitted that England had reached "rock bottom", saying "if it was a boxing match it would have been stopped".

Nasser Hussain, whose 2002-03 team avoided a 5-0 scoreline by winning the corresponding "dead" rubber in Sydney, was scathing towards Cook's leadership on the trip.

"We keep hearing he is a good learner," Hussain said. "He has been out-captained, he has not learnt one iota from first game to last." He urged Cook to stand up to senior players tactically, to "go with your gut instinct, and if he does not have one then give the job to someone else".

**Buying The Times:** Austria €4.80; Belgium €4.00; Bulgaria BGN7.50 Cyprus €4.00; North Cyprus YTL8.00; Denmark DKK 30.00; France €4.00; Germany €4.00; Gibraltar £2.00; Greece €4.00; Italy €4.00; Luxembourg €4.00; Malta €4.00; Morocco MAD 36.00; Netherlands €4.00; Norway NOK 42.00; Oman OMR 1.50; Portugal €4.00; Spain €4.00; Sweden SEK 35.00; Switzerland CHF 6.80; Turkey TL9.00; UAE AED18

*The headlines got bigger as the defeats got heavier for England in 2013–14*

## FIFTH TEST, THE OVAL, 2013

MIKE ATHERTON,
CHIEF CRICKET CORRESPONDENT

*August 24*. Certainly there was little in the cricket to light the spectators' fire yesterday, although Pietersen and Michael Clarke did their best to fan some flames with a volley of verbals ten minutes before tea.

Mysteriously, it was the arrival of Ian Bell, after Jonathan Trott's dismissal to Mitchell Starc's first ball with the second new ball, that initiated the spat. Pietersen wandered down to warn Bell that the ball was swinging, prompting Clarke to remind Pietersen that Bell was a batsman with 20 Test hundreds to his name, and that he didn't need babysitting. On and on they went then, shouting at each other at a respectable distance, like two boys in the schoolyard, Clarke from second slip, Pietersen at the non-striker's end, with Aleem Dar doing his best matronly peacemaker's impression in between.

All good fun for a while – and Clarke spent much time thereafter aligning his field a foot from Pietersen's backside – but an indication, perhaps, that Clarke has had a gutful of losing and that we may see a little more of the Aussie mongrel in him during the return series.

Sporting

OW ENGLAND KEPT ASHES

VO GREAT HEARTS OVERTHROW AUSTRALIA

England beat Australia by five wickets in the fourth Test match at delaide yesterday and so, gaining a lead of three matches to one in the ies, have retained the Ashes. In an interview after the match L. Hutton, e England captain, paid a tribute to the younger members of the side. Much of the credit, he thought, should go to J. B. Statham, F. H. Tyson, M. C. Cowdrey and P. B. H. May, together with the wicket-keeper, T. G. Evans.

From Our Special Correspondent

ADELAIDE, FEB. 2

Many years from now young Cowdrey will point to his broken nose and tell boys yet unborn that he was at Adelaide on February 2, 1955, when England won the Test match and kept the Ashes. And the boys will think him wondrous lucky.

the catch. (We asked Hutton afterwards what he thought of Miller's bowling. Hutton thought Miller ought to concentrate much more on batting.) England 10 for 2. In comes the battered Cowdrey. Miller hits him twice running on the pads and appeals, and everybody here who isn't English appeals too. What a man is Miller. He comes in from a shortish run, loose of limb like an African, hair streaming, and as he pulls up the hair goes on and falls about his face.

Meanwhile May has begun driving, and Johnson has gone from mid-off to square-leg. For Cowdrey Miller brings fine-leg up to third slip, and Cowdrey cover drives classically for 4. Miller heaves his shoulders over even faster, and Cowdrey is taken by Archer at first-slip. England 18 for 3. Four Meteor jets fly over at 200ft.; they look and sound quite tame beside this wild man … His figures now are 3 overs, no … runs, 3 wickets.

ngland all too obliging … eaches new heights of greatnes

One that got away: Gilchrist misses a stumping chance off Warne to give Pietersen an extra life, but it was to make little difference

High five: Warne acknowledges the Melbourne crowd after his haul ripped the heart out of England's fragile batting

six, but Chris Read for Geraint Jones was the only change. As the best player in the team, Pietersen needs to bat at four. Since Paul Collingwood shared the only partnership of any substance with Strauss — 57 for the third wicket — it may appear that England's strategy, to keep him away from the new ball, had worked again, but to have Pietersen batting with the tail repeatedly is not satisfactory.

Sporting News

ENGLAND HAVE LAST WORD

THREE YEOMEN FOIL AUSTRALIA

GREAT STAND BY WATSON AND BAILEY

FROM OUR CRICKET CORRESPONDENT

Out of darkness, through fire into light. Thus did England yesterday rise like some Phoenix from the ashes of apparent defeat to save the second Test match at Lord's and so gain a … draw against Australia with … seven wickets, … original aim fo…

Ponting run out (Flintoff) 66

P Siddle c Flintoff b Harmison 10

…iant leap

S Clark c Cook b Harmison 0

for proud S…

36 TUESDAY AUGUST 1 1989

THE TIMES First published 1785

England's abject surrender marks new low in series

By Alan Lee, Cricket Correspondent

Inglorious procession at Old Trafford

10-1: Curtis c Boon b Alderman 0

25-2: Robinson lbw b Lawson 12

27-3: Smith c Healy b Alderman 2

28-4: Gooch c Alderman b Lawson 13

38-5: Botham lbw b Alderman 4

59-6: Gower c Marsh b Lawson 15

SCOREBOARD FROM OLD TRAFFORD

Gower unfairly blamed for failings of others

Simon Barnes

Border rewarded for hard labour

Only two men so far decline

Was this English … most desperate …

SPORT…

Cricket

# BRICKBATS

THE TIMES SATURDAY JUNE 11 1938

A GOOD BEGINNING BY ENGLAND

4

Sporting News

LAKER'S SUPREME PART IN RETAINING THE ASHES

ALL TEN AUSTRALIAN WICKETS AND 19 IN MATCH

From Our Cricket Correspondent

England won the fourth Test match against Australia at Old … yesterday by an innin… retaining the … achiev…

pitch perked up and the ball showed signs of misbehaving.

At luncheon McDonald and Craig were still together. They had then added only 59, but the important thing was that they had each been batting for more than four hours. Ahead of them stretched another four and only 15 minutes of these had ticked away when Laker stru… blow. Craig, still …

THE TIMES

LOCOMEN'S BAN BOUND TO CAUSE GREATER … TODAY

HOW THE AUSTRALIANS WERE SKITTLED OUT AT LORD'S

Gaullists may get back with clear majority

… BETRAYS A NOTE OF REGRET

Inquiry over bank chief's salary

Police alerted by strike ship

Railways must act alone, Marsh says

13 die in Swi… rail crash

…ped aiming to hit Mallett over the hill, and the end draws nearer.

… dismally surrender Ashes

TEST MATCH

BRADMAN 309 NOT OUT

ALL RECORDS BROKEN

*The Third Test Match between England and Australia was begun at Leeds yesterday. A. P. F. Chapman, for once, lost the toss and Australia went in to bat on a perfect batsman's wicket. By the end of the day they had scored 458 runs for the loss of three wickets …*

## JAMES ANDERSON

### FIRST TEST, BRISBANE, 2006–07

CHRISTOPHER MARTIN-JENKINS, CHIEF CRICKET CORRESPONDENT

*November 24.* James Anderson bowled too many short balls all day. Only briefly, during the early afternoon when he helped his captain to apply some consistent pressure on Ponting and Damien Martyn, did he look like making up for the absence of Simon Jones, or indeed look a better bet than Sajid Mahmood, but it is a fair bet, alas, that his Lancashire colleague would have been just as expensive. Anderson did bowl one of the few balls to get past Ponting, one that cut back between bat and pad, but his form and rhythm still seems to come and go like clouds on a windy day.

## AUSTRALIA

### FOURTH TEST, ADELAIDE, 1954–55

A.G. MOYES

*February 3.* The Australian batting was again the weakest point and without question it lacks the qualities of certainty, pugnacity, and determined attack; virtues which were once Australian pride and glory. No one ever seemed likely either to hold the fort or develop a devastating attack once wickets began to fall and today's batting was enough to make spectators weep as batsman after batsman played across the ball and paid the penalty. Only Maddocks kept his bat straight and only Davidson seemed capable of meeting Tyson and Statham who obtained amazing success with the old ball on a dead pitch.

Without doubt this should not have happened. Both bowled with great heart and admirable control, but it must be said that they were aided by batting which was so out of true Australian character as to be really pitiful.

### FOURTH TEST, OLD TRAFFORD, 1956

JOHN WOODCOCK, CRICKET CORRESPONDENT

*July 30.* It was not, as might be supposed, that conditions became impossible for the 55 minutes astride the tea interval, the period when Australia lost their whole side, and that before and after this they were perfectly satisfactory. The answer, as every objective Australian will admit, was hysterical batting, sans spirit, sans skill, sans everything, in the face of some fine off-break bowling. [...]

Yet this issue runs deeper than the competence or otherwise of Australian batsmen to play a turning ball. Everyone is of one mind that this is something at which they do not excel. Where the controversy begins is over the preparation of the pitches at Headingley and Old Trafford. In Australia, as well as England, the clouds of dust that blew away from the groundsman's besom last Friday as be was making ready for Australia's first innings have made front page news. There have been indignant cries that Mr Flack was instructed to produce a wicket to help Laker and Lock so that England might take advantage of Australia's shortage of good spin bowling. This, one is convinced, was not so.

## THIRD TEST, TRENT BRIDGE, 1977

JOHN WOODCOCK,
CRICKET CORRESPONDENT

*August 3.* Watching it on television Mr Packer can have been left in no doubt that the Australian side he has purchased is playing at the moment like a job lot. He would accept too, I am sure, that nothing he can stage will ever compare for drama and tension and suffering and excitement with Test cricket such as it was played at Trent Bridge. The first four days took place before full houses in warm, often sunny weather, on a good pitch and an historic ground. It is this that is the real thing.

## SECOND TEST, LORD'S, 2013

MIKE ATHERTON,
CHIEF CRICKET CORRESPONDENT

*July 22.* Australia did not just lose a Test match yesterday, they lost some self respect, conceding the second-biggest winning margin (in terms of runs) to England in Ashes history. Only once before, in Brisbane in the 1928-29 series, have Australia been beaten by a bigger runs margin than the 347 runs they lost by here. A shellacking, annihilation, a walloping; whatever you want to call it, this was it. One side was playing cricket, the other not, as was said in a different context many years ago.

# KEN BARRINGTON

## FOURTH TEST, HEADINGLEY, 1968

JOHN WOODCOCK,
CRICKET CORRESPONDENT

*July 29.* Barrington took three hours to make 49. By the time he was sixth out at 235 he had convinced himself, and one or two others, that the pitch precluded anything in the way of positive batsmanship. If this is how Barrington sees it as his duty to play, with England trailing in the series, there is little point, for all his qualities, in having him in the side.

# IAN BOTHAM

## THIRD TEST, TRENT BRIDGE, 1985

JOHN WOODCOCK,
CRICKET CORRESPONDENT

*July 15.* For 10 minutes after Botham had had Ritchie given not out on Saturday he was in a rage. He followed through down the pitch and was warned for that; he bowled one petulant bouncer after another, which eventually brought him a second warning; and despite what Gower said afterwards he should have had a third warning for what at Wimbledon they might call 'abusing the conventions of the game'. To put it kindly, Botham behaved grotesquely, though Gower said he thought he had done nothing excessive.

### FIFTH TEST, EDGBASTON, 1985

JOHN WOODCOCK,
CRICKET CORRESPONDENT

*August 16.* What play there was revolved, not for the first time, around Botham, whose performance would have been considered bizarre even in a pub knockout. I hardly think it is ever likely to happen again that the first over of a Test match against Australia, with England in the field, will be bowled by someone with a new blond rinse, wearing a Rastafarian wristband, and operating to two long legs. We know Botham is a law unto himself, but this was a bit much even for him. He took one of the two wickets to fall and missed a catch into the bargain.

I am afraid it reflects no better on Gower than on Botham if he thinks that the way to take wickets on this Edgbaston pitch is with long hops – for that is all they were. True, Wood and Hilditch both like to indulge a weakness for the hook shot, but are Botham and Gower so bankrupt of ideas that this is the best they can do with a new ball at the start of a Test match against Australia? It was a ridiculous piece of cricket, which Alec Bedser, as one of the England selectors, must have watched with disbelief.

### FOURTH TEST, OLD TRAFFORD, 1989

ALAN LEE, CRICKET CORRESPONDENT

*July 28.* Then Botham committed a sin for which he can present no defence. Tempted unforgivably by the first sight of flight from Hohns, he charged recklessly, head in air, aiming an outlandish slog and hearing the stumps rattle behind him. It would have been a bad shot for a man on 100, let alone on nought. He clutched his head as the red mists dispersed, but it was too late.

---

## DON BRADMAN

### THIRD TEST, MELBOURNE, 1928–29

ROY CURTHOYS

*January 1.* While White was on the batting became almost absurd in its caution, both Bradman and A'Beckett treating it with such care that the pitch might easily have been a really difficult one. It is a sad reflection on present-day Australian cricket that two young men, having been in quite long enough to see the ball as though it were a balloon, played such a hopelessly stodgy game.

### SECOND TEST, MELBOURNE, 1932–33

ROY CURTHOYS

*December 31.* Bradman's failure was inexplicable; he slogged at the first ball with the impetuosity of a novice or an overconfident player. It was the crudest of strokes, for he pulled the ball feet back into his wicket.

*He may have been the idol of every English schoolboy, but Denis Compton was not above being ticked off by* The Times

## STUART BROAD

### FIRST TEST, BRISBANE, 2010–11

MIKE ATHERTON,
CHIEF CRICKET CORRESPONDENT

*November 26.* The hat-trick ball was rapid, full and straight, and it hit Broad on the boot, whereupon not even the Decision Review System could save him. Broad thought he had hit the ball, although increasingly he gives the impression of thinking nothing is out when he bats and everything is when he bowls.

## DENIS COMPTON

### THIRD TEST, MELBOURNE, 1946–47

NEVILLE CARDUS

*January 8.* The sad mishap or folly of the day occurred just after half past 2. Compton drove exquisitely to the off, was nearly stumped off McCool, and then he hit again with grace and speed to the off-side near cover point and dashed for a run, even though the ball went quickly near to Miller, a superb fieldsman whose pick-up and return to Tallon left poor, misguided Compton swinging his heart, soul, and body round in an agonized attempt to retrieve his impetuosity. Not for worlds would the present writer chide Compton for impulsiveness in the right place and moment; today it was his duty to absent himself from felicity awhile. England's position here was one in which runs were a vanity, and boundaries mere baubles.

## NICK COOK

### FIFTH TEST, TRENT BRIDGE, 1989

JOHN WOODCOCK

*August 12.* I must try not to labour the point, and I know the modern player, like the modern selector, does what he does for what he thinks to be the best. But only when Cook threw the ball up yesterday and rid himself of that pestilential silly point, did he have any success and yet, for over after boring over, there that confounded fielder was, reducing the game to stalemate. And jumping like a jack in the box for fear of being hit.

## JOE DARLING

### FIRST TEST, TRENT BRIDGE, 1905

R.H. LYTTELTON

*May 31.* Mr Darling put on Mr Armstrong at the pavilion end, and he bowled without a break for upwards of two and a half hours No doubt it was of the most material importance, from the Australians' point of view, to check the run-getting; and Mr Armstrong succeeded with a vengeance, and Mr Darling cannot be blamed for keeping him on so long; but that such a policy can be the proper one is much to be regretted in the interests of the game. Mr Armstrong bowled nearly every ball outside the batsman's legs, and at just the length that makes it almost impossible to hit and equally impossible, unless attempts are made to hit, for the batsmen to get out. The result was that for two hours or so the melancholy spectacle was seen of maiden after maiden being bowled with no prospect of either runs or wickets. There were three short-legs and a deep square-leg; and so monotonous became the cricket that it cannot be a matter of surprise that the crowd threatened to become unruly. Although not to the same extent, Mr Macleod's swinging ball, going away to the off-side with the field carefully and skilfully placed, made things the same at the other end, and consequently five hours and a half was taken up in making 318 runs, although at times the run-getting was fast. Such a state of things is not the fault of the players, but that such a procedure is correct is not healthy, least of all in such a match as a Test match.

## TED DEXTER

### FIFTH TEST, THE OVAL, 1961

JOHN WOODCOCK, CRICKET CORRESPONDENT

*August 22.* Mackay was presented next with Dexter's wicket off a long hop. It was the first ball of Mackay's second over and Dexter could have dispatched it in the direction of his choice. There must have been two or three acres of untenanted ground between mid-on and the long leg area where Gaunt was standing in front of the Vauxhall scoreboard.

With the deadliest aim Dexter hooked the ball to Gaunt, who needed to move neither forward nor backward nor sideways. Like the Australian rules footballer that he is, he made the catch above his head. And, as if the gods could stand no more of this ineptitude, it soon began to rain, nothing more being possible until four o'clock.

## BILL EDRICH

### SECOND TEST, LORD'S, 1938

R.B. VINCENT, CRICKET CORRESPONDENT

*June 24.* Again it was a rather short ball, but straight, and Edrich must be found guilty of taking a liberty in trying to hook the ball before he had had time to get a sight of it. It was a mistake which no doubt he will grow out of.

## ENGLAND

### FOURTH TEST, OLD TRAFFORD, 1905

R.H. LYTTELTON

*July 25.* A word of protest may fairly be made against the inordinate length of time taken for tea. The day was by no means hot, nor was the pace of run-getting fast, and in these circumstances 25 minutes seems a long time to take for 5 o'clock tea. It would seem that in a short time this meal will soon take up nearly as much time as luncheon, and this is hardly suitable or proper for a day's play, which cannot in any circumstances occupy more than six and a quarter hours.

### FOURTH TEST, HEADINGLEY, 1953

GEOFFREY GREEN,
CRICKET CORRESPONDENT

*July 29.* England yesterday saved their face at Headingley and so are left to look forward to the Oval for a last chance of the Ashes after four drawn games. But unlike the prince and princess in the fairy story they cannot live entirely happily even in the coming three weeks let alone for ever. For in saving their face they also lost some face last evening as they were shown how to play cricket. Even the sun came out to smile and to watch as Australia, confronted with a final target of 177 for victory in a space of five minutes under two hours, fell only 30 short of their mark gloriously. Indeed, an Australian score of 147 for four in that contracted span, following England's second innings of 275 in nearly 10 hours, represented a heaven of delight and a revival of faith after the grim struggle and negation that preceded it. Here in fact at the last was plenty in the midst of poverty.

### SECOND TEST, LORD'S, 1961

JOHN WOODCOCK,
CRICKET CORRESPONDENT

*June 26.* What is so thoroughly depressing from an English point of view is the extent to which we have been outfought. When, on paper, there is nothing to choose between two sides the deciding factors are courage, common sense and character, assuming that the luck breaks even. In this case England, had they been more fortunate in the field, might have earned a lead themselves. But their batting, for the umpteenth time in recent years, has been wretchedly irresolute.

In their last seven meetings with Australia England have been outplayed; in that time they have passed 300 only once in 13 innings. With the exception of the second innings at Edgbaston, collapse has followed collapse until now they are expected. When the heat has been turned on, in fact, the English temperament has failed.

### FIRST TEST, BRISBANE, 1970–71

JOHN WOODCOCK,
CRICKET CORRESPONDENT

*November 28.* For anyone who cares for English cricket the following account of the first day's play in the first Test match between England and Australia will make melancholy reading. In 74 eight-ball overs Australia made 308 for two wickets and England at no time seemed competent to stop them. From morning until night Stackpole pounded the English bowlers, his innings of 175 not out being by some way the highest of his career.

It was as though none of the lessons of the past month have been heeded. In length and line England's bowling was manifestly unintelligent. Shuttleworth's opening spell was the poorest I have seen in an Anglo-Australian Test match – he improved as the day went on – and although England had the early encouragement of Lawry's wicket, Australia soon recovered. D'Oliveira was ineffectual and Illingworth was again all too reluctant to bowl. Of the 73 runs which Underwood conceded, 50 came on the legside which is an indictment of the line of his attack.

## FIRST TEST, OLD TRAFFORD, 1972

JOHN WOODCOCK,
CRICKET CORRESPONDENT

*June 9.* As so often in recent years England's batsmen made their profession look almost impossibly difficult when the Test series began at Old Trafford yesterday. After the first 90 minutes had been lost while the ground dried out from overnight rain, they endured four hours and a half of unrelieved embarrassment.

No doubt they are all short of practice: no doubt it was wretchedly cold: no doubt the ball moved about off the seam and came through at varying heights: no doubt the fact that Boycott had to retire hurt after being hit on the arm by Lillee, and was in obvious discomfort when he came back, was a severe handicap: no doubt the size of the crowd (4,500) was dispiriting. Yet when all that is said, England's batting displayed a startling lack of quality.

## THIRD TEST, TRENT BRIDGE, 1972

JOHN WOODCOCK,
CRICKET CORRESPONDENT

*July 18.* It is part of a cricketer's day to have a cup of tea before the start of play. Yesterday, whatever was served up in the England dressing room should have been sent to the analyst, judging by the way they bowled and fielded. Theirs was the poorest display of out-cricket I have seen from an England side. At a time when their main purpose should have been to make runs as scarce as possible, they were prodigal in the extreme. Full tosses, long hops, and overthrows abounded, to the delight of Edwards and Greg Chappell.

## THIRD TEST, HEADINGLEY, 1981

JOHN WOODCOCK,
CRICKET CORRESPONDENT

*July 18.* The local view was that a Bradford League side would have bowled better than England did yesterday morning. Their line was dreadful. Although it was Dilley, who took the only wicket to fall, when he removed Bright, the nightwatchman, no-one was less straight, all day, than he.

Most counties, with the help of their overseas players, would have bowled better than this. I imagine even that an attack of Hendrick, Jackman, Selvey and Allott, or of Arnold, Lever, Jarvis and Jesty would have been disappointed to let Australia declare. Of one thing you may be fairly sure – Australia will bowl more accurately than England did.

## FOURTH TEST, EDGBASTON, 1981

JOHN WOODCOCK,
CRICKET CORRESPONDENT

*July 31.* It was a glorious day for batting – cloudless, warm and sunny. At last, we thought, we were in for a batsman's match. Yet one after another the England side found ways of getting out by playing not as though this was a five-day Test against Australia but one of countless one-day games, which take up so much of the calendar.

Brearley, Gower, Gooch, Gatting and Willey all had good reason, whatever they may say (and they do not take kindly to criticism), for feeling when they got out that they had played strokes unworthy of the occasion.

## FIRST TEST, HEADINGLEY, 1989

ALAN LEE, CRICKET CORRESPONDENT

*June 14.* Rumours of the rebirth of English cricket were, it seems, greatly exaggerated. For, by embracing defeat yesterday, when it was apparently untouchable, England displayed a spineless inadequacy, depressing in its familiarity.

Given the relatively straightforward task of batting for five hours for safety on a pitch devoid of treachery, they managed to lose this First Cornhill Test match by 4.45pm, with 28 overs unused. The last seven wickets fell for 57 runs. This, remember, after Australia had amassed 831 runs, declared twice, and lost only 10 wickets in the match.

Australia's bowling, allegedly an amalgam of ageing impotence unlikely ever to bowl England out twice, bankrupted such arrogant theories at the first attempt. Terry Alderman, taking 10 wickets in a match for the first time in his roller-coaster Test career, was the deserving hero of a victory, which was as merited as it was unexpected.

If England have suffered a darker day, against anyone but West Indies, it stretches the boundaries of memory. The brave new dawn, heralded by the advent of Ted Dexter and the return of David Gower, has suffered a false start so incomprehensible it beggars belief.

## FOURTH TEST, OLD TRAFFORD, 1989

JOHN WOODCOCK

*July 31.* Although the Ashes were at stake, there was no due sense of combat and that is a sad thing to have to say. For better or worse, of the 267 Test matches to have been played between England and Australia, this is the 112th I have reported. That comes to something like 550 days' Test cricket, and Saturday struck me as being just about the first to have no special flavour.

The weather may have had something to do with that and it is a disappointingly slow pitch. But mainly it was because there was neither tone nor acumen to England's cricket. It was self-consciously second-rate.

## FOURTH TEST, ADELAIDE, 1990–91

ALAN LEE, CRICKET CORRESPONDENT

*January 24.* England, by comparison, are playing largely for pride, the quantity they seem to have found most elusive during this tour. It is too easy to infer that they do not care; individually, of course they do. But all too often, a hint

THE TIMES

First published 1785

# England's abject surrender marks new low in series

By Alan Lee, Cricket Correspondent

*OLD TRAFFORD: England, with four second-innings wickets in hand, are 64 runs behind Australia*

Just when it seemed safe to assume that things could not possibly get any worse for the England cricketers, they perpetrated a batting shambles horrible enough to bring them nightmares.

This may be understating the case for, even if he did wake up screaming during Sunday night, David Gower is unlikely to have been dreaming anything quite so calamitous as the collapse which yesterday presented the Ashes to Australia on a silver salver.

The rain which swept across Old Trafford at tea time, under appropriately funereal skies, granted England a stay of execution in this fourth Cornhill Test match. It was more than they deserved having slid, with white flag raised high, to 28 for four and then 59 for six as they approached the task of scoring 187 to make Australia bat again with all the inclinations of men anxious to escape the scene of their crime.

Ted Dexter had somehow located grounds for congratulating his players on Saturday. He believed they had fought back commendably. His words, which seemed to strain credulity at the time, are now exposed as the misplaced loyalty of a chairman to whom platitudes are no longer allies.

Dexter must surely assert himself, both publicly and in private, to bring about the changes necessary to maintain his own credibility and to persuade those observing this miserable summer that complacency has not taken root.

If this means accepting Gower's resignation as captain, then so be it. The disease, however, runs deeper than leadership and a new captain is as likely, in isolation, to inspire prolonged improvement as the treatment of a terminally sick patient with aspirin.

Dexter must now address himself to the present crisis and accept that the players who appeared to be the best available are no longer mentally or technically equipped for the job.

Any remaining doubts on this score vanished in yesterday's carnage. And yet, given the hopelessness of the situation, it was a day which had begun with a glimmer of promise.

First, Australia's tenth wicket pair were prevented from adding to the tail-end insults already regularly issued to England's bowlers during this series. In the second over, Geoff Lawson was bowled off his pads by Angus Fraser, who must share

More cricket ..........34

with Russell and Smith the distinction of being the only men from this side certain of their places on the Caribbean tour.

England received further encouragement when Graham Gooch took 10 runs from Lawson's opening over. It could not last. Terry Alderman, doubtless stung by his rare failure to take a first innings wicket, lost no time in correcting any impression that his powers were waning. Curtis survived a confident leg-before shout first ball but haplessly nudged his second to forward short leg.

Robinson avoided a pair but promised little more. He had managed 12 when Lawson exposed his lack of footwork and also confirmed that his technical flaws against high class bowling made his re-selection futile.

Worse was to come. Robin Smith, so admirably disciplined during his first innings century, now fell within an over to a wholly unnecessary shot. Chasing a legside ball from Alderman he could profitably have left alone, and edging a catch to the wicketkeeper.

Gower, can hardly have feared he would be called upon as early as midday – nor, that within a few balls of his arrival he would be watching the retreating back of the man most likely to play the long, delaying innings.

The truth is that even Gooch seems to have lost the heart for this battle. Twice, earlier in the series, he batted heroically under pressure but now, as Lawson probed outside off stump, he slid the ball to first slip with a crooked bat.

Botham entered with no helmet and, if he was honest, no pretentious bravado. He must have known, after his refusal to tour, that his place hangs on a slender thread and he played as if intent on obliterating the memory of that awful first-innings slog. Within five overs, however, he was gone to a classical piece of swing bowling from Alderman, deceiving Botham first one way and then, decisively, the other.

Gower lingered for 79 minutes. There was just a hint or a prayer of the kind of face-saving, job-saving century he had made at Lord's. But, two overs after lunch he cut hard at Lawson and Marsh, who has dropped more than he has caught this summer, hung on grimly at squarish gully. Gower marched off purposefully to a dressing room which now contained Dexter, hot foot from London. The result of their discussions may be known later today.

It could be said that this was when England began to bat as if there was a match to be saved rather than a train to be caught. Russell, who has endeared himself with the bat as much as the gloves, was friskly determined and Emburey quirkily effective. They had more than doubled the score when the promised rain arrived. Border had even felt obliged to bowl himself.

He knows, however, that a fine day today should be all that is needed to apply the humane killer to an England squad which has outlived its value.

## Inglorious procession at Old Trafford

HUGH ROUTLEDGE

10-1: Curtis c Boon b Alderman 0

25-2: Robinson lbw b Lawson 12

27-3: Smith c Healy b Alderman 1

28-4: Gooch c Alderman b Lawson 13

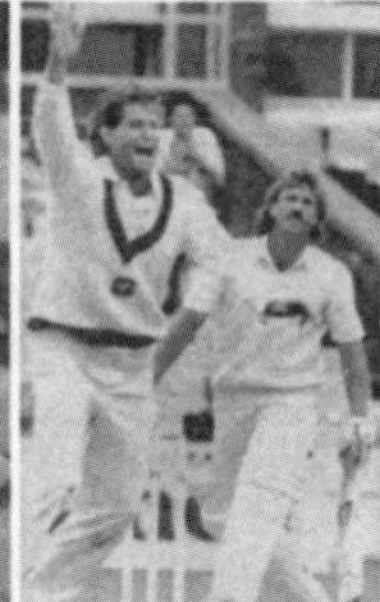

38-5: Botham lbw b Alderman 4

59-6: Gower c Marsh b Lawson 15

## SCOREBOARD FROM OLD TRAFFORD

England won toss

### ENGLAND

First Innings: 260 (R A Smith 143; G F Lawson 6 for 72).

Second Innings

| | | 6s | 4s | Mins | Balls |
|---|---|---|---|---|---|
| G A Gooch c Alderman b Lawson | 13 | – | 2 | 51 | 23 |
| T S Curtis c Boon b Alderman | 0 | – | – | 5 | 2 |
| R T Robinson lbw b Lawson | 12 | – | 1 | 31 | 28 |
| R A Smith c Healy b Alderman | 1 | – | – | 5 | 8 |
| *D I Gower c Marsh b Lawson | 15 | – | 1 | 67 | 40 |
| I T Botham lbw b Alderman | 4 | – | – | 24 | 23 |
| †R C Russell not out | 47 | – | 6 | 126 | 109 |
| J E Emburey not out | 23 | – | 5 | 82 | 71 |
| Extras (lb 3, w 2, nb 3) | 8 | | | | |
| Total (6 wkts, 50 overs) | 123 | | | | |

A R C Fraser, N A Foster and N G B Cook to bat.

FALL OF WICKETS: 1-10, 2-25, 3-27, 4-28, 5-38, 6-59.

BOWLING: Lawson 17-4-46-3; Alderman 13-1-38-3; Hohns 12-8-11-0; Hughes 5-0-22-0; Border 3-1-3-0.

### AUSTRALIA

First Innings

| | | 6s | 4s | Mins | Balls |
|---|---|---|---|---|---|
| M A Taylor st Russell b Emburey | 85 | – | 10 | 179 | 160 |
| G R Marsh c Russell b Botham | 47 | – | 5 | 156 | 100 |
| D C Boon b Fraser | 12 | – | 2 | 40 | 40 |
| *A R Border c Russell b Foster | 80 | – | 10 | 312 | 266 |
| D M Jones b Botham | 69 | 1 | 7 | 173 | 141 |
| S R Waugh c Curtis b Fraser | 92 | – | 7 | 283 | 174 |
| †I A Healy lbw b Foster | 0 | – | – | 1 | 1 |
| T V Hohns c Gower b Cook | 17 | – | 2 | 62 | 64 |
| M G Hughes b Cook | 3 | – | – | 9 | 6 |
| G F Lawson b Fraser | 17 | – | 3 | 31 | 29 |
| T M Alderman not out | 6 | – | – | 12 | 22 |
| Extras (b 5, lb 7, w 1, nb 6) | 19 | | | | |
| Total (167.5 overs) | 447 | | | | |

FALL OF WICKETS: 1-135, 2-143, 3-154, 4-274, 5-362, 6-362, 7-413, 8-423, 9-423.

BOWLING: Foster 34-12-74-2; Fraser 36.5-4-95-3 (nb 6); Emburey 45-9-118-1; Cook 28-6-85-2; Botham 24-6-63-2 (w 1).

Umpires: B J Meyer and J H Hampshire.



## Gower unfairly blamed for failings of others

Simon Barnes

No one with a heart could fail to mourn for poor David Gower yesterday. He is a perfectly charming man. He is an exquisite cricketer. He has led England to a series win from 1-0 down in India, and he won the Ashes in 1985. He has never provoked a diplomatic incident, never screamed at an umpire of any race, never played for the South African Breweries.

He has a nice sense of humour, and what is more, he loves both champagne and wildlife, and these two things prove beyond all possible doubt that he is a good sort. But failure this summer has brought his life to a point of crisis. It is a peculiarly public crisis, of the kind that few other professions could offer.

Imagine, say, a teacher who found that his daily doings had become the stuff that fascinated the tabloid press. "Now Teach loses control of Lower Four Science!" "Teach must Go!"

Or perhaps a doctor whose every surgery was part of a patient-by-patient radio broadcast: "I'm nonplussed! The young doctors of today have no idea – look what he's just prescribed! In my day we'd have used leeches and let me tell you, them leeches never failed."

And yet what has Gower done wrong? It is not his fault that his batsmen got out to poor shots yesterday, and that they have done so throughout this series. When every bowler you turn to sends down half-volleys and long-hops, it is hard to come up with an inspired bowling change. And you cannot blame the captain for the quality of the opposition, either.

But Gower is blamed, and blamed quite furiously. The Benaud dictum on captaincy is that you must take all the praise you can when it's going, no matter how little you deserve it . . . because you'll get all the blame when anything at all goes wrong.

Gower feels the weight of this unfair blame quite dreadfully. Gower, a man who looks diffident even in his pomp, now looks like Captain Sisyphus. He is quite bowed down: yet another victim of the mystique of captaincy.

"What can Gower do now?" Allan Border was asked on Saturday night. "All he can do is make runs," Border said, in his common-sense, ornery way. Border knows all about being a captain of a hopelessly inferior side. How did he cope? "I just tried to get as many runs as I personally could."

Gower made 15 yesterday. So much for Plan A. Now what options are left to a captain?

One of the great disappointments of my life was reading Mike Brearley's *The Art Of Captaincy*. Not that it is a bad book, far from it. It is just that I expected it to take me into another dimension of cricketing consciousness. Instead, I learnt that Brearley's secret was that he had no secret. Take out good luck and good sense, and there is not a whole lot left.

A cricket captain has a great deal of control, more than any other individual in any other team game except perhaps a quarterback in American football, but it is an illusion to think that he has the game and all his players in the palm of his hand.

The captain may fall into that illusion in victory, but in defeat, it is his own impotence that leaves the strongest taste.

I asked Border about Gower's captaincy before the series began: "In 1985, I always felt under pressure. There was never any let-up." Was this good captaincy from Gower, weak captaincy from Border, or just an overwhelming difference in the quality of the two sides? For certainly the situation has been completely reversed, this time, and Gower has felt under pressure from the first day of this series.

There *are* many things a captain can be praised for: Brearley's seeking to make things happen: Fletcher's rapport with his dressing-room. But it seems to me that the finest possible quality he can have is to lead the right team at the right time. Napoleon wanted his generals above all to be lucky. Brearley had something of that. Not the incumbent, not in this series. Alas, poor David.

## Border rewarded for hard labour

By John Woodcock

Australia played 10 Test matches in 1988, and in only one of them – against Sri Lanka in Sydney – did they reach 400. For most of the year every innings they embarked upon was a tortuous and potentially disastrous affair. The Australian Press fulminated much as England's does now.

The present Test at Old Trafford is Australia's sixth in 1989 (two against West Indies and four against England), and in none of them have they been bowled out for under 400. The only country ever to have chalked up more totals of over 400 in successive Tests is Pakistan, who reached seven in 1982-83. Not even in the Bradman era did Australia do it, nor West Indies when the three Ws were in their prime, nor India on pitches on which it is difficult to get out.

When Australia were routed yet again by West Indies at Melbourne on December 27 last year – they were bowled out for 114 – Allan Border cut no less disconsolate a figure than David Gower has at Old Trafford. Border and his side were both mentally and physically scarred. But they were not broken, and today they have inherited the earth.

They have pulled through by hard work, a proper respect for the text book, the best running between wickets of any current Test side and through being spared for seven months the merciless attentions of the West Indian fast bowlers on awkward pitches. They have made 401 at Sydney (where the West Indians were let down by their spinners), 515 at Adelaide (where the West Indians were wanting to get home), 601 for seven declared at Headingley, 528 at Lord's, 424 at Edgbaston and 447 at Old Trafford. Their bowlers, especially in the present series have given confidence to their batsmen, and vice-versa.

Just how long it takes these days to become a Test batsman, other than against the weakest opposition (namely England and Sri Lanka), can be seen from the fortunes of Waugh. Anyone watching him this summer will have recognized an unusual talent. The way he is playing at the moment suggests that he is destined for true greatness. Yet when he arrived in England in April he had played 41 Test innings without making a 100. In Pakistan last autumn he could not get a run; but his failure was a part of the learning process. Having come early into the Australian side, he is still only 24 – a daring yet orthodox player, a rare and burgeoning talent.

But it is for Border that Australia's run of overdue success must be especially rewarding. No one has suffered more or taken more knocks. At times he has been near the end of his tether. It is not the man himself so much as his example that has been an inspiration – plus the fact, that he, too, is a mighty good player.

## Only two men so far decline

By Alan Lee

Thursday is the deadline for the 30 players who have been asked about their availability for England's winter tours and the Test and County Cricket Board confirmed yesterday that anyone who has not replied will be assumed unavailable.

I understand that 20 had replied by the weekend, and of these only two have officially ruled themselves out. One is a player outside the present squad and the other is Mike Gatting, who may yet be requested to change his mind.

Graham Gooch has joined the list of those available but there has been no reply from Ian Botham, whose decision against touring was transmitted via his newspaper column.

The board's problem is that players are being asked to make a statement of intent, not to sign a binding contract, and the suspicion will persist that some may plead loyalty only until the end of the season.

A further 12 players are to be carded about their intentions this week, with a later deadline. The urgency of the inquiries has, of course, been created by the acknowledgement that an unofficial tour of South Africa this winter is certain and an announcement from the Republic can be expected within days.

So far, only the gifted young Glamorgan batsman, Matthew Maynard, and the semi-retired wicketkeeper, Jack Richards, have admitted receiving approaches for the tour. Several England players are in negotiation, and the main fear of Ted Dexter's management team is that some of the younger generation, waiting to break into Test cricket, will also be tempted.

● Colin Moynihan, the Minister for Sport, advised England cricketers not to join the rebel tour of South Africa. "My message to any cricketer is not to go, whatever the money," he said. "The implications if they do tour go far beyond cricket. All British sports could be hit as well as the Commonwealth Games in Auckland next year.

"I am simply repeating the message I gave to rugby players who were thinking of joining South African centenary celebrations – don't go. The British Government plans to stick firmly to the terms of the Gleneagles Agreement."

## Morrell takes 1,500m place at Gateshead

By Pat Butcher, Athletics Correspondent

Tony Morrell has quietly crept up on the inside, and pipped the old favourites, Sebastian Coe and Steve Ovett, as replacement for the injured Steve Cram and the indisposed Steve Crabb in the European Cup 1,500 metres in Gateshead this weekend.

Crabb decided that his stomach virus would leave him vulnerable, so he opted out. But, although Morrell has run faster than Coe, and more consistently than Ovett, he is still a controversial choice.

He is a novice at 1,500 metres, and is not known as a winner. He was even serving as a pacemaker to Abdi Bile on the grand prix circuit two weeks ago. Those are hardly the credentials for getting a European Cup place.

It would seem that Ovett's poor run in Belfast two weeks ago, when he could only finish 10th in a mile, outside four minutes, militated against him. For that was his only run in front of the selectors.

But Coe was not approached yesterday, officials relying on advice from his father that he has not done the preparation for 1,500 metres. Coe was indeed asked if he would be reserve for the European Cup 800 metres two weeks ago, which he declined, saying he wanted a definite race, which will be an 800 metres in Viareggio tomorrow. But, in contrast to Morrell, Coe, the double Olympic 1,500 metres champion, has won all his four races this season.

## SPORT IN BRIEF

### Swansea to go to court

The third division club, Swansea City, wants to take legal action to win compensation from Bradford City after the Yorkshire club poached its manager, Terry Yorath. A Football League committee yesterday upheld the £10,000 fine imposed on Bradford for breaching League regulations by inducing Yorath to break his contract last January.

Swansea are still unhappy and are to go to court seeking compensation.

### Stadium plan

Notts County, of the third division, want to leave Meadow Lane after 79 years and move to a £5 million multi-purpose stadium on the outskirts of Nottingham.

Lopez: 41st victory

### Classic Lopez

Nancy Lopez scored a one-under-par 69 on Sunday to win the Atlantic City Classic golf tournament by one stroke for her 41st career victory on the LPGA tour. Lopez beat her American compatriots, Chris Johnson and Vicki Fergon, who registered 71.

### Thorp rides

Paul Thorp, of Bradford, will partner the England speedway captain, Kelvin Tatum, in the World pairs final in Poland on Saturday. He replaces Simon Cross, of Cradley Heath, who has dislocated a shoulder.

### Gomer loses

Sara Gomer, the British tennis No. 1, last night lost in the first round of the Great American Bank women's Classic in San Diego 5-7, 6-2, 6-1 to Isabelle Demongeot, of France.

### Pyatt at No. 2

Chris Pyatt, the Leicester light-middleweight, has been named No. 2 contender for the WBC title held by the Ugandan, John Mugabe.

D 2

*** ☆☆☆

*A procession of wickets, the Ashes lost and the English game in crisis at Old Trafford in 1989* of turbulence has led to a cry of 'abandon ship' rather than a willingness to fight through adversity. The batting has been feeble, the bowling and fielding only spasmodically adequate.

## THIRD TEST, PERTH, 2001–02

CHRISTOPHER MARTIN-JENKINS, CHIEF CRICKET CORRESPONDENT

*December 2.* Neither a recognition of Australia's excellence, nor sympathy for the succession of injuries, is sufficient, however, to account for the mental disintegration that lay behind the surrendering of the Ashes for an eighth successive time and the loss of the series in only 11 playing days.

This was not an England side facing unassailable odds. They could and should have done much better than they did. Despite another stout effort by Key, a fine innings, after being dropped first ball, by the captain and a defiant if gung ho piece of cultured hitting by Stewart, England played yesterday not like a side determined not to be beaten but like one that already was.

They talk of planning and discipline in theory but in practice all they have offered in both innings of this game has been seeming recklessness. This is not, surely, the same as being positive, as Hussain firmly believed they had to be. He pointed to the fact that Australia's batsmen hooked and cut with abandon themselves. Indeed they did, but not against bowlers who harry the batsmen with such calculated aggression and accuracy as McGrath, Gillespie, Lee and Warne. The lesson taught by New Zealand last year, that patience is the only way, went unheeded.

It seemed to this observer that the right strategy, for once, was simply to try to occupy the crease and thereby tire the bowlers until scoring became easier late in the day. [...] time and again, attacking shots were aimed with no account either of field settings or the pace of the pitch. It was the kind of desperation that makes a gambler put his last money on a 50-1 outsider when the only rational strategy is to rebuild little by little.

## FIRST TEST, TRENT BRIDGE, 2013

SIMON BARNES

*July 11.* It all happened because the England cricket team are the worst favourites in the history of sport. They are the worst front-runners since Devon Loch.

One hint of triumphalism and they have gone in the fetlock, gone in the brain, gone in the heart. As soon as they succeed in climbing to any summit whatsoever, they make the fearful error of looking down. That is when they come over queer. Fit of the vapours. Do you mind if I have a little lie-down?

## THIRD TEST, OLD TRAFFORD, 2013

GIDEON HAIGH

*August 5.* Time yesterday set Alastair Cook a different predicament, and his men set out to fill it every which way, in a kind of variation on Parkinson's Law, overs expanding to fill the maximum time allowable for their completion. Had strategy meetings lasted any longer someone would have been appointed to keep minutes. Bowlers trudged to their marks. Fielders never took a shortcut when there was a long way round.

England contrived to bowl 22.3 overs in an afternoon session shortened ten minutes by rain, and 6.3 overs in the next 36 minutes. Species have evolved faster.

The quickest England moved all day was at 4.26pm, when the umpires decided that the light was an issue, whereupon they set PBs for spontaneous ground evacuation and feet upputting – Andy Flower has probably had them practising it.

## FIRST TEST, BRISBANE, 2013–14

MIKE ATHERTON,
CHIEF CRICKET CORRESPONDENT

*November 23.* And for all the talk from this epoch-making team, of their toughness and ability to withstand pressure, there was the unmistakable whiff of panic as they were bowled out for 136 – England's fifth lowest total at the Gabba.

The soft cricket played in the weeks building up to this game was no preparation for this cauldron and some ferocious fast bowling from Johnson. Mind you, there is a pattern that followers of English cricket in recent times will not be slow to recognise, that of a poor first-innings performance in the first Test of an overseas series, the Gabba now joining the below-par efforts in Galle, Ahmedabad, Dunedin and the United Arab Emirates. More food for thought – and not mung beans or tofu, either – for a backroom staff that has had to answer similar questions before.

## FIFTH TEST, SYDNEY, 2013–14

MIKE ATHERTON,
CHIEF CRICKET CORRESPONDENT

*January 6.* The surprise was the lack of resilience and competitive heart, whose beating got more faint with every passing game and finally stopped once and for all on the final afternoon in Sydney. Maybe these players were not quite as good as they believed themselves to be, maybe not quite as tough, either. Certainly, in the face of some withering fast bowling from Johnson, they played like timid schoolboys who had been asked to join a men's game for the first time.

## C.B. FRY

### FOURTH TEST, OLD TRAFFORD, 1905

R.H. LYTTELTON

*July 25.* Mr Fry had 25 minutes' batting before luncheon, but only scored one run, and after luncheon he went on at the same rate and took just an hour making 17 runs. Every batsman plays the right game when he carefully plays himself in, but it is unfortunate that Mr Fry should require such a long time for this object, for valuable time is absorbed, and few Test matches can be finished in England.

## TOM GODDARD

### FOURTH TEST, OLD TRAFFORD, 1930

R.B. VINCENT, CRICKET CORRESPONDENT

*July 26.* Chapman was not content with negative tactics, and when 10 runs had been scored in half an hour he put on Goddard at the City end and let Tate change over to the other. Goddard placed three men close in at short leg and treated them rather unkindly by bowling no-balls at culpably frequent intervals. Each time he presented the batsman with an opportunity to kill a fielder without risk to himself.

## GRAHAM GOOCH

### SIXTH TEST, THE OVAL, 1989

ALAN LEE, CRICKET CORRESPONDENT

*August 26.* England had begun their reply to a relatively modest Australian score of 468 in November gloom. The lights of the pavilion were glaring but umpire Bird, to whom this would traditionally present a persuasive case for hurrying the cast off the field, remained unmoved. With Gooch facing Alderman, there are no prizes for guessing what happened next.

Gooch faced three balls and did not lay his bat on any of them. Two were out-swingers he had no need to play, the third was ducked into his pads. Gooch was creasebound and playing the wrong line but the ball did look to be passing harmlessly down the leg side. Umpire Ken Palmer disagreed.

This was the fifth time in eight Test innings this summer that Gooch has been dismissed leg-before and it was not the first decision open to doubt. He may be suffering from a sense of familiar expectation; after successive scores of 0, 8, 11, 13 and 0 he may also be suffering from self-doubt which could yet influence his willingness to tour the West Indies.

## DAVID GOWER

### SECOND TEST, LORD'S, 1989

ALAN LEE, CRICKET CORRESPONDENT

*June 26.* It was not simply a bad day, it was a catastrophe, and the captain should, actually, have had rather a lot to say about it, even if he feels press conferences to be an encumbrance.

Gower was appointed in the well-founded belief that he possesses the wherewithal to cope articulately with the ever-increasing public relations side of being England captain. I supported his nomination and even detected a new, aggressive edge to his utterances, which was no bad thing.

He let himself down here, however, in a way which cannot pass without comment. His testy attitude and premature exit would have been more pardonable had he been returning to the dressing-room to debate where things went so badly wrong. Instead, he was heading to the theatre. Make what you will of the fact that his choice of entertainment was 'Anything Goes'.

### SIXTH TEST, THE OVAL, 1989

JOHN WOODCOCK

*August 29.* For 45 minutes yesterday morning Gower played exquisitely. I can think of no one – Sir Frank Worrell, Neil Harvey, Martin Donnelly, Colin Cowdrey, Denis Compton, Mushtaq Ali, Majid Khan and Graeme Pollock included – who had a more perfect sense of timing than David Gower. It hardly seems fair that anyone can hit so hard and yet so effortlessly.

*David Gower is about to lose patience and make a hasty exit from a press conference at Lord's in 1989. He had tickets in the West End*

I thought the same when I saw Gene Littler, the American golfer and seemingly a slip of a man, just feather the ball the best part of 300 yards down the middle. The best stand-off halves, the best fishermen, the best hockey players, the best shots, the best footballers seem always to have this precious gift of timing, and to do what they will with time to spare.

Yet how maddeningly typical it was – as maddening, surely, for him as it was for us – that Gower got out as he did, caught down the leg side flicking at a harmless ball from Alderman. It is partly because he will not learn from his mistakes, because of the casual way that he plays, that he has a good deal to answer for this summer. If the captain is not going to get his head down, what sort of an example is there to the others?

On the one hand he has this great talent; on the other he has never made quite enough of it. As a cameo the 36 runs he added yesterday to the 43 he had made on Saturday were fit to compare with such brief but brilliant exhibitions as Hutton's 37 against Australia at Sydney on the 1946–1947 tour and the occasional little jewel that Graveney might produce. Gower has much in common with Graveney; but Hutton, he had the steel as well.

## FOURTH TEST, ADELAIDE, 1990–91

ALAN LEE, CRICKET CORRESPONDENT

*January 28.* In the final over of the morning, bowled by Craig McDermott, Gower had already survived one top-edged pull and an attempted run-out. With one ball to come, and England's hopes resting squarely on his alliance with Graham Gooch, circumspection did not seem too much to ask.

Instead, tempted by a ball straying outside leg stump, Gower pivoted, picked it up in that familiar, flicking motion and watched in hypnotised horror as it looped gently and precisely into the hands of Hughes, at long leg.

Not for the first time in this series, Gooch wore the most eloquent expression on the field. He was 80 not out and England had still been placed to ponder a first-innings lead. One thoughtless piece of cricket had compromised hours of diligence. No wonder the captain looked angry.

Gower would be disingenuous if, this time, he excused himself by saying this is just the way he is. It was an acceptable response to the relatively harmless escapade in a Tiger Moth aircraft last week, an incident which Gower is unwisely prolonging by lodging an appeal against the severity of his fine, but on a matter of basic cricketing sense and professionalism, he has no such defence.

No one on either side has scored more runs in this series than Gower; at times he has played inimitably well. His batting, now as ever, is akin to flying by the seat of his pants and there is no value in judging either his brilliance or his blind spots by conventional standards.

But there is a time and a place for even the most eccentric extremes, and the last ball before lunch does not qualify. It was a moment which justified, more than the fly-past which provoked it, that management accusation of being 'immature, ill-judged and ill-timed'.

## TOM GRAVENEY

### SECOND TEST, SYDNEY, 1954–55

JOHN WOODCOCK, CRICKET CORRESPONDENT

*December 21.* It might have been better for the more dependable Cowdrey to come in now, but, as it was, Graveney made his fleeting appearance. His third ball was straight in flight, a foot or more wide of the off stump, and he drove at it as though he were well set in a September festival at Weston-super-Mare. It was an unaccountable stroke at this juncture – Graveney seems unable to apply himself to make the most of his many talents in a Test match – and England's spirits were low when luncheon was taken.

## TONY GREIG

### THIRD TEST, TRENT BRIDGE, 1972

JACK FINGLETON

*July 14.* Even if Greig were a good Test bowler, which he is not, it would not condone his immature histrionics. I dislike the way my countrymen leap and embrace when a wicket falls. I thought the same of Greig's antics yesterday when the ball beat the bat and when he got a solitary wicket.

### SECOND TEST, PERTH, 1974–75

JOHN WOODCOCK, CRICKET CORRESPONDENT

*December 18.* Greig hit the first ball of the first over this morning to third man for four, off the middle of the bat. It gave him false ideas. He seems to think at the moment that he can launch into an attack without needing to play himself in. His arrogance is in danger of becoming a disadvantage. The sixth ball of the day was pitched well up, Greig drove it without bothering to get his foot to the ball and Greg Chappell at first slip held a good head-high catch.

## STEPHEN HARMISON

### FIRST TEST, BRISBANE, 2006–07

SIMON BARNES

*November 24.* Normally, when the first ball of the series gets into the hands of second slip, it is a matter for rejoicing. But alas, the ball went to Andrew Flintoff straight from Harmison's hand, as wide a wide as you could hope to see in professional cricket.

## EDDIE HEMMINGS

### THIRD TEST, SYDNEY, 1990–91

ALAN LEE, CRICKET CORRESPONDENT

*January 7.* Eddie Hemmings, a man approaching 42, behaved like a spoiled schoolboy here on Saturday. Worse, he did so in front of the world's leading

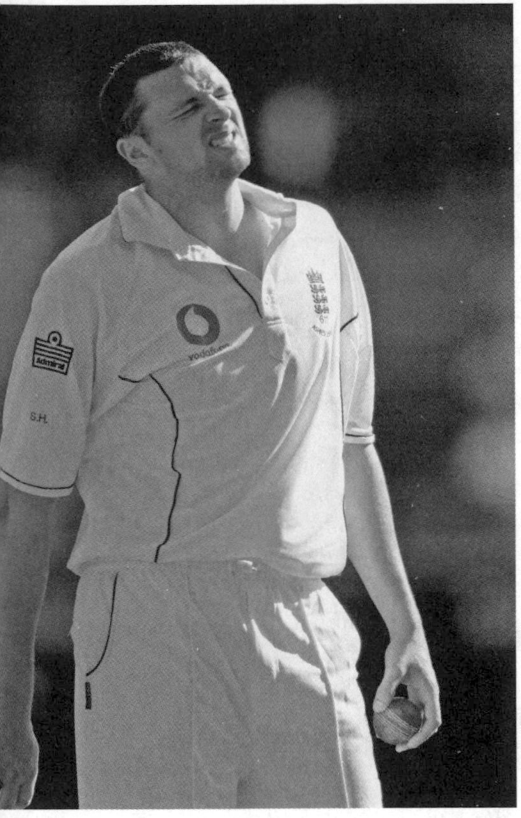

*Stephen Harmison endured a torrid Test match at the Gabba in 2006–07*

cricket administrators, who are gathered in Sydney to debate the adoption of an international code of conduct.

Hemmings's ill-mannered reaction to a properly rejected appeal for a bat-pad catch was to kick the ball lustily in the direction of the umpire, Peter McConnell. Luckily for him, it hit the stumps before it could hit the umpire.

It was inexcusably immature behaviour, even allowing for England's parlous position in the third Test match. It provoked booing in the crowd and embarrassment among the English delegates to the meeting of the International Cricket Council in Melbourne this week.

## JACK HOBBS

### THIRD TEST, HEADINGLEY, 1926

A.C.M. CROOME,
CRICKET CORRESPONDENT

*July 13.* Hobbs looked like proceeding methodically to his hundred. He had got nearly half way and then, making quite sure of the single which he needed to reach 50, he dealt gently with a long hop which might have been hooked for a 4 and cocked it up to short leg. The scoring boards now in use have much to answer for.

## MITCHELL JOHNSON

### FIRST TEST, BRISBANE, 2010–11

MIKE ATHERTON,
CHIEF CRICKET CORRESPONDENT

*November 29.* It was the kind of day, toiling for no reward and, more than that, never looking like getting any, that brought to mind the Cambridge University team of my vintage. To keep spirits up we used to have a fines session at the end of each day's play.

There was always a fine for a 'noncon', for the person who contributed least to the day's play – and in this match Mitchell Johnson is winning that award hands down. He went wicketless in England's first innings, scored a tentative blonger when he batted and he remained wicketless at the close of the fourth day's play. He left the field smiling with his team-mates in close attendance, in a kind of faux bonhomie, but it fooled no one. He has had a bad match so far.

## GERAINT JONES

### SECOND TEST, EDGBASTON, 2005

MICHAEL HENDERSON

*August 5.* Plucked from obscurity last year, and given every encouragement to make the No.7 spot his own by making runs, his career has stalled. If he is not making scores, he is not worth his place in the team because, behind the stumps, he wears gloves that might have been forged in a Black Country foundry.

## MARTIN McCAGUE

### THIRD TEST, TRENT BRIDGE, 1993

MICHAEL HENDERSON

*July 3.* Where nationhood is concerned battle lines can be hard to draw. After all, [Bob] Hope was born in Eltham, as we are reminded every time he returns (home), but to call him English on account of this accident of birth is like claiming the Liberty Bell for ourselves because it was forged in Whitechapel. Nevertheless, we can be sure of one thing. For the first time in Test history, England took the field yesterday with two fast bowlers, McCague and Caddick, who are English only in the most marginal sense. Every day a little death: the notion of Englishness, if we really care about it, has died a little here.

Of all the heat generated by McCague's conversion from Australian to stout man of Kent, the views of the three men closest to his selection bear consideration. First, Ted Dexter: 'We must be proud of our multi-national background.' Next Keith Fletcher: 'We acted within the rules.' Finally McCague: 'I owe Australia nothing.'

Why English cricket lovers should take pride in being represented by a bowler unable to win a place in his own country's side is unclear. As for rules, the unwritten one is commonsense, which has not been applied in this case. A student who felt he owed his lecturers nothing would be considered a most ungrateful chap.

McCague has argued that England has absorbed too many foreigners for his selection to be newsworthy. He is missing the point by a mile. By using the Union Jack as a flag of convenience, McCague is helping to diminish the sense of communality which binds a team. In any meaningful estimation, he is Australian. He knows it. The Australians know it. County cricketers know it. Most important, the spectators know it. All the wickets and catches in the world cannot alter that central fact.

## CRAIG McDERMOTT

### FOURTH TEST, MELBOURNE, 1986–87

JOHN WOODCOCK,
CRICKET CORRESPONDENT

*December 29.* McDermott, who improved his bowling figures by taking the last three England wickets, may wonder in years to come, when he watches a film of the day's play, how he was not in the hands of a psychiatrist. Not even Lillee at his worst used to behave with a more reckless passion when bowling for Australia.

*Craig McDermott launches a typically aggressive appeal in 1990–91*

### THIRD TEST, SYDNEY, 1994–95

JOHN WOODCOCK

*January 2.* When Crawley came in yesterday England were 20 for three with Gooch, Hick and Thorpe already out, McDermott in full cry and the ball swinging all over the place on a hot and humid morning. McDermott may not be as good as Miller and Lindwall to my mind, he never will be so long as he bowls in a watch ...

## DEVON MALCOLM

### FIFTH TEST, TRENT BRIDGE, 1989

JOHN WOODCOCK

*August 11.* It was not until the late afternoon that Malcolm lived up to his reputation as the wild bull of the Derbyshire Dales. His opening spell had been fast and presentably accurate. I suppose he might just about get into the Windward Islands side but not the Leewards, who must have dozens as good.

## EDDIE PAYNTER

### SECOND TEST, LORD'S, 1938

R.B. VINCENT,
CRICKET CORRESPONDENT

*June 29.* Paynter again edged a ball through the slips, but things were improving from England's point of view when Paynter, attempting a second run of a stroke to fine leg, had his wicket thrown down. At this state of the game, when a stolen run was of little importance and when a wicket meant everything to Australia, it was a stupid thing to have done.

## KEVIN PIETERSEN

### FIFTH TEST, THE OVAL, 2005

PAT GIBSON

*September 9.* It was a clever piece of bowling but it was a dreadful shot and Pietersen, who spends an awful lot of time with Warne, would do well to reflect that it is not the colour of a cricketer's hair that matters but what goes on underneath it.

*Kevin Pietersen and his ill-advised 'skunk' hairstyle*

## RICKY PONTING

### FOURTH TEST, MELBOURNE, 2010–11

GIDEON HAIGH

*December 28.* Every man has his weakness. With Shane Warne, it's blondes. With Ian Chappell, it's Ian Botham – and vice versa. With Ricky Ponting, it's umpires. Other players suffer white line fever; he has white coat fever. Few cricketers, and certainly no present international captain, has a poorer reputation: in the presence of officialdom that has somehow crossed him, he is never knowingly outstropped.

## DEREK PRINGLE

### SIXTH TEST, THE OVAL, 1989

ALAN LEE, CRICKET CORRESPONDENT

*August 25.* Pringle looked what he has always been – an effective county bowler ill-equipped for Test pitches.

## HERBERT STRUDWICK

### SECOND TEST, LORD'S, 1926

A.C.M. CROOME,
CRICKET CORRESPONDENT

*June 28.* The out-cricket of the England team would have been amazingly good if Strudwick had touched his own high standard of safety and brilliancy. He has recently written a book in which he sets out the principles of the art which he has practised so long and so successfully. On Saturday he was prone to violate one of them. Time and again he snapped at the ball and failed to gather it. Mr Macartney, soon after he came in, gave him a chance to stump him off a leg-ball from Tate. Admittedly, that chance was extremely difficult. But Strudwick and his few peers have in their time taken dozens of the kind. Mr Bardsley all through his long innings was never immune from the danger of edging the off-ball, and twice at least Strudwick failed to catch him.

## FRED TRUEMAN

### FIRST TEST, EDGBASTON, 1961

JOHN WOODCOCK,
CRICKET CORRESPONDENT

*June 12.* Trueman, on the other hand, showed less spirit for the struggle, which is disturbing news at this stage in the series. Off his shorter run he was neither fast nor threatening; indeed, as a Yorkshireman said, he looked as though he was growing old before his time. If a fast wicket comes along he will no doubt be a different proposition, but it is more a mark of greatness to bring life out of a lifeless pitch.

## ALEX TUDOR

### FOURTH TEST, MELBOURNE, 1998–99

MICHAEL HENDERSON

*December 28.* It is a pity that young Alex Tudor was not available to share the new ball. Pencilled in to play, he withdrew 40 minutes before the scheduled start on Boxing Day with what was described as a 'hip niggle', though it was said, rightly or wrongly, that he wanted to play and was dissuaded from confirming his fitness by unnamed others.

One hopes that he did want to play. It beggars belief that a 21-year-old, faced with the prospect of playing in a Christmas Test match at the MCG, pulled out because his hip was giving him some gyp. Tudor's fitness record, for a man who has played so little cricket, is appalling. Short of breaking a leg, there is no real excuse for not wanting to take part in an occasion like this. The last thing he wants to cultivate at so tender an age is a reputation as a namby-pamby.

## DEREK UNDERWOOD

### SECOND TEST, OLD TRAFFORD, 1977

JOHN WOODCOCK,
CRICKET CORRESPONDENT

*July 12.* I wish I could say the trusty Underwood. Trusty he was today, trusty he always has been; but he is off to Mr Packer very soon, to receive none of the plaudits that he did now and none of the pride either.

## SHANE WARNE

### SECOND TEST, ADELAIDE, 2002–03

CHRISTOPHER MARTIN-JENKINS,
CHIEF CRICKET CORRESPONDENT

*November 25.* Warne, the maestro, probed away for over after over, from round the wicket into the rough, often behaving outrageously and being allowed a little too much indulgence by Steve Bucknor, the umpire. It is time he was told to shut up occasionally as he oohs and aahs, chatters to his colleagues about the troubles of the batsman while he rubs his hand on the pitch and appeals with histrionic venom, running backwards down the pitch as he does so.

Sporting
HOW ENGLAND KEPT THE ASHES
TWO GREAT HEARTS OVERTHROW AUSTRALIA
England beat Australia by five wickets in the fourth Test match at Adelaide yesterday and so, gaining a lead of three matches to one in the series, have retained the Ashes. In an interview after the match L. Hutton, the England captain, paid a tribute to the younger members of the side. Much of the credit, he thought, should go to J. B. Statham, F. H. Tyson, M. C. Cowdrey and P. B. H. May, together with the wicket-keeper, T. G. Evans.
From Our Special Correspondent
ADELAIDE, FEB. 2
Many years from now young Cowdrey will point to his broken nose and tell boys yet unborn that he was at Adelaide on February 2, 1955, when England won the Test match and kept the Ashes. And the boys will think him wondrous lucky.
the catch. (We asked Hutton afterwards what he thought of Miller's bowling. Hutton thought Miller ought to concentrate much more on batting.) England 10 for 2. In comes the battered Cowdrey. Miller hits him twice running on the pads and appeals, and everybody here who isn't English appeals too. What a man is Miller. He comes in from a shortish run, loose of limb like an African, hair streaming, and as he pulls up the hair goes on and falls about his face. Meanwhile May has begun driving, and Johnson has gone from mid-off to square-leg. For Cowdrey Miller brings fine-leg up to third slip, and Cowdrey cover drives classically for 4. Miller heaves his shoulders over even faster, and Cowdrey is taken by Archer at first-slip. England 18 for 3. Four Meteor jets fly over at 200ft.; they look and sound quite tame beside this wild man
Ashes Fourth Test
England all too obliging as Warne reaches new heights of greatness
Australia v England
One that got away: Gilchrist misses a stumping chance off Warne to give Pietersen an extra life, but it was to make little difference
High five: Warne acknowledges the Melbourne crowd after his haul ripped the heart out of England's fragile batting
Sporting News
ENGLAND HAVE LAST WORD
THREE YEOMEN FOIL AUSTRALIA
GREAT STAND BY WATSON AND BAILEY
FROM OUR CRICKET CORRESPONDENT
Out of darkness, through fire into light. Thus did England yesterday rise like some Phoenix from the ashes of apparent defeat to save the second Test match at Lord's and so gain a
for proud
36 TUESDAY AUGUST 1 1989
THE TIMES
England's abject surrender marks new low in series
By Alan Lee, Cricket Correspondent
Inglorious procession at Old Trafford
SCOREBOARD FROM OLD TRAFFORD
Gower unfairly blamed for failings of others
Simon Barnes
Border rewarded for hard labour
By John Woodcock
Only two men so far decline
By Alan Lee
Was this English most desperate

# CAPTAINS

THE TIMES SATURDAY JUNE 11 1938
A GOOD BEGINNING BY ENGLAND
THE TIMES
LOCOMEN'S BAN BOUND TO CAUSE GREATER
HOW THE AUSTRALIANS WERE SKITTLED OUT AT LORD'S
Gaullists may get back with clear majority
Inquiry over bank chief's salary
Police alerted by strike ship
Railways must act alone, Marsh says
13 die in Swiss rail crash
Sporting News
LAKER'S SUPREME PART IN RETAINING THE ASHES
ALL TEN AUSTRALIAN WICKETS AND 19 IN MATCH
From Our Cricket Correspondent
dismally surrender Ashes
TEST MATCH
BRADMAN 309 NOT OUT
ALL RECORDS BROKEN
The Third Test Match between England and Australia was begun at Leeds yesterday. A. P. F. Chapman, for once, lost the toss and Australia went in to bat on a perfect batsman's wicket. By the end of the day they had scored 458 runs for the loss of

# WARWICK ARMSTRONG

## THIRD TEST, HEADINGLEY, 1921

F.B. WILSON

*July 5.* Mr Armstrong changed his bowling like the master he is – sometimes one can almost believe him the superior of Mr M.A. Noble as a captain, as many Australians declare him to be …

## FIFTH TEST, THE OVAL, 1921

A.C.M. CROOME

*August 17.* Mr Armstrong took up his position on the farthest boundary, by the Vauxhall entrance, and declined to move either at the end of an over, or when the ball came his way. But he did once run quite fast, when Mr Fender hit a 'balloon' off Mr Mailey. He got under the ball and brought off a distinctly good catch. None can say whether he continued to direct the tactics of his side telepathically, or whether the bowlers put themselves on by lot.

# MIKE ATHERTON

ALAN LEE, CRICKET CORRESPONDENT

*July 27, 1993.* Ted Dexter, the chairman, was yesterday in contact with Micky Stewart, Ossie Wheatley and Alan Smith to convene a meeting and, although a compromise decision on an outsider cannot entirely be discounted, the issue is likely to rest between Michael Atherton, Alec Stewart and Mike Gatting.

Sporting Index, the bookmakers, yesterday opened a market on the captaincy and made Stewart their 6-4 favourite, with Atherton at 7-4 and Gatting at 7-2. In recent days, however, the lobby for Atherton has grown. The only candidate with an entirely clean licence in conduct terms, Atherton is an intelligent, self-contained character, stronger than often perceived and likely to flourish with the responsibility. At 25, he is young enough to be a long-term investment and would give the team the fresh, untainted outlook now so plainly needed. Stewart can be considered seriously as captain only if he no longer keeps wicket, and Fletcher, a Gatting devotee, has made it plain he wants him to continue in the role.

ALAN LEE, CRICKET CORRESPONDENT

*July 29, 1993.* Sociable, communicative but extremely determined, Atherton will bring a refreshing approach to the job. He will also bring a different, more relaxed character. He said he 'slept like a baby' after being told the news. If he can go on avoiding sleepless nights, he might do this job for years.

## SIXTH TEST, THE OVAL, 1993

MICHAEL HENDERSON

*August 24.* However ably he handled his players during his first Test win as England captain, Michael Atherton's savoir faire at the subsequent press conference exceeded the normal call of duty.

An encounter with a tabloid journalist who appeared to be under the misapprehension that he was questioning the manager of a lower division football club, represented the greatest chasm of IQ since Isaiah Berlin last greeted his dustmen.

## THIRD TEST, SYDNEY, 1994–95

JOHN WOODCOCK

*January 4.* On Saturday, Atherton and Crawley did England, Manchester Grammar School and the ancient universities proud. Yes, the ancient universities, inferentially derided by Raymond Illingworth whenever he sees the chance. Having been to Cambridge, he said, and never done a day's work of a certain kind, Atherton was not best equipped to 'gee-up' his side.

The chairman of selectors approves of Atherton. It just is that he has a thumping great chip as well. It is, of course, no more admissable to imply that Atherton is not qualified to pull England together because he went to Cambridge than it is to say that Gough played the innings he did on Monday because he is a Yorkshireman. The trademark of Illingworth's England's captaincy was deliberation, not motivation; the trademark of Atherton's is tenacity. Atherton can, in fact, take much credit for England's revival and Illingworth will get round to telling him so, I am sure.

# ALLAN BORDER

JOHN WOODCOCK

*August 26, 1989.* Although Australia won only three of the first 25 Test matches they played under the captaincy of Allan Border, he himself became in that time his country's most popular sportsman. It was not that he had the charisma of a Benaud or the tactical sagacity of a Bradman or the genius of a Chappell: what appealed to the Australian public was his determination always to stand his ground; his courage, in fact, in face of the fastest and shortest bowling, however desperate Australia's plight.

For match after match Border gave his all, more often than not in an unavailing cause; and now, at last, he can feel that it was all worthwhile. He has seen the side which he and Bobby Simpson built up give England the mother and father of a beating, and for an Australian captain life has nothing sweeter to offer than that.

# IAN BOTHAM

## FIRST TEST, TRENT BRIDGE, 1981

JOHN WOODCOCK, CRICKET CORRESPONDENT

*June 20.* Still unrecognizable as the irrepressible bowler and brilliant catcher of a year ago, Botham's performance must finally have convinced the selectors, for his own good, to make a change. They must turn to Boycott.

# DON BRADMAN

## FIFTH TEST, THE OVAL, 1948

R.B. VINCENT, CRICKET CORRESPONDENT

*August 18.* The score was then 64, but Bradman, apparently not quite satisfied, brought Ring on in place of Lindwall. Bradman's captaincy has a reason in it which only the cultured observer can follow.

## MIKE BREARLEY

### FOURTH TEST, EDGBASTON, 1981

JOHN WOODCOCK,
CRICKET CORRESPONDENT

*August 4.* The selectors have a few days yet to decide what changes, if any, to make. Like all other Englishmen last night they were content to rejoice at England's remarkable success. For this Brearley must take no small part of the credit.

The best thing that has happened to Botham since Brearley gave up the captaincy last year was when Brearley was prevailed upon to take it on again. After 12 Tests in a row without a victory England's bowlers, under Brearley's leadership, have emerged to play a memorable part in this royal summer. Once again yesterday Brearley's tactical astuteness, with so few runs to play with, was a source of strength.

## ARTHUR CARR

### SECOND TEST, LORD'S, 1926

A.C.M. CROOME,
CRICKET CORRESPONDENT

*June 28.* An eminent cricketer has publicly suggested that Mr Carr's captaincy, otherwise admirable, was blameworthy in respect of his selection of slip fielders. It is alleged that practically every member of the side drifted into the slips at one time or another. The truth is that Sutcliffe crossed from first slip to first slip

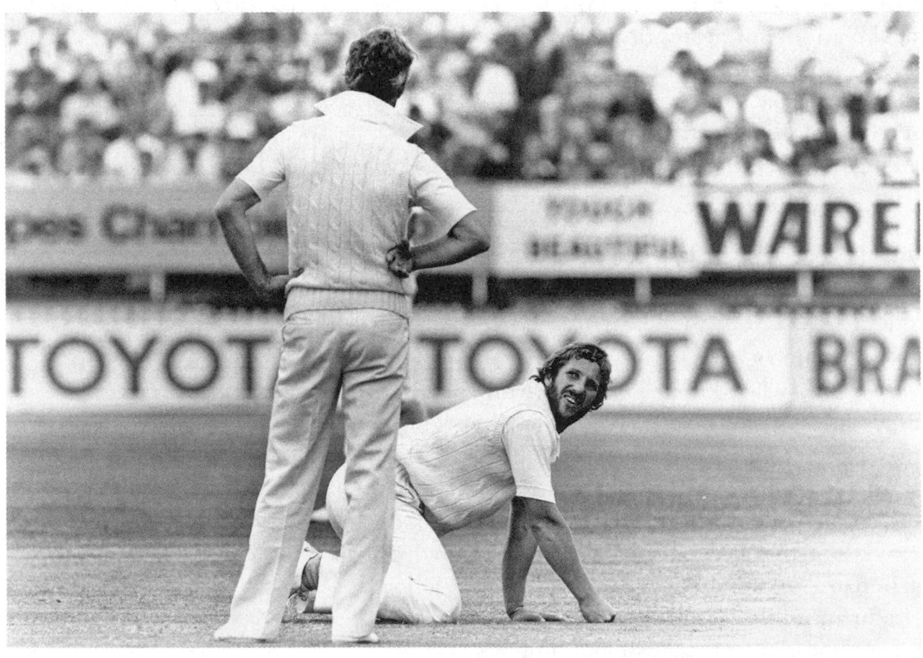


*Advice gratefully received. Mike Brearley passes on some words of wisdom to Ian Botham at Edgbaston in 1981*

throughout the day, and when Kilner was bowling Mr Chapman and Hendren had to run considerable distances in order to take up their positions beside Sutcliffe at the end of the over. Even Woolley, who has caught as many slip catches as any other man now playing for England, was never called upon to save them this exertion. Mr Carr's critic, Balaamlike, has blessed where he was expected to curse, and the captain fully deserves the supreme compliment involved in the mis-statement of facts. Mr Carr not only placed his men wisely; he also set them an excellent example of diligent, efficiency. It is a nice question whether he or Hendren, when their turn comes to bat, will go in credited with the larger number of runs saved.

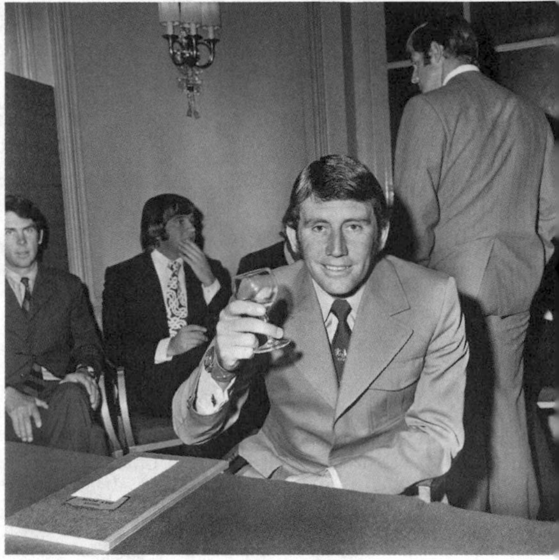

*Ian Chappell, despite an empty glass, wishes for a successful summer in 1972. The 2-2 draw marked the start of a new beginning for Australian cricket*

## PERCY CHAPMAN

### FIRST TEST, TRENT BRIDGE, 1930

R.B. VINCENT,
CRICKET CORRESPONDENT

*June 16.* For A.P.F. Chapman too it was also a great day. His generalship in the changing of his bowling was superb, but not more remarkable than the wonderful spirit which he instilled in the whole team, for every man on the side was on the tip-toe of expectancy. His fielding was extraordinary, and on today's showing alone he is proclaimed a great captain who can get the utmost out of his team.

## IAN CHAPPELL

### FOURTH TEST, THE OVAL, 1975

JOHN WOODCOCK,
CRICKET CORRESPONDENT

*September 1.* Unless someone talks him out of it Chappell seems to have decided that this shall be his last Test match as Australia's captain, though not as an ordinary member of their side. Since first taking over, against England at Sydney in 1971, he has met with outstanding success. There is a real toughness about him, a side to his character which has no time for compromise: it is this which makes him unlikely to change his mind about withdrawing from the captaincy and well capable of putting England in again, if he sees that as the best way of discomforting Greig.

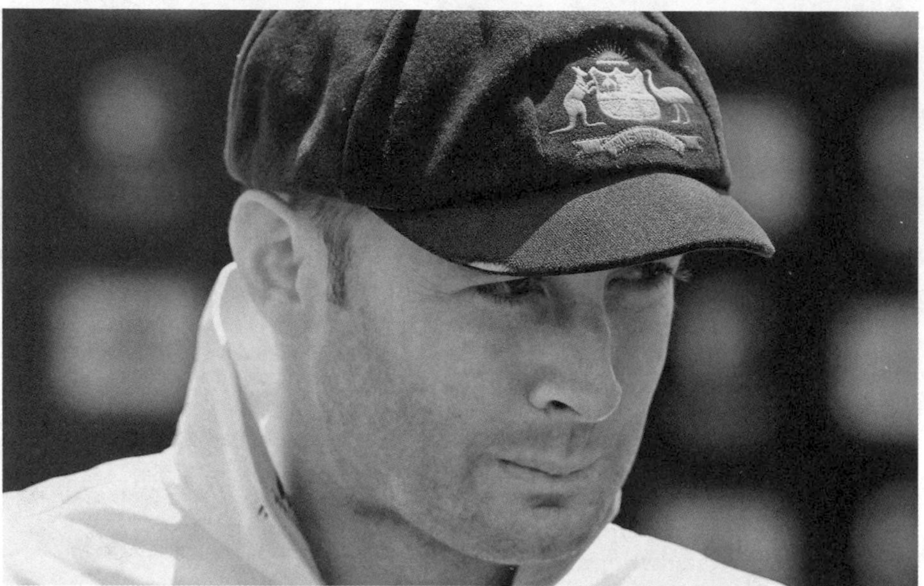

*Baggy green and bowed; Michael Clarke finds the going tough at Sydney in 2010–11*

## MICHAEL CLARKE

### FIRST TEST, BRISBANE, 2013–14

MIKE ATHERTON,
CHIEF CRICKET CORRESPONDENT

*November 23.* An advert was doing the rounds before the start of this match, touting for business from those with defective eyesight. 'Struggling to tell the difference between Michael Clarke and Alastair Cook,' went the jingle, 'then you know where to go.'

On the second afternoon, as Clarke orchestrated his potent attack with masterly expertise, there could have been no confusion. What a turnaround this was for him. The image of Clarke the batsman undone by a Stuart Broad sucker punch on day one, was replaced by Clarke the all-knowing on day two; Clarke the sorcerer, Clarke the aggressor, as he stood by the stumps under his sunhat, directing the field, seemingly in control of his destiny once again.

## MIKE DENNESS

JOHN WOODCOCK,
CRICKET CORRESPONDENT

*December 24, 1974.* For the past week Denness has been unable to pick up a paper without seeing himself 'rubbished', as they say in Australia. If it has not been by a critic it has been by Snow, who is commenting on the series ('Colin (Batman) Cowdrey … never quite unleashed his zap, pow and bam' is from one of Snow's offerings), or even by Close, whose verdict on Denness, pronounced from halfway across the world, was published yesterday. Last night Sir Donald Bradman, the best of all judges, told me that he thought Denness was 'a nice player. Not as tight as some, but a good player'. If any sportsman needs special wishes for a joyful Christmas it is England's captain.

## GRAHAM GOOCH

ALAN LEE, CRICKET CORRESPONDENT

*July 27, 1993.* One of Gooch's achievements, on that tour, was to instil a strict and proper sense of discipline among players who had been permitted too much theatrical licence by his predecessors. This was to be a theme of his leadership; transgressors, such as Hussain and Tufnell, were dealt with sharply and anybody who wanted to sulk or malinger on the field was left in no doubt about his responsibilities.

Gooch the captain believed that his example which was consistently impeccable should be enough for anybody to follow. What he could or would not do was make allowances for those whose ways were different. This alienated Gower and Tufnell, among others, and led to suspicions that Gooch's England was a mechanical side, stripped of joy for the sake of conformity.

That he punished his own, ageing and creaking body was evident to all. Only last week, Allan Border shook his head as he described arriving at a ground to find Gooch, already changed, running around the square in his batting pads. 'Graham has his own way of preparing,' Border said, 'and some of it may be pretty strange for a 40-year-old. But what he cannot bear is to see others less committed than he is.' Gooch identified this trait in this summer's first Test and, yes, he could not bear it. He might have resigned on the spot and he almost did, after the second Test at Lord's. Headingley was one let-down too many.

## TONY GREIG

LEADING ARTICLE

*August 16, 1977.* That the tables have been so completely turned lies largely to the credit of Greig. He took over a side being compared with the very worst in England's cricketing history, made its members believe in their individual and collective abilities, and by his own flamboyant, perhaps over-aggressive example instilled confidence into a team that had become accustomed to losing. In particular, his insistence on the importance of good fielding has paid handsome dividends. The superb athleticism and sticky fingers of the English side contributed in large measure to its success.

## LEN HUTTON

### FOURTH TEST, ADELAIDE, 1954–55

A.G. MOYES

*February 2.* Hutton threw Appleyard into attack after Statham had bowled only two overs and bowled him into the end where Johnson had worried the English batsmen. The difference was, and Hutton that shrewd campaigner knew it, that Johnson was too slow to take full advantage of the pitch, whereas Appleyard, who pushed the ball through much faster, would succeed.

STEWART HARRIS

*February 3.* After lunch Appleyard is given two overs from the Cathedral end, both of which are maidens. Then Hutton takes him off and puts on Wardle, and we all ask why. And Wardle explains by getting Davidson l-b-w with his second ball. Well done, Hutton, once again.

---

## RAYMOND ILLINGWORTH

### FIRST TEST, BRISBANE, 1970–71

JOHN WOODCOCK,
CRICKET CORRESPONDENT

*November 28.* On a day when England were never in greater need of strong and forthright leadership, Illingworth was seldom conspicuous. If, through it all, he was thinking shrewd thoughts he was not acting on them. Rightly or wrongly Cowdrey at slip appeared to be taking a keener interest in the tactical implications of the play.

### SEVENTH TEST, SYDNEY, 1970–71

JOHN WOODCOCK,
CRICKET CORRESPONDENT

*February 17.* Illingworth played a true captain's part in all this. Throughout the day he had shown no signs of the knee injury which came into its own on the rest day. He ran for himself this morning, and this evening it was he who removed Redpath and Stackpole. Illingworth knew then that, barring unforeseen resistance from the Australian tail, he should return to England with his mission completed.

THE TIMES THURSDAY FEBRUARY 18 1971

Cricket

**Illingworth's triumph as England regain the Ashes**

From John Woodcock
Cricket Correspondent
Sydney, Feb. 17

Just after half past twelve here today England regained the Ashes and Ray Illingworth their captain was carried off the field on the shoulders of John Edrich and John Hampshire. Australia had lost the seventh Test match by 62 runs, the victims of an impressively calculating performance.

It is high time the Ashes changed

each with a different arm in a sling. It must have embarrassed the Australians to see it. Yet, ironically, it was Snow's absence which obliged Illingworth to bowl more than he otherwise might have done and to return the principal figures. His victims, Stackpole, Redpath and Greg Chappell, were all good ones.

For English cricketers from the village green to the Sydney Cricket Ground the winning of the Ashes

*February 18, 1971 and an English winter is cheered by a triumph in Australia*

### FOURTH TEST, HEADINGLEY, 1972

JOHN WOODCOCK,
CRICKET CORRESPONDENT

*July 31.* Illingworth's handling of the whole operation was shrewd and efficient. He is to be warmly congratulated on keeping the Ashes, and especially on his part in this match. His batting, bowling, fielding and field placing all showed him for what he is – an outstanding competitor on the big day.

---

## DOUGLAS JARDINE

### SECOND TEST, MELBOURNE, 1932–33

ROY CURTHOYS

*December 31.* The tactics of England were entirely successful, D.R. Jardine's leadership being the outstanding feature of the day. He conceived the idea that the surest way to succeed was with consistent pace in attack, and so he began with Larwood and Voce, followed by G.O. Allen and Bowes, with Hammond as support. Judicious changes from the off to the leg theory, careful and scientific placing of the field and intense concentration rendered the batting impotent and ineffective. It was, in fact, a triumph for Jardine, who continually encouraged and advised his bowlers.

## BILL LAWRY

### FIFTH TEST, MELBOURNE, 1970–71

JOHN WOODCOCK,
CRICKET CORRESPONDENT

*January 26.* Lawry is one of those captains who seldom departs from the conventional. Imaginative bowling changes are not a part of the pattern, though there must have been lots of people who had been wondering why, in order to break the deadlock, he did not try Ian Chappell. Even more surprising, especially with Duncan unable to take part because of an injured heel, was Lawry's refusal to make use of Walters, whose bowling he consistently underrates. Cricket, as Lawry and Illingworth play it, is less full of surprises than it need be.

## RICKY PONTING

### FIRST TEST, CARDIFF, 2009

GIDEON HAIGH

*July 11.* Ponting's leadership still attracts plenty of criticism in Australia, particularly from former players who remember their era as one of non-stop flair and innovation. For sure, there remains some truth to the assertion that he does not deviate far from basics. But captaincy is in the main not a public event – it is the leadership in a dressing room, in a hotel, on a team bus, at training. And in this respect Ponting is, from all accounts, far better than he was.

Ponting is no arm-around-the-shoulder captain with a degree in people, the famous Bachelor of Brearleyism. In his early years he could be terse, gruff, not from lack of feeling, but because the expression of it did not come naturally.

## ANDREW STRAUSS

### FOURTH TEST, MELBOURNE, 2010–11

MIKE ATHERTON,
CHIEF CRICKET CORRESPONDENT

*December 30.* […] this England team carry all the hallmarks of their leader. They are diligent, committed, intensely competitive and incredibly well organised. It is in the disciplined batting of Jonathan Trott and Alastair Cook, rather than the flair of Pietersen, that Strauss's England can best be sighted, a discipline that has extended to the bowling throughout this series from, principally, James Anderson but latterly Chris Tremlett and Tim Bresnan. Not that jokers, such as Graeme Swann, are undervalued.

Few doubted Strauss's ability to succeed here, because this tour has not necessarily been his hardest challenge. Thrust into the job at short notice after a couple of periods of babysitting, he had to work in the opening few months to create a culture of self-sufficiency. It is ironic how this tour has come to be seen as the apotheosis of the culture of coaching, but Strauss's first message to the players was that they had become too soft and too reliant on outside help. That was necessary, though, because seeking help is one thing, taking responsibility quite another.

## FIFTH TEST, SYDNEY, 2010–11

ED SMITH

*January 8.* Where more conspicuously ambitious men have fallen by the wayside, victims of impatience, Strauss has bided his time. He has never cared about walking into a room like a natural-born leader. Impressing people has never been important to him; what matters to Strauss is getting things done.

Able but not intimidating, assured but not overbearing, analytical but not fretful, amenable but not compliant, Strauss is a master of moderation. His greatest political talent is not appearing to be overly political. He is at ease in most company, from the dressing room to the boardroom. Even his batting eschews the limelight. He is not strikingly effortless like David Gower, nor scorched with the scars of bravery like Mike Atherton. Instead, he is halfway between the two, helped by his strength of character but not defined in by it.

*Andrew Strauss's leadership was at its best in the triumphant 2010–11 series in Australia*

## LIONEL TENNYSON

### THIRD TEST, HEADINGLEY, 1921

F.B. WILSON

*July 5.* Mr J.C. White was bowled for a single, and then the England captain came in to join his Second in Command. He received a tremendous ovation, for in Yorkshire, though they may be partisan, they can and do always realize a sportsman.

Mr Tennyson must have been jarred by some of the strokes he played: but he is essentially a right-handed hitter, using his right wrist, forearm, and body to drive with and using his left hand only, as a guide. It seemed as if the injury to his hand was encouraging him, in vulgar language 'to get his own back.' He hit extremely hard when he got the right ball to hit and went through with every stroke without a sign of flinching on the forcing strokes. With the pair apparently well set the follow-on seemed to be averted. Quite unexpectedly, however, Colonel Douglas was deceived in the flight of a ball from Mr Armstrong and bowled. [...]

Mr Tennyson, the worst averted, was caught in the slips. He batted only 85 minutes for his runs and hit 10 4's. It was an innings which will be remembered by those who saw it as one of the greatest exhibitions of determination and opportunism ever seen in a Test: match; determination, because he was advised not to bat; opportunism, because he had to score quickly and pick out the exact ball which could be hit without a fatal hurt.

More memorable and ever to be admired as a precedent, however, was his coming out to field after his innings. Here indeed he showed the spirit in which cricket should be played. A batsman who can make over 50, and make them quickly, can also field; or if he cannot do so, and particularly if he is captain of a side, he has no right to a substitute. The action of Mr Tennyson was, indeed, worthy of an England captain.

Sporting ...

# ...OW ENGLAND KEPT TH... ASHES

## ...WO GREAT HEARTS OVERTHROW AUSTRALIA

England beat Australia by five wickets in the fourth Test match at Adelaide yesterday and so, gaining a lead of three matches to one in the series, have retained the Ashes. In an interview after the match L. Hutton, the England captain, paid a tribute to the younger members of the side. Much of the credit, he thought, should go to J. B. Statham, F. H. Tyson, M. C. Cowdrey and P. B. H. May, together with the wicket-keeper, T. G. Evans.

From Our Special Correspondent

ADELAIDE, FEB. 2

Many years from now young Cowdrey will point to his broken nose and tell boys yet unborn that he was at Adelaide on February 2, 1955, when England won the Test match and kept the Ashes. And the boys will think him wondrous lucky. A ma... should dip his pen in blood to write ... is day. Let no one talk and ...

... the catch. (We asked Hutton afterwards what he thought of Miller's bowling. Hutton thought Miller ought to concentrate much more on batting.) England 10 for 2. In comes the battered Cowdrey. Miller hits him twice running on the pads and appeals, and everybody here who isn't English appeals too. What a man is Miller. He comes in from a shortish run, loose of limb like an African, hair streaming, and as he pulls up the hair goes on and falls about his face. Meanwhile May has begun driving, and Johnson has gone from mid-off to square-leg. For Cowdrey Miller brings fine-leg up to third slip, and Cowdrey cover drives classically for 4. Miller heaves his shoulders over even faster, and Cowdrey is taken by Archer at first-slip. England 18 for 3. Four Meteor jets fly over at 200ft.; they look and sound quite tame beside this wild man ... His figures now are 3 overs, no ... runs, 3 wickets.

Sporting News

# ENGLAND HAVE LAST WORD

## THREE YEOMEN FOIL AUSTRALIA

## GREAT STAND BY WATSON AND BAILEY

FROM OUR CRICKET CORRESPONDENT

Out of darkness, through fire into light. Thus did England yesterday rise like some Phoenix from the ashes of apparent defeat to save the second Test match at Lord's and so gain a ... draw against Australia with ... seven wickets, ... original aim fo...

The age of ... yet past, nor c... cany scarce f... dramatic and ... a match alrea... But within t... longest and ... of a match it... that last spa... back with le... yeomen of ... nearly the w...

The yeom... were Watso... greatest of ... Yorkshirem... order, was ... rearguard ... twentieth ...

...e Ashes Fourth ...

# ...ngland all too obliging ... eaches new heights of greatnes...

One that got away: Gilchrist misses a stumping chance off Warne to give Pietersen an extra life, but it was to make little differen...

High five: Warne acknowledges the Melbourne crowd after his haul ripped the heart out of England's fragile batting

... by Warne's legendary accuracy and a lush outfield, they ran poorly between the wickets, chose the wrong balls to try to hit in the air and failed to justify the decision to bat.

"We didn't expect conditions to change dramatically over the first day and a half," Strauss said, "but it seamed about more than we expected." It did so slowly but Glenn McGrath, Stuart Clark and Brett Lee all got enough past the bat to suggest that the wrong option had been taken.

Australia missed two catches, two clear run-out opportunities and a gaping stumping, but still bowled England out for 159 after they had been 101 for two. Very few Test matches are won after such a start. All of Warne's wickets were taken by flight and dip, as batsmen spied what they believed to be boundary opportunities. Only Kevin Pietersen got anywhere near the boundary as he attempted to drive Warne straight for six, but by now he was, as usual, batting with the tail.

Even he needed 70 balls for 21 runs, having come close to running out Andrew Flintoff for six as, for the third Test in succession, he attempted a ridiculous single in order to get off the mark. He had only made four when he also survived a simple stumping chance offered to Adam Gilchrist after charging Warne and missing.

England, we all know, have too long a tail, but tweaking it made no difference. Matthew Hoggard is back where he started, No 11, pushing Monty Panesar and Stephen Harmison up a place each, which reflects their various abilities with the bat. It is higher up, however, that the balance is wrong. Ed Joyce or Jamie Dalrymple should have played ... six, but Chris Read for Geraint Jones was the only change.

As the best player in the team, Pietersen needs to bat at four. Since Paul Collingwood shared the only partnership of any substance with Strauss — 57 for the third wicket — it may appear that England's strategy, to keep him away from the new ball, had worked again, but to have Pietersen batting with the tail repeatedly is not satisfactory. In any case Collingwood might have been leg-before to Clark for nought, one of four apparently plumb leg-before decisions turned down by Rudi Koertzen.

Panesar was the other, ...

... Australia's recent practice of not using a nightwatchman.

Ponting said that Australia too, would have chosen to bat first, but it was one of those tosses that either captain would prefer to have lost. Play was delayed by rain for half an hour and only 16 overs were bowled before an early lunch was taken. Alastair C...

...nting run out (Flintoff) 66

P Siddle c Flintoff b Harmison 10

S 37 343-9 S Clark c Cook b Harrison 0

...iant leap

for proud S...

36 TUESDAY AUGUST 1 1989

THE TIMES

First published 1785

# England's abject surrender marks new low in series

By Alan Lee, Cricket Correspondent

## Inglorious procession at Old Trafford

10-1: Curtis c Boon b Alderman 0

25-2: Robinson lbw b Lawson 12

27-3: Smith c Healy b Alderman 1

28-4: Gooch c Alderman b Lawson 13

38-5: Botham lbw b Alderman 4

59-6: Gower c Marsh b Lawson 15

SCOREBOARD FROM OLD TRAFFORD

## Gower unfairly blamed for failings of others

Simon Barnes

## Border rewarded for hard labour

By John Woodcock

## Only two men so far decline

By Alan Lee

# Was this English most desperate

...ding

... night issued a dramatic ... et Union to make a positive ... te. He said that unless the ... epared to help to achieve an ... ategic arms limitations, he would ... tional funds of more than

# PITCHES

THE TIMES SATURDAY JUNE 11 1938

H: A GOOD BEGINNING BY ENGLAND

4

Sporting News

LAKER'S SUPREME PART IN RETAINING THE ASHES

ALL TEN AUSTRALIAN WICKETS AND 19 IN MATCH

From Our Cricket Correspondent

pitch perked up and the ball showed signs of misbehaving.

At luncheon McDonald and Craig were still together. They had then added only 59, but the important thing was that they had each been batting for more than four hours. Ahead of them stretched another four and only 15 minutes of these had ticked away when Laker struck

THE TIMES

HOW THE AUSTRALIANS WERE SKITTLED OUT AT LORD'S

LOCOMEN'S BAN BOUND

Gaullists may get back with clear majority

Inquiry over bank chief's salary

Police alerted by strike ship

Railways must act alone, Marsh says

dismally surrender Ashes

TEST MATCH

BRADMAN 309 NOT OUT

ALL RECORDS BROKEN

The Third Test Match between England and Australia was begun at Leeds yesterday. A. P. F. Chapman, for once, lost the toss and Australia went in to bat on a perfect batsman's wicket. By the end of the day they had scored 458 runs for the loss of three wickets and

## FIRST TEST, TRENT BRIDGE, 1921

A.C.M. CROOME

*May 30.* During that time Mr Carter, standing back, was only once obliged to jump in order to reach a bumper, and two or three times he was yorked on the second bounce by balls which came on from the pitch with unexpected mildness. The comfort of the wicketkeeper is a pretty good criterion by which spectators may estimate the character of the pitch. It was a different story after luncheon when the sun was shining on the ground dampened by morning showers. Then Rhodes in particular had a most unpleasant time. A ball from Mr Macdonald grazed the peak of his cap, and thereafter neither bowler showed excessive consideration for his feelings.

## FIRST TEST, TRENT BRIDGE, 1926

*June 12.* In spite of the amount of rain that has fallen this week, it may be quite possible for the present match to be fought out on a hard wicket. The ground at Trent Bridge has seldom been in better condition generally, and Marshall, the groundsman, hopes and expects to have a first-rate pitch available. He has worked on it all through the winter with the greatest care. When yesterday afternoon a shower, which was of brief duration, broke over Nottingham there had been no rain in the district for more than 24 hours. The pitch then had already been covered, and unless there is a heavy downpour conditions should certainly favour batsmen.

## SECOND TEST, LORD'S, 1926

A.C.M. CROOME,
CRICKET CORRESPONDENT

*June 29.* The hydrant at the north-west corner of the 'Square' at Lord's was found to be running in the small hours of Monday morning by White, who was telepathically disturbed in his sleep, and went round to the ground, anxious about he knew not what. He was able to stop the flow of water before the damage was irreparable, but the start of play yesterday was delayed while sacks of sawdust were spread on the quagmire in front of mid-off, and there was a patch of wet turf about two yards wide across the exact middle of the Test match pitch. Indeed, Larwood's second ball failed to carry the water hazard, and came on so slowly that Mr Oldfield had ample time to hook it for four.

## SECOND TEST, LORD'S, 1930

R.B. VINCENT,
CRICKET CORRESPONDENT

*June 27.* There is surely rain about somewhere, and it would be comfortable to have a nice large parcel of runs made and stacked before the rain reaches St John's Wood. If it never gets there the pitch may be trusted to last for the whole four days. In fact, the side which goes in first may have a little the worse of it. White has eliminated much of the waywardness from the turf at Lord's, but it can still behave eccentrically. One has often seen conditions more favourable to batsmen on the second day of a match than on the first. It is some years since a wicketkeeper found it more difficult at Lord's than on other famous

*Mike Atherton and coach David Lloyd inspect the Lord's wicket with groundsman Mick Hunt in 1997*

grounds to discover the place where he could most conveniently stand to take the fast bowling. Time was when one ball was liable to fly over his head, another to york him on the second bounce. How White has tamed the turf he alone knows. There is no mention of Nottingham marl or liquid manure in the published accounts of the M.C.C., and White will tell you, if you have the privilege of his acquaintance, that he does not pay for these materials out of his own pocket.

## FIRST TEST, TRENT BRIDGE, 1938

DUDLEY CAREW

*June 15.* At the same time a cricket match is supposed to be a contest between bat and ball, and the more even the balance the better the match. When the pitch is such as it was from Friday to yesterday, then the game ceases to have its proper balance and significance. Not only is the bowling barred from its rightful privilege, a fair and equitable pitch that is, but the batsman who has a conscientious pride in his cricket suffers almost as much as the bowler with a pride in his. It might have been a great, and heroic, feat for the Australians to have avoided defeat yesterday, but it was turned by the pitch into a worthily and patiently performed piece of honest craftsmanship, for which W.A. Brown and D.G. Bradman deserved the praise suitable to the comparatively mild difficulties with which they had to contend.

## SECOND TEST, LORD'S, 1938

R.B. VINCENT,
CRICKET CORRESPONDENT

*June 24.* There is nothing, apart from a chance of rain falling, to suggest that the Test match which is to be begun at Lord's today will provide any hope of a completed game. So long as two teams so strong in batting are allowed the use of pitches manufactured to a type of such excellence, and the games are restricted to four days, the bowlers must be content with the poor compliment that they are a necessary component part of the game. Someone has to supply the batsman with fodder or there would be no more 'records', and that would be fatal to so-called 'Test match' cricket.

In all conscience enough runs were scored at Trent Bridge, but I shudder to think how many will be made at Lord's. Yesterday afternoon I gazed in wonder at the wicket on which this match is to be played, and my heart bled for the bowlers – for all the bowlers, that is, except O'Reilly, who I believe could make the ball rise and spin off a bed of feathers.

## FIFTH TEST, THE OVAL, 1938

JOHN WOODCOCK

*August 22, 2001.* The first Test I watched at the Oval was, in fact, timeless, though it took England less than four days to win it. It was Len Hutton's match in 1938, when 'Bosser' Martin, the groundsman, bound the pitch with liquid manure and you could almost smell it from Oval station. The Health and Safety people would no doubt put a stop to that today.

## FIRST TEST, BRISBANE, 1954–55

JOHN WOODCOCK,
CRICKET CORRESPONDENT

*November 27.* This may be an omen, but one's opinion is that Hutton's decision, when he won the toss in the presence of innumerable cameramen at five minutes past 11, was not only justified but made almost inevitable by circumstances and the constitution of his side.

Hutton staked everything on the wicket being damp and lively, as it was for M.C.C.'s match with Queensland a week ago. Soon, however, he was faced with the horrible realization that the pitch was dry and lifeless and that he had thrown Australia a considerable advantage and condemned his own side to batting in the fourth innings.

## FIRST TEST, TRENT BRIDGE, 1956

JOHN WOODCOCK,
CRICKET CORRESPONDENT

*June 7.* It is thought that the pitch is the same as that on which Trent Bridge Test matches have been fought out for many years with the important difference that it has been heavily rolled and given no dressing. The impression is that the ball may be turning by the third day. At all events the toss will probably be a most valuable one to win, for with the covers remaining on until the first ball is bowled the pitch will begin easy. After that it is open to the elements and anything may come to change its character.

## FOURTH TEST, OLD TRAFFORD, 1956

JOHN WOODCOCK,
CRICKET CORRESPONDENT

*July 26.* Yet perhaps the factors which may again have more influence than any on the meeting of two well-balanced sides are the weather and the wicket. Yesterday the sky became gradually more clouded as one drove north, and because of Manchester's climate Old Trafford Test matches are notoriously unpredictable. The estimable and original intention of the authorities was to prepare the fastest possible wicket and they are still confident of doing so. In appearance it is green and firm and the hope is that the recent persistent rains will not have taken toll of too much of its speed. The covers have been on since last weekend and the result could well be a true and lasting pitch very similar to that on which South Africa beat England in a thrilling finish last year. One writes, of course, on the perhaps improbable assumption that it will not rain. If it does so, then the winning of the toss may be just as important as it was at Leeds.

## SECOND TEST, LORD'S, 1961

JOHN WOODCOCK,
CRICKET CORRESPONDENT

*June 26.* The groundsmen at Lord's have had trouble with their wickets for as long as most memories last. I arrived there on Friday morning to be told by Mr Neville Cardus that when England met Australia in 1921 he trembled in his seat for the batsmen's safety. There have been years, of course, when the balance has been reversed, such as in 1930, when four fine days brought 1,600 runs. More recently, however, the batsmen have walked in peril of their lives. It was so in 1955, when the South Africans were black and blue by the time the match was done, and again in 1957 against West Indies.

The prevailing wicket, which is so misplaced in this of all years, deceived even England's own selectors. They chose their side in the expectation that the spinners would play a full part in the game. In the event Australia had bowled close on 150 overs before Simpson was called into action and in Australia's innings Statham, Trueman, and Dexter took nine wickets between them. On Thursday and Friday the 'ridge' at the Nursery end seemed like some Loch Ness monster, causing the ball to shoot or fly. Yet on Saturday, when England set out on their second innings, the fire had all but died away.

## THIRD TEST, HEADINGLEY, 1961

JOHN WOODCOCK,
CRICKET CORRESPONDENT

*July 7.* Without doubt, however, it must be one of the worst pitches ever prepared for a big match. As an Australian said, it may produce plenty of incident, but it reduces the game to a farce. It is bone dry and bare and already the fast bowlers are picking out thimblefuls of earth where they pitch. Certainly it is no better than that on which Laker took 19 wickets at four apiece in 1956, and the reason given that there has been a drought in Leeds hardly holds water, if one may be excused the metaphor. In two months Yorkshire have had only two county matches on the ground so that there should have been ample opportunity to put the hoses on the square.

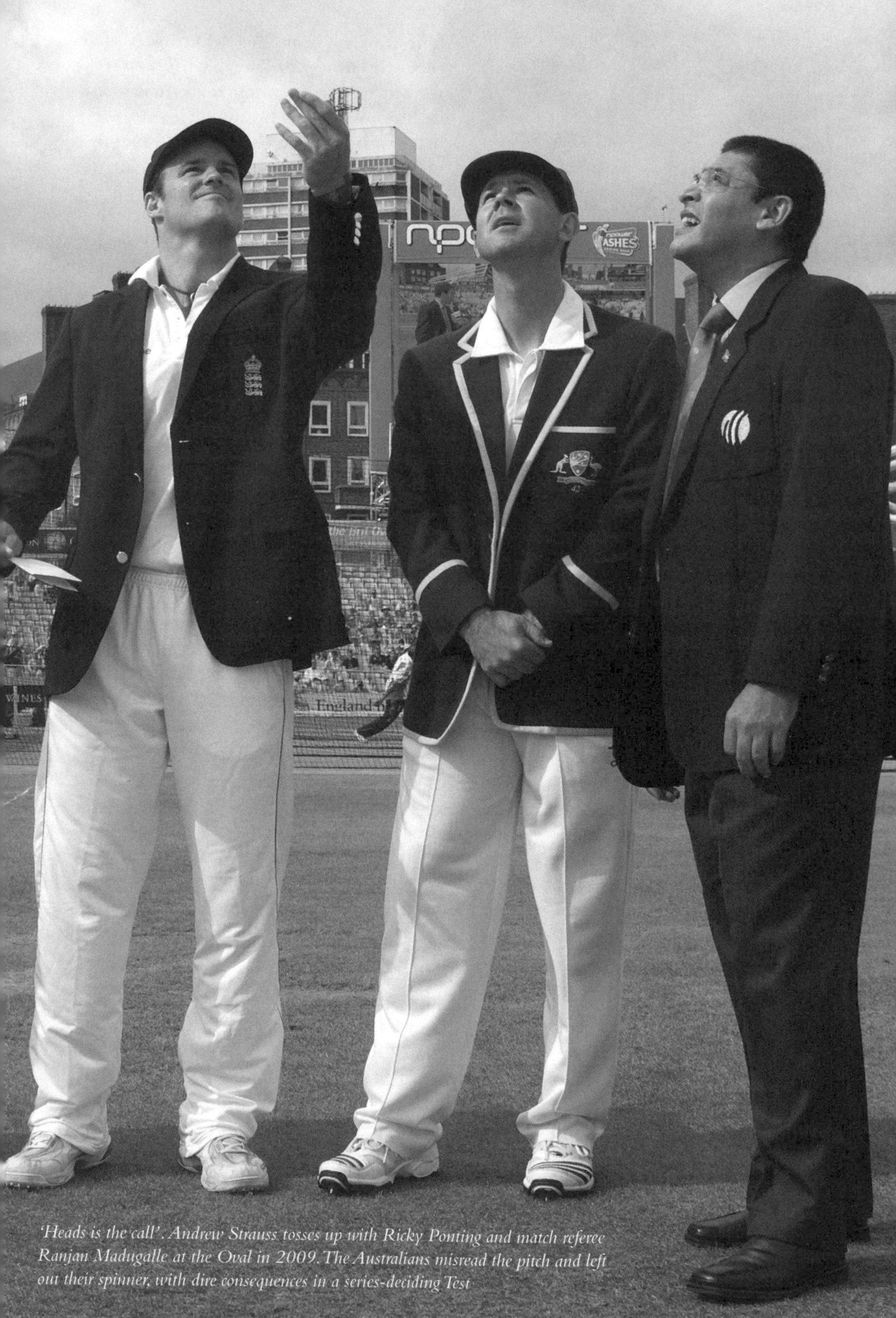


*'Heads is the call'. Andrew Strauss tosses up with Ricky Ponting and match referee Ranjan Madugalle at the Oval in 2009. The Australians misread the pitch and left out their spinner, with dire consequences in a series-deciding Test*

## THIRD TEST, TRENT BRIDGE, 1972

JACK FINGLETON

*July 14.* There were several prognosticating groups around the Trent Bridge pitch yesterday morning when I looked at it. A pre-match pitch is an interesting study. Old cricketers like to probe it, study it and then prophesy what it will or will not do.

Stackpole anxiously bounced a ball on the side of it to try to gauge its pace. Recently, in Durban, Bacher won the toss from Lawry, decided to bat, and then had the groundsman cut the pitch. This seemed strange. A pitch should be as it is when the skippers toss. I saw Illingworth, at Perth during the last series, bounce the ball to try to gauge that pitch. I wonder if the players should be entitled to do this.

I did not think highly of this pitch. It had some slight tufts on it on a good length. If the ball, I reckoned, hit the up part of the tuft it would rise. If it hit the other side it would keep low. So I thought before play began, and I thought also that runs would never be too easy to come by on this pitch.

## FOURTH TEST, HEADINGLEY, 1972

JOHN WOODCOCK, CRICKET CORRESPONDENT

*July 31.* Beating Australia at cricket and thereby retaining the Ashes should be the greatest possible fun. On Saturday it was not quite that, the reason being a pitch hopelessly unsuited to a five-day match. With more than two full days left England won the fourth Test by nine wickets.

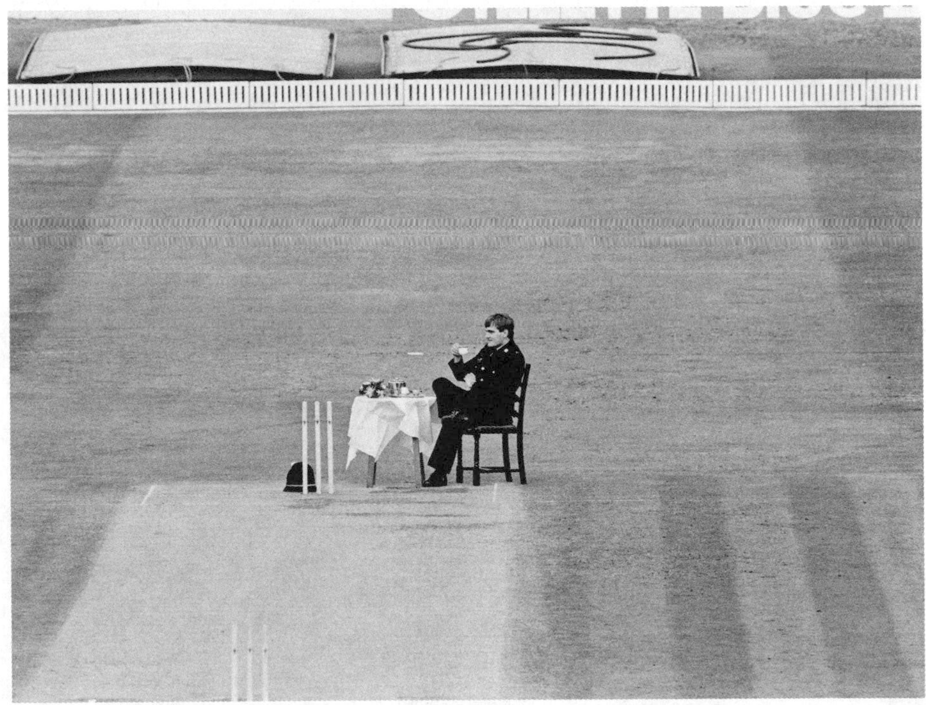

*The Headingley pitch – often the source of heated debate – gets a police guard during the first Test in 1985*

Ray Illingworth is a functionalist, who calls a stump a stump. When the match was over he said that he thought 250 would have been a useful score on the first day and that 150 would have taken a good deal of getting on the third. Which, to my way of thinking, condemns the pitch.

## FIRST TEST, BRISBANE, 1974–75

JOHN WOODCOCK,
CRICKET CORRESPONDENT

*November 29.* The idea of playing four fast bowlers has, I think, been finally discarded, not least because the pitch can be nothing but slow. At the ground this afternoon there was even a mystery as to precisely where the pitch was to be. The Lord Mayor-cum-groundsman, who will decide that, had left to prepare for a reception which he was giving the two teams. In the ordinary way on the day before a Test match the pitch is ready and waiting, the clearly defined culmination of a groundsman's year. In Australia, as a rule, it looks more like a pavement than a pitch on which a blade of grass would be an oasis. There is nothing like that here. What the ground staff were rolling this afternoon was a strip which looked like the rest of the square, still soft underfoot after Tuesday night's storm, not especially flat, and in parts thickly grassed. Other than that, it is sure to be slow, but no one knows quite what to expect. Because there will still be some moisture there in the morning whoever wins the toss will have to consider fielding first.

## FIFTH TEST, ADELAIDE, 1974–75

JOHN WOODCOCK,
CRICKET CORRESPONDENT

'By half past two she'll be a beaut', Redpath said as he took his pads off, and he was right. He was referring not to any of the attractive young things for which the Adelaide Oval is renowned, but to the pitch.

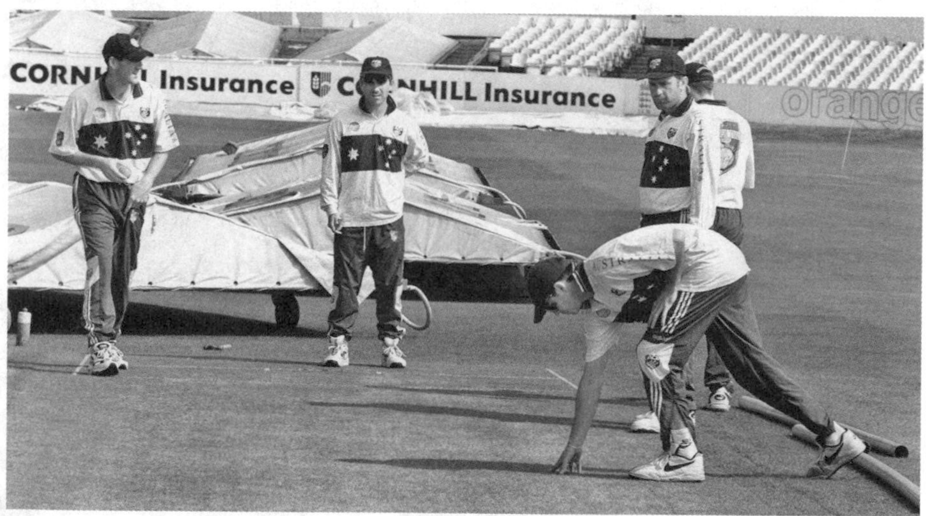


*The Australians take a close look at the much-discussed Headingley pitch before the fourth Test in 1997*

## FIRST TEST, EDGBASTON, 1975

JOHN WOODCOCK, CRICKET CORRESPONDENT

*July 11.* That the groundsman, after so much dry weather, has produced a pitch so devoid of bounce is disappointing. It will all look different when Australia bowl, no doubt, but yesterday the views of Arnold and the rest of them on the pace of the Edgbaston pitch would have been unprintable.

## SECOND TEST, OLD TRAFFORD, 1977

JOHN WOODCOCK, CRICKET CORRESPONDENT

*July 7.* Lancashire have been having trouble on their ground. The man they appointed to look after it, in succession to Bert Flack, who retired last winter, stayed for only a few weeks. This left them, a month ago, without a groundsman in what has been a difficult season for pitch-making. Last year's drought, followed by a poor spring growth, means that the grass has no depth to it.

Another Flack, Bernard, of Edgbaston (who might have gone to Old Trafford instead of Bert but for a case of mistaken identity), has been active as a consultant in the preparation of today's pitch. Although one of the best in the business he is not as familiar with the soil and the surface of the Old Trafford square as he would like to be.

## FIFTH TEST, EDGBASTON, 1993

JOHN WOODCOCK

*August 6.* So that the two sides in a series should be tested at every point there is much to be said for having a variety of pitches; a fast true one, and a fast and frisky one, and a green one, and a drying one, and an absolutely plumb one, and one which looks from a distance, like this one, as though it could have been lifted from the beach at Weston-super-Mare.

## SECOND TEST, LORD'S, 2013

GIDEON HAIGH

*July 19.* Rumour has it that on Wednesday the ECB was keen for Marylebone's groundsman, Mick Hunt, to shave the pitch of its five o'clock shadow of grass.

Nobody issues orders to cricket's Duchy of Grand Fenwick, however, and Australia were not displeased to have the first opportunity at checking it out.

Sporting

# W ENGLAND KEPT TH ASHES

## O GREAT HEARTS OVERTHROW AUSTRALIA

England beat Australia by five wickets in the fourth Test match at laide yesterday and so, gaining a lead of three matches to one in the es, have retained the Ashes. In an interview after the match L. Hutton, e England captain, paid a tribute to the younger members of the side. uch of the credit, he thought, should go to J. B. Statham, F. H. Tyson, M. C. Cowdrey and P. B. H. May, together with the wicket-keeper, T. G. Evans.

From Our Special Correspondent

ADELAIDE, FEB. 2

Many years from now young Cowdrey will point to his broken nose and tell boys yet unborn that he was at Adelaide on February 2, 1955, when England won the Test match and kept the Ashes. And the boys will think him wondrous lucky.

the catch. (We asked Hutton afterwards what he thought of Miller's bowling. Hutton thought Miller ought to concentrate much more on batting.) England 10 for 2. In comes the battered Cowdrey. Miller hits him twice running on the pads and appeals, and everybody here who isn't English appeals too. What a man is Miller. He comes in from a shortish run, loose of limb like an African, hair streaming, and as he pulls up the hair goes on and falls about his face.

Meanwhile May has begun driving, and Johnson has gone from mid-off to square-leg. For Cowdrey Miller brings fine-leg up to third slip, and Cowdrey cover drives classically for 4. Miller heaves his shoulders over even faster, and Cowdrey is taken by Archer at first-slip. England 18 for 3. Four Meteor jets fly over at 200ft.; they look and sound quite tame beside this wild man ... His figures now are 3 overs, no ... runs, 3 wickets.

# England all too obliging ... reaches new heights of greatness

One that got away: Gilchrist misses a stumping chance off Warne to give Pietersen an extra life, but it was to make little difference as ...

High five: Warne acknowledges the Melbourne crowd after his haul ripped the heart out of England's fragile batting

"We didn't expect conditions to change dramatically over the first day and a half," Strauss said, "but it seamed about more than we expected." It did so slowly but Glenn McGrath, Stuart Clark and Brett Lee all got enough past the bat to suggest that the wrong option had been taken.

Australia missed two catches, two clear run-out opportunities and a gaping stumping, but still bowled England out for 159 after they had been 101 for two. Very few Test matches are won after such a start. All of Warne's wickets were taken by flight and dip, as batsmen spied what they believed to be boundary opportunities. Only Kevin Pietersen got anywhere near the boundary as he attempted to drive Warne straight for six, but by now he was, as usual, batting with the tail.

Even he needed 70 balls for 21 runs, having come close to running out Andrew Flintoff for six as, for the third Test in succession, he attempted a ridiculous single in order to get off the mark. He had only made four when he also survived a simple stumping chance offered to Adam Gilchrist after charging Warne and missing.

England, we all know, have too long a tail, but tweaking it made no difference. Matthew Hoggard is back where he started, No 11, pushing Monty Panesar and Stephen Harmison up a place each, which reflects their various abilities with the bat. It is higher up, however, that the balance is wrong. Ed Joyce or Jamie Dalrymple should have played

six, but Chris Read for Geraint Jones was the only change.

As the best player in the team, Pietersen needs to bat at four. Since Paul Collingwood shared the only partnership of any substance with Strauss — 57 for the third wicket — it may appear that England's strategy, to keep him away from the new ball, had worked again, but to have Pietersen batting with the tail repeatedly is not satisfactory. In any case Collingwood might have been leg-before to Clark for nought, one of four apparently plumb leg-before decisions turned down by Rudi Koertzen.

Australia's recent practice of not using a nightwatchman.

Ponting said that Australia, too, would have chosen to bat first, but it was one of those tosses that either captain would prefer to have lost. Play was delayed by rain for half an hour and only 16 overs were bowled before an early lunch was taken, Alastair Cook

Ponting run out (Flintoff) 66

P Siddle c Flintoff b Harrison 10

5.37 343-9 S Clark c Cook b Harmison 0

...iant leap ... for proud S...

## Sporting News

# ENGLAND HAVE LAST WORD

## THREE YEOMEN FOIL AUSTRALIA

## GREAT STAND BY WATSON AND BAILEY

FROM OUR CRICKET CORRESPONDENT

Out of darkness, through fire into light. Thus did England yesterday rise like some Phoenix from the ashes of apparent defeat to save the second Test match at Lord's and so gain a ... draw against Australia with ... seven wickets, ... original aim fo... The age of ... yet past, nor c... cany scarce fo... dramatic and ... a match alrea... But within t... longest and ... of a match it... that last spa... back with le... yeomen of ... nearly the w...

The yeom... were Watso... greatest of ... Yorkshirem... order, was ... rearguard ... twentieth ...

36 TUESDAY AUGUST 1 1989

THE TIMES

# England's abject surrender marks new low in series

By Alan Lee, Cricket Correspondent

## Inglorious procession at Old Trafford

18-3: Curtis c Boon b Alderman 0

25-2: Robinson lbw b Lawson 12

27-3: Smith c Healy b Alderman 1

28-4: Gooch c Alderman b Lawson 11

59-6: Gower c Marsh b Lawson 15

SCOREBOARD FROM OLD TRAFFORD

## Gower unfairly blamed for failings of others

Simon Barnes

## Border rewarded for hard labour

By John Woodcock

## Only two men so far decline

By Alan Lee

# Was this English c... most desperate d...

# GREAT BATTING: ENGLAND

THE TIMES SATURDAY JUNE 11 1938

CH: A GOOD BEGINNING BY ENGLAND

4

Sporting News

LAKER'S SUPREME PART IN RETAINING THE ASHES

ALL TEN AUSTRALIAN WICKETS AND 19 IN MATCH

From Our Cricket Correspondent

England won the fourth Test match against Australia at Old ... yesterday by an innings ... retaining the ... achieve...

pitch perked up and the ball showed signs of misbehaving.

At luncheon McDonald and Craig were still together. They had then added only 59, but the important thing was that they had each been batting for more than four hours. Ahead of them stretched another four and only 15 minutes of these had ticked away when Laker struck ... blow. Craig, still ...

THE TIMES

LOCOMEN'S BAN BOUND TO CAUSE GREATER ... ON TODAY

HOW THE AUSTRALIANS WERE SKITTLED OUT AT LORD'S

Gaullists may get back with clear majority

EF BETRAYS A NOTE OF REGRET

Inquiry over bank chief's salary

Police alerted by strike ship

Railways must act alone, Marsh says

13 die in rail c...

TEST MATCH

BRADMAN 309 NOT OUT

ALL RECORDS BROKEN

*The Third Test Match between England and Australia was begun at Leeds yesterday. A. P. F. Chapman, for once, lost the toss and Australia went in to bat on a perfect batsman's wicket. By the end of the day they had scored 458 runs for the loss of three wickets and D. G. B...*

... stumped aiming to hit Mallett over the hill, and the end draws nearer.

dismally surrender Ashes

England came so close to ... a bumper, there being no love lost between them. The next, according to one of the Australian slips, was Lillee's fastest ball for a long time, but wide of the off stump. Lillee bowled faster here, and better, than at any time in the series.

Cowdrey looks to me as though he could be becoming affected by special pressures of almost ... less speed. To be being washed in fact.

# IAN BELL

## SECOND TEST, LORD'S, 2013

MIKE ATHERTON,
CHIEF CRICKET CORRESPONDENT

*July 19.* Once again England were indebted principally to Bell, reprising his role from Trent Bridge as the man for a crisis and as comfortable in his position as a senior batsman as he can ever have been. He scored his nineteenth Test hundred and third in as many matches against Australia, playing beautifully – languid without being loose and eager to score without taking on risk. A proper knock, by a proper player. [...]

Two balls before Bairstow's piece of good fortune, Bell had demonstrated the perfect on drive, with his top hand and top elbow directing the blade through the line of the ball. He is as technically accomplished a batsman as England possess, a quality adorned in the past two innings by a glinting hardness that has not always been apparent, and when he pushed a ball from Shane Watson into point, an hour before the close, to bring up his hundred, Lord's rose to acknowledge it.

GIDEON HAIGH

... Ian Bell has enough technique for two batsmen. His bat hardly departs its groove. When he plays a defensive shot, the ball drops like a shot partridge. When he strokes the ball off the back foot, the additional effort is virtually imperceptible.

He expressed satisfaction before the match at his improvement in 'grinding out innings'. Yesterday, as at Trent Bridge, he ground pure filet mignon.

## FOURTH TEST, CHESTER-LE-STREET, 2013

MIKE ATHERTON,
CHIEF CRICKET CORRESPONDENT

*August 12.* Kevin Pietersen does not walk in the shadow of many batsmen, but yesterday afternoon, during a partnership with Ian Bell that pushed England firmly into the ascendancy, he was forced to do just that.

Such a sentence, which could not have been written during the 2005 series when both these players made their Ashes debuts, is a measure of Bell's development, which has reached its apotheosis in this series.

He made his twentieth Test hundred yesterday, brought up in the closing moments of the day as the sun embellished a glorious northern scene. It is a statistic that places him in the very highest rank of England batsmen, the style and grace of his play, as well as the numbers, being suitable companions for such an assessment.

*Ian Bell salutes the dressing room and the England supporters after his brilliant hundred at Sydney in 2010–11*

As with his other hundreds in the series, these were vital runs, fashioned in circumstances that were far from straightforward, and without them England would have been in the soup. As it was, they finished the day 202 runs to the good and their eyes on the prize.

---

## IAN BOTHAM

### THIRD TEST, HEADINGLEY, 1981

JOHN WOODCOCK,
CRICKET CORRESPONDENT

*July 21.* The third Test match, sponsored by Cornhill, contained a most joyous surprise at Headingley yesterday. England were heading for an innings defeat when, against all the signs, they took their score from 135 for seven to 351 for nine in only 35 overs, Botham making 145 not out with as magnificent a display of attacking batsmanship as can ever have graced the ground.

When Dilley joined Botham, Lillee and Alderman, with Lawson relieving each of them in turn, had been working their way through England's second innings as inexorably as they did through the first. Boycott had had to be dug out, as you would expect, and Willey had played a few good strokes before falling into a trap. But England still needed another 92 runs to make Australia bat again when Dilley came shuffling to the wicket.

The way, after that, the ball rocketed to the boundary, not from one end but from both, was in startling contrast to everything that had gone before. Botham was already under way, playing much as he had on Saturday but with a shade more discretion. His previous highest Test score was also at Headingley. That, too, was a superb innings, played, though, not against a rampaging Australian side but against India's medium pace. [...]

Until Botham cut loose, Dilley outscored him; once Botham had done so he bestrode the field. He went from 36 to 100 with 14 fours, a six and two singles. It was a marvellous piece of savagery, acknowledged, when he reached his seventh Test century, with a standing ovation. By close of play he had batted for three hours and a half and hit 26 fours and one six, a straight drive off Alderman made from down the pitch. [...]

When at 6 o'clock, he came in, the crowd gathered round the pavilion to cheer him as though he had won the match for England, rather than having given them what amounts to an outside chance of victory. Whoever wins, to have Botham looking himself again makes the remainder of the summer and the rest of the series an altogether more cheerful prospect. [...]

When, with only three runs added, Taylor was caught at short leg, making a poor effort to fend off a short ball from Alderman, England had taken fifty overs to score 135 for 7. As they were entitled to be, the Australians were cock-a-hoop. They would dispose of Dilley in no time, Old was no good against pace, and Botham would soon be left high and dry. Instead, Dilley found unexpected strength. And Old played his part. And Botham batted like Jessop. And the game is still alive.

### FIFTH TEST, OLD TRAFFORD, 1981

JOHN WOODCOCK,
CRICKET CORRESPONDENT

*August 17.* Ian Botham's innings was, of its kind, perhaps the greatest ever played and the chart details its progress. It began just before half past two in the fifth Test match at Old Trafford on Saturday afternoon, when England, in their second innings, were 104 for five after starting the day at 70 for one. With a relentless display of tight fielding and accurate bowling, Australia had recovered from an apparently hopeless position to one from which they could well win.

In 34 overs, Boycott, Gower, Gatting and Brearley had fallen to Alderman and Lillee, while a mere 34 runs were being scored. Although still in, and batting with the utmost resolution, Tavare, England's No. 3, had made only nine runs in the two hours of the morning, and another two in the first 20 minutes of the afternoon. The light was grey, the pitch not unhelpful to the faster bowlers.

When Botham walked out to bat he left an England dressing room in which few could bring themselves to watch the play. There is nothing worse for England cricketers than to see a hard won advantage against Australia being gradually whittled away. Contrasting with England's abject surrender was Australia's uncontrollable joy.

The cheers which greeted Botham were of desperate encouragement, the position scarcely less fraught than at Headingley where he made his historic 149 not out. His 118 on Saturday was an even finer innings. It was more calculated for one thing, and less chancy. At Headingley, he played a wonderful, unforgettable slog, but it was also a lucky one. On Saturday, with a full sense of responsibility, he played himself in. If Brearley said anything to him as they passed on the pavilion steps, other than the customary 'Good luck', it might simply have been: 'Now, take your time' – and to the Australians it must have been increasingly worrying the way he did so.

Of his first 32 balls Botham scored five runs. With a new ball available in only 17 overs from the time he took guard, Bright was soon bowling at one end and Whitney at the other. When Alderman did take the new ball, immediately it was due, Botham had made 28 from 53 balls. At the other end, Tavare was taking good care of himself, not scoring much but relieving Botham of the anxiety of seeing a partner in distress. Of the 149 they added together, Tavare's share was 28.

Botham had been in for 65 minutes when the new ball was taken. At 150 for five, one or two of the England side were to be seen watching the cricket again. Tavare, wrapped in his cocoon, had completed the slowest half century ever made in a Test match in England. Then, suddenly, the floodgates opened.

Rather than finishing off the England innings, as they were expected to do, Lillee and Alderman took a dreadful hammering. Lillee had already bowled 14 overs in the day and Alderman 16. If they had lost their edge, it would not have mattered had it not been for Botham.

When, 13 overs later, Botham was caught at the wicket, he had made another 90 runs in 49 balls. Off Alderman's first over with the new ball he took seven; off Lillee's, 19. In the remaining nine overs in which he received a ball he made six and 10 off Alderman, five, six and 13 off Lillee, eight and seven off Bright and one and eight off Whitney. I refuse to believe that a cricket ball has ever been hit with greater power or rarer splendour.

Where England's earlier batsmen apart from Tavare, had found survival impossible, Botham made the boundaries seem far too short and the wicket far too good. When Lillee bowled bouncers to him he hooked them off his eyebrows for six. When Alderman tried one it was pulled to mid-wicket for six. The crowd became

# THE TIMES

No 61,007 — MONDAY AUGUST 17 1981 — Price twenty pence

## More talks to avert rail strike

Hopes of averting the national rail strike, due to start on August 31, may rest on talks with the two unions involved later this week. But with British Rail adamant on productivity concessions before paying the full 11 per cent awarded by Lord McCarthy's tribunal, there is little scope for resolving the deadlock. British Rail's financial plight will be highlighted tomorrow when the first half-year results are expected to show a loss exceeding £50m. On the same day the leaders of both unions meet officials of the miners and steelmen's unions to seek guarantees of active support within the "triple alliance" for the projected strike Page 2

## Four policemen still in hospital

Four of the 15 police injured during the two and a half-hour demonstration in Toxteth, Merseyside, on Saturday were still in hospital yesterday. The protest march was held to demand the removal of Mr Kenneth Oxford, Chief Constable of Merseyside. It involved about 2,000 people, with 3,000 officers in attendance Page 2

## Mitterrand's revolution

M François Mitterrand was elected President of the French Republic 100 days ago, since when he has launched the country on a silent revolution. On the whole, its impact has been positive, though some initiatives provoke misgivings, a poll shows Page 4

## Fungus threat to cereals

Severe attacks of fungus diseases have blighted hopes for cereal crop yields in many southern areas. But in the north and west, and in Scotland and Wales the harvest outlook is not so gloomy, despite storm damage earlier in the summer Page 10

## Queen told of plot talks

Lord Mountbatten of Burma told the Queen about the conversation that led to accusations of a plot to oust the Harold Wilson government, Lord Cudlipp, who took part in the conversation, says. Lord Mountbatten asked him to delete reference to the talk in his book because the remarks were made in utmost confidence Page 2

## First national TV top ten

Gardeners' World, Top Crown, and Bringing Up Baby, all BBC 2 programmes, have entered the national top ten television listings for the first time now that the BBC and ITV have set up joint audience research by the Broadcasters Audience Research Board. Instead of the Jictar top ten the new list gives separate billings for BBC 1, BBC 2 and ITV Information Service, back page

## Fear of fall in tobacco sales

cigarette sales by early autumn may be 14 per cent down on last year, and the decline could ... are passed on by retailers. Cigarettes have risen by nearly 30 per cent in almost six months Page 15

## Nato in tatters

A rising tide of opposition to nuclear weapons in Europe, fuelled by America's decision to proceed with the neutron bomb, threatens the foundations of the Atlantic alliance. In the first of three articles, John Barry argues that Nato's nuclear policy is in tatters, with little credibility left Page 8

## Deadly rivalry

In the early years of the century the cosmetics industry was dominated by two names—Elizabeth Arden and Helena Rubinstein. In the first extract from her book *Selling Dreams*, Margaret Allen examines the deadly rivalry between these two extraordinary women Page 11

| | | | |
|---|---|---|---|
| Home News | 2, 3 | Lucie cartoon | 6 |
| Overseas | 4-6 | Obituary | 10 |
| Appts | 10, 16 | Premium Bds | 24 |
| Arts | 7 | Property | 21 |
| Book serial | 11 | Religion | 10 |
| Business | 15-18 | Science | 2 |
| Church | 10 | Sport | 12-14 |
| Court | 10 | TV & Radio | 23 |
| Crossword | 24 | Theatres, etc | 23 |
| Diary | 8 | 25 Years Ago | 10 |
| Events | 22 | Universities | 10 |
| Features | 6, 8 | Weather | 24 |
| Letters | 9 | Wills | 10 |

Times Information Service, back page

## Soviet Union to defer repayment of Polish debt

Moscow, August 16.—The Kremlin has announced measures to ease Poland's financial crisis after a summit meeting between Soviet and Polish leaders; but has withheld judgment on the political course taken by Warsaw.

Rallies and marches planned for tomorrow to protest against the detention of political prisoners in Poland were called off tonight, thus averting what could have been a major confrontation with the authorities.

The organizers of the rallies in five towns, which were to have been followed by a march on Warsaw unless three anti-Communist dissidents were released from detention, announced that all protests were suspended for the time being.

The march had been condemned by Solidarity, the independent union movement, and the Roman Catholic Church. The Government had promised to stop it with all available means.

The Solidarity branch in Plock, west of Warsaw, which was to have been one of the assembly points for the march, said about 500 extra police with armoured vehicles had been brought into the town.

A full communiqué on the summit talks in *Pravda* today showed Moscow has pledged to postpone repayment of about $4,200m (now worth about £2,300m) in credits until the mid-1980s, and raise supplies of raw materials and consumer goods to Poland.

Western diplomats said the measures would be a significant boost to the attempts of Mr Stanislaw Kania, the Polish party leader, to revive the country's economy.

They said, however, that the communiqué showed Mr Kania and general Wojciech Jaruzelski, the Prime Minister, had failed to gain Soviet endorsement for their handling of the Polish crisis when they met President Brezhnev at his summer retreat in the Crimea on Friday.

The communiqué said Mr Brezhnev was told that the Polish Communist Party had formulated a plan to overcome the crisis at a congress in Warsaw last month, and would strengthen its leading role in the country.

Replying to the Polish leaders' comments and their promises to fight the threat of counter-revolution, Mr Brezhnev said only that Moscow was "following the events in the Polish People's Republic with close attention".

He added that the Soviet Union wanted Poland's communists "to implement successfully the decisions of the party congress aimed at strengthening the Polish United Workers' Party as a Marxist-Leninist party and consolidating the position of socialism in society".

Diplomats said that amounted to Soviet approval for only a part of the congress decisions and did not suggest Moscow shared Mr Kania's view that it had plotted a course out of the country's difficulties.

It also indicated the Kremlin was still dissatisfied with the Polish party's pledges to continue policies of liberalization and reform, an important part of the programme put forward at the congress.

The communiqué's description of the climate at the talks also indicated that the two sides remained seriously divided on basic policy questions.

It said the meeting was held in an atmosphere of "fraternal friendship and comradely mutual understanding". Usually Soviet block leaders are said to have reached "full unity of views" at such meetings. Diplomats said the wording used for the Crimean talks was at least as cool as the official description of the last Polish-Soviet summit in March.

After that meeting, which was termed "cordial", Moscow released a statement saying Mr Brezhnev had called on Mr Kania to change the course of events in Poland following months of political liberalization.

The communiqué made clear that Mr Brezhnev told Mr Kania and General Jaruzelski he considered events in Poland posed a threat to its place in the Warsaw Pact alliance. Mr Brezhnev and the Polish leaders were agreed, however, about the inviolability of the alliance between their countries.

Mr Brezhnev was quoted as saying that opponents of Poland's communist system both inside and outside the country were now turning to anti-Soviet actions in an attempt to "dig a trench between People's Poland and the Soviet Union".

The financial aid announced by Mr Brezhnev amounted to postponement of Poland's debt repayments until the next five-year plan period, which begins in 1986.

Moscow gave Warsaw credits worth $4,200m between August, 1980 and June this year, nearly a quarter of which was in hard currency. It has already rescheduled debts of more than $620m granted between 1976 and 1979.—Reuter.

Crimea text, page 4

## Kremlin warning on collision with US

Washington, Aug 16.—One of President Brezhnev's chief aides, Mr Georgi Arbatov, said today that Moscow and Washington were on a collision course. It was time for the Soviet Union and the United States to resume the real dialogue of the 1970s and to stop accusing and threatening each other.

"If we go in that direction I think then we are on a collision course which will bring us to very, very serious troubles," he said in a television interview broadcast from

optimistic" about next month's New York meeting between Mr Haig and Mr Gromyko.

Soviet-American relations were in a very bad state not improved by President Reagan's decision to stockpile the neutron bomb.

"At a time when we just were groping for our way to start very cautious preliminary talks of what to do with them and similar Western weapons, suddenly the United States introduces a new weapon to be regarded as a good development," he said.

"With the increase in military budget, with some other new programmes, it shows a trend, a very bad trend, a very dangerous trend".

☐ Moscow: Western Europe must soon decide whether to follow Washington to collective suicide or hold separate arms talks, the Soviet news agency Tass said today.

It said the United States was abandoning détente and taking a course which could lead to

missiles overseas, it said in a commentary on American policies.

"And if these start a nuclear missile war, the entire arsenal of weapons stockpiled in the past years will be put to use with all the ensuing consequences," Tass said.

In such a situation each West European leader had to consider if he was prepared to follow the United States course, it said.—Reuter.

Sakharov attack, page 4

## Israel to get American jets next week, says Begin

From Moshe Brilliant, Tel Aviv, August 16

Mr Menachem Begin, the Israeli Prime Minister, said F16 and F15 aircraft, whose delivery is being held up by the United States, were expected to reach Israel next week, but he unequivocally denied the Israelis had undertaken not to use the jets for attack missions across the borders.

Interviewed as he left the weekly Cabinet meeting in Jerusalem, Mr Begin reacted sharply to American news reports that the release of the aircraft was being made possible by an unwritten Israeli pledge to refrain from using them in missions such as the bombing of the nuclear reactor in Baghdad or Palestinian terrorist headquarters in Beirut.

"There is not a word of truth in the report", the Prime Minister said.

Claiming the embargoed American-made aircraft were already Israeli property, Mr Begin said that their detention was tantamount to demanding the return of jets already in Israel, because the United States disapproved of certain Israeli actions.

The deliveries were suspended after the Israelis used American-made F16s to bomb the Iraqi atomic reactor in Baghdad last month, and to attack Palestinian guerrilla headquarters in Beirut.

The Prime Minister also revealed he plans to meet President Sadat in Alexandria on August 25. He said the talks would centre on the renewal of the negotiations for autonomy in the West Bank and Gaza which have been stalled since May last year

Reagan arms decision, page 4



## Was Botham's innings the greatest ever?

By John Woodcock, Cricket Correspondent

Ian Botham's innings was, of its kind, perhaps the greatest ever played and the chart details its progress. It began just before half past two in the fifth Test match at Old Trafford on Saturday afternoon, when England, in their second innings, were 104 for five after starting the day at 70 for one. With a relentless display of tight fielding and accurate bowling, Australia had recovered from an apparently hopeless position to one from which they could well win.

In 34 overs, Boycott, Gower, Gatting and Brearley had fallen to Alderman and Lillee, while a mere 34 runs were being scored. Although still in, and batting with the utmost resolution, Tavaré, England's No 3, had made only nine runs in the two hours of the morning, and another two in the first 20 minutes of the afternoon. The light was grey, the pitch not unhelpful to the faster bowlers.

When Botham walked out to bat he left an England dressing room in which few could bring themselves to watch the play. There is nothing worse for England cricketers than to see a hard won advantage against Australia being gradually whittled away. Contrasting with England's abject surrender was Australia's uncontrollable joy.

The cheers which greeted Botham were of desperate encouragement, the position scarcely less fraught than at Headingley where he made his historic 149 not out. His 118 on Saturday was an even finer innings. It was more calculated for one thing, and less chancy.

At Headingley, he played a wonderful, unforgettable slog, but it was also a lucky one. On Saturday, with a full sense of responsibility, he played himself in. If Brearley said anything to him as they passed on the pavilion steps, other than the customary "Good luck", it might simply have been: "Now, take your time"—and to the Australians it must have been increasingly worrying the way he did so.

Off his first 32 balls Botham scored five runs. With a new ball available in only 17 overs from the time he took guard, Bright was soon bowling at one end and Whitney at the other. When Alderman did take the new ball, immediately it was due, Botham had made 28 from 53 balls. At the other end, Tavaré was taking good care of himself, not scoring much but relieving Botham of the anxiety of seeing a partner in distress. Of the 149 they added together, Tavaré's share was 28.

Botham had been in for 65 minutes when the new ball was taken. At 150 for five, one or two of the England side were to be seen watching the cricket again. Tavaré, wrapped in his cocoon, had completed the slowest half century ever made in a Test match in England. Then, suddenly, the floodgates opened.

Rather than finishing off the England innings, as they were expected to do, Lillee and Alderman took a dreadful hammering. Lillee had already bowled 14 overs in the day and Alderman 16. If they had lost their edge, it would not have mattered had it not been for Botham.

When, 13 overs later, Botham was caught at the wicket, he had made another 50 runs in 49 balls. Off Alderman's first over with the new ball he took seven; off Lillee's, 19. In the remaining nine overs in which he received a ball he made six and 10 off Alderman, five, six and 13 off Lillee, eight and seven off Bright and one and eight off Whitney. I refuse to believe that a cricket ball has ever been hit with greater power or rarer splendour.

Where England's earlier batsmen, apart from Tavaré, had found survival impossible, Botham made the boundaries seem far too short and the wicket far too good. When Lillee bowled bouncers to him he hooked them off his eyebrows for six. When Alderman tried one it was pulled to mid-wicket for six. The crowd became a mass of dancing people and waving flags. Never before in Anglo-Australian Tests has anyone hit six sixes in an innings. Having reached his hundred with one, a sweep off Bright, Botham drove Bright over the sight screen for another. He also hit 13 fours.

The fastest hundred in Test cricket, in terms of balls received, was by the West Indian, Roy Fredericks, at Perth in 1975. It took him 71 balls. In 1902 the mighty Jessop scored 102 against Australia at the Oval in 75 balls. On Saturday, with the Ashes in the balance, Botham's hundred took 86 balls (one fewer than at Headingley), though he went from five to 118 in 70 balls.

It was an innings that could have been played in the first place only by a man of astonishing power. Botham's attack on the new ball was a mixture of crude strength and classical orthodoxy.

At Trent Bridge in 1938, while Stan McCabe was scoring 232, Bradman called from the balcony to those in the dressing room: "Come out here, you may never see the like of this again."

So it was on Saturday. Botham, as McCabe occasionally did, is able to scale heights beyond the reach of ordinary men.

Test report, page 12
(Chart by Wendy Wisbush)

## Cardinal attacks Thatcher for 'lack of priority' on Ulster

From Christopher Thomas, Belfast

Dr Garret FitzGerald, the Irish Prime Minister, and the Roman Catholic Church in Ireland rounded on the British Government yesterday over the Maze prison crisis, amid mounting anxieties over the spread of tensions from Northern Ireland into the republic.

There is increasing fear about the eventual destabilization of normal government in the republic if the affair is not resolved. In Dublin and other big cities nearly every policeman is on regular compulsory overtime to cope with the almost endless protests over the H-block issue.

Dr FitzGerald was not especially robust in his criticisms yesterday, which suggests that he is anxious to put Anglo-Irish relations on a steadier course after last weekend's severe criticisms by Mr Michael O'Leary his deputy, who strongly attacked Mrs Margaret Thatcher.

The Roman Catholic Church, which is now consistently calling on the hunger strikers to end their fast, was sharply

Catholic Primate of All Ireland, was particularly harsh about Mrs Thatcher, whom he met in Downing Street last month. He confirmed they had clashed and added: "I was not terribly impressed by her knowledge of Irish history or her interpretation of events which occurred in the past, nor by her understanding of the present crisis.

"Particularly I felt she did not realize the impact that the hunger strike deaths were having on the Catholic youth of Northern Ireland."

He said that while Mrs Thatcher would like to see the problem solved, he did not feel it impinged much on her political activities or that Northern Ireland was high on her list of priorities.

Dr FitzGerald, speaking in Dublin on the *Face the Press* programme for Independent Television, also expressed fears about violence in the South as a result of the fast. The IRA had gained greatly in strength by increased fund raising in America and by the way they

he was puzzled why the Government had allowed the Fermanagh and South Tyrone by-election to be held now.

"The election has produced a polarization again between two extremes and has had a damaging effect on moderate minority opinion in Northern Ireland, and probably on moderate loyalists", he said.

It was unfortunate that the Social Democratic and Labour Party was not standing but he could understand their dilemma.

Dr FitzGerald claimed that British politicians of all parties privately recognized it was desirable to bring North and South together and for Britain to disengage. It would help if they said that publicly because northern unionists were often misled into believing there was a strong feeling for the union in Britain.

☐ Jackie McMullan, aged 25, is to join the hunger strike at the Maze jail in place of Thomas McIlwee, who died on

## Laker asks banks for more time to pay

By Peter Wainwright

Sir Freddie Laker, chairman of Laker Airways, the independent airline that pioneered cut-price transatlantic travel, wants his bankers to postpone asking for repayment of dollar loans until the pound recovers.

In January his group signed a $131m loan package provided by a consortium of 13 leading banks led by Midland Bank International. The total of loans at issue is thought to be £130m. The money was borrowed to pay for five DC10s and three A300 Airbuses, and was negotiated at exchange rates of between $2.10 and $1.80.

Sir Freddie wants the banks, which include Eximbank, to put a new "release and recapture" clause into the existing agreements. This would, if accepted, allow him to postpone repayment for six months with, if the pound recovers, no exchange-rate penalty.

The chairman said: "There is no question of us not making our repayments. We are attempting to get the banks to be more flexible when dealing with an industry like ours, which is highly cyclical".

## Economists call for a new strategy

By Melvyn Westlake

Three leading economists today called on Mrs Thatcher and her Government to make a U-turn on economic policies.

The economists, Professor Sir Bryan Hopkin, of University College, Cardiff, Professor Marcus Miller, of the University of Warwick, and Professor Brian Reddaway, of the University of Cambridge, all have wide experience in advising on economic policy.

In today's statement called *Outline Of An Alternative Economic Strategy*, they blame the Government for the present slump.

They also claim that government policies, which have caused so much damage, offer little hope of anything much better in the future.

Part of the academics' alternative strategy is that the Government should boost demand by driving down the pound's exchange rate against other currencies and by cutting indirect taxes on consumer goods.

In March last year the three professors were among 364 economists who signed the statement attacking the theoretical basis of the Government's economic strategy. This was in turn criticized for being negative and offering no alternative. Today's statement is partly intended to meet that criticism. More details, page 15

## World war not inevitable says Graham Greene

Mr Graham Greene, in a long interview in the Soviet weekly newspaper, *Literaturnaya Gazeta*, says he believes that a new world war can be avoided. He contrasts this feeling with the "*greater shadow hanging over us*" in the 1930s.

He also expresses scepticism about the influence writers can have on politics.

The most renowned living English novelist was interviewed for the publication of the Writers' Union by the Soviet writer most widely known in the West, the poet Yevgeny Yevtushenko.

In this interview, Mr Greene carefully side-stepped questions which invited him to take an explicitly political stand. He is also quoted as saying that if he had not become a writer "I would have become a criminal" in order to conquer boredom.

**Yevtushenko:** In 1933, the year Hitler came to power, you wrote an essay about Hans Christian Andersen. Do you remember how the little girl Gerda courageously fought for her brother's heart which was being turned into ice by the breath of the Snow Queen?

**Greene:** I'd quite forgotten about that article, and the fairy tale, too, but no, it's coming back to me.

**Q:** Fascism is a sort of freezing of hearts. Back then in 1933 did you sense the danger of a world war brought about by Fascism?

**A:** Yes. I was aware of that danger from 1933 to 1939. We sensed there was going to be a war. Its shadow hung over us. We felt a greater shadow hanging over us than we do today. Now there is the threat of nuclear war. It is quite frightening for the younger generation, and this threat will probably be hanging over them all their lives. But I personally do not sense such an absolutely inescapable shadow hanging over me now as I did between the years 1933 and 1939.

**Q:** Do you believe that a new world war can be avoided?

**A:** Yes. I still continue to believe that it can be avoided. But in 1933 I didn't have that faith.

**Q:** What, in your view, is the cause of world wars?

**A:** Before the start of the Second World War there was a madman, who somehow managed to capture the imagination of many people. The madness spread from one person to another, like hysteria. Have you never observed how someone's hysteria begins to suck you into its vortex. Thus, Hitler, the madman, dragged people into the vortex of his hysteria. But today thank God, there is nothing like that.

**Q:** But dragging nations into war—albeit the cold war—nevertheless is still going on. Nowadays the cold war, like the Snow Queen, causes freezing of

Continued on back page, col 6



*Ian Botham makes the front page again in 1981 after his extraordinary Old Trafford innings*

a mass of dancing people and waving flags. Never before in Anglo-Australian Tests has anyone hit six sixes in an innings. Having reached his hundred with one, a sweep off Bright, Botham drove Bright over the sight screen for another. He also hit 13 fours.

The fastest hundred in Test cricket, in terms of balls received, was by the West Indian, Roy Fredericks, at Perth in 1975. It took him 71 balls. In 1902 the mighty Jessop scored 102 against Australia at the Oval in 75 balls. On Saturday, with the Ashes in the balance, Botham's hundred took 86 balls (one fewer than at Headingley), though he went from five to 118 in 70 balls. It was an innings that could have been played in the first place only by a man of astonishing power. Botham's attack on the new ball was a mixture of crude strength and classical orthodoxy.

At Trent Bridge in 1938, while Stan McCabe was scoring 232, Bradman called from the balcony to those in the dressing room: 'Come out here, you may never see the like of this again.'

So it was on Saturday. Botham, as McCabe occasionally did, is able to scale heights beyond the reach of ordinary men.

## FIRST TEST, HEADINGLEY, 1985

JOHN WOODCOCK,
CRICKET CORRESPONDENT

*June 17.* But the most spectacular contribution came from Botham, who bludgeoned 60 in 51 balls.

Two or three years ago on a visit to Duncan Fearnley's bat factory, the Middlesex players saw propped up against a wall something in the shape of a bat but which was incredibly heavy even for these days. When Edmonds decided that he would like to see what he could make of it, a grip was fitted so that he might and he had some success with it.

Recently, when Botham saw it, he decided to try it himself, which he did on Saturday – to such effect that his defensive pushes carried through mid-wicket for four and his more violent blows created panic among the spectators.

Sitting to my right even Ted Dexter, himself one of the great strikers of a cricket ball, shook his head in awe and smiled in disbelief. This was not batting, it was butchery. Though Botham's straight drives back over the bowlers' heads were strokes of classical outline, and once when the stave gave way to the scalpel, he ran a late cut down to third man with a lovely touch.

Those wanting to see a cricket ball hit harder than possibly ever before must go and watch Botham this summer. With this new weapon, and if the right ball comes along, he will clear the pavilion at Lord's next week, something only ever done by Albert Trott, batting for M.C.C. against the Australians in 1899.

## FIRST TEST, BRISBANE, 1986–87

JOHN WOODCOCK,
CRICKET CORRESPONDENT

*November 17.* There is unlikely to be a better piece of batting on the tour than Botham's 138 on Saturday. Coming in after England had lost their two overnight batsmen, Lamb and Athey, without a run added, and finding Gower in all kinds of trouble, he simply took charge of the game. He has such huge strength and so adaptable a batting method that he remains, when he can be bothered, a mighty threat against anything less than the best bowling (for example, the West Indian attack).

*Ian Botham's calculated attack on the Australian bowling at Brisbane helped to set the tone for England's dominance of the series*

This, though, was no slog. That was the most impressive and, for Australia, the most ominous thing about it. It was a brilliant innings, not because of the great blows that it contained but for the judgment and the unwonted restraint that went into it. With England in danger of squandering their hard-won advantage of the opening day, and falling back into the slough of the previous week, it was as though Botham rose and said: 'Leave it to me.' By lunch-time, he had even ushered Gower, dropped at slip before scoring, into some sort of form.

# GEOFFREY BOYCOTT

## FOURTH TEST, HEADINGLEY, 1977

JOHN WOODCOCK,
CRICKET CORRESPONDENT

*August 12*. 'Go to it; Geoff', the headline exhorted, in the local evening paper. A broadsheet it is, and Boycott's photograph took up most of the front page. Well, Geoff went to it all right, reaching the hundredth hundred of his career in the fourth Test match against Australia at Headingley yesterday, and so making the whole of Yorkshire deliriously happy. At close of play Boycott was 110 not out.

The climax came just before 6 o'clock when he drove Greg Chappell straight for four, and the hats went in the air. The day had been building up to that. Here he was, Yorkshire's one great player of the day, back in the England side after three years of self-imposed and self-conscious exile. Whatever the rights and wrongs of that, there could have been few people on the ground yesterday who were not moved by the long struggle before them.

At lunch Boycott was 36; at tea, he was 79. With an hour to go he was 88. He had had his bad moments, being dropped once and surviving certainly one appeal for a catch at the wicket which the Australians thought was palpably out. It was a perfect day for cricket – warm, and blue, and just sufficiently breezy. From tea-time onwards 25,000 people broke the silence only to cheer Boycott's every run. They crossed their fingers and sweated it out; for all I know, they said a tribal prayer.

When at last Boycott claimed his kingdom, the crowd, now standing, cheered and cheered and cheered. Those who invaded the ground to lay their hands on him will have to be forgiven. When Boycott emerged from underneath them, his cap was missing. By the time that had been returned and he had taken his final bow seven or eight minutes had been lost. Not that it was really lost. It was too famous an occasion for that, and one made more emotional by the fact that, in Yorkshire at any rate, the man is a martyr.

Boycott is the 18th batsman to score a century of centuries, and the first to make the one hundredth of them in a Test match. After this, he can forget his grievances. Yesterday was a personal triumph such as few cricketers enjoy. This was his 645th first-class innings. Only Bradman (295), Compton (552) and Hutton (619) have taken fewer innings to reach the landmark. Sutcliffe, the other Yorkshire opening batsman, besides Hutton, to get there took 700 innings. W.G. Grace took 1,113; Cowdrey, who got there two years ago, took 1,035; Edrich, who made it only last month, took 945. Sutcliffe went on to make 149 hundreds, Hutton to make 129, Hobbs to make 197; Boycott could well have another 50 in him.

By 11 o'clock the gates were closed – just after Brearley had won the toss for England. Nowhere in the world is there a better place for batting than Headingley, on such a morning as this. You can name all the great run-getting grounds, such as Adelaide and Kingston, and Cape Town and Karachi, and Kanpur, but on none of them is the light better than it was now, the temperature more suitable, the outfield faster or the pitch more accommodating. It was a wretched toss to lose for a side already two matches down in the series.

Yet England lost Brearley in the first over of the match, caught at the wicket off a fine ball from Thomson that moved from leg to off. From the way he turned his back on the appeal, Brearley must have disagreed with the decision. That his was the only wicket to fall before lunch was due partly to Woolmer's knack of playing and missing outside the off stump. Though less often than it often does on the first morning of a match, the ball still moved about.

While Woolmer and Boycott were adding 82 for the second wicket, Boycott looked the sounder and Woolmer the more fluent. Not many runs were scored in front of the wicket. Those that were came mostly from cover drives by Woolmer. When Boycott was 22, and the score 48, he survived a difficult chance to Marsh, diving low to his right, off Walker; when he was 26, a boisterous appeal for a catch at the wicket off Pascoe was turned down on the grounds that the ball had brushed Boycott's forearm.

At lunch, England had scored 76 for one off 28 overs. In the fourth over of the afternoon Woolmer, found out again outside the off stump, was caught low down at first slip, Chappell making the catch look much easier than it was. It was not until Randall had taken three fours to third man that Chappell placed a fielder there for the first time in the day. Just as his brother did, when he was Australia's captain, Greg Chappell believes in keeping his slips and gullies intact for as long as he reasonably can. To break them up must seem like conceding the initiative.

When Randall was leg-before, though, aiming at midwicket, Australia were doing well. Three or four times, too, they might have picked Greig up early on. It was 20 minutes or so before the ball began to go where Greig intended. Some imperious drives came to nothing. Then he hooked Chappell for six, just over long leg's head, and drove both Thomson and Pascoe for four. Boycott, meanwhile, kept plodding along, taking infinite care not only in the production of his strokes, but in checking his guard, clearing out his block, and making sure that nowhere was there a buckle loose. To watch Boycott was to see the perfectionist at work.

When Bright bowled only his second over of the day, at 167 for three, Boycott hit two of the first three balls for four. Off the last ball of the over all those fielders near the bat claimed a legside catch to Marsh, an appeal which grew more passionate the clearer it became that umpire Alley was unmoved. Bright having an admonitory finger wagged at him by Alley. At tea, England were 185 for three.

Afterwards, as the clouds built up, the ball began to move about again, especially for Walker. Walker will bowl no better on another Test day than be did now, and yet finish with five wickets. When he came off, with Boycott in the nineties, he was given a reception which suggested that that was what he had done. Greig had been bowled by then, driving hugely at Thomson. Boycott's partner, therefore, when he went to his hundred was Roope, always a fidgety starter, and yesterday a lucky one. Half a dozen times Walker must have beaten him. But he avoided running Boycott out, thank goodness. Had Roope done that we might not have had a crowning to report, but a riot.

*August 13*. During the day I sought the opinion of the man who has watched probably as much Yorkshire cricket as anyone in the past 50 years on the relative merits of Sutcliffe, Hutton and Boycott. In conditions like those that have applied at Headingley over the past two days he thought Sutcliffe would have been the most likely of the three to reach his hundred and that Hutton would have given the purest display of batsmanship. Neither would have been as clinical as Boycott, or any more thorough.

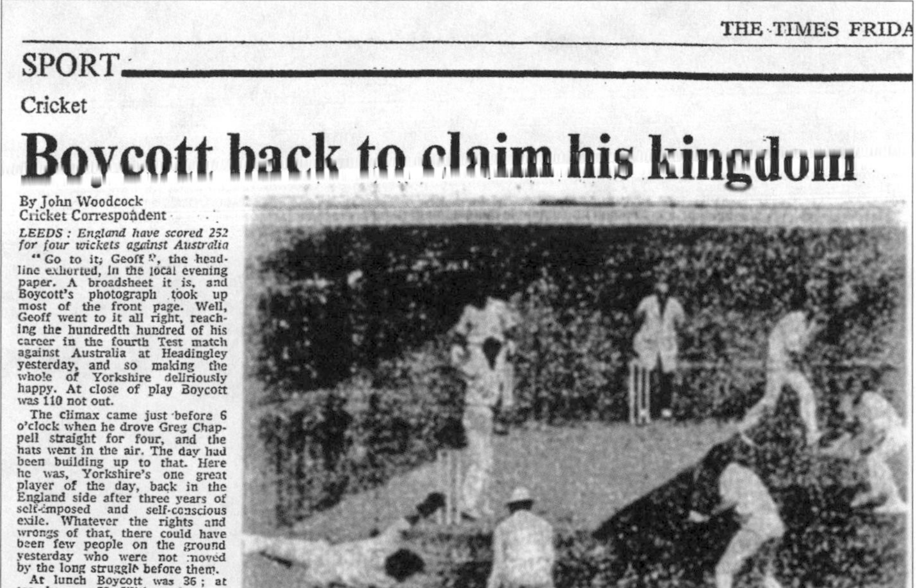

THE TIMES FRIDA

SPORT

Cricket

**Boycott back to claim his kingdom**

By John Woodcock
Cricket Correspondent

*LEEDS: England have scored 252 for four wickets against Australia*

"Go to it, Geoff !", the headline exhorted, in the local evening paper. A broadsheet it is, and Boycott's photograph took up most of the front page. Well, Geoff went to it all right, reaching the hundredth hundred of his career in the fourth Test match against Australia at Headingley yesterday, and so making the whole of Yorkshire deliriously happy. At close of play Boycott was 110 not out.

The climax came just before 6 o'clock when he drove Greg Chappell straight for four, and the hats went in the air. The day had been building up to that. Here he was, Yorkshire's one great player of the day, back in the England side after three years of self-imposed and self-conscious exile. Whatever the rights and wrongs of that, there could have been few people on the ground yesterday who were not moved by the long struggle before them.

At lunch Boycott was 36; at tea, he was 79. With an hour to go he was 88. He had had his

*Geoffrey Boycott completes a century of centuries at Headingley and Yorkshiremen everywhere celebrate*

## CHRIS BROAD

### FOURTH TEST, MELBOURNE, 1986–87

JOHN WOODCOCK,
CRICKET CORRESPONDENT

*December 29.* It was a good total for Melbourne, built on another hundred by Broad and exceeded by England in only three of the 16 Test matches they have now played here since the war. Gatting had the utmost difficulty getting to 40; Lamb's 43 was hard work; and Botham, who batted for 85 minutes, was never able to cut loose.

Broad, however, soldiered on, joining in the process Hobbs and Hammond as the only other Englishman to have made centuries in three successive Tests in the same rubber. Woolmer also got three in three Tests against Australia, but in two different series.

*England opener Chris Broad was the surprise package of the 1986–87 triumph with three centuries, including this one in the third Test at Adelaide*

This is a remarkable achievement by Broad, based on a good temperament, application, opportunism, a workmanlike technique and the height to scotch the extra bounce of Australian pitches. It is simple enough to point to the lack of quality in the Australian attack as being another factor, but it was nothing like so weak on Saturday as to be easy meat.

---

# MARK BUTCHER

## FIRST TEST, BRISBANE, 1998–99

ALAN LEE, CRICKET CORRESPONDENT

*November 23.* His second century in three Tests was a marvel of self-belief, for hitherto his tour had been a string of indignities. Struck on the head in Perth three weeks ago, then a victim of a training collision with Peter Such, he was a walking accident zone, with more stitches than he had scored runs.

Yet, in a situation of high stress for the team and heavy overtones for himself, he struck his fifth ball for four and proceeded to play as if his preparation had been perfect. He required painkilling tablets after suffering another freakish complaint – ricking his back as his boot-studs caught in the crease – but nothing could disturb his calm concentration.

## FOURTH TEST, HEADINGLEY, 2001

CHRISTOPHER MARTIN-JENKINS, CHIEF CRICKET CORRESPONDENT

*August 21.* The odds were 16-1 against when England set out yesterday morning at Headingley to try to score 311 more runs to win the fourth Test. Such was the alarming, almost frightening bounce of some of the balls bowled by Glenn McGrath and Jason Gillespie in the first half-hour of a sunny morning, that they might have been 500-1 as they were here in 1981.

At 33 for two, Australia could easily have bowled them out for 120, but the chestnuts were pulled from the fire by an innings of astonishing brilliance by Mark Butcher. Nasser Hussain's determination, phlegmatic approach and skill helped his third-wicket partner to play his natural game to such effect that when he was out with 101 still needed, Butcher went joyously on to win the game in the face of all expectations. Against high-class bowling and athletic fielding, he cut and drove his way to 173 not out with a six and 23 fours.

As the ball became softer and the variations in bounce less, the prospect of victory became steadily more credible. It was achieved in the end at 5.20pm on a tide of boundaries to which Mark Ramprakash and, briefly, young Usman Afzaal, contributed. As many as 21 overs were left unbowled, leaving the crowd that had packed Headingley for a fifth successive day – the gates were closed 20 minutes before lunch – pinching themselves with pleasure that England had pulled off the second highest winning fourth-innings score in their history.

It has denied Australia their dream of a 5-0 clean sweep but nothing became them so much as the manner in which they took their defeat. To a man they applauded Butcher when he reached his hundred and again when he had won the match. Adam Gilchrist, the stand-in captain, had declared to set England their target, as he might not have done if the Ashes had still been at stake but this was, nonetheless, a wonderful consolation for England after a summer in which luck had hitherto deserted them. Headingley restored it, as it so often has.

*Mark Butcher departs at Headingley in 1997. Four years later, on the same ground, he would play one of the great Ashes innings*

In 30 previous Tests there had been only hints that Butcher was capable of quite so commanding an innings. He has always been an impressive player of fast bowling; brave, a shrewd leaver of the ball but with all the shots needed and a straight bat in defence. What he has lacked has been a secure method against the best spin bowlers and the concentration to move on from promising starts, despite his two previous centuries – at Brisbane against Australia in the last Ashes series and at Headingley against South Africa the following season.

'It will be remembered for a long time', Hussain said of his innings with understatement. In fact, it will be remembered as long as cricket is played. In the circumstances it was scarcely less remarkable than Ian Botham's 149 not out in 1981. If not in quite the exalted class of Graham Gooch's 154 not out to beat West Indies on a worse pitch in 1991, it will certainly be mentioned in the same breath. It is, too, a happy coincidence that his score matches Bradman's on the day that Australia scored 404 to win at Headingley in 1948. [...]

It was the courage of Butcher and Hussain in playing every ball on its merits that was so impressive. Hussain, who has played better in this match than at any time since his first tour in charge in South Africa, cover-drove the first half-volley he received for four and put his bat under his arm as if it were a rolled-up newspaper about to be read in the sunshine on a park bench. Butcher was no less inclined to bow before Australian pressure that lost nothing in its fierceness by comparison with the previous Tests. A hook for four off McGrath persuaded Gilchrist to bring on Shane Warne for the first time at 59 for two. When, an over later, Gillespie was given a turn up the hill, Hussain swivelled to pull him high over square-leg and the wall that separates the ground from Cardigan Road.

These were moments that changed the mood. Batting became easier. The snicks refused to go to hand as they had earlier in the series. At lunch England were 118 for two and the third-wicket pair had put on another 96 in the face of a furious and sustained spell by Brett Lee. In one over he exceeded 90 mph with every ball but it was Gillespie who eventually claimed Hussain to a catch down the leg side.

Ramprakash played no less well in Butcher's support, getting firmly forward and showing not a trace of his supposed temperamental frailty. The game was all but won when he edged Warne so low to Waugh at slip that replays suggested, once again, that the ball had touched the ground first. Ramprakash walked without waiting for the television verdict, but it was in keeping with a delightful match that had defied the weather, been played highly competitively but without a moment of nastiness.

*Paul Collingwood, determination personified, was a rare bonus among England batsman during the 2006–07 whitewash*

## PAUL COLLINGWOOD

### SECOND TEST, ADELAIDE, 2006–07

CHRISTOPHER MARTIN-JENKINS,
CHIEF CRICKET CORRESPONDENT

*December 2.* As Paul Collingwood was struggling at the start of his second innings in Brisbane last week, a group of mischievous and somewhat cynical cricket pundits began scouring the records in pursuit of other possible candidates for the 'worst' batsmen to have represented England in the prime position of second wicket down.

By the end of that innings of 96, he had left them feeling a trifle sheepish, and by the close of the first, intriguing day of the second Test in Adelaide yesterday, embarrassment had turned to guilt. With great self-confidence, character and understated competence, he first rescued, then bound together, a faltering team.

Coming in at 45 for two, he finished the day 98 not out, on the brink of a third Test hundred, having kept the wolves from the entrance to the pen like a protective shepherd for more than 4½ hours.

## DENIS COMPTON

### FIRST TEST, TRENT BRIDGE, 1948

R.B. VINCENT,
CRICKET CORRESPONDENT

*June 15.* Compton having achieved his century, Barnett was caught at second slip, so that half the side were out for 264 and a terrible drag against the collar to fight against. This was Compton's moment, and a better display of confident batting could not be imagined. The ball was met fully in the middle of the bat – and occasionally it was turning just enough to be awkward – and always there was the perfectly timed and placed stroke to the off which even the adroit captaincy of Bradman could not check. Once he had to get his head out of the way of a full toss from Miller which went first bounce into the hands of the wicket-keeper standing back, just after a short ball had been struck to the square-leg boundary. [...]

The clouds cleared and at one time there was even a peep of sunshine, soon dimmed by fog or mist or whatever it may be called. Gradually the score advanced with Compton seemingly playing better, if such could be the case, over after over. Bradman worked a nice variety of bowlers and they all responded well to their task, though Compton was in no mood to be deterred from his driving to the off and he remained attentive to the end to the probabilities of spin. When Evans came in at the end of the day to help Compton to clear off those shocking arrears, spirits rose to end the day with a great acclamation for Compton.

*Even a superstar can find time for the public. Denis Compton signs an autograph for a docker at Tilbury as England prepare for their voyage aboard the Stratheden in 1950–51*

## THIRD TEST, OLD TRAFFORD, 1948

R.B. VINCENT,
CRICKET CORRESPONDENT

*July 9.* Yet Lindwall and Johnston, without except on very rare occasions making the ball rear, were able to get that touch of speed which now seems to flabbergast our batsmen. It was unfortunate that Compton's innings was interrupted by a blow on the forehead, for his temporary absence left a crack in the batting just at the moment when it required stiffening. […]

Compton then reappeared, and a Compton moreover at his very best. Where others had plodded Compton played fully out to the ball or, waiting for it, chopped it down to third man or deflected it to the finest of fine legs. Yardley was playing his part handsomely enough in an attempt to recover lost ground until suddenly he hit a ball a shade short of a length into the hands of mid-wicket. Compton found a cheerful and willing partner in Evans, who treated himself to four boundaries in his first 20 runs. Compton, having reached his 50, was missed at the wicket low down wide to the offside off Lindwall, who must be reckoned particularly unlucky since he was patiently bowling to take that particular wicket in that particular way. […]

Still there remained Compton, unperturbed by Lindwall's faster ball or by a much slower one which he introduced two or three times, or by Johnston, who towards the end of the innings was bowling round the wicket.

*July 10.* When England started batting in the morning the score stood rather feebly at 231 for seven wickets. But Compton was there, happily recovered from his injury of the day before, and magnificently he used this opportunity to pull his side out of trouble. He was nobly aided by Bedser, and the pair of them, it must be admitted, were abetted by an unusual amount of fumbling by the fieldsmen. Compton was soon at work with his perfectly timed deflections to long leg. […]

Toshack and Johnson, when they bowled to Compton, had no slip fieldsmen, distributing their forces square and deep to the off side with a semi-deep third man. Compton duly reached his century with an on-drive off Toshack which also sent up the 300. When the cheering had died down the game was a while held up by the intrusion of the traditional Test match dog who, no doubt, wishes to pay his personal respects to the hero of the moment, but was eventually escorted from the ground under the arm of a policeman. […]

When Johnson came on after luncheon Compton attacked him fiercely and the answer was a few overs from Lindwall in his most hostile mood. To the balls which did not rise too high Compton played back with extreme composure; the others he left alone.

# ALASTAIR COOK

## FIFTH TEST, SYDNEY, 2010–11

MIKE ATHERTON,
CHIEF CRICKET CORRESPONDENT

*January 6.* To Cook first, who played so well and so freely that his struggles last summer against Pakistan might well have been imagined. To watch him so secure in defence, so certain in attack, it is hard to imagine it is the same player. Until his lapse at the end, his discipline outside off stump was the fundamental upon which this latest exhibition of Test-match batting was based, because it forced bowlers to bowl at him, with the result that 68 of his first 100 runs were scored through the on side.

As he batted on, his footwork so smooth it could have been fashioned in

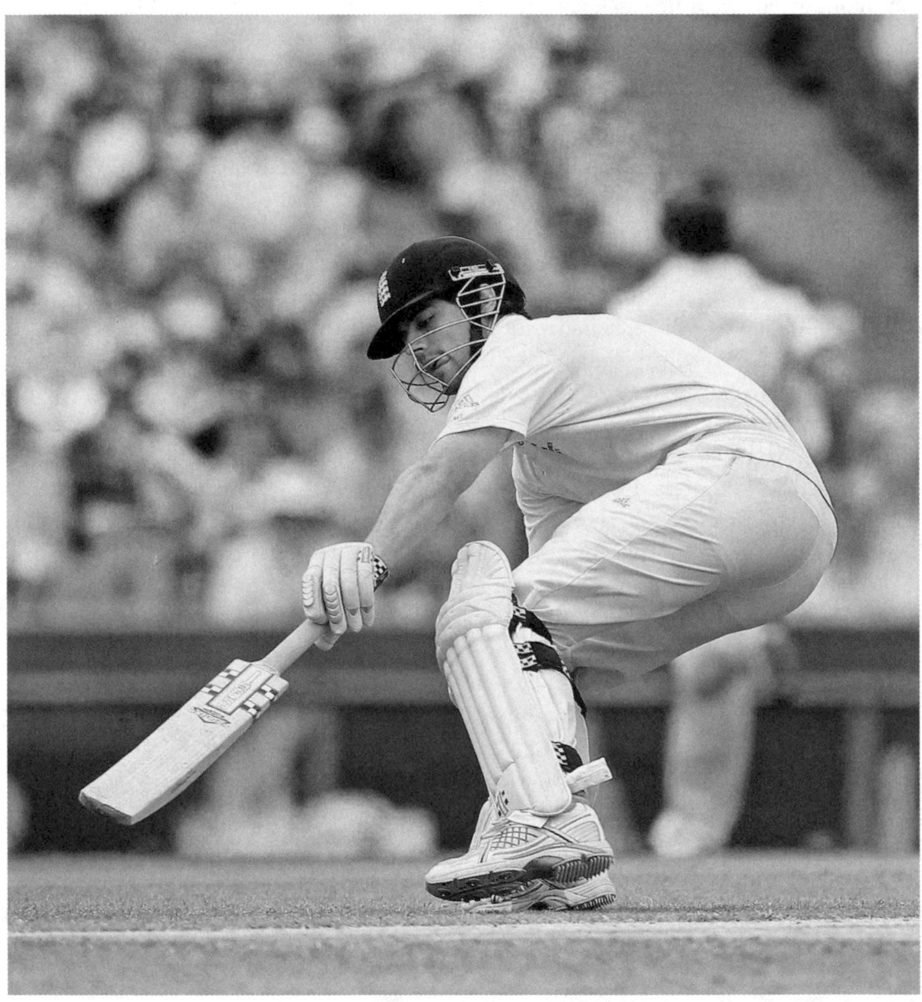

*Alastair Cook turns for two during his relentless pursuit of records at Sydney in 2010–11*

a blender, records fell to him as readily as autumn leaves into the gutter. One by one he passed the great names of English batting who had pounded Australia's bowlers in previous Ashes series: past John Edrich's total in 1970–71; past Geoffrey Boycott in the same series; past the great Jack Hobbs in 1911–12; and when he cut Shane Watson for four just after 2 o'clock in the afternoon, past Herbert Sutcliffe's 734-run tally in Australia in 1924–25. Nineteen runs later he had gone past the great Denis Compton, who famously tucked into South Africa's attack for 753 runs in 1947. Cook has 766 runs in this series and even if he suffers a duck in the unlikely event of a second innings, he will end with an average in it of more than 100. He has been immense. Only Wally Hammond's run-glut in the 1928–29 Ashes series, when he scored 905 runs, stands above Cook's effort for the number of runs scored by an England batsman in any series. Apologies for the stat-fest, but rarely in cricket do numbers tell the whole story, as they do here.

GIDEON HAIGH

*January 6.* 'Knowing where your off stump is' is one of those cricket expressions that sounds perennially mysterious to the uninitiated. After all, doesn't it just sit there alongside the other two?

Cook the expositor unravels its meaning: by letting go balls that compel no stroke, he draws bowlers into his pads, coaxes them to pitch the ball farther up for driving, and generally tires them, little by little. He makes the non-stroke into a kind of stroke, silence into a kind of statement.

## COLIN COWDREY AND TREVOR BAILEY

### FIRST TEST, BRISBANE, 1954–55

JOHN WOODCOCK,
CRICKET CORRESPONDENT

*November 30.* Slowly a revival began. At one end was Bailey of the iron nerve in the dead bat act which he made so famous in 1953 and who, with his slippers on 40 minutes earlier, had been filming Hutton going out to bat, as he hoped, for the day; at the other was Cowdrey, asserting some authority by twice hitting Johnson back over his head to the sightscreen and at once looking a player of Test match status, better by far than anything that had gone before.

At teatime, when the score was 52, Cowdrey had been in for 90 minutes and Bailey for an hour, and in the first 25 minutes of the evening session they added 40 runs, not feverishly but off loose balls from Benaud and Johnston. Thrice Cowdrey drove the latter through the covers with all the grace and majesty of Hammond, and thrice Bailey hit Benaud for 4 in an over, two long hops hooked and a deflection past slip. In Cowdrey's first 32 were seven boundaries, yet his defence looked as solid as a rock and suddenly, in spite of the variety of attack and the change of seeing slow bowlers in action after days of speed, the pitch again seemed dead, as, of course, it always had been.

Certainly, after their burst of scoring, the fifth wicket pair added only 10 runs in the next 70 minutes, but neither looked like getting out, and gradually the close drew near. They had been together for two hours 40 minutes and Cowdrey had been in for more than three hours when eventually Johnston, began his last fatal over. Cowdrey prodded cautiously at the second ball, boot and bat together, and first slip took a catch. Cowdrey seemed in some doubt as to whether he had made contact, but the umpire adjudged him out and there it was, a sad ending to a sad day. He had played a masterly innings in what must surely be his first of many Test matches.

# COLIN COWDREY

## THIRD TEST, MELBOURNE, 1954–55

JOHN WOODCOCK,
CRICKET CORRESPONDENT

*January 1.* Thus it was left to the rest to salve what they could from the wreckage, and Cowdrey, with the help first of Bailey and then of Evans, did a magnificent job.

That Cowdrey is soon going to rank as a Test match player of the very first magnitude seems as certain as anything can be in cricket. Yet he will play few finer innings than he did today. For the fifth time in five Test innings he came in at a time of crisis, the score being 21 for two, and he quickly lost Hutton and Compton.

A century against Australia is the ambition of every cricketer; to get one in a crisis out of 158 runs and before nearly 70,000 people at Melbourne at the age of 22 makes it a great achievement. J.W. Hearne was only 20 when he made 114 on the same ground in 1911, and Cowdrey is the youngest M.C.C. century maker in Australia since then, being a few months younger than the Nawab of Pataudi when the latter made 102 at Sydney in 1932. Bradman, incidentally, was 21 when he made his first Test match 100 in England. One will not soon forget the ovation which Cowdrey had when, with his score at 97, he turned Archer for 3. [...]

As it was, at 41 for four the innings was dreadfully broken and now as at Brisbane when they came together at 15 for four, Cowdrey and Bailey began their rescue work. At Brisbane they added 82, today 74, and when, half an hour before tea, Bailey was eventually caught the pitch had become so utterly placid that there seemed little reason why the pair should not have gone on for a considerable time. Bailey mishooked a long hop on to his pad, whence it lobbed to Maddocks – a luckless end which was not deserved after he had batted well through the worst.

When this misfortune came Cowdrey had been becalmed for 40 minutes, and he remained so for another 20. It was the one time in his innings when he was not master of the bowling, and during it he scored only four runs. After luncheon he had gone easily to his 50 made out of 69 in 100 minutes, and in the overs before tea he crashed three handsome boundaries off Johnson and Johnston to make his score 68.

Cowdrey began the evening by driving and sweeping Johnston majestically for two 4's in the same over and then driving Lindwall for another, and with Evans showing welcome discretion together with some good leg-side strokes, the score was soon jogging along, 35 coming in 40 minutes. Cowdrey was the figure to watch in the centre of the great arena as he neared his 100, and he overshadowed Miller, who came on for two bustling overs, his only others apart from his devastating spell. At 169 Cowdrey lost Evans, but within 10 minutes he had retaliated by scoring the 10 runs he needed for his 100. A delicious late cut off Johnson, then off Archer a terrific straight drive for his fifteenth 4 and at 179 his 3 to leg.

## THIRD TEST, HEADINGLEY, 1961

JOHN WOODCOCK,
CRICKET CORRESPONDENT

*July 8.* As a general criticism Australia bowled too short, and their direction was not all it might have been. Yet the fact remains that Cowdrey's was the innings of a master. His wonderful technique must have made the Australians despair. He had a few of those broody spells which are inseparable from his batting and he survived chances at 22 and 70, the first to mid-wicket off Simpson, the second when he glanced McKenzie to Davidson at backward short leg. Davidson by then was feeling the burden of the day and stooped rather wearily for the catch.

For the remainder of his four hours and a quarter at the wicket Cowdrey's judgment could scarcely be faulted. He came in at 59 for one and left at 223 for four, caught far away down the leg side by Grout as he hooked at a short one from McKenzie. Cowdrey's last gesture was as noble as his batting. Within a stone's throw of his first century against Australia in England he walked away to the pavilion although Langridge seemed undecided whether or not to give him out. The Australian team applauded him most of the way in as a mark of their admiration.

# TED DEXTER

## FIRST TEST, EDGBASTON, 1961

JOHN WOODCOCK,
CRICKET CORRESPONDENT

*June 14.* A defiant innings of 180 by Dexter, with shafts of brilliance darting through it, saved the first Test match against Australia at Edgbaston yesterday. England, having begun the day 215 behind, were leading by 80 at the end, with six wickets still in hand. Since last Friday afternoon, in fact, when O'Neill and Harvey were running riot, the wheel of fortune had turned about.

From Australia's point of view the result must be a crushing disappointment after they had seemed to have victory in their grasp on Saturday, and their day was darkened further by the realization that Benaud at the moment can hardly get his arm above his shoulder. As Australia's chief threat to England he bowled only nine uncomfortable overs for 38 runs, which, among other things, must have been a great relief to Dexter. The rest of the Australian attack were powerless to overcome the pitch, which showed none of the malice expected of it. […]

Australia's problems are suddenly more numerous than England's and by a strange twist of fate it was Dexter who batted for five hours and a half and did most to deny them the victory they so much desired.

On Monday it was impossible to find an Australian with any noticeable respect for Dexter's cricketing ability. Both on tour in Australia and against them here this season he has struck them as having feet of clay. In spite of his outstanding record in the West Indies he was their idea neither of a Test match batsman nor a Test match bowler. Failure yesterday might have led to his omission: yet here he was making the second highest score against Australia by an English batsman since Hutton's famous innings in 1938. Strangely enough, he never stung them with quite the fullest powers of his driving. He was hitting the ball too much into the ground for that, and the pitch was a shade too slow. There was, however, an aggression and an authority about his play that revealed to the Australians a batsman of singular strength and style. His detachment, amounting almost to disdain, must have maddened his opponents. He was concentrating on laying a bogy, upon overcoming an inferiority complex against leg spin bowling, and in doing so he gave no chance until his score was 179.

Had Dexter got out at any time before 3 o'clock, Englishmen might have been gnawing at their nails for much longer than they were. Instead, he found a balance between attack and defence and conveyed an air of permanency which surprised even those who knew his talents. When Barrington dropped anchor as his partner for the fourth wicket, in a stand of 161, Australia ceased to look capable of winning, and the tension eased. One day I hope to see Dexter play an even greater innings against Australia; one that will help to win a match rather than save one.

## BASIL D'OLIVEIRA

### FIFTH TEST, THE OVAL, 1968

JOHN WOODCOCK, CRICKET CORRESPONDENT

*August 24.* D'Oliveira set himself on automatic steering. He batted until five o'clock with the minimum of effort, never a hair or a nerve out of place. He was impassive and assured; his best shots were powerful but seldom physical. On yesterday's form he should go back to South Africa this winter, as a member of the M.C.C. team: his batting far surpassed anything he did in the West Indies earlier this year. His hundred was his second for England and the continuation of a most successful run as a Test match batsman in this country. Obviously he plays better for getting away from the Worcester wicket.

## PERCY FENDER

### FOURTH TEST, OLD TRAFFORD, 1921

A.C.M. CROOME

*July 26.* During the spell of fierce hitting Mr Armstrong kept the runs down at one end by bowling a couple of feet wide of the leg stump. Mr Fender was the more resourceful of the two batsmen, for, in dealing with Mr Armstrong, he contrived at times to get away and place the ball on the deserted off side. He once shifted his hands on the handle of his bat and pulled him back-handed across the wicket to the place where cover-point generally stands.

## ANDREW FLINTOFF

### FOURTH TEST, TRENT BRIDGE, 2005

CHRISTOPHER MARTIN-JENKINS, CHIEF CRICKET CORRESPONDENT

*August 26.* … but it was Flintoff who dominated the scene in the morning and thereby defined the mood of the day. He has played many a violent and spectacular innings for England in the last two years, many a valuable one too, but none so pure or coolly impressive as this. To the quick bowlers he offered the full face of his newly altered Woodworm bat, one with a bowed blade, thick edges and a thick toe.

Against Shane Warne, who bowled the first ten overs from the Pavilion End and gave the ball generous air to try to entice his once impetuous opponent into something self-destructive, Flintoff waited on the back foot unless he was absolutely sure he could get to the pitch of the ball to drive. He escaped one early leg-before appeal but never looked bothered afterwards, picking off fours through the covers before going down on one knee to launch his first and only six.

The new ball merely offered the chance to punish Shaun Tait with strokes of effortless power. This time, Ricky Ponting's cautious fields, with always three, sometimes four men on the boundary, merely offered large gaps and a feeling of freedom. Not until he had nudged Warne to square leg to reach his first hundred against Australia, off 121 balls, did Flintoff offer a reminder of his youth, hitting across the line and falling leg-before.

## MIKE GATTING

### FOURTH TEST, ADELAIDE, 1994–95

ALAN LEE, CRICKET CORRESPONDENT

*January 28.* As recently as a week ago, there was no reason to think that Mike Gatting would play again on this tour. He admits as much himself. Yesterday, however, he added to the extreme circumstances that restored him once again to the England side, his first Test century since 1987.

The curtain calls for Gatting have been many and varied, but this is the one that he will remember. On the ground where he last made an overseas hundred for England, in December 1986, he battled through almost seven hours for 117. His tortured progress through the nineties, a journey that occupied 78 minutes and created a level of tension through inactivity that only Test cricket can contrive, held the attention of the second-day crowd in this fourth Test.

Gatting's pursuit of the century, England's first in this series, almost brought the match to a standstill. Yet the tenacity with which he clung to his wicket, against magnificent fast bowling from Craig McDermott and a teasing spell by Shane Warne, told how much it meant to him. Once the England innings had come to an abrupt and unsatisfactory end and Australia had begun their reply with ominous haste, Gatting explained the deeper reasons.

Among his many virtues are loyalty and sensitivity. He remembers those who have been good to him and he cares for them. So when, yesterday, the death of one good friend and influence coincided with the funeral of another, Gatting was driven as much by melancholy as by the state of the tour and the generally unflattering assessment of his part in it.

Harry Sharp, the Middlesex scorer throughout Gatting's time at the county and a man he loved dearly, was buried yesterday. Hours earlier had come the death of Fred Bennett, one of Australian cricket's most genial administrators, who had brought Gatting into Sydney grade cricket with Balmain in the late 1970s. Instead of savouring his triumph last night, Gatting was stating his sadness and dedicating his innings appropriately. [...]

Coming to the crease at 93 for one meant he could bat with less pressure than of late, and he prospered for it. He enjoyed the short square boundaries, flexing those powerful forearms with some of the old purpose, but, when he resumed yesterday on 50, his passage was not untroubled.

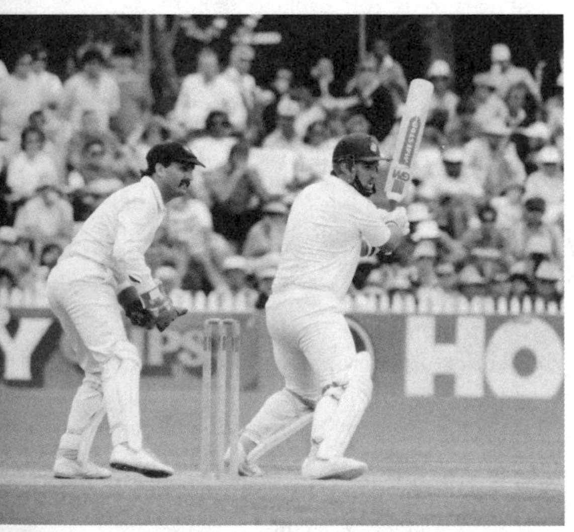

*Mike Gatting made a century at the Adelaide Oval as captain in 1986–87, and returned to make another in very different circumstances in 1994–95*

Running between the wickets is not a strong point of his game, and he was fortunate to survive a single to Blewett when 64. Almost immediately, an imploring leg-before appeal from McDermott went unanswered. McDermott, who had bowled Gatting with a no-ball when he had made only 19, wore the exasperated look of a man who suspects that it will not be his match. [...]

When Chris Lewis was out to a characteristically thoughtless pull, Gatting had reached 99 by way of 35 minutes rooted on 95. The final run was to come no more easily, as he played French cricket against Warne and simply survived against McDermott, who was entering the eleventh over of a spell in the hottest part of the day when Gatting jabbed a short ball to the left of Steve Waugh at gully.

He set off with confidence for the run, only to see the doubt in his partner's eyes. 'Daffy [DeFreitas] was a bit reticent; we had to negotiate in the middle of the pitch," Gatting said. Selflessly, DeFreitas ran on, but the pair had barely crossed when Waugh's throw, after a superb stop, missed the stumps. Gatting reached sanctuary with a sigh of relief and then, with unusual ostentation, kissed the crown on his helmet.

## TOM GRAVENEY

### FIFTH TEST, SYDNEY, 1954–55

JOHN WOODCOCK,
CRICKET CORRESPONDENT

*March 2.* Let one at once congratulate Graveney on his century. It was a lovely innings, true though it is that he could have asked for no more favourable circumstances in which to display his talents.

*Bowling like a man possessed, Shane Warne fought to deny England on the final day at the Oval in 2005 (Marc Aspland)*

*Nasser Hussain illuminated a magnificent England victory at Edgbaston in 1997 with a commanding double century (Marc Aspland)*

*All smiles at Edgbaston as England go 1-0 up in 1997. Left to right, Stewart, Hussain, Gough, Atherton, Croft and Malcolm (Marc Aspland)*

*A wet welcome to England for the 1956 Australians aboard the* The Himalaya. *Left to right: Jim Burke, Peter Burge, captain Ian Johnson, Pat Crawford, Jack Wilson (just visible), Len Maddocks, Ken Mackay and John Rutherford (*The Times *picture library)*

*James Anderson's mastery of swing was never better demonstrated than in England's series-clinching win at the SCG in 2010–11 (Marc Aspland)*

*Paul Downton, right, drinks a toast to the return of the Ashes at the Oval in 1985 as David Gower and Ian Botham celebrate (Graham Morris)*

*Just as in 1981, England rallied around an inspirational all-rounder in 2005. In Andrew Flintoff England finally found a hero to match Botham (Marc Aspland)*

*Stephen Harmison was part of a formidable England pace attack in 2005. In the first Test at Lord's he was at his most hostile (Marc Aspland)*

An 18-year-old Brian Close and the Lancashire spinner Bob Berry on the deck of the *Stratheden* at the start of the 1950–51 tour (*The Times* picture library)

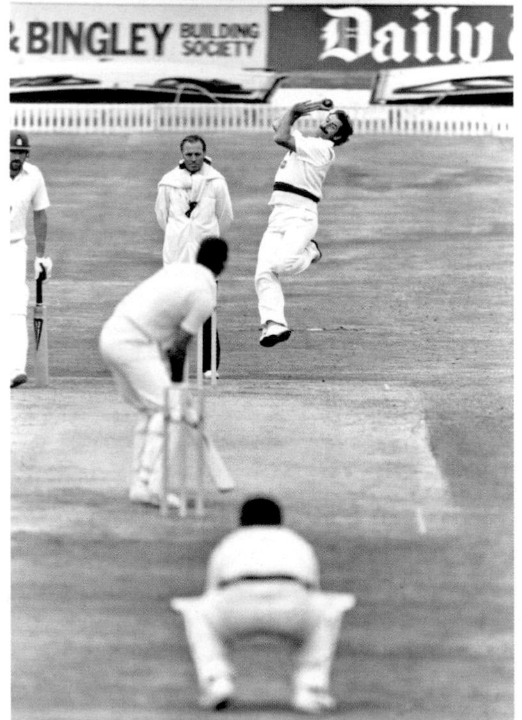


*Still an intimidating sight even towards the end of his great career, Dennis Lillee charges in during the 1981 series (*The Times* picture library)*

*David Gower seldom batted better than in the summer of 1985. At Edgbaston in the fifth Test he made a superb double century (Chris Cole)*

*The milestones came thick and fast for Alastair Cook in 2010–11. He celebrates another one during his 189 at Sydney (Marc Aspland)*

*Ian Botham helps out with promotional duties for the BBC's video of his epic exploits in 1981 (*The Times *picture library)*

*Smart suits and slim ties are the uniform choice for Bill Lawry's 1968 team as they pose outside the Waldorf Hotel (*The Times *picture library)*

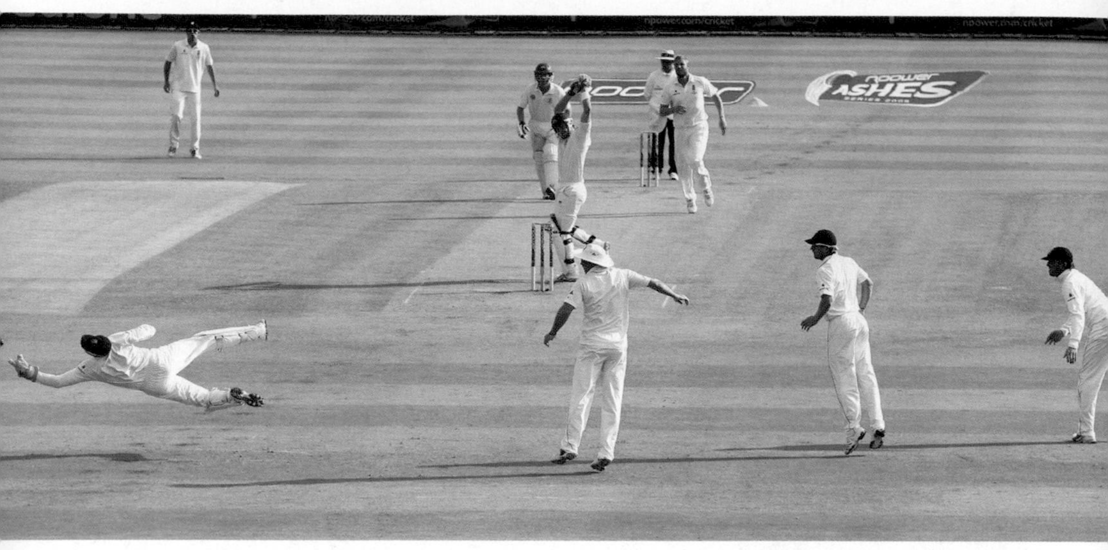


*Matt Prior takes off in pursuit of a wide and wild delivery from Andrew Flintoff at Edgbaston in 2009 (Marc Aspland)*

*A period of unprecedented Australian dominance has begun as Allan Border's superbly drilled team celebrate a 4-0 victory at the Oval in 1989 (Graham Morris)*

*England captain Mike Atherton conducts a press conference from an unusual angle during the 1997 series (Graham Morris)*

*The maestro and his adoring public: Shane Warne celebrates his 700th Test wicket at the MCG on Boxing Day 2006 (Graham Morris)*

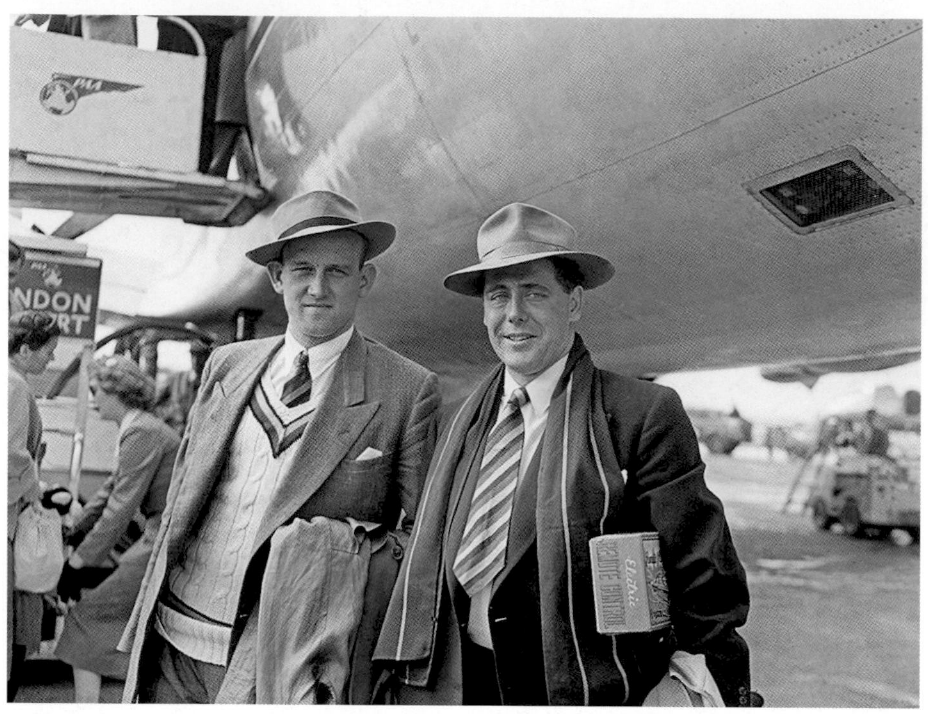

*Home with the Ashes. Frank Tyson and Trevor Bailey arrive back in England after the triumph in Australia in 1954–55 (*The Times *picture library)*

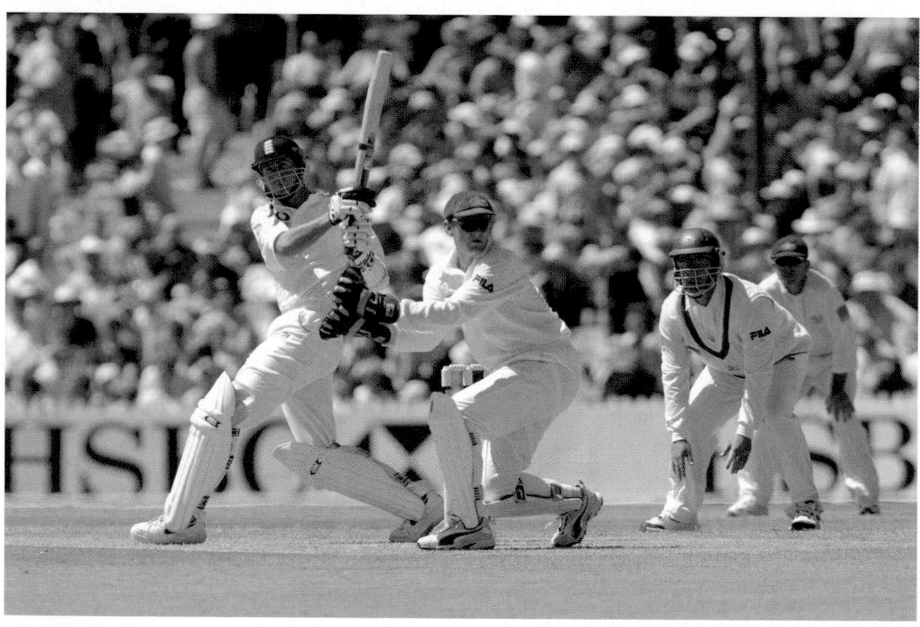


*Michael Vaughan hits Shane Warne for a boundary during his century at the Adelaide Oval on his outstanding 2002–03 tour (Graham Morris)*

*A century on debut and the beginning of a fine Test career: Graham Thorpe is congratulated by Nasser Hussain at Trent Bridge in 1193 (Graham Morris)*

*In a golden spell on the final evening, Stuart Broad rips through the Australian batting to take England to a series-clinching victory at Chester-le-Street (Graham Morris)*

*Darren Gough begins the celebrations and there is Ashes joy at last for Alec Stewart as England pull off a remarkable 12-run victory at the MCG in 1998–99 (Graham Morris)*

*After waiting an age for the DRS decision, Brad Haddin is given out and an ecstatic England go 1-0 up in the 2013 series at Trent Bridge (Graham Morris)*

*Kevin Pietersen acknowledges the applause after his extraordinary innings on the final day at the Oval in 2005 (Marc Aspland)*

*Matt Prior's sweat-stained cap is testament to England's Ashes-winning efforts at Sydney in 2010–11 (Marc Aspland)*

*A windy and chilly welcome for the 1953 Australians at Southampton. Left to right: Arthur Morris, Jack Hill, Alan Davidson, Colin McDonald, Gil Langley, Arthur James, Keith Miller, Neil Harvey and Ian Craig (*The Times *picture library)*

The pitch was a beauty, the bowling approaches were brown and sodden, and there was not the tension that there generally is when England meet Australia. But for all that England lost Hutton to the fourth ball of the match and Johnson had sought the initiative by putting England in to bat. This no doubt, he saw as the only possible way in which he might bundle England out twice in the 13 hours 10 minutes which remained for play when the umpires left their Ark.

Watching Graveney today it seemed absurdly incongruous that England should have turned him down for three Test matches on this tour. Of his natural ability there has never been the slightest doubt. Yet the fact is that this was the first time he has passed 50 in a first-class match on the Australian mainland, although eight times out of 11 he has got as far as 20.

His innings was one that Edrich, whose place he took, could not have played. Indeed, for sheer elegance, it was one that few batsmen in the world could have played. But until this match Hutton has backed Edrich's temperament against Graveney's potentialities, and the Ashes have been won. It is simply a great pity that Graveney cannot more often be relied upon to make the most of his skill when playing for England, and perhaps now that he has this achievement under his belt he will.

There was no Archer, who had been left out of the Australian side to give Burge and Watson the chance to sample the atmosphere of a Test match, or what there was of it, and only Benaud won much esteem from the batsmen. He danced for a couple of leg-before appeals when Graveney was 67 and 73, and then he put his fingers to a drive from Graveney when the latter was 80. This hit came as though from a gun – only the smell of grapeshot was missing – and 55 more runs came in as many minutes before drinks were taken.

Graveney then was 85 and in the next over he careered to his 100, made out of 166, with four boundaries off Miller. Three drives and a sweep took him there after batting for two and a half hours and hitting 13 4's, testimony to the power of his strokes over a heavy ground. The Australians congratulated him as though he had won one of their national lotteries, and he celebrated by sweeping Johnson majestically for 4.

## TONY GREIG

### FIRST TEST, BRISBANE, 1974–75

JOHN WOODCOCK,
CRICKET CORRESPONDENT

*December 2.* Greig's hundred was his sixth in Test matches, his first against Australia. It was more than an innings, it was an expression of defiance, a rallying call. He came in at 57 for four, with England on the run before the Australian fast bowlers. Right from the start he carried the fight to the Australian camp. He riled them with his antics. He got the 'aggro' going, with no one more than Lillee. This was a case of one giant bearding another. When Greig crashed Lillee through the covers for four, he signalled the boundary himself with a flourish which there was no way of Lillee missing. To do that kind of thing you have to be good enough, and confident with it. Mohammad Ali is. In this innings so was Greig.

First thing today he slashed wildly two or three times at the fast bowlers, chasing them outside the off stump as though determined to get after them wherever they bowled. But his judgment for the most part was wonderfully good, and, however fast the bowling, he never flinched. As an example to the side it was just what was needed. The crowd took to him too. Efforts are already being made, I believe, to persuade him to play for Queensland next year. When he was caught at the wicket off Lillee, having just stormed past his 100, Greig was given a most generous reception.

The day had began with Edrich who had played with much courage yesterday, being caught at slip off Thomson. In the previous over Lillee had hit him on the finger (Edrich did not field this evening, though nothing was broken) and it was off a tentative stroke to a short ball that he was out. Early this morning, therefore, England had only Knott and the four bowlers to come as prospective partners for Greig, and of these Knott and Lever were quite soon gone, Knott caught in the gully off one of his less good strokes, Lever caught at slip.

When Underwood came in England were 168 for seven. Although he has been batting above his known form on this tour, it seemed to be expecting too much that he should do so now. But he did. Regularly encouraged by Greig, between overs, and presenting a straight bat, at times a flashing one, Underwood was England's answer to Walker, who made 41 not out at the end of Australia's first innings. Underwood's opening shot was a stroke through the covers off Walker, reminiscent of Dexter. He stayed for 75 minutes, adding 58 with Greig, every run an irritation to Australia. In the end, playing too soon at the first ball of a relieving spell by Walters, after seeing off the new ball, Underwood was caught at extra cover.

Greig was 93 by now. Off the third over with the new ball he and Underwood had hit Thomson for 15, each getting four for a slash over the slips. This prompted Ian Chappell to move as deep at first slip as anyone since Bill Edrich fielded there to Frank Tyson out here in 1954. Greig went to his 100 with two magnificent strokes through the covers off Lillee and then lofted Walters first over mid-on, then over cover point for two more fours before Lillee put an end to his tormentor. Greig had batted for five hours and given one chance, a low one to Jenner in the gully, just before Edrich was out this morning.

Greig used his height to scotch the bounce, which the others found so disconcerting, especially yesterday, either that or he swayed out of the line like a poplar in the breeze. One must be careful about calling an innings 'great' but in all the circumstances Greig's, I think, was.

## THIRD TEST, MELBOURNE, 1974–75

JOHN WOODCOCK,
CRICKET CORRESPONDENT

*December 27.* With a drive over long-off for six off Mallett, Greig announced that all was not over. This was a stupendous hit. I can remember Dexter driving Veivers straight for six here, a low one-iron shot that was still rising when it cleared the sightscreen, but this, I think, was a rarer stroke of Greig's. At 231 for eight, by when Greig and Willis had added 49, the new ball was taken, which produced two of the finest pieces of cricket of the day – a pair of cracking off drives by Greig, both saved by Ross Edwards at deep mid-off, one diving to his right, the next to his left, like a wing three-quarter hurling himself at the line.

Greig had reached 50 by now, acknowledging it with a provocative wave of his cap to those who either love or hate him in the crescent of the southern stand. An on drive for four by Greig off Lillee was another fine stroke. This was not batting so much as inspiration.

## DAVID GOWER

### THIRD TEST, SYDNEY, 1990–91

ALAN LEE, CRICKET CORRESPONDENT

*January 8.* Nothing, however, could upstage the lordly manner in which Gower seized the initiative from the Australian bowlers at the start of play. It never seemed to occur to him that anything other than his third century in six Tests was awaiting, and nor was he inclined to wait very long for it.

Gower hit three fours in the first over of the day from Alderman and after 35 minutes play he had struck five more in scoring 37 of the 38 runs added. Atherton, who resumed on 94, was no more than a spectator as Gower recalled the days when his cricket wore no cares or no tension, when his gift of eye-to-hand coordination and exquisite timing produced batting of peerless fluency.

The century he made at the Oval in late August not only installed him on this tour but re-emphasised the huge affection in which Gower is held in England. His two centuries in this series have indicated he is no less popular in Australia and if, once or twice on tour, he has shown a testiness suggesting that he appreciates that age imposes precarious new demands, it is no bad thing. By mood and deed he has made it clear that nobody will take his place without a fight.

## W.G. GRACE

### ONLY TEST, THE OVAL, 1880

LEADING ARTICLE

*September 9.* What the people lacked in elegance they made up in enthusiasm. A goodly share of it fell to Dr W.G. Grace on his return from the wickets. Everyone is pleased that Dr Grace should have made 150 runs in a match when runs were peculiarly expected of him. The Grace family in cricket have come to be almost a national institution, and it was gratifying to find the head of the clan working well, like other British institutions, in a time of trial.

*A wheelchair-bound Percy Fender was the oldest England player to make the journey to Melbourne for the Centenary Test in 1977*

## THIRD TEST, THE OVAL, 1886

*August 13*. England won the toss and were batting the whole day. Dr W.G. Grace, who until recently held the record for the highest individual total against Australian bowling in this country, treated the spectators to a fine display of batting. He got within 16 of Maurice Read's score on the Oval a fortnight ago and beat Shrewsbury's innings at Lord's by six runs. He gave several chances, despite which his innings will rank among the best he has played. Mr Scott should have caught him at slip when the total was only six, and it is needless to say how terribly expensive this error proved to the visitors. [...]

With his figures at 60 Dr Grace was missed low down at long-off by Mr Bruce, who started very late, or might have easily affected the catch. This mistake was from Mr Spofforth, whom the Gloucestershire captain next drove twice to the on for four each, the second ball falling on the top of the stand. [...]

Shrewsbury aided Dr Grace, who, after some slow cricket, drove Mr Palmer to the off for four, and hit him to leg with a like result. Dr Grace increased his score to 160 at five minutes past 5. Mr Spofforth then bowled in lieu of Mr Palmer at 192, but Dr Grace continued his free hitting, and after bringing up 200 at a quarter-past 5, he increased his score to 168 – four better than Shrewsbury's innings at Lord's. Shortly afterwards he was nearly caught and bowled, but he had only added a single when he was splendidly taken at the wicket. He had been batting four and a half hours, and despite the chances mentioned had hit very finely. Among his contributions were 22 fours, four threes, and 17 twos. He had scored 170 out of 216.

## WALTER HAMMOND

### SECOND TEST, SYDNEY, 1928–29

FROM OUR SPECIAL CORRESPONDENT*

*December 18.* The promise previously given by Hammond that when the Test matches came to be played he would reveal the form which had compelled his inclusion in the team to take part in the tour, as was the case years ago with Hobbs, was fully realized here today. Hammond batted the whole day long, and at the close was still unbeaten, having put together the second highest English individual score in Test matches against Australia.

In a wonderful display of steadiness, combined with dazzling off-side strokes, Hammond's uncertain hits could be numbered on the fingers of one hand. A difficult return chance to Ryder and an apparent chance of stumping were the only real blemishes, but the former was due to his getting his feet mixed up with his pads, while in the latter case the ball hit his pad and was deflected too wide for Oldfield to gather it and put down the wicket. He was never actually in any real difficulty, even when Blackie, with cleverly disguised changes of pace, was bowling better than he had ever done before against the M.C.C. team. Hammond waited for the loose ball, and then made delightful strokes past cover point and occasionally stepped back to cut the ball, the pace at which it travelled giving the fieldsmen no chance. Naturally he became tired during the last three-quarters of an hour, but he never lost his form in a display of the highest class. During this period the Australian bowlers distinctly made the ball spin and turn, but both Hammond and Larwood, the latter again showing his great value as a batsman, continued to hit the ball in the middle of the bat.

* *The Times* archivist has not been able to identify the author of this report

### THIRD TEST, MELBOURNE, 1928–29

ROY CURTHOYS

*January 3.* As at Sydney, his innings extended over one whole day and part of two others, and was marked throughout by unerring judgment in stroke play. He never once pulled; indeed he sets his face rigidly against that form of scoring, holding that control of direction is lost by the use of a horizontal bat. Mostly he exploited the drive, either square or straight, and his strong forcing strokes off the right leg were also a pronounced feature of his play. Particularly good, too, was the manner in which he chopped down on balls at the last moment. Twice he did this to Grimmett when the slow bowler looked to have got through his defence with balls that kept low.

### FIRST TEST, SYDNEY, 1932–33

DELAMORE MCCAY

*December 5.* Hammond's was a great display; he mastered Grimmett, his footwork being perfect, and he drove him powerfully. He scored his first 50 runs in 57 minutes, and has so far hit 13 4's. He played some perfect forcing strokes, and his innings, which was of a very high class, was greatly appreciated.

## FIFTH TEST, SYDNEY, 1932–33

DELAMORE MCCAY

*March 1.* Hammond abandoned his waiting policy after the interval and proceeded to attack the bowling. With his score at 17 he made one of the biggest hits in the history of the Sydney cricket ground, an on-drive off O'Reilly, sending the ball down the steps leading to the grandstand luncheon room. This he followed up by driving O'Reilly to the boundary and then hit Ironmonger to the boundary. Woodfull took O'Reilly off in favour of Alexander at 98, but the 100 went up in two hours and 21 minutes. At this point Ironmonger had his first rest, Lee, the slow to medium bowler, coming on in his place. Wyatt now began to score freely and kept pace with Hammond. Woodfull made some quick changes in the hopes of separating the batsmen, but Wyatt and Hammond went on their way to win the match with a glorious finish. Wyatt sent Lee to the boundary twice in succession, and in the same bowler's next over Hammond scored a boundary off the first ball and then scored the winning hit with a magnificent off-drive into the stand for a 6. A spectator seized the ball as a souvenir.

## SECOND TEST, LORD'S, 1938

R.B. VINCENT,
CRICKET CORRESPONDENT

*June 25.* The first day's play in the second Test match at Lord's yesterday will be remembered by all those who were lucky enough to be there for a display of batting by Hammond which can seldom have been surpassed. He has done great things in Australia, but it is certain that in a Test match in this country he has never approached such grandeur. At the close of play England had scored 409 runs for the loss of only five wickets, which is pretty reading on paper, but without Hammond one shudders to think what the total would have been.

The fact that he scored more than half the runs speaks for itself; it was the combination of batting technique and cricket brain, supported by physical endurance, which was so amazing. He took command from the moment that he went in; never put a foot wrong; refused to be tempted to achieve the brilliant; and patiently waited for the game to swing round in England's favour. It was an innings which many years hence will be referred to as a classic example of a batsman's elegant triumph over difficulties. The King arrived at the end of the luncheon interval, and both teams were presented to him in front of the Pavilion before the game was continued. [...]

Hammond, therefore, entered at a most gloomy period, which was to become even darker when at 31 Barnett played a rising ball down on to his thigh, from where it bounded into the hands of a crouching short-leg. He was certainly unlucky, for he had played the ball down well enough, but for all that McCormick had done his duty nobly as a fast bowler – not that he is particularly fast – in taking these three quick wickets. Paynter at first seemed a little uneasy, both to McCormick and McCabe, but left-handed batsmen, even the best of them, are liable to give that impression at the beginning of the innings.

Hammond nursed Paynter carefully, he himself finding no difficulty in playing any kind of ball. Fleetwood-Smith was soon put on at the Nursery end, and O'Reilly, who had a short-leg and three other men on the on-side when bowling to Hammond, gave Paynter two more uncomfortable overs. Gradually the precept and dominance of Hammond gave his partner the encouragement he required, and the Australian bowling sagged. O'Reilly bounded away, but the life had left the wicket. McCabe could do little more than bowl the ball into the middle of Hammond's bat, and Chipperfield's leg-breaks lost their break in Hammond's mastery. Hammond still had to fight after that miserable start, and never for one second was his technique at fault. His batting lost nothing of the glamour associated with his name, but behind it there was a security which killed even O'Reilly's normal venom. Hammond in one over hit him away to the square-leg boundary, which he followed with a gorgeous off-drive, also for four.

Paynter had one more piece of luck when he snicked a ball off Fleetwood-Smith over the head of slip. McCormick, when he came on again, looked to have lost all his pace and ferocity, and he was still further tamed by Hammond. Paynter also found plenty of time to cut him square, and was making runs almost as quickly as Hammond at one time … Hammond just before luncheon unloosed a battery of strokes and the interval score of 134 for three was a sign of the first stage of a recovery.

Fleetwood-Smith began the bowling after luncheon from the Nursery end, Hammond greeting him with a grand delayed drive to the boundary past third man and a sweep, following the break, to long leg. Hammond reached his century at 3 o'clock, a century which might have been marked on the scorecard from the moment he went in. Fleetwood-Smith was bowling untidily, offering far too many cheap runs, but there was always the danger that his unorthodoxy might gain an unexpected wicket. Hammond, still scoring at a rate of nearly a run a minute, never played the semblance of a loose stroke, while Paynter was hitting the ball with immense power for so small a man on the off side, lying right back and disengaging his left leg to give himself plenty of room in which to make the stroke.

Bowling changes were made every few overs, with O'Reilly moved from end to end until he can scarcely have known which way he was facing. The attack by all the bowlers except McCabe was concentrated on the leg stump, with a bunch of short legs, but Hammond was not to be drawn into the error of attempting to play balls which went a foot wide of the wicket. The balls which were straight he forced off his legs away to parts of the field where there was no green cap to be seen, although it must be admitted that the field was very tightly placed to save runs […]

Hammond, who, still without taking any risks played every ball he meant to with the full blade and force of the bat.

As with Paynter he preferred that Ames should not at first have too much of the bowling until he had had time to have a look at it. When once Ames was settled down he allowed him his full share, Hammond himself on a hot day no doubt being glad of some respite so long as he knew he had a trustworthy partner.

Small wonder that by 6 o'clock the Australian bowling wilted, although towards the end of the evening O'Reilly rose in his might and bowled as good an over as he had done all the long and tiring day. Hammond reached his 200 still batting as he had done before luncheon, and Ames had scored 50 before the Australians were allowed the solitude and restfulness of their dressing room.

Mead came in to join Hearne, who had made 85. The total rose slowly, but since the dismissal of Rhodes the batting had become much less interesting. Hearne, with a leg hit for 2 off Dr Hordern's bowling, put the English total ahead of the Australian's first innings score amid applause all round the ground, which broke out again very soon afterwards when Hearne completed his 100.

---

# JACK HOBBS

## SECOND TEST, MELBOURNE, 1911–12

*January 4.* The M.C.C. had to make 219 runs in their second innings to win the match, and they batted with the utmost confidence from the start. Hobbs played a magnificent innings of 126 not out in his best style. He was batting for three hours and a half, and he did not give anything approaching a chance. The Australian bowling was completely mastered, Mr Whitty (who, it will be remembered, was mainly instrumental in bringing about the defeat of the South Africans in the corresponding game a year ago) being the only one who ever looked at all dangerous. [...]

The crowd were now awaiting Hobbs's century and when he reached three figures with a cut off Mr Whitty's bowling past point for a single, there was a great burst of cheering. Frequent changes were made in the bowling, but the score continued to rise at a good rate. Hobbs made the winning hit and then ran straight to the pavilion amid enthusiastic cheering.

## THIRD TEST, ADELAIDE, 1911–12

*January 15.* Then with a drive for a single off Mr Armstrong's bowling he equalled his score at Melbourne in the second Test match. A little later he cut a ball from Mr Cotter to the boundary, and repeating the stroke in the next over for a single he made his individual score equal to the Australian first innings total, the fact being noticed and cheered by the crowd.[...]

Several more changes were made in the bowling, and the last of them – Mr Minnett for Mr Kelleway – was immediately successful, Hobbs being caught at point by Dr Hordern off the new bowler for 187. During his stay of 6hrs 34min he gave five chances but played a splendid all-round innings, the chief feature of which was magnificent driving. The cheering when he returned to the pavilion was extraordinary, the Australian players all joining in the applause.

## FIRST TEST, TRENT BRIDGE, 1930

R.B. VINCENT,
CRICKET CORRESPONDENT

*June 17.* For England Hobbs once again declared himself to be indispensable, this time not as the plodder we have now come to accept him, but as the brilliant attacking batsman of former years. One shudders to think what the state of the game would have been without Hobbs and Sutcliffe [...]

---

# JACK HOBBS AND

## HERBERT SUTCLIFFE

### FIFTH TEST, THE OVAL, 1926

A.C.M. CROOME, CRICKET CORRESPONDENT

*August 18*. The story of the third day's play begins with the tropical rain which fell in the small hours of Tuesday morning and awakened thousands of England's supporters to blasphemy. For the first hour of play the sky was cloudy and the light dull. Hobbs and Sutcliffe were fairly comfortable during this period. Then the sun came out, and the pitch from noon to half-past 1 was horrid. Mr Grimmett, Mr Macartney, Mr Richardson, and Mr Mailey, to name them in the order of their going on, bowled on it each of them as well as he knows how. But our two opening batsmen remained masters of their fate throughout. Their artistry in manipulation of the bat was consummate, their judgment infallible, their patience inexhaustible. Before they started their performance I should, if I had been given my choice of all the pairs who have ever gone in first for England, have selected Dr W.G. Grace and Shrewsbury to bat for my side in the existing circumstances. Now I consider reincarnation unnecessary. I also consider that I have done my best to render to Hobbs and Sutcliffe the gratitude due to them from the community of English cricketers.[…]

It was very instructive to note the way in which Hobbs dealt with Mr Richardson. He stood nearly a foot wide of his leg stump, so that the bowler could not range on his pads. Then, when he had detected the length and pace of the ball, he glided – sometimes ran – into position for the appropriate stroke. […]

I find I have omitted to enumerate Sutcliffe's brilliant scoring strokes. They constitute the least important feature of his innings. What every one who saw it will remember to his dying day is the graceful solidity of his defence, his subordination of self to side, and his almost uncanny wisdom.

## NASSER HUSSAIN

### FIRST TEST, EDGBASTON, 1997

ALAN LEE, CRICKET CORRESPONDENT

*June 7*. Hussain, perhaps the most vulnerable of the England top six when the game began, secured his spot for the summer with the innings that his disrupted Test career has long promised but never previously delivered. He became only the seventh Englishman to score 200 against Australia and did so in a befittingly lordly manner. Some of his driving stood comparison with the finest of any generation.

# LEN HUTTON

## FIFTH TEST, THE OVAL, 1938

R.B. VINCENT,
CRICKET CORRESPONDENT

*August 23.* Hutton's innings was the perfect continuation of the task he had set himself when he went in on Saturday morning. In so long an innings mistakes are expected to creep in here and there; yet Hutton seems to have found a method of eliminating to the greatest possible extent such errors. His range of stroke play is sufficient for any reasonable purpose – none of the Australian bowlers in this match could curb it – and he has the quiet confidence which would remain undisturbed in any circumstances. [...]

Hutton as he was approaching R.E. Foster's score edged one ball off O'Reilly past first slip, a false stroke which obviously vexed so accurate a batsman, but he continued on his way afterwards with never the suggestion of a mistake.

*August 24.* For Hutton himself the match has been a triumphant one, and when once the reason of a time-limitless match is recognized it must be said that no one could have played his part more adequately. Throughout his innings, while making it his main object to remain as long as possible at the wicket, he took every opportunity which he considered safe to score runs. Whether this is a desirable form of cricket is a matter of opinion, but the majority of a crowd of 31,000 who were at the Oval yesterday seemed thoroughly to enjoy it. [...]

*Len Hutton gets used to life in the media spotlight after his record-breaking innings at the Oval in 1938*

Hutton was certainly taking his time in compiling his record-shattering runs, for he scored 21 runs only during the first hour of play, but he sent the 700 up with a late cut off Waite which flew away down to the pavilion railings. He wanted only four more runs when O'Reilly provided him with a no-ball, but he missed it, and he had to wait some considerable time before he received a ball which he considered safe to cut and to pass Bradman's 334. This was the occasion for a great demonstration of praise, combined with relief; the entire crowd rose to its collective feet, the cheering was prolonged, and the Australian team, led by Bradman, who for some time had been lurking close to Hutton's bat, shook hands with him. The opportunity was taken for a waiter to bring out some refreshments, and thereafter the business of the time-limitless Test match was continued.

4

Sporting News

**ENGLAND DECLARE AT 903 FOR 7**

**HUTTON BREAKS ALL RECORDS**

**BRADMAN OUT OF THE MATCH**

**Hours of Play, 11.30 to 6.30.**

FROM OUR CRICKET CORRESPONDENT

The Test Match at the Oval made considerable progress yesterday, for after England's innings had been declared closed with their score standing at 903 for seven wickets the Australians lost three good wickets for 117 runs. For Australia it was indeed an unlucky day, as D. Bradman when running up to the wicket to bowl fell down and sustained a fracture of

*Len Hutton's feats at the Oval in 1938 were big news*

## FIRST TEST, TRENT BRIDGE, 1948

R.B. VINCENT,
CRICKET CORRESPONDENT

*June 14.* Not because it was a revival for England, but because it was to produce the finest stroke play so far of the whole match, one welcomed an hour of Hutton at his true best. It was an awkward, very bad position for England. Australia had made their runs according to a plan never very exhilarating, and Hutton, when all seemed to be lost, came to the relief of our eyes and spirits with strokes of immense grandeur.

# STANLEY JACKSON

## FOURTH TEST, OLD TRAFFORD, 1902

ERNEST WARD,
CRICKET CORRESPONDENT

*July 26.* But above everything else, the batting of Mr Jackson was the feat of the match. Mr Jackson was always, from his Harrow days, a great batsman, full of resource, courage, and nerve, but in his long series of success he has never done better than he did yesterday. He forced the game at the proper time; he went in when England were in an almost hopeless position, and he got his runs without a bad stroke. His late cutting was wonderful, and his shortened off drive just beyond cover point was worthy of Dr Grace.

### THIRD TEST, HEADINGLEY, 1905

E.H. LYTTELTON

*July 4.* The rest of the day's cricket may be summed up in one word – 'Jackson'. He was batting for the whole day after the first hour and a half, and not until he had scored 117 did he give a chance, when Mr Kelly missed stumping him off Mr Laver, and he hardly made a bad stroke. He was batting for five hours and a quarter, and scored freely when he was once set, although Mr Armstrong kept him quieter than the others. When he went in England had distinctly the worst of the game, and he was the cause of the averting of a bad collapse. He cut magnificently, and at no time did he seem to be in difficulties. The wicket was never easy, and considerable power was necessary to hit the ball to the boundary, for the ground is large and rather slow. Altogether it was perhaps the greatest of Mr Jackson's many great feats. Hirst gave him good assistance at a very critical time, and he received useful help from Lilley, Haigh, Mr Bosanquet, and Warren. It was essentially a one man's innings that of England, and the enthusiasm of the huge Yorkshire crowd was unbounded.

## MAURICE LEYLAND AND BOB WYATT

### THIRD TEST, ADELAIDE, 1932–33

E.W. PARISH

*January 14.* Leyland and Wyatt then began their invaluable, dogged partnership. They batted aggressively and enterprisingly and scored 156 runs before they were separated. Wyatt and Leyland, in fact, saved a complete disaster and eventually mastered the bowling, scoring easily off every bowler. It was evident that the wicket had lost its earlier pace and the Australian bowlers, particularly Grimmett, came in for much punishment. Wyatt lifted Grimmett into the stand twice within a few minutes and, later, he hit a short ball from Wall out of the ground. The partnership put on 156 in 145 minutes.

Leyland was the first to go. After an appeal for leg-before-wicket had not been sustained O'Reilly bowled him. He had made 83 in three hours, hitting 13 4's in a fearless innings. The fifth-wicket stand of 156 runs was 36 runs short of the English record. Paynter then joined Wyatt, who was soon caught by Richardson off Grimmett. Wyatt had made his highest score in the Tests. He batted for 164 minutes, and hit three 6's and three 4's. It was a magnificently confident innings.

## PETER MAY

### THIRD TEST, MELBOURNE, 1954–55

A.G. MOYES

*January 4.* May's cricket was splendid. Before tea he drove mostly off the back foot but after tea he hit off the front foot with gloriously controlled power, hitting the ball so hard that sometimes cover-point and mid-off heard rather than saw it. Johnson's shrewdly placed field stopped many and the fielders' hands must have tingled, but plenty burst through the inner ring and found the boundary fence. A lovely innings.

## COLIN MILBURN

### SECOND TEST, LORD'S, 1968

JOHN WOODCOCK,
CRICKET CORRESPONDENT

*June 22.* Milburn's innings gave more people more satisfaction than any for a long time. The last to cause the spectators at Lord's to rise when it was over, with such warmth and gratitude, was Ted Dexter's 70 against West Indies in 1963. Until now there has, I think, been a tendency not to take Milburn's batting seriously as a Test force, in spite of a very presentable technique.

Milburn is unhindered by an excess of theory. Born with a gentle nature and a gift for pounding a cricket ball, he refuses to compromise himself. As he matures, so his attacking judgment improves. Yesterday he silenced the doubters. It was remarkable stuff. Australia took the field hopeful of exploiting a drying wicket. Instead they were scattered by one man's aggression.

McKenzie, who had given the big fellow such a torrid time of it on Thursday, was driven and hooked in his first over, each time for four, so that after two overs Lawry withdrew him from the attack. Connolly was forced ruthlessly for four and hooked for another. And when after half an hour Cowper came on, Milburn pulled his first ball on to the Grandstand balcony just below the secretary's box. In six overs Cowper was hit for 28, most of them by Milburn. At Old Trafford, in England's first innings, Cowper bowled 26 overs for 48 runs.

We knew now that if Cowper bowled a half volley or a long hop he would regret it. Milburn, having dispatched them, would hitch up his trousers in readiness for the next. When Gleeson bowled after 70 minutes Milburn and Boycott, his admirable foil, had added 84 runs, 65 of them to Milburn. He, by then, had the run of the field; he could have had the freedom of the ground.

*Tony Greig rose to the challenge of the England captaincy with 96 on his first day in office at Lord's in 1975*

## KEVIN PIETERSEN

### FIFTH TEST, THE OVAL, 2005

SIMON BARNES

*September 13.* How lucky was Pietersen yesterday? As lucky as a cricketer can be. He was dropped on nought, a quarter chance between wicketkeeper and slip. On 15 he gave a routine slip chance, shoulder high. He missed being run out by a fraction and was dropped again on 60, a diving attempt just in from the boundary. He went on to make 158 in an innings of neurotic violence, of eccentric watchfulness, of brainless impetuosity and incontinent savagery. It was an extraordinary innings, a masterpiece, and it secured the Ashes for England.

How does it feel to drop the Ashes, Shane? How brutally cruel that it should be Warne. Warne took on England near as damn it single-handed over the course of the summer. He had 40 wickets, bowled with brilliance, batted with courage and played every match with a glorious, shining will for victory. Yet he it was who made the error that, in the end, decided both match and series.

England would have been done for had that catch stuck. But as it was, Pietersen was able to play his innings to its conclusion, an innings that began in the tensest circumstances that cricket can provide and ended with the cheery bullying of a beaten side.

Pietersen was brought into the team along with a lot of sucking of teeth and wagging of heads: a mere one-day hitter unsuited to the longer game. He is from South Africa and has something of a show pony in his make-up, and these are things that make a man mistrusted. He is also twitchy, jumpy and speedy, prone to constant movement and a notoriously nervy starter. But he has the finest eye for a cricket ball I have seen – one straight pull for four was one of the most extraordinary shots played in Test cricket – and with it a gormandising taste for the big stage.

It turned out that the final battle of this endless summer of twists within twists within twists was between Warne and Pietersen. One man hungry to play the biggest of big games and another whose hunger for such games is unsated even after all these years. And it was Pietersen, with the matchless combination of luck and eye, who prevailed, sometimes kicking Warne away, sometimes offering a huge play-and-miss, sometimes launching him for towering sixes when more conventional souls would have played an innings dominated by defence.

Pietersen gave the final polish to a wonderful summer.

JOHN WOODCOCK

*September 14.* For its temerity alone, Pietersen's innings was breathtaking. But it was brilliant too. There were, almost inevitably, other slices of luck, but that was no more than he deserved. His 158 is the score that Basil D'Oliveira made in 1968, against Australia at the Oval, an innings that also left an impression, of a very different kind, on the rich pattern of the game.

Pietersen and D'Oliveira have quite a lot in common, not only because of their South African background. Timing, eye, bottle and body strength apply to them both, as well as what golfers call club-head speed. Pietersen and D'Oliveira do not rate as strokers of the ball, like Colin Cowdrey and Frank Worrell and David Gower, or Ernie Els and Colin Montgomerie, so much as strikers of it: at the moment of impact their contact

*Kevin Pietersen played one of the great Ashes innings and virtually guaranteed the draw England needed on the final day at the Oval in 2005*

with the ball is lightningly fast. It would have had to be late in the evening, though, for the demurring D'Oliveira to have displayed any of Pietersen's apparent brashness.

## SECOND TEST, ADELAIDE, 2010–11

MIKE ATHERTON,
CHIEF CRICKET CORRESPONDENT

*December 6*. Pietersen likes it here, as most batsmen do, but it was the occasion as much as anything that has lifted his game out of the furrow of mediocrity that he has ploughed of late. Like Heineken, the Ashes can reach the parts other series cannot.

This was the man, remember, who admitted to a shocking loss of confidence last summer, so much so that he was dropped from the team for the first time at the end of the season. Twenty-one months is a long time to go without a Test hundred for anyone, let alone for a man of his ability.

He was back to his swaggering, sumptuous best here, attacking Australia's bowlers without the fear that had seemingly crept into his game in the last few months. He began the day on 85, and needed only 20 minutes to reach three figures, which he did with a neat tuck off his hip, followed by an extravagant celebration.

All the Pietersen TM shots were there, except the switch hit, which he no doubt felt unnecessary against a bowler of Doherty's modest ability. The flamingo reappeared, though, as if a litmus test of his health, when Ricky Ponting and Doug Bollinger hatched a cunning 7-2 offside plan; Pietersen simply walked across his crease and 'flamingoed' him away.

GIDEON HAIGH

*December 6.* All the same, Australians saw again the qualities in Pietersen that first caused them discomfiture. A Pietersen playing soberly is still like a conventional batsman spontaneously brainstorming. Thanks to wrists that rotate like gimbals, he scores in more areas of the field than perhaps any other contemporary batsman. He does not have one sweep, for instance, but many. He swung Doherty as fine as 40 degrees behind square leg, then North as much as 30 degrees in front, all along the ground.

## FIFTH TEST, THE OVAL, 2013

MIKE ATHERTON, CHIEF CRICKET CORRESPONDENT

*August 26.* To win Test matches in such circumstances, you need players who possess a little something out of the ordinary, and in Kevin Pietersen, England certainly have one. He came to the crease after Cook had given his team a perfect platform playing sensibly and positively without being frenetic, so that there was little danger of England losing the match by the time he walked across his crease to Faulkner and fell leg-before.

The stage was set: a full house, a sunlit evening, a ground where Pietersen has excelled in the past and a match to win; hard to think of a situation that did not suit him and his ego more. And right from the start, when he whipped Faulkner through mid-wicket, then drove him hard past mid-off, it was clear that Pietersen meant business. A sign that Pietersen is on the go is when his follow-through is so excessive that it smacks his own behind, and time and again, after thrashing the ball, bat came into contact with his backside.

He played some extraordinary shots and began to dominate Australia's young bowlers so that the thought occurred that much of their good work through the series was being undone.

Clarke's declaration was brave and generous – whether it was doing his fragile young team any good is another matter. When Pietersen took 15 off an over by Mitchell Starc, the left-armer visibly wilted.

Clarke shuffled his pack desperately, but could not prevent Pietersen going to his half-century in 36 balls, the quickest by an English batsman in Ashes history, the second quickest from either side. It needed Ryan Harris, the rock-solid Harris, brought back in desperation by Clarke despite a niggle, to end Pietersen's dash, although any fast bowler will not want to be reminded of a dismissal that reads caught long-on.

## TIM ROBINSON

### FIRST TEST, HEADINGLEY, 1985

JOHN WOODCOCK,
CRICKET CORRESPONDENT

*June 15.* Robinson's batting in his first home Test was a revelation. There was the odd alarm outside the off stump, and he survived a chance to slip, but his timing through the covers and off his toes was wonderfully good. It is quite something to be able to follow a long defensive rearguard such as he conducted at Delhi with a free and attractive innings such as yesterday's.

## WILLIAM SCOTTON

### THIRD TEST, THE OVAL, 1884

*August 14.* England were mainly indebted to Scotton and Mr Read for the creditable draw they made with Australia yesterday at Kennington Oval. It will long remain in the minds of those who witnessed Scotton's batting how he defied the various attacks of his opponents and the elegant manner in which he defended his wicket when matters were looking anything but bright for the mother country. Perhaps a finer display than that of the Nottinghamshire professional has seldom, if ever, been witnessed in a match of such importance. Had it not been for him England might possibly have suffered a severe defeat. He went in first, but received little assistance beyond that given by Mr Steel before being joined by Mr Read with the score at 181 for eight wickets. Runs were then obtained very fast, as may be judged from the fact that during the partnership 21 fours were made. The aspect of the game was completely changed and the innings realized 345.

## ARTHUR SHREWSBURY

### SECOND TEST, LORD'S, 1886

*July 20.* Three of their great batsmen – Messrs Grace, Read and Steel – failed; but Shrewsbury enabled the spectators to witness a splendid defensive innings. He was at the wickets upwards of four hours, and, with the exceptions mentioned in the details, did not make a mistake. [...]

Six overs were sent down without a run being scored. Shrewsbury, however, then enlivened the play by hitting a ball from Mr Spofforth to the leg boundary and scoring two by an off-drive.

*July 21.* The second day's play of the match will long be remembered for the brilliant innings by Arthur Shrewsbury. His 164 is the largest individual total ever scored against the Australian bowlers in this country. The 1880 match at the Oval furnishes the previous best innings – Dr W.G. Grace's 152. Shrewsbury's perfect style of batting is so familiar to most followers of the game that it is almost unnecessary to say that he played in masterly form during the whole time he was in. His performance is rendered all the more creditable from the fact that the wicket materially assisted the bowlers.

## ROBIN SMITH

### FIFTH TEST, TRENT BRIDGE, 1989

ALAN LEE, CRICKET CORRESPONDENT

*August 14*. Smith came to the crease with England having made a start grotesque even by their own standards. Alderman had taken two wickets in his first over. Smith's response was to take 10 runs off his second, setting the rebellious tone of one of the most thrilling innings I have seen from an England player in many years.

The scene when it ended was equally impressive. Smith had savaged his century out of only 144 runs from the bat in an England innings which, without him, would have been an embarrassment. Yet when he departed to a rare misjudgement, one would have sworn he had made nought. He walked distraught through a standing ovation before slumping in his dressing-room chair, head in hands, inconsolable.

## ANDREW STRAUSS

### SECOND TEST, LORD'S, 2009

MIKE ATHERTON, CHIEF CRICKET CORRESPONDENT

*July 17*. Andrew Strauss, a man very much in the prime of his career, went through to 150 and then, shortly after that, walked back to the pavilion, still undefeated with 161 to his name. He played superbly and without him England would not be looking forward to the second day with any optimism.

The Lord's effect, eh? During all the pre-match talk about how the ground has inspired the Australians to great deeds, it had been forgotten that England's top six have drawn plenty of inspiration of their own from this historic turf. Before yesterday they had scored 12 hundreds at Lord's, three of which had come from the blade of Strauss, who passed 5,000 career Test runs. The England captain likes to tuck in at Lord's.

He never looked like not adding a fourth yesterday. As badly as Australia bowled to him – and, my, they bowled badly – the England captain gave off an air of utter assurance at the crease, powerfully cutting anything short, clipping clinically off his hips when the bowlers erred in line, his concentration unwavering. His hundred came off the penultimate ball before tea and was celebrated with that usual overhead swing of the bat that belongs on the Centre Court at Wimbledon, and a golden smile.

*Andrew Strauss was capable of attacking innings when the situation required*

# ANDREW STRAUSS AND ALASTAIR COOK

## FIRST TEST, BRISBANE, 2010–11

MIKE ATHERTON,
CHIEF CRICKET CORRESPONDENT

*November 29.* Australia have had nearly four years to get over the retirement of two of the game's greatest bowlers, yet on days such as yesterday a certain wistfulness hangs in the air. Oh, my Shane Warne and Glenn McGrath not so long ago. Instead, yesterday Ricky Ponting had to make do with a rookie finger spinner and a strike bowler suffering an identity crisis and, on a pitch as flat as the Nullarbor Plain, my, how England took advantage on a day that must rank alongside their very best in Test cricket.

The visiting team began the day deep in the red and finished it with their account showing a glowing profit and there were very few shocks to the system along the way. Only one wicket fell, that of Andrew Strauss, but not before the England captain had put two singles in front of the nought he made in the first innings.

This was the performance of a man with an iron constitution, for walking out to bat on a pair in the first Ashes Test of a five-match series is no picnic. His stock, already high in England, will have grown a notch or two in Australia where, before today, he had never posted a score of note.

The runs were important, of course, but it was the way Strauss scored them that sent a message of confidence, conviction and optimism ringing around the Gabba. He did not set about reducing England's deficit by putting his nose to the grindstone, rather he went after Australia's bowling as if the thought of defeat had never entered his mind; and more than that, as if victory was still a possibility. His hundred came up in 184 balls, a decent lick given the circumstances.

It was clearly a message that resonated with the team. When Strauss departed, stumped after skipping down the pitch to Marcus North, England's forward momentum did not stall. Any stand between Jonathan Trott and Alastair Cook has the potential to reduce the scoring rate to a crawl, but they, too, rattled along, their hundred partnership coming in only 165 balls.

Anybody visiting the Gabba yesterday for the first time in this Test match would have been hard pressed to nominate Australia as the team in the ascendancy.

Strauss took the lead in this regard, driving the ball through the off side as fluently as he can ever have done, and, a nod to Mike Hussey's treatment of Graeme Swann this, refusing to allow Xavier Doherty to settle. Strauss has never been a natural down-the-pitch player of spin, nor a particularly good hitter over the top, but he did both in the left-arm spinner's opening spell and when he back cut the spinner in the afternoon to bring up his hundred, he let out a roar that revealed what the innings meant to him.

Normally a phlegmatic soul, Strauss has been unusually emotional in this game, badgering the umpires, reacting with disbelief to the occasional decision and engaging in a little chit-chat with Brad Haddin.

His desire rubbed off on Cook, who played as well and as securely yesterday as he has done for two years. His back-foot play has never deserted him in times of drought, but now he is moving smoothly into the ball; feet, head and body working as one again rather than battling against each other. The word is that Cook has abandoned much of the tinkering to his technique of the past few months and gone back to a method that feels more natural and instinctive – further evidence, if evidence was needed, of the dangers of over-coaching.

Theirs was a significant partnership, in the course of which Strauss and Cook became the most prolific of all England opening combinations, overhauling in aggregate terms Hobbs and Sutcliffe. When Cook brought up his hundred, also with a cut, it was the first time for 72 years that both England openers had scored hundreds in the same innings against Australia.

## HERBERT SUTCLIFFE

### FIFTH TEST, THE OVAL, 1930

R.B. VINCENT, CRICKET CORRESPONDENT

*August 19.* It is impossible to over-estimate the worth of Sutcliffe's innings; or to over-praise the moral virtues which enabled him to play it. From the start he set himself to hold up one end for England. During nearly seven hours he never relaxed his concentration or lost sight of his objective. If once, when he off-drove a ball from Wall for 4, he played a stroke which gave him acute physical pleasure, that should not be accounted to him for unrighteousness. Occasionally he hit Grimmett to square leg for four, but boundary strokes were not a salient feature of his innings. Sutcliffe has now made nearly 2,000 runs for England against Australia, with an average of 73.

## GRAHAM THORPE

### THIRD TEST, TRENT BRIDGE, 1993

ALAN LEE, CRICKET CORRESPONDENT

*July 6.* Gooch did not, of course, cope alone. Graham Thorpe ensured he did not have to try. Coming in at the fall of the implacable Andy Caddick 70 minutes into the day, Thorpe batted through to the close, when he was unbeaten on 88. Gooch and the other selectors, derided for choosing Thorpe to make his debut with an average of 25 this season, can feel thoroughly vindicated.

Left-handed, a virtue that the selectors have been slow to acknowledge in the series, Thorpe is, more importantly, strikingly composed. Unfussy of style, he played far more than a stooge's role in a sixth-wicket stand of 150 with Gooch, which may, in weeks to come, be identified as a turning point of the summer [...]

Gooch made just 21 of the 54 runs in the session but no wicket was lost and Thorpe had by now begun to look a genuine Test player.

He was unruffled by anything the Australians confronted him with, which yesterday appeared to include none of the verbal aggression which earned them an official reprimand on Saturday. Having accelerated through the final session, by the close Thorpe was batting as he does when setting up a declaration for Surrey. He may not have known that England are seldom in a position to think of such luxuries.

# MICHAEL VAUGHAN

## SECOND TEST, ADELAIDE, 2002–03

CHRISTOPHER MARTIN-JENKINS,
CHIEF CRICKET CORRESPONDENT

*November 22.* Whatever the result of the second Test match, Michael Vaughan will never forget November 21, 2002 and his first experience of the glorious Adelaide Oval. In perfect weather and a marvellous, unpolluted, pellucid light, he reached what he said was the pinnacle of his career to date: 177 – his first Test hundred against Australia, scored in Australia, against what he described as 'a fantastic attack who were always asking questions'.

He did not exaggerate. It was a performance the more remarkable both for the context in which it occurred – a tour that could easily have hit the rocks yesterday and never broken free – and for the fact that it might easily have been made impossible by his late withdrawal from the game.

Shortly before the toss, during fielding practice, Vaughan strained the knee only recently recovered from an operation. Rumours that he would not be able to play filtered through the crowd like a bad smell. Nasser Hussain, the England captain, had to ask him if he was fit as his knee was being re-strapped (it has been for all his matches on the tour) and he said that he was; but not, it seems, with absolute conviction.

Eight hours later, not only had he scored his first Test hundred against Australia but also his fifth since May and the highest by any England player on the ground since Walter Hammond's identical score in 1929. In the end, triumph was tinged with regret because he was out only three balls before the night's rest that might have preceded a further cultured attack on Australia's bowling on the second day. Still, only Jack Hobbs's 187 in 1912 stands higher. Immortal names; immortal deeds.

It would be premature and unwise to put this lean and stylish batsman, claimed both by Manchester, where he was born, and Sheffield, where he was raised, anywhere near the Hobbs-Hammond class just yet. It is not too soon, however, to say that he may get close one day. As a prophet is without honour in his own country, so people (or those, at any rate, of a certain age) tend to underestimate the star performers of their own era.

Vaughan is a stylist of the classical school in an age of heavy bats and shots, invariably perfectly balanced and equally good off either foot. He is more likely, perhaps, to be bracketed by the end of his career with fine players such as, say, Dennis Amiss, Mike Gatting, Allan Lamb or Alec Stewart rather than the exalted elite, but he bats so very much as all coaches would like their charges to bat – going back when the ball is short, forward when it is well pitched up, leading with the left shoulder for the vertical strokes and lifting through the line with a straight bat – that it would be a tonic for all the young cricketers in England if his recent improvement continues and he goes on to become one of the great players.

In 21 Test innings in 2002 he has now scored 1,241 runs, an aggregate bettered only by Sachin Tendulkar (who has played one more innings for 51 more runs). In doing so he has left an indelible impression on those who have watched him: of leaning drives through extra cover and thunderous pulls over square leg.

He was true to the image yesterday, scoring most freely in those areas and thereby exploiting to the full the

*Michael Vaughan hit a glorious run of form in Australia in 2002–03*

short square boundaries that contrast so sharply with the long straight ones at Adelaide. Fortune rewarded his boldness more than once, two sharp chances and a potential run-out being unaccepted by the Australians. When 19, too, he would surely have been given out caught at cover were it not for the television replays that encourage a batsman to stand his ground unless it is blindingly obvious that he is out. He got some 'verbals' after that; no more, he said, than usual.

His opponents were notably less churlish than, regrettably, England sides have been for far too long. They clapped him at each of his landmarks and when he left the field ahead of the rest to a standing ovation. But how those chivalrous Australians had rejoiced when finally he edged to slip in the last over of the day.

## THIRD TEST, OLD TRAFFORD, 2005

SIMON BARNES

*August 12.* You see mistakes all the time in sport, at every level. It is the ability to profit from the mistake that counts. And England in general, and their captain in particular, gave us ... well, it was a feast for the gods, let's not be half-hearted about this. It was a day straight from a cricketing Elysium. Vaughan went from 41 to 166 with as majestic a display of batting as this ground has seen.

Before this match, everyone was worrying about Vaughan's technique. He had been clean-bowled three times in four innings this series. But it wasn't coaching he needed: it was a sign. It came in that glorious double let-off [he had been dropped and then bowled by a no ball], and Vaughan was a man transformed.

Even before that, Vaughan was beginning to look like a man finding his touch. He can look lanky, vague, uncoordinated, but yesterday he made a dramatic transition to elegance, power and purpose. It was a miraculous transformation: from anxiety to confidence, from gawkiness to grace, from 'never mind he's a great captain' to what might, in the context, be seen in mid-September as an innings of historic significance.

There was something of Roger Federer in the perfection of it all, and I can't think of higher praise. Australia came into the match rejoicing that McGrath and Brett Lee were fit to play and Vaughan played as if the two bowlers were actively seeking to showcase his talents. He played Shane Warne on his merits, while Jason Gillespie – running in like Boxer on his way to the knackers – was treated like a net bowler.

---

## BOB WOOLMER AND DEREK RANDALL

### SECOND TEST, OLD TRAFFORD, 1977

JOHN WOODCOCK,
CRICKET CORRESPONDENT

*July 9.* The partnership between Woolmer and Randall provided the best piece of English batsmanship to come from both ends simultaneously for a long time. Both were missed, Randall when he was six, Woolmer at 43 and 39, but because of the way they played they deserved to be. They chose attack as the best method of defence. They brought the best out of each other and the best of both of them is uncommonly good.

We are inclined to say that Australians and West Indians hit their way out of trouble, but not Englishmen. Well, these two put bat to ball to such effect that the time came when the Australian attack looked threadbare and their fielders rattled. With an hour to go Australia were rather hanging their heads.

---

## FRANK WOOLLEY

### SECOND TEST, LORD'S, 1926

A.C.M. CROOME,
CRICKET CORRESPONDENT

*June 29.* From that point to the finish we saw some batting that was most exhilarating. At one end Woolley, making himself up to his full height, would block three balls and send the fourth to the boundary with a perfectly timed back-stroke. At intervals he made a full-shouldered leg hit, or a powerful square cut, and once at least he leaned forward and drove Mr Gregory all along the ground to the boundary behind him.

Sporting N…

# …OW ENGLAND KEPT THE ASHES

## …VO GREAT HEARTS OVERTHROW AUSTRALIA

England beat Australia by five wickets in the fourth Test match at …delaide yesterday and so, gaining a lead of three matches to one in the …ries, have retained the Ashes. In an interview after the match L. Hutton, …ne England captain, paid a tribute to the younger members of the side. Much of the credit, he thought, should go to J. B. Statham, F. H. Tyson, M. C. Cowdrey and P. B. H. May, together with the wicket-keeper, T. G. Evans.

From Our Special Correspondent

ADELAIDE, FEB. 2

Many years from now young Cowdrey will point to his broken nose and tell boys yet unborn that he was at Adelaide on February 2, 1955, when England won the Test match and kept the Ashes. And the boys will think him wondrous lucky. A ma… should dip his pen in blood to write … is day. Let no one talk and writ… …ket and explain away the … …ms more fit for …al in dull …d!

the catch. (We asked Hutton afterwards what he thought of Miller's bowling. Hutton thought Miller ought to concentrate much more on batting.) England 10 for 2. In comes the battered Cowdrey. Miller hits him twice running on the pads and appeals, and everybody here who isn't English appeals too. What a man is Miller. He comes in from a shortish run, loose of limb like an African, hair streaming, and as he pulls up the hair goes on and falls about his face.

Meanwhile May has begun driving, and Johnson has gone from mid-off to square-leg. For Cowdrey Miller brings fine-leg up to third slip, and Cowdrey cover drives classically for 4. Miller heaves his shoulders over even faster, and Cowdrey is taken by Archer at first-slip. England 18 for 3. Four Meteor jets fly over at 200ft.; they look …d sound quite tame beside this wild man … His figures now are 3 overs, no …2 runs, 3 wickets.

…Ashes Fourth Test

# …ngland all too obliging as … …eaches new heights of greatnes…

…a v England

…st day of five; England …ralia, with eight …kets in hand, are 111 …and

…artin-Jenkins …orrespondent

One that got away: Gilchrist misses a stumping chance off Warne to give Pietersen an extra life, but it was to make little difference

High five: Warne acknowledges the Melbourne crowd after his haul ripped the heart out of England's fragile batting

…by Warne's legendary accuracy and a lush outfield, they ran poorly between the wickets, chose the wrong balls to try to hit in the air and failed to justify the decision to bat.

"We didn't expect conditions to change dramatically over the first day and a half," Strauss said, "but it seamed about more than we expected." It did so slowly but Glenn McGrath, Stuart Clark and Brett Lee all got enough past the bat to suggest that the wrong option had been taken.

Australia missed two catches, two clear run-out opportunities and a gaping stumping, but still bowled England out for 159 after they had been 101 for two. Very few Test matches are won after such a start. All of Warne's wickets were taken by flight and dip, as batsmen spied what they believed to be boundary opportunities. Only Kevin Pietersen got anywhere near the boundary as he attempted to drive Warne straight for six, but by now he was, as usual, batting with the tail.

Even he needed 70 balls for 21 runs, having come close to running out Andrew Flintoff for six as, for the third Test in succession, he attempted a ridiculous single in order to get off the mark. He had only made four when he also survived a simple stumping chance offered to Adam Gilchrist after charging Warne and missing.

England, we all know, have too long a tail, but tweaking it made no difference. Matthew Hoggard is back where he started, No 11, pushing Monty Panesar and Stephen Harmison up a place each, which reflects their various abilities with the bat. It is higher up, however, that the balance is wrong. Ed Joyce or Jamie Dalrymple should have played…

six, but Chris Read for Geraint Jones was the only change.

As the best player in the team, Pietersen needs to bat at four. Since Paul Collingwood shared the only partnership of any substance with Strauss — 57 for the third wicket — it may appear that England's strategy, to keep him away from the new ball, had worked again, but to have Pietersen batting with the tail repeatedly is not satisfactory. In any case Collingwood might have been leg-before to Clark for nought, one of four apparently plumb leg-before decisions turned down by Rudi Koertzen.

Panesar was the other, … …ly out to Warne before … out instead, but it was … turned down when … Hayden was hit on … front of the stu… …gard, the first … the other who… more signif… captain's … when Ju… ball …

Australia's recent practice of not using a nightwatchman.

Ponting said that Australia, too, would have chosen to bat first, but it was one of those tosses that either captain would prefer to have lost. Play was delayed by rain for half an hour and only 16 overs were bowled before an early lunch was taken, Alastair Coo…

…ointing run out (Flintoff) 66

…8 P Siddle c Flintoff b Harmison 10

5.37 343-9 S Clark c Cook b Harmison 0

…iant leap

for proud S…

# Sporting News

## ENGLAND HAVE LAST WORD

### THREE YEOMEN FOIL AUSTRALIA

### GREAT STAND BY WATSON AND BAILEY

FROM OUR CRICKET CORRESPONDENT

Out of darkness, through fire into light. Thus did England yesterday rise like some Phoenix from the ashes of apparent defeat to save the second Test match at Lord's and so gain a … …draw against Australia with … seven wickets, … original aim fo…

The age of … yet past, nor c… cany scarce fo… dramatic and … a match alrea… But within t… longest and … of a match it… that last spa… back with le… yeomen of … nearly the w…

The yeom… were Watso… greatest of … Yorkshirem… order, was … rearguard … twentieth …

THE HUNDRED UP.—…

HUTTON, the young Yorkshire batsman, …

36 TUESDAY AUGUST 1 1989

THE TIMES

First published 1785

# England's abject surrender marks new low in series

By Alan Lee, Cricket Correspondent

## Inglorious procession at Old Trafford

18-1: Curtis c Boon b Alderman 0

25-2: Robinson lbw b Lawson 12

27-3: Smith c Healy b Alderman 1

28-4: Gooch c Alderman b Lawson 13

38-5: Botham lbw b Alderman 4

59-6: Gower c Marsh b Lawson 15

SCOREBOARD FROM OLD TRAFFORD

ENGLAND

AUSTRALIA

## Gower unfairly blamed for failings of others

Simon Barnes

## Border rewarded for hard labour

By John Woodcock

## Only two men so far decline

By Alan Lee

# Was this English … most desperate …

…ding…

…night issued a dramatic … …et Union to make a positive … He said that unless the … …epared to help to achieve an … …tegic arms limitations, he would … …onal funds of more than …

…less. People will … The Franks … …mended the replacem… …tion two of the Act, while … "catch-all" measure design… …prevent the unauthorized … …disclosure and transmission of … official information, by …

# GREAT BATTING: AUSTRALIA

THE TIMES SATURDAY JUNE 11 1938

A GOOD BEGINNING BY ENGLAND

4

Sporting News

LAKER'S SUPREME PART IN RETAINING THE ASHES

ALL TEN AUSTRALIAN WICKETS AND 19 IN MATCH

From Our Cricket Correspondent

England won the fourth Test match against Australia at Old Trafford yesterday by an innings ... retaining the ... achieve...

pitch perked up and the ball showed signs of misbehaving.

At luncheon McDonald and Craig were still together. They had then added only 59, but the important thing was that they had each been batting for more than four hours. Ahead of them stretched another four and only 15 minutes of these had ticked away when Laker struck ... blow. Craig, still ...

THE TIMES

LOCOMEN'S BAN BOUND TO CAUSE GREATER ... TODAY

HOW THE AUSTRALIANS WERE SKITTLED OUT AT LORD'S

Gaullists may get back with clear majority

Inquiry over bank chief's salary

Police alerted by strike ship

... BETRAYS A NOTE OF REGRET

Railways must act alone, Marsh says

13 die in ... rail crash

...mped aiming to hit Mallett over the hill, and the end draws nearer.

... dismally surrender Ashes

TEST MATCH

BRADMAN 309 NOT OUT

ALL RECORDS BROKEN

*The Third Test Match between England and Australia was begun at Leeds yesterday. A. P. F. Chapman, for once, lost the toss and Australia went in to bat on a perfect batsman's wicket. By the end of the day they had scored 458 runs for the loss of three wickets ...*

## WARREN BARDSLEY

### SECOND TEST, LORD'S, 1926

A.C.M. CROOME,
CRICKET CORRESPONDENT

*June 28.* It remains to speak of Mr Bardsley's innings, for which the Australians must be eternally grateful. Technically it was by no means flawless, since he has lost most of his strokes in front of the wicket on the off side. Only once in many attempts did he succeed in driving past cover-point to the boundary. On the other occasions he either missed the ball or snicked it to, or through, the slips; when he had scored about 30 Sutcliffe made a supreme effort to catch him off Tate but the ball dropped inches short of his hands. But he is still master of the on-side, which for him includes the line to his leg and middle stumps. So surely as the bowler sent down a ball on, or outside, his pads he was made to pay for it. And late in the day he began to cut. When he did he seldom failed to get right on top of the ball and beat third man. He was batting for approximately six hours and did not seem appropriately tired at the end of the day. He made more than half the runs scored after the fall of the sixth wicket, and in the last half-hour he was no slower between wickets that he had been when play was started.

## RICHIE BENAUD

### SECOND TEST, LORD'S, 1956

JOHN WOODCOCK,
CRICKET CORRESPONDENT

*June 26.* Until yesterday Benaud in Test matches had been a player of glittering promise but sparse achievement. When first he came to England in 1953 one look at him showed a cricketer with a burning enthusiasm for the game, and enough natural ability to enable him to scale the heights. But ability without judgment and concentration merely brings frustration, and this has been so in Benaud's case. Yet one day he was always likely to play a devastating innings in a Test match, an innings to have a considerable influence on the course of the game, and it happened to come yesterday. On Saturday evening he walked into the middle of a stirring English counter-attack, but when he strode back to the pavilion soon after luncheon yesterday he had made 97 out of 117 in two hours and 20 minutes.

It was as superb a display of crisp hitting as has been seen in a big match at Lord's for a long time. Last year McLean made a fine century there for South Africa. But that was dotted with chances. Benaud did not once hit the ball to hand, and apart from the first 20 minutes of his innings he attacked with almost complete certainty. He began by playing like a man in a desperate hurry. For three or four overs it seemed only a matter of minutes before he would take a risk too many. He sliced Trueman just over cover point's head, twice he nearly gave a catch to short-leg, and once the umpire, Lee, could only just have given him the benefit of the doubt in a leg-before-wicket appeal. But gradually his temperature subsided and discretion tempered aggression.

With a full and graceful flow of the bat Benaud hit straight off the front foot, with a forester's action he hooked contemptuously, and with all the strength of his broad shoulders he pulled to leg. One remembers particularly an early hook for 6 off a ball none too short which Trueman could only applaud. He reached his 50, made in 73 minutes, with a pull for 4 off Bailey, who was doing what he could to quench this ravaging fire of batsmanship. The next two balls both went to the boundary, and so it went on.

There were thoughts of 100 runs by one man before luncheon; in fact there were 90, and at the other end the remarkable Mackay was in permanent occupation. [...]

When Benaud was 96 the new ball was taken and he had added only a single off Trueman when, aiming a huge hook, he mis-hit the ball off the top edge of the bat and skied it to Evans. Had this stroke come off it would have been a glorious gesture and an ideal culmination to a memorable innings. But it was not to be, and the rest of Australia's innings without him was inevitably something of an anti-climax.

*Richie Benaud is congratulated on a successful tour as he and his team board the Strathmore and head for home in 1961*

## DAVID BOON

### FOURTH TEST, ADELAIDE, 1990–91

ALAN LEE, CRICKET CORRESPONDENT

*January 29.* For tuition in this regard, they could do no better than study the methods employed by David Boon in making the ninth Test century of his underrated career. It was launched unpromisingly at one for one, proceeded under severe restraint while Australia courted disaster at 25 for three, and was allowed to flourish only after three hours of diligence had banished all possible risk of defeat.

Boon is an oddball in an Australian team which revels in its fitness and its image. But if forced to choose anyone in the world to bat for one's life, he would be a strong candidate.

The frail and compulsive strokes which marred his game on England's last tour, four years ago, have long since been eliminated and Boon is a much more formidable opponent these days than when he saved his place with a century of painful uncertainty on this same ground. Yesterday's 121 brought his aggregate for this series up to 436 at an average of 73. No one talks of leaving him out any more.

# ALLAN BORDER

## SECOND TEST, LORD'S, 1985

JOHN WOODCOCK,
CRICKET CORRESPONDENT

*July 1.* Border's 196 deserves the epithet 'great', chiefly because of what it meant to his side. Had he failed, the chances are that they would have lost the match and, before long, surrendered the Ashes. Now the greater likelihood is that they will win here and level the series.

After starting the tour with four successive hundreds, Border had gone a little off the boil, so that he had first to re-find his touch. Once he had done this he made wonderfully few mistakes. On Saturday, as on Friday, the gates were closed, and the reception given to Border was as generous as I have heard anywhere.

Border's was his thirteenth Test hundred and his highest. He could have been out to what would have amounted to a brilliant fluke had Gatting caught him at short leg, as he nearly did on Friday. Border was then 87. And he was not far past his 100 on Saturday morning when he edged Allott to where a second slip would have been. These, though, were isolated blemishes.

Border has not so much a style as a *modus operandi*. He is utterly practical, playing each ball on its merits; when he goes down the pitch he does it quickly and decisively. Give him anything loose and it goes for four. He has hidden strength, physically and mentally. It shows in the way he watches the ball and the power with which he dispatches it.

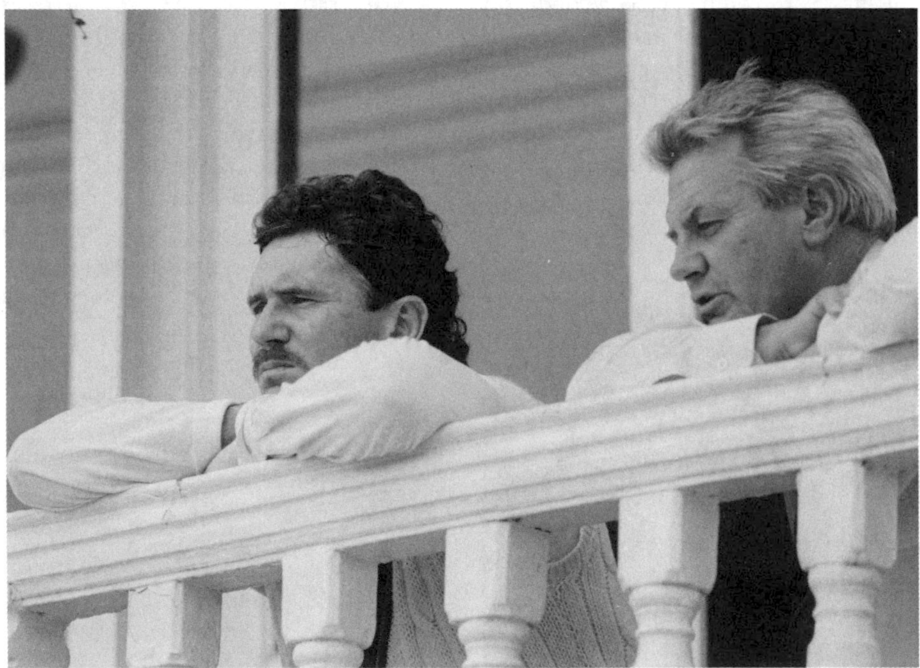

*The tension shows for Allan Border and tour manager Bob Merriman at Trent Bridge in 1985*

## DON BRADMAN

### SECOND TEST, LORD'S, 1930

R.B. VINCENT,
CRICKET CORRESPONDENT

*June 30.* He [Ponsford] should derive some consolation for his failure to make his 100 from the knowledge that the King was thereby enabled to see more of an innings which must be destined to be famous as long as the game is played.

To do justice to D. Bradman's batting it is necessary to use the language of superlatives and compare it with the acting of Miss Marie Tempest. Both are so exquisitely right in the general design and in the polished execution of every detail. Bradman on Saturday was as audacious as Macartney in the second innings of the Lord's Test match of 1926. His cutting was as safe and brilliant as that of Duleepsinhji on the previous day. He played the ball on the leg side as deftly as Hendren had, and Woolley for all his advantage in height was not so very much the more powerful off-driver. Bradman's innings began, so to speak, in the middle, for he had no need to play himself in. He was still in the middle of it when stumps were drawn, for he had not begun to lift the ball off the ground as those who propose to get on or got out when it makes no difference which of their alternative objects they achieve. He has, in fact, played the first part of an extremely steady innings, treating each ball sent down to him strictly on its merits as he discerns them. And yet he has scored 155 runs in 2½ hours.

If one were to begin particularizing his strokes there would be no end to this account, but one of them must be specially noted. Hammond was put on at the Pavilion end to bowl defensively, and was doing his job quite well. Naturally he had a defensive field, with only one man in the slips. He sent down a fast, good-length ball which broke back viciously at the top of the off and middle stumps. Bradman met it with an orthodox-looking back stroke which had the effect of a late cut. The ball flew, and clearly was meant to fly, wide of the solitary slip and fine enough to beat the deep third-man. White, who was so successful in slowing down the scoring in Australia, could do nothing with him. He *chasseed* out to the pitch of the good-length balls, and altered the direction of them as well as their length to suit his purpose, so that he could drive them where the fieldsmen were not. The crowd twice paid him unusual but well-deserved compliments. They gave Tate one of the loudest rounds of applause heard during the afternoon when he succeeded in bowling a maiden over to him. And once when he shaped to cut at a dangerous ball from that bowler some 2,000 people appealed for the expected catch at the wicket, and were badly scored off when he checked his stroke.

*July 1.* Play began punctually at 11 o'clock, and at 11.15 D. Bradman, attempting to play a leg glance off Hammond, snicked the ball past short slip's right hand. That was the only incident of note which had occurred, and it becomes noteworthy merely because it was the first time that Bradman had omitted to strike the ball with the exact part of the bat which he intended to apply to it. [...]

We had visions of a third new ball being required to take the third wicket, and we were tolerably certain that Bradman would achieve the object, which was obviously in his mind, of cutting the late R.E. Foster's record of 287. But Bradman at long last made a mistake, and by the mercy of providence the resulting catch went to Chapman at extra-cover. Bradman did not quite get to the pitch of an off ball and hit it apparently very hard, and only just within reach of the fieldsman's right hand. But there was less pace on the ball than the stroke had indicated, and Chapman had to take it at the extreme of his telescopic reach and also at the second intention. How long Bradman batted and how many 4's he hit are matters of little moment. He had played one stroke otherwise than as he had intended, and his intentions had always been of copybook correctness. That might be a description of an innings by W.G. Grace himself.

## THIRD TEST, HEADINGLEY, 1930

R.B. VINCENT,
CRICKET CORRESPONDENT

*July 12.* But whatever may happen during the next three days this has been Bradman's match, for by scoring 309 not out he has made the highest individual score which has ever been made in a Test match, so, at long last, beating the 287 made by R.E. Foster at Sydney during the tour of 1903–1904. That he would achieve this feat before the end of this tour was expected by all who have seen him play. He came near to it at Lord's, and in every game of importance he has shown a sureness of scoring power to which there has seemed no limit. How high he ranks among the greatest batsmen the world has ever known is not yet established, but at the moment, and at his age, his promise has been exceeded by none. It is idle to compare him with his great predecessors, Victor Trumper, who was no doubt more graceful, or C. Macartney, who was more impertinently shattering, but for sheer and continual efficiency his performances are truly astounding. Today he pulverized the English bowling not with the abandon of Macartney, who, like Bradman, also scored 100 runs before luncheon on the same ground, but by a display of batsmanship which in ease of scoring combined with absolute security could not be surpassed. To mention the strokes from which he scored most of his runs is to go through the whole range of strokes known to a modern batsman. Once or twice he demonstrated an idea which is not generally understood, but at no time did he take anything approaching a risk, and he cannot have hit the ball in the air more than three times during the day. It was in fact an innings so glorious that it well might be classed as incomparable, and how the Yorkshiremen loved it. […]

Bradman, without in any sense forcing the pace or taking any liberties, at once took runs whenever they were offered. He scored 11 runs in one over from Larwood, which included a beautiful stroke past cover-point in which he lay right back to place the ball through the opening and a stroke off his legs to the on boundary. […]

Geary had to be brought on again at the other end to steady the game. Bradman greeted him with the first really impudent stroke he had so far played, an amazing hook only just wide of mid-on from a ball outside the off stump. This he followed with a square cut, also for 4, and at 1 o'clock the English bowlers bore every appearance of hoping that a batsman would get out, rather than of suspecting that they would get him out. Hammond was given a trial, but he did not bowl so well then as he did in the afternoon, and Bradman reached his 100 out of

16 THE TIMES, SATURDAY, JULY 12, 1930

# BRADMAN'S NEW TEST MATCH RECORDS ETON V. HARROW

AUSTRALIA'S BIG SCORE.—More Test Match records were made at the Headingley ground, Leeds, yesterday, when the third Test Match between England and Australia was begun. Bradman was again the hero of the day, and his score of 309 not out is the largest ever made in any Test Match. The game opened sensationally, Jackson being caught by Larwood when only two runs had been scored. The second wicket, however, did not fall until 194 was reached, when Woodfull was bowled by Hammond for a patient 50. At the close of play Australia had scored 458 for three. Our photograph shows the game in progress.

BRADMAN IN PLAY.—Bradman playing a ball from Tate during his wonderful innings at Leeds yesterday. He reached 105 before lunch, a feat which had only twice previously been accomplished in Test Matches. During the time he made his 105 Woodfull had scored only 29.

AFTER THE FIRST HUNDRED.—Spectators applauding Bradman on his return to the pavilion at the lunch interval. Behind him is Woodfull, followed by Hobbs and other English players.

FOR CANADA.—The launch of the destroyer Saguenay at Southampton yesterday. It is the first of two being built for the Royal Canadian Navy, and was launched by Mrs. G. J. Desbarats, wife of the Deputy Minister of National Defence of Canada.

THE SCENE AT LORD'S.—There was a large gathering at Lord's yesterday to see the opening day of the Eton and Harrow match, and away from the playing area the scene was reminiscent of a garden party. Eton had the advantage of the day's play, being only 18 runs short of the Harrow total of 199 with four wickets in hand.

HARROW'S TOP SCORER.—J. M. Stow and N. B. Clive going out to bat after lunch. Stow's 64 was the top score for Harrow.

JEWS AT THE WAILING WALL.—A photograph taken in 1916 of Jews at the Wailing Wall. It will be noted that many are seated on benches, a point on which stress has been laid in the evidence given to the League of Nations Commission.

## SERVICES TO-MORROW

### FOURTH SUNDAY AFTER TRINITY

*Cricket dominates* The Times' *picture page on Saturday, July 12, 1930. Bradman at Headingley, top hats at Lord's*

128 runs scored from the bat when he had been in for only 85 minutes, and that without ever suggesting that he was in a hurry. At the luncheon interval the total was 136, of which Woodfull's share, though only 29, had been of the greatest value.

Both Bradman and Woodfull hit Geary, who started the bowling after the interval, square for 4 and so Hobbs was moved back from cover-point to the boundary, a defensive move which was indicative of what was to follow. Bradman played one superb late cut off Larwood, but in the same over he played the first bad stroke of his innings and was lucky to see the ball sail in the air safe out of reach of second and third slip. […]

Bradman scored his 200 out of 268 on the board, but two minutes later he should have been caught off a skier by Tate at mid-on, but Tate was curiously slow in starting to make the catch. Kippax also had an escape when he had scored 24, but this was a very hard chance, high up to Leyland at mid-off, and England had no manner of consolation until a wicket fell in the only way one was likely to fall – a glorious catch by Chapman at backward point dismissing Kippax, who is as good a No.4 as his captain is a No.1. Just before this Bradman had made his record-breaking stroke, and no ground in the world, not even his own Sydney, could have offered him such sincere and prolonged congratulations as did the crowd at Leeds.

*July 14.* Five minutes afterwards there was a roar which could have been heard in Sheffield when Tate and Duckworth, between them, rid themselves of the young terror. But that howl of relief was a whisper compared with the uproar which followed as Bradman quite composedly ambled back to the pavilion. The entire crowd – and the Headingley ground looked to be packed – rose to give acknowledgment of an innings the like of which they may never see again. Bradman had batted in all for about six and a quarter hours, had scored 334 runs out of 506 on the board, and had, among other details, hit 46 4's. He had a very lucky escape when he had made 202, and again, at 273, he should have been caught at the wicket, but he had made cricket history and had established a new era in the game.

## THIRD TEST, ADELAIDE, 1932–33

E.W. PARISH

*January 19.* The only bright feature of the match from the Australian point of view was Bradman's bright innings today. In a little over an hour he showed his best form. He hit the bowling hard at a critical period, and he made it look playable, which other Australians have hitherto failed to do. The crowd applauded heartily while Jardine kept his bowlers to the off theory, but when he reverted to leg theory against Bradman, who seemed to be getting the better of the bowling, they howled and hooted loudly. Except for Bradman, who practically threw his wicket away through over-eagerness, no Australian played the bowling with any confidence […]

## FOURTH TEST, HEADINGLEY, 1934

R.B. VINCENT,
CRICKET CORRESPONDENT

*July 23.* When the English team went on the field at 11 o'clock in the morning, escorted by an immense sergeant of police, they must have known that Bradman was coming in at once. In any case they soon found it out, for the last two balls of an over which Bowes had not completed on Friday were each forced to the boundary, the first straight and the next to long-on.

## FIRST TEST, TRENT BRIDGE, 1938

DUDLEY CAREW

*June 18.* So long as Bradman was in and so long as he had a partner who could score at a normal rate the possibility of Australia's snatching a wonderful victory was a very real one, but the partners did not stay quite long enough. When Bradman himself was bowled it was clear that Australia's heroic effort would fail.

In all conscience, however, even with Larwood unable to bowl, a score of 335 in the fourth innings was a great performance, and of Bradman in particular it is impossible to speak too highly. So long as he was batting he controlled the game, never hurrying himself when a ball occasionally did enough to suggest that one end of the pitch was crumbling. He himself caused certain changes in the bowling and was invariably to the fore where danger was threatening.

## SECOND TEST, LORD'S, 1938

R.B. VINCENT,
CRICKET CORRESPONDENT

*June 29.* Farnes welcomed Bradman by nearly decapitating him with a vicious ball, and Bradman's answer was immediate and typical of him, two fours to leg and a square cut also for four off consecutive balls. Moreover he continued in that vein, and it was clear that he was going to make another Test match century if time and weather allowed. [...]

Verity, when he came on, bowled one good over to Brown, and Wright, in his turn, made even Bradman for a short time seem a trifle hesitant. Certainly he beat him once, but in the meantime Bradman's score, chiefly composed of 4's, many of them slashing drives off the back foot past cover-point, was accumulating runs at an alarming pace. He hopped from 20 to 70 so quickly that one wondered whether the mechanism of the scoring board was not at fault.

## FIRST TEST, TRENT BRIDGE, 1948

R.B. VINCENT,
CRICKET CORRESPONDENT

*June 12.* Surprisingly therefore, whatever the scoreboard can show we have seen England bowl much better than they have batted. Not so surprising was the fact that Bradman played his way composedly to gather a century, the 18th that he has made in his career in Test matches against England. Some opinions have been offered comparing the Bradman of today with the man we knew before the war. There can be no doubt that if some of that fierce attack has dimmed – he spent half an hour at one time yesterday in scoring one run – the brain still controls a method approaching to certitude. Occasionally that triumphant drive through the covers emerged and there was always that forcing stroke off the back foot which would want two mid-ons and two long-ons to prevent the ball from reaching the boundary. In any case it is always good to see Bradman score a century and more.

# GREG CHAPPELL

## SECOND TEST, PERTH, 1970–71

JOHN WOODCOCK, CRICKET CORRESPONDENT

*December 14.* Today's most memorable achievement was Greg Chappell's, the brother of Ian and a grandson of Victor Richardson, a former Australian captain. For the first three hours of his innings he kept England at bay before scattering them this evening with a dazzling exhibition of stroke play. His second 50 took only 58 minutes and when at five o'clock he joined the band of famous batsmen who have made centuries on their first appearance in Anglo-Australia Test matches, he became his country's idol. For a young man of 22 first his temperament and then his confidence were remarkable.

## SECOND TEST, LORD'S, 1972

JOHN WOODCOCK, CRICKET CORRESPONDENT

*June 24.* Greg Chappell's is already the best innings I have seen played by an Australian since he and Ian Redpath each made hundreds at Perth in the second Test match of the last tour. It is the kind of innings which has been conspicuously absent from recent chapters in Australian cricket. Too often their batsmen have seemed not to fight it out. With a bang and a crash, they have come and gone. Now, in the crisis, Greg Chappell produced an innings that owed as much to a fine technique as to a firm temperament. His running between wickets showed how calm he was keeping, and in Edwards he found, for two hours and a half, the partner he had to have. [...]

Chappell's strokes off the back foot held the power of perfect timing and he could have been beaten no more

*Greg Chappell, elegance personified, added another brilliant hundred at the Oval to his one at Lord's in 1972*

than half a dozen times. Price, emerging it seemed from the writing room in the pavilion, with that absurd run of his, was driven for the best boundary of the day.

## FOURTH TEST, SYDNEY, 1974–75

JOHN WOODCOCK,
CRICKET CORRESPONDENT

*January 9.* In just over four hours Greg Chappell gave only one chance, and that late in his innings and out of carelessness. When he was 136 he hit a full toss to deep long leg where Underwood dropped it. Always well balanced, invariably with the right stroke, always with time to spare, Chappell's was a model innings. At the age of 26 he is now a batsman to rank with the postwar best. With as safe a pair of hands as there is in Australia he is a marvellously good cricketer, with a temperament to match.

---

# GREG CHAPPELL AND IAN CHAPPELL

## FIFTH TEST, THE OVAL, 1972

JACK FINGLETON

*August 12.* They are a phlegmatic, laconic pair, these Chappell brothers, Ian rising 29 years, and Greg, rising 24. Never in Test history has there been a more illustrious pair of brothers and I warn that today I intend to be more than usually Australian. I owe it to Vic Richardson, the most pleasant Australian skipper I played under, who was the proud grandfather of Ian and Greg.

It was at Taunton in 1968 that I told Ian I would like to meet his young brother. Greg was playing his first season with Somerset and only because John Inverarity, who was to teach at Millfield and play with Somerset, was a last-minute inclusion in Bill Lawry's side for England. Greg summoned his brother and we yarned on the top of the Taunton pavilion. There was no brotherly blurb with them, though one could appreciate the regard of one for the other. They were as natural as Adam and Eve, if I may be allowed to use an illustration from another context.

So it was yesterday down the long, brilliant day of sunshine at the Oval [...]

So Australia were well up against it at 34 for two, but the drama-packed situation brought out the full, cool cricket character of the Chappells. Greg hit his first ball from Snow for a mid-on boundary, turning his back on it as soon as he had hit the ball. He knew its worth. Greg was never in doubt apart from a snick at 79 off Arnold which streaked narrowly past his stumps for four. If there was another dubious stroke, I never saw it.

Greg Chappell's century was a thing of absolute cricket joy. I have never, over many years, seen a batsman his equal on the leg-side. He gets his front foot out of the way and positions his body beautifully for every angle from mid-on to fine leg. His forces are glorious. Illingworth, in desperation, as Greg hit Snow and Arnold repeatedly for fours on the leg side, finally had to put three men on that side in front of the umpire. This was the apt tribute to Greg Chappell's greatness. He also plays the pull to perfection.

There is not a single speck of exhibitionism about either Chappell. Not a single word passed between them. There was never a mid-pitch conference. There was no need. Each appreciated his job.

When brother Greg got his delectable century Ian did not walk the pitch and shake his hand. Neither even looked at the other. The job was still in hand. The closest they got together was at 4.40 when they were some four yards apart patting the pitch. I could imagine the conversation: 'All right?' from Ian – 'Yeah, all right', from Greg. 'Bit hot' from lan – 'Yeah, a bit hot', from Greg.

The only piece of emotionalism, if it could generously be called that, was when Ian patted his bat in tribute as Greg walked past him on the way back to an unforgettable reception for an unforgettable century.

This, unfairly, is mostly about Greg. Ian shuffles his feet. He is not so composed in the middle. He was in trouble often against Underwood, but he had the character – or 'guts', which is a more descriptive word – to battle it through. He would never give up.

## MICHAEL CLARKE

### THIRD TEST, OLD TRAFFORD, 2013

MIKE ATHERTON,
CHIEF CRICKET CORRESPONDENT

*August 2*. 'Maximise your career potential' counselled the advertising board from the University of Salford, high up to the left of the façade of the old Victorian pavilion, and few could argue that Michael Clarke, a batting wonder of the age, has not done that. He had failed to stamp his authority on this series, though, something he put right on the opening day at Emirates Old Trafford with his 24th Test hundred.

Having yo-yoed up and down the batting order throughout this series, Clarke was back at No.4 yesterday, ignoring the overwhelming statistical evidence, which suggests that No.5 suits him more, recognising instead the requirement for a captain of a besieged team to lead from the front. [...]

There was a delicious contest between Clarke and Swann that was the day's most enjoyable theme, one that delighted the cricketing cognoscenti among a capacity Old Trafford crowd. The closeness of the result at Trent Bridge notwithstanding, the comparison between this series and that of 2005 has not been a flattering one as the quality of the play, eight years down the line, has been significantly poorer. Yesterday, though, as Clarke and Swann confronted each other, we were given again a glimpse of cricket of the highest class.

Clarke and Swann are cricketers who would command a place in any world XI of the moment. The conditions, although favouring Clarke, allowed a chance to both, there being some turn and bounce for the spinner, but as well as Swann teased and taunted Clarke, varying his pace and line with immaculate control, it was the Australia captain who came off best.

He really is a brilliant player of spin, something that first came to notice on his debut hundred in Bangalore, when he took to India's spinners as if he had grown up playing on the maidans of Mumbai. Quick feet, a sure touch and a willingness to attack are the hallmarks of his game, although he had to be watchful as well when Swann moved to attack him on the leg-stump line that had brought the batsman's downfall in the previous Test at Lord's.

It was a single from Swann, dabbed into the leg side, that brought up his hundred in the final session of the day, and it was fitting that Allan Border, an Australia captain who embodied leadership from the front, was present to witness it.

## SYD GREGORY

### FIRST TEST, SYDNEY, 1894–95

*December 17.* When play was over the Hon G.H. Reid, the Premier of New South Wales, who had been an interested spectator of the match, presented to Gregory the sum of 100 Guineas, which had been collected in the members' reserve, for his splendid play.

## NEIL HARVEY

### FOURTH TEST, HEADINGLEY, 1948

R.B. VINCENT,
CRICKET CORRESPONDENT

*July 26.* That was three wickets down for 68 and accordingly a great moment for the young Harvey, who came in next, to show his mettle. And magnificently he acquitted himself. Assuredly here is a batsman of the new generation who can be expected to have a great future. While Harvey and Miller were in together one saw batting which obscured the normal idea of Test match cricket. Strokes came one after the other, full blooded and delightful. [...]

Harvey had made one nice stroke to the off to Pollard's bowling before he played just one streaky shot down to third man. This he followed with a drive away to long off, and throughout his innings he perpetually found runs with a stroke which beat the offside fieldsmen in the neighbourhood of cover point. [...]

Harvey, having driven Bedser to the offside boundary, reached a century – the first he has yet made against England, but no doubt to be succeeded by many more – out of 273 runs on the board. Loxton, now fiendishly busy, reached his 50 with a straight drive for 6 off Cranston, but Harvey's grand innings came to an end when he was bowled hitting a little too jubilantly to leg.

### FIRST TEST, TRENT BRIDGE, 1956

JOHN WOODCOCK,
CRICKET CORRESPONDENT

*June 12.* [...] and yet it was Harvey who gave us the finest batting of the day. Australia stood or fell by him when Lock and Laker were threatening to tear them apart during the morning, and by dint of great courage and his uncanny quickness of reaction and movement he defied them for three hours, 20 minutes, and the game has become such that minutes are every bit as important as runs.

## NEIL HARVEY AND NORMAN O'NEILL

### FIRST TEST, EDGBASTON, 1961

JOHN WOODCOCK,
CRICKET CORRESPONDENT

*June 10.* Fortune favoured Australia at Edgbaston yesterday in that no rain impeded them, and, on a perfect wicket, they reacted with batting so uninhibited that it might not have been a Test match. In five hours and a half they made 359 for five in reply to England's meagre score of 195, and with three days to go that looks a watertight position.

The highlight of the day was a partnership of masterly accomplishment between Harvey and O'Neill, worth 146 in 117 minutes. It was a display of attacking batsmanship that must have thrilled the 20,000 people who were there to see it. It was the classical way of clinching their initiative and it laid bare England's limitations in the field.

Harvey made his twentieth Test match century, a number exceeded only by Bradman and Hammond and in his many innings against England I have never seen him in more convincing form. It begins to look as though he is as great a force as ever. He takes fewer chances now than in his more precocious days, especially outside the off stump, yet his footwork is just as quick and his stroke-play no less decisive. He batted yesterday for three hours and 35 minutes, accompanying Australia from 47 for one to 299 for four, and when O'Neill was at the other end England were driven from pillar to post.[...]

The details of the third-wicket partnership between Australia's two great batting champions gives an idea of the momentum they gathered. When they came together Australia were 89 behind. Within 78 minutes they were ahead. During the afternoon there were 19 boundaries and 149 runs, which represented a kind of punishment England have not known for many years. The new ball, at four o'clock, made no difference to Harvey and O'Neill. They went on playing with a freedom that approached abandon; indeed, they batted with such refreshing brilliance that even the most bigoted Englishman could not forbear to cheer.

O'Neill's end came at 4.50 on a sunlit evening, when everyone expected him to enjoy himself for the remainder of the day. Aiming to cut Statham. he chopped the ball on to his stumps. He had batted for 117 minutes and hit 11 fours, and of the innings I have seen him play this year this was his best. Its power and elegance were too much for England's struggling bowlers as his bat echoed round the ground.

## MATTHEW HAYDEN

### FIRST TEST, BRISBANE, 2002–03

CHRISTOPHER MARTIN-JENKINS,
CHIEF CRICKET CORRESPONDENT

*November 11.* Hayden's second innings was even more impressive than his first, when he admitted to problems of concentration caused, he felt, because he had not eaten enough to combat first day nervousness. This time there were no drags to leg off the front foot. The hooks came out of the middle of the bat and far from the reach of fielders. He is a superb player in the form of his life. Waugh, the last to score two hundreds in an Ashes Test, said afterwards: 'I've not seen a better player.'

## ARCHIE JACKSON

### FOURTH TEST, ADELAIDE, 1928–29

FROM OUR SPECIAL CORRESPONDENT*

*February 4.* ... after White had bowled Kippax with a well-flighted ball Jackson and Ryder set about improving the position by some splendid batting. Jackson might well have been forgiven for failing in such a crisis, but he rose superbly to the occasion, and gave a most delightful display of high-class, polished, resourceful batting.

He possesses the inestimable advantage of playing with a perfectly straight bat and without the two-eyed stance. Indeed, his position at the wicket is admirable, and he showed command of a rare variety of strokes, being particularly good on the leg-side. He played Larwood better than any one has done during this tour, bringing his left foot well across and playing the ball in the middle of the bat every time, except one, when Hobbs, had he started earlier, might have caught him. Twenty years of age and with a delightful style, Jackson is a batsman of whom much is to be expected in the future. Little, indeed, should be beyond his powers, and all being well both he and Bradman will be seen in England with the next Australian team.

* *The Times* archivist has not been able to identify the author of this report

## BILL LAWRY

### SECOND TEST, LORD'S, 1961

JOHN WOODCOCK, CRICKET CORRESPONDENT

*June 24*. The epithet 'great', referring to an achievement on a sporting field, is heavily overworked. It can, however, be justifiably applied to an innings by Lawry in the second Test match at Lord's which has given Australia a real chance of winning. He made 130 out of a score of 286 for eight, batting for just over six hours and enabling Australia to lead England by 80 runs with two wickets left.

Lawry's was indeed a great achievement. He excels not in stroke-play, nor was there anything remarkable about his technical resources. What helped him to endure from half past five on Thursday until 20 to six yesterday evening was his lion heart and his inexhaustible patience. When, on a fiery, ill-natured wicket, a man can shield and outshine batsmen far more gifted, he relies on temperament and courage. These are qualities that make the Test match cricketer whom a captain values beyond esteem. When at last he was out, having slowly steered the match in favour of his side, the whole ground rose to him. This is a tribute seldom paid, and now it was thoroughly deserved. [...]

Lawry was at once a picture of tenacity. He is tall, angular, even ungainly, but what matters most is his iron resolution. However hard he was hit he moved implacably into line for the next ball, and if he saw the chance to hook he was always game.

## CHARLES MACARTNEY

### FIRST TEST, TRENT BRIDGE, 1921

A.C.M, CROOME

*May 30*. We were then treated to about 20 minutes of Mr Macartney at his best. Mr Macartney sometimes is found to be in an unorthodox position at the finish of a stroke which has failed to find the ball, but his bat is always perfectly poised in time for the stroke, and it must be a matter of pure guesswork for the bowlers to discover where he will be when the ball pitches. His footwork enabled him to make Howell seem slow, and to cut Richmond as if the ball had considerable pace on it. Colonel Douglas did his side a good turn when he went on at the far end and got him out leg-before-wicket.

## SECOND TEST, LORD'S, 1926

A.C.M. CROOME,
CRICKET CORRESPONDENT

*June 30.* Mr Macartney came in to play what, with all respect to Hendren, I take leave to regard as the finest innings of the match. It seemed almost incredible that he and Mr Collins should be taking part in the same game. Mr Collins placed his bat and pads correctly for some three hours, and let the ball hit one or the other. He did once condescend to cut a rank long hop, and then did not hit the ball hard enough to make it reach the boundary. For the rest of the time he scored an occasional single on the leg side under protest.

Mr Macartney, on the contrary, was his own impudent self, dealing with half a dozen similar balls in half a dozen different ways as if he were picking experimental strokes in a net. By the way, he made an experiment in running before the total reached 30, which would have been fatal to Mr Collins if Larwood, after fielding the ball smartly, had thrown it straighter to Strudwick. After this even long singles were declined. But Mr Macartney kept the score mounting largely by pushing or gliding to leg balls which many respectable players would be proud to stop. He was equally daring on the off side. He has a stroke which is purely individual. When the bowler pitches wide of the off stump he deflects the ball past the slips with a sort of sliced chop as no other living cricketer can. In defending his wicket he brings his wrists into his stroke so late that it is difficult to anticipate the line which the ball will take. And it is useless to go by the position of his feet. He can hit as easily off the wrong foot as off the right. Yesterday they could not place the field for him.

## THIRD TEST, HEADINGLEY, 1926

A.C.M. CROOME,
CRICKET CORRESPONDENT

*July 12.* After his escape Mr Macartney completely dominated the English bowlers. Nothing like his innings has been seen since Mr Victor Trumper made 100 before luncheon for Australia against England at Manchester in 1904. Only Tate looked capable of bowling him a good ball. If I describe his batting as insolent or contemptuous I do so with the desire to pay the highest possible compliment to his technique, not to impugn his sense of proportion. They could not set the field for him on Saturday. His twinkling feet and the telescopic reach of his arms enabled him to meet two similar balls at different stages in their careers, and to send them to points in the boundary separated by fifty yards. One remembers, too, that he scored several 4's by getting up on his toes and playing the back strokes as Dr W.G. Grace used to play them.

To carry the comparison between a large man and a small one a stage further, Mr Macartney's ordinary forward stroke counted 4, and the bowler acquired merit if he could oblige him to play half-cock to the ball.

---

# STAN McCABE

## FIRST TEST, SYDNEY, 1932–33

DELAMORE MCCAY

*December 5.* McCabe played an amazing innings this morning, making 60 out of the 70 runs scored in 55 minutes, his stand for the last wicket with Wall adding 55 runs in 33 minutes. He cut, hooked, and drove with equal certainty and power. One over from Voce produced 14 runs and the next eight, and the over between from Larwood cost nine runs. His is the highest score which has been made by a batsman for Australia at Sydney since S.E. Gregory made 201 in 1894. He was twice dropped wide in the slips, and while he was battering the attack the English team appeared to be rattled. He scored freely off the leg-theory bowling, and proved that it is possible to hit that type of bowling.

## FIRST TEST, TRENT BRIDGE, 1938

DUDLEY CAREW

*June 14.* Whatever happens in this Test match of records at Trent Bridge the name of S.J. McCabe must imperishably be associated with it. Figures are often uninformative, but sometimes they have a way of speaking the truth with utter clarity and conviction, and yesterday McCabe actually scored 213 runs out of 273 in three hours and three-quarters. In all he made 232 and hit one 6 and 30 4s. Considering the pace at which he went and the risks which he most laudably and legitimately took in the interests of his side, the mis-hits were astonishingly few and there was not a chance in the whole course of the great and historic innings.

The Australians went in shortly before 4 o'clock needing 247 runs to save the innings defeat. J.H. Fingleton and W.A. Brown scored 89 runs for the first wicket, and when stumps were drawn D.G. Bradman was not out, the score was 102 for one wicket, and there was the feeling of a draw in the air.

It was obvious that the first hour yesterday morning was going to be of great importance, and the crowd, when play was begun, seemed even bigger than it had been on the Saturday morning, and it was not long before the gates were closed. W.R. Hammond opened the bowling with K. Farnes, who had two slips and a gully, and Wright, who had one slip and a forward short-leg. England got the quick wicket they wanted, but it was not the important one, as it was F.A. Ward, and not McCabe, whom Farnes bowled. This happened after only six runs had been added to the overnight score of 138, and seven runs later they suffered a really formidable casualty in the person of A.L. Hassett. Hassett went out to drive Wright through the covers, did not get his left leg quite far enough across, and the ball flew off the edge of the bat to Hammond at first slip.

The rest of the morning was dominated by McCabe. His side were struggling for their lives, and the English bowling and fielding were reinforced with a proper hostility and confidence. The out-cricket was altogether more formidable and better organized than that of Australia had been, but never for a moment did McCabe play like a member of a losing side. His batting was cool, upright, and aggressive enough to earn him 88 runs off his own bat before luncheon.

Once he mistimed an on-drive and lifted the ball, but generally the ball came off the bat as he intended it to. He placed Sinfield down to the boundary at fine-leg and a cut for 3 off the same bowler got him his 50. When Hammond came on he forced successive balls off his legs to the boundary, both strong handsome shots, brought up the 200 by hooking Farnes, and in the same over he played a lovely forcing shot off his back foot through the covers. Shortly before this, however, he had lost C.L. Badcock. Wright had been bowling his leg-breaks at something not

16 THE TIMES SATURDAY JUNE 11 1938

# THE FIRST TEST MATCH: A GOOD BEGINNING BY ENGLAND

THE HUNDRED UP.—Barnett scoring a fine boundary to the off and bringing England's total up to 100 in the Test Match at Trent Bridge yesterday. O'Reilly is the bowler and Hutton is at the other end. These two players gave England a splendid start, and before they were separated, when Barnett was bowled with his score at 126, they had made 219 together, a record opening stand for these encounters in this country. When stumps were drawn for the day England had made 422 for 4 wickets.

HUTTON, the young Yorkshire batsman, driving a ball from Fleetwood-Smith in the course of his innings of 100 against the Australians yesterday. It was his first appearance in a Test Match against Australia.

BARNETT of Gloucestershire, who played forceful and confident cricket from the start, making the boundary hit which gave him his century immediately after the luncheon interval.

O'REILLY bowling to Barnett with Hutton backing up. He worked very hard in the earlier part of the day without success, but was rewarded later with two valuable wickets, those of Edrich and Hammond, both of whom he bowled.

ADVANCE ON SUCHOW.—A Japanese tank travelling up a steep incline in the old town of Yungcheng during the advance on Suchow.

THE WIGHTMAN CUP.—Miss K. E. Stammers gave England a good start by beating Miss A. Marble, the American champion, 3—6, 7—5, 6—3. She and Miss Marble are seen leaving the court. America won the other Singles match and also the Doubles.

AT ST. MARGARET'S.—Mr. E. A. H. Legge-Bourke, Royal Horse Guards, and Miss Catherine Jean Grant were married at St. Margaret's, Westminster, yesterday. The bride and bridegroom.

IN PLAY.—A photograph taken of Miss Stammers during her match with Miss Marble. To-day the contest will be concluded at Wimbledon, the programme including three Singles and one Doubles.

## SERVICES TO-MORROW

### TRINITY SUNDAY

*The start of a run-filled Test match at Trent Bridge dominates the picture page on Saturday, June 11, 1938* far from medium in pace, and bowling them with a most commendable accuracy, and when Badcock had made nine he produced a devastating googly which completely deceived Badcock, who tried to cut it and which came in to hit the top of the off-stump.

Hammond did not take the new ball, and Verity did not appear until the time was five minutes past 1. He could make nothing of the pitch, and did not look as dangerous as either Sinfield or Wright. McCabe duly reached his 100 and added two runs before luncheon, when the score was 261 and B. A. Barnett's contribution a highly important 20. It was a little grim to reflect that at lunch-time on the third day only 14 wickets had fallen.

The weather afterwards was hot and sultry, and McCabe, who, goodness knows, had been severe enough on the bowling before luncheon, became brutal to it afterwards. He soon lost Barnett, but the fall of the wicket seemed to encourage him to take the game into his hands. His attack was terrific in its power and virility, and at the end of an hour of it an England team which had looked assured of victory wilted, and wilted not without cause. The 4's came faster than an agitated pencil could note them down. Three of them came in one over off Farnes, and then the unfortunate Wright felt the full force of his wrath. Two successive balls were driven straight and handsomely to the boundary, and the fact that neither W.J. O'Reilly nor E.L. McCormick could help him very much mattered not at all.

Nine wickets were down for 334, but such was his attack in the next 20 minutes or so that the English bowling began to look as though it would find Fleetwood-Smith's wicket, let alone McCabe's, difficult to take. Wright played his part well, taking the Australians' innings as a whole, and the fact that he lost his length under the lash of McCabe's driving, cutting, and hooking should not unduly upset him – McCabe, as he was yesterday, would have upset greater bowlers. Three times in one over McCabe dismissed the ball superbly to various parts of the field, and then he scored 16 runs off four successive balls from Wright, first an on-drive, then a full-pitch – full-pitches in this match have not been conspicuous by their absence – pulled round to square-leg to give him his 200, then that shot off the right foot through the covers, and finally a hook off a long-hop.

When eventually he lifted a ball from Verity to extra cover-point he could retire with the knowledge that if his side were to save the match that devastating 75 minutes after luncheon would be mainly responsible.

---

## KEITH MILLER

### FIRST TEST, BRISBANE, 1946–47

NEVILLE CARDUS

*December 2.* And now for half an hour or so Miller played the finest cricket of the match so far; freedom of swing in his strokes with wrist work added, head and body inclined over the ball as though taking part in the direction of his hits, lifted the cricket temporarily above the level of perspiring competence. This was cricket of blood, and we could almost see the red carpet laid on the pitch. The plebeian origins of the match yesterday and all the heavy bottled beer were temporarily forgotten; this was champagne of sorts. Miller is no merely dashing batsman; he keeps near and over the ball.

# ARTHUR MORRIS

## FIFTH TEST, THE OVAL, 1948

R.B. VINCENT,
CRICKET CORRESPONDENT

*August 17.* Morris is so quick on his feet that he can afford to walk across his stumps with the certitude that he is in the exact position to play the ball as late as he requires – so late, in fact, that he can treat himself to a chop off the off-stump which can be taken either as a defensive stroke to the turning ball or a deflection to score one run down to third man. Equally so in his attacking strokes to the offside he finds time to cover the ground and to strike the ball at the last possible moment away through the most carefully placed field. He is, in fact, a batsman of genius, but of a genius born to the soundest principles in batsmanship.

When Hollies, who throughout the innings had insisted on careful attention, came on Morris reached his century with a perfectly timed stroke to the offside for three runs, and when Young came on at the Pavilion end he greeted him at once with an off drive bang to the boundary.

[…] and then at last Morris was out – run out – the only way that one could see that he ever would be out. Tallon played a ball down to deep backward-point, Morris ran and Simpson, the substitute, had the ball back to Evans to enforce the penalty for a run which was never there. Morris, whose innings had combined exquisite stroke play with perfect judgment, had batted for six hours and three-quarters, and had hit 16 fours. Those are facts; the true value of his innings can be best judged by those who had to bowl to him. The humble spectator felt that this is a young man who will cause England's bowlers a deal of trouble for years to come.

# NORMAN O'NEILL

## FIFTH TEST, THE OVAL, 1961

JOHN WOODCOCK,
CRICKET CORRESPONDENT

*August 19.* Australia's splendid progress began when O'Neill set out to show cricketers in this country how he has acquired his reputation. He had the fortune which favours the brave, being dropped when he was 19 and playing several false strokes as he conquered the England bowling. His century was the fastest of the series, lasting for three hours 20 minutes, and of its kind was the finest.

At lunch time Benaud may have exhorted O'Neill to go out and give the crowd a treat. Without the Ashes to worry about he was less jumpy than in his earlier innings, and once Barrington had let him off he plundered the bowling. Every boundary that he hit must have been a stab of pain to Barrington, but to Londoners starved of stroke play it was wonderfully refreshing.

When O'Neill came in, Australia were 15 for two. His reaction to this was to add 50 in an hour with Simpson, and when Simpson was out he launched such a counter-attack that Flavell and Allen hardly knew what had hit them. With Burge playing second fiddle and giving O'Neill all he could of the strike, the 75 minutes before tea brought 78 runs and saw O'Neill to the brink of his hundred.

Watching him make such an auspicious first appearance against MCC in Perth almost three years ago, I little thought he would not make a century against England until his 15th innings. He has scored four others in the meantime, against West Indies, India and

Pakistan, and he will give pleasure with many more. [...]

Australia's running between wickets was twice as good as England's. O'Neill runs the first one flat out in the hope of a second, rather as Bradman used to do. With few exceptions the Englishmen settle for a single as soon as they see the ball heading for third man. When Statham came off, O'Neill loosened up against Allen with a glorious cover drive and after batting for 100 minutes he reached his 50 with two late cuts and a resounding straight hit. When Flavell had a spell in mid-afternoon he was struck for 25 in six overs.

After 45 minutes O'Neill and Burge had made 50, 45 of them to O'Neill. For an hour or so only Lock commanded much respect. The score was 135 for three before he was called upon and his first eight overs cost only eight runs. When the last over before tea began and ended O'Neill was 99, Lock having bowled a maiden with the young master straining at the leash. In the second over after the interval O'Neill went to his hundred, scored out of 160 in 168 minutes. His last 68 had taken only 25 overs and it occupied Australia only three hours and 40 minutes to score as many runs as England made in six hours on Thursday.

---

## BILL PONSFORD

### FOURTH TEST, HEADINGLEY, 1934

R.B. VINCENT,
CRICKET CORRESPONDENT

*July 23.* [...] even if that terrible Bradman has made 271 excellent runs, it was by common consent Ponsford's day. No one can fail to be an admirer of Ponsford as a stroke player – who will ever forget his innings at the Oval in 1930? – but on Saturday for sheer workmanship he excelled himself. Winding himself up with the appearance sometimes of entwining himself round that huge bat of his he met the ball consistently full in the middle of the blade. His attacking strokes were made with such judgment that he could find a hole on a densely packed off-side field, and his defensive strokes, with men waiting almost under his green cap cocked over his left ear, were played with an utterly dead bat. It was a superb display of the type which the big occasion demands ...

---

## RICKY PONTING

### FOURTH TEST, HEADINGLEY, 2001

CHRISTOPHER MARTIN-JENKINS,
CHIEF CRICKET CORRESPONDENT

*August 17.* The toss was of no great importance, the new ball swung dangerously, the pitch had an unevenness of bounce that can only increase but still England could not prevent Australia taking such a grip on the fourth Test that already it is hard to imagine any result other than an Australia victory.

This time it was Ricky Ponting's turn to play the vital innings. Saved from a third-ball duck by a blade or two of Headingley grass and a fuzzy action replay, he proceeded with hawk-eyed, quick-footed brilliance to his eighth Test hundred and his second on this ground.

Bradman, too, used to make a habit of scoring hundreds at Headingley. Ponting may be not much larger and he apparently picks the ball up every bit as quickly, but in most respects they are chalk and cheese. The young pretender will never have the same concentration, unyielding defence or calculated approach. He is a gambler on and off the field, is aptly nicknamed 'Punter' and is an entertainer par excellence.

He reached three figures yesterday in nine minutes under three hours with three sixes and 11 fours. It was the pulled sixes that told, above all, what a wonderfully good eye he has. Mark Waugh, his patient and unselfish partner in a third-wicket stand of 221 in 46 overs, had a distinctly uncomfortable time when Gough and, especially, Caddick began peppering him with short balls in a not unsuccessful effort to unsettle him. Waugh was eventually caught off the splice off a ball that lifted in the final over of the day.

Yet Ponting simply swivelled inside anything short and lifted it over the square-leg boundary with the ease of a walker idly knocking the head off a thistle with his stick. Once past a hundred he enjoyed himself even more in the evening sunshine, blazing nine more fours off the back foot on both sides of the wicket as England's bowlers failed to appreciate that this is one batsman to whom bowling short of a length really is a waste of time.

Finally defeated eight overs from the close by a ball from Alex Tudor that lifted and left him, Ponting's was an innings of great importance to him after a series of cheap dismissals both before and after his promotion to first wicket down. In all probability his 144, the first time that he has passed 17 in 12 Test innings, will prove decisive to the outcome of this game.

### THIRD TEST, OLD TRAFFORD, 2005

RICHARD HOBSON

*August 16.* There was character as well as strokeplay about this innings. A short, wiry man, Ponting is deceptively strong and his currant-like eyes burn with pride. He is a combination of the best of the Chappell brothers: he scraps like Ian but can bat with the grace of Greg. The Ashes will have to be torn from his grip, finger by finger.

This did not seem like a great defensive innings because he never allowed himself to be bogged down. Right from the start he drove signature-style between mid-wicket and mid-on. To those who have seen Ponting at his best these were ominous strokes indeed. 'Faced with the situation we were in it is probably one of my best knocks', he said.

## MICHAEL SLATER

### SECOND TEST, LORD'S, 1993

ALAN LEE, CRICKET CORRESPONDENT

*June 18.* Taylor was on 85 then, but Slater was long past his century, a milestone he recorded by punching the air repeatedly, kissing his green helmet and throwing his arms around Taylor.

Slater's strength is speed of footwork, so nimble he looks to be on wheels. It gets him in position uncommonly early, so his favourite on-drive is played from perfect position, no matter the length of the ball.

## FIRST TEST, BRISBANE, 1994-95

ALAN LEE, CRICKET CORRESPONDENT

*November 26.* Slater habitually bats with the appetite of one so ravenous that he has one wide eye on the dessert trolley even as the main course is being served. His restless desire to hit every ball for four is occasionally self-destructive, but, on days such as this, when pitch and bowling are equally obliging, he presents entertainment on a scale beyond most batsmen.

The fourth century of his brief Test career was also his biggest. His range of strokes was wondrous, his footwork so slick that, eventually, even well-directed balls were being treated as half-volleys and pummelled through mid-on. Having made 105 by tea, he was well on course for a second century in the final session when he mistimed an off-drive and fell victim to a collector's dismissal: caught Gatting bowled Gooch.

*Michael Slater, on the offensive as always, against Peter Such at the Gabba in 1998–99*

## STEVEN SMITH

### FIFTH TEST, THE OVAL, 2013

MIKE ATHERTON, CHIEF CRICKET CORRESPONDENT

*August 23.* Until now, Steven Smith has been a poster boy for the new generation of Australian cricketer: overpaid and underachieving; multitalented, without ever being quite sure which of those talents should be the making of him. At 4.15pm yesterday, he answered that question emphatically, becoming the youngest Australian to make a hundred in an Ashes Test since Ricky Ponting at Headingley 16 years ago.

He got there in style, too, not nervously and with a hint of desperation as Chris Rogers had done in Durham, but with confidence and no little bravado. Having given away the chance of a first Test hundred at Old Trafford earlier in the summer, Smith was determined not to fret his way through the nineties, smashing Jonathan Trott majestically over long-on for six before turning to the dressing room for confirmation of his new-found standing.

Picked for his first Ashes Test in Perth because, they said at the time, of his upbeat nature, as well as his talent, the joke was now very much on England. [...]

After heavy overnight rain and morning drizzle had delayed the start by 3½ hours, Smith moved from his overnight score of 66 and into the nineties with some lovely shots: a back-foot force, with a touch of Caribbean flair, and a leg-side flick off Stuart Broad initially; a pulled four with full extension of the arms to the mid-wicket fence off Chris Woakes, and a calm steer to third man off James Anderson.

## MARK TAYLOR

### FIRST TEST, OLD TRAFFORD, 1993

ALAN LEE, CRICKET CORRESPONDENT

*June 4.* His method remains unfussy, economical, for he is a tradesman, not a craftsman. But as the cherished on-drive began to work with ease and the stray leg-stump balls were dismissed with contempt, English memories stirred and hearts sank.

## VICTOR TRUMPER

### SECOND TEST, LORD'S, 1905

E.H. LYTTELTON

*June 17.* On going in to bat the Australians at once showed they had made up their minds to play a free game, thinking that the wicket would be difficult and runs more likely to come by running a certain amount of risk. Haigh and Rhodes began the bowling to Mr Trumper and Mr Duff, and the batting was of a most attractive nature, both batsmen hitting hard, and, considering the slowness of the wicket, better hitting has seldom been seen. Mr Duff drove Haigh clean into the pavilion, while Mr Trumper made a most unique leg hit over the boundary off what looked a fairly good length ball from Haigh. The ball was not hooked but hit with an almost straight bat; but it was one of the most remarkable hits in the history of cricket, and it is doubtful if any other batsman in the world could have made it.

## MARK WAUGH

### FOURTH TEST, ADELAIDE, 1990–91

ALAN LEE, CRICKET CORRESPONDENT

*January 26.* With an innings of infinite charm and fluency, Waugh changed the course of the day and charted the course of his future. His twin brother, Steve, may have beaten Mark into the Australian side by five years, but he had to wait 27 Tests for his first century. Mark needed just one majestic innings. The long wait is over. A new and engaging star is here to stay.

This was the 26th century of Waugh's career and his third in successive games. If he goes on to make a hundred, which well he might, he will struggle to play better. He offered England no chances, indeed scarcely a false shot, as he scored 106 of the unbroken sixth-wicket stand of 145 with Greg Matthews.

When the 25-year-old reached his century, in under three hours, with a typically assured square-cut four, 17,000 people rose and roared their approval as one, a deafening gesture of acclaim. Out in the middle, Gooch plodded stoically over to his erstwhile county colleague, patted him on the back and said: 'Well done, boy.' If it was said through gritted teeth, Gooch could not be blamed.

### SECOND TEST, LORD'S, 2001

CHRISTOPHER MARTIN-JENKINS, CHIEF CRICKET CORRESPONDENT

*July 21.* Mark Waugh's 108 at Lord's yesterday was an innings of unyielding discipline by a singular genius. Building as it did on another formidable feat of fast bowling by Glenn McGrath, it went a long way towards winning both the second Test and the Ashes for Australia but a moment of inspiration in the field by Darren Gough and a bouncer by Dominic Cork that skimmed Steve Waugh's left glove and finally gave some justification for a surfeit of short-pitched bowling, brought limited consolation for England late in the day. [...]

Waugh's innings left seasoned observers wondering if there has ever been a right-handed batsman who has played off his legs with silkier timing, or, indeed, a team – even an Australia team – that has pursued Test victories with a more voracious hunger than this one. Australia's bowlers allow no margin for error, their fielders have caught every legitimate chance in this match and the batsman whose innings formed the centrepiece of the day yesterday has a way of hitting fours off even the most blameless balls.

## STEVE WAUGH

### SECOND TEST, LORD'S, 1989

ALAN LEE, CRICKET CORRESPONDENT

*June 26.* It already seems incomprehensible that Waugh made his maiden Test century only a fortnight ago. Here, he played with the assurance of a man who has been scoring hundreds for years, instead of one who undoubtedly will be scoring them for years to come.

Waugh is 329 not out for the series and the frightening thing is that he can get in no higher than No.6. His confidence inspired the tail outrageously and the stand of 130 with Lawson was England's greatest embarrassment of many already suffered in this series.

*After making his long-delayed first Test century at Headingley, Steve Waugh was unstoppable in 1989*

The classical correctness of Waugh contrasted with a painful evening session in which three England batsmen demonstrated their technical problems.

## THIRD TEST, OLD TRAFFORD, 1997

ALAN LEE, CRICKET CORRESPONDENT

*July 4.* Only two Australians resisted for long and one of these, Matthew Elliott, might have been out to almost every ball he faced in the opening hour. His 40, occupying 32 overs and almost as many moral defeats, was a triumph of survival, but Waugh, making his thirteenth Test century, gave a lesson in technique.

Throughout the day, the ball moved extravagantly off the pitch. At times, especially on a still afternoon, it also swung and the problems were exacerbated by occasional steep bounce and a desperately slow outfield. These were disagreeable circumstances for any batsman, but Waugh, predominantly on the back foot, played with hawk-eyed vigilance. Periodically, there was a poised drive through mid-on or extra cover; otherwise, the innings was one of pushes, deflections and watchful defence.

Without him, Australia would have been out for a pittance.

## FIRST TEST, EDGBASTON, 2001

CHRISTOPHER MARTIN-JENKINS, CHIEF CRICKET CORRESPONDENT

*July 7.* If Billy Woodfull was the unbowlable, Steve Waugh is surely the unbreakable. Conditions were thoroughly inimical to batsmen when he walked to the wicket for the eighth ball of the second morning of the first Test match yesterday. Thursday's hero, Michael Slater, had lost his off stump driving at Darren Gough's first ball, the light was gloomy, the air heavy with mist. If England had got him out quickly, the advantage would have moved their way. But he would not and did not let it happen, moving with all his renowned resolution and carefully honed craft to his ninth hundred in 39 innings as the Australia captain.

In difficult batting conditions in a match of such significance, it was one of the finest of the 26 centuries he has now scored for his country. It was completely without chance, virtually without flaw or anxious moments, and Waugh himself rated it as 'among my best six'.

To some extent, England missed a chance in what looked like ideal conditions for swing bowling, but the ball did not move as they had hoped, the only slip catch offered was dropped and, essentially, Waugh was too good for them, literally and faultlessly playing every ball on its merits.

By the time that he had shared a fourth-wicket partnership of 133 with his far less comfortable brother, Mark, and another of greater fluency later with an assured looking Damien Martyn, the indomitable captain had taken Australia not only into the lead but also into a position from which they will almost certainly win the game. [...]

It is asking for the impossible, perhaps, for every half-chance to be taken, but these are the moments on which series after series have turned towards Australia. Such is the balance of power, they can afford to make more mistakes than England.

Not that Steve Waugh looked like making any yesterday. He ducked the short balls, of which there was no shortage at all as the fast bowlers strove in vain to exploit such uneven bounce as there was; he met those that had to be defended with unyielding resolution and the straightest of bats; and those he knew he could punish, he hit to his designated scoring areas with unerring placement and compact power, his body low to the ground and surging into the stroke like a tug butting through the waves.

Exploiting a rapid and immaculate outfield, he needed only 164 balls and a little less than four hours to reach his latest landmark, preceding the obligatory punch of the air with a clip off his hip to send a ball from White skimming backward of square leg for his thirteenth four.

Most of his other boundaries were hit, as usual, through extra cover or between mid-wicket and mid-on, his favourite areas. When he did get a ball to cut he never missed the chance, his bat coming hard down on top of the bounce. It was the innings of a pragmatist, a hard, clear-minded man and a technician of the highest quality.

## FIFTH TEST, SYDNEY, 2002–03

CHRISTOPHER MARTIN-JENKINS, CHIEF CRICKET CORRESPONDENT

*January 4.* In more prosaic words, it seemed when Hobbs was at his best that the bowler was operating simply so that he should be able to display his mastery. It was like that here yesterday: first the fall of wickets early in Australia's innings to set up the sort of sticky situation that Waugh loves; then a superb exhibition of simple batting in which the impression was given that bowlers who were bursting blood vessels to try to get him out were merely putting the ball in the right places for him to play his favourite strokes.

They did not, in fact, bowl very well, especially the disappointing Matthew Hoggard, but the truth is that when Waugh is in the mood, he makes bowlers dance to his tune. This was one of the finest of the 29 Test hundreds he has scored since 1989, when he made his first two in successive Tests in England. In all the circumstances, it was possibly the most remarkable of them all. Certainly it was the innings that has set his legend in stone.

There is no doubt that his future as a Test batsman was at stake. He may yet announce his retirement on Monday, but somehow it seems more likely that he will have forced the selectors to retain him as captain. If so, he will pass Allan

Border's record number of Test caps (156) for any country in April and begin the chase towards 11,000 Test runs.

He went past 10,000 yesterday, only the third man to do so after Border and Sunil Gavaskar, with a crisp back-foot force off Richard Dawson, hit against the spin to the cover boundary. He had come in to yet another standing ovation when Australia were genuinely in trouble at 56 for three, spent ten minutes getting his bearings and began hitting the ball with those astonishingly fast hands, through extra cover and mid-wicket off the front foot and through cover point off the back.

His method is so simple and, yes, it draws the bowlers in. He looks vulnerable to the short ball but never hooks, so they try to get him caught in the slips, where, again, he looks likely to fall because he stays inside the line until the last minute. But as soon as there is width, the ball is laced through the off side for four; when it is dead straight, he gets behind the line and plays with the full face; and when they stray even inches to the leg side, he punches through mid-wicket or square leg.

As the end of the day approached and the attempt to make his hundred by the close seemed to recede, he accelerated, even taking risks with running between the wickets. The match had become an irrelevance: this was Waugh's Test. Moving into the 90s just in time to make it possible, he came haring back for a second run to long leg off Andrew Caddick in the penultimate over and would have been run out by Steve Harmison's throw if it had not missed the stumps by inches. Then he dashed a quick single to get the strike for the final over.

It was bowled by Dawson, and well bowled, too. On 95 at its start, Waugh was obliged to play careful defensive strokes to the first three balls; but he was not to be denied. He drove the fourth through extra cover, for once not out of the middle and not sufficiently well-timed to reach the boundary. Adam Gilchrist, however, his belligerent and brilliant but now almost forgotten partner, worked a single to mid-wicket to leave the final ball for his captain: not just his captain but all Australia's captain.

Nasser Hussain, for a moment Douglas Jardine reincarnate, set his field fastidiously as an impatient crowd booed. But it did not have long to wait. Waugh took a firm step forward and drove Dawson's length ball just outside off stump through the gap at extra cover before lifting his arms to a crowd in seventh heaven. Every member of the England team hurried to shake him by the hand before he left the field with that Chaplinesque walk, to climb the steps of the pavilion that Bradman once climbed in triumph. They are equal on 29 centuries for Australia now.

---

## DAVID WARNER

### THIRD TEST, PERTH, 2013–14

MIKE ATHERTON,
CHIEF CRICKET CORRESPONDENT

*December 16.* As Broad has been broken, so have England. For Warner, the opposite is true. His star is in the ascendant and his transformation has had much to do with Australia's resurgence. He spent the English summer in the dog house, courtesy of his late-night fracas with Joe Root, and never has a man looked more determined to atone for his errors, and make his enemies pay. He scored his second hundred of the series, celebrated with an exaggerated run towards Matt Prior, and in doing so put England's limp batting efforts into sharp perspective.

Warner, true to his instincts as a natural-born Twenty20 cricketer, began aggressively, almost swinging himself off his feet against two of the first three balls he received. The adrenalin was flowing, as he stared down Tim Bresnan, taking the new ball instead of Broad, picked a verbal fight with Ian Bell at gully and was warned by Marais Erasmus of the possible consequences should his erratic behaviour continue.

That warning, a good example of proactive umpiring, did the trick. Warner then settled down, if that term can ever be applied to his batting, to show his best side. Bresnan was cut hard to the fence, and pummelled back over his head at the start of his second spell, and Graeme Swann was slog-swept into the crowd. He was missed badly by Prior off Swann on 13, as the spinner's second ball turned past Warner's charge, and then again by Prior, in similar fashion, on 89. Generally, though, Warner played Swann superbly, one more transformation from the summer, when left-handers were fodder for England's off spinner. Swann was reduced to bowling wide of off stump in defensive mode.

---

## JACK WORRALL

### THIRD TEST, HEADINGLEY, 1899

ERNEST WARD,
CRICKET CORRESPONDENT

*June 30.* The Australians on the slow, treacherous wicket of the morning had a difficult struggle for runs, and when Kelly, Noble, and Gregory were all out without a single between them, and the score stood at 24, there seemed a sensational day in store. But Worrall hit with a brilliance that recalled that prince of Australian batsmen on bad wickets, the late Percy McDonnell, who so long divided with Hugh Massie the honour of being the most brilliant batsman Australia had ever sent to this country. Worrall hit with wonderful precision. Here and there would come a snick, but he timed the ball splendidly. He got nearly all his runs in front of the wicket, and his driving and cutting were equally good. He did all this, too, when things were going greatly against his side. His only partner of any substance was Hill, who helped to add 71 in an hour for the fourth wicket. Then came the running out of Worrall, who made his 76 out of 95 in an hour and a half. The vigour of his batting may be gathered from the composition of his innings, which included 14 fours, two threes, two twos, and singles. Beyond the careful batting of Hill, who went in third wicket down at 24, and was seventh out at 132, there was nothing else worthy of comment in the Australian batting.

---

## GRAHAM YALLOP

### FIFTH TEST, OLD TRAFFORD, 1981

JOHN WOODCOCK,
CRICKET CORRESPONDENT

*August 17.* Against England at Sydney in 1978–79, in an innings of 121 out of a total of 198, Yallop showed how uncommonly well he is capable of playing. There is a flowing quality about his strokes when at his best, which contrasts strangely with his rather stilted gait. Yesterday was his sixth Test hundred and his third against England, and it was with some relief that England, at 198 for three, uprooted him. He had made his 114 in just under three hours and hit 17 fours.

Sporting

# HOW ENGLAND KEPT THE ASHES

## TWO GREAT HEARTS OVERTHROW AUSTRALIA

England beat Australia by five wickets in the fourth Test match at Adelaide yesterday and so, gaining a lead of three matches to one in the series, have retained the Ashes. In an interview after the match L. Hutton, the England captain, paid a tribute to the younger members of the side. Much of the credit, he thought, should go to J. B. Statham, F. H. Tyson, M. C. Cowdrey and P. B. H. May, together with the wicket-keeper, T. G. Evans.

From Our Special Correspondent

ADELAIDE, FEB. 2

Many years from now young Cowdrey will point to his broken nose and tell boys yet unborn that he was at Adelaide on February 2, 1955, when England won the Test match and kept the Ashes. And the boys will think him wondrous lucky. A man should dip his pen in blood to write of this day. Let no one talk and write of cricket and explain away ...

the catch. (We asked Hutton afterwards what he thought of Miller's bowling. Hutton thought Miller ought to concentrate much more on batting.) England 10 for 2. In comes the battered Cowdrey. Miller hits him twice running on the pads and appeals, and everybody here who isn't English appeals too. What a man is Miller. He comes in from a shortish run, loose of limb like an African, hair streaming, and as he pulls up the hair goes on and falls about his face. Meanwhile May has begun driving, and Johnson has gone from mid-off to square-leg. For Cowdrey Miller brings fine-leg up to third slip, and Cowdrey cover drives classically for 4. Miller heaves his shoulders over even faster, and Cowdrey is taken by Archer at first-slip. England 18 for 3. Four Meteor jets fly over at 200ft.; they look and sound quite tame beside this wild man ... His figures now are 3 overs, no ... runs, 3 wickets.

The Ashes Fourth ...

# England all too obliging ... reaches new heights of greatness

Australia v England

One that got away: Gilchrist misses a stumping chance off Warne to give Pietersen an extra life, but it was to make little difference

High five: Warne acknowledges the Melbourne crowd after his haul ripped the heart out of England's fragile batting

"We didn't expect conditions to change dramatically over the first day and a half," Strauss said, "but it seamed about more than we expected." It did so slowly but Glenn McGrath, Stuart Clark and Brett Lee all got enough past the bat to suggest that the wrong option had been taken.

Australia missed two catches, two clear run-out opportunities and a gaping stumping, but still bowled England out for 159 after they had been 101 for two. Very few Test matches are won after such a start. All of Warne's wickets were taken by flight and dip, as batsmen spied what they believed to be boundary opportunities. Only Kevin Pietersen got anywhere near the boundary as he attempted to drive Warne straight for six, but by now he was, as usual, batting with the tail.

Even he needed 70 balls for 21 runs, having come close to running out Andrew Flintoff for six as, for the third Test in succession, he attempted a ridiculous single in order to get off the mark. He had only made four when he also survived a simple stumping chance offered to Adam Gilchrist after charging Warne and missing. England, we all know, have too long a tail, but tweaking it made no difference. Matthew Hoggard is back where he started, No 11, pushing Monty Panesar and Stephen Harmison up a place each, which reflects their various abilities with the bat. It is higher up, however, that the balance is wrong. Ed Joyce or Jamie Dalrymple should have played.

six, but Chris Read for Geraint Jones was the only change. As the best player in the team, Pietersen needs to bat at four. Since Paul Collingwood shared the only partnership of any substance with Strauss — 57 for the third wicket — it may appear that England's strategy, to keep him away from the new ball, had worked again, but to have Pietersen batting with the tail repeatedly is not satisfactory. In any case Collingwood might have been leg-before to Clark for nought, one of four apparently plumb leg-before decisions turned down by Rudi Koertzen.

Australia's recent practice of not using a nightwatchman. Ponting said that Australia, too, would have chosen to bat first, but it was one of those tosses that either captain would prefer to have lost. Play was delayed by rain for half an hour and only 16 overs were bowled before an early lunch was taken. Alastair Cook ...

... Ponting run out (Flintoff) 66

... P Siddle c Flintoff b Harmison 10

5.37 343-9 S Clark c Cook b Harmison 0

... giant leap ... for proud S...

# Sporting News

## ENGLAND HAVE LAST WORD

### THREE YEOMEN FOIL AUSTRALIA

### GREAT STAND BY WATSON AND BAILEY

FROM OUR CRICKET CORRESPONDENT

Out of darkness, through fire into light. Thus did England yesterday rise like some Phoenix from the ashes of apparent defeat to save the second Test match at Lord's and so gain a ... draw against Australia with ... seven wickets, ... original aim fo...

The age of ... yet past, nor c... cany scarce fo... dramatic and ... a match alrea... But within t... longest and n... of a match it... that last spa... back with le... yeomen of ... nearly the w...

The yeom... were Watso... greatest of ... Yorkshirem... order, was ... rearguard ... twentieth ...

36 TUESDAY AUGUST 1 1989

THE TIMES

# England's abject surrender marks new low in series

## Inglorious procession at Old Trafford

By Alan Lee, Cricket Correspondent

10-1: Curtis c Boon b Alderman 0

25-2: Robinson lbw b Lawson 12

27-3: Smith c Healy b Alderman 1

28-4: Gooch c Alderman b Lawson 13

38-5: Botham lbw b Alderman 4

59-6: Gower c Marsh b Lawson 15

SCOREBOARD FROM OLD TRAFFORD

## Gower unfairly blamed for failings of others

Simon Barnes

## Border rewarded for hard labour

By John Woodcock

## Only two men so far decline

By Alan Lee

THE F...

SPOR...

Cricket

# Was this English ... most desperate ...

... night issued a dramatic ... Union to make a positive ... He said that unless the ... prepared to help to achieve an ... strategic arms limitations, he would ...

# GREAT BOWLING: ENGLAND

## JAMES ANDERSON

### THIRD TEST, EDGBASTON, 2009

RICHARD HOBSON

*August 1.* Figures still fail to do justice to the bowler that Anderson has become. His seventh haul of five or more in a Test innings, on his 40th appearance, leaves him with an overall record of 139 wickets at an average of 33.61. But a statistical nicety at Edgbaston means that Anderson really does have a career of two halves.

His defining recall at Wellington last year now marks the midway point of his England experience. In the 20 Tests starting with his debut he had taken 62 wickets at 39.20 apiece. In the 20 since his comeback, including this one, he has 77 victims at 29.10. That last figure represents better the performer he is today.

In conditions that swing, Anderson is devastating. His wrist and seam position give him every chance to hoop the ball whichever way he chooses. He can make batsmen look worse than they are, delivering from wide of the stumps, shaping it in to invite attempts to play through leg only for late swing to take it towards off.

Graham Manou, on debut, will not receive a better ball if he plays another hundred Tests.

*A master at work. Jimmy Anderson torments the Australians at Edgbaston in 2009*

## SECOND TEST, ADELAIDE, 2010–11

MIKE ATHERTON,
CHIEF CRICKET CORRESPONDENT

*December 4.* The opening moments of any Ashes Test are always pregnant with tension. Anxiety and nervousness, as well as excitement, are the overwhelming emotions of any cricketer involved, regardless of age or experience.

These heightened sensations bring opportunities for the team and the individuals best able to channel those feelings into something resembling normality. Yesterday that team were England and the individual was James Anderson.

The leader of Australia's attack may be sitting this game out, but there is no question about the health of England's.

Anderson has taken to his responsibilities superbly and he led an outstanding all-round display, with the ball and in the field, so that on a blameless Adelaide pitch England bowled out Australia for 245, an outcome beyond the imaginings even of this confident team. After Anderson's luckless display at the Gabba, it felt just that the wheel of fortune should turn so quickly here.

## FOURTH TEST, MELBOURNE, 2010–11

MIKE ATHERTON,
CHIEF CRICKET CORRESPONDENT

*December 27.* England's bowlers were excellent, led by James Anderson, who, in a nine-over spell from the Members End either side of lunch, found the kind of sweet rhythm that comes to bowlers all too rarely and often only in their dreams. Twelve rhythmical paces to the crease; lithe and whippy in his action and with masterful control, he reduced Australia's batting line-up to rubble, taking the key wicket of Mike Hussey on the stroke of lunch and adding Michael Clarke, Steven Smith, and Johnson just after. There was no way back for the home side from that.

## FIRST TEST, TRENT BRIDGE, 2013

MIKE ATHERTON,
CHIEF CRICKET CORRESPONDENT

*July 11.* Clarke had no answer to Anderson five balls later, though: angling in, and moving away late, the Lancastrian produced the ball to win the day's beauty contest, one of which Fred Trueman, whose 307 Test wickets Anderson has now passed, would have been proud.

---

# SYDNEY BARNES

## FIRST TEST, SYDNEY, 1911–12

*December 20.* Mr Foster, Mr Douglas, and Barnes did most of the work. The two amateurs met with more success than the professional, but Barnes maintained his length in a way that was really wonderful in the circumstances; he bowled for an hour and 34 minutes – from the time the game was continued after luncheon until the tea interval – bareheaded in a blazing sun. During that time he took one wicket and only 23 runs were hit off his bowling.

## SECOND TEST, MELBOURNE, 1911–12

*January 1.* Some sensational cricket was witnessed today in the second Test match of the M.C.C. tour, the first six Australian wickets falling for 38 runs. After this, however, the 'tail' saved the side from a bad collapse, and the last four wickets added 146 runs to the total. Barnes bowled magnificently throughout, and in the early stages of the game, he was almost unplayable. At one time he had secured five wickets for six runs. He kept a perfect length, swinging in from the off and turning back.

---

# ALEC BEDSER

## FIRST TEST, TRENT BRIDGE, 1953

GEOFFREY GREEN,
CRICKET CORRESPONDENT

*June 15.* Events stood out exciting and clear as the balance of a remarkable match was swung once more by the wonderful bowling of Bedser. Whatever happens, his superhuman efforts will never be forgotten. When Australia went to the crease again, one over before luncheon, with a comfortable first-innings lead of 105, the same question was heard on every side: 'Can he do it again?' The afternoon and the man gave up their answer, and that first faint flicker of hope spurted into a consuming fire as Australia was stripped of her authority.

Bedser indeed even surpassed his figures of Friday, though the intrinsic quality of his performance was perhaps not quite on the same exalted level, for the Australian batting, Morris apart, now curiously lacked its traditional application. Yet the fact remains that by taking another seven wickets to gain the almost unbelievable match analysis of 14 for 99 – this on a pitch that offered little material help – Bedser has turned away, momentarily at least, the finger of defeat that was so close upon England's shoulder. In doing so he passed S.F. Barnes's record of 189 Test match wickets, and now only C.V. Grimmett, the Australian, is ahead of him with 216. [...]

Bedser, with the pavilion his background, again was the executioner, destroying all but the inspired Morris. First he hit Hole's off stump behind an attempted forcing stroke to the off. That was at half-past two, with the total 28. An hour later the scoreboard showed 68 for five, with Morris 50 not out. The atmosphere was electric as: the packed assembly, living every ball, itself touched the very heartbeat of the quickening tussle.

After Hole there came the diminutive Hassett. Outwardly he remained calm, but soon he was troubled and then dispatched by Bedser as England's giant pounded the ball up off an indefinable spot. Hutton took the simple catch in the leg trap from the shoulder of the bat. Harvey, the menace, soon had his fangs drawn, finely caught off a hook, also close in Bedser's leg trap, by Graveney, who had been moved there astutely by Hutton. The great Miller, surprised by a full pitch, tossed his head in disgust as he hit the ball straight to Kenyon at mid-wicket. When Benaud at once lost his leg stump Australia, half the side gone, once more were bowed before Bedser. Only Morris, past 50 and resplendent in stroke play, had stood up to the storm as the Surrey man at last put on his sweater, having taken wickets in his fourth, seventh, ninth, 11th, and 12th overs for 28 runs.

Sporting News

**BEDSER AGAIN HUMBLES THE AUSTRALIAN BATSMEN**

**ENGLAND'S GREAT CHANCE IF RAIN HOLDS OFF**

**From Our Cricket Correspondent**

England this day expects every batsman to do his duty at Trent Bridge. The signal is hoist and the aim clear. Kenyon alone is gone with 42 scored, but Hutton and his lieutenants remain, left with 187 runs to gather for a famous Test match victory over Australia.

The task may prove to be a mountain or a molehill. Yet so far the Nottingham pitch, its character blackened by Australian totals of 249 and 123 and an England innings of 144, has really been its benign self; and 48 overs

Bedser as England's giant pounded the ball up off an indefinable spot. Hutton took the simple catch in the leg trap from the shoulder of the bat. Harvey, the menace, soon had his fangs drawn, finely caught off a hook, also close in Bedser's leg trap, by Graveney, who had been moved there astutely by Hutton. The great Miller, surprised by a full pitch, tossed his head in disgust as he hit the ball straight to Kenyon at mid-wicket. When Benaud at once lost his leg stump Australia, half the side gone, once more were bowed before Bedser. Only Morris, past 50 and

*Alec Bedser dominates the headlines at Trent Bridge in 1953*

## BERNARD BOSANQUET

### FIRST TEST, TRENT BRIDGE, 1905

R.H. LYTTELTON

*June 1.* The Australians are hardened, seasoned players, and yet it is hardly too much to say that no public school eleven could display more nervousness than did these experienced players. They must have had terror put into them by Mr Bosanquet's bowling when playing in Australia against Mr Warner's team. They were afraid to hit except when full pitches and long hops, such as Mr Bosanquet alone knows how to bowl, came at no very rare intervals. Mr Bosanquet's success, hitherto, has been owing to his power of making the ball come from the off, with the same action as when making it come from leg; but yesterday the wickets were all got with leg breaks as far as could be seen; but the batsmen, anticipating the break from the off, became completely bewildered, and did nothing more. Mr Bosanquet does not try to bowl maidens, and therefore could try every device he was capable of, and the result was almost comic. Close observers who watched the play before luncheon all agreed that Mr Darling and Mr Duff were never at home to him, and they had good hopes of England's gaining a victory; and Mr Bosanquet rose to the occasion.

## IAN BOTHAM

### FOURTH TEST, EDGBASTON, 1981

JOHN WOODCOCK,
CRICKET CORRESPONDENT

*August 3.* Once again Ian Botham was in the very thick of the action. When Australia must still have been fancying their chances of pulling it off – they reached 100 for four in the sort of glorious sunshine they are accustomed to in Sydney and Perth – Botham came on and took their last five wickets for one run in 26 balls. Bowling like a man possessed, he gave England a lead of two matches to one in a series which they seemed only recently to be on the point of losing.

## JOHNNY BRIGGS

### SECOND TEST, LORD'S, 1886

*July 22.* English cricketers will be highly gratified at the brilliant victory gained by their representatives at Lord's yesterday. Briggs's bowling proved even more effective than that of the previous day. To this professional the English side was mostly indebted for the rapid manner in which the game was finished off. Yesterday morning he started bowling from the nursery wicket, but was subsequently put on at the pavilion end, and the change proved beneficial, as, after some good batting by Messrs Palmer, Trumble, and Jones, wickets fell to his bowling In quick succession. Altogether in the match he claimed 11 wickets (seven clean bowled) for 74 runs.

## STUART BROAD

### FIFTH TEST, THE OVAL, 2009

MIKE ATHERTON,
CHIEF CRICKET CORRESPONDENT

*August 22.* In an astonishing spell that lasted throughout the middle session, Broad took five for 37 in 12 overs of swing and cut, destroying the cream of Australian batsmanship in the process, confirming his position as the heir to Fred's throne and his place in Ashes folklore.

There was little in the morning session to suggest that such a collapse was in the offing. Sure, the occasional ball had dusted the top and Shane Watson had given off an early air of impermanence before settling to his task with Katich, that doughty fighter, for company. Flintoff, relegating Stephen Harmison to first change and bowling urgently with the new ball, might have had Watson leg-before twice but for umpiring intransigence before Australia went to lunch, three minutes early because of some light rain, at 61 without loss.

After a break of 55 minutes while the showers cleared and the groundstaff dried the outfield, Strauss decided to replace Graeme Swann with Broad and that was the catalyst for the procession that followed: Watson was trapped on the crease in Broad's first over; in his third Ricky Ponting dragged on from wide; the next over Mike Hussey was palpably leg-before, playing with pad and not bat to a ball nipping back; in Broad's next over, Michael Clarke played too soon and into the hands of Jonathan Trott at short extra cover; and in his ninth over Brad Haddin played all around a full, swinging ball, the death rattle confirming his worst fears.

## FOURTH TEST, CHESTER-LE-STREET, 2013

MIKE ATHERTON,
CHIEF CRICKET CORRESPONDENT

*August 13.* Not cricket's longest day, perhaps, but certainly one of the most dramatic.

The full stop to it all was fittingly applied by Stuart Broad taking his sixth wicket of the innings, his eleventh of the match, when Peter Siddle drove to mid-off where James Anderson took a simple catch and hurled the ball high before the celebrations began. As tight as the cricket has been at times, the scoreline is now a crushing one.

Moments afterwards, as Australia's last pair walked off disconsolate after an astonishing collapse that saw them lose nine wickets in a session, the sun disappeared behind the clouds for the final time. It cloaked the ground in the kind of darkness that had prevented Alastair Cook from bowling his fast bowlers, just as he had the opportunity to take the extra half-hour. For a while, then, it looked as though Australia might survive the off spin of Graeme Swann and Joe Root, but then the sun popped out briefly.

Broad had produced a brilliant spell of fast bowling after tea, getting on the same type of roll, bowling fast and full and straight, as he had at the Oval against Australia in 2009, when he first came to public attention. After Bresnan breached the dam by dismissing David Warner, Broad rushed through, responding to the mood by taking five wickets in a hypnotic nine-over spell. Chief among the wickets was that of Michael Clarke, undone by the kind of ball – moving late to clip off stump – that was his undoing by Anderson at Trent Bridge.

It has been a seam bowlers' match. Ryan Harris took nine wickets, but he was trumped when Broad flattened Nathan Lyon's middle stump in the last over of his spell and celebrated with a charge to cover, arms outstretched in aeroplane mode. In between Clarke and Lyon, Broad dismissed Steven Smith, pulling on to his stumps, Brad Haddin and Harris, both leg-before, to take his match haul to ten, the second time he has achieved such a feat in Test cricket. The eleventh would come, albeit after an agonising wait.

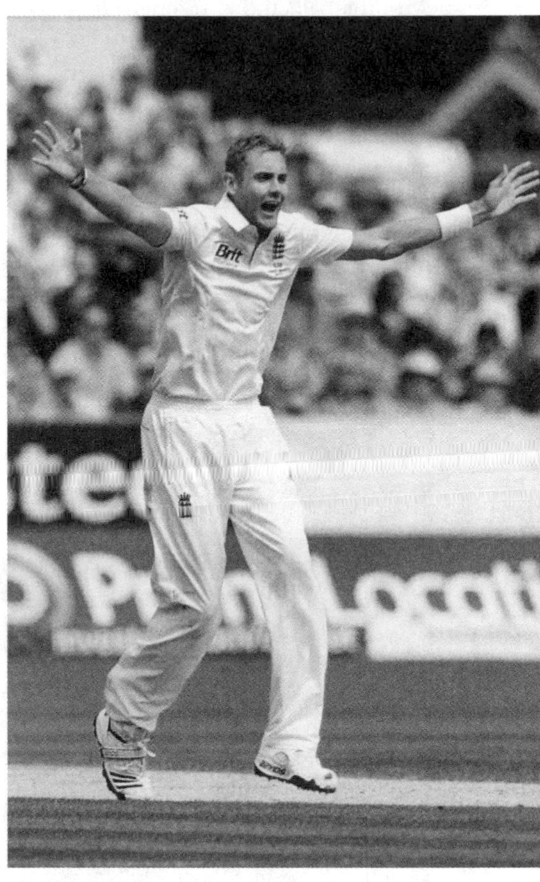


*Stuart Broad appeals for the wicket of Australia captain Michael Clarke in the fourth Test at Chester-le-Street in 2013*

## ANDREW CADDICK

### FIFTH TEST, SYDNEY, 2002–03

CHRISTOPHER MARTIN-JENKINS, CHIEF CRICKET CORRESPONDENT

*January 7.* Caddick, bowling in conditions and a situation ideal for him, took five more wickets yesterday and seven for 94 to enhance his reputation as a second innings, and in particular a fourth-innings, specialist. On the yellowy-white pitch with the ball cutting through the top, his steep bounce was nasty in the extreme for batsmen, no matter what their class. Already past Darren Gough to become England's seventh-highest wicket-taker, this was Caddick's sixth five-wicket haul in the last innings of a match.

His faults and virtues are well enough known by now. He can be infuriatingly wayward when the pressure is on him to perform early in a match with the new ball, as it was, for example, in Brisbane in the crucial first match of the series, but he has been a match-winner more times than any other man still bowling for England. They must continue to take the rough with the smooth and be grateful for the smooth.

## RICHARD ELLISON

### FIFTH TEST, EDGBASTON, 1985

JOHN WOODCOCK, CRICKET CORRESPONDENT

*August 20.* When, almost immediately, Emburey dropped Wessels at first slip off Taylor Australia may have thought that their luck had changed. But Ellison, coming on at 31 for one, embarked on a spell of bowling which he will always be remembered for.

*Richard Ellison removes Allan Border in the midst of a golden match-winning spell at Edgbaston in 1985*

In his third over he had Wessels caught at the wicket and then, next ball, Holland, the intended nightwatchman, was leg-before. Thinking better of sending in a second nightwatchman, Border set forth himself to try to inspire a rearguard action.

His partner was Wood, and he would have been pleased to see him still there, having batted already for 70 minutes. But in Ellison's fourth over, trying to play a ball away to the on-side, Wood got a leading edge and was caught off a half-skier in the covers. Finally, wonder of wonders, Border was bowled off his pads. In 25 minutes Australia had plummeted from 30 for one to 37 for five. Ellison pitched a full length, moved the ball a little, mostly late and in the air, and made the batsmen play.

A good crowd so warmed to this big, shambling, hirsute fellow, a bowler of a traditional English type, that they roared their heads off in his support.

---

# ANDREW FLINTOFF

## SECOND TEST, LORD'S, 2009

MIKE ATHERTON, CHIEF CRICKET CORRESPONDENT

*July 21.* Miracles rarely happen in sport – just ask Tom Watson. Making more runs to win than any team have made in the fourth innings of a first-class game proved beyond Australia yesterday. They bowed down not to history, though, but to Andrew Flintoff.

Flintoff was the plot, the subplot, the chapter headings and the footnotes of the 21 overs it took England to bury 75 years of Ashes hurt at Lord's. Bowling unchanged for ten overs from the Pavilion End, as quickly and with as much hostility as any England bowler has mustered in recent times, he took three of the last five wickets to fall, giving him his first five-wicket haul at Lord's.

The sight of Australia batsmen clearly brings out the best in him, as do the grandest of occasions. It was at the Oval in 2005, when the Ashes were decided, that Flintoff last took five wickets in an innings of any match and there has been no grander stage for him since than yesterday morning, with Lord's bursting at the seams and Australia at England's mercy.

For some reason, even though the touring team began the day five wickets down and 209 runs adrift, it was felt to be squeaky bum time. They couldn't lose this, could they? To ease frayed overnight nerves, England needed a strong start and Flintoff and James Anderson, who bowled a superb opening over to Michael Clarke, gave them just that, as they had throughout the game.

It took Flintoff only four balls to strike, moving one fractionally up the hill to find the edge of Brad Haddin's bat, the wicketkeeper unable to add to his overnight score. A wicket maiden. Nine more Flintoff overs followed, each as hostile and as threatening as the last. Clarke took a blow to the back of the head, Mitchell Johnson numerous to the arms, shoulder and body. A thunderbolt burst through Matt Prior's gloves.

When Nathan Hauritz shouldered arms and heard the clatter of leather on stump, Flintoff stood in the middle of the pitch, legs splayed, arms raised aloft. He was mobbed. When, 25 runs later, he castled Peter Siddle with a similar ball, to ensure that his name would be on the honours board for posterity, he knelt down on one knee in the middle of the pitch, head bowed, as if about to be knighted. He was mobbed again. He rose up through the clamour of his team-mates and saluted each corner of the ground, with a special nod to the Grand Stand where the WAGs were sitting.

---

## FRANK FOSTER

### THIRD TEST, ADELAIDE, 1911–12

*January 13.* The English bowlers, however, by sheer merit, held the upper hand throughout the innings. Mr Foster bowled splendidly and quite up to his best English form. He varied his pace very cleverly, and often made the ball swerve considerably. His five wickets were obtained for a fraction over seven runs apiece. Barnes was very accurate, and was distinctly unlucky. He and Mr Foster did nearly all the bowling, but Mr Douglas and Hitch also bowled very well, and the ball with which the latter dismissed Mr Trumper was a particularly good one.

---

## ANGUS FRASER

### SECOND TEST, MELBOURNE, 1990–91

ALAN LEE, CRICKET CORRESPONDENT

*December 29.* Angus Fraser sometimes seems to wear the cares of the world on his sloping shoulders as he puffs and plods his way through over after over. But the trust England have heaped on this endearingly ordinary young man was handsomely repaid in a monumental spell of bowling here yesterday.

Fraser took six Australian wickets at a cost of only 23 runs, completing the best analysis of his young but already mature England career and gaining for his side an unexpected and precious first-innings lead of 46 in the second Test.

Only 197 runs were scored on a day when batting became steadily more complicated. But the pitch's sluggish pace and its erratic bounce do not entirely account for some shocking lapses by the Australian batsmen. Most of the credit for these must lie with the most purposeful, disciplined bowling performance by an England side since the Trinidad Test in March.

Fraser was at the sharp end of the operation, as, these days, he always will be. The burden on him is heavy for one playing only his tenth Test, and there have recently been times when it has told on him. But yesterday he was magnificent, taking six consecutive wickets as Australia declined from 224 for three, in mid-afternoon, to 306 all out just before the scheduled close.

In the day, Fraser bowled 26 overs for figures of six for 34, but if the word inexhaustible springs readily to mind, forget it. With the job done, Fraser was just about able to lead the team off the MCG before collapsing onto his dressing-room bench, dehydrated and weary beyond words.

---

## DARREN GOUGH

### THIRD TEST, SYDNEY, 1994–95

ALAN LEE, CRICKET CORRESPONDENT

*January 4.* Australia, scrambling undeservedly past the follow-on figure, were bowled out for 116. Optimists will discern a symbolism in the fact that this was their lowest score against England since the Headingley Test of 1981, the launch pad of a magical transformation in an

*A rarity in the 1990s – England in command as Darren Gough removes Mark Waugh at Edgbaston in 1997*

Ashes series. Romantics will also point to Ian Botham's role in that victory and relate it to Darren Gough.

This is unfair, not so much to Botham as to Gough. England's tiro requires no comparisons with the past for he is refreshingly different. Yesterday, he took six Australia wickets for 49 to add to his ebullient 51 on Monday. 'I am on the honours board now,' he announced proudly, having received congratulations in writing from Ray Lindwall and on the telephone from Harold Larwood.

No England player has scored a half-century and taken five wickets in an innings in a single Test since Chris Lewis at Edgbaston in 1991. For Lewis, this was one more false dawn to a career chained by introspection. It is difficult to believe the same fate will befall Gough, for already he enjoys the affection of the public and the grudging respect of the opposition.

Taking five wickets for the first time meant a great deal to him, but it was the way he took his fifth that said so much about the man. Mark Taylor had batted through the innings with clear and increasing irritation as eight wickets fell at the other end. On 49, Gough confounded him with a leg break. 'I once got a wicket with one in a benefit match,' he explained artlessly. 'But I've bowled it four times out here and taken two wickets.' There is no inhibition to a young bowler who can do this to the Australia captain.

# GEORGE HIRST AND WILFRED RHODES

## FIRST TEST, EDGBASTON, 1902

R.H. LYTTELTON

*May 31.* The Australians began with Trumper and Duff, and the Yorkshiremen Hirst and Rhodes led off the bowling. The first noteworthy incident was a bad miss by Braund at short slip off Hirst, giving Duff a life when the score was seven. Directly afterwards Braund went on at Hirst's end, but only for one over, and Hirst and Rhodes changed ends. Duff was caught off Rhodes by point standing forward. Hill came in, but after a single was out to a grand catch at short slip by Braund off Hirst, a splendid bit of cricket. Gregory came in, and was l-b-w to Hirst for *nil*; and the Colonials, like their opponents on the previous day, had lost three, good wickets for 14. Darling succeeded, but was soon out, caught at cover-point off Rhodes. Four for 17. The English bowling and fielding, as might be expected, were first-rate. The wicket did not appear difficult at first, but seemed to get so as time went on. Noble then came in and was stumped off Rhodes. Trumper was batting beautifully, but Armstrong was caught at the wicket off Rhodes's first ball,and six wickets were down for 25. Rhodes was now bowling admirably, with excellent length and making the ball turn a great deal. After some quiet play by Trumper and Hopkins, Trumper was clean bowled by Hirst with a lovely ball, which came with the bowler's arm. Seven for 31. The wicket now seemed to favour the bowlers, and the two famous Yorkshiremen were evidently very difficult to play. Kelly was badly missed by Jackson at cover point off Rhodes, but the fielding generally was very good. Hopkins was caught at the wicket off Rhodes. Eight wickets were down for 35, and with Jones caught first ball at cover-point and Howell caught by Fry in the long field, both off Rhodes, the innings closed for 36 runs, the lowest score ever recorded in a test match. The Australians were undoubtedly very unlucky in having all the worst of the wicket, and in addition the light was far from good; but at the same time the bowling was very fine. Rhodes bowled an excellent length and kept the ball well up – an invaluable policy on such a wicket. He had the extraordinary analysis of seven wickets for 17; Hirst's three only cost 15, and he got the two best wickets, Trumper and Hill. Trumper showed the highest qualities as a batsman while he was getting his 18, and indeed nothing could have been better than his style of play. Shortly after the Australians began their second innings the umpires stopped play on account of the light; rain began to fall, and a melancholy day ended in wet and darkness.

The match so far has, of course, been, spoilt by the weather and by the fact that all the luck has been on one side. In the first place, it was impossible to estimate the loss of Trumble, who is, according to some good judges, the best bowler in the world. In the second place the wicket was at its worst during the Colonial batting, while the intense cold must have affected the Australians after the hot weather of their own country.

## JIM LAKER

### FOURTH TEST, OLD TRAFFORD, 1956

JOHN WOODCOCK,
CRICKET CORRESPONDENT

*July 28.* One of the most amazing batting collapses in the 80 years of Test cricket took place in the fourth match between England and Australia at Old Trafford yesterday, and as a result it is virtually certain that for the next 18 months the Ashes will be in England's keeping. Only unyielding rain can save Australia now from overwhelming defeat, for last night they were 322 runs behind England with nine second innings wickets to fall, having been bowled out once for 84 and made to follow on in face of England's total of 459.

At five minutes to four Australia's score was 48 for no wicket and McDonald and Burke, if they were not exactly making light of the bowling of Laker and Lock, at least were suggesting that England would have to work hard for victory. Eighty minutes later Australia's first innings was over. They had capitulated to the spin of Laker, whose off-breaks they had found unplayable. His remarkable figures are eloquent enough. In his last nine overs he had taken nine wickets for 16 runs, and after tea he had claimed a victim, seven in all, with every third ball he bowled.

There has never been anything like it before, and the Australians came one by one to the slaughter convinced, it seemed, before they took strike that they had not long to live. All 10 wickets tumbled while 36 runs were being made and the villain of the piece, one felt, was not only the pitch. Nor was Laker's brilliant exploitation of it wholly responsible for what happened. Psychology played its part; for the batsmen, once the storm had broken, made little effort to seek an answer to England's spin, and in thinking there was not one they were wrong. It was a nasty wicket certainly; but had not England scored freely on it? And the fact, too, that Lock bowled 22 overs for only one wicket and that between them Lock and Laker toiled for 18 overs before they struck at all shows that it was far from impossible. The ball turned, sometimes more quickly than another, but generally it came through at an even height. A side of well-organized English batsmen accustomed to the ball deviating might have made 250 against Laker and Lock. Several Huttons, Mays, and Baileys might have made more. But Australia, although they have had lessons on their tour, knew not what it was all about and this, the fact that England were crushing them in such conditions, must have taken some of the gilt from England's gingerbread.

There is no doubt that this is a bad pitch for a five-day Test match and the Australians may even feel that it is an unfair one. Yet in one's own mind one is sure that the groundsman did not know what, as it were, was coming out of the hat. It so happens that when it comes to spinning a way to victory Australia are left far behind, and yesterday morning, when Benaud made an occasional ball bite, one knew that Laker and Lock would in all likelihood have the winning of the match in their power. Statham and Bailey had no chance of doing much, and when Australia began their first innings these two bowled only as a formality.

After 40 minutes Laker replaced Bailey, and Lock Statham, but not until they changed ends half an hour later was the innings hurled into confusion. Then the disasters came thick and fast, and one must recall them as they occurred. At 48

McDonald, pushing forward to Laker, was caught off the inside edge of his bat at backward short leg, and three balls later Harvey was bowled by what to him was a beastly leg break. At this moment of crisis young Craig came out to play his first Test innings against England, and the crowd received him more warmly than anyone else so far during the match.

But Craig needed more than the moral support of cricket lovers and understanding mothers, and although he looked, as he always does, neat and full of talent, this was more than he could cope with. He was undefeated, it is true, at tea, but he was leg-before playing back to an off-break in the second over afterwards. Before that, Burke, pushing forward at Lock, had been nicely caught by Cowdrey low to his right at slip and at the same score Mackay, his bat dangling like a lifeless pendulum, was caught in the gully. Oakman stooped in the manner of a giraffe for this low catch and he did the same, five minutes later, to catch Miller in Laker's leg trap.

A drive for 6 by Miller had been a lone defiant stroke. Indeed this and a cover shot by Archer stood like standards in Australia's surrender. But Archer soon flung his bat wildly at Laker, Benaud was caught on the boundary, and, to finish things off, Laker bowled Maddocks and Johnson in the same over. Laker returned happy in his triumph, Johnson was a picture of dejection and he must have had the sympathy of many.

The wicket had not suddenly deteriorated as the course of the innings might suggest. Rather had Australia's spirit been broken by Laker, and in 10 minutes they were out there struggling again. They did so in fact with some success, for in the 55 minutes left they lost only Harvey. McDonald had just retired with temporary knee trouble and Harvey hammered his first ball, a full pitch from Laker, straight to Cowdrey standing 20 yards out in the direction of mid-wicket. Poor Harvey tossed his bat in the air; he had completed a pair of spectacles all in four balls and within an hour. Perhaps this is a record of some sort. But the record that mattered was Laker's and now he stands to break several more today.

*August 1.* This match will always be talked about as much as any of the 171 played between England and Australia before, if not only because of Laker's analysis but also because there arose on the second day a widespread controversy over the condition of the pitch. Then the ball spun from dry turf. Yesterday it did so after persistent rain and the batsmen's task grew progressively harder with the passing of time. Yet for a long while it seemed that the grass would not dry sufficiently or quickly enough for England to win and as nothing was foregone the play was full of tension. One knew that the turn would not have to be ridiculously awkward for England's purpose and during the long partnership between Craig and McDonald the batting was so good that the art was made to seem perfectly feasible. As soon as Craig was out, it was made at times to look impossible. In reality it was somewhere between the two when the game finally hurried to its conclusion. [...]

Play was begun only 10 minutes late, although it had rained heavily through the night until 5 o'clock, and before luncheon the pitch was too saturated to be of any use to anyone. May explored every move. He began with Bailey, who was inclined to bowl too short, and later he gave Oakman a turn. Statham, too, tried with the new ball to hammer some life from the pitch. But of course the attack was based primarily on Laker and Lock, and what they wanted most of all was some sunshine to dry the turf. There was a stiff wind, which sent the many lowering clouds scudding over the ground, but that was not enough, and towards the end of the morning some blue sky began to appear. And with it the pitch perked up and the ball showed signs of misbehaving.

At luncheon McDonald and Craig were still together. They had then added only 59, but the important thing was that they had each been batting for more than four hours. Ahead of them stretched another four and only 15 minutes of these had ticked away when Laker struck his first blow. Craig, still showing a full sense of duty after 259 minutes, played back where he might have been better advised to go forward, and was leg-before. Several other Australians were to do the same and the departure of Craig revealed a hollow middle to Australia's innings. Mackay splashed about in deep water until he sank pushing forward at Laker and being caught off the edge of the bat at second slip. Miller undermined himself, by choosing to take everything he could on the pads. One has never seen him so completely dispossessed and he was out at 130 lunging myopically at a ball he might have made into a full pitch. Archer at once was caught by the middle of three backward short legs playing back to Laker and the day was not yet half run. The sun, too, was now blessing the scene, the threat of showers was fading and as Laker's spin quickened it seemed that there might be a collapse of the kind that had been witnessed on Friday.

Perhaps if Benaud had fallen at once there would have been, for Mackay, Miller, and Archer had not scored a run between them and between 25 past two and five to three four wickets had gone for 16 runs. But McDonald stood immensely determined amid this crumbling world, and now Benaud stayed with him until tea. That was for 80 minutes, and it began to seem again as though England might be thwarted. Benaud carried gamesmanship almost to an extreme by asking for guard in every over, and slowly and deliberately taking a botanical interest in the pitch after every ball. It is fair enough to repair each divot mark which the ball makes, but Benaud's way of doing it irritated the crowd, just as his admirable powers of resistance must have worried England.

When the final two hours of the evening started, whichever side was to win still had a long way to go. Someone was going to be denied and the likelihood that it would be Australia increased when McDonald's monumental vigil of 337 minutes was ended by the second ball after tea. He pushed forward at an off-break and Oakman at backward short leg took his fifth catch of the match. The next two balls from Laker must have settled any doubts that had been sown in English minds. Both of them turned viciously and now it was only a matter of time and a question of whether Laker could take the last three wickets himself.

4

Sporting News

**LAKER'S SUPREME PART IN RETAINING THE ASHES**

**ALL TEN AUSTRALIAN WICKETS AND 19 IN MATCH**

**From Our Cricket Correspondent**

England won the fourth Test match against Australia at Old Trafford yesterday by an innings and 170 runs, so retaining the Ashes, and Laker made the achievement possible by taking all 10 wickets in Australia's second innings. Either feat is notable enough; but when one leads to the other a mockery is made of all laws of probability. Last Friday pitch perked up and the ball showed signs of misbehaving.

At luncheon McDonald and Craig were still together. They had then added only 59, but the important thing was that they had each been batting for more than four hours. Ahead of them stretched another four and only 15 minutes of these had ticked away when Laker struck his first blow. Craig, still showing a full sense of duty after 259 minutes, played back where

*Jim Laker's record-breaking feat at Old Trafford was a sensation*

This was suddenly a fabulous possibility, and three-quarters of an hour later it was an accomplished deed. First Benaud was forced back on to his stumps and bowled by a generously flighted off-break, then Lindwall was snapped up in the leg trap, and finally Maddocks was trapped leg-before. Australia were beaten, and in a trice the crowd flooded the ground, there were smiles and handshakes, and the hero jogged off the field as though nothing very much had happened. Close behind him was May, who could feel justly proud at having led England to the Ashes at his first attempt. His splendid efforts must not be overlooked, but this now was Laker's hour, and here to end with and for all time are his figures. In Australia's second innings he took 10 for 53, in the match 19 for 90 in 68 overs, and yesterday eight for 26 in 36 faultless overs. Surely there may never again be anything like it.

---

## JIM LAKER AND TONY LOCK

### FIFTH TEST, THE OVAL, 1953

GEOFFREY GREEN,
CRICKET CORRESPONDENT

*August 19.* That set the stage for an afternoon of upheaval. There is no need to decorate the truth. All that followed was no dream. It was hard reality, an age of exploration and discovery as the expansive crowd sat agog, thrilled by the quick current of a new life. In a word, Australia crumpled up before spin on a dusty surface made for men like Lock and Laker, who took nine wickets between them.

But here one fact requires some clarification. The reason Bailey and his lesser henchmen were able to live through the long morning, adding 71 runs for their last three wickets, was that the sharp showers of early dawn had helped lay the dust and cool the fiend's brow over a vital period. In this period the left-handed Johnston, at slower spinning pace, Australia's most suitable weapon for the occasion, was denied a maximum support, though even he was a character, through force of circumstances, called upon to play a makeshift part. He is not the true left-hand spinner of tradition. Thus Australia's attack was largely bereft.

As the day's sun took its warming effect, the pitch later on cried out with open arms to be caressed and used to the full. England were able to answer the call after only two nominal overs each by Trueman and Bedser. Here, in fact, was virtue at last. With the score 19 and Hassett and Morris temporarily on a calm sea, Laker appeared at the Vauxhall end. In his first over he beat Hassett's back stroke with a vicious off-break to gain an l.-b.-w. appeal. Australia 23 for one, their most dependable man, their captain, gone, and still eight behind. Now was the value of Bailey's earlier effort with the bat really to be measured as Laker and Lock began to make the ball turn and fizz.

That was the beginning of Australia's slide down the hill. A crisis clearly was at hand, but it was not reached until a quarter-past three when, with Morris already showing signs of attack as the only antidote, the score had reached 59 for one. Yet within the next quarter of an hour the heart was torn out of the innings as Hole, Harvey, Miller and Morris fell to the spin of Lock and Laker in 16 balls for two runs. In a twinkling Australia had gone from 59 for one to 61 for five. Here was Australian batting shown up in all its nakedness on a turning wicket. Poor technique and stabs and prods were punished to the full.

## FIRST TEST, TRENT BRIDGE, 1956

JOHN WOODCOCK,
CRICKET CORRESPONDENT

*June 12.* There ensued the most significant period of the day. Lock and Laker were on the rampage, the batsmen were being tortured almost as much by their own apprehensions as the material horrors of the pitch, and for 20 minutes, with the total lodged at 36, there was even a possibility that Australia might not get the 68 they needed to avoid following on. For a while Archer looked as though he might be out any ball. Twice he nearly played on, the jaws of Laker's short legs were wide open with anticipation, and Lock's leg-breaks were fizzing past the bat. Harvey, too, must have been perilously near to being leg-before to Lock. There was no escaping it, Australia were in dire distress.

## THIRD TEST, HEADINGLEY, 1956

JOHN WOODCOCK,
CRICKET CORRESPONDENT

*July 14.* When May called up Laker at 10 past four the close of play score seemed utterly improbable. Trueman, after capturing his one wicket, had bowled fast but not well, and Burke and Harvey had seemed to be at home. Even when Burke cocked up Lock's first ball to where a forward short leg would have been, the cloud on Australia's horizon seemed little bigger than a man's hand. Yet in an hour it hung heavily over the innings.

At five to five the score was 38 for one, when Lock joined Laker in attack, and at once the collapse began. At 40 Harvey glanced Lock's sixth ball to backward short leg, where Trueman took a straightforward catch; at 59 Burge played back once too often to a good length ball from Laker and was leg before; and in the next over Burke, who had batted admirably, was leg-before playing back to Lock's in-swinger.

Mackay by this time was trying rather pathetically to unravel the mysteries of Laker. His contortions were very strange, and it always seemed only a matter of minutes before he gave gully a catch as he lunged at a leg-break. He did so via his pad at 63, and then Archer, after one defiant lofted drive, was bowled trying to cut an off-break and hearing the ball clip his off-bail. Five wickets had fallen in 75 minutes while Australia were adding 30 runs, and 10 minutes later Miller and Benaud thankfully withdrew to the safety of the pavilion.

Lock and Laker had struck as few others could have done. From the time in his opening over, when Laker filled Burke's mind with apprehension, Australia had been in constant danger, and if England can now enforce the follow-on there must be a chance that in quite a short time the Surrey pair will complete their destruction.

# HAROLD LARWOOD

## FIRST TEST, BRISBANE, EXHIBITION GROUND, 1928–29

FIRMIN MCKINNON

*December 4.* While Australia were occupying less than an hour and a half in completing a very doleful innings every one was interested to see how Larwood would follow up his astounding bowling of Saturday. He duly rose to the occasion, dismissed three more men, and with his record of six wickets for 32 runs accomplished, in the conditions, probably the finest performance ever achieved by an English fast bowler in Test matches in Australia. He maintained a great pace, and made the ball come off the pitch very fast, so that at no time did anyone play him with anything like the confidence that Hendren had exhibited in dealing with Gregory. Chapman managed his bowling with great judgment, giving Larwood just the requisite spells of rest required, so that he was always fresh in an innings that lasted, less than two hours and a half.

## FIRST TEST, SYDNEY, 1932–33

DELAMORE MCCAY

*December 7.* Larwood was slightly troubled by a strain to his left side, and left the field for plaster. But he stuck to his task in great style and maintained a great pace. He must be given credit for a great bowling performance which has won the game for England. It would be a tragedy if he should break down, but this is not suggested. The Australians were uncomfortable to the leg theory, it being most awkward to get runs off Larwood when he was bowling to his leg field.

*Fresh home from Australia and anointed as a national hero, Harold Larwood passes on advice to some starstruck youngsters in 1933*

R.B. VINCENT,
CRICKET CORRESPONDENT

*December 8.* In recent years Test matches in Australia have resolved themselves into a prolonged trial of endurance between two sets of batsmen, with the unfortunate bowler, bowl he never so well, merely providing an incidental name in the scoring book when, at long last, a batsman faltered and got out. Succeeding editions of evening papers were bought to learn to what terrific heights individual and collective scores had risen. But now that suddenly a bowler, Larwood, has come into his own, and has dominated the play, with the support of the others, Voce and Hammond in particular, we find that the full force of attack has returned to its proper place in cricket. There has been nothing like this seen in Australia since the days of F.R. Foster and Barnes in 1911–1912, and at once Test match cricket has awakened from the sloth of the last 10 years and is again a glorious game.

### FOURTH TEST, BRISBANE, 1932–33

DELAMORE MCCAY

*February 13.* Larwood, finding a better length, continued to bowl at a great pace, and his efforts were rewarded when he got Bradman's wicket at 264. Bradman, who had never been comfortable when facing Larwood today, played over an extra fast ball in Larwood's third over and turned round to see his leg-stump knocked back. Bradman, who was almost timid in his inability to play the ball on the leg side, was at the wicket 31 minutes while adding five to his overnight score.

*February 15.* Larwood was brought on again at 55. Bradman twice hit him through the cordon of fieldsmen on the leg side. He frequently drew away to leg, leaving his wicket unprotected, and hit several balls cleverly to the off. He also pulled to leg with such force that Larwood had to set his fieldsman deeper. Bradman stepped away to cut the last ball of Larwood's ninth over, and when he failed to get hold of it properly Mitchell at deep point made a splendid catch.

## ALFRED LYTTELTON

### THIRD TEST, THE OVAL, 1884

*August 13.* So completely was the English bowling mastered at Kennington Oval yesterday and Monday that every member of the team was tried. It was when the score stood at 532 for six wickets, however, that Mr Lyttelton, who had been tried overnight, went on again with lobs and brought about the rapid downfall of the remaining four batsmen. His position as wicket-keeper was occupied by Dr Grace. The first ball Mr Lyttelton sent down had the desired effect, Mr Midwinter being well caught at the wicket amid tremendous applause. Following up this success the renowned wicket-keeper got rid of Mr Blackham, leg-before-wicket, at 545, and bowled Mr Spofforth at 409, while at 551 Mr Boyle was caught from a delivery of the same bowler. Only eight runs had been scored from his bowling.

## BRIAN STATHAM

### SECOND TEST, SYDNEY, 1954–55

JOHN WOODCOCK,
CRICKET CORRESPONDENT

*December 22.* Australia needed 223 to win, there were 25 minutes to go before tea, and soon Statham, as though determined to win the match alone, was letting fly a tremendous opening over. Favell nearly played the first ball on, and all Sydney and most of the English team appealed for leg-before against him off the second. The fifth was a fierce, two-handed catch to Edrich at first slip which went for two runs, and the eighth was a snick to fine leg for 4. For the bowler it was a cruel over, and he seemed to be showing the effects of the second. But with the sixth ball of his third, just before tea and when 27 had come in 25 minutes, he had Morris leg-before after beating him four times in the preceding five balls. It was a magnificent piece of fast bowling and ended an unbelievably irresponsible innings from Australia's captain, whose batting in the face of such hostility became completely disorganized.

*David Sheppard, Reg Simpson and Trevor Bailey aboard the Stratheden, ready for the long voyage to Australia for the 1950–51 series*

## GRAEME SWANN

### FOURTH TEST, MELBOURNE, 2010–11

MIKE ATHERTON,
CHIEF CRICKET CORRESPONDENT

*December 29.* Swann's spell from the Great Southern Stand End was mesmeric, 22 overs' worth, fully half of them maidens, and this on a pitch with precious little wear and tear and therefore next to no turn. But the off spinner is a master of his art and he varied his pace and angle of attack so that he conceded only 23 runs in all and caused continual problems for all Australia's batsmen. They could not get him away, nor did they look secure in keeping him out, even though he took only the one wicket, that of Michael Clarke.

## FRED TRUEMAN

### THIRD TEST, HEADINGLEY, 1961

JOHN WOODCOCK,
CRICKET CORRESPONDENT

*July 7.* At tea Harvey had made 66, O'Neill 27, but Trueman, as soon as he got the new ball in his hands, had

O'Neill caught by Cowdrey in the gully. O'Neill reached defensively forward and Cowdrey took the catch low down and two-handed. This was no more than a pleasant surprise, but an even richer prize came England's way in Trueman's next over when Harvey was beautifully caught by Lock. The ball skimmed off the inside edge as Harvey pushed out on the leg-side and Lock swooped to his left to make the catch.

Australia now were 192 for four with Mackay emerging instead of Simpson. The next excitement was a hot return chance to Trueman from Burge which went to ground, followed shortly by Burge's departure. This was another bootlace catch by Cowdrey, taken with complete economy of effort, Jackson being the bowler. Trueman's third victim came in his fourth over with the new ball. Simpson being leg before as he pushed tentatively forward. That was 203 for six, with the crowd of 20,000 on their feet as their hero was surrounded by his colleagues.

Without a run added Mackay was leg before to a shooter from Jackson and at 204 Benaud was bowled first ball by Trueman. Australia's captain stayed only long enough to give the pitch a somewhat sour and penetrating stare. Grout, on the other hand, survived for 10 minutes before being caught by Murray off Trueman as he made to drive. Trueman at that time had taken five for 16 in six overs with the new ball and Australia had lost seven wickets for 21 runs in 50 minutes.

*July 10.* As Trueman returned, Australia, with eight wickets left were 37 on and moving resolutely forward. At that moment the match was desperately close, and yet from May's decision to recall Trueman sprang destiny.

All through the day pace for pace's sake bad been worth little. However quickly the ball travelled through the air it came slowly off the ground, so that Trueman was prompted to shorten his run and reduce his speed. Control was guaranteed this way and there was always the pitch to help in providing the unexpected. Thus it was that the match reached its explosive climax, with Trueman achieving a spell of bowling beyond his wildest hopes and even more conclusive than on Thursday. In 24 balls between 3.50 and the tea interval he took the wickets of O'Neill, Harvey, Simpson, Benaud, and Mackay without conceding a run. In 25 minutes all the sweat and toil of one side was rewarded, all the ambitions of another were dashed, by a spell of destruction seldom equalled by an Englishman against Australia.

The first Australian to fall was Harvey, caught in the covers off a ball that stopped and lifted. This was Trueman's third ball, and in the next over from Allen Burge was leg before to a nasty off-break. Without a run added, O'Neill scooped Trueman to Cowdrey at close short leg and at 105 Simpson was utterly bowled by Trueman. At 109 Benaud completed a 'pair', and off the last ball before tea Mackay was caught by Murray. Australia had plunged from 99 for two to 109 for eight, and never did a cricketer get a greater reception than Trueman from his Yorkshire crowd.

Twenty minutes after tea Australia were all out, the innings being ended by a brilliant diving catch at second slip by Cowdrey. Davidson was the batsman and like O'Neill earlier he waited for the umpire to confirm that he was out. Trueman in the match had taken 11 for 88 and in good time before the close England secured their victory.

## DEREK UNDERWOOD

### FIFTH TEST, THE OVAL, 1968

JOHN WOODCOCK,
CRICKET CORRESPONDENT

*August 28.* There were 40 minutes to go when Illingworth began what seemed like just another over from the Vauxhall end. The draw by then had been accepted as inevitable. Australia had five wickets still in hand. Yet within moments we were involved in a climax no less desperate than that at Georgetown earlier this year when England themselves were in a corner. In this over from Illingworth, Inverarity survived a tumbling chance to Dexter, one of 10 vultures perched round the bat. The next ball fizzed past the shoulder of Inverarity's bat to show that the anaesthetizing effect of the rain was wearing off.

In the next over, from D'Oliveira, Jarman, playing no stroke, was bowled, the ball just trimming the off bail. Underwood replaced D'Oliveira at the pavilion end, and in his first over he took the wickets of Mallett and McKenzie. Mallett, Monday's hero, prodded a catch to Brown, fielding forward of the bat as one of five short legs. Five balls later, Brown, in the same position, dived forward to catch McKenzie, a fine left-handed effort scooped off the very pitch itself.

There were 27 minutes left when Gleeson made his way in, walking at a sporting pace. When Underwood bowled him, there were 12 minutes to go; when Connolly, the last man, took guard, there were 10. There was a hush across the ground. Connolly survived the last ball of Underwood's over. In the

*A great partnership reunited – when Fred Trueman heard of Brian Statham's financial difficulties in 1989 he organised two fundraising dinners*

next over from Illingworth, Inverarity took a single off the fourth ball and Connolly played the last two with the whole world, it must have seemed, against him.

At five minutes to six, off the third ball of the next over, Inverarity was leg-before, offering no stroke to Underwood. The fateful decision was umpire Elliott's; the crowd surged once more across the Oval with an English victory to cheer. It was not as historic a moment as 1926 or 1953, when the Ashes were regained. Even so, it was one to savour.

## HEDLEY VERITY

### THIRD TEST, ADELAIDE, 1932–33

E.W. PARISH

*January 19.* Another big hit in Verity's next over resulted in a six over the on-boundary. Verity, however, had lured Bradman into a false sense of security. Bradman tried a big hit off the next ball, failed to time it properly, and only succeeded in returning the ball to the bowler, who made a fine catch.

### SECOND TEST, LORD'S, 1934

R.B. VINCENT,
CRICKET CORRESPONDENT

*June 26.* No two opinions will agree on the exact state of the pitch at Lord's yesterday. It was inclined to pop in the morning; after an hour's play it became easier; and in the afternoon, playing appreciably faster, it took spin much more to the bowler's fancy. Certainly it was never anything approaching to a sticky wicket, and Verity, the great and undisputed hero of the match, had all the time to make the Australian batsmen believe that it was just a little more unkind than in fact it really was.

Helped as he was by a queer lack of confidence among the Australians, to whom the very sight of sawdust may suggest unknown horrors, Verity's achievement must be written down as one of the greatest in the whole story of Test match cricket. In the first innings he took seven wickets for 61 runs in 36 overs, and in the second innings eight wickets for 43 runs in 22 overs. Only one bowler before has taken 15 wickets in a match between England and Australia, W. Rhodes at Melbourne in the tour of 1903–1904.

For the greater part of the day yesterday he bowled from the Pavilion end with three slips to the right-handed batsmen and three short-legs to Darling and Bromley, and during all this time one saw only one ball which was pitched not of the length he meant. Continually he made the batsman play to the ball, whether going with his arm, or coming back to offer a catch to Hammond at third slip and Hendren at silly mid-off. It was indeed a great bowling performance, a left-handed bowler taking just the slight chance that was offered him.

It may sound unkind to the Australians, and perhaps a trifle ungenerous to Verity, but, if the truth must be told, the batting was a little feeble. Woodfull in the second innings, by putting the whole of his body between the pitch of the ball and the stumps, did his noble utmost to keep one end intact, and Chipperfield played two gallant innings, but the Australians themselves would be the first to try to forget some of the meagre strokes that were offered. No one who saw it can ever forget the crude manner in which the great Bradman gave his wicket away when so much depended upon him. For all that, bad strokes or not, it was a great victory for England, and now all is again to be played for. [...]

Verity can always make the ball stand up, and it was therefore not surprising to see him pack the slips, with Hammond moved first from short to second, and then second to third slip. [...]

O'Reilly afterwards did his utmost to allow Chipperfield to make the runs, but at 284 he let loose at a well-pitched-up ball, missed it, and was bowled. Wall, without a run added, was leg-before-wicket, and so Australia followed on 156 runs behind.

... it was not long before Wyatt showed the full force of his attack by putting Verity on at the Pavilion end with Hammond at the other to relieve a patently tiring Bowes. McCabe twice in one over from Verity was lucky to escape being caught in the slips, and Woodfull once put the edge of his bat at the last moment to a ball from Hammond which might have hit his middle stump, but which went for four runs.

Verity, even when bowling to McCabe, was now well on top, and the turn of the game came when McCabe drove a ball hard at Hendren at silly mid-off. The catch was held, and the bottom was knocked out of Australia's batting. Bradman, rather in the manner of the Bradman of 1930, played some workmanlike strokes until, with the score at 57, he suddenly perpetrated the worst stroke he has ever made in his life. He slashed, crooked bat, against the break to Verity, and, skying the ball, was caught by the wicketkeeper. Darling was all but bowled by the first ball he received from Verity, who by now was merely waiting for wickets, and at 94 the Australians suffered their final blow when Woodfull, playing back to a leg-break, was caught at extra slip. He had not made many impressive strokes, but so long as he was there Australia was alive.

Darling at 94 was bowled by Hammond, who most certainly had deserved a wicket, and one run later Verity took a good catch off his own bowling, high and to the right, to get rid of Bromley. Then the cheering broke out full-hearted and the wickets fell accordingly. Oldfield, who might have been a nuisance, was leg-before-wicket: Grimmett, who also can be tiresome, was caught at third slip from the first ball he had; and Chipperfield, who had had a nasty blow from Hammond, was caught at first slip.

Verity was bowling to batsmen whom he knew he could get out, and the end came when Hendren, rolling on his back, caught Wall close in under his bat.

## SECOND TEST, LORD'S, 1938

R.B. VINCENT,
CRICKET CORRESPONDENT

*June 27.* Verity was put on to check Bradman's exuberance, but Bradman's answer was two quick steps down the wicket to make the ball a half-volley. Verity had two slips to Bradman, hoping for a mistake to the leg break, but the 100 was up in 90 minutes and Brown was by then firmly established. Suddenly the unbelievable happened: Bradman dragged a ball well wide of the off stump from Verity on to his stumps and the crowd, having recovered from their first moment of astonishment, roared with delight. Some, maybe, were genuinely sorry, for they had travelled far to see Bradman bat.

## JOHNNY WARDLE

### FIFTH TEST, SYDNEY, 1954–55

JOHN WOODCOCK,
CRICKET CORRESPONDENT

*March 4.* The man to tie Australia into all sorts of knots was Wardle. He wheeled away from the 'Hill' end for more than four hours with a catholic collection of orthodox left-arm leg-breaks, googlies and Chinamen, all thrown well into the air. Wardle, it is true, seldom lets a Test match go by without making a useful contribution of one sort or another, but by and large his bowling in Australia has lacked the flight or the imagination to trouble the better batsmen. Nor has he been able to do more than straighten his ordinary leg-break.

Between leaving Perth and arriving here for the recent state match he dismissed three batsmen who went in before number seven in the order in first class matches. These figures must reflect a certain harmlessness, although generally he has been used in a defensive capacity. Today he experimented widely with the unorthodox, and looked an altogether different bowler. The pitch was not unsympathetic to genuine spin, and from McDonald to Lindwall the Australians stood in their creases and groped myopically whenever Wardle turned his wrist over. Having looked bad against speed in the last three Tests they now looked little better against spin, and one wondered what such cricketers as Sir Donald Bradman, S.J. McCabe, and A.F. Kippax, all of whom were watching or listening to the match, must have been thinking of it all. This was how Englishmen used to play S. Ramadhin in 1950, and it must be a long time since an Australian side has been made to look so shabby and inept as has this one these past three days.

Sporting

OW ENGLAND KEPT THE ASHES

VO GREAT HEARTS OVERTHROW AUSTRALIA

England beat Australia by five wickets in the fourth Test match at elaide yesterday and so, gaining a lead of three matches to one in the ries, have retained the Ashes. In an interview after the match L. Hutton, e England captain, paid a tribute to the younger members of the side. Much of the credit, he thought, should go to J. B. Statham, F. H. Tyson, M. C. Cowdrey and P. B. H. May, together with the wicket-keeper, T. G. Evans.

From Our Special Correspondent

ADELAIDE, FEB. 2

Many years from now young Cowdrey will point to his broken nose and tell boys yet unborn that he was at Adelaide on February 2, 1955, when England won the Test match and kept the Ashes. And the boys will think him wondrous lucky. A ma... should dip his pen in blood to write ... is day. Let no one talk and writ... ket and explain away the ... ms more fit for ... al in dull

the catch. (We asked Hutton afterwards what he thought of Miller's bowling. Hutton thought Miller ought to concentrate much more on batting.) England 10 for 2. In comes the battered Cowdrey. Miller hits him twice running on the pads and appeals, and everybody here who isn't English appeals too. What a man is Miller. He comes in from a shortish run, loose of limb like an African, hair streaming, and as he pulls up the hair goes on and falls about his face.

Meanwhile May has begun driving, and Johnson has gone from mid-off to square-leg. For Cowdrey Miller brings fine-leg up to third slip, and Cowdrey cover drives classically for 4. Miller heaves his shoulders over even faster, and Cowdrey is taken by Archer at first-slip. England 18 for 3. Four Meteor jets fly over at 200ft.; they look and sound quite tame beside this wild man ... His figures now are 3 overs, no ... 2 runs, 3 wickets.

ngland all too obliging ... eaches new heights of greatnes

ia v England

...artin-Jenkins ...orrespondent

One that got away: Gilchrist misses a stumping chance off Warne to give Pietersen an extra life, but it was to make little difference

High five: Warne acknowledges the Melbourne crowd after his haul ripped the heart out of England's fragile batting

...egendary accuracy and a lush outfield, they ran poorly between the wickets, chose the wrong balls to try to hit in the air and failed to justify the decision to bat.

"We didn't expect conditions to change dramatically over the first day and a half," Strauss said, "but it seamed about more than we expected." It did so slowly but Glenn McGrath, Stuart Clark and Brett Lee all got enough past the bat to suggest that the wrong option had been taken.

Australia missed two catches, two clear run-out opportunities and a gaping stumping, but still bowled England out for 159 after they had been 101 for two. Very few Test matches are won after such a start. All of Warne's wickets were taken by flight and dip, as batsmen spied what they believed to be boundary opportunities. Only Kevin Pietersen got anywhere near the boundary as he attempted to drive Warne straight for six, but by now he was, as usual, batting with the tail.

Even he needed 70 balls for 21 runs, having come close to running out Andrew Flintoff for six as, for the third Test in succession, he attempted a ridiculous single in order to get off the mark. He had only made four when he also survived a simple stumping chance offered to Adam Gilchrist after charging Warne and missing.

England, we all know, have too long a tail, but tweaking it made no difference. Matthew Hoggard is back where he started, No 11, pushing Monty Panesar and Stephen Harmison up a place each, which reflects their various abilities with the bat. It is higher up, however, that the balance is wrong. Ed Joyce or Jamie Dalrymple should have played six, but Chris Read for Geraint Jones was the only change.

As the best player in the team, Pietersen needs to bat at four. Since Paul Collingwood shared the only partnership of any substance with Strauss — 57 for the third wicket — it may appear that England's strategy, to keep him away from the new ball, had worked again, but to have Pietersen batting with the tail repeatedly is not satisfactory. In any case Collingwood might have been leg-before to Clark for nought, one of four apparently plumb leg-before decisions turned down by Rudi Koertzen.

Panesar was the other, ... ly out to Warne before ... out instead, but it was ... turned down when ... Hayden was hit on ... front of the stu... gard, the first ... the other whe... more signif... captain's ... when Ju... ball ... seco...

Australia's recent practice of not using a nightwatchman.

Ponting said that Australia, too, would have chosen to bat first, but it was one of those tosses that either captain would prefer to have lost. Play was delayed by rain for half an hour and only 16 overs were bowled before an early lunch was taken. Alastair Cook

Sporting News

ENGLAND HAVE LAST WORD

THREE YEOMEN FOIL AUSTRALIA

GREAT STAND BY WATSON AND BAILEY

FROM OUR CRICKET CORRESPONDENT

Out of darkness, through fire into light. Thus did England yesterday rise like some Phoenix from the ashes of apparent defeat to save the second Test match at Lord's and so gain a ... draw against Australia with ... seven wickets, ... original aim fo...

The age of ... yet past, nor c... cany scarce f... dramatic and ... a match alrea... But within t... longest and ... of a match it... that last spa... back with le... yeomen of ... nearly the ...

The yeom... were Watso... greatest of ... Yorkshirem... order, was ... rearguard ... twentieth ...

36 TUESDAY AUGUST 1 1989

THE TIMES

First published 1785

England's abject surrender marks new low in series

By Alan Lee, Cricket Correspondent

Inglorious procession at Old Trafford

10-1: Curtis c Boon b Alderman 0

25-2: Robinson lbw b Lawson 12

27-3: Smith c Healy b Alderman 3

28-4: Gooch c Alderman b Lawson 13

38-5: Botham lbw b Alderman 4

59-6: Gower c Marsh b Lawson 15

SCOREBOARD FROM OLD TRAFFORD

ENGLAND

First innings

AUSTRALIA

First innings

Gower unfairly blamed for failings of others

Simon Barnes

Border rewarded for hard labour

By John Woodcock

Only two men so far decline

By Alan Lee

THE F...

THE HUNDRED UP.—Barnett scoring a four boundary to the off ... Trent Bridge yesterday. O'Reilly is the bowler and Hutton is at the ...

...iant leap

for proud S...

5.37 343-9 S Clark c Cook b Harmison 0

P Siddle c Flintoff b Harmison 10

ponting run out (Flintoff) 66

1 S Katich lbw b

SPOR...

Cricket

Was this English ... most desperate ...

...ding

night issued a dramatic ... Union to make a positive ... He said that unless the ... prepared to help to achieve an ... strategic arms limitations, he would ... additional funds of more than ... new nuclear

# GREAT BOWLING: AUSTRALIA

THE TIMES SATURDAY JUNE 11 1938

H: A GOOD BEGINNING BY ENGLAND

4

Sporting News

LAKER'S SUPREME PART IN RETAINING THE ASHES

ALL TEN AUSTRALIAN WICKETS AND 19 IN MATCH

From Our Cricket Correspondent

pitch perked up and the ball showed signs of misbehaving.

At luncheon McDonald and Craig were still together. They had then added only 59, but the important thing was that they had each been batting for more than four hours. Ahead of them stretched another four and only 15 minutes of these had ticked away when Laker stru

THE TIMES

LOCOMEN'S BAN BOUND CAUSE GREATER ON TODAY

HOW THE AUSTRALIANS WERE SKITTLED OUT AT LORD'S

Gaullists may get back with clear majority

Inquiry over bank chief's salary

Police alerted by strike ship

Railways must act alone, Marsh says

13 die in S rail crash

mped aiming to hit Mallett over the hill, and the end draws nearer.

dismally surrender Ashes

TEST MATCH

BRADMAN 309 NOT OUT

ALL RECORDS BROKEN

*The Third Test Match between England and Australia was begun at Leeds yesterday. A. P. F. Chapman, for once, lost the toss and Australia went in to bat on a perfect batsman's wicket. By the end of the day they had scored 458 runs for the loss of three wickets and D. G. Brad*

## JASON GILLESPIE

### FOURTH TEST, HEADINGLEY, 1997

SIMON WILDE

*July 26.* Exactly who is Jason Gillespie? That is the question which the England players were privately asking themselves after they had felt the heat of another of his 'hot streaks' yesterday. It was Gillespie, remember, who triggered their second-innings collapse at Old Trafford, when he claimed the wickets of Atherton, Hussain and Butcher in the space of 20 minutes.

*Jason Gillespie devastated England with seven for 37 at Headingley in 1997. Darren Gough becomes another victim*

Whoever he is, he bowls fast and very well. In taking six wickets in the space of 47 balls yesterday morning he reaped the sort of havoc of which every fast bowler dreams but few achieve at Test level. Spurred by claiming the wicket of Headley, the nightwatchman, with his first ball of the day, he upped his pace and finished with the best figures achieved for Australia at Headingley.

Before yesterday, the best-known thing about Gillespie was his spectacular unwillingness to communicate. He rarely gives interviews and even those who spend time close to him have failed to melt the ice. 'He's either very simple or very complex,' an Australian journalist, who is following the tour, said. 'We've never managed to find out which.'

## JOHN GLEESON

### FIRST TEST, OLD TRAFFORD, 1972

JACK FINGLETON

*June 9.* Gleeson bowled the first over after tea and it was one of the most remarkable seen in many a Test day. In it, he thrice beat Edrich completely and also had him dropped by Stackpole at first slip. Edrich's composure deserted him. He had several long mid-pitch talks with D'Oliveira and obviously it was decided D'Oliveira would keep Gleeson.

Gleeson gets the credit from me for Edrich's run out. He had scattered Edrich's aplomb and it was a bad call by Edrich that led to his run out.

## CLARRIE GRIMMETT

### FIRST TEST, TRENT BRIDGE, 1930

R.B. VINCENT,
CRICKET CORRESPONDENT

*June 14.* The first day of the first Test match has left all the honours with the Australians, and with C.V. Grimmett in particular. Rain held up play for a time in the afternoon, but that England at the end of the day had scored only 241 runs for the loss of eight wickets was in the main due to Grimmett's truly wonderful bowling before the luncheon interval, when the conditions were all in favour of the team who had first use of a beautiful pitch. [...]

Bad light after luncheon and a long pause afterwards (while the crowd pondered on the miseries of 1926) were only incidental to a day's cricket in which the glory lay in Grimmett's bowling. He was called upon when only 13 runs had been scored, and from that moment he controlled the game. Hobbs he kept quiet without trying any pranks, and to the others he offered just the ball to which they would play the false stroke. [...]

Hammond played two strokes, each for 4, one forced off his body to the on and one through the covers, before Grimmett produced his great achievement of the morning and, in fact, of the day. He first bowled one through with top spin, which had Hammond out leg-before-wicket, and he then bowled a ball of which anyone might dream – a googly to a left-hander of such perfect length that Woolley had to lean out to it and, quite properly, was stumped. The Australians were then quite naturally chuckling with joy, and Hendren, who was never at his ease, stayed for only a very short duel with Grimmett, who made him run up and down the pitch before he bowled him.

### SECOND TEST, LORD'S, 1930

R.B. VINCENT,
CRICKET CORRESPONDENT

*July 1.* 'Trouble began when Grimmett came on as first change,' is a phrase kept permanently in type in the offices of all respectable newspapers. It must be used once more, for, coming on at the Nursery end as soon as the shine was off the ball, he got two immensely valuable wickets. Hobbs must have made a complete miscalculation, for he walked in front to play a half-volley to leg, and was bowled round his pads. He could hardly believe it. Woolley also had to be informed that he was out. He stepped a long way back to turn a shortish ball to leg, hit it to the boundary and carefully swung his left leg, the dangerous one, clear of his wicket, but his right foot must have slipped, for the heel touched the leg stump and dislodged a bail.

## DR HERBERT HORDERN

### FIRST TEST, SYDNEY, 1911–12

*December 19.* Hearne, who made top score of the English side, played a very fine innings. He was occasionally troubled by Dr Hordern's bowling in the later stages of his innings, but found little or no difficulty with the other bowlers. Although D. Hordern took five wickets for 85 runs his bowling was not of the same class as in the matches against the South African team last season; late in the innings, however, he sent down some very puzzling 'googlies'.

*December 21.* Dr Horden's bowling, especially between luncheon and tea, was exceedingly good. He made the ball break both ways and several times beat the wicket-keeper as well as the batsman … Hearne played the 'googlies' in both innings better than anyone else on the English side, and good judges here express the opinion that he will develop into a really great batsman.

… the score was still 141 when Rhodes was well caught by Mr Trumper at square-leg off Dr Hordern's bowling; he received only five balls from the 'googlie' bowler and four of them beat him.

## BOB MASSIE

### SECOND TEST, LORD'S, 1972

JACK FINGLETON

*June 24.* The press box at Lord's is between cover and mid-off, which does not give one an impression of what the bowlers are doing. So I went in the morning to the top of the Pavilion, directly behind the bowler's arm to watch the new ball and felt exceedingly sorry for Illingworth. He got one from Massie that whipped in late from the off. I would call it unplayable. As at Manchester, Illingworth got runs when much needed.

*Keith Stackpole is applauded in after Australia's eight-wicket win at Lord's in 1972, a match forever associated with Bob Massie*

Snow got a similar ball and over went his stumps. Massie, with eight wickets, returned to a scene which he will never forget. To gain eight wickets in any match sends a warm tingle down a bowler's spine. To do so at Lord's for Australia against the old enemy, England, and in one's first appearance on this immortal ground, is something which no young bowler would dare envisage. And certainly not one as modest as this likable young man of 25 from Perth.

Massie is beautifully built, strong hips, powerful shoulders yet with a lithe body that gives him a smooth run to the crease. He is medium paced. He knows how to use the stitches for swing so that every ball moves in the air. When it does, it is late, the hardest of all to play, and he moves both ways. He, too, changes his pace with no alteration of action.

So the Pavilion rose to this manly young Australian, he bowled much around the stumps here, possibly aiming to get the most out of the downward slope.

## GLENN McGRATH

### SIXTH TEST, THE OVAL, 1997

MICHAEL HENDERSON

*August 22.* Hail the conquering hero. When all is said and done about the death-wish fulfilment of the England batting, you have to give Glenn McGrath nine out of ten. He compressed his life story as a fast bowler into two shattering sessions, revealing Australian cricket at its most resolute and exposing the flabbiness that masquerades as defiance in the English game.

It was a high-class performance of bowling, fast, straight and relentless, by a man whose fingerprints are all over this series. He has taken 36 wickets this summer at less than 19 a time. Only the notable West Australian firm of Lillee and Alderman have been more successful in a series over here and they are within his sights when he bowls later in the match.

Why not a full ten? Well, he must be deducted one mark for his childish abuse of the tailenders and, if he is fair-minded, he will admit it made an unedifying spectacle. Other than that it was a superb performance, yet another one. England have nobody within a thousand miles of him, and when Devon Malcolm served up tripe at tuppence a pound after tea, on what was apparently the same pitch, it was hard to keep a straight face.

McGrath has everything except absolute pace, which is given to few. To batsmen who seek to break him, and England have discussed at some length how best to take him on, he must be a real pest, as he nags away at that off-stump line. Like Lillee before him, he is a true leader of the attack, a champion.

### FIRST TEST, LORD'S, 2005

RICHARD HOBSON

*July 22.* McGrath's 500th Test wicket was something special in itself. To remove another four batsmen inside 31 balls represented bowling of the highest order. And how did he wreak such havoc? All he did was put the ball in the right place and wait for batsmen to make a mistake. There you have the career of Glenn McGrath. [...]

It was a rare display of ostentation – or, more likely, testament to the ingenuity of sponsors – that he should change into a pair of boots bearing the number 500 stitched in gold after reaching the landmark. 'I am not normally much of a show pony but I think I deserved it,' he said.

*A great bowler in full cry on his favourite hunting ground; Glenn McGrath dismisses Matthew Hoggard at Lord's in 2005*

He reverted to modest kind when he considered his success. 'There is no secret,' he said. 'I reckon that if I can put the ball where I want to 99 times out of 100, then I do pretty well. The complicated thing about cricket is to keep everything simple and over the course of my career I have done that.'

## GRAHAM McKENZIE

### SECOND TEST, LORD'S, 1961

JOHN WOODCOCK, CRICKET CORRESPONDENT

*June 27.* The Australian side, as they left the field to set about the formal task of winning, allowed McKenzie to lead them off. This young giant from Perth had enjoyed a triumph in his first Test. His great physical strength enables him to surprise the batsmen with his pace. His approach is deceptively casual, but his promise is abundant.

## SHANE WARNE

### SECOND TEST, OLD TRAFFORD, 1993

ALAN LEE, CRICKET CORRESPONDENT

*June 5.* As soon as Warne did appear, 80 for one quickly became 123 for four. Gatting was the unfortunate recipient of that outrageous first ball and his reaction suggested he expected to wake up and find it had never happened.

He stood rooted to the crease, staring at the spot where the ball had pitched and wearing an expression of disbelief matched only by the umpire at Warne's end, Harold Bird. By the time Gatting had persuaded himself to depart, Robin Smith was well on his way from the dressing-room.

MICHAEL HENDERSON

*June 5.* For all his defiance and Graham Gooch's under-stated mastery until he slapped a full toss to mid-on, the day will be recalled years from now for the ball Warne found, first up, for Mike Gatting. That dismissal Simpson freely admitted altered the balance of the innings and consequently of the match.

If he lives to be a hundred Warne will still see that ball in his dreams. As for Gatting, whose forward defensive push was utterly confounded by the deviation of a ball which spun a good yard to hit the top of his off stump, he stood transfixed like Macbeth before the floating dagger.

Bob Taylor, the world record holder for dismissals by a wicket keeper and a sound judge of the extravagance of turn, recalled a similar ball by John Gleeson which bamboozled Brian Luckhurst on the 1970-71 tour of Australia. Other than that he couldn't think of one which fizzed as Warne's did. Not bad for a loosener!

## FIFTH TEST, EDGBASTON, 1993

ALAN LEE, CRICKET CORRESPONDENT

*August 9.* An over later, the wicket on which the day had always seemed to depend, fell to a ball as outrageous as anything seen in the game.

Graham Gooch, whose technique against turn was as masterful as others had been miserable, thrust out his left pad when Warne, from round the wicket and wide of the crease, pitched fully two feet outside leg stump. The ball snaked past the back of Gooch's leg to hit middle and leg stump. Warne was lost in euphoria at this wizardry; England simply looked lost.

SIMON BARNES

*August 9.* Shane Warne, the suicide blond – dyed by his own hand – has done it again. Yesterday, he called a crisis into being. It was a crisis that more or less ruled out England's hopes of a draw, and it took place in a burst of three wickets for six runs in six hot overs before lunch.

That is Warne's great gift: to exploit the sense of crisis. It is the very essence of the match-winning bowler's art: an ability to entrap an entire cricket ground your fielders, the batsmen, the umpires and the spectators all in a web of disaster.

An extraordinary fellow, this Warne. He mixes the eternal mysteries of leg spin with a name straight out of *Neighbours*. Never one to bear the enigmatic countenance traditionally worn by the purveyors of his craft, he is a heart-on-sleeve appealer, as intense and as emotional as any fast bowler that ever drew breath.

Nor is he truly subtle. He does not seek to entrap each batsman in a web of deceit, building up the tensions with bluff and counter-bluff. He just runs in and rips it, like a quickie trying to kill the batsman with every single delivery.

Each extravagant, wildly turning leg-spinner is Warne's own kind of throat-ball, intended as an utterly destructive ball, aimed viciously at the batsman's mind. Tim May, his off-spinning colleague, is a classic worker and whittler, a man of guile and patience, who was Warne's perfect complement. May tweaked it; Warne ripped it.

Robin Smith's mind-scrambled performance against him was positively

*Old Trafford, 1993 – Shane Warne has just made the most dramatic start to an Ashes career in history with a bewitching delivery that became celebrated as 'the ball of the century'*

Keatonesque. It was finally terminated by the umpire more on aesthetic grounds than any serious likelihood that the ball would have hit off stump. Alec Stewart was roasted and burned with a leg spinner; again a few eyebrows were raised at the decision. There is, perhaps, a desire in umpires to give brilliance its due reward. And it is a part of a great bowler's crisis-management.

In between the two came the ball that did for Graham Gooch, and with it, almost certainly, for England. The ball did not so much beat him as virtually dismember him. He was bowled behind his back, clean missing with both pads as he attempted to pad up. A protractor on the pitch might have read the angle of turn at 90 degrees or even more: Warne pushes the laws of physics to their limit.

He has also taken cricket's dress code into new and exciting areas, wearing more zinc cream on cloudy days than when the sun is out. He always steps on to the pitch looking as if he had just woken up after passing out in the ice-cream.

He affects that *bete noire* of modern cricket, the *eejit's* sunglasses, but, to his lasting credit, he seldom actually wears them and then only in overcast weather when there are five lights shining from the scoreboard light meter. No, Warne wears sun glasses on his hat, which is about as smart as wearing your shoes on your ears, and every bit as attractive.

He looks less like a professional athlete than some members of the press-box, with his puddingy face and his amply-insulated frame. Warne proves what is proved again and again that the game is a vehicle of excellence for all sorts of men.

Phil Edmonds, another singular fellow, once said: 'Mentally, my stock

*Warne disappears behind celebrating team-mates as Gatting wonders what happened. Both men were destined to be asked to relive the moment again and again*

ball pitches leg and hits the top of off.' He was, of course, exaggerating wildly. But with Shane Warne, this is literally true. Well, actually, his stock ball pitches a couple of feet outside leg before making the cobra-lunge at the off stick. Such extravagance with such extraordinary control is more or less unheard of in cricket.

To give him yet more credit, he did, for once, lose control in the first innings and his full-bungers and near-double-bouncers got walloped. He came back to cause England total dismay.

He is the man of the series, in the wickets he has taken and in the seeds of self-doubt he has sown among the England side. From the first ball he bowled, he has had them in a state of shattered disbelief. How can a refugee from *Neighbours* win the Ashes? But he has.

## SECOND TEST, MELBOURNE, 1994–95

ALAN LEE, CRICKET CORRESPONDENT

*December 30.* Hat tricks in Test cricket are rare and nobody had taken one in an England-Australia game since Hugh Trumble, also at Melbourne, in the 1903–04 series. But the way things are right now, it was a certainty that Warne would put that right. As, most unusually, he had taken none of the first six England wickets to fall, here was the ideal opportunity.

It came with the last three balls of an over, which was a shame for him as he might have needed only one ball at Tufnell to make it four in four. The cast list DeFreitas, Gough and Malcolm is undistinguished and resistance was negligible but that did not bother Warne.

4X

Such and Warne provide spectac

**England spin out of control on freak pitch**

BY ALAN LEE, CRICKET CORRESPONDENT

*OLD TRAFFORD (second day of five): England, with two first-innings wickets in hand, are 87 runs behind Australia*

ANY idle fancy that England might have entertained of securing a winning position in the first Cornhill Test yesterday was rudely shattered when Shane Warne's first ball pitched a foot outside Mike Gatting's leg stump and hit the top of off. It was a freak and told us we were watching big matches, was obviously the key figure in the match.

England were suitably grateful for the reprieve. As soon as Warne did appear, 80 for one quickly became 123 for four. Gatting was the unfortunate recipient of that outrageous first ball and his reaction suggested he expected to wake up and find it had never happened.

He stood rooted to the crease, staring at the spot where the ball had pitched deceived by both the leg break and the "flipper" when he did face up.

His judgment saw him through, however, and when he picked the googly, last ball before tea, and struck it high to the long-on boundary, the spell was briefly broken. Gooch's dismissal has often, in recent years, been the beginning of the end for England. Now, though he had batted gallantly for three hours, he had not made

*Shane Warne announces his arrival on the back page of June 5, 1993*

DeFreitas was leg-before on the back foot to one that kept low and hurried on and Gough was caught behind off a looping leg break. As Malcolm trudged out, Warne went across to Damien Fleming, who took a hat-trick on his Test debut in Pakistan in October. 'I asked him what I should do,' Warne said. 'He said he just closed his eyes and bowled his stock ball, so I did the same.'

Malcolm, groping blindly, nudged the ball low to the right of short leg, where David Boon plunged for a fine catch before being enveloped by a joyful Warne. The leg spinner has now taken 20 wickets for 190 in the first two Tests of this series and Jim Laker's Ashes record of 46, set in 1956, is no longer safe. 'I suppose I'll wake up soon,' Warne said.

JOHN WOODCOCK

*December 31.* None of the great wrist spinners of the past has combined, to the same extent, Warne's accuracy and power of spin. His control is astonishing, his versatility exceptional and, when bowling into the rough from round the wicket to the right-handers, he makes currency out of what is, in theory, a negative tactic.

## THIRD TEST, OLD TRAFFORD, 1997

ALAN LEE, CRICKET CORRESPONDENT

*July 5.* What happened next would have beggared belief had we not seen Warne do similar things several times over.

Stewart was first to depart, and if his feet were crease-bound and his stroke diffident, it was still a fine piece of bowling. Warne, pitching around leg stump, obtained such bounce and turn that it took an outside edge at the top of the bat and was expertly caught by Taylor at slip.[…]

Hussain twice lapped Warne fine for four and the pressure eased, but England could not afford another loss before tea and when Thorpe used his favoured, full-blooded sweep against Warne and was caught at slip off inside edge and pad, the balance had shifted dramatically inside 40 minutes.

The worst was yet to come, for it was clear that the tea interval had done nothing to calm England's rising sense of paranoia, a familiar affliction when Warne is in such a mood. Hussain and Crawley offered tame, hypnotised prods, sacrificial to Warne's leg break. So hard were they trying to open their shoulders, the latest technical ploy impressed upon the England batsmen, that they ended up looking as exposed and inept as schoolboys playing French cricket.

## FIRST TEST, EDGBASTON, 2001

RICHARD HOBSON

*July 6.* His introduction to the bowling attack yesterday was not quite as dramatic as his first ball in Ashes cricket at Old Trafford eight years ago. He did not strike until his second delivery this time, and nor with the venomous spin that accounted so memorably for Mike Gatting. Yet, that wicket of Mark Butcher proved to be the most significant turning point of an enthralling day.

Warne's thoughts might have started to drift towards the toasted cheese sandwiches that form his staple lunch when he eventually joined the bowling attack. Back in 1993, fresh and naive, he would begin by ripping the leg break as far as he could. These days he prefers to settle on a length and build from there.

His first ball, thus, landed on the ideal spot, but Butcher could not get close enough to the pitch of the second to smother the turn and supplied a low catch to silly point via his pad instead. England never looked as solid thereafter.

In *The Times*, Warne had referred to a new ball that he claims to have added to his arsenal and christened the 'slider' or 'skidder'. Doubtless there is an element of gamesmanship about his alleged discovery, but when he can still spin his leg break as violently as the one that beat Usman Afzaal's attempt to drive, he has no need to expand his repertoire.

It spun into the debutant left-hander probably as far as the 'Gatting Ball' and recalled the words of Charlie Macartney to describe a particular ball from Syd Barnes that undid Victor Trumper, a colleague in the Australia team before the First World War: 'It was the sort a man might see if he was dreaming or drunk.'

There were several occasions thereafter when Warne threatened to bowl right-handed batsmen around their pads going around the wicket.

Rumours of his demise in India this year, when his ten wickets cost an average of 50.5 apiece, clearly have been exaggerated. So is the idea that his role in the side is now as an entirely defensive foil for Glenn McGrath, Brett Lee and Jason Gillespie.

## THIRD TEST, TRENT BRIDGE, 2001

CHRISTOPHER MARTIN-JENKINS
CHIEF CRICKET CORRESPONDENT

*August 4.* The genius of Shane Warne turned a thrilling third npower Test match at Trent Bridge Australia's way with stunning suddenness yesterday evening. In a day prolonged by frequent showers for an hour and a half beyond its scheduled close, Warne produced a spell of four for 11 in 36 balls to turn a promising-looking England total of 115 for two into a perilous 144 for six. They lead by only 139.

To some extent it was a case of batsmen buckling under the high pressure of having to make a decent second-innings total in a match that they have to win, but Warne has always been a master of exploiting not just a pitch that helps him but also any tension in his opponents, like a dog who knows that the postman is nervous of being bitten.

The variations are nowhere near as baffling as they used to be before his two operations but the mesmeric accuracy, the natural cunning and the biting turn of his leg break were all in evidence as he followed up the vital wicket of Michael Atherton by bowling Alec Stewart off an inside edge, having Mark Ramprakash stumped as he danced down the pitch in an ill-judged attempt to turn the tide and finally claiming Craig White to a low catch off inside edge and pad.

Sporting …

# [H]OW ENGLAND KEPT TH[E] ASHES

## [T]WO GREAT HEARTS OVERTHROW AUSTRALIA

England beat Australia by five wickets in the fourth Test match at Adelaide yesterday and so, gaining a lead of three matches to one in the series, have retained the Ashes. In an interview after the match L. Hutton, the England captain, paid a tribute to the younger members of the side. Much of the credit, he thought, should go to J. B. Statham, F. H. Tyson, M. C. Cowdrey and P. B. H. May, together with the wicket-keeper, T. G. Evans.

From Our Special Correspondent

ADELAIDE, FEB. 2

Many years from now young Cowdrey will point to his broken nose and tell boys yet unborn that he was at Adelaide on February 2, 1955, when England won the Test match and kept the Ashes. And the boys will think him wondrous lucky. A ma… should dip his pen in blood to write … s day. Let no one talk and … ket and explain away …

… the catch. (We asked Hutton afterwards what he thought of Miller's bowling. Hutton thought Miller ought to concentrate much more on batting.) England 10 for 2. In comes the battered Cowdrey. Miller hits him twice running on the pads and appeals, and everybody here who isn't English appeals too. What a man is Miller. He comes in from a shortish run, loose of limb like an African, hair streaming, and as he pulls up the hair goes on and falls about his face. Meanwhile May has begun driving, and Johnson has gone from mid-off to square-leg. For Cowdrey Miller brings fine-leg up to third slip, and Cowdrey cover drives classically for 4. Miller heaves his shoulders over even faster, and Cowdrey is taken by Archer at first-slip. England 18 for 3. Four Meteor jets fly over at 200ft.; they look and sound quite tame beside this wild man … His figures now are 3 overs, no … 2 runs, 3 wickets.

# [E]ngland all too obliging … [r]eaches new heights of greatnes[s]

One that got away: Gilchrist misses a stumping chance off Warne to give Pietersen an extra life, but it was to make little difference

High five: Warne acknowledges the Melbourne crowd after his haul ripped the heart out of England's fragile batting

… legendary accuracy and a lush outfield, they ran poorly between the wickets, chose the wrong balls to try to hit in the air and failed to justify the decision to bat.

"We didn't expect conditions to change dramatically over the first day and a half," Strauss said, "but it seamed about more than we expected." It did so slowly but Glenn McGrath, Stuart Clark and Brett Lee all got enough past the bat to suggest that the wrong option had been taken.

Australia missed two catches, two clear run-out opportunities and a gaping stumping, but still bowled England out for 159 after they had been 101 for two. Very few Test matches are won after such a start. All of Warne's wickets were taken by flight and dip, as batsmen spied what they believed to be boundary opportunities. Only Kevin Pietersen got anywhere near the boundary as he attempted to drive Warne straight for six, but by now he was, as usual, batting with the tail.

Even he needed 70 balls for 21 runs, having come close to running out Andrew Flintoff for six as, for the third Test in succession, he attempted a ridiculous single in order to get off the mark. He had only made four when he also survived a simple stumping chance offered to Adam Gilchrist after charging Warne and missing.

England, we all know, have too long a tail, but tweaking it made no difference. Matthew Hoggard is back where he started, No 11, pushing Monty Panesar and Stephen Harmison up a place each, which reflects their various abilities with the bat. It is higher up, however, that the balance is wrong. Ed Joyce or Jamie Da[l]rymple should have played … six, but Chris Read for Geraint Jones was the only change.

As the best player in the team, Pietersen needs to bat at four. Since Paul Collingwood shared the only partnership of any substance with Strauss — 57 for the third wicket — it may appear that England's strategy, to keep him away from the new ball, had worked again, but to have Pietersen batting with the tail repeatedly is not satisfactory. In any case Collingwood might have been leg-before to Clark for nought, one of four apparently plumb leg-before decisions turned down by Rudi Koertzen.

Panesar was the other, … ly out to Warne before … out instead, but it was … turned down when … Hayden was hit on … front of the stumps … gard, the first …

… Australia's recent practice of not using a nightwatchman.

Ponting said that Australia, too, would have chosen to bat first, but it was one of those tosses that either captain would prefer to have lost. Play was delayed by rain for half an hour and only 16 overs were bowled before an early lunch was taken. Alastair Coo[k] …

… S Katich lbw b …

… unting run out (Flintoff) 66

…8 P Siddle c Flintoff b Harmison 10

5.37 343-9 S Clark c Cook b Harmison 0

…iant leap

for proud S…

Sporting News

# ENGLAND HAVE LAST WORD

## THREE YEOMEN FOIL AUSTRALIA

## GREAT STAND BY WATSON AND BAILEY

FROM OUR CRICKET CORRESPONDENT

Out of darkness, through fire into light. Thus did England yesterday rise like some Phoenix from the ashes of apparent defeat to save the second Test match at Lord's and so gain a … draw against Australia with … seven wickets, … original aim fo… The age of m… yet past, nor c… cany scarce f… dramatic and … a match alrea… But within t… longest and m… of a match it… that last spa… back with le… yeomen of … nearly the w…

The yeom… were Watso… greatest of … Yorkshirem… order, was … rearguard … twentieth …

36 TUESDAY AUGUST 1 1989

THE TIMES

First published 1785

# England's abject surrender marks new low in series

By Alan Lee, Cricket Correspondent

## Inglorious procession at Old Trafford

10-1: Curtis c Boon b Alderman 0

25-2: Robinson lbw b Lawson 12

27-3: Smith c Healy b Alderman 1

28-4: Gooch c Alderman b Lawson 13

38-5: Botham lbw b Alderman 4

59-6: Gower c Marsh b Lawson 15

SCOREBOARD FROM OLD TRAFFORD

England won toss

ENGLAND

First innings: 260 (R A Smith 143; G F Lawson 6 for 72)

AUSTRALIA

First innings

## Gower unfairly blamed for failings of others

Simon Barnes

## Border rewarded for hard labour

By John Woodcock

## Only two men so far decline

By Alan Lee

# Was this English most desperate

… night issued a dramatic … Union. He said that unless the … prepared to help to achieve an … strategic arms limitations, he would … additional funds of more than … new nuclear …

# GREAT WRITING

## MIKE ATHERTON

### FIRST TEST, CARDIFF, 2009

*July 10.* England are employing a 'buddy' system, where a top-order player is given the responsibility of improving the batting of a designated tailender. Paul Collingwood is the unfortunate minder for Panesar, who was the only England player not to make double figures. Poor Colly, if he can improve Panesar's batting, he can expect to trade in his MBE for something better.

### SECOND TEST, LORD'S, 2013

*July 18.* For Alastair Cook, the England captain, the only alarm yesterday was the fainting of a young female journalist during his press conference. Did she swoon? Was she suffering in the heat and humidity? Or, as Cook intimated in self-deprecating manner, was she bored by his answers?

*July 19.* Her Majesty had seen enough. The Royal Standard was lowered, the fawning members of the M.C.C. committee shuffled the deckchairs and allowed the Queen room to move and she departed the scene. At 28 for three she cannot have been impressed, although as head of state for both countries, she was on to a good thing whichever side were on top. A bob each way, she might have thought, as someone who likes a flutter.

### FIFTH TEST, THE OVAL, 2013

*August 22.* Australia are playing five seamers; England two spinners. It is a bit like walking into a party dressed as Elvis Presley and the first person you see is in black tie. You know that one of you has got things wrong.

*August 26.* Someday, somewhere, it may be possible to explain how a game, struggling to assert itself in the modern world, can injure itself so grievously. At a little past 7.30pm, on a late summer's evening, with a full house enthralled, floodlights on and England 21 runs short of a victory target that would have given them an historic triumph, the umpires walked both sets of players from the field.

They did so to boos, and received a security escort into the pavilion for their pains. It must be emphasised that the umpires were not at fault, they were merely carrying out the playing regulations that state that consistency above all else is adhered to, and since they had gone off at 7.26pm on Thursday evening in similar light, they had to again. My, my, though, in the context of a game being marginalised, the regulations struck a blow for petty mindedness over common sense.

At some stage, the I.C.C. will realise how much damage they are doing to the game. They act on the small things, such as dishing out a fine to Darren Lehmann, the Australia coach, for a ridiculous radio interview, but do nothing about the dilatory over-rates that both teams were guilty of from time to time.

In Manchester and at the Kia Oval, England's over-rate at times was appalling, as was Australia's towards the end of the day as Michael Clarke hoped for the intervention that prevented a 4-0 scoreline. Dealing with that, and an urgent adoption

*The game is poised on a knife edge, but despite the blazing floodlights the umpires rule that the light is unfit and the Australians troop off the Oval in 2013*

of play at all times under floodlights rule must be of prime consideration.

Clarke was also booed to the podium during the presentation ceremony, which seemed a little small-minded and short-sighted from a crowd that would have had little to shout about had most other captains been in charge.

---

## SIMON BARNES

### FIRST TEST, LORD'S, 2005

*July 21.* There is a chapter in one of Enid Blyton's Famous Five books entitled 'A lovely day with a horrid end'. That was England's first day of the Ashes series. An heroic bowling performance enabled England to get rid of Australia in 40 overs, but they were then horrifically punished for getting above themselves. It was tears after teatime for England.

### SECOND TEST, ADELAIDE, 2010–11

*December 4.* Clarke made an ugly shove at the ball, it caught the edge and Swann made the catch. Some time later, Australia got another run. That made the score three for three, or if you happen to be Australian, three for three.

---

## NEVILLE CARDUS

### FIRST TEST, BRISBANE, 1946–47

*December 2.* From a negative point of view the English bowlers and fieldsmen may be said to have done well today, and the Australian rate of scoring was at any rate kept down to less than the tempo that threatens a massacre. But it is difficult to deduce from the modern batsman's methods whether he is on the defensive by compulsion or by habit. It is, indeed, difficult to explain on what principle boundary hits are made at all by our contemporary heroes. For hours they are passive and unfruitful; then suddenly a ball is hit severely, and the eye of the spectator can see nothing to mark it off from many balls which, for hours have been cautiously inspected and treated. There is probably some deep-seated periodic law at the bottom of all this; perhaps it is the influence of the moon that governs the ebb and flow of the tides.

---

## DUDLEY CAREW

### FIRST TEST, TRENT BRIDGE, 1938

*June 15.* The wicket did not fall, however, and once all was saved Bradman perhaps might have given the crowd some 6's in the way an indulgent uncle might give some rich, and not particularly wholesome, sweets to a child.

---

## JACK FINGLETON

### FOURTH TEST, HEADINGLEY, 1968

*July 27.* What constitutes time is an interesting study. It was explained to me theologically recently as a continuation of creation, but England seemed in the morning not to be interested in the subject.

**thetimes.co.uk**
No 1 for the Ashes

**9.30am**
Listen to Mike Atherton's verdict on day one and read his report
**Plus**
Analysis from Simon Barnes and Gideon Haigh

**Noon**
All the rumblings from Down Under in our Aussie press wrap

**4pm**
Tomorrow's tactics today, with Hawk-Eye

**Midnight**
Follow every ball of day two, with commentary, scores and interactive analysis

**On the iPad edition**

Full live match service
Swipe through stunning pictures from Marc Aspland
Follow the news, gossip and banter on Twitter

*In the 21st century, Ashes coverage became a round-the-clock business*

## GEOFFREY GREEN

### SECOND TEST, LORD'S, 1953

*June 26.* All things considered the scales are not too unevenly balanced at this moment. Certainly from an English aspect the scoreboard at the end wore a softer look than it might have done, and certainly less harsh and tidier than the edges of Lord's green stage where the scattered flotsam of a capacity crowd lay behind as mute reminder of a hard battle, grimly fought.

### FOURTH TEST, HEADINGLEY, 1953

*July 28.* The weather man would seem to have overlooked the month of April in the calendar and has been trying to rectify the omission at Headingley. Yesterday again there were showers which lost two more hours of the fourth Test match against Australia between brief snatches of sunshine. Before luncheon indeed there came even flashes of lightning and some trumpetings of thunder. All that was missing was a rainbow. And it is a rainbow that England now need.

## GIDEON HAIGH

### THIRD TEST, EDGBASTON, 2009

*August 1.* During a form trough in the mid-1990s, Hussey was so despondent about his batting for Western Australia that he wrote to Steve Waugh pleading for insights into 'mental toughness' – the psychological certification that came almost to bear Waugh's watermark. Waugh told Hussey he was too intense, which sounds like being scolded by Dylan Thomas for taking a dram too many.

### FIRST TEST, BRISBANE, 2010–11

*November 27.* The Channel 9 protractor, which measures the alleged deviation of balls after pitching and is studied as seriously as ballistics testimony before the Warren Commission, had had little to do before lunch, at least until James Anderson bent one away subtly from Shane Watson.

### SECOND TEST, ADELAIDE, 2010–11

*December 6.* When Doherty resumed to Pietersen after lunch, it was with six men deep: Peter Siddle at deep mid-on, Shane Watson deep mid-off, North deep mid-wicket, Bollinger deep backward square, Ryan Harris deep point and Ponting deep trouble.

### FIRST TEST, TRENT BRIDGE, 2013

*July 13.* Shane Watson also bowled some invaluable 'dry overs', adding to the inertia he induced by a heavy-booted trudge to his mark at half the pace of anyone else in this game, his back as it receded resembling a fridge being pushed slowly down a narrow hallway on casters.

### THIRD TEST, PERTH, 2013–14

*December 14.* To Swann, Smith kept springing down the pitch two or three times an over, even if it was to play defensively. Most modern batsmen use their feet to spinners as though fearful of tripwires and booby traps, preferring the security of the crease and the comfort of their thick-edged cudgels. Smith is so relaxed, he might almost be humming a tune as he does so. For all the time he spends out of his crease, he has been stumped only once in 29 Test innings.

---

## STEWART HARRIS

### FOURTH TEST, ADELAIDE, 1954–55

*February 1.* But your Correspondent must also report that from half an hour after luncheon until Hutton was out, and again from half an hour after tea until the customary quiescent period before stumps were drawn, he reflected thankfully that, unlike 40,000 other souls, he was being paid to watch.

---

## MICHAEL HENDERSON

### FIRST TEST, OLD TRAFFORD, 1993

*June 5.* This was a day to forget about sponsored sightscreens, logos on the outfield, low-grade nationalism (braying from a popular side containing what may be termed 'Oslo elements') and other detachable parts of the modern game. Anyone who failed to stir yesterday should not bother to watch another day's Test cricket.

### THIRD TEST, TRENT BRIDGE, 1993

*July 2.* Perversely, for such an assertive batsman, Robin Smith's five-year journey towards international maturity has been consumed by more self-doubt than even Julie Andrews endured in the von Trapp household. Although he averages 47 over 43 Tests, his bold public manner has often run counter to private uncertainty.

Less than two months ago, the Australian off spinner, Tim May, snared him twice at Lord's, when his anguish could not have been more evident. Here Smith ran free, like Maria through the Alpine meadows. One could almost hear him sing: 'When the ball bites, when the pitch spins, when my footwork's bad, I simply remember my favourite things and then I don't feel so sad.'

### FIRST TEST, EDGBASTON, 1997

*June 7.* For two hours yesterday morning, a small and not terribly distinguished part of a big and not awfully nice city was transformed into a land of milk and honey. So superbly did Master Hussain and Master Thorpe bat, more mellifluously even than they had played the previous evening, that one wanted to stand on the nearest rooftop and shout (extremely loudly): 'Hurrah!'

It was Sydney Smith, the 18th-century parson-wit, who famously described his idea of heaven as 'eating pate de foie gras to the sound of trumpets'. For many of his countrymen, watching two Englishmen bat against Australia as this pair did, over nearly five hours, evokes almost equally celestial visions. In the view of many spectators last night, not all of them sober, admittedly, Hussain and Thorpe stood only slightly lower than the angels.

### THIRD TEST, OLD TRAFFORD, 1997

*July 8*. There are many reasons for taking pride in being English. Here are a few: *The Book of Common Prayer*, King's College Chapel, *The Lark Ascending*, *Nicholas Nickleby*, Timothy Taylor's Landlord bitter, *The Prelude*, Stephenson's Rocket, Double Gloucester, Peter Simple, the Penny Black, Giles's grandma, the Oscar Wilde sketch, Brunel, *Dad's Army*, *Greensleeves*, the E-type Jag, battered haddock, the Shell guides, Frankie Howerd, Newton, *The Bash Street Kids*, fig rolls, *The Mikado*, *Penny Lane*, Chatsworth House, *Scoop*, Mrs Worthington, Screaming Lord Sutch, *Lucky Jim*, *The Owl and the Pussycat*, Inigo Jones, afternoon tea, the V-sign, *The Fighting Temeraire*, 617 Squadron, Ken Dodd, Basil Brush, Landseer's Lions and some cock from Stratford whose name quite escapes me.

I am sure the people who chant 'Ashes coming home … it's [*sic*] coming home' can supply their own list, but first they should brush up on their grammar.

---

## RICHARD HOBSON

### FOURTH TEST, MELBOURNE, 2010–11

*December 27*. But perhaps Andrew Strauss and Andy Flower really had been

*A gathering of Times cricket correspondents at Longparish in 2008. Mike Atherton, John Woodcock, Alan Lee and Christopher Martin-Jenkins*

persuaded that sledging brought defeat. This time, England behaved like gentlemen in the field.

They offered not a hint of a snarl or a send-off, although with wickets falling so often, any finger-pointing towards the dressing room would have resulted in repetitive strain injury.

### LEADING ARTICLE

*October 11, 1933.* On the other hand, the particular kind of fast leg bowling that has been the source of controversy is likely to be dropped. It will not be dropped because it is illegal; it will not even be dropped because it is against the spirit of the game. It will be dropped because it interferes with our Australian friends' enjoyment of cricket – and consequently with our own.

---

## ALAN LEE

### FIRST TEST, HEADINGLEY, 1989

June 13. [...] Border looked last night like a man intent on going off the high board to find out if there is any water in the pool.

### SECOND TEST, LORD'S, 1989

*June 24.* Although Boon gave a chance to gully off the luckless Jarvis, there was little to suggest that England would restrict the total to less than 450. In mid-afternoon, the public address summoned the Bishop of Croydon to the Pavilion; doubtless, the selectors were waiting to consult him.

*June 27.* Shortly after tea yesterday, 25,000 partisans at Lord's exploded into prolonged, euphoric cheering. England had avoided an innings defeat. Within minutes, the royal ensign was lowered from the pavilion flag pole as if the Queen had nodded her personal approval of a momentous happening and moved on to other business. [...]

Gower's century occupied 253 minutes, included 15 fours and was rapturously received, nowhere more so than in the private box occupied by Tim Rice and the cast of Anything Goes, the musical to which he had felt obliged to dash on Saturday evening.

### THIRD TEST, EDGBASTON, 1989

*July 11.* When Border turned to Hohns, his leg-break bowler, Botham removed his helmet and handed it to Russell in the style of a butler taking the master's coat before pistols at dawn. The duel had great potential but Botham, to his evident disgust, fell at the other end, swinging lustily at Hughes and losing his off stump.

### FIFTH TEST, EDGBASTON, 1993

*August 10.* It ended with a trademark four from Boon, guided through midwicket with the minimum of fuss and provoking the now familiar songs of victory from the Australian dressing-room. England may have a song of their own for such occasions; if so, they have probably forgotten the words.

ROYAL EDITION
TUESDAY JUNE 25 1968
NO. 57,286 NINEPENCE

# THE TIMES

DE KAT'S FULL STORY, WRITTEN SPECIALLY FOR THE TIMES, P. 10

## LOCOMEN'S BAN BOUND TO CAUSE GREATER CONFUSION TODAY

Anxious commuters studying the notice board at Cannon Street station, London, last night.

### Government refuses to interfere

**The situation on the railways is expected to deteriorate sharply today after yesterday's decision by the Associated Society of Locomotive Engineers and Firemen to join the work-to-rule from midnight last night.**

**Main line services, most of which ran yesterday with only minor delays, are likely to suffer widespread cancellations, and Southern Region commuters, who were the worst affected yesterday, face far greater disruption today as a result of the decision by the drivers' and firemen's union.**

**Mr. Marsh, Minister of Transport, said yesterday that he would *not* interfere in the dispute. The railways' management were on their own and could expect no help from the Government.**

**Sir Henry Johnson, chairman of the Railways Board, said last night: "The Aslef decision will complicate the situation further. It must be worse tomorrow. We are hoping all the time that we shall find a way out."**

### Police shut station gates

BY A STAFF REPORTER

In spite of conspicuous little knots of police in all the London main line stations, last night's rush-hour passed without serious incident. A senior police officer at Victoria said it had gone exceptionally well.

The worst crowd scenes occurred at Cannon Street, where at one point early in the rush-hour police closed the station gates because of the crush inside. But this was a temporary measure, and the press of angry bowler hats soon thinned out. Ironic cheers greeted each train announcement.

The information clerk at Cannon Street said no one had been particularly rude, though his colleague showed me that he had kept a poker under the counter.

West End theatregoers ignored the curtailed train timetables and many theatres reported full houses yesterday in spite of their being warned to take trains getting them home by 10 p.m.

But theatre managers fear that if late trains continue not to run audience figures will be hit.

A spokesman for the London Palladium said: "I don't think it has fully sunk in yet that some people may have difficulty getting home. If the present situation continues some theatres could certainly feel the pinch."

**Because of the railwaymen's dispute *The Times*, in conjunction with other newspapers, has had to make alternative arrangements for distribution. We apologize if copies are received late in some areas.**

#### More time for GCE exam

The University Entrance and School Examinations Council at London University said yesterday that it had advised schools whose pupils arrived late to sit their G.C.E. examinations that they should be allowed extra time so that they had the full three hours for the papers. Special consideration would also be given to such papers, an official said.

Five thousand railway workers and their wives and families might be forced to make fresh travel arrangements for their annual holiday, which starts this weekend, because of the work to rule by their colleagues. The men, who make and service locomotives at the Crewe locomotive works, have been told that the traditional special trains laid on for the West Country and other holiday centres might have to be axed.

[illegible] yesterday telling them that their train had been cancelled.

Mr. Michael Abbott, secretary of the Bromsgrove Passenger Action Committee, said he thought it was a "very nice gesture".

#### 'Not according to rule'

Yesterday was not without its flashes of humour. A train from Littlehampton to Victoria had made one of its many extra stops and was pulling out of a station when the brakes were suddenly applied. Passengers saw the guard, who had almost missed the train, running along the platform shouting at the driver. "This is not according to rule".

The smallest public railway in the world, which operates between Hythe and Dungeness, Kent, was running to time. A spokesman for the company which runs the mini-sized trains said: "Our men are quite independent . . . it's business as usual for us."

### ASLEF BETRAYS A NOTE OF REGRET

By MICHAEL BAILY, Transport Correspondent

Announcing Aslef's decision to bring forward its go-slow a week, Mr. Ray Buckton, assistant general secretary, said after a three-hour meeting at the union's headquarters at Hampstead yesterday: "My executive have given very serious consideration to all the circumstances. They are very firm in their attitude that our just claim for an increase in rates of pay should be considered as separate and apart from the efficiency and productivity jobs.

"If the board say there is extra money for our people in these pay and efficiency talks, then we fail to see why they cannot indeed make a proposal to give a percentage to our member grades, even if this is subsequently to be taken into consideration in the finalization of pay and efficiency talks."

Apparently betraying a note of regret over yesterday's decision, Mr. Buckton said Aslef would try not to worsen the difficulties of commuters and business people, but with about 60 per cent of rest days being worked, Southern Region was bound to be badly disrupted.

The first day of the go-slow went off a good deal more smoothly than had been expected. Some overnight expresses were cancelled, and commuters, especially on the Southern Region, suffered overcrowding and irregular services. But the main flows of both passengers and freight were successfully moved, and traffic in London was not badly obstructed by commuters taking to their cars.

Sir Henry Johnson, British Railways chairman, said during the afternoon that the effects so far had not been as bad as had been feared. It appeared that there was little working to rule, although the men's refusal to work overtime and on rest days was obviously having its effect.

In a statement on the B.B.C. programme *The World at One*, Sir Henry said he could offer little hope of an early end to the dispute while the railwaymen demanded an increase across the board.

*Michael Thomas writes*:—One reason why services were not even worse affected yesterday was simply that more than two-thirds of the men defied their union's instructions and worked overtime or on their rest days as usual. Only a handful worked to rule in the sense that they carried out their duties in an abnormal way.

The British Railways Board may consider today whether to suspend the railwaymen's guaranteed week agreement. This would make it possible to send home men left without work by the industrial action of others and save the cost of their wages.

Sir Henry Johnson, chairman of the board, said last night that disciplinary action could not be taken against men for working to rule or for declining to volunteer for overtime, but it could be taken against any man who refused to obey legitimate instructions.

New proposals on train manning, an issue which reached deadlock in the productivity negotiations, were sent to both unions yesterday with an invitation from British Railways to discuss them today. Affecting some 80,000 footplatemen and guards, they would cost £2m. a year to introduce, but this would be offset by savings. One proposal is that drivers' milage bonuses should be replaced by a flat weekly allowance. Another attempts to break the deadlock over the manning of locomotives by men apart from drivers.

Even if talks take place on these proposals they are unlikely to settle the main dispute, which is over the unions' demand for an immediate all-round increase without productivity conditions.

**Southern Region cuts, page 2.**

### Railways must act alone, Marsh says

FROM OUR CORRESPONDENT—Carlisle, June 24

Mr. Marsh, Minister of Transport, said here today [illegible] British Railways affairs.

"The situation is totally different from any previous dispute", he said. "The management of British Railways must deal with this dispute. They are on their own. They can expect no help from the Government.

He added: "At the very time when British Rail has a shiny future, it is faced with a dispute which can not only damage it financially but which can have very serious implications indeed for the people who work for British Rail."

Earlier Mr. Marsh had opened a £100,000 extension to the seat-belt manufacturing plant of Kangol Magnet Ltd. in the city.

*Our Political Correspondent writes*:—

Tory backbenchers protested in the Commons yesterday when a private notice question on the disruption of rail services addressed to Mr. Marsh was answered by Mr. Carmichael, one of the parliamentary secretaries. Mr. Peter Walker had put in the question half-way through the morning. By that time [illegible] Swingler, Minister of State, Ministry of Transport. He was in Lancashire for the day, speaking in the Nelson and Colne by-election campaign.

Without the facts, several parliamentarians on both sides of the House thought Mr. Marsh had his priorities wrong, for the question dealt with what the Ministry is doing "to minimize inconvenience to public and industry".

Mr. Carmichael made a holding statement decribing the day's events, and did not allow himself to be drawn into controversy about the dispute.

Mrs. Castle, Secretary of State for Employment and Productivity, went to 10 Downing Street last night to discuss the work-to-rule with Mr. Wilson, but Government quarters went out of their way to emphasize that the discussion did not presage any possibility of Government intervention to bring about a settlement on terms that conflict with incomes policy. Mr. Wilson and Mrs. Castle are said to be standing firm in their view that the Government's incomes policy has been brought under direct challenge and they have no intention of surrendering to the pressure from the railway unions.

**Parliamentary report, page 14.**

### HOW THE AUSTRALIANS WERE SKITTLED OUT AT LORD'S

**England dismissed Australia for 78 in their first innings at Lord's yesterday. Good fast bowling supported by magnificent close-catching combined to put out the Australians for their lowest score in a Test match in this country since 1912. At the close of play Australia had scored 50-0 in their second innings. Report page 15.**

W. M. Lawry, c. Knott, b. Brown .. .. 0

I. R. Redpath, c. Cowdrey, b. Brown .. .. 4

R. M. Cowper, c. Graveney, b. Snow .. .. 8

K. D. Walters, c. Knight, b. Brown .. .. 26

A. P. Sheahan, c. Knott, b. Knight .. .. 6

I. M. Chappell, l.b.w., b. Knight .. .. 7
G. D. McKenzie, b. Brown .. .. .. 5

J. W. Gleeson [illegible]

B. N. Jarman retired hurt .. .. 0

N. J. N. Hawke, c. Cowdrey, b. Knight .. .. 2
A. N. Connolly, not out .. .. .. 0
Extras .. .. .. .. 6
Total .. .. .. .. 78

### Gaullists may get back with clear majority

From CHARLES HARGROVE—Paris, June 24

The victory of the Gaullist party in the first ballot of the French parliamentary elections yesterday could turn into a landslide in the second vote next Sunday. Even on the most conservative estimates the Gaullist majority in the new Assembly will be much more substantial than it was in the last.

The Government can even look forward to the possibility of having an absolute majority in its own right without having to rely on the qualified and critical support of M. Giscard d'Estaing's Independent Republicans.

On the first vote the Government has recovered three-fifths of the seats it held in Parliament, with another 333 to be filled. Very few of its candidates have failed to obtain the 10 per cent of votes cast in the first ballot that they need to remain in the second, and a substantial number are very well placed to win under mutual withdrawal arrangements which will be struck with Independent Republican candidates.

A new development came tonight when M. Pompidou suggested a similar arrangement to candidates of the centre—offering to withdraw the Gaullist candidate if the centrist had emerged in a better place in the first ballot whenever there was risk that a communist might win.

He went even further. He said that he was prepared to withdraw the Gaullist candidate in favour of a better placed candidate of the centre even if there were no communist threat.

M. Pompidou said: "I think that such a union for the second ballot is made all the more necessary because we know how decisive the second ballot is, that it is never settled in advance, and that the experience of the past few years, particularly of last year, shows that hopes formulated after the first ballot can sometimes be disappointed."

He added that he hoped that the electorate "remains vigilant and on the alert, and that no one imagines the game is won; and that on June 30, in the evening, and only then, Frenchmen may quietly and optimistically think about their holidays."

The Gaullist leaders are remembering March, 1967, when through over-confidence they lost in the second ballot much of the ground they had won in the first.

They also wish to avoid provoking the voters into switching their support between now and next Sunday through fear that the Gaullist party might emerge too powerful and therefore insensitive to the need for reform.

The victory is remarkable for a party which had been in power uninterruptedly for 10 years and for a leader aged 77. The Gaullists undoubtedly cashed in handsomely on the climate of fear engendered by demonstrations, riots, and strikes; and the Opposition's clumsy and ill-timed bid for power before it had in fact been relinquished.

The party kept before the electorate the spectre of further disorder and unrest if the opposition came to office. It won back many votes from the centre which last time, in protest against its style of government and its refusal of discussion, had gone to the left. These elections have proved once again, as in 1848, 1871 and on other occasions throughout recent French history, that in times of stress the reaction of this country is overwhelmingly conservative, and that the chance of the left only comes in times when the voters feel that the institutions and the foundations of the social structure are not threatened.

#### Swing from left

But this does not altogether explain the extent of the Gaullist success. The failure of the opposition to propose a convincing alternative also played a part. Many votes won by the Gaullists were communist or left-wing votes.

The danger would be for Gaullism to imagine that it was back in the halcyon days of 1962, with its absolute "unconditional" majority, and to act as though the events of last May had merely been an unpleasant episode which yesterday's poll had effaced. Half of France still supports the Opposition.

**Gaullist gamble pays off, page 6; leading article, page 11.**

### Inquiry over bank chief's salary

BY OUR POLITICAL STAFF

Payment of a £4,279 increase in director's remuneration to Mr. Jocelyn Hambro chairman of Hambros Bank is being investigated by the Department of Employment and Productivity. Mr. Walker, Parliamentary Secretary to the Ministry, said in the Commons yesterday.

He told Mr. Allaun, Labour M.P. for Salford East, that the Prices and Incomes White Paper made it clear that the principles of the policy applied to directors' remuneration.

"The Government expect directors to show the same sense of responsibility towards these principles as is being asked of wage and salary earners", he said. "We will be keeping the question of directors' remuneration under close review, as details become increasingly available through the operation of the Companies Act, 1967."

Mr. Allaun said in his question that the chairman of Hambros had a rise of from £20,866 to £25,145 a year in the past 12 months, besides share dividends.

**Business News, page 21.**

### Police alerted by strike ship

FROM OUR CORRESPONDENT
DOVER, JUNE 24

For five hours today members of the crew of the Israel ship Avocadocore (18,433 tons) argued with officials as the vessel lay at anchor in the middle of the fog-shrouded harbour at Dover. Police stood by on shore.

The ship, sailing to Bremerhaven with a cargo of fruit was diverted to Dover to land eight members of the crew who were refusing [illegible]

[illegible] immigration officers went out by launch to board the ship a radio message asked Kent police to stand by. The message said some of the seamen were armed with knives and wire hawsers. A convoy of vehicles took police to the pierhead, but they were later withdrawn.

### 13 die in Swiss rail crash

FROM OUR CORRESPONDENT
GENEVA, JUNE 24

Thirteen people were killed and 119 injured, some seriously, when two trains collided head-on on a single-track stretch of the main line from Lake Geneva to the Simplon tunnel today.

**Picture, page 7.**

### Woman's body near camp

FROM OUR CORRESPONDENT
GUILDFORD, JUNE 24

A murder hunt began tonight after the body of a woman in her early twenties had been found naked and mutilated on a track near the Women's Royal Army Corps depot at Guildford, Surrey. She had been strangled and also attacked with a blunt instrument.

Joan de Kat in the fishing boat to which he was transferred after leaving the Jagona at Skagen.

### Saved sailor slips quietly ashore

SKAGEN, DENMARK, June 24.—M. Joan de Kat, the French yachtsman saved from the Atlantic by an international rescue operation, slipped quietly ashore here today.

M. de Kat, a 27-year-old artist whose trimaran Yaksha broke up in mid-ocean while he was taking part in the single-handed transatlantic yacht race, was picked up by the Norwegian cargo ship Jagona.

He came ashore today in a fishing boat.—*Reuter.*

**Alone on the Atlantic, page 10.**

### Hancock dies in Sydney

SYDNEY, Tuesday morning.—Tony Hancock, the British comedian, was found dead today in a flat in the Sydney suburb of Bellevue Hill. Police announced his death but gave no further details.

Mr. Hancock, who was 47, had his greatest success in a B.B.C. television series *Hancock's half-hour*.—*United Press International.*

On Friday, Tony Hancock's wife was granted a decree *nisi* in the Divorce Court in London, on the grounds of cruelty and adultery.

#### ON OTHER PAGES


**David M. Davies**: Plight of farmers in the Mekong Delta 11

**The North-West**: Eight-page special report

| | | | |
|---|---|---|---|
| Arts and Entertainments | 13 | Parliament | 14 |
| Business News | 21-30 | Pictures | 36 |
| Course of Nature | 12 | Sale Room | 12 |
| Court, Social | 12 | Science report | 8 |
| Crossword | 20 | Sports | 15-17 |
| Engagements | 12 | TV and radio | 18 |
| Home News | 2, 4, 5 | *The Times* Diary | 10 |
| Law report | 9 | 25 Years Ago | 12 |
| Letters | 11 | University news | 5 |
| Obituary | 12 | Weather | 18 |
| Overseas News | 6-8 | Wills | 12 |
| | | Women's Page | 9 |




*A dramatic 1968 front-page with pictures of all ten Australian wickets at Lord's*

### FIRST TEST, BRISBANE, 1994–95

*November 26.* There are many ways, kind and cruel, of conveying the message that the first day of the Ashes series at the Woolloongabba yesterday was not a raging success for England, but perhaps the most pointed is the fact that their two most effective overs were bowled, deep into the final hour, by Graham Gooch.

### FIFTH TEST, TRENT BRIDGE, 1997

*August 8.* In the final session, the Hollioakes were in tandem for a while, offering the surely unprecedented spectacle of two Australians bowling to two more Australians in a Test match.

## CHRISTOPHER MARTIN-JENKINS

### FIFTH TEST, SYDNEY, 2002–03

*January 6.* Australia have been undone in this match by the absence of Glenn McGrath and Shane Warne; the loss of the toss and therefore the requirement to bat last on a pitch that has worn rapidly; the strange psychology by which England play towards the end of an Ashes series twice as well as they do when it matters most; and, above all, the supreme form of Vaughan.

His innings was no more nor less a joy than all of the seven Test hundreds that preceded it, based upon a rare natural poise, a straight bat, a classical sideways-on technique and an eye that spots a short ball as surely as an owl detects a shrew.

### FIRST TEST, LORD'S, 2005

*July 22.* No novelist or playwright would have dared, so early in the plot, to pack together dramatic events of such relentless intensity as the cricketers of England and Australia contrived on a dry and grassy Lord's pitch on the opening day of the series for the Ashes yesterday. The excitement was contained yet tangible among spectators who, in some cases, had begun queueing, even with tickets in their pockets, on Wednesday evening, simply to be sure of a prime view. It became almost feverish from the moment that Stephen Harmison's second ball lifted into Justin Langer's right elbow and continued unabated until Glenn McGrath led Australia from the field with figures of five for 21.

## R.B. VINCENT

### FIFTH TEST, THE OVAL, 1930

*August 16.* In 1890 Turner and Ferris were going through England's batting on a Turner and Ferris wicket like water through a sieve. James Cranston held up one end while Maurice Read hit, and eventually England got home by two wickets. Martin, of Kent, and Sharpe, of Surrey, England's last two batsmen on that day, were of the class whose best chance of scoring is to run to short leg and appeal for a wide.

## FOURTH TEST, HEADINGLEY, 1938

*July 25.* […] both bowlers, keeping a good length, tied down Fingleton, who hardly raised his bat high enough for a field mouse to squeeze its way underneath it. […]

England was granted a great mercy, for the great McCabe was late to a ball from Farnes and had his off stump knocked out of the ground. When the illustrious depart it is as well that the business should be done thoroughly.

*July 26.* The joy of the Australians could be both seen and felt, but possibly not even they could predict how near they were already to winning the match. The field crowded so close to Paynter that it was difficult to see him from a distance. What one did see of him, however, was good.

## FIFTH TEST, THE OVAL, 1938

*August 25.* The absence of Fingleton rubbed in the hopeless handicap under which Australia were labouring, for he could have been relied upon to give some stability to a side which was beginning to bear the appearance of a clock when a small boy has begun to pull its inside to pieces.

## SECOND TEST, LORD'S, 1948

*June 30.* In the same over Coxon walked across his wicket, as if he had an appointment with someone on the ring side, and was given out leg-before-wicket.

## FOURTH TEST HEADINGLEY, 1948

*July 24.* By this time the tea interval had arrived, and no sooner had the spoons stopped rattling than Evans was caught at square-leg.

---

# JOHN WOODCOCK

## SECOND TEST, LORD'S, 1961

*June 26.* Ten minutes later Illingworth was caught at backward short leg off Simpson's googly – to a leg spinner he is like clay in a potter's hands …

## FIRST TEST, OLD TRAFFORD, 1968

*June 6.* The bookings for the match are disappointing, being down in terms of cash on 1964, although the tickets are now costing more. The weather, of course, has had a lot to do with this, and also the fact that Manchester is a city consumed with football.

I am told that no cricket match here this year has attracted the same interest as the one between Manchester City and Manchester United for Ken Higgs's benefit. Yesterday, on the eve of England against Australia, the boys were kicking footballs about in the car park behind the cricket pavilion. They might have been throwing stones at an altar.

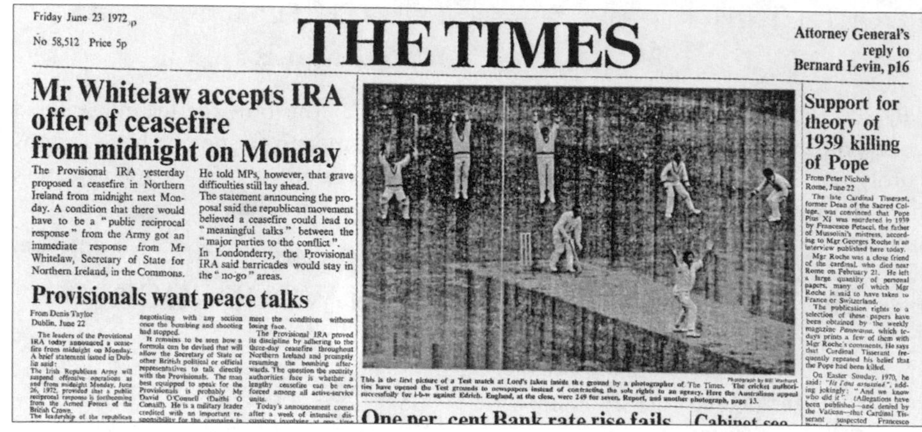

Friday June 23 1972

No 58,512 Price 5p

**THE TIMES**

**Attorney General's reply to Bernard Levin, p16**

**Mr Whitelaw accepts IRA offer of ceasefire from midnight on Monday**

The Provisional IRA yesterday proposed a ceasefire in Northern Ireland from midnight next Monday. A condition that there would have to be a "public reciprocal response" from the Army got an immediate response from Mr Whitelaw, Secretary of State for Northern Ireland, in the Commons.

He told MPs, however, that grave difficulties still lay ahead.

The statement announcing the proposal said the republican movement believed a ceasefire could lead to "meaningful talks" between the "major parties to the conflict".

In Londonderry, the Provisional IRA said barricades would stay in the "no-go" areas.

**Provisionals want peace talks**

From Denis Taylor
Dublin, June 22

The leaders of the Provisional IRA today announced a ceasefire from midnight on Monday. A brief statement issued in Dublin said:

The Irish Republican Army will suspend offensive operations as and from midnight Monday, June 26, 1972, provided that a public reciprocal response is forthcoming from the Armed Forces of the British Crown.

The leadership of the republican ... negotiating with any section once the bombing and shooting had stopped.

It remains to be seen how a formula can be devised that will allow the Secretary of State or other British political or official representatives to talk directly with the Provisionals. The man best equipped to speak for the Provisionals is probably Mr David O'Connell (Daithi O Conaill). He is a military leader credited with an important responsibility for the campaign in ... meet the conditions without losing face.

The Provisional IRA proved its discipline by adhering to the three-day ceasefire throughout Northern Ireland and promptly resuming the bombing afterwards. The question the security authorities face is whether a lengthy ceasefire can be enforced among all active-service units.

Today's announcement comes after a week of intensive discussions ...

Photograph by Bill Warhurst

This is the first picture of a Test match at Lord's taken inside the ground by a photographer of The Times. The cricket authorities have opened the Test grounds to newspapers instead of contracting the sole rights to an agency. Here the Australians appeal successfully for l-b-w against Edrich. England, at the close, were 249 for seven. Report, and another photograph, page 13.

**Support for theory of 1939 killing of Pope**

From Peter Nichols
Rome, June 22

The late Cardinal Tisserant, former Dean of the Sacred College, was convinced that Pope Pius XI was murdered in 1939 by Francesco Petacci, the father of Mussolini's mistress, according to Mgr Georges Roche in an interview published here today.

Mgr Roche was a close friend of the cardinal, who died near Rome on February 21. He left a large quantity of personal papers, many of which Mgr Roche is said to have taken to France or Switzerland.

The publication rights to a selection of these papers have been obtained by the weekly magazine *Panorama*, which todays prints a few of them with Mgr Roche's comments. He says that Cardinal Tisserant frequently repeated his belief that the Pope had been killed.

On Easter Sunday, 1970, he said: *"Ils l'ont assassiné"*, adding jokingly: "And we know who did it". (Allegations have been published—and denied by the Vatican—that Cardinal Tisserant suspected Francesco ...

**One per cent Bank rate rise fails** | **Cabinet see...**

*An historic moment at Lord's in 1972 as Times photographer Bill Warhurst takes the first Test match action picture exclusively for use in the paper. Previously only photographic agencies had been allowed to cover international matches in England*

## SECOND TEST, LORD'S, 1968

*June 20.* The original Test match between England and Australia was played in Melbourne 92 years ago. Today, at Lord's, the 200th game in the series is due to start. It is a great occasion, quite apart from being the high point of the Australian tour.

For all cricketers, not only visiting sides, this is the sweet of the year. Wickets are fast and runs plentiful: Thomas Lord's historic ground is full; in the fields there is a delicious smell of hay; and on the lawns there is elegance and style. The life of a cricket correspondent has many compensations. The pleasure of turning into the Grace Gates on the morning of a Test match is not the least of them.

## THIRD TEST, TRENT BRIDGE, 1972

*July 15.* With all the confidence of Jack Fingleton and myself setting out to cross the Atlantic in a punt, Edrich and Luckhurst began England's innings 10 minutes before luncheon in the third Test match at Trent Bridge yesterday.

## FIRST TEST, EDGBASTON, 1975

*July 12.* Australia had five wickets left when the day began. The first of these fell after 40 minutes when Marsh was caught at the wicket, following any amount of coming and going, and fussing and frowning. Eight overs had been bowled with the new ball when it lost its shape. Off went umpire Bird, who always has to be at the centre of these affairs, in search of a comparable one.

After bringing out a full box of possibilities and deciding with umpire Fagg that none was sufficiently like the

*Perhaps the only unrecorded statistic of Don Bradman's career was the number of autographs he gave. Here, at a lunch at the start of the 1948 tour, he signs for Eric Holmes, a page at the Savoy.*

one in use, he asked Alan Oakman, the Warwickshire coach, to take a new one to the nets, and in the fastest possible time to bowl eight overs with it. This was done, the scene evidently resembling a film that was being run at too fast a speed. Whitehouse, of Warwickshire, batted, Brown and others bowled.

Marsh, meanwhile, was at once caught at the wicket when play restarted, not off the ball that had gone out of shape but one that Fagg had been carrying in his pocket and had had something like 20 overs bowled with it. Marsh's brother, at Carnoustie, could hardly have looked angrier than Rodney had he found a perfect drive trodden into the fairway. When, breathlessly, the ball that had been through the sausage machine was rolled out to Bird, he kept going with Fagg's, which was used for the rest of the innings.

## FOURTH TEST, THE OVAL, 1975

*August 28.* Anyone wanting to plan an attack on the pitch should be careful. The Oval was a prisoner-of-war camp in the last war and was being as carefully guarded last night as it was then, dogs and all.

## FIRST TEST, LORD'S, 1977

*June 21.* Woolmer had batted for four hours 10 minutes and hit 13 fours, some of which in outline looked like Colin Cowdrey specials. It was under Cowdrey that Woolmer came into the Kent side and in build they are not unalike, in so far as a cruiser is not unalike a battleship.

Wednesday August 20 1975
No 59,479
Price ten pence

THE TIMES

The right to choose schools for our children, page 9

**Ford warning to Russia on more arms spending**

President Ford last night issued a dramatic challenge to the Soviet Union to make a positive gesture over détente. He said that unless the Russians were prepared to help to achieve an agreement on strategic arms limitations, he would ask Congress for additional funds of more than $2,000m (about £1,000m) for new nuclear weapons.

**US sees Portugal as test of détente**

From Fred Emery
Washington, Aug 19

President Ford today warned the Soviet Union that unless a satisfactory agreement on strategic arms limitation was forthcoming he would ask Congress for additional funds of up to $3,000m (£1,428m) for new nuclear weapons.

At the same time Mr Ford expressed strong support for the anti-communist forces in Portugal, saying he hoped their "sheer weight of numbers . . . will prevail in this conflict of ideologies."

He reminded Mr Brezhnev, the Soviet party leader, that Portugal was one of a number of "serious situations" the United States was watching to see whether the Russians put détente principles into practice.

"Peace is crucial, but freedom must come first", he said.

The occasion for this tough talk about national defence and détente was the convention of the American Legion in Minneapolis. Seeing Mr Ford sporting a legionnaire's forage cap, many would conclude his remarks were tailored for his audience. There is, of course, a lot of politics to it.

Mr Ford is under direct and indirect fire from three sides for being "soft" on the Russians, or letting them get too carefully watching some serious situations for indications of the Soviet attitude towards détente and cooperation in European security. The situation in Portugal is one of them. We are deeply concerned about the future of freedom in Portugal, as we have always been concerned about the freedom of people throughout the world."

Mr Ford said the reality in Portugal was apparent to all. "The wishes of a moderate majority have been subverted by forces more determined than representative. We are hopeful that the sheer weight of numbers, the 80 per cent of the Portuguese people who support the democratic process, will prevail in this conflict of ideologies. But they must find the solution in an atmosphere that is free from the pressures of outside interests".

Mr Ford managed to leave out Vietnam in his quick celebration of the Allied salvation of civilization since the Second World War.

"The free world, as we define it, is essentially intact after 30 years of an uneasy peace", he said, insisting that the lessons learnt must not be forgotten.

First was his commitment to that "parity" derided by Mr Wallace, but expressed in Mr

**Mr Jenkins seeks to limit secrets Act**

By Peter Hennessy

Mr Jenkins, Home Secretary, is expected to seek the replacement of section two of the Official Secrets Act, 1911, during the next session of Parliament with legislation that will go far beyond the recommendations of the Franks report of 1972.

"It will be a measure of extreme liberality", a Whitehall source said. "It will open up to the press the power, more or less, of total investigation. People will be surprised by it."

The Franks report recommended the replacement of section two of the Act, which is a "catch-all" measure designed to prevent the unauthorized disclosure and transmission of all official information, by a more limited Act covering only the most sensitive aspects of foreign, financial, defence and security matters, and all Cabinet documents. The committee's brief did not cover section one of the Act concerned with espionage.

The new measure will place the burden of proof firmly on the authorities. They will have to advance strong reasons for withholding official information that is not classified as "top secret", "secret", or "defence—confidential".

The new legislation and its expected place in the crowded timetable for the next session of Parliament owe much to the personal conviction of Mr Jenkins, whose libertarian views on such matters are well known and were expressed at length in his evidence to the Franks committee. He received support in the Cabinet from Mrs Williams, Mr Lever, Mr Foot and Mr Crosland.

The repeal of section two is likely to receive a good measure of bipartisan support in the House of Commons. Mr Gilmour, shadow Home Secretary, has for long been a critic of excessive secrecy in government operations. "The Tory party appreciates that section two of the Official Secrets Act needs amendment. It is one of the great blunderbusses that can seldom be used", he said.

The feeling in Whitehall is that, for all its liberality, Mr Jenkins's proposed Bill will neither change the daily lives of civil servants nor lead to a greater degree of open government. It will not provide for the public scrutiny of the flow of documents in and out of departments in the manner of the

**Yard inquiry into conviction of minicab driver after vandals wreck Leeds Test match pitch**

By Clive Borrell

Scotland Yard said yesterday that it would make an immediate independent investigation into the case of George Davis, who is serving a 20-year prison sentence.

The move came after the cricket pitch had been spoilt at Headingley, Leeds, causing abandonment of the third Test match between England and Australia. Friends who maintain that Mr Davis is innocent claimed responsibility for the vandalism.

Mr Davis, aged 34, a minicab driver, was convicted in April last year for his alleged part in a £7,700 robbery in which a policeman was shot and injured. His appeal is pending. Since he was sent to Albany prison, Isle of Wight his family and friends have campaigned for his release

Detective Superintendent Jack Moulder, of Hertfordshire CID, travelled to London yesterday to take charge of the investigation at the invitation of Mr Colin Woods, Deputy Commissioner of the Metropolitan Police. He will recruit his own staff from Hertfordshire and will be helped by detectives from Scotland Yard's A10 branch, which investigates complaints against the police.

Four detectives from Leeds travelled to London last night to assist the Metropolitan police.

Last night detectives were trying to find several men who are believed to have travelled to Leeds from the East End.

Three-inch holes were made in the pitch with kitchen knives and forks, and oil was poured over one end of the wicket. The high walls round the ground were daubed with slogans demanding the release of Mr Davis.

One slogan apologized to spectators for the spoiling of the match, upon which the tenure of the *Ashes* depended. It was later declared a draw, thus depriving England of a possible victory and ensuring Australia's retention of the trophy.

Mr Colin Dean, a brother-in-law of Mr Davis, said last night on Thames Television that four people, two of whom had watched the cricket all Monday afternoon, were responsible for spoiling the pitch. On Monday night, he said, they bought a gallon of oil from a motorway service area and took knives and forks from the restaurant

Ian Chappell (left) and Tony Greig, the rival captains, examining the spoilt wicket

Early yesterday, according to Mr Dean, two of them climbed a wall into the ground, made their way to the centre, and crept under the pitch covers.

Police patrol cars passed the ground regularly during the night. A police constable hired by Yorkshire County Cricket Club and told to guard the wicket went off duty at 6.30 am, unaware of the damage.

Shortly afterwards Mr George Cawthray, the head groundsman, arrived to inspect the wicket. Later he described his discovery as follows:

It was drizzling a bit and we were in no hurry to get the covers off. In fact, I had got half the covers off before I noticed anything wrong. When I saw it at first it did not sink in. I was amazed. I thought I should be able to repair the holes but it was the oil that did the damage.

The umpires, the captains and the team managers were called to the ground, and after a brief discussion it was decided that the match could not continue. The heavy rain later in the morning would almost certainly have prevented a decisive result in any case.

Mr Peter Chappell, one of the leaders of the campaign to free Mr Davis, said yesterday that the pitch had been spoilt because more than a year of frustration had failed to get a proper inquiry into the case. He added:

We are all sorry for the disappointment this has caused to thousands of cricket fans, but a man serving 20 years for a crime he did not commit is far more important than a game of cricket. The responsibility for George Davis is borne by everyone in this country. Everyone must realize that this case is their concern.

Continued on page 2, col 1

**English marmalade joins the Community**

From David Cross
Brussels, Aug 19

British visitors ordering marmalade with their breakfast in other EEC countries are less likely in future to be presented with a nondescript jam because of proposals announced today by the European Commission in Brussels.

The British definition of marmalade as a product made exclusively from citrus fruits would be extended to the whole Community, except Denmark, where the term is used in a generic sense for all types of jam.

The suggested measures, which are being sent to member governments for a final decision, are designed to provide more informative labelling for consumers and to permit free trade in jams and similar products throughout the Community.

The Commission says that the present rules on contents labelling are confusing and tend to hamper the free movement of these products.

Under the proposed standards jams and jellies would be labelled "first quality" or "standard quality", depending on their fruit content, which would have to be marked on every container. Products not measuring up to these standards would continue to be manufactured and marketed, but would not be allowed to bear the "quality" labels.

This is the Commission's second attempt to standardize jam qualities. A proposal made 10 years ago failed to meet the requirements of member governments. The Commission expects the new, more flexible rules to be more acceptable to the Nine. Most interested parties have been consulted and have raised no serious objections.

At present, in countries like France and West Germany, terms like "confiture" and "marmelade" are both used to describe jams, irrespective of the kind of fruit they contain.

**Royal warrant display**

*Front-page sensation at Headingley in 1975 as campaigners dig up the Test pitch*

## SECOND TEST, OLD TRAFFORD, 1977

*July 9.* Australia had batted for almost seven hours and a half, England had bowled their overs at under 14 to the hour. To keep pace with the tempo drinks were taken on a cool morning with nine wickets down. That was like being held up by the signals just outside the station when the train is already late.

## THIRD TEST, TRENT BRIDGE, 1977

*July 28.* If Derek Randall were to be given the choice, he would probably plump for Roope on the grounds that the more batsmen England have the better. Randall has played two championship matches at Trent Bridge this season. He made nought and one in the first, against Northamptonshire, but was less successful in the second, against Middlesex.

## SECOND TEST, LORD'S, 1981

*July 6.* On Saturday morning when play was due to start a pall hung over the ground, with no wind to blow it away. Anyone opening his eyes and seeing the covers in place and the forecourt full would have suspected at once that this was Lord's and England were playing Australia. Upon espying Kerry Packer talking to Irving Rosenwater he might have closed them again.

Sporting …

# …OW ENGLAND KEPT TH… ASHES

## …WO GREAT HEARTS OVERTHROW AUSTRALIA

England beat Australia by five wickets in the fourth Test match at …elaide yesterday and so, gaining a lead of three matches to one in the …ries, have retained the Ashes. In an interview after the match L. Hutton, …e England captain, paid a tribute to the younger members of the side. …Much of the credit, he thought, should go to J. B. Statham, F. H. Tyson, M. C. Cowdrey and P. B. H. May, together with the wicket-keeper, T. G. Evans.

From Our Special Correspondent

ADELAIDE, FEB. 2

Many years from now young Cowdrey will point to his broken nose and tell boys yet unborn that he was at Adelaide on February 2, 1955, when England won the Test match and kept the Ashes. And the boys will think him wondrous lucky. A ma… should dip his pen in blood to write … day. Let no one talk and writ… …cket and explain away the… …ms more fit for … …al in dull …

… the catch. (We asked Hutton afterwards what he thought of Miller's bowling. Hutton thought Miller ought to concentrate much more on batting.) England 10 for 2. In comes the battered Cowdrey. Miller hits him twice running on the pads and appeals, and everybody here who isn't English appeals too. What a man is Miller. He comes in from a shortish run, loose of limb like an African, hair streaming, and as he pulls up the hair goes on and falls about his face. Meanwhile May has begun driving, and Johnson has gone from mid-off to square-leg. For Cowdrey Miller brings fine-leg up to third slip, and Cowdrey cover drives classically for 4. Miller heaves his shoulders over even faster, and Cowdrey is taken by Archer at first-slip. England 18 for 3. Four Meteor jets fly over at 200ft.; they look and sound quite tame beside this wild man … His figures now are 3 overs, no … runs, 3 wickets.

# …ngland all too obliging … …eaches new heights of greatnes…

One that got away: Gilchrist misses a stumping chance off Warne to give Pietersen an extra life, but it was to make little difference

High five: Warne acknowledges the Melbourne crowd after his haul ripped the heart out of England's fragile batting

… legendary accuracy and a lush outfield, they ran poorly between the wickets, chose the wrong balls to try to hit in the air and failed to justify the decision to bat.

"We didn't expect conditions to change dramatically over the first day and a half," Strauss said, "but it seamed about more than we expected." It did so slowly but Glenn McGrath, Stuart Clark and Brett Lee all got enough past the bat to suggest that the wrong option had been taken.

Australia missed two catches, two clear run-out opportunities and a gaping stumping, but still bowled England out for 159 after they had been 101 for two. Very few Test matches are won after such a start. All of Warne's wickets were taken by flight and dip, as batsmen spied what they believed to be boundary opportunities. Only Kevin Pietersen got anywhere near the boundary as he attempted to drive Warne straight for six, but by now he was, as usual, batting with the tail.

Even he needed 70 balls for 21 runs, having come close to running out Andrew Flintoff for six as, for the third Test in succession, he attempted a ridiculous single in order to get off the mark. He had only survived a four when he also survived a simple stumping chance offered to Adam Gilchrist after charging Warne and missing.

England, we all know, have too long a tail, but tweaking it made no difference. Matthew Hoggard is back where he started, No 11, pushing Monty Panesar and Stephen Harmison up a place each, which reflects their various abilities with the bat. It is higher up, however, that the balance is wrong. Ed Joyce or Jamie Dalrymple should have played six, but Chris Read for Geraint Jones was the only change.

As the best player in the team, Pietersen needs to bat at four. Since Paul Collingwood shared the only partnership of any substance with Strauss — 57 for the third wicket — it may appear that England's strategy, to keep him away from the new ball, had worked again, but to have Pietersen batting with the tail repeatedly is not satisfactory. In any case Collingwood might have been leg-before to Clark for nought, one of four apparently plumb leg-before decisions turned down by Rudi Koertzen.

Panesar was the other, …

… Australia's recent practice of not using a nightwatchman. Ponting said that Australia, too, would have chosen to bat first, but it was one of those tosses that either captain would prefer to have lost. Play was delayed by rain for half an hour and only 16 overs were bowled before an early lunch was taken. Alastair Cook …

… S Katich lbw b …

… onting run out (Flintoff) 66

P Siddle c Flintoff b Harmison 10

5.37 343-9 S Clark c Cook b Harmison 0

…iant leap

for proud S…

Sporting News

# ENGLAND HAVE LAST WORD

## THREE YEOMEN FOIL AUSTRALIA

### GREAT STAND BY WATSON AND BAILEY

FROM OUR CRICKET CORRESPONDENT

Out of darkness, through fire into light. Thus did England yesterday rise like some Phoenix from the ashes of apparent defeat to save the second Test match at Lord's and so gain a … draw against Australia with … seven wickets, … original aim fo… The age of … yet past, nor c… cany scarce f… dramatic and … a match alrea… But within t… longest and m… of a match it… that last spa… back with le… yeomen of T… nearly the w…

The yeom… were Watso… greatest of … Yorkshirem… order, was … rearguard … twentieth …

36 TUESDAY AUGUST 1 1989

THE TIMES

# England's abject surrender marks new low in series

By Alan Lee, Cricket Correspondent

## Inglorious procession at Old Trafford

10-1: Curtis c Boon b Alderman 0

25-2: Robinson lbw b Lawson 12

27-3: Smith c Healy b Alderman 1

38-4: Gooch c Alderman b Lawson 13

38-5: Botham lbw b Alderman 4

59-6: Gower c Marsh b Lawson 15

SCOREBOARD FROM OLD TRAFFORD

England won toss

ENGLAND

First Innings: 260 (R A Smith 143; G F Lawson 6 for 72)

Second Innings

AUSTRALIA

First Innings

## Gower unfairly blamed for failings of others

Simon Barnes

## Border rewarded for hard labour

By John Woodcock

## Only two men so far decline

By Alan Lee

# Was this English … most desperate …

… night issued a dramati… …et Union to make a positive …e. He said that unless the …epared to help to achieve an …tegic arms limitations, he would … additional funds of more than …

# WEATHER

THE TIMES SATURDAY JUNE 11 1938
A GOOD BEGINNING BY ENGLAND
Sporting News
LAKER'S SUPREME PART IN RETAINING THE ASHES
AUSTRALIAN WICKETS AND 19 IN MATCH
From Our Cricket Correspondent
THE TIMES
HOW THE AUSTRALIANS WERE SKITTLED OUT AT LORD'S
Gaullists may get back with clear majority
Inquiry over bank chief's salary
Police alerted by strike ship
Railways must act alone, Marsh says
dismally surrender Ashes
TEST MATCH
BRADMAN 309 NOT OUT
ALL RECORDS BROKEN
The Third Test Match between England and Australia was begun at Leeds yesterday. A. P. F. Chapman, for once, lost the toss and Australia went in to bat on a perfect batsman's wicket. By the end of the day they had scored 458 runs for the loss of three wickets

## FIRST TEST, OLD TRAFFORD, 1884

*July 11.* Owing to the heavy rain yesterday at Manchester it was found impossible to make a commencement in this match – the first of three representative contests arranged between picked elevens of Englishmen and Australians. The public waited about until after luncheon, when the weather showed some signs of improvement. An inspection of the ground about a quarter to 4, however, precluded any idea of play for the day, and it was accordingly agreed to postpone the start until this morning.

## FIFTH TEST, MELBOURNE, 1894–95

*March 6.* No rain fell today, but the cricket was spoiled both for players and spectators, of whom some seven thousand were present at the opening of play, by one of the stifling dust storms peculiar to Australia. Clouds of hot dust constantly blew over the ground, causing great discomfort.

## FIRST TEST, EDGBASTON, 1902

R.H. LYTTELTON

*May 31.* During Thursday night there was some rain at Birmingham, but no large quantity. At 11 o'clock this morning there was practically no rain falling, but the weather was cold and the whole outlook depressing. The wicket was not affected to any considerable extent, but cricket in these days appears to be out of the question if there is a suspicion of rain, and for some reasons, which to older cricketers seemed altogether inadequate, no attempt was made to begin the game before luncheon. After luncheon the umpires ordered the game to be resumed at a quarter to 3. Their decision appears difficult to account for on any logical or consistent principles. It must be remembered that no rain to speak of had fallen since 10 o'clock in the morning, and there was practically very little difference in the condition of the wicket at 11 and at 3. Even if there was a little improvement in the condition of the wicket it cannot have been sufficient to justify play in the afternoon, assuming that play was really impossible in the morning. It may be that 30 years ago too little attention was paid to the condition of the wicket, and in those days when rain stopped play was resumed immediately but we are now erring in a contrary direction. Howell and Noble began the bowling, and Lockwood and Rhodes continued their innings, in the chilliest and bleakest weather, before about 6,000 spectators.

## SECOND TEST, LORD'S, 1902

R.H. LYTTELTON

*June 13.* The weather of this so-called summer recalls that of 1860, 1879, and 1888. After three or four fairly fine days, rain began to fall about 7 o'clock yesterday morning and continued till nearly 12, and the umpires at Lord's ordered play in the second test match to begin after luncheon. Rain had then stopped, but the weather was very cold and of the gloomiest description. [...]

There is every probability that the match will be ruined by the weather, as the day closed with a most gloomy appearance. Great coats were in universal use, as the temperature was more like January than June; but nevertheless there was an attendance of about 8,000.

## FIRST TEST, SYDNEY, 1911–12

*December 18*. The weather was much more pleasant when the game was continued, but the wind was still very strong, and spectators' hats, players' caps, and bits of paper were flying about all over the ground.

## FIFTH TEST, THE OVAL, 1926

ALAN ROBBINS

*August 19*. There could be no doubt that, on the day's play, victory went to the better side, but on the final day England was able to add to her team a 12th player in the rainstorm which broke over the ground before lunch, and a 13th in the hot sun which followed during the aftemoon. England on the other hand had had an equally difficult time to survive on the previous morning, and yesterday she grasped every opportunity which came her way.

No Test match this summer would have been complete without some interruption owing to rain, but few of the spectators who groaned when the English innings was interrupted realized that the decisive moment of the match had been reached. Just before midday rain was falling heavily in some parts of London, but the Oval escaped lightly and it was possible to start play at 12.15. An appreciative crowd, which included during the day the King of Iraq, Prince Arthur of Connaught, and the Prime Minister, settled down to see what the remaining English batsmen would do, and what task Australia would finally be called on to accomplish.

## THIRD TEST, OLD TRAFFORD, 1938

R.B. VINCENT,
CRICKET CORRESPONDENT

*July 9*. It may have been a comforting, and profitable, day for cinema proprietors in Manchester yesterday, but it was unsuitable for anyone who wanted to see any play in the third Test Match between England and Australia. It had rained hard on Thursday, although the wind which blew later in the afternoon offered some hope of drying the ground. During most of the night rain fell again, although those who were called early had half an hour's peep at the sun.

That apparently was a sure sign that more rain was to come, and come it did in earnest at 9 o'clock. Some few made the trek to Old Trafford, and having arrived there soon returned. Some armed with tickets actually entered the ground. They were rewarded with the amusement of watching the groundsmen take the covers off the pitch and make an attempt to mop up casual pools, but they knew full well in their hearts that there was never a chance of seeing any cricket.

Luncheon over, the captains walked to the centre of the ground and immediately walked back, and one minute after a loud-speaker announced, 'Play abandoned for the day.' I am told by one who is old enough to understand Manchester that the bad spell of weather is broken, and that there are to be some days of beautiful sunshine. If he proves to be correct we can expect some entertaining cricket before the match is over.

R.B. VINCENT,
CRICKET CORRESPONDENT

*July 11*. Rain again prevented any play in the third Test Match at Old Trafford on Saturday, and when the first ball will be bowled no man can tell. The weather has so often promised to clear only to prove fickle that those who have bought tickets for reserved seats have probably by now consigned them to the dustbin.

The wicket was sodden on Friday night, but a high wind without rain might have dried it. By breakfast time the streets were dry and a glimpse of sunshine made tongues wag recklessly in discussing what the captain would do who had the luck to win the toss. Foolish talk it turned out to be when it became known throughout the hotels of Manchester that the captains had gone to Old Trafford and had formed a very poor idea of the hope of any play. That was not to dishearten the groundsman and his staff, who removed the wet turf near the pitch and replaced it with virgin grass. Thus they hoped to make it both secure and handsome, but they could not remove the covers from the wicket.

So the unhappy ticket-holders sat patiently until 4 o'clock, when the captains again trod and prodded the ground. Apparently they disagreed, for the umpires were in turn sent out to form an opinion. Their inspection was little more than formal, for it was soon announced that play was abandoned for the day, and with that the Salford Town band, who had nobly given of Gilbert and Sullivan, packed up their trombones and went home. As the crowd passed out of the ground the rain fell again in earnest as if to support the judgment of umpires and captains. If a beginning is possible today the match will be played under the rule governing two-day games.

R.B. VINCENT,
CRICKET CORRESPONDENT

*July 13*. The third Test match that should have been was abandoned at Old Trafford yesterday without a ball having been bowled. The weather had cleared on Monday evening, but yesterday morning the rain fell in torrents, and only those who find pleasure in a journey on a Manchester tramcar made the excursion to look at a water-logged pitch. [...]

The matter may not have been put officially, but for all that the whole question of Test matches in this country is a matter of comment, and even cricket spectators must be allowed freedom of speech. There is need for an adjustment between Test match and County Cricket. Obviously a team which has travelled 13,000 miles expects some reward for the journey in their principal matches, which are Test matches. They are expected to provide the most advanced and efficient form of cricket available, and to give some indication of the comparative standard of cricket in the two countries. In those respects they are both interesting and instructive.

To form the English team the selectors have to rely upon the counties who for their very existence sometimes have to rely upon the proceeds of Test match cricket. Test match cricket, accordingly, cannot survive without the goodwill of the counties in sparing their men for so many matches in the season, and county cricket would fade away unless it were for the money it receives in return.

The present state of affairs is manifestly unsatisfactory, and demands serious consideration by the authorities. If the number of Test matches were reduced from five to three, and each played to a finish, the visiting team at least would have a definite result at the end of their tour, and the counties would not be called upon to make so-great a sacrifice.

At present each of the five Test matches breaks into two county fixtures, and a Test match without time limit could do no more damage. Two of the games could be played in London, at Lord's and at the Oval, and one match alternately at Leeds and Old Trafford.

Anything would be an improvement upon the present state of affairs.

## FIRST TEST, BRISBANE, 1946–47

NEVILLE CARDUS

*December 3.* And I have a purely personal objection to rain in Brisbane; it brings the mosquitoes out in whole symphonies in the night.

*December 5.* Another miracle was performed this morning at Brisbane; the match began as usual at noon. The waters had subsided, and the fig tree was green in the leaf. It was like playing cricket in the Old Testament.

## FIRST TEST, TRENT BRIDGE, 1953

GEOFFREY GREEN, CRICKET CORRESPONDENT

*June 16.* What the future holds and how the pitch will behave it is impossible to forecast. All depends on the unpredictable weather of these islands. It seems odd, somehow, or perhaps typical, that it took the English to invent this beautiful but highly complicated game of cricket so utterly unsuited to their own strange climate.

*A first speech of the tour for Australia captain Ian Johnson as the newsreel cameras greet the 1956 touring party*

## THIRD TEST, OLD TRAFFORD, 1953

GEOFFREY GREEN, CRICKET CORRESPONDENT

*July 11.* A meteorological expert is the need for Manchester, where no finish against Australia has been achieved since 1905.

Old Trafford, indeed, is a desolate scene, grey, glistening, and misty in the wet. The flotsam of a crowd that earlier sat patiently around the boundary's edge lies dank and soggy, hugged by the soaked turf. It tests the spirit. Yet this same rain, should it continue, may save England in the end, for Australia surely now stand in little danger of defeat.

## FIFTH TEST, SYDNEY, 1954–55

JOHN WOODCOCK, CRICKET CORRESPONDENT

*March 1.* Never before in Australia have the first three days of a Test match had to be completely abandoned. Tonight, for those who like the hard facts, it is still raining a steady slanting drizzle and the field is as waterlogged as at any previous time. There will have to be a change of wind if there is to be any play tomorrow.

## FOURTH TEST, OLD TRAFFORD, 1956

JOHN WOODCOCK, CRICKET CORRESPONDENT

*July 31.* It was as though someone had arranged a game of cricket in mid-winter, with a few spectators huddled miserably in their seats and clinging frantically to their hats. Not surprisingly the play was comparably unrealistic, and England in their frustration must feel that this is a match which they are not ordained to win.

Through the weekend the thunder had roared, the rain streamed down, and yesterday morning as the wind howled round the city of Manchester there seemed little chance of any play at all. From time to time great storms kept bursting over the ground, yet amazingly enough the pitch was sufficiently dry for action to begin at a quarter to three.

## FIRST TEST, EDGBASTON, 1961

JOHN WOODCOCK, CRICKET CORRESPONDENT

*June 13.* The weather man who predicted yesterday morning that the spectators at Edgbaston might need their coats to sit on but not to wear was a long way off the mark. At half past two the players were driven in by rain with England's second innings score at 106 for one. At a quarter past four all action was abandoned, leaving England appreciably nearer to safety than they were at the start of the day.

## FOURTH TEST, OLD TRAFFORD, 1961

JOHN WOODCOCK, CRICKET CORRESPONDENT

*July 27.* Yesterday it was grey and cool and windy, but the glass, I gather, was surprisingly high and Mr G. Duckworth, who, as a Lancashire farmer as well as a Lancashire wicketkeeper, should know the climate, reckoned that if it rained it would hardly be enough 'to wet the floor'.

*A chance to put their feet up for Alan Davidson, Bobby Simpson and Peter Burge as they leave for home aboard the Strathmore in 1961*

## SECOND TEST, LORD'S, 1968

JOHN WOODCOCK, CRICKET CORRESPONDENT

*June 21.* At half past two yesterday afternoon a canal some five yards wide joined the grandstand with the Mound stand, bisecting the pitch as it went. The decision by the umpires to 'look again' at four o'clock before abandoning play for the day raised only the caterer's hopes. Their inspection, anyway, was preceded by a second cloudburst.

JACK FINGLETON

The only previous time I have seen a pitch under so much hail and water was in Brisbane in 1946 in that city's most damaging storm. Stumps floated to the surface and that artful dodger, Sid Barnes, caused English eyes to open even wider when he surreptitiously slid a block of ice out of the team's ice-box down the pavilion lawn among the huge hailstones.

## FIRST TEST, OLD TRAFFORD, 1972

JOHN WOODCOCK,
CRICKET CORRESPONDENT

*June 12.* It has been rather like playing a Test match in the depths of an English winter. Even on a grey November day the Manchester skyline could have made no bleaker sight, and yesterday, as the Australians wondered how they could possibly escape with a draw, there was still no permanent sign of the warmth and sunshine that might clear the air and purify the pitch.

## FIFTH TEST, THE OVAL, 1972

JOHN WOODCOCK,
CRICKET CORRESPONDENT

*August 14.* A capacity crowd had a vexing afternoon. For between luncheon and tea it was they rather than the players who were in possession of the field – in rain, at times so fierce that Fischer and Spassky might have played in it without noticing. On the committee balcony the Prime Minister sat without oilskins.

But there is a custom in cricket that, except upon the insistence of both captains, play shall not start while it is raining. On Saturday, with their backs to the wall, England would not have wanted a damp ball to add to their problems. For much of the time the rain was too slight to have driven the players off the field had they been on it, but sufficient to deter the umpires from leading them back on. To make it more galling, when the rain did stop it was announced that the players were having tea. Tempers, like the kettle, boiled at that, and it was not surprising.

JOHN WOODCOCK,
CRICKET CORRESPONDENT

*January 22, 1975.* The weather has been lovely these last few days in Sydney. At the start of the tour it rained on 25 of the first 31 days. For the last three or four days there has been hardly a cloud in the sky, Lillee and Thomson have been far enough away not to hinder our enjoyment of the oysters, and the harbour has looked beautiful beyond words. Sir Neville Cardus once wrote that he could live in Sydney, at Watson's Bay or Vaucluse, and be happy, given a gramophone and Test matches only once every four years. Today you would have known what he meant.

## FIRST TEST, LORD'S, 1977

JOHN WOODCOCK,
CRICKET CORRESPONDENT

*June 16.* The first Test match begins at Lord's this morning on a pitch affected by floods but with the promise of brighter weather ahead. In the middle of last Monday night Jim Fairbrother and three of his ground staff were battening down the covers, in conditions which he, as a wartime sailor, described as sounding and seeming like a naval engagement.

## FIRST TEST, BRISBANE, 1986–87

JOHN WOODCOCK,
CRICKET CORRESPONDENT

*November 19.* England's one piece of luck was with the weather. There had been a confident forecast of afternoon showers and at 2.30 word came that it was raining hard down the road (which could mean a couple of hundred miles away in Australia) and would be doing so at the Gabba by four o'clock. When four o'clock came, we looked like getting another 10 minutes' play at the most; but the clouds broke up and in the end there was a full day, lasting until 5.30.

## FIFTH TEST, PERTH, 1990–91

ALAN LEE, CRICKET CORRESPONDENT

*February 1.* The hottest day in the history of this city was a trial to everyone, not least the England cricketers, who spent much of their time sheltering in their air-conditioned hotel, anxiously tuned in to weather forecasts for today's start of the fifth and final Ashes Test.

The temperature here did not fall below 26C on Wednesday night and, shortly after two o'clock yesterday afternoon, the record was set at 45.8C, almost 115F. One can hardly expect sympathy reporting such facts to a Britain suffering frost and snow, but it is a fact that to be in Perth yesterday was to be unpleasantly incarcerated in an oven.

Bush fires raged all around the area, destroying homes and animals, almost 2,000 cars broke down through overheating in the city and the water board, not to be outdone by the statistics of the day, reported a record consumption. Stocks of fans, hats and suncream dwindled rapidly in the shops and, at the WACA ground, practising cricketers battled against conditions few of them can have experienced before.

Australian players wore sunglasses, not simply against the glare but to protect their eyes from burning. England players adopted a version of legionnaire's hats, tucking handkerchiefs in their caps to keep the sun off their necks. Dehydration was a serious factor, even at practice, and one England player, drenched with perspiration and parched in his throat after a fielding session, was properly piqued to find that the team's drinks supply had been raided by spectating tourists.

Had the Test match started yesterday, there would have been a genuine health risk involved and while I doubt if any Test has ever been halted by heat, I similarly doubt if one has been played in such searing heat as this. Thankfully, a change is evidently on the way; the weathermen say it might struggle to reach 100F today.

## THIRD TEST, SYDNEY, 1994–95

ALAN LEE, CRICKET CORRESPONDENT

*January 3.* The grey skies that had been brooding over Sydney all morning began doing their worst during the lunch interval, and although the Australian reply did start, 25 minutes late, it was into only its fourth over when more serious and persistent rain interrupted, perhaps even deleted, this developing story line.

Sydney suffers more rain-ruined days of cricket than any other Australian city – a fact Manchester mischievously used in its propaganda when bidding for the Olympic Games of 2000 – but the weather has seldom turned with such unkind timing, not only for England's lingering hopes of reviving this series but for the second crowd of 30,000 in successive days. Even the holidaying solicitors and self-confessed dropouts who make up the motley and noisy 'Barmy Army', England's travelling fan club, were subdued and bedraggled by the time play was abandoned.

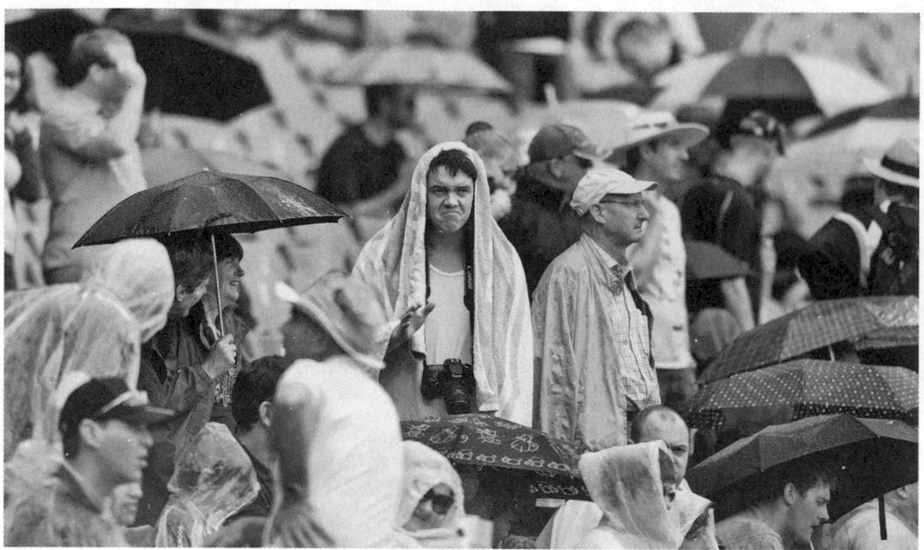

*A soggy end to the day at the SCG in 2010–11*

## FOURTH TEST, MELBOURNE, 1998–99

ALAN LEE, CRICKET CORRESPONDENT

*December 28.* There was no rain yesterday, but nothing else had improved. A city that sweltered in a temperature of 38C on Christmas Day now shivered in the low teens. It was a case of scarves and overcoats for the 25,000 spectators and three sweaters for the players. A chill and blustery wind swirled rubbish around the outfield and the palm trees across the park might have been transplanted from an alien planet.

## FIFTH TEST, THE OVAL, 2005

PAT GIBSON

*September 10.* There is usually nothing more frustrating for a cricket-lover than to watch the players leave the field because of bad light, nothing more depressing than to see the rain set in, the groundstaff drag on the covers and tarpaulins and the umpires announce that there will be no more play for the day.

Now it is different. There were a few jeers and a half-hearted attempt at a slow handclap when Justin Langer and Matthew Hayden accepted the umpires' offer to go off with rather more alacrity than one would expect from a side trying to hang on to the Ashes, but the jeers promptly turned to cheers when the crowd realised that they were actually helping England's cause.

Never mind that they were watching one of the most enthralling series in the history of the game. Never mind that Langer and Hayden had finally shown why they are the most prolific opening partners of modern times. Never mind that the ball was 33 overs old and starting to reverse swing. All that most of them cared about was that the more it rained, the better England's chances of drawing the Test and thereby winning the series would be.

*The use of floodlights at major Test grounds has made interruptions for bad light far less common. Play continues at the SCG on a murky afternoon in 2010–11*

## FIRST TEST, BRISBANE, 2013–14

GIDEON HAIGH

*November 25.* Johnson was not the only natural force on display during the day. A storm in these parts is a Storm, and as the players evacuated ahead of the weather at 2pm, the big screen flashed an official warning, urging patrons in the event of rain to 'follow instructions from Gabba staff and seek shelter from exposed areas of the venue'. There was no request to assume the brace position or offer of an oxygen mask, although perhaps this was understood. In fact, the crowd rather relished it, roaring approval at the first sign of hail and enjoying the veritable blizzard as though it was part of the in-game entertainment.

They relished even more that the ground was bathed in sunshine within 25 minutes.

Sporting

# OW ENGLAND KEPT TH ASHES

## VO GREAT HEARTS OVERTHROW AUSTRALIA

England beat Australia by five wickets in the fourth Test match at Adelaide yesterday and so, gaining a lead of three matches to one in the ries, have retained the Ashes. In an interview after the match L. Hutton, he England captain, paid a tribute to the younger members of the side. Much of the credit, he thought, should go to J. B. Statham, F. H. Tyson, M. C. Cowdrey and P. B. H. May, together with the wicket-keeper, T. G. Evans.

From Our Special Correspondent

ADELAIDE, FEB. 2

Many years from now young Cowdrey will point to his broken nose and tell boys yet unborn that he was at Adelaide on February 2, 1955, when England won the Test match and kept the Ashes. And the boys will think him wondrous lucky. A ma ... should dip his pen in blood to writ ... his day. Let no one talk and writ ... ket and explain away the ... ms more fit for ...

the catch. (We asked Hutton afterwards what he thought of Miller's bowling. Hutton thought Miller ought to concentrate much more on batting.) England 10 for 2. In comes the battered Cowdrey. Miller hits him twice running on the pads and appeals, and everybody here who isn't English appeals too. What a man is Miller. He comes in from a shortish run, loose of limb like an African, hair streaming, and as he pulls up the hair goes on and falls about his face.

Meanwhile May has begun driving, and Johnson has gone from mid-off to square-leg. For Cowdrey Miller brings fine-leg up to third slip, and Cowdrey cover drives classically for 4. Miller heaves his shoulders over even faster, and Cowdrey is taken by Archer at first-slip. England 18 for 3. Four Meteor jets fly over at 200ft.; they look and sound quite tame beside this wild man ... His figures now are 3 overs, no ... runs, 3 wickets.

# ngland all too obliging ... eaches new heights of greatnes

One that got away: Gilchrist misses a stumping chance off Warne to give Pietersen an extra life, but it was to make little difference

High five: Warne acknowledges the Melbourne crowd after his haul ripped the heart out of England's fragile batting

Australia's recent practice of not using a nightwatchman. Ponting said that Australia, too, would have chosen to bat first, but it was one of those tosses that either captain would prefer to have lost. Play was delayed by rain for half an hour and only 16 overs were bowled before an early lunch was taken. Alastair Cook

Sporting News

# ENGLAND HAVE LAST WORD

## THREE YEOMEN FOIL AUSTRALIA

## GREAT STAND BY WATSON AND BAILEY

FROM OUR CRICKET CORRESPONDENT

Out of darkness, through fire into light. Thus did England yesterday rise like some Phoenix from the ashes of apparent defeat to save the second Test match at Lord's and so gain a ... draw against Australia with ... seven wickets, ... original aim fo ... The age of m ... yet past, nor c ... cany scarce fo ... dramatic and ... a match alrea ... But within t ... longest and m ... of a match it ... that last spa ... back with le ... yeomen of ... nearly the w ...

The yeom ... were Watso ... greatest of ... Yorkshirem ... order, was ... rearguard ... twentieth ...

Ponting run out (Flintoff) 66

P Siddle c Flintoff b Harmison 10

5.37 343-9 S Clark c Cook b Harmison 0

iant leap

for proud S

36 TUESDAY AUGUST 1 1989

THE TIMES

First published 1785

# England's abject surrender marks new low in series

By Alan Lee, Cricket Correspondent

## Inglorious procession at Old Trafford

18-1: Curtis c Boon b Alderman 0

25-2: Robinson lbw b Lawson 12

27-3: Smith c Healy b Alderman 1

38-4: Gooch c Alderman b Lawson 13

38-5: Botham lbw b Alderman 4

59-6: Gower c Marsh b Lawson 15

SCOREBOARD FROM OLD TRAFFORD

## Gower unfairly blamed for failings of others

Simon Barnes

## Border rewarded for hard labour

By John Woodcock

## Only two men so far decline

By Alan Lee

# Was this English ... most desperate

# BEYOND THE BOUNDARY

THE TIMES SATURDAY JUNE 11 1938

...H: A GOOD BEGINNING BY ENGLAND

4

Sporting News

LAKER'S SUPREME PART IN RETAINING THE ASHES

ALL TEN AUSTRALIAN WICKETS AND 19 IN MATCH

From Our Cricket Correspondent

THE TIMES

HOW THE AUSTRALIANS WERE SKITTLED OUT AT LORD'S

Gaullists may get back with clear majority

Inquiry over bank chief's salary

Police alerted by strike ship

Railways must act alone, Marsh says

...dismally surrender Ashes

TEST MATCH

BRADMAN 309 NOT OUT

ALL RECORDS BROKEN

*The Third Test Match between England and Australia was begun at Leeds yesterday. A. P. F. Chapman, for once, lost the toss and Australia went in to bat on a perfect batsman's wicket. By the end of the day they had scored 458 runs for the loss of three wickets...*

## ONLY TEST, THE OVAL, 1880

*September 7.* Long before the time appointed for commencing hostilities had arrived streams of spectators could be seen wending their way to the Oval at Kennington, and by 10 o'clock there were about 10,000 persons present. Extra accommodation had been provided, and on the western side of the ground a stand had been erected with chairs to seat from 1,200 to 1,500 spectators. The utmost enthusiasm was shown, and there has probably never been so large and appreciative an audience present at any match in England before; at one time there were over 25,000 persons on the ground.

The crowd had arranged themselves in a very orderly manner before 11.30, and five minutes afterwards the Australians, who had lost the toss, entered the field. Drs E.M. and W.G. Grace appeared on behalf of England; Messrs Boyle and Palmer conducted the attack.

## ONLY TEST, THE OVAL, 1882

*August 29.* The fact of an 'England' team proving itself competent to dispose of the Australians for the meagre total of 63 was received with considerable gratification by the sightseers, who, by the way, were by no means grudging of their cheers at any noteworthy piece of play on the part of the Australians.

*August 30.* Yesterday afternoon a painful sensation was caused among a large number of the spectators of the cricket match at Kennington Oval by a very sudden death that occurred. It seems that immediately after the conclusion of the the innings of the Australian players, one of the spectators, who it was afterwards ascertained was George Eber Spendlen, of 101, Brook-street, Kennington, complained to a friend who was with him of feeling unwell, and left the seat which he had for some time occupied. Scarcely had he done so, however, when he fell to the ground and blood commenced to flow freely from his mouth. He was at once conveyed to a room adjoining the pavilion, where he was examined by several medical men, who pronounced life extinct, the cause of death being attributed to a broken blood-vessel.

## SECOND TEST, LORD'S, 1884

*July 23.* The interest taken in the Australian cricketers remains unabated. Probably there has never been so numerous and appreciative a crowd at Lord's than that which yesterday assembled to witness the play of the Colonial team against the combined talent of England. The official record shows that 16,388 paid for admission, and, taking into consideration the number of members and others, it is computed that there were over 20,000 persons present.

## FIRST TEST, ADELAIDE, 1884–85

*January 21.* By far the most important engagement of Shaw's team of English cricketers was against the representative Eleven of Australia. It began on Friday, December 12, at the Oval, Adelaide. The company was very numerous, and, indeed, the match engrossed so much interest that it was made the occasion of an almost general holiday. Among those present were his Excellency the Governor and Lady Robinson, the Misses Robinson, Sir Henry Wrenfordsley, the Hon J. Forrest, C.M.G., and Mrs Forrest, and a large number of the leading citizens. The weather was very fine, and the wicket played perfectly true.

## SECOND TEST, LORD'S, 1886

*July 22.* No better illustration of the popularity of cricket could be afforded than the immense company of spectators which assembled at Lord's yesterday. Unlike the fashionable matches, when the promenade is a feature, everybody yesterday seemed bent on securing a view of the game.

## FIRST TEST, LORD'S, 1888

*July 17.* A more perfect contrast to last week could scarcely be found than that afforded at Lord's yesterday. The fashionable array of spectators that graced the ground on Friday and Saturday were replaced by a compact circle – in places eight and ten deep – of cricket enthusiasts. The wicket on examination in the morning was found to be in such a saturated state as to cause any idea of play to be given over until after luncheon. A placard to this effect was posted outside the gate. When the gate was at length opened the rush was so sudden as to cause a block. However, the road gradually became cleared, and the seats in the covered terraces, which were nearly all thrown open to the public, were soon occupied. The company at one time numbered about 14,000.

## SECOND TEST, THE OVAL, 1888

*August 14.* The Oval yesterday presented a scene which is only witnessed when representative matches are in progress. Since the great contests of 1880 and 1882 the Oval itself has undergone great improvement, and spectators are now able to get a better view of the game than they were in those days. Yesterday the terraces all round the ground were packed, as was every position from which a glimpse of the play could be caught. It was an ideal cricket crowd. The manner in which the spectators discriminated between good and bad play was noticeable. They were very impartial and not grudging in their applause, yet they seemed well pleased with the excellent position secured by the Englishmen at the close.

## FIRST TEST, SYDNEY, 1894–95

*December 17.* The match between Mr Stoddart's team and an eleven representing All Australia was continued today. On account of the half holiday the assemblage of spectators was immense. It numbered early in the forenoon over 10,000; after luncheon it had increased to 23,000 and before the end of the afternoon it reached 26,000 – a record total for Sydney. The money takings amounted to £1,300.

## FIFTH TEST, THE OVAL, 1902

E.H. LYTTELTON

*August 12.* An appreciable number of Australian soldiers in their picturesque uniforms formed an attractive group at the south-east corner of the pavilion, and the hitting of Mr Keely at the end of the day gave great delight to these gallant Volunteers.

## FIFTH TEST, THE OVAL, 1905

LEADING ARTICLE

*August 17.* None the less we have learnt by long experience to respect our Colonial antagonists so heartily, we know them to be capable of such great things when fortune favours them ever so little, that the public interest in the fifth Test match, which began last Monday at the Oval, was if possible greater than that shown in any of the other four. A crowd of at least twenty-five thousand persons assembled to see the game; a typical 'Oval crowd,' which comes there on foot or omnibuses and trams – a crowd of serious men and lads out for a serious holiday, a crowd of past and present cricketers and would-be cricketers. Among them were not a few sweethearts and wives, intent on the game, and, what one is always glad to see at a good cricket match, a strong sprinkling of town and country clergy, full of the memories of school and college and conscious perhaps of the indisputable truth that few things make an English parson more respected and more efficient in his parish than a good knowledge of the game and a power of inspiring the lads of his village or of his town club with a keen interest in it.

## FIRST TEST, SYDNEY, 1911–12

*December 18.* The greatest interest was taken in the second day's play of the first Test match of the M.C.C. tour. During the day 35,526 people were admitted to the ground, and the takings amounted to £2,054: The behaviour of the crowd has been excellent throughout the two days, and the absence of annoying 'barracking' has been greatly appreciated by the visiting team.

## SECOND TEST, LORD'S, 1921

A.C.M. CROOME

*June 13.* The crowd, although well-behaved, was frankly partisan. Once, when Mr Haig hit Mr Pellew on the pads, several thousand voices yelled, 'How's that?' And it is unlikely that all who appealed habitually keep wicket on Saturday afternoons. There were other indications that desire for an English victory was single in the hearts of the watchers. But decorous applause greeted the more brilliant strokes of the Australian batsmen when they were making the last two hours of the day an interval for taking tea. And, indeed, the quality of the cricket played by Mr Armstrong and his men was such as to command respectful admiration.

## FIFTH TEST, THE OVAL, 1926

GEORGE CRAIG

*August 19.* Among the large crowd which had gathered outside the Oval excitement became intense as the match drew to a close, and it rose to a climax when, at two minutes past 6, a roar of cheers from the spectators announced the fall of the last Australian wicket. There was a rush for the main entrance to await the players, but the spectators inside the grounds had the first claim upon them. For over half an hour continuous cheering could be heard,

The Times *marketing department gets in on the act at Edgbaston in 1997*

varied by choruses of 'We want Hobbs and Sutcliffe,' 'We want the team,' and then, 'We want the Australians.' At length the players, having escaped from the thousands of persistent hero-worshippers in the grounds, made their way out in motor-cars. Although they were in mufti, they were recognized by the waiting crowds, and they had an enthusiastic ovation as they drove away.

## SECOND TEST, SYDNEY, 1928–29

FROM OUR SPECIAL CORRESPONDENT*

*December 17.* By the general interest the present team has aroused, all attendance records have gone by the board, and never in the history of cricket has such a remarkable sight been witnessed as that of nearly 60,000 people watching every ball on a muggy, sultry afternoon with the closest possible attention. The famous Hill was an extraordinary sight, with its serried ranks of hatless enthusiasts packed so tightly that by comparison the proverbial sardine would seem to be lolling in luxury.

* *The Times* archivist has not been able to identify the author of this report

## FIFTH TEST, THE OVAL, 1930

R.B. VINCENT,
CRICKET CORRESPONDENT

*August 19.* The Surrey crowd has often been unjustly abused. It should, therefore, be recorded that at the close of England's innings, again at the end of the luncheon interval, and again when the rain and bad light interrupted play, the 30,000 spectators showed a most excellent self-restraint. Throughout their manners were altogether admirable. It must have been quite a relief to the Australians to play without the accompaniment of the noise to which they are accustomed at home. The crowd even took without protest what may have seemed to them an unnecessary appeal against the light, and when the umpires came out to resume play cleared the ground without persuasion by the police.

## SECOND TEST, MELBOURNE, 1932–33

ROY CURTHOYS

*December 31.* The constant trouble Larwood was having with his boots – he only had one pair – amused and irritated the spectators in turn. They laughed heartily when, at 100, he showed them the offending boot as he left the field.

## FOURTH TEST, BRISBANE, 1932–33

DELAMORE MCCAY

February 11. When Larwood began bowling his leg theory a section of the crowd became hostile, but after the batsmen had obtained a mastery precisely that same section of the crowd tauntingly implored Jardine to keep Larwood on.

## FOURTH TEST, HEADINGLEY, 1934

R.B. VINCENT,
CRICKET CORRESPONDENT

July 23. The ground looked full enough on Friday, but that was a mere sprinkling compared with the 38,000 who were there on Saturday, packed solidly but cheerfully one against the other, with the

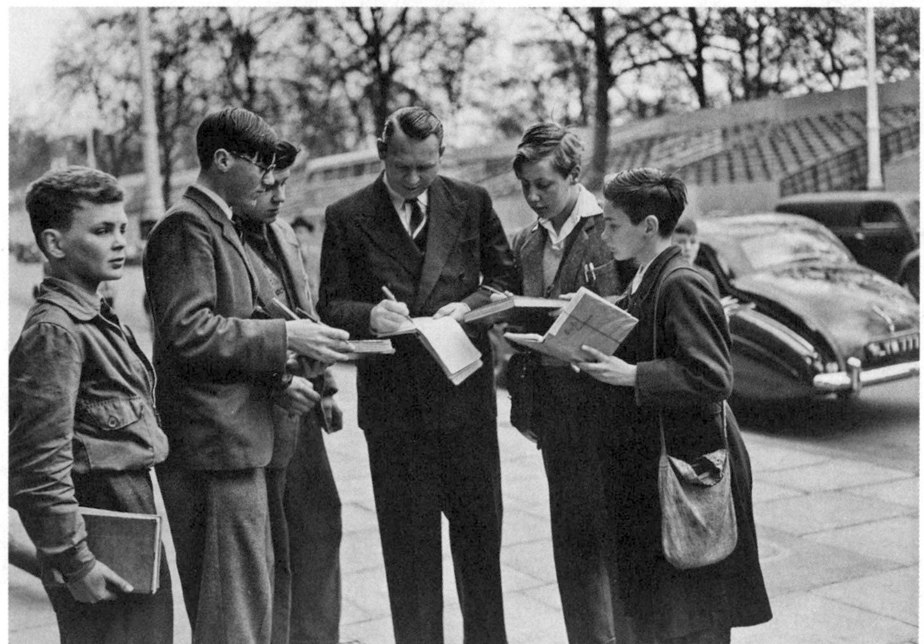

*Doug Ring is kept busy by autograph hunters waiting outside the Australians' hotel in 1953*

more adventurous sitting on the sharp angled roofs of sheds and swarming up trees. The crowd, which is said to be the biggest that has ever watched a Test match in this country, and which saw the largest partnership for any wicket which has ever been made in a Test match, Ponsford and Bradman easily surpassing the 323 made by Hobbs and Rhodes at Melbourne during the tour of 1911–12, reflected by their behaviour the day's play admirably – as is usual on a Yorkshire ground.

## SECOND TEST, LORD'S, 1938

*June 23.* A map showing garage facilities and the roads and streets leading to Lord's Cricket Ground for the Test Match has been issued by the Automobile Association in conjunction with the M.C.C. As the map is designed for use all through the season, a fixture list of other matches at Lord's is given, as well as the names, addresses, and telephone numbers of nearby garages which have agreed to charge standard rates during the summer. Negotiations between the A.A. and Motor Agents' Association have ensured that prices will not be increased on days of special matches. Copies of the map can be obtained free of charge by members from the Association's Headquarters, Fanum House, New Coventry Street, W.1, or through any A.A. branch office.

R.B. VINCENT,
CRICKET CORRESPONDENT

*June 24.* And so we await what, in all probability, will be a feast of runs, while buns, cakes, sandwiches, and bottles in their thousands are being unloaded in the ground for the needs of a crowd which –

again if the rain holds off – will fill every available inch of space.

## FIRST TEST, TRENT BRIDGE, 1948

R.B. VINCENT,
CRICKET CORRESPONDENT

*June 12.* England's bowling certainly did not flag even if there was a cynical note when a musician tootled out *Land of Hope and Glory* during the tea interval with the score 215, and Bradman having already made 78. Hassett scored his runs immaculately and casually, unperturbed by advice offered by some of the spectators to 'get on with it'. And it was noticeable that, Bradman having reached his century, there was marked movement for the gates and home.

*June 14.* So far the cricket had been pleasant to watch on a nice summer day at Trent Bridge. It finished unhappily, and stupidly, but it must be recorded that Miller incurred the most hostile and most unseemly criticism from the crowd that it could be one's displeasure to hear. Booing it was, and booing continued until the teams left the field on their way into the pavilion. Certainly when he put his full vigour into his bowling he was occasionally short of a length. Once he did hit Hutton on the shoulder. That was his business, and a perfectly reasonable challenge to a batsman who was playing altogether too well. The utmost that can be said from the other point of view is that Miller was a little naughty, petulant, call it what you may. But surely cricketers, even in these standardized days, may indulge in some personal liberty of thought and action.

## FIRST TEST, BRISBANE, 1950–51

R.C. ROBERTSON GLASGOW

*December 4.* A night rainfall of nearly an inch at Brisbane, followed by intermittent showers, prevented any cricket on the second day of the first Test match.

In one sense this was a pity, because the Saturday three-quarter holiday and the sudden boom in English cricket stock had together promised a large crowd. Some of the disappointed spectators expressed their feelings by throwing pies and abuse at the turnstiles.

## FIFTH TEST, THE OVAL, 1953

GILBERT WOOD

*August 20.* But there were also women and girls in extraordinary numbers. Some followed the game, ball and stroke, with intensity; others, all of school age, set themselves the curious holiday task of keeping the score in exercise books, as though the rudimentary record of a match card was too bare for them.

There were also, not in the crowd but of it, as their punctual cheers and applause to approve a shot or a neat piece of fielding showed, the thousands outside the ground who occupied all the windows and points of vantage that Oval architecture affords. Also outside, of course, were the crews of pantechnicons and brewers' lorries, who turned their vehicles into vantage points as the England score moved, after luncheon, towards victory. Taxi-drivers also gave up looking for fares and stood on tiptoe on their rooftops to command a view over the 12ft wall; and the youngsters of the neighbourhood found perches on everything from trees and the sign-post of

*No room inside the Oval, but crowds still gather outside to hear news of the action in 1953*

'The Cricketers' to the dull green bulk of the famous gasholder, from whose summit flew the British and Australian flags.

JEROME CAMINADA

*August 20.* Everything has its setting, its meaning, and even its use. Take the wall, for example, the encircling wall. It was not so forbidding as to stop six south London urchins from coming over it, with the help of some incorrigible grown-up, and here they all are, on the ground beside us, cheeky, noisy, dirty, each with a packet of sandwiches, and even with a bottle of water between them. They chatter like monkeys, and beat back with rapier tongues any foolish adult who tries to silence them. And this decent crowd, this good-humoured, tolerant, helpful crowd – some of it Cockney, and some of it not – puts up with them, even when they fight over the water and throw jammy crusts about. Just so long as they *sit down.*

## FIRST TEST, BRISBANE, 1954–55

LEADING ARTICLE

*November 26.* The thoughts we entertain in the early morning remain for the most part unrevealed, for as a nation we are notoriously uncommunicative until the breakfast things have been cleared away. Whatever may go on behind those inexpressive features as they greet the new day it is certain that today the thoughts of many will have been with our Test players in Australia. Before daylight has asserted itself the hand of the cricket enthusiast emerges from the bedclothes to grope for the switch on his wireless set and to satisfy a powerful curiosity. For weeks he has followed the triumphs and failures of our players. The last time they were in Australia he was plagued by news of injuries. If it was not Compton's knee it was Wright's neck or Bailey's shoulder. This year the casualty list has been shorter and the achievement already substantial, but he has been kept on tenterhooks by the in-and-out form of the English batsmen. Now the rehearsals are finished. The captains, the teams, and the umpires have been picked; the pitch has been appraised for the last time, the coin has been tossed, and in the cold light of breakfast time speculation gives way to fact.

The news may not always be to the audience's liking – in 1946 Bradman was already on his way to a double century after the first day's play – but the score is not everything. The hard figures of the day's play may be heard in later bulletins, but nothing can quite destroy the fascination of listening to the ebb and flow of the commentator's voice as he describes, from the other side of the world, Lindwall running in to bowl or a sweep to leg by Compton. So absorbing can this become that the whole routine of a household may temporarily be set at naught. The listener wanders about distractedly, carrying cups of tea and listening for the quickening of the commentator's voice as it tells of a boundary or the muffled roar that greets a fallen wicket. Sustenance is taken not necessarily at the breakfast table but wherever the loudspeaker stands. Children are hushed into silence. Sooner or later the passage of time forces the listener back into the rhythm of another working day, but before he slips on his overcoat he will have relished the sound of cheers from an Australian crowd on whom – or so he imagines – the sun is beating pitilessly down.

## THIRD TEST, MELBOURNE, 1954–55

JOHN WOODCOCK,
CRICKET CORRESPONDENT

*January 5.* Soon after five o'clock a spectator in his shirt sleeves, with a sense of occasion and filled still with the various spirits of the season, saw the field as his stage and Nijinsky as his model – or perhaps the strain of the match was too much for him and he felt his help was needed. There were three or four hilarious minutes before the arm of the law apprehended him in the covers.

## SECOND TEST, LORD'S, 1961

JOHN WOODCOCK,
CRICKET CORRESPONDENT

*June 22.* However moderate the bowling and however clouded the outlook this remains, of course, one of the great occasions of an English summer. In the cricket world there is nothing quite to match the meeting of England and Australia at the game's ancestral home. All manner of men will have woken up this morning with a special sense of pleasure. Making one's way to Lord's it will be as though the flags are out; as the ground fills up and the players cross over to the Nursery nets the pulse will quicken.

## THIRD TEST, MELBOURNE, 1970–71

JOHN WOODCOCK,
CRICKET CORRESPONDENT

*January 2.* The temperature today has been in the low 50s. The ground is saturated, the streets have been awash, and there is an open fire burning in the Melbourne club. Those poor people, who have flown from England to fulfil a life's ambition and watch a Test match in Australia must feel as though they have been robbed. They were attracted by the prospect of sunshine and sport; yet by a quarter to twelve this morning all hope of play had been abandoned. One of them was said to be looking for someone to sue.

## THIRD TEST, MELBOURNE, 1974–75

JOHN WOODCOCK,
CRICKET CORRESPONDENT

*December 28.* The best fun after that was the appearance of two young Australians, dressed, as the umpires always are out here, in white shoes, black trousers, white shirts with the sleeves rolled down, and broad white hats. They came out during the break for bad light, marching in step, which is again the thing to do, and taking everyone in. By the time they were rumbled they were halfway to getting the game restarted, which most people thought should be happening anyway.

## FOURTH TEST, SYDNEY, 1974–75

JOHN WOODCOCK,
CRICKET CORRESPONDENT

*January 8.* The last three days have been as much an ordeal for England as a game of cricket. I have watched many Test matches in Sydney without ever seeing or hearing anything to compare with what has been happening on the Hill. By the afternoon, when the beer is taking effect (on a cool day they drink beer to keep warm, if it is hot they drink it to keep cool), there are all the signs of mass hysteria. Lillee reckoned that it put two yards on his speed on Sunday afternoon to be bowling with the thousands wedged on the Hill baying him on. For the England side it is like being brainwashed at the same time as facing two fast and fearsome bowlers. The Hill is not a place for old-fashioned barracking any more, or for subtleties, but for taking as many cans of beer as an 'esky' (a portable icebox) can carry and consuming them until each voice becomes louder than the next, each remark more obscene. There are thus the same pressures as if you were playing, not for a mere 90 minutes, but for six hours on a packed football ground, and batting, if you are English, against two bowlers who have been allowed to get away for most of the present series with a surfeit of short-pitched bowling.

## FOURTH TEST, EDGBASTON, 1981

JOHN WOODCOCK,
CRICKET CORRESPONDENT

*August 3.* The crowd, another good one, did all they could for England. With increasingly less reserve they cheered them on, sending Willis and Botham in to bowl on such waves of chauvinism as are seldom heard on English cricket fields. In Barbados yes; at Sydney certainly; in Calcutta always; at Wembley of course: but the English are usually more staid than this in the way they watch the game of bat and ball.

## FIRST TEST, HEADINGLEY, 1989

ALAN LEE, CRICKET CORRESPONDENT

*June 12.* The enduring memories of the first Test match in this summer's Ashes series ought to be of vivid, attacking batting. Sadly, those who were present at Headingley on Saturday will have taken home some altogether more disturbing images.

I will not forget, as anyone with an interest in cricket's welfare should not forget, how a moronic element in the near-capacity crowd found ways to interrupt the game and spoil everyone's enjoyment.

I will not forget the leering, fist-shaking demeanour of a menacing gang strutting around the ground, utterly indifferent to the cricket.

They looked as if they were filling in a quiet Saturday while awaiting the arrival of Vinny Jones at Leeds United; and yet, when Allan Lamb completed his marvellous century, they lurched and swaggered on to the ground, revelling in their own stupidity. [...]

Play was first delayed when another rendition of the Mexican wave, that mental aberration which cricket should have long since discouraged, was accompanied by a confetti storm of torn-up paper.

David Gower, who was batting at the time, diplomatically called it 'a minor annoyance we could well have done without'.

Play was delayed again when spectators, clutching pints of beer, clearly not their first of the day, tottered in front of the sightscreens at the bowling end. They were not all youngsters. Sponsored guests, emerging from three-hour lunches, were equally to blame.

Finally came the predictable pitch invasion. One of the galloping goons who buffeted Lamb and scuffed across the pitch flumped to the ground as he retreated and needed four stewards to carry him off.

## THIRD TEST, SYDNEY, 1994–95

ALAN LEE, CRICKET CORRESPONDENT

*January 5.* Much worse behaviour followed in the final session, as the self-styled 'Barmy Army' of England followers showed that their noisy antics are not exclusively harmless. Some beery clashes with Australian supporters on what used to be the Hill led to a line of police and stewards separating the rival groups.

What a pity, on a day when the crowd of 22,812 lifted the match attendance above 100,000 and was the highest fourth-day crowd on this ground for ten years. Test cricket is thriving again in this country, but the kind of warlike behaviour that so damagingly infected football some years ago should be discouraged.

## FIRST TEST, EDGBASTON, 2001

CHRISTOPHER MARTIN-JENKINS, CHIEF CRICKET CORRESPONDENT

*July 6.* But in the 79 balls that intervened, Alec Stewart and Andrew Caddick turned a patently unsatisfactory England total of 191 for nine into one that gave their bowlers at least a sporting chance on a dry pitch. Their last-wicket partnership of 103 was battered out to roars of patriotic fervour by the crowd that resounded like a long echo of those that in the past few days have hailed the deeds of Tim Henman and the British Lions.

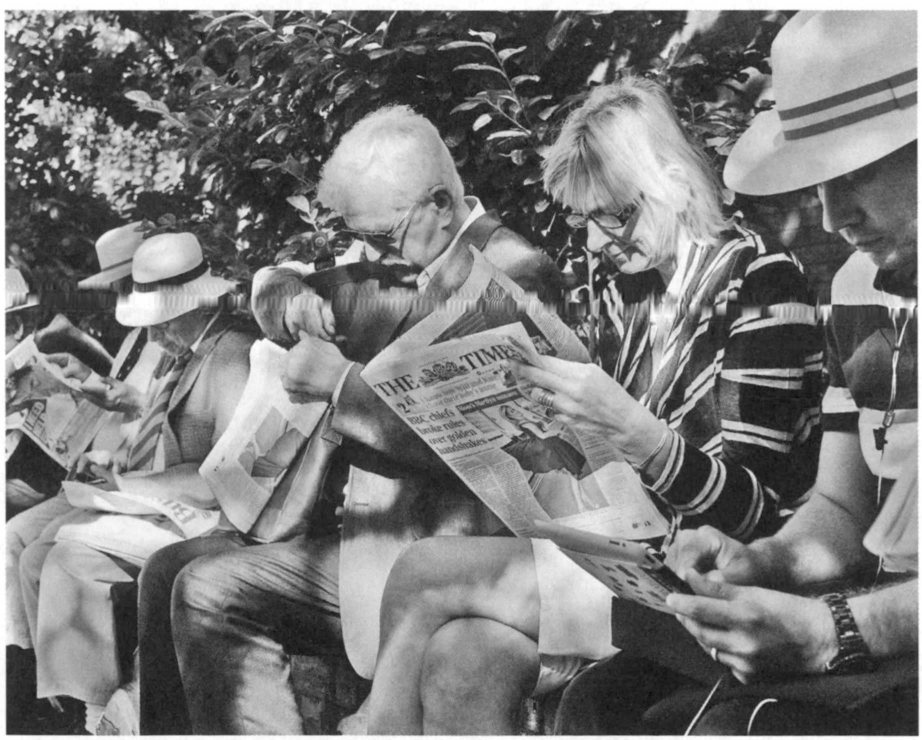


The Times *is essential reading in the early morning queue outside Lord's in 2013*

## SECOND TEST, LORD'S, 2001

ALAN LEE

*July 20.* Quite the most surprising thing about a Lord's Test is how early the day starts. By 7am, under sullen skies, the queue had swelled beyond 100 but, inside, all was bustling activity. In the Edrich Stand, sat in subordinate silence as if already watching Atherton bat, hundreds of temporary stewards were receiving instructions. Out on the square, groundstaff were sweeping rainwater from the covering with the morose air of those who knew there was more to come.

It would be another two hours before the gates were opened for the daily sprint to the best pavilion seats and the M.C.C. equivalent of the towels-on-sunbeds routine, an uproarious cabaret that involves many elderly members moving at a speed they last achieved in schooldays.

Yesterday's race was won by a man clutching a holdall in one hand and punching the air with the other, while the also-rans included a Corporal Jones lookalike thrusting his umbrella before him like cold steel and an elderly gent with a shopping bag who slowed to mutter: 'We're all bloody mad, every one of us.'

## FOURTH TEST, HEADINGLEY, 2001

RICHARD HOBSON

*August 18.* You can take a man from the Western Terrace but not, it seems, take the Western Terrace wholly out of the man. Yorkshire have begun their £10 million redevelopment of Headingley by replacing the most notorious structure at a cricket ground in England but it does not appear to have eradicated the behaviour that gave it such a bad name.

As if the county does not have great players in its past to honour, the replacement has been unimaginatively christened the West Stand. Steeper banking has improved the lines of sight and there is more space between the rows. Part of the thinking is that spectators will not become as hot, bothered and aggressive as in the past.

Unfortunately, in this age of the soundbite, it seems as though a section of the crowd cannot sit and watch cricket for a whole day. On Thursday evening, a fight broke out, apparently between a husband and wife. Elsewhere, police were showered with beer and plastic glasses. Six people were ejected.

'It is all very well creating more space under the stand,' one steward said, 'but it just gives them more room to drink beer all day.' During the final session yesterday evening, spectators tried to create a chain of empty pint pots from the back row to the front. They were stopped in their efforts by an official.

Few would argue that the new stand is not an improvement and there has been a certain improvement in manners. Women have taken their seats without being invited to bare their breasts 'for the lads'. There has even been evidence of courtesy among stewards, although not from the man who asked to check my ticket on re-entry when I stepped a few feet outside the ground to view the new Sir Leonard Hutton Gates. Do these people have to look as if they are enjoying their job so much?

*Another Kevin Pietersen six lands in the crowd during his thrilling innings at the Oval in 2005*

## FOURTH TEST, MELBOURNE, 2006–07

CHRISTOPHER MARTIN-JENKINS, CHIEF CRICKET CORRESPONDENT

*December 27*. This final milestone [Shane Warne's 700th Test Wicket] for a charismatic genius was witnessed at the ground by Michael Newman, a 63-year-old property developer from Wimbledon who was also at Old Trafford as a schoolboy 50 years ago to see every one of Jim Laker's 19 wickets.

For all the uncertainty of Manchester's weather throughout that fabled game, Newman believes that he has never been colder at a cricket match. It was a rather different temperature when he was also at the Recreation Ground in Antigua in 1986 to see the fastest Test century, by Viv Richards, and at the same ground in April 2004 when Brian Lara made the highest Test score of 400 not out. Not a bad four-timer for half a lifetime's cricket-watching.

## FIFTH TEST, SYDNEY, 2010–11

GIDEON HAIGH

*January 8*. So the role of the armies of spectators behind England this time, Barmy and otherwise, cannot be underestimated. Acting as rousers, revivers and karaoke machine, they were recognised yesterday, when Strauss's men made a beeline for the serried ranks of red and white.

Sporting

OW ENGLAND KEPT T
ASHES

VO GREAT HEARTS OVERTHROW AUSTRALIA

England beat Australia by five wickets in the fourth Test match at delaide yesterday and so, gaining a lead of three matches to one in the ries, have retained the Ashes. In an interview after the match L. Hutton, he England captain, paid a tribute to the younger members of the side. Much of the credit, he thought, should go to J. B. Statham, F. H. Tyson, M. C. Cowdrey and P. B. H. May, together with the wicket-keeper, T. G. Evans.

From Our Special Correspondent

ADELAIDE, FEB. 2

Many years from now young Cowdrey will point to his broken nose and tell boys yet unborn that he was at Adelaide on February 2, 1955, when England won the Test match and kept the Ashes. And the boys will think him wondrous lucky. ... should dip his pen in blood to ... this day. Let no one talk and ... ket and explain away ...

the catch. (We asked Hutton afterwards what he thought of Miller's bowling. Hutton thought Miller ought to concentrate much more on batting.) England 10 for 2. In comes the battered Cowdrey. Miller hits him twice running on the pads and appeals, and everybody here who isn't English appeals too. What a man is Miller. He comes in from a shortish run, loose of limb like an African, hair streaming, and as he pulls up the hair goes on and falls about his face.

Meanwhile May has gone from mid-off to square-leg. For Cowdrey Miller brings fine-leg up to third slip, and Cowdrey cover drives classically for 4. Miller heaves his shoulders over even faster, and Cowdrey is taken by Archer at first-slip. England 18 for 3. Four Meteor jets fly over at 200ft.; they look ... sound quite tame beside this wild man ... His figures now are 3 overs, no ... 2 runs, 3 wickets.

ngland all too obliging
eaches new heights of greatnes

One that got away: Gilchrist misses a stumping chance off Warne to give Pietersen an extra life, but it was to make little difference

High five: Warne acknowledges the Melbourne crowd after his haul ripped the heart out of England's fragile batting

legendary accuracy and a lush outfield, they ran poorly between the wickets, chose the wrong balls to try to hit in the air and failed to justify the decision to bat.

"We didn't expect conditions to change dramatically over the first day and a half," Strauss said, "but it seamed about more than we expected." It did so slowly but Glenn McGrath, Stuart Clark and Brett Lee all got enough past the bat to suggest that the wrong option had been taken.

Australia missed two catches, two clear run-out opportunities and a gaping stumping, but still bowled England out for 159 after they had been 101 for two. Very few Test matches are won after such a start. All of Warne's wickets were taken by flight and dip, as batsmen spied what they believed to be boundary opportunities. Only Kevin Pietersen got anywhere near the boundary as he attempted to drive Warne straight for six, but by now he was, as usual, batting with the tail.

Even he needed 70 balls for 21 runs, having come close to running out Andrew Flintoff for six as, for the third Test in succession, he attempted a ridiculous single in order to get off the mark. He had only made four when he also survived a simple stumping chance offered to Adam Gilchrist after charging Warne and missing.

England, we all know, have too long a tail, but tweaking it made no difference. Matthew Hoggard is back where he started, No 11, pushing Monty Panesar and Stephen Harmison up a place each, which reflects their various abilities with the bat. It is higher up, however, that the balance is wrong. Ed Joyce or Jamie Da... rymple should have played

six, but Chris Read for Geraint Jones was the only change.

As the best player in the team, Pietersen needs to bat at four. Since Paul Collingwood shared the only partnership of any substance with Strauss — 57 for the third wicket — it may appear that England's strategy, to keep him away from the new ball, had worked again, but to have Pietersen batting with the tail repeatedly is not satisfactory. In any case Collingwood might have been leg-before to Clark for nought, one of four apparently plumb leg-before decisions turned down by Rudi Koertzen.

Panesar was the other, ...

Australia's recent practice of not using a nightwatchman.

Ponting said that Australia, too, would have chosen to bat first, but it was one of those tosses that either captain would prefer to have lost. Play was delayed by rain for half an hour and only 16 overs were bowled before an early lunch was taken. Alastair Cook

iant leap

for proud S

Sporting News

ENGLAND HAVE LAST WORD

THREE YEOMEN FOIL AUSTRALIA

GREAT STAND BY WATSON AND BAILEY

FROM OUR CRICKET CORRESPONDENT

Out of darkness, through fire into light. Thus did England yesterday rise like some Phoenix from the ashes of apparent defeat to save the second Test match at Lord's and so gain a ... draw against Australia with ... seven wickets, ... original aim fo...

The age of ... yet past, nor c... cany scarce f... dramatic and ... a match alrea... But within t... longest and ... of a match it... that last spa... back with l... yeomen of ... nearly the w...

The yeom... were Wats... greatest of ... Yorkshirem... order, was ... rearguard ... twentieth ...

36 TUESDAY AUGUST 1 1989

THE TIMES

First published 1785

England's abject surrender marks new low in series

By Alan Lee, Cricket Correspondent

Inglorious procession at Old Trafford

16-1: Curtis c Boon b Alderman 0

25-2: Robinson lbw b Lawson 12

27-3: Smith c Healy b Alderman 1

38-4: Gooch c Alderman b Lawson 13

38-5: Botham lbw b Alderman 4

59-6: Gower c Marsh b Lawson 15

SCOREBOARD FROM OLD TRAFFORD

England won toss

ENGLAND

AUSTRALIA

First Innings

Gower unfairly blamed for failings of others

Simon Barnes

Border rewarded for hard labour

By John Woodcock

Only two men so far decline

By Alan Lee

Was this English c
most desperate c

night issued a dramatic ... Union to make a positive ... He said that unless the ... to help to achieve an ... additional funds of more than

# THE FAST MEN

THE TIMES SATURDAY JUNE 11 1938

H: A GOOD BEGINNING BY ENGLAND

4

Sporting News

LAKER'S SUPREME PART IN RETAINING THE ASHES

ALL TEN AUSTRALIAN WICKETS AND 19 IN MATCH

From Our Cricket Correspondent

England won the fourth Test match against Australia at Old ... terday by an innin... retaining the A... achieve...

pitch perked up and the ball showed signs of misbehaving.

At luncheon McDonald and Craig were still together. They had then added only 59, but the important thing was that they had each been batting for more than four hours. Ahead of them stretched another four and only 15 minutes of these had ticked away when Laker struck ... blow. Craig, still ...

THE TIMES

HOW THE AUSTRALIANS WERE SKITTLED OUT AT LORD'S

LOCOMEN'S BAN BOUND TO CAUSE GREATER ... TODAY

Gaullists may get back with clear majority

Inquiry over bank chief's salary

Police alerted by strike ship

Railways must act alone, Marsh says

13 die in S... rail crash

... mped aiming to hit Mallett over the bill, and the end draws nearer.

... dismally surrender Ashes

TEST MATCH

BRADMAN 309 NOT OUT

ALL RECORDS BROKEN

*The Third Test Match between England and Australia was begun at Leeds yesterday. A. P. F. Chapman, for once, lost the toss and Australia went in to bat on a perfect batsman's wicket. By the end of the day they had scored 458 runs for the loss of three wickets ...*

## BILL BOWES

### FOURTH TEST, HEADINGLEY, 1934

R.B. VINCENT, CRICKET CORRESPONDENT

*July 21.* Ponsford was most assiduous in looking for runs, and there was every appearance of the evening wearing out with a typical Australian opening partnership when Wyatt had the idea of putting Mitchell on in place of Bowes, whom he transferred to the other end.

The move was at once successful, Bowes knocking Brown's off stump back, and in the next over having Oldfield caught at the wicket. Oldfield, whether he was sent in out of his proper position or not, is always a nice man to have back in the pavilion, for he is inclined to be a perfect nuisance towards the end of an innings. When Oldfield fell there were only five minutes left for play, and it was great for England, but perhaps sad for many who admire a brave gesture, that Woodfull who himself came in next, played a ball on to his wicket. But the roar of acclamation to Bowes was worth going all the way to Leeds to hear.

*July 24.* If Ponsford and Bradman on Saturday by their great partnership had carried the honours of the day, it was Bowes yesterday who was the undisputed hero. His bowling has often been criticized in the past, chiefly because of an apparent laziness in his run up to the wicket. Yesterday he had shaken off all suggestion of lethargy. He ran, instead of ambling, up to the bowling crease, and he positively thundered the ball down to hit the stumps with a crack which could be heard all over the ground. He was, in fact, a fast bowler in the true meaning of the word …

## WALTER BREARLEY

### FOURTH TEST, OLD TRAFFORD, 1905

R.H. LYTTELTON

*July 27.* Mr Brearley bowled really well all through. He had, for these days, comparatively few overs to bowl; but he has a very fine swing of arm and shoulder, and does not take such an exaggerated run as most fast bowlers do now.

## STUART BROAD

### FOURTH TEST, CHESTER-LE-STREET, 2013

GIDEON HAIGH

*August 13.* Dennis Lillee's fitness guru, Frank Pyke, once said that the ideal fast bowler would be a 'beautifully co-ordinated giant', not only because of the advantage of his height but the length of his arms, thereby providing the leverage conducive to real pace. No bowler on either side fits this bill better than Broad, 6ft 6in in his socks he reveals during one of his periodic pitstops to adjust his boots. He is best appreciated from side on, where the sweep of his arms and the brace of his front leg can be seen levering off one another, generating the speeds that yesterday clocked more than 90mph.

Broad can be loath to bowl full, hating to be driven down the ground, but when everything clicks it is like he is earthing an electric current. Once he attacked the stumps after tea, he threatened them with every ball.

# THE TIMES

35p

No. 65,909 FRIDAY JUNE 6 1997 5L

**EXAM FAMILY FEVER**
Why the whole household suffers
PAGE 20

**BUCKLEY'S END**
Caitlin Moran on the genius who walked into the Mississippi
PAGE 37

TOMORROW
**JOHN WOODCOCK'S 100 GREATEST CRICKETERS OF ALL TIME**
100
**JANE MACQUITTY'S 100 BEST SUMMER WINES**
MAGAZINE

Beef imports threatened

## 'Mad sheep' fears prompt slaughter

By Michael Hornsby, Agriculture Correspondent, and Nigel Hawkes

THE Government is to extend "mad cow" controls to sheep because of fears that they may also have become infected with the fatal brain disease, and will order the compulsory slaughter of all sheep suspected of having scrapie.

Jack Cunningham, the Agriculture Minister, said he was acting on scientific advice that BSE (bovine spongiform encephalopathy) might have jumped to sheep from cattle and be disguised as scrapie, a closely related brain disease.

"I must emphasise there is no scientific evidence there is any BSE in the sheep flock," he said. "What we are taking are sound, precautionary measures to avoid any possible risk to consumers, no matter how remote."

Dr Cunningham also announced that the Government will ban beef imports from other countries which have had cases of BSE in their cattle herds and do not apply the same controls against the disease as Britain. At present only Ireland, among European Union member states, has full safeguards.

The rest of the EU would be given until July 22 to come into line. "I would much prefer to have Europe-wide regulations enforced, but if agreement cannot be reached at the council of agriculture ministers on that date, I will have to act unilaterally," he said.

"This is no game. This is no bluff. I am in earnest in making this announcement. The draft orders are in my briefcase. It is nothing to do with protectionism. It is based on very important advice to safeguard public health."

He added: "I thought it was an absurd situation that, with all the rigorous controls on beef in this country, we are importing beef not subject to the same safeguards."

European Commission officials insisted last night that, if Britain acted on its own, it would be illegal. Gerry Kiely, spokesman for Franz Fischler, the Agriculture Commissioner, said: "As in all cases where a Government does something which is not in conformity with EU law, you start out with infringement procedures and possibly end up in the Court of Justice".

He said that Herr Fischler would soon put forward proposals for uniform application of abattoir controls, but a majority of member states rejected similar proposals last December.

Dr Cunningham said four weeks of consultation would be held with farmers on how best to conduct the sheep slaughter. Farmers would be offered compensation equal to the average market price for culled ewes to provide an incentive to notify animals suspected of having scrapie.

In addition, spinal cords would have to be removed at the abattoir from all sheep and goats more than a year old, and spleen would have to be removed from all sheep and goats of any age. Heads are already banned for human consumption or animal feed.

The Spongiform Encephalopathy Advisory Committee (SEAC) first suggested in July of last year that these organs could pose a public health risk because of the possibility that BSE might have passed to sheep in feed containing meat and bone meal derived from infected cattle remains.

Its head, Professor John Pattison, said the only reason his committee had not recommended that spinal cord be removed then was that abattoirs did not have the necessary equipment for doing this in sheep at the time. Such equipment was now available.

The new moves to control sheepmeat are likely to arouse suspicion among consumers. Scrapie has been in the British flock for at least 200 years, yet not until August last year were any restrictions placed on the consumption of the tissues most likely to be infected. The altered advice reflects a changed perception about how BSE may have arisen. When it first appeared, it was assumed to be a modified form of scrapie, caused in cattle fed on material that included sheepmeat. Scrapie itself appears to pose no threat. There is another possibility: BSE itself could exist in sheep, either as a spontaneous change in the scrapie infective agent, or by recycling material from infected cows.

Establishing that any particular strain of scrapie is identical to BSE is a lengthy procedure, since there is no quick test to distinguish between strains. The recommendations are therefore prudent but are unlikely to lead to the complete elimination of scrapie in sheep in Britain.

In Iceland, where this has been attempted, infected flocks have been slaughtered but new flocks introduced later to the same pasture land developed the disease.

**How the pride of Australia fell as they were put to the test**

11-1 — Matthew Elliott is the first to go

15-2 — . . . quickly followed by Mark Taylor

26-3 — Mark Waugh is bowled by Gough

28-4 — . . . and Greg Blewett is caught for 7

48-5 — Steve Waugh got into double figures

48-6 — . . . but Ian Healy was out first ball

48-7 — Michael Bevan caught by Ealham

54-8 — . . . and Gillespie is lbw to Caddick

110-9 — Michael Kasprowicz's resistance ends

118 all out — . . . as does that of top scorer, Warne

*Alan Lee's match report, page 52. John Woodcock and Michael Henderson, page 50*

## Conservative membership falls by half in five years

By Peter Riddell

THE state of the Tory party at the grass roots is even worse than suspected, according to an exclusive survey for *The Times* showing that membership has fallen by nearly a half in the past five years.

Tory membership is now a maximum of 350,000 to 400,000, and possibly very much less. This is the first time that the Tories have had fewer members than Labour, which has boosted its membership by two thirds since 1992, to 420,000. The findings provide powerful ammunition for the growing debate among candidates for the party leadership about how to revive its battered organisation.

The results have emerged as John Major has made known that he plans to remain active in Tory affairs after he gives up the leadership in a fortnight. He will urge a sweeping reform of party organisation, a central membership list and a broader franchise for the election of the party leader.

In many inner cities, in Glasgow and the Welsh Valleys, the Tory party has virtually ceased to exist and is mainly kept going by a tiny handful of elderly stalwarts.

The survey has been conducted for *The Times* by Michael Pinto-Duschinsky, a leading expert on party organisation and senior research fellow at Brunel University. His estimate of total membership is based on statistics — many of which are not known to Conservative Central Office — collected from 340 local Tory associations. He concedes that even these lower figures may have been padded, for instance by failing to exclude former and even dead members.

This shows that a fifth of the constituencies surveyed had memberships of 100 or fewer, often down to a couple of dozen or less. The Rhondda party was defunct for part of last year and was re-formed for the general election. Moreover, membership has even dropped sharply in the party's heartlands which it managed to retain in the election. In ten of the strongest associations, membership has dropped by two fifths over the past three years.

Survey report, Peter Riddell, page 15
Lilley interview, page 21
Matthew Parris, page 22

*"Having roamed the planet since the beginning of time the Tory party, at the end of the 20th century, suddenly became extinct"*

‘Peter Lilley's instincts are the soundest and the surest in this field . . . he has our support’
*Leading article, page 23*

ENTER TODAY
WIN 21 FORD CARS
TOKEN - Page 32

**Putting the bite on the euro**

Some commentators are suggesting that the Franco-German [illegible] (hard on the outside, soft inside) may be replaced by the Dolcelatte version (softer all through and riddled with green veins of corruption). Anatole Kaletsky thinks the likelihood of either is fast diminishing.

Economic View, page 31

**Net plan delay**

British Telecom cancelled an announcement on the plan to connect schools to the internet after hearing that Oftel had not yet approved ...... Page 27

The Times on the Internet
http://www.the-times.co.uk

23
9 770140 046350

## Compromise likely on Camelot pay

By Jon Ashworth

CAMELOT was holding talks with the Government last night in a last-minute attempt to break the impasse over "fat cat" pay.

[illegible] Secretary, [illegible] has demanded [illegible] lot, claiming that high levels of pay at a time of declining sales threaten to damage public [illegible] in the draw.

There were signs that a deal satisfactory to both sides would be done today when a Camelot board meeting is scheduled. A government source said: "I think everyone is ready to bury the hatchet."

It has been suggested that Camelot's three top directors, including Tim Holley, the chief executive, might resign rather than give up their personal bonuses.

It is understood that sources at a high level within the Government made contact with Camelot yesterday afternoon to expressed concern.

The resignation of key Camelot directors would plunge the National Lottery into uncertainty and threaten a knock-on effect for the privatised electricity and water companies, which have been criticised over high levels of boardroom pay. The Institute of Directors said government meddling in private enterprise sent a worrying signal to wider business. Mr Holley and his colleagues, David Rigg, director of communications, and Peter Murphy, finance director, have threatened to resign at today's [illegible]

Mr Smith has [illegible] that the Camelot directors hand back their bonuses. Mr Holley, 56, received a bonus of £127,000 and a long-term incentive payment of £176,000, taking his overall 1996 package to £590,000. Mr Rigg, 49, and Mr Murphy, 40, each got £170,000 in bonuses.

Camelot has offered to pay an amount equivalent to the bonuses to charity from its own profits, but Mr Smith wants the directors to make a personal sacrifice. In further concessions, Camelot has pledged to pay £6 million in interest earned on its prize fund shortfall to good causes, and has agreed to consider ways of running the lottery on a "not for profit" basis.

The Department of National Heritage refused to say what it would do if Mr Holley and his colleagues were to resign. The Office of the National Lottery (Oflot), which regulates Camelot, said it could not comment until it knew the outcome of today's meeting.

Running out of luck, page 31

Make your dreams come true.

"CŒURS" Collection from £ 575

Van Cleef & Arpels

Fine Jewellery Room, Ground Floor Exclusively at

Harrods KNIGHTSBRIDGE

Harrods Limited, Knightsbridge, London SW1X 7XL. Telephone 0171-225 6520

| | | | |
|---|---|---|---|
| TV & RADIO ........ 50, 51 | LETTERS ........ 23, 31, 47 | ARTS ........ 35-38 | SPORT ........ 42-50, 52 |
| WEATHER ........ 26 | OBITUARIES ........ 25 | CHESS & BRIDGE ........ 45 | EDUCATION ........ 41 |
| CROSSWORDS ........ 26, 52 | MATTHEW PARRIS ........ 22 | COURT & SOCIAL ........ 24 | LAW REPORT ........ 39 |

*A remarkable first day at Edgbaston in 1997 as Australia are blown away by Andrew Caddick, Darren Gough and Devon Malcolm gets gleeful front-page treatment*

## TIBBY COTTER

### FIRST TEST, TRENT BRIDGE, 1905

R.H. LYTTELTON

*May 30.* The first two hours the batsmen had to fight hard for runs; but this was due to the excellent length of Mr Laver's bowling and the terrific speed of Mr Cotter's. Mr Cotter has no idea of length and very little of direction; he is not tall and has not a high delivery, but the way he made the ball bump was a revelation to many. Frequently the wicketkeeper standing back had to extend his arm to its full length above his head to stop the ball. It was simply a case of pace, and if he had any method, it was to bowl three or four bumping long hops and then a 'yorker', and in this way he disposed of Hayward.

## BILL EDRICH

### THIRD TEST, OLD TRAFFORD, 1948

R.B. VINCENT, CRICKET CORRESPONDENT

*July 8.* To support Bedser there will be Pollard and Edrich as men of some pace. One wonders whether Edrich would not do better in his first over or two to bowl at a quieter pace, then winding himself up to his full pace. At the moment he seems to expend too much energy in his first over, a mistake never committed by Australia's bowlers, past or present.

## FRANK FOSTER

### FIFTH TEST, SYDNEY, 1911–12

*February 29.* A criticism of Mr Foster's bowling has been published here, in which the writer accuses him of bowling at the batsmen instead of at the wicket. There has been considerable comment on the frequency with which batsmen have been temporarily disabled while facing him. Mr Foster indignantly denies that there is the smallest truth in the suggestion.

## JACK GREGORY AND TED McDONALD

SYDNEY PARDON
CRICKET CORRESPONDENT

*May 28, 1921.* On a hard wicket Mr E.A. Macdonald [*sic*] is a really good bowler. He makes the ball come two paces off the wicket. Some of them come off very fast indeed and break back sharply, and he has a fine slow ball, well held back. Mr J.M. Gregory is fast in the air and, coming as he does from a great height, he makes the ball get up most awkwardly from the pitch. Mr Armstrong has abandoned his leg theory – an exasperating but not very terrible form of attack to the seasoned batsman – for a much more formidable style of bowling. Nobody has accused him of bowling the googly maliciously, but he does do so.

## STEPHEN HARMISON

### FIRST TEST, LORD'S, 2005

SIMON BARNES

*July 22.* And yet until tea, it seemed so obvious that it was England's day, and Stephen Harmison's in particular. The fast bowler was immense – surely the *mot juste*. He gave us two sessions of sustained and unrepentant menace. He sent the first ball of the day fizzing past Justin Langer's bat, the second cracked him on the elbow, a blow that required lengthy treatment. Unabashed, Harmison then hit Matthew Hayden on the helmet and blasted one through the visor of the Australia captain, Ricky Ponting. Ten balls afterwards, Ponting fended Harmison apologetically to slip. [...]

After terrorising the top order, he skittled the lower order. It was a fast bowler's performance, an exhibition of perfect supremacy, and England went back to the pavilion bursting with pride and joy.

## MITCHELL JOHNSON

### FIRST TEST, BRISBANE, 2013–14

GIDEON HAIGH

*November 23.* Johnson is frustrating and formidable for the same reasons – the sheer unpredictability of his variations from that sidewinding arm, the inconstancy of the seam's influence as the ball saucers through the air.

Even his bounce is unlike that obtained by other fast bowlers. Not for him the vertical take-off of a ball from, say, Glenn McGrath; more the rise up a steep ramp,

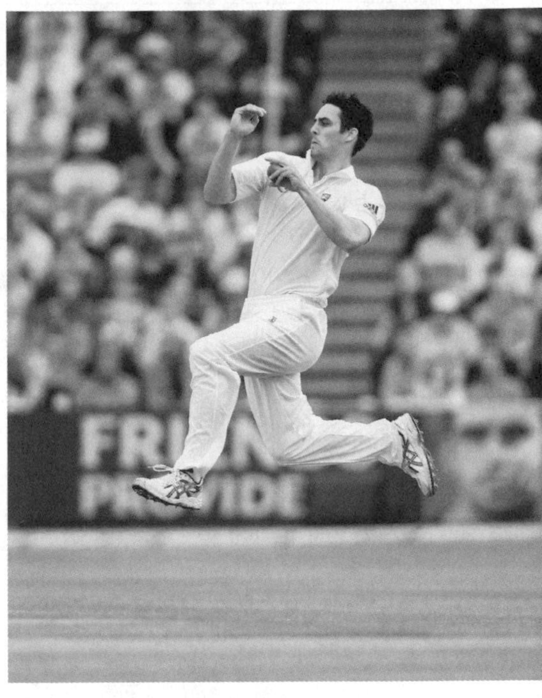

*Mitchell Johnson hurls himself into the delivery stride at Edgbaston in the third Test in 2009*

where the ball keeps coming and coming, so that sternum height becomes clavicle height becomes mandible height, as your hands struggle to adjust.

Again, when Johnson resumed to Carberry an hour later, round the wicket with a short leg, it hardly took a mind-reader to penetrate anyone's thoughts. Carberry had left the ball composedly all day but slipped subtly into a rut, unable to add to his total in 25 balls.

Recoiling after a blow to the chest, Carberry offered a hazy hook, then neither quite played nor quite left as the ball crossed his airspace. At the point of release, the ball was probably outside the return crease; at the end of its flight, it was in second slip's hands. Carberry would not have seen a lot of that in county cricket.

## HAROLD LARWOOD

### FIFTH TEST, THE OVAL, 1930

R.B. VINCENT,
CRICKET CORRESPONDENT

*August 21.* Tate at the other end could get little or nothing out of the turf but when Larwood took over from him neither batsman was anxious to run a sharp single in order to secure the privilege of playing him. After one or two shortish balls had flown head high, Bradman definitely declined to stand up to him. He retired to short-leg and sparred dangerously at the rising balls. He either missed them completely or knocked them down safely to third man. Jackson was more ready to stand up to his bat as the books recommend, and received a nasty blow on the fingers, for which the four runs accruing from his glance to the boundary at fine-leg were inadequate compensation.

## GEOFF LAWSON

### SECOND TEST, LORD'S, 1981

JOHN WOODCOCK,
CRICKET CORRESPONDENT

*July 3.* By perhaps a couple of yards Lawson was the fastest of the Australian bowlers. He came first to our attention in Sydney two and a half years ago when he put the wind up Boycott: since when he has been propositioned by Lancashire, where he had a season in the league, and overshadowed by Lillee, Pascoe and Hogg. He got the last bowling place in this Australian party ahead of Thomson, and yesterday he showed why.

*The Australians celebrate after bringing the 1985 series level at 1-1 at Lord's. Geoff Lawson, centre, had another good match after his fine performance in 1981*

# DENNIS LILLEE AND JEFF THOMSON

## FIRST TEST, BRISBANE, 1974–75

JOHN WOODCOCK,
CRICKET CORRESPONDENT

*December 3.* Conversation here today – the rest day in the first Test match between England and Australia – has turned to the proper use of fast bowling. There has been so much of it in the past three days, a lot of it so short, that it is on everyone's mind, not least the batsmen's.

The pitch has had a lot to do with this. Although not fast by Australian standards, the bounce is sufficient and sufficiently unpredictable for one thunderbolt from Lillee to have gone for four byes over the head of Marsh, standing a longish way back. This is all the encouragement the fast bowlers have needed to bowl as consistently short as I have seen in a Test match since Procter and Peter Pollock gave the Australians such a bad time of it in South Africa in the early part of 1970. Before that it must have been Hall and Griffith in England in 1963.

For Lever and Willis there has been the further encouragement of seeing the bouncer get wickets. In Australia's first innings five batsmen were out hooking the fast, short-pitched balls. In England's, no one was. The difference is easily explained. Even Greig found Thomson and Lillee too fast and awkward to hook. Both, when they really let fly, are a couple of yards faster than anything England has. They are as strong as two horses – and a lot younger than Lever.

So far, mercifully, no one has been badly hurt. Wally Edwards was hit on the side of the head last night by Willis, a horrible blow to which Willis's reaction was to walk back to the end of his run while the stars were clearing before his victim's eyes. Having been hit in the ribs himself, as well as in the box, Willis was out for revenge. Edrich was struck on the finger by Lillee, but that was not quite a bouncer. Others have been bruised, but if this goes on, and there is as much pace in the pitch at Perth as there can be, it will be surprising if no one ends up in hospital. If Boycott has been watching on television he may be thinking himself to be well out of it all.

In the present match only Lever has been spoken to by the umpires, for bowling three bouncers in succession at Jenner. Had I been Amiss, or Luckhurst, or Edrich, watching this, I would have been just as cross, as Jenner was, knowing that they would all come back and more, not at Lever, but at the batsmen on the England side. Four years ago when Snow was warned in three of the Test matches for bowling too short, Australia were not adequately armed to retaliate. This time they are. Denness, I believe, pressed for Snow's inclusion in his present side. He has probably been wishing today that he had got his way. Yet Snow, at 33, like Lever, at 34, would be giving vital years away to Thomson and Lillee.

It is unlikely, I think, once we have passed through Perth, where the second Test match starts on December 13, that this short bowling will continue to be the menace it is now. Either the sides will have come to their senses, or the umpires will have taken a hand, or the pitches at Melbourne and Adelaide will be less responsive than this one. Until then though, I shall find the cricket too rugged to be much fun to watch – at any rate, when one's friends are facing Thomson, fresh and out for blood.

*December 5.* The day began to the echo of some unedifying remarks made by Lillee on television last night. The idea of the bouncer, as he uses it, is to hit the batsman 'somewhere between the rib cage and the stomach'. That is what he said, and he had written it previously in a book. Thomson is already on record as saying that he enjoys felling a batsman with a bouncer. This is the talk of the underworld, not of Test cricketers. It has to be said that to some extent M.C.C. have brought their present troubles upon themselves. There was Snow on the last tour to Australia, there have been Lever and Willis on this one. There was bodyline of odious memory. 'The evil that men do …' […]

Thomson was the fastest bowler, in the match. Often by some way. I was reminded of Arthur Morris telling me in 1954 that to face Statham after facing Tyson was like facing Bailey after facing Statham.

Cowdrey's observations from having watched the first Test match on television are interesting. He admits that seeing just the 'highlights' can be misleading, but even in 1954-55, when England had Tyson and Statham and Australia had Lindwall, Miller and Davidson, he remembers nothing to compare with Brisbane '74 for bumpers. I would go farther than that and say that there were more of them there than in any Test match in which England have been involved since the war.

*December 17.* What cannot possibly be afforded is another collapse tomorrow as dismal as Friday's or any more injuries. If there is the same failure to get into line as there was then, the same lack of technical resource and physical determination, we shall need not only a bomb disposal expert, which in a sense Cowdrey was, but a psychiatrist as well.

## SECOND TEST, PERTH, 1974–75

JOHN WOODCOCK,
CRICKET CORRESPONDENT

*December 12.* For the match to be as enjoyable as it should be to watch, let alone play in, there will need to be much less short-pitched bowling than in Brisbane. Willis and Lever have a lot to answer for in this respect. It was they who started it, before Thomson made their efforts look like childsplay. England in Brisbane were hoist, with their own petard. I am making no excuses for the defeat there but the umpires I thought were at fault in not taking a firmer line over the surfeit of short bowling. The same two umpires are standing here, and may, I hope, have had a directive to guard more carefully the spirit and letter of the law.

## FIFTH TEST, ADELAIDE, 1974–75

JOHN WOODCOCK,
CRICKET CORRESPONDENT

*January 28.* Being square to the wicket, rather than behind the bowler's arm, the dressing rooms and press box here give an unusual view of the game. For the England players it was a new angle from which to be daunted by the speed of Thomson and Lillee before going out to face them. The length of Lillee's run adds to the impression of violence conveyed at the start of an English innings. […]

Ken Barrington, who is here having his first view of Thomson, says that all it has done is to make him cable his mother-in-law to put his pads and gloves that much higher up the attic.

SPORT

Cricket

Greig, England's top scorer, is stumped aiming to hit Mallett over the hill, and the end draws nearer.

**England dismally surrender Ashes**

From John Woodcock
Cricket Correspondent
Sydney, Jan 9

With some more dismal batting England surrendered the Ashes to Australia here today, losing the fourth Test match by 171 runs with only 4.3 of the last 15 overs left. It was four years ago, on this

That England came so close to saving themselves was due in the end to Edrich, who played with a courage and determination unmatched by the other batsmen. This morning his first ball was a short one from Lillee. Ducking into it he was hit a nasty blow in the ribs, bad enough for him to

a bumper, there being no love lost between them. The next, according to one of the Australian slips, was Lillee's fastest ball for a long time, but wide of the off stump. Lillee bowled faster here, and better, than at any time in the series. At times, to Thomson, Marsh reckoned he stood

Cowdrey looks to me as though he could be becoming affected by the special pressures of almost ceaseless speed. To be being brainwashed in fact.

He played no positive stroke of any kind today. For three-quarters of an hour this afternoon, while Knott and Greig were together,

*Inspired by Lillee and Thomson, Australia won back the Ashes emphatically in 1974–75*

## SIXTH TEST, MELBOURNE, 1974–75

JOHN WOODCOCK,
CRICKET CORRESPONDENT

*February 14.* Sir Donald Bradman gave two opinions in Adelaide after England had lost the Ashes there. These may help to put things in perspective. He thought that only Tyson, of the bowlers he had seen or played against, was consistently faster than Thomson (I was surprised how adamant he was about this) and that no side in his time would have coped easily with Thomson and Lillee bowling in partnership. With two umpires unwilling to do more than throw out the occasional threat to curb the short-pitched bowling, England's batsmen found themselves confronted with much more than they had bargained for.

# DENNIS LILLEE

## FIRST TEST, OLD TRAFFORD, 1972

JOHN WOODCOCK,
CRICKET CORRESPONDENT

*June 9.* Boycott was hit not once but four or five times about the body by Lillee, whose pace and bounce were as testing as anything he had met in a Test match. By the time Boycott's Test career began Hall and Griffith were past their peak.

### FIRST TEST, TRENT BRIDGE, 1981

JOHN WOODCOCK, CRICKET CORRESPONDENT

*June 19.* Lillee bowled beautifully in short spells. He is a magnificent athlete and a great bowler. Only his occasional ball was genuinely fast. For the most part he was brisk. All the time, though, he bristled with aggression.

---

## RAY LINDWALL AND KEITH MILLER

### FIRST TEST, BRISBANE, 1954–55

JOHN WOODCOCK, CRICKET CORRESPONDENT

*November 30.* The question that many at home will be asking is how, if England's fast bowlers could get nothing out of the wicket, did Lindwall – who had been at the crease all morning – Miller, and Archer demolish England's early batting? The answer is not difficult to find. It lies in the much fuller length to which they bowled. Where Statham, Tyson, Bailey, and even Bedser, had allowed the batsmen to play back, the Australians were always setting problems on the front foot, and brilliantly they did it.

Lindwall, one knew, was still a great fast bowler and a master of the art of movement and change of pace, but the class of Miller's opening spell came at something of a surprise. The former it was who undermined the whole English effort when, to a tumultuous roar which was, in a way, an expression of respect for England's master, he had Hutton caught at the wicket off the seventh ball of the first over.

Hutton, after waiting for more than three days to bat, had hit the first ball for 4 past gully; the seventh was a late, seductive outswinger which he felt for to hit into the covers, and there, as Langley threw the ball aloft, was the whole Australian side dancing jigs and prancing around like children.

### THIRD TEST, MELBOURNE, 1954–55

JOHN WOODCOCK, CRICKET CORRESPONDENT

*January 1.* There were two villains, Miller and the pitch, and the volatile one exploited the mischievous other to produce a destructive and brilliant piece of bowling. Miller professes not to like bowling, probably, one feels, with his tongue in his cheek, and it was generally thought that after his knee trouble he was unlikely to bowl unless things were running badly for Australia. But not a

*Ray Lindwell and Keith Miller get a first look at England as their ship arrives at Southampton in 1953*

bit of it. He bowled as he always does, like a man who was born to bowl, with abounding verve and dash, and within 37 balls he got rid of Edrich, Hutton, and Compton for five runs. No two successive balls were alike, many were spitefully fast, and almost all were to a full length.

At the other end was Lindwall, who for an hour while the pitch was malicious was little less fierce a proposition. The ball was not moving alarmingly in the air, but for about a dozen overs it kept lifting horribly. All along one knew that the dampness would soon go, and that if only England could fight through resolutely and reasonably unscathed until luncheon all should be comparatively calm afterwards. It was easy to see, by the way they threw everything into their effort, that Miller and Lindwall knew this too, and England could not resist them.

## RAY LINDWALL

### SECOND TEST, LORD'S 1948

R.B. VINCENT,
CRICKET CORRESPONDENT

*June 29.* When when the game did settle down one saw the value of fast bowling, both Lindwall and Johnston making the ball rise fearsomely off the pitch. Both Washbrook and Hutton took some hard knocks, and Hutton, flourishing an optimistic bat, was missed in the slips off Johnston before he had scored. They stood up with a good heart to this battering, and had made 42 – Washbrook always the more secure of the two – when Hutton drew away to play a ball on the rise and was accordingly caught in the slips. Lindwall had certainly bowled in the manner of a true fast bowler, and if he was liable every now and then to let the ball slip away to the leg side, the one he bowled on the off stump wanted a deal of careful watching and quick anticipation.

### FIFTH TEST, THE OVAL, 1948

R.B. VINCENT,
CRICKET CORRESPONDENT

*August 18.* One must go back many years to the time of Richardson and Lockwood, later through that period when Macdonald and Gregory skittled batsmen out, with Larwood of pace and accuracy, to find a peer to Lindwall. He surely is one of the great fast bowlers of all time, perfect in action – you must stand square to the wicket to see the full joy of his follow-through – wise in the exact moment to loose off that frightfully fast ball, and above all continually accurate in length. If this English summer has allowed us nothing else it has granted the sight of Lindwall bowling.

## KEITH MILLER

### FIFTH TEST, THE OVAL, 1948

R.B. VINCENT,
CRICKET CORRESPONDENT

*August 18.* Crapp was never happy to Miller, who bowled every kind of ball, fast, medium, even slow, delayed from the back of his hand, and once made Crapp duck his head and be hit on his cap to one which could have risen little above bail high.

## FOURTH TEST, ADELAIDE, 1954–55

STEWART HARRIS

*February 3.* Then Miller commits *lese-majeste* by making Hutton hurry. The ball flies from a length and Davidson, at second slip, takes the catch. (We asked Hutton afterwards what he thought of Miller's bowling. Hutton thought Miller ought to concentrate much more on batting.) England 10 for 2. In comes the battered Cowdrey. Miller hits him twice running on the pads and appeals, and everybody here who isn't English appeals too. What a man is Miller. He comes in from a shortish run, loose of limb like an African, hair streaming, and as he pulls up the hair goes on and falls about his face.

Meanwhile May has begun driving, and Johnson has gone from mid-off to square-leg. For Cowdrey Miller brings fine-leg up to third slip, and Cowdrey cover drives classically for 4. Miller heaves his shoulders over even faster, and Cowdrey is taken by Archer at first-slip. England 18 for 3. Four Meteor jets fly over at 200ft; they look and sound quite tame beside this wild man bowling. His figures now are 3 overs, no maidens, 12 runs, 3 wickets.

## SECOND TEST, LORD'S, 1956

JOHN WOODCOCK,
CRICKET CORRESPONDENT

*June 23.* At 5 o'clock Crawford, after bowling five overs all but a ball, left the field with a pulled thigh muscle which will prevent him from bowling again in this match. At two minutes past, Richardson, feeling for an outswinger from Miller, was taken at the wicket, and at 17 minutes past, Graveney was bowled between bat and pad, also by Miller.

The irrepressible Miller had made his noble mark again. He was bounding up to bowl like a youngster, and making the ball come off with a will. Here was a short spell of bowling to store in the memory and talk about in years to come, and before he withdrew he almost added May to his victims. The latter came within an inch or two of playing on before he had scored, but soon Miller began to wane. Cowdrey stood up and drove him superbly through the covers, and May forced him to square leg for four, and then cut him like lightning for another. This was cricket fit for any Test match; the challenge of a crucial situation had been answered, and when Miller put on his sweater the heat of the battle died.

# TOM RICHARDSON

## FIRST TEST, SYDNEY, 1894–95

*December 15.* The opening was remarkable. In the second over, Lyons's leg stump was sent flying by Richardson. Darling, a left-handed man, came in, and was bowled first ball with a yorker from the same end. Iredale joined Trott, and a few runs were made, Trott hitting Richardson for a four and a two in the same over. But the first ball of the next over from Richardson found its way to his wicket, which it struck with such force that the head of the off stump was knocked clean off.

*Fast bowlers Fred Trueman and Peter Loader are seen off at St Pancras by David Sheppard, by then the Rev David Sheppard, before the fateful 1958-59 tour*

## JOHN SNOW

### THIRD TEST, TRENT BRIDGE, 1972

JOHN WOODCOCK,
CRICKET CORRESPONDENT

*July 14.* But Snow came to his rescue, as he has such a wonderful way of doing when playing for England.

Before luncheon Snow bowled six rather plain overs for 13 runs and no wicket. After that he removed the Chappells, Walters and Edwards, three of them by making the ball fly on a basically slow pitch. Long before the end Snow was the idol of the crowd of 18,000. With a self-conscious thumbs-up he acknowledged cheers when, after taking a wicket, he returned to his corner of the ground.

## FRED TRUEMAN

### FIFTH TEST, THE OVAL, 1953

GEOFFREY, GREEN,
CRICKET CORRESPONDENT

*August 17.* Yet, drawing a dark veil temporarily over the catching sins of the evening, the day brought forth one heartening event. Trueman was a success.

From his very first spell at the morning's beginning, with the pavilion at his back, he breathed a challenging ferocity allied to a fairly strict regard to length and direction. With the last ball of his very first over, in fact, he might have had the scalp of Morris, whose late glance eluded the two-handed clutch of the diving Compton at short fine leg. Although Trueman had to wait until half past two for his first success, when his pace at last beat Harvey's intended hook – this was a fine catch by Hutton, moving away from the wicket at square leg – it was none the less heartening to see Australian players uncomfortable and at times beset by a ring of seven fieldsmen around and behind the bat.

## FRANK TYSON

### SECOND TEST, SYDNEY, 1954–55

JOHN WOODCOCK,
CRICKET CORRESPONDENT

*December 23.* There have been many Test matches in which the technical standard has been higher, and, for that matter, several in which the margin of victory has been smaller. But few can have followed a more winding course or reached so great a climax as did this one. And in few can there have been so courageous and sustained a piece of fast bowling as Tyson's today. For four days England's cricket alternated between the pit of depression and, very occasionally, the heights of expectation, until this morning it seemed that Australia would most likely win.

**THE TIMES THURSDAY DECEMBER**

Sporting News

**TYSON LEVELS TEST SERIES FOR ENGLAND**

**HARVEY ALONE HIS EQUAL**

**From Our Cricket Correspondent**

SYDNEY, DEC. 22

At Brisbane, tragedy; at Sydney, triumph. Here this afternoon England won a memorable victory by 38 runs after one of the most exciting Test matches for many years. At 10 minutes past three Tyson and Statham, heroes at the

began the bowling and the former bowled Archer in his second over. The ball fairly whipped back off the pitch and Australia, with four wickets to go, still needed 101 to win. One had lurking fears of Davidson and Lindwall, both of whom are highly inflammable drivers, and yet before Harvey could get at the bowling to shield and prepare them they had gone. Davidson was the victim of

*Australia are swept away by a typhoon called Tyson in 1954–55*

Indeed it had seemed that way since England were bowled out for 154 in their first innings. But Tyson, with a bump on the back of his head the size of an egg, swung the balance after 15 minutes today with two shattering yorkers in an over. Thereafter England fought like lions, paralysing all Australia's batsmen except Harvey. Statham supported Tyson with great heart and determination, Appleyard got a valuable wicket, and Evans took a staggering catch. Nor must one forget the batting of May and Cowdrey or England's last wicket partners. Yet one feels that the match should be remembered more than anything for Tyson's fast bowling today on an easy wicket.

Only last week at Melbourne he changed to a shorter, more controlled, run. Now he has also learnt the value of a full length by watching Lindwall, and 10 wickets in a Test match is the result. He is strong, and it is difficult to see how a man can bowl much faster than he did at times today. Within a fortnight he has acquired for himself a considerable ascendancy over Australia's leading batsmen through being genuinely too good for them.

## THIRD TEST, MELBOURNE, 1954–55

JOHN WOODCOCK,
CRICKET CORRESPONDENT

*January 6.* Englishmen should raise their glasses and drink the health of Tyson, their fastest bowler. In 51 balls and 80 minutes here this morning he took six Australian wickets for 16 runs and initiated one of the most extraordinary collapses in the history of Test match cricket. Between noon and 20 minutes past one Australia lost their last eight wickets for 36 runs on a hard pitch and England stampeded to victory in the third Test match by 128 runs. If any of the fifty thousand witnesses did not realize it before they must know now that fact can be stranger than fiction.

Sporting …

# …OW ENGLAND KEPT TH… ASHES

## …VO GREAT HEARTS OVERTHROW AUSTRALIA

England beat Australia by five wickets in the fourth Test match at …delaide yesterday and so, gaining a lead of three matches to one in the …ries, have retained the Ashes. In an interview after the match L. Hutton, …e England captain, paid a tribute to the younger members of the side. Much of the credit, he thought, should go to J. B. Statham, F. H. Tyson, M. C. Cowdrey and P. B. H. May, together with the wicket-keeper, T. G. Evans.

From Our Special Correspondent

ADELAIDE, Feb. 2

Many years from now young Cowdrey will point to his broken nose and tell boys yet unborn that he was at Adelaide on February 2, 1955, when England won the Test match and kept the Ashes. And the boys will think him wondrous lucky. A ma… should dip his pen in blood to write … Let no one talk and … explain away …

the catch. (We asked Hutton afterwards what he thought of Miller's bowling. Hutton thought Miller ought to concentrate much more on batting.) England 10 for 2. In comes the battered Cowdrey. Miller hits him twice running on the pads and appeals, and everybody here who isn't English appeals too. What a man is Miller. He comes in from a shortish run, loose of limb like an African, hair streaming, and as he pulls up the hair goes on and falls about his face. Meanwhile May has begun driving, and Johnson has gone from mid-off to square-leg. For Cowdrey Miller brings fine-leg up to third slip, and Cowdrey cover drives classically for 4. Miller heaves his shoulders over even faster, and Cowdrey is taken by Archer at first-slip. England 18 for 3. Four Meteor jets fly over at 200ft.; they look …d sound quite tame beside this wild man … His figures now are 3 overs, no … runs, 3 wickets.

Sporting News

# ENGLAND HAVE LAST WORD

## THREE YEOMEN FOIL AUSTRALIA

## GREAT STAND BY WATSON AND BAILEY

FROM OUR CRICKET CORRESPONDENT

Out of darkness, through fire into light. Thus did England yesterday rise like some Phoenix from the ashes of apparent defeat to save the second Test match at Lord's and so gain a … draw against Australia with … seven wickets, … original aim fo… The age of … yet past, nor c… cany scarce f… dramatic and … a match alrea… But within t… longest and … of a match it… that last spa… back with l… yeomen of … nearly the w… The yeom… were Watso… greatest of … Yorkshirem… order, was … rearguard … twentieth …

# …ngland all too obliging … reaches new heights of greatness

One that got away: Gilchrist misses a stumping chance off Warne to give Pietersen an extra life, but it was to make little difference

High five: Warne acknowledges the Melbourne crowd after his haul ripped the heart out of England's fragile batting

…legendary accuracy and a lush outfield, they ran poorly between the wickets, chose the wrong balls to try to hit in the air and failed to justify the decision to bat.

"We didn't expect conditions to change dramatically over the first day and a half," Strauss said, "but it seamed about more than we expected." It did so slowly but Glenn McGrath, Stuart Clark and Brett Lee all got enough past the bat to suggest that the wrong option had been taken.

Australia missed two catches, two clear run-out opportunities and a gaping stumping, but still bowled England out for 159 after they had been 101 for two. Very few Test matches are won after such a start. All of Warne's wickets were taken by flight and dip, as batsmen spied what they believed to be boundary opportunities. Only Kevin Pietersen got anywhere near the boundary as he attempted to drive Warne straight for six, but by now he was, as usual, batting with the tail.

Even he needed 70 balls for 21 runs, having come close to running out Andrew Flintoff for six as, for the third Test in succession, he attempted a ridiculous single in order to get off the mark. He had only made four when he also survived a simple stumping chance offered to Adam Gilchrist after charging Warne and missing.

England, we all know, have too long a tail, but tweaking it made no difference. Matthew Hoggard is back where he started, No 11, pushing Monty Panesar and Stephen Harmison up a place each, which reflects their various abilities with the bat. It is higher up, however, that the balance is wrong. Ed Joyce or Jamie Dalrymple should have played six, but Chris Read for Geraint Jones was the only change.

As the best player in the team, Pietersen needs to bat at four. Since Paul Collingwood shared the only partnership of any substance with Strauss — 57 for the third wicket — it may appear that England's strategy, to keep him away from the new ball, had worked again, but to have Pietersen batting with the tail repeatedly is not satisfactory. In any case Collingwood might have been leg-before to Clark for nought, one of four apparently plumb leg-before decisions turned down by Rudi Koertzen.

Panesar was the other, …ly out to Warne before … out instead, but it was … turned down when … Hayden was hit on … front of the stu… gard, the first w… the other whe…

Australia's recent practice of not using a nightwatchman. Ponting said that Australia, too, would have chosen to bat first, but it was one of those tosses that either captain would prefer to have lost. Play was delayed by rain for half an hour and only 16 overs were bowled before an early lunch was taken, Alastair Cook …

…onting run out (Flintoff) 66

…8 P Siddle c Flintoff b Harmison 10

5.37 343-9 S Clark c Cook b Harmison 0

…iant leap

for proud S…

36 TUESDAY AUGUST 1 1989 THE TIMES First published 1785

# England's abject surrender marks new low in series

By Alan Lee, Cricket Correspondent

## Inglorious procession at Old Trafford

18-1: Curtis c Boon b Alderman 0

25-2: Robinson lbw b Lawson 12

27-3: Smith c Healy b Alderman 1

28-4: Gooch c Alderman b Lawson 13

38-5: Botham lbw b Alderman 4

59-6: Gower c Marsh b Lawson 15

More cricket

SCOREBOARD FROM OLD TRAFFORD

England won toss

ENGLAND

First Innings: 260 (R A Smith 143; G F Lawson 6 for 72)

Second Innings

AUSTRALIA

First Innings

## Gower unfairly blamed for failings of others

Simon Barnes

## Border rewarded for hard labour

By John Woodcock

## Only two men so far decline

By Alan Lee

THE F…

SPOR… Cricket

# Was this English … most desperate …

…ding

…night issued a dramatic … …ct Union to make a positive … …te. He said that unless the … …epared to help to achieve an … …tegic arms limitations, he would … …ditional funds of more than … …new nuclear

# FIELDING

THE TIMES SATURDAY JUNE 11 1938

H: A GOOD BEGINNING BY ENGLAND

4

Sporting News

LAKER'S SUPREME PART IN RETAINING THE ASHES

ALL TEN AUSTRALIAN WICKETS AND 19 IN MATCH

From Our Cricket Correspondent

England won the fourth Test match against Australia at Old ... terday by an innin... retaining the A... achiev...

pitch perked up and the ball showed signs of misbehaving. At luncheon McDonald and Craig were still together. They had then added only 59, but the important thing was that they had each been batting for more than four hours. Ahead of them stretched another four and only 15 minutes of these had ticked away when Laker struck... blow. Craig, still...

TEST MATCH

BRADMAN 309 NOT OUT

ALL RECORDS BROKEN

The Third Test Match between England and Australia was begun at Leeds yesterday. A. P. F. Chapman, for once, lost the toss and Australia went in to bat on a perfect batsman's wicket. By the end of the day they had scored 458 runs for the loss of three wickets...

THE TIMES

LOCOMEN'S BAN BOUND ... CAUSE GREATER ... ON TODAY

HOW THE AUSTRALIANS WERE SKITTLED OUT AT LORD'S

Gaullists may get back with clear majority

Inquiry over bank chief's salary

Police alerted by strike ship

Railways must act alone, Marsh says

13 die in Swi... rail crash

...ped aiming to hit Mallett over the hill, and the end draws nearer.

dismally surrender Ashes

## ONLY TEST, THE OVAL, 1880

*September 8.* [...] Mr Bonnor, who had played with tolerable care, was at length induced to 'let out' to a ball of Shaw's, and it was exceedingly well judged by Mr G.F. Grace at long-field-on.

LETTER TO THE EDITOR

*June 16, 1930.* Sir, Comparatively few can recall that catch of G.F. Grace by which he disposed of G.J. Bonnor. I was standing close to where G.F. Grace was fielding. The ball ought to have gone right out of the ground, but was just mistimed. So high did the ball travel that the roar of the crowd had time to die down, and an extraordinary silence and stillness followed. Meanwhile, Grace stood quite still, having moved scarcely a yard, apparently the coolest man on the ground. I wonder how many seconds it was, it seemed minutes, before he caught and tossed up the ball as easily as if it had been poked to him at point. What a loss to cricket-loving enthusiasts was his early death!

Yours truly,
H. Summerhays
Bromfield Vicarage, Ludlow, Shropshire

## FIRST TEST, OLD TRAFFORD, 1886

*July 6.* The Englishmen's fielding was remarkably good and some fine catches were made. A glance at the score will show the excellence of the wicket-keeping, a wide being the only 'extra'.

## SECOND TEST, THE OVAL, 1888

*August 14.* Messrs O'Donnell and Bannerman opened the Australian batting, while Lohmann led off the attack from the pavilion end. His field was disposed as follows:- Dr Grace, mid-off; Mr Read, point; Mr Shuter, short mid-on; Wood, wicket; Sugg, long field straight; Barnes, extra slip; Abel, slip; Briggs, cover-point, Peel, extra mid-off; and Ulyett, third man. Nothing came from the first over. Peel had charge of the bowling at the other end, with his field as follows:- Dr Grace, mid-off; Mr Shater, cover-point; Mr W.W. Read, point; Wood, wicket; Sugg, third man; Barnes, short mid-on; Abel, long-off; Briggs, extra mid-off; Lohmann, slip; Ulyett, deep on the off side. [...]

In batting, bowling, and fielding the Englishmen were seen to great advantage. Lohmann's two marvellous catches at slip were among the features of the day's cricket. The great Surrey bowler was loudly applauded for a most remarkable feat. [...]

With his third ball Peel got the Australian captain brilliantly caught at slip by Lohmann, who dropped on his knee and made the catch wide with his left hand. [...]

From his third ball there was another brilliant catch at extra slip by Lohmann, who secured the ball almost on the ground with his right hand. Again he was most heartily cheered.

*St Peter's cathedral provides a scenic backdrop as England go through their fielding drills at the Adelaide Oval in 2002–03*

## THIRD TEST, OLD TRAFFORD, 1888

*September 1.* Dr Grace's catch which sent back Mr Edwards was remarkable, and should silence the criticism sometimes heard that the veteran is no longer able to get down to the ball as of old.

## FOURTH TEST, OLD TRAFFORD, 1902

ERNEST WARD,
CRICKET CORRESPONDENT

*July 26.* Next Mr Darling and Mr Gregory were together, and the score was only 16 when Mr Darling was badly missed at deep square-leg, almost on the boundary, by Tate, who after judging the ball well and making it look quite an easy catch, dropped it. Braund and Lockwood were bowling with great judgment, but the bad miss altered the aspect of the game. The batsmen played very steadily after this.

## FIFTH TEST, THE OVAL, 1902

R.H. LYTTELTON

*August 13.* Mr Trumper then played a ball tolerably hard to Mr Jessop's left hand and started to run; Mr Duff refused to go, and Mr Trumper, who slipped in trying to return, was easily run out. He would probably have been run out in any case, for Mr Jessop is the last fieldsman in the world to run risks with.

## FOURTH TEST, OLD TRAFFORD, 1905

R. H. LYTTELTON

*July 27.* Rhodes made two splendid catches, the first at extra slip and the second at short leg. The one at extra slip, dismissing Mr Darling, was one of the finest that it is possible to make; the ball came like lightning, very low to his right-hand side, Rhodes being a

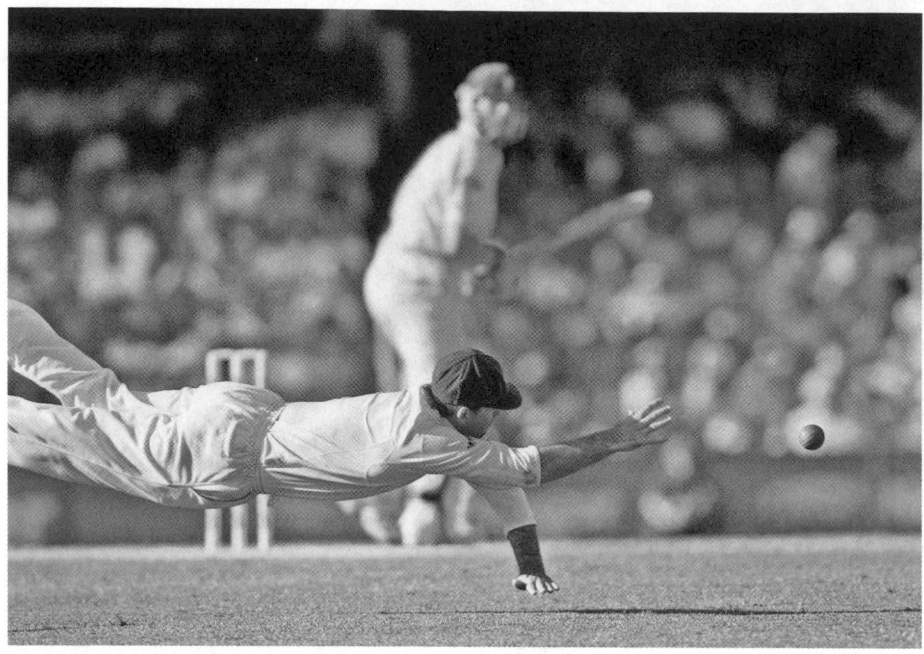

*Ricky Ponting was a brilliant fielder in several positions. He makes a flying stop at Sydney in 2006–07*

left-handed man, and he caught it a few inches from the ground. No prettier bit of cricket has been seen this season.

## THIRD TEST, HEADINGLEY, 1926

A.C.M. CROOME,
CRICKET CORRESPONDENT

*July 13.* He [Richardson] was run out in the next over by a wonderful bit of combination between Macaulay and Strudwick. Macaulay had taken over the bowling from Tate. Mr Richardson hit one back hard and wide to his right hand. Macaulay reached it somehow and threw, which is one of the things he can do; Strudwick gathered the ball on the half, half-volley, and Mr Richardson, who had started to run, could not get back.

## SECOND TEST, MELBOURNE, 1932–33

ROY CURTHOYS

*December 31.* Richardson made a pull to the boundary off Voce, but at 188 he glanced a ball from Voce to short-leg and Hammond made a splendid catch. He clutched at the ball with both hands, lost it, but just got hold of it again with his right hand a few inches from the ground.

## FOURTH TEST, BRISBANE, 1932–33

FIRMIN MCKINNON

*February 16.* Darling's fine innings was brought to an end in a most unfortunate manner at 169. Love hesitated after playing a ball from Larwood towards mid-on, and then called Darling for a run. The latter ran, but he was only half-way down the pitch when Larwood picked the ball up smartly and threw it to Mitchell, who broke the wicket with Darling well beaten. Love had had time to sacrifice his own wicket, but realised it too late. He was obviously distressed at his unfortunate mistake. It was an ill-deserved ending to what promised to be a fine innings.

## FIFTH TEST, SYDNEY, 1932–33

DELAMORE MCCAY

*February 28.* Allen attempted a big hit, which would have completed his 50, partly mis-hit the ball and lofted it over cover point's head. Bradman, running at full speed along the boundary, took a brilliant catch, which is likely to be remembered in Sydney for many years to come.

## FOURTH TEST, HEADINGLEY, 1938

R.B VINCENT,
CRICKET CORRESPONDENT

*July 26.* Fourteen of these were provided in one over of Verity's, four of them from an overthrow, and four more because Bowes at mid-on allowed a ball to pass him without apparently noticing its whereabouts. This disgusted the crowd ...

## FIRST TEST, BRISBANE, 1946–47

NEVILLE CARDUS

*November 30.* Bedser then found his rhythm, and compelled strokes which batsmen prefer not to make. Morris's bat was drawn to an outswinger which discovered the edge, and Hammond held the catch with all his old grace.

*Intense concentration from Graeme Swann, barely suppressed excitement from the crowd, as he takes a catch at the Oval in 2013*

## FOURTH TEST, HEADINGLEY, 1948

R.B. VINCENT,
CRICKET CORRESPONDENT

*July 27.* Washbrook soon after reached his 50, but with the score at 129 the first wicket fell when Harvey, at deep long-leg, held a catch on his bootlaces offered to him by Washbrook. The fielding of Harvey and his return to the wicket, whether at deep third man or at long-leg, were a feature of the day's cricket.

## FIRST TEST, BRISBANE, 1950–51

R.C. ROBERTSON-GLASGOW

*December 2.* Harvey did not long survive his gay companion, for Evans brilliantly ended a brilliant innings with a catch on the leg side of the wicket. He also whipped off the bails 'just to show 'em'. [...]

Just before tea Evans made the second of his two remarkable catches. Brown found a teasing length with his leg-spinners. Loxton snicked one wide and hard. The ball bounced to the right from Evans's gloves, but before it reached the ground he had plunged like Nijinsky and caught it.

## SECOND TEST, LORD'S, 1953

GEOFFREY GREEN,
CRICKET CORRESPONDENT

*June 30.* But at 20 minutes to 1, shortly after Hutton had dropped his third chance in the game, now at slip off Wardle to Morris, a great acrobatic catch by Statham brought succour to parched lips. Hutton, in desperation, put on Compton at the nursery end, hoping that his left-handed 'chinaman' might work some sort of oriental charm. It did. Morris, apparently set for a century, swung to leg; Statham ran fully 30 yards, leapt high, turned a somersault and landed on his head, but held on superbly to the ball.

*Two great wicket-keepers of the 1970s, Alan Knott and Rod Marsh, in direct competition at the Oval in 1972*

## FIRST TEST, BRISBANE, 1954–55

JOHN WOODCOCK,
CRICKET CORRESPONDENT

*November 29.* Within 20 minutes, and just after a hard chance to mid-off, Harvey, in full cry, had been magnificently caught by Bailey at square leg off a full-blooded hook, the fielder hurling himself to his left and holding the ball near the ground in both hands, and Archer had been well taken in the gully by Bedser off Statham, who again bowled extremely well all day.

What mockery it seemed that Bailey should now hold such an incredible catch, when 316 runs back, he had dropped one so straightforward from Morris off the same stroke and before the innings had set its course.

A.G. MOYES

*November 29.* The plain fact is that England lacks specialist fielders, which is not Hutton's fault but makes his task infinitely harder, even to using fast bowlers as outfielders, which is foreign to the Australian practice, because we believe that bowling fast under a hot Australian sun is a big enough task without chasing the ball round the boundary as well.

## SECOND TEST, SYDNEY, 1954–55

JOHN WOODCOCK,
CRICKET CORRESPONDENT

*December 18.* Hutton played another legitimate deflection off the back foot and the middle of the bat which he must have thought worth 4. The ball flew as quick as a bird but Davidson threw himself, like a cat, full length to his right and caught the ball in his right, or unnatural, hand. Few other fielders in the world would have got anywhere near the ball. Hutton looked understandably flabbergasted, and England never recovered. Indeed, a pathetic procession started.

## FIRST TEST, TRENT BRIDGE, 1956

JOHN WOODCOCK,
CRICKET CORRESPONDENT

*June 8.* The score was seven when Cowdrey played a ball past Davidson in the covers. There was a disagreement over a second run, and as Davidson's return reached Langley, a yard or so wide of the stumps, Richardson was on his back in the middle of the pitch and Cowdrey, with 10 yards to go, was heading for the wicketkeeper's end.

The chances at that moment of either batsmen escaping were too long to be worth quoting. Yet first Langley fumbled the ball and Cowdrey, intending obviously to sacrifice himself, instead found that he was safe. Richardson was now rising, and Langley threw a reasonable catch to Miller standing over his stumps. Miller, with all the time in the world, gathered the ball and then somehow dropped it. By the time he went to regain it Richardson, his bat lost in the rush, was sprinting for his life, and as he breasted the tape so Miller, shorn of all his self-possession, desperately swept the wicket to the ground. As umpire Buller shook his head it was hard to believe that both players were reprieved, and it seemed to leave everyone shaking with reaction.

## SECOND TEST, LORD'S, 1956

JOHN WOODCOCK, CRICKET CORRESPONDENT

*June 23.* Three-quarters of an hour remained, Mackay began to bowl, a disarming and self-conscious sight, and the crisis seemed over when, at 60, the majestic Cowdrey was wonderfully caught in the gully. And who should be the bowler but Mackay? Cowdrey could not have been quite at the pitch of the ball, which he made to drive, for it flew towards the gully at the speed of sound. There Benaud held it in his hands stretched above his head. That he touched it at all was remarkable, that he actually caught it was almost beyond belief.

*June 25.* England, indeed, were being left behind when, at a quarter to 4, the game, as it burned peacefully, was fanned into a flaming conflagration. For 10 minutes there was hardly time to think. McDonald was brilliantly snapped up low and right handed in the gully by Cowdrey off Bailey. Harvey, driving at his first ball, gave a technical chance to Cowdrey, also in the gully, and also off Bailey. At the time he stood to make a pair of spectacles, and the way in which he hit the next two balls for 4 suggested that he would make England pay for their error – if error it was. But a single by Burke brought him to face Trueman, whose first ball he glanced delightfully round the corner. Nineteen times out of 20 it would have been a boundary, but there was Bailey elongating himself to his right and catching an incredible catch. Poor Harvey! The dismayed way in which he threw his hands in the air and disbelievingly shook his head was so expressive.

## FIFTH TEST, THE OVAL, 1956

JOHN WOODCOCK, CRICKET CORRESPONDENT

*August 25.* Late on Thursday evening the rain had come down in sheets, and the pitch must still have been wet. Already the seamers had found some response and it was pretty certain that Laker and Lock would do the same. May clearly thought so, for he called up Laker after Statham had bowled only two overs. But by then McDonald had been wonderfully caught at leg slip by Lock off Tyson. This was in Tyson's first over, which began with two fierce, short balls as a reminder that he has lost none of his hostility since last he unleashed his thunderbolts against Australia. His fifth ball, one of the few which he pitched well up to the bat in this spell, was glanced legitimately enough by McDonald. More often than not it was a boundary, but now Lock nonchalantly took a catch with his right hand as though he was stooping to pick up a coin that had slipped out of his pocket. The speed of the ball alone frustrated the eyesight, the dexterity of the man was almost past belief.

## FIFTH TEST, THE OVAL, 1968

JOHN WOODCOCK, CRICKET CORRESPONDENT

*August 27.* Lawry had hit his first ball through the covers for four. The next cocked up off bat and pad to the on side, where Milburn, diving like a porpoise to his right, took the vital catch only a few feet from the bat. If the England side could have thrown Milburn aloft they would have done.

## FOURTH TEST, SYDNEY, 1970–71

JOHN WOODCOCK,
CRICKET CORRESPONDENT

*January 15.* In Snow's second over, Lever threw himself to his left for a chance from Stackpole and, in his third over, Willis made an even more spectacular leap to get rid of Marsh. Lever's catch was one-handed, Willis's two-handed. No one else in the England side would have had the height to make the ground that Willis did. He could go through a whole football season with Corinthian Casuals, whose goal he keeps when he is in England, without making a better catch than this.

## FIRST TEST, OLD TRAFFORD, 1972

JACK FINGLETON

*June 10.* It was England's turn to spill the slip catches yesterday. Poor Arnold, who was to get justice later, had the mortification of seeing Stackpole go down off successive balls (Greig and Snow) and then Greig spilt Francis in the slips in D'Oliveira's first over. I made it that Australia dropped four in the English innings, all in the slips. Though the dull light makes sighting difficult, it is not to be ignored that coloured advertisements strung along the fences at slip catch height, could make a background somewhat difficult. At the least, it is a good excuse.

## SECOND TEST, LORD'S, 1972

JOHN WOODCOCK,
CRICKET CORRESPONDENT

*June 22.* […] and the slips, you might say, are aptly named. In a letter yesterday a friend quoted the 91st psalm with reference to England's slip fielding at Old Trafford: 'A thousand shall fall beside thee, and ten thousand at thy right hand.'

JACK FINGLETON

*June 23.* Francis made a bad miss when he dropped Knott at 16 off Lillee. This cost Australia dear. The sun was out at this time and I wondered if the uncapped Francis was handicapped. Only Gleeson and Marsh in this side continuously wear the baggy Australian caps. The vogue of long hair has kept the cap in the dressing room because the cap will not sit on long hair.

JOHN WOODCOCK,
CRICKET CORRESPONDENT

*June 24.* One of the highlights of the day was Smith's catch to send back Ian Chappell. Hooking again, and hooking up, as he will, Chappell sent a high ball towards long leg, where Smith was some time sighting it. Only after it had cleared the rim of the Warner Stand, and shown against the sky, could he make for the catch, and even then he reached it only by falling forward and rolling over. Never at Twickenham, in the heat of an international match, did he make a better catch than this.

## FIRST TEST, BRISBANE, 1974–75

JOHN WOODCOCK,
CRICKET CORRESPONDENT

*November 30.* As it was, we were into the last hour and Ian Chappell and Edwards had added 87 before Chappell was out. Within 10 runs of his 13th Test hundred he hooked at a bouncer from Willis – that compulsive hook again – and skied it high above the Gabba. With Greig, from square leg, and Knott both converging on it, it was even money a collision, but Knott backed off just in time, leaving Greig to hold the catch. That he did so in a position of genuflexion was not inappropriate.

## SECOND TEST, PERTH, 1974–75

JOHN WOODCOCK,
CRICKET CORRESPONDENT

*December 18.* [...] the last wicket fell, aptly enough, to another marvellous catch by Greg Chappell, running and tumbling at wide long-off. This gave him a record for Test cricket of seven catches in a match by a fieldsman other than a wicket-keeper. Several players have held six catches, including Cowdrey and also Vic Richardson, the grandfather of the Chappells.

## FIRST TEST, LORD'S, 1977

JOHN WOODCOCK,
CRICKET CORRESPONDENT

*June 16.* I doubt, for a start, if England have ever put out a much better fielding side. That is the sort of thing one writes and is immediately confounded by a succession of dropped catches and missed run-outs but, as they fielded in India and again in the one-day Prudential trophy matches, England are uncommonly good, with Barlow, Randall, Lever and Old in the highest class.

*June 17.* In the best light they can have enjoyed for a week and across a quickening outfield, Randall and Woolmer took their third wicket partnership to 98 before Randall was marvelously caught at first slip by Chappell. As though expecting a chance and that if he dropped it he could do himself a nasty injury, Chappell had just sent for a box. He caught it somewhere near his midriff, the ball travelling at lightning speed.

## THIRD TEST, TRENT BRIDGE, 1977

JOHN WOODCOCK,
CRICKET CORRESPONDENT

*July 29.* Off the first ball of the next over, Hookes was marvellously caught at third slip by Hendrick off Willis. The ball went low and far to Hendrick's left. How he got a hand to it was remarkable, how he got two to it was more so, how he held it was miraculous.

## FIRST TEST, TRENT BRIDGE, 1981

JOHN WOODCOCK,
CRICKET CORRESPONDENT

*June 20.* With catching that would have put a girls' school to shame, England allowed Australia to get within 19 runs of their first innings total, with one wicket left, in the first Test match, sponsored by Cornhill, at Trent Bridge yesterday. Five chances went astray, three of them easy, which, if England lose, could be

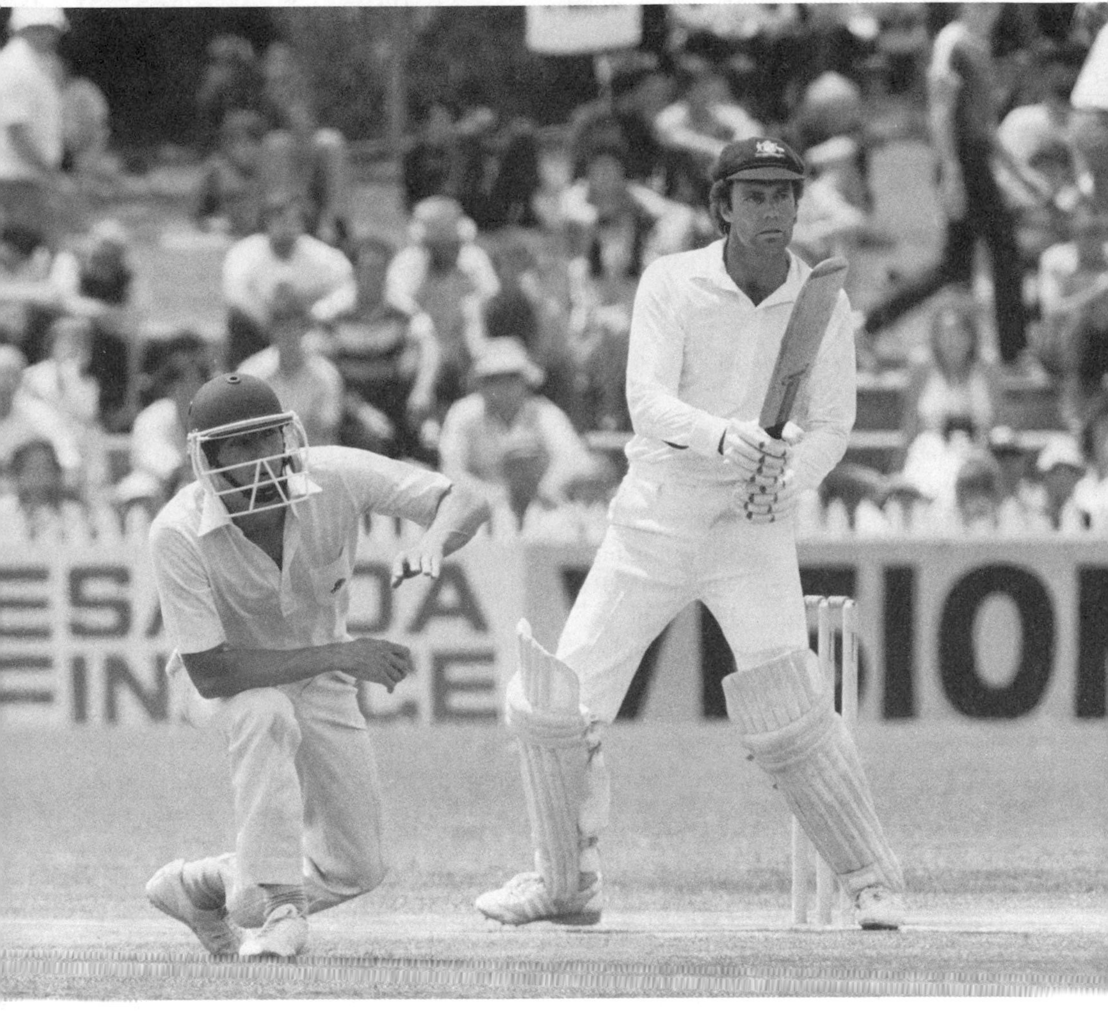

*Derek Randall, brilliant in the covers early in his career, finds himself in a helmet at short leg in Australia in 1982–83*

the reason why. Drizzle and bad light reduced the playing time from six hours to just under four.

Besides the runs they cost, England's fielding errors had a significant psychological effect. Apart from cheering the Australians up when they badly needed it, they undermined the English bowling, which was less good than it had been on Thursday evening.

## SECOND TEST, LORD'S, 1985

JOHN WOODCOCK,
CRICKET CORRESPONDENT

*June 29.* Then there was an extraordinary incident in which England literally threw away the chance of Border's wicket. Border, who was 87 at the time, took a step to Edmonds and hit him firmly at

Gatting, fielding no more than three yards away at short leg. Fearlessly, yet more by luck than judgment, Gatting captured the ball, albeit fleetingly, between his legs; then when it escaped, he clutched it again. In his delight at doing this he made to throw it aloft, as is the modern custom. Instead it fell feebly to the ground

## SECOND TEST, MELBOURNE, 1994–95

JOHN WOODCOCK

*December 31.* Because England are slower in the field than Australia, I read that a prerequisite for anyone wishing to become a genuine Test cricketer in future will be a high degree of 'athleticism'. Rod Marsh, maverick turned Academy guru, is among those who have been saying so.

Presumably, therefore, all potential Alec Bedsers, Colin Milburns, Herbert Sutcliffes, Jim Lakers and Maurice Tates, or Bill O'Reilly's for that matter, need not apply. What nonsense! It helps of course it does to have a few greyhounds in the field and between the wickets, but temperament and flair and judgment and competence and guts and concentration and good bowlers and, above all, confidence are what win cricket matches, not acrobatics.

## FIFTH TEST, PERTH, 1994–95

ALAN LEE, CRICKET CORRESPONDENT

*February 7.* Sometimes a single moment can encapsulate a game of cricket. It happened here yesterday when, in an expression of disgust that degenerated into self-parody, England surrendered their interest in this Test series and prepared for humbling defeat.

Ten minutes after lunch, Graham Thorpe dropped a slip catch. It was his second miss of the innings and, astonishingly, England's tenth of the match. Thorpe could take no more. He aimed an angry kick at the ball and sent it wide of cover for two bizarrely donated runs.

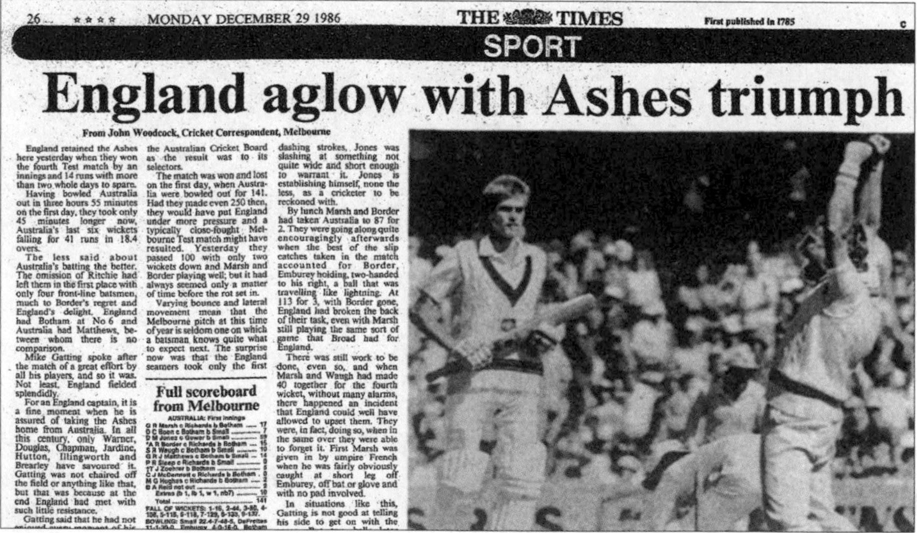

26 ★★★★ MONDAY DECEMBER 29 1986 THE TIMES First published in 1785

SPORT

# England aglow with Ashes triumph

**From John Woodcock, Cricket Correspondent, Melbourne**

England retained the Ashes here yesterday when they won the fourth Test match by an innings and 14 runs with more than two whole days to spare.

Having bowled Australia out in three hours 55 minutes on the first day, they took only 45 minutes longer now, Australia's last six wickets falling for 41 runs in 18.4 overs.

The less said about Australia's batting the better. The omission of Ritchie had left them in the first place with only four front-line batsmen, much to Border's regret and England's delight. England had Botham at No 6 and Australia had Matthews, between whom there is no comparison.

Mike Gatting spoke after the match of a great effort by all his players, and so it was. Not least, England fielded splendidly.

For an England captain, it is a fine moment when he is assured of taking the Ashes home from Australia. In all this century, only Warner, Douglas, Chapman, Jardine, Hutton, Illingworth and Brearley have savoured it. Gatting was not chaired off the field or anything like that, but that was because at the end England had met with such little resistance.

Gatting said that he had not ...

... the Australian Cricket Board as the result was to its selectors.

The match was won and lost on the first day, when Australia were bowled out for 141. Had they made even 250 then, they would have put England under more pressure and a typically close-fought Melbourne Test match might have resulted. Yesterday they passed 100 with only two wickets down and Marsh and Border playing well; but it had always seemed only a matter of time before the rot set in.

Varying bounce and lateral movement mean that the Melbourne pitch at this time of year is seldom one on which a batsman knows quite what to expect next. The surprise now was that the England seamers took only the first ...

**Full scoreboard from Melbourne**

AUSTRALIA: First innings

G R Marsh c Richards b Botham 17
D C Boon c Botham b Small 7
D M Jones c Gower b Small 59
*A R Border c Richards b Botham 15
S R Waugh c Botham b Small 10
G R J Matthews c Botham b Small 14
P R Sleep c Richards b Small 0
†T J Zoehrer b Botham 5
C J McDermott c Richards b Botham 0
M G Hughes c Richards b Botham 2
B A Reid not out 2
Extras (b 1, lb 1, w 1, nb7) 10
Total 141

FALL OF WICKETS: 1-16, 2-44, 3-80, 4-108, 5-118, 6-118, 7-129, 8-133, 9-137.

BOWLING: Small 22.4-7-48-5, DeFreitas 11-1-30-0, Emburey 4-0-16-0, Botham ...

... dashing strokes, Jones was slashing at something not quite wide and short enough to warrant it. Jones is establishing himself, none the less, as a cricketer to be reckoned with.

By lunch Marsh and Border had taken Australia to 87 for 2. They were going along quite encouragingly afterwards when the best of the slip catches taken in the match accounted for Border, Emburey holding, two-handed to his right, a ball that was travelling like lightning. At 113 for 3, with Border gone, England had broken the back of their task, even with Marsh still playing the same sort of game that Broad had for England.

There was still work to be done, even so, and when Marsh and Waugh had made 40 together for the fourth wicket, without many alarms, there happened an incident that England could well have allowed to upset them. They were, in fact, doing so, when in the same over they were able to forget it. First Marsh was given in by umpire French when he was fairly obviously caught at short leg off Emburey, off bat or glove and with no pad involved.

In situations like this, Gatting is not good at telling his side to get on with the ...

*Victory at Melbourne means the Ashes are retained by Mike Gatting's team in Australia*

Michael Atherton, the captain, dropped to his haunches, head in hands; Devon Malcolm, the suffering bowler, ranted inaudibly and kicked imaginary backsides in mid-pitch.

## SECOND TEST, ADELAIDE, 2002–03

CHRISTOPHER MARTIN-JENKINS, CHIEF CRICKET CORRESPONDENT

*November 25.* Vaughan and Stewart had played him well and the stand of 74 was getting troublesome when Vaughan finally took a risk and paid the penalty. Going down on one knee to pick up a flighted ball pitched on his stumps, he was wonderfully well caught by McGrath, who ran some 15 yards along the square leg boundary and threw himself towards the descending ball, catching it in his right hand in the instant before it dropped to earth. It was typical of Australia's commitment and of their ability to find someone to do something special whenever they seemed to be starting to struggle.

## THIRD TEST, PERTH, 2010–11

MIKE ATHERTON, CHIEF CRICKET CORRESPONDENT

*December 17.* Cue Ponting, and three swift boundaries, two crisp ones through the leg side and one squirted in the air off Tremlett to where fourth slip should have been. His tenth ball was short and wide and in his eagerness Ponting played firmly but with a crooked bat. It went towards fourth slip again, and in the nanoseconds it took observers to utter obscenities in the direction of the England captain for not learning his lesson, there appeared Collingwood, at full stretch, back arched, springs apparently attached to his heels, to pluck the ball out of the air.

By any estimation, this was one of the great slip catches ...

Sporting …

# …OW ENGLAND KEPT THE ASHES

## …WO GREAT HEARTS OVERTHROW AUSTRALIA

England beat Australia by five wickets in the fourth Test match at Adelaide yesterday and so, gaining a lead of three matches to one in the series, have retained the Ashes. In an interview after the match L. Hutton, the England captain, paid a tribute to the younger members of the side. Much of the credit, he thought, should go to J. B. Statham, F. H. Tyson, M. C. Cowdrey and P. B. H. May, together with the wicket-keeper, T. G. Evans.

From Our Special Correspondent

ADELAIDE, FEB. 2

Many years from now young Cowdrey will point to his broken nose and tell boys yet unborn that he was at Adelaide on February 2, 1955, when England won the Test match and kept the Ashes. And the boys will think him wondrous lucky. A ma… should dip his pen in blood to write… his day. Let no one talk and …

… the catch. (We asked Hutton afterwards what he thought of Miller's bowling. Hutton thought Miller ought to concentrate much more on batting.) England 10 for 2. In comes the battered Cowdrey. Miller hits him twice running on the pads and appeals, and everybody here who isn't English appeals too. What a man is Miller. He comes in from a shortish run, loose of limb like an African, hair streaming, and as he pulls up the hair goes on and falls about his face. Meanwhile May has begun driving, and Johnson has gone from mid-off to square-leg. For Cowdrey Miller brings fine-leg up to third slip, and Cowdrey cover drives classically for 4. Miller heaves his shoulders over even faster, and Cowdrey is taken by Archer at first-slip. England 18 for 3. Four Meteor jets fly over at 200ft.; they look and sound quite tame beside this wild man … His figures now are 3 overs, no … runs, 3 wickets.

Sporting News

# ENGLAND HAVE LAST WORD

## THREE YEOMEN FOIL AUSTRALIA

## GREAT STAND BY WATSON AND BAILEY

FROM OUR CRICKET CORRESPONDENT

Out of darkness, through fire into light. Thus did England yesterday rise like some Phoenix from the ashes of apparent defeat to save the second Test match at Lord's and so gain a … draw against Australia with … seven wickets, … original aim fo… The age of … yet past, nor … cany scarce … dramatic and … a match alrea… But within … longest and … of a match it… that last spa… back with le… yeomen of … nearly the … The yeom… were Watso… greatest of … Yorkshirem… order, was … rearguard … twentieth …

# …ngland all too obliging … eaches new heights of greatnes…

One that got away: Gilchrist misses a stumping chance off Warne to give Pietersen an extra life, but it was to make little difference

High five: Warne acknowledges the Melbourne crowd after his haul ripped the heart out of England's fragile batting

… legendary accuracy and a lush outfield, they ran poorly between the wickets, chose the wrong balls to try to hit in the air and failed to justify the decision to bat.

"We didn't expect conditions to change dramatically over the first day and a half," Strauss said, "but it seemed about more than we expected." It did so slowly but Glenn McGrath, Stuart Clark and Brett Lee all got enough past the bat to suggest that the wrong option had been taken.

Australia missed two catches, two clear run-out opportunities and a gaping stumping, but still bowled England out for 159 after they had been 101 for two. Very few Test matches are won after such a start. All of Warne's wickets were taken by flight and dip, as batsmen spied what they believed to be boundary opportunities. Only Kevin Pietersen got anywhere near the boundary as he attempted to drive Warne straight for six, but by now he was, as usual, batting with the tail.

Even he needed 70 balls for 21 runs, having come close to running out Andrew Flintoff for six as, for the third Test in succession, he attempted a ridiculous single in order to get off the mark. He had only made four when he also survived a simple stumping chance offered to Adam Gilchrist after charging Warne and missing.

England, we all know, have too long a tail, but tweaking it made no difference. Matthew Hoggard is back where he started, No 11, pushing Monty Panesar and Stephen Harmison up a place each, which reflects their various abilities with the bat. It is higher up, however, that the balance is wrong. Ed Joyce or Jamie Dalrymple should have played six, but Chris Read for Geraint Jones was the only change.

As the best player in the team, Pietersen needs to bat at four. Since Paul Collingwood shared the only partnership of any substance with Strauss — 57 for the third wicket — it may appear that England's strategy, to keep him away from the new ball, had worked again, but to have Pietersen batting with the tail repeatedly is not satisfactory. In any case Collingwood might have been leg-before to Clark for nought, one of four apparently plumb leg-before decisions turned down by Rudi Koertzen.

Panesar was the other, …

… Australia's recent practice of not using a nightwatchman.

Ponting said that Australia, too, would have chosen to bat first, but it was one of those tosses that either captain would prefer to have lost. Play was delayed by rain for half an hour and only 16 overs were bowled before an early lunch was taken. Alastair Coo…

6-1 S Katich lbw b …

…onting run out (Flintoff) 66

…-8 P Siddle c Flintoff b Harmison 10

5.37 343-9 S Clark c Cook b Harmison 0

…iant leap

for proud S…

7-6 B Hadd…

One…

36 TUESDAY AUGUST 1 1989

THE TIMES

# England's abject surrender marks new low in series

By Alan Lee, Cricket Correspondent

## Inglorious procession at Old Trafford

28-3: Curtis c Boon b Alderman 0

25-2: Robinson lbw b Lawson 12

27-3: Smith c Healy b Alderman 1

28-4: Gooch c Alderman b Lawson 13

38-5: Botham lbw b Alderman 4

59-6: Gower c Marsh b Lawson 15

SCOREBOARD FROM OLD TRAFFORD

## Gower unfairly blamed for failings of others

Simon Barnes

## Border rewarded for hard labour

By John Woodcock

## Only two men so far decline

By Alan Lee

# Was this English … most desperate …

…ding

# SELECTION

THE TIMES SATURDAY JUNE 11 1938
A GOOD BEGINNING BY ENGLAND
THE TIMES
LOCOMEN'S BAN BOUND
CAUSE GREATER
HOW THE AUSTRALIANS WERE SKITTLED OUT AT LORD'S
Gaullists may get back with clear majority
Inquiry over bank chief's salary
Police alerted by strike ship
Railways must act alone, Marsh says
4
Sporting News
LAKER'S SUPREME PART IN RETAINING THE ASHES
ALL TEN AUSTRALIAN WICKETS AND 19 IN MATCH
From Our Cricket Correspondent
dismally surrender Ashes
TEST MATCH
BRADMAN 309 NOT OUT
ALL RECORDS BROKEN
The Third Test Match between England and Australia was begun at Leeds yesterday. A. P. F. Chapman, for once, lost the toss and Australia went in to bat on a perfect batsman's wicket. By the end of the day they had scored 458 runs for the loss of

## SECOND TEST, MELBOURNE, 1884–85

*February 11.* England v Australia. The second match under this title, began on New Year's Day on the Melbourne Cricket Ground, differed materially from the contest a few weeks previously at the Oval, Adelaide. On the latter occasion the whole of the Australians had been seen on English cricket fields; but in the match at Melbourne only two in the Eleven had visited England. The game, however, possessed great interest for a large number of colonials as a test of the merits of a team of Australians other than the celebrated Eleven of which Mr Murdoch was captain, and the attendance on the Melbourne Ground was consequently very large.

6

**SPORTING INTELLIGENCE.**

**CRICKET.**

**ENGLISH VICTORY IN AUSTRALIA.**

**MELBOURNE, MARCH 6.**

**At a quarter past 4 this afternoon the great match between Mr. Stoddart's Eleven and the All Australia team ended in a victory for the Englishmen by six wickets. The result is a disappointment here, but it is conceded that the better team won. At the same time the selection of the colonial eleven is criticized, and it is urged by some that a good fast bowler ought to have been included. A drizzling rain fell during the earlier hours of the morning, but it ceased shortly after play began and did not affect the wicket at all. For the rest of the day the weather was fine and warm, though the sky was overcast. Ward and Stoddart, the overnight not-outs, resumed their innings, Henry Trott and Giffen being the bowlers. To the very first ball of Trott's the English captain was out leg-before-wicket, and the Australian hopes rose high. But Brown came in, and, after scoring 11 off Giffen's first over, continued to play with the greatest spirit, hitting the bowling to every part of the field, while Ward kept up his wicket and scored slowly. The hundred went up a few minutes after 1, Ward's total being 21 and Brown's 60. The bowling was constantly changed, and by lunch-time, when the board showed 145—Ward being 41 and Brown 80—no fewer than six bowlers had been tried—Henry Trott,**

*By 1894–95 improved communications meant reports from Australia appeared the following day*

## SECOND TEST, THE OVAL, 1888

*August 14.* Dr W.G. Grace captains the English side, in which there are five Surrey men (Mr Read, Mr Shuter, Abel, Lohmann, and Wood), two Yorkshiremen (Ulyett and Peel), two Lancastrians (Briggs and Sugg), and Barnes, from Nottinghamshire. Much adverse criticism was heard of several of the selections, but under the circumstances the team, in Mr A.G. Steel's absence, could scarcely have been altered for the better.

## THIRD TEST, ADELAIDE, 1911–12

*January 13.* There has been a good deal of disagreement this season between Mr P. McAlister, Mr C. Hill, and Mr F. Iredale, who were appointed to select the Australian teams for the Test matches. For this match Mr McAlister urged the inclusion of Mr Matthews; Mr Hill, on the other hand, preferred Mr Macartney, and finally Mr McAlister sent the following telegram to Mr Hill from Melbourne: 'If you will include Macartney, better leave yourself out.'

## FIRST TEST, TRENT BRIDGE, 1921

SYDNEY PARDON,
CRICKET CORRESPONDENT

*May 28.* The England team for today's match at Nottingham has been so fully discussed that little remains to be said on the subject. No one would pretend that the side compares for a moment with the great elevens we have had in the past, notably, to give only one example, at Birmingham in 1902. Lilley, England's wicket-keeper on so many occasions, regards that Birmingham team as the finest for which he ever had the honour of playing. Exactly the same combination took the field at Lord's when rain limited cricket to two hours or so on the first day.

According to their judgment the Selection Committee have done their best with the material available, handicapped as they were by the enforced absence of Hobbs and Hearne. I take it that the necessity of ensuring, if possible, fine fielding accounts for the fact of both Mr Fry and Mead having been passed ever. Other batsmen, more likely to save runs as well as to get them, have been chosen in preference. The team as it stands would be good enough to meet all comers in a series of matches such as the Australians are playing, apart from the Test games, but the task today is for obvious reasons exceptionally difficult.

SYDNEY PARDON,
CRICKET CORRESPONDENT

*July 2.* No one, I am certain, wishes to find fault with the members of the Selection Committee. They have been faced by unexampled difficulties. Never before have we been in the lamentable position of not having a single bowler fit to step unchallenged into the England team. I am thinking, of course, of bowlers pure and simple. Colonel Douglas is indispensable, but he is an all-round man. If he did not bowl at all, his claims as a batsman of unfailing nerve would have to be considered. In days long before Test matches with Australia were even dreamed of, the county of Nottinghamshire alone could have furnished us with a far more dependable set of bowlers than we shall have at Leeds today. Every bowler picked for England this year is an experiment.

## FIRST TEST, TRENT BRIDGE, 1926

A.C.M. CROOME,
CRICKET CORRESPONDENT

*June 14.* At breakfast time a local newspaper informed us that Holmes would play for Yorkshire at Leeds. The inclusion of Rhodes in that same Yorkshire team came as an unpleasant surprise and gave a handle to those critics who hold that professionals should not be included in the Selection Committee. A selector's advice is likely to be of less value to his colleagues at their future meetings if he does not see in action the team which he has helped to choose. For the first Test match an amateur can at any moment withdraw from his county eleven to do work of national importance. A professional must, if required, fulfil his contract with his employers.

## THIRD TEST, HEADINGLEY, 1926

A.C.M. CROOME,
CRICKET CORRESPONDENT

*July 12.* A few minutes later the captains tossed, and Mr Carr sent Australia in to bat. If ever in the last 20 years appearances have justified that policy this was the occasion. The sun was shining fiercely on a damp marled wicket, and the weather seemed to be set fair, but there would seem to have been some lack of coordination between the captain and his colleagues of the selection committee, for it was illogical to omit Parker and subsequently put the other side in.

## SECOND TEST, LORD'S,1938

R.B. VINCENT,
CRICKET CORRESPONDENT

*June 24.* Consequently, always provided there is no immediate threat of rain, I believe that Verity, who on a perfect wicket can do little more than keep runs down – and time is the chief ally of the Australians – should make room for the more hostile Wellard. If rain should have fallen, then, of course, Verity's place in the team is all-important. But if the wicket is firm it must be remembered that Wellard is capable of making runs exceedingly fast, as a hard-hitting batsman and not as a wild slogger. The composition of the team in fact depends entirely on whether the selectors fancy themselves as weather prophets, and perhaps, after all, they will consider the best thing to do is to leave well alone. [...]

There were fears at one time that Fleetwood-Smith would not be able to play, but it turned out in the end that he had suffered no greater calamity than having a tooth taken out, a good example of what a fine all-round player Rumour is in a season of Test matches.

## FOURTH TEST, HEADINGLEY, 1938

R.B. VINCENT,
CRICKET CORRESPONDENT

*July 22.* The English selectors, who have no doubt in their minds about the possibilities the limitations of the Australians, have chosen the batsmen they consider most likely to make as big a score as possible; they have picked the most suitable bowlers; and the two ends of the team have been joined together regardless of whether there is a tail to the batting. For this they have invited, and received, criticism. But surely, at a time when all-round cricketers of real ability are not to be found, there is reason in the argument that if the chosen batsmen cannot make enough runs between them you cannot expect fast bowlers and their like to do it for them.

## SECOND TEST, LORD'S, 1953

GEOFFREY GREEN,
CRICKET CORRESPONDENT

*June 25.* For not only is there more potential variety in the attack but there are also two all-rounders in Bailey and Brown who is about to make an historic return to Test cricket – historic in the sense that he is the first chairman of selectors to extend his activities to the field of play during a term of office.

## SECOND TEST, SYDNEY, 1954–55

JOHN WOODCOCK,
CRICKET CORRESPONDENT

*December 18.* To begin with England omitted Bedser, the old and faithful servant and the last survivor of the four bowlers who won the Ashes for England in 1953, from their side. Then came Morris's bold decision; he smiled and put his arm round Hutton when asking him to bat.

When the selectors omitted Bedser they took a momentous step. Since the war he has not missed a Test match against Australia and in the 11 matches since December, 1950, he has averaged almost four wickets an innings. One knows that Bedser cannot have been lightly discarded and it may be only a temporary measure, but one would not call it a decision fully justified by the evidence for neither Wardle nor Appleyard has shown any sustained promise since the tour began.

## SECOND TEST, LORD'S, 1956

JOHN WOODCOCK,
CRICKET CORRESPONDENT

*June 22.* Test matches these days have a way of opening with surprises. At Nottingham Statham's last minute withdrawal was unavoidable. Yesterday the dropping of Lock was voluntary, and one rather thinks that a fly on the wall of the Australian dressing-room might have observed some incredulous and relieved expressions when the news came through. Wardle for Laker, yes; but Wardle for Lock, was something that no one had expected. Lock is the most aggressive spin bowler in the world, and a tiger in the field. Wardle is sometimes more effective on a good wicket, and one can only think that it was this that moved the selectors to what someone described as midsummer madness.

## FOURTH TEST, HEADINGLEY, 1972

JOHN WOODCOCK,
CRICKET CORRESPONDENT

*July 31.* In 52 overs Underwood took 10 wickets for 92 runs. The last time he played against Australia in England, at the Oval in 1968, he took seven for 50 and won the match. In Australia he played no small part in helping England regain the Ashes. In New Zealand, immediately afterwards, he took 17 wickets in two Test matches for 205 runs.

Yet since then he had played, until this one, in only two Test matches against Gifford's seven. It is like asking Robin Marlar or David Acfield to play in seven Test matches and Jim Laker in two: or John Pulman to play seven frames and Joe Davis only two.

## SECOND TEST, PERTH, 1974–75

JOHN WOODCOCK,
CRICKET CORRESPONDENT

*December 5.* There seems no end to the ups and downs of Colin Cowdrey's cricketing career. Having been rejected by the England selectors in 1971, and passed over for lesser players and lesser captains both before and since, he has now accepted a Mayday call from here to come and help MCC out on as tough an assignment as any of their recent sides have faced.

'We considered him but not seriously,' said Alec Bedser, then chairman of selectors and now touring manager, when asked, upon announcing the MCC party, whether Cowdrey had come near to being chosen. Now he is back, having resisted, perhaps, a temptation to turn the invitation down. Had he done so it would have been unlike him. He is not made the same way as Boycott. It is an open secret that Boycott would have come to Australia had Denness not been captain. Yet how much more reason Cowdrey has to feel that he himself should have had the captain's job. But that is by the way. Cowdrey will leave on Saturday morning and be in Perth Sunday lunchtime. It has taken only until the first Test match for the imbalance of the original selection to be exposed.

*December 7.* The SOS for Cowdrey has taken most Australians by surprise. They would have had someone younger, they say. He comes out, though, on a wave of goodwill and with at least as good a chance of success as anyone else who might have been sent for. He will arrive here on Sunday in time for a net on Monday and Tuesday. Whether, if he is to play in the Test match, he should fly the 300 miles to Geraldton for a one-day match on Wednesday or be kept at work in the nets here in Perth is a decision for next week. My own view is that a couple of hours in the middle is worth half a week at the nets. The rumour that Cowdrey has been told to pad up in the aircraft is unconfirmed. [...]

We find ourselves in Perth, where the plan was always to discomfort Australia with speed, with Arnold having taken only four wickets on the tour, and Old giving away runs at the rate of five an over, and Lever needing support for an injured back, and Hendrick with a virus on him, with Snow due at any moment to comment on the tour (what an irony!) and with an extra spinner more than likely to play.

LEADING ARTICLE
*December 18, 1974.* Mrs Thatcher will probably stand, but the Conservative Party does not seem to want a woman leader and has taken a minor gaffe about the tins in her larder as an excuse for crossing her off the list. Sir Keith Joseph has made worse gaffes than Mrs Thatcher and has crossed his name off as completely as Mr du Cann. Mr Whitelaw will not stand against Mr Heath and Mr Prior will not stand against Mr Whitelaw. Lord Carrington is in the House of Lords and Sir Christopher Soames is in Brussels. At the moment the spectacle of Mr Heath's potential rivals is like that of the English cricket team in Australia. All the best people are either in the wrong country, have retired hurt or have got themselves out by kindergarten strokes.

## THIRD TEST, EDGBASTON, 1989

ALAN LEE, CRICKET CORRESPONDENT
*July 6.* For those who have understandably lost track of England's problems, this is the latest bulletin. From the originally selected 12, delete Smith and Lamb, prepare to omit Foster and Gatting and add Curtis, Tavare and Jarvis.

This will hopefully add up to 11 men available to resume the Cornhill series this morning, although it would be wise if the manager made an early check to ensure no one has fallen foul of the hotel stairs.

## FIFTH TEST, TRENT BRIDGE, 1989

ALAN LEE, CRICKET CORRESPONDENT
*August 10.* The team fielded for today's fifth Cornhill Test match will increase England's turnover for the series to 26 players, three more than were used amid the disruption of last summer's multi-captained defeat by the West Indies. There are only three survivors from the team humbled in the opening Test at Headingley and, most remarkably, only two men, David Gower and Jack Russell have appeared throughout the series. [...]

Mike Atherton, Devon Malcolm and Greg Thomas were, however, produced for the obligatory photographs and managed the kind of forced smiles usually seen on passport snaps of conscripts.

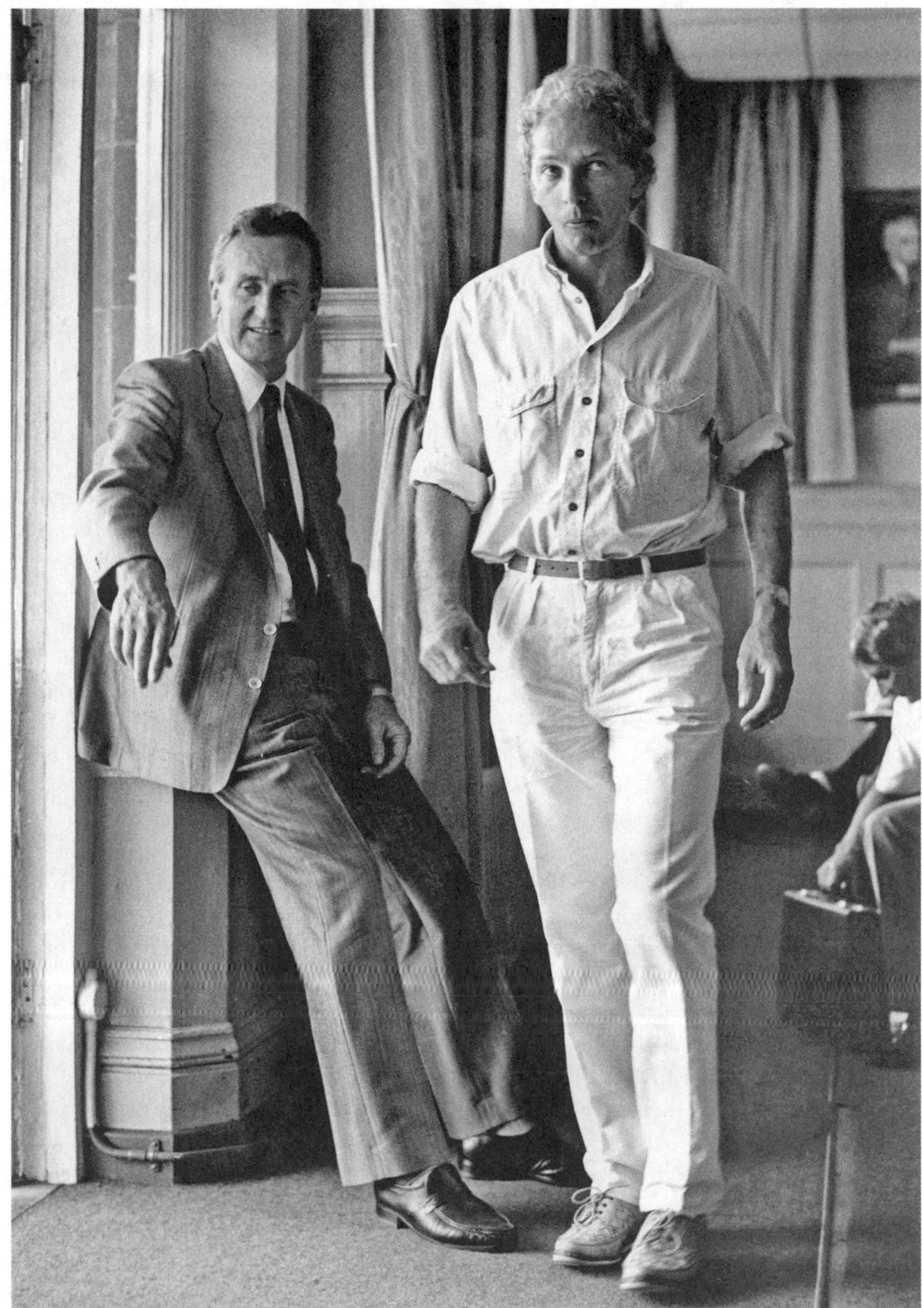

*The partnership of Ted Dexter and David Gower was supposed to bring a new dawn for England in 1989 – but that's not how it worked out*

## SIXTH TEST, THE OVAL, 1989

ALAN LEE, CRICKET CORRESPONDENT

*August 24.* Alan Igglesden, aged 24, the 6ft 6in Kent fast bowler, can hardly have known whether to feel honoured or insulted as he heard Micky Stewart, the England team manager, explain that 16 candidates had been crossed off before the nomination came his way. [...]

Igglesden's washing machine had broken down when he took the SOS call from Stewart at his home in Westerham. Before leaving to join the England party he had to enlist the help of a neighbour to mend it so that he could wash his kit. It was a farce somehow symbolic of all that has occurred this week since, paradoxically, England picked their most adventurous Test team in years.

## FIRST TEST, OLD TRAFFORD, 1993

MICHAEL HENDERSON

*June 3.* Is DeFreitas worthy? After 32 Tests he ought to be but, as everyone knows, his international career has been afflicted by more false trails than a Clouseau investigation. To be called up when Alan Igglesden pulled out, and then given the nod over Mark Ilott, who was a first-choice pick, devalues the selection process.

## THIRD TEST, TRENT BRIDGE, 1993

JOHN WOODCOCK

*July 1.* Should the ludicrous situation arise whereby England's bowling is opened by a product of New Zealand cricket (Caddick) at one end and of Australian cricket (McCague) at the other, we may see whether Gooch tolerates intemperance of the kind shown by Hughes to the same extent that Border does. This is because McCague is said to be Hughes's mirror image.

The muddle the England selectors have got themselves into is indescribable. It comes from having allowed the captain and manager far too much say for far too long. They have tended to see only what they have wanted to see. Let me give just one example of how Australians are better served by their own more traditional, less arbitrary system, in which, except of course on tour, neither Border nor his cricket manager, Bobby Simpson, is a Test selector. These two have their say, but the final choice rests with others who are not so close to the canvass.

Early last year Border was so put out at not being allowed to keep his old cobber, Geoff Marsh, in the Australian side for the last Test against India that he went into hiding for 24 hours. There is every chance that if Border had had his way Slater would not have been at Lord's a month ago to play the innings he did. Marsh had done Australia proud, but in his previous 30 Test innings, going in first, he had not scored a hundred. Border's loyalty was misguided, though he found that hard to accept. In a similar situation Gooch, until recently, would have had his way.

So Australia today have a nice blend of youth and experience, while England, desperate to escape their ever-worsening plight, put into the field a side so speculative and unrepresentative that it would probably struggle to win the county championship.

## FIFTH TEST, TRENT BRIDGE, 1997

ALAN LEE, CRICKET CORRESPONDENT

*August 7*. As Malcolm cannot be trusted as one of two fast bowlers, his inclusion would mean the younger Hollioake misses out and the tail begins at No.7. Otherwise, Hollioake minor would have to play as third seam bowler, a heavy responsibility even for such a self-possessed teenager.

The ballyhoo around Ben shows no sign of abating. Yesterday, he was photographed with Brian Close standing over him in a grandfatherly way. Close, thus far the only teenager to have played Test cricket for England, had played 15 first-class games before his debut, scored more than 600 runs and taken 66 wickets. Hollioake's figures are 11 games, 422 runs and 21 wickets. On experience alone, he is England's greatest gamble, but the first of four capacity crowds would regard his exclusion with dismay.

## FIRST TEST, LORD'S, 2005

TIM DE LISLE

*July 23*. In ditching him, the selectors showed admirable faith in the future – and threw 12 years' hard-earned know-how into the bin. Their mistake was to let it boil down to Thorpe v Kevin Pietersen. It was like choosing between salmon and raspberries.

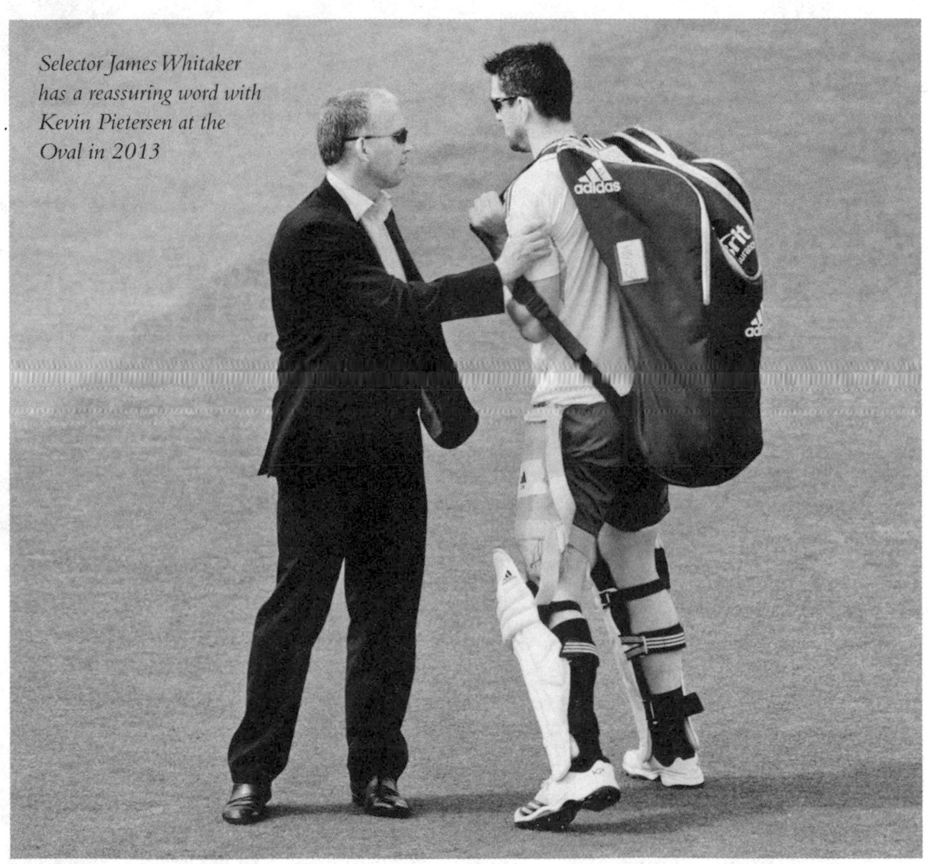


*Selector James Whitaker has a reassuring word with Kevin Pietersen at the Oval in 2013*

Sporting News

HOW ENGLAND KEPT ASHES

TWO GREAT HEARTS OVERTHROW AUSTRALIA

England beat Australia by five wickets in the fourth Test match at Adelaide yesterday and so, gaining a lead of three matches to one in the series, have retained the Ashes. In an interview after the match L. Hutton, the England captain, paid a tribute to the younger members of the side. Much of the credit, he thought, should go to J. B. Statham, F. H. Tyson, M. C. Cowdrey and P. B. H. May, together with the wicket-keeper, T. G. Evans.

From Our Special Correspondent

ADELAIDE, FEB. 2

Many years from now young Cowdrey will point to his broken nose and tell boys yet unborn that he was at Adelaide on February 2, 1955, when England won the Test match and kept the Ashes. And the boys will think him wondrous lucky. A ma... should dip his pen in blood to write ... day. Let no one talk and ... ket and explain away ... more fit for ... in dull ...

... the catch. (We asked Hutton afterwards what he thought of Miller's bowling. Hutton thought Miller ought to concentrate much more on batting.) England 10 for 2. In comes the battered Cowdrey. Miller hits him twice running on the pads and appeals, and everybody here who isn't English appeals too. What a man is Miller. He comes in from a shortish run, loose of limb like an African, hair streaming, and as he pulls up the hair goes on and falls about his face. Meanwhile May has begun driving, and Johnson has gone from mid-off to square-leg. For Cowdrey Miller brings fine-leg up to third slip, and Cowdrey cover drives classically for 4. Miller heaves his shoulders over even faster, and Cowdrey is taken by Archer at first-slip. England 18 for 3. Four Meteor jets fly over at 200ft.; they look and sound quite tame beside this wild man ... His figures now are 3 overs, no ... 2 runs, 3 wickets.

England all too obliging ...

... reaches new heights of greatness

One that got away: Gilchrist misses a stumping chance off Warne to give Pietersen an extra life, but it was to make little difference ...

High five: Warne acknowledges the Melbourne crowd after his haul ripped the heart out of England's fragile batting

... legendary accuracy and a lush outfield, they ran poorly between the wickets, chose the wrong balls to try to hit in the air and failed to justify the decision to bat.

"We didn't expect conditions to change dramatically over the first day and a half," Strauss said, "but it seamed about more than we expected." It did so slowly but Glenn McGrath, Stuart Clark and Brett Lee all got enough out of the pitch to suggest that the wrong option had been taken.

Australia missed two catches, two clear run-out opportunities and a gaping stumping, but still bowled England out for 159 after they had been 101 for two. Very few Test matches are won after such a start. All of Warne's wickets were taken by flight and dip, as batsmen spaced what they believed to be boundary opportunities. Only Kevin Pietersen got anywhere near the boundary as he attempted to drive Warne straight for six, but by now he was, as usual, batting with the tail.

Even he needed 70 balls for 21 runs, having come close to running out Andrew Flintoff for six as, for the third Test in succession, he attempted a ridiculous single in order to get off the mark. He had only made four when he also survived a simple stumping chance offered to Adam Gilchrist after charging Warne and missing.

England, we all know, have too long a tail, but tweaking it made no difference. Matthew Hoggard is back where he started, No 11, pushing Monty Panesar and Stephen Harmison up a place each, which reflects their various abilities with the bat. It is higher up, however, that the balance is wrong. Ed Joyce or Jamie Dalrymple should have played six, but Chris Read for Geraint Jones was the only change.

As the best player in the team, Pietersen needs to bat at four. Since Paul Collingwood shared the only partnership of any substance with Strauss — 57 for the third wicket — it may appear that England's strategy, to keep him away from the new ball, had worked again, but to have Pietersen batting with the tail repeatedly is not satisfactory. In any case Collingwood might have been leg-before to Clark for nought, one of four apparently plumb leg-before decisions turned down by Rudi Koertzen. Panesar was the other, ...

... Australia's recent practice of not using a nightwatchman. Ponting said that Australia, too, would have chosen to bat first, but it was one of those tosses that either captain would prefer to have lost. Play was delayed by rain for half an hour and only 16 overs were bowled before an early lunch was taken, Alastair Cook ...

S Katich lbw b ...

... Ponting run out (Flintoff) 66

... P Siddle c Flintoff b Harmison 10

5.37 343-9 S Clark c Cook b Harmison 0

... iant leap

for proud S...

Sporting News

ENGLAND HAVE LAST WORD

THREE YEOMEN FOIL AUSTRALIA

GREAT STAND BY WATSON AND BAILEY

FROM OUR CRICKET CORRESPONDENT

Out of darkness, through fire into light. Thus did England yesterday rise like some Phoenix from the ashes of apparent defeat to save the second Test match at Lord's and so gain a ... draw against Australia with ... seven wickets, ... original aim fo... The age of m... yet past, nor c... cany scarce fo... dramatic and ... a match alrea... But within t... longest and m... of a match it... that last spa... back with le... yeomen of ... nearly the w...

The yeom... were Watso... greatest of ... Yorkshirem... order, was ... rearguard ... twentieth ...

36 TUESDAY AUGUST 1 1989

THE TIMES

England's abject surrender marks new low in series

By Alan Lee, Cricket Correspondent

Inglorious procession at Old Trafford

10-1: Curtis c Boon b Alderman 0

25-2: Robinson lbw b Lawson 12

27-3: Smith c Healy b Alderman 1

28-4: Gooch c Alderman b Lawson 13

38-5: Botham lbw b Alderman 4

59-6: Gower c Marsh b Lawson 15

SCOREBOARD FROM OLD TRAFFORD

Gower unfairly blamed for failings of others

Simon Barnes

Border rewarded for hard labour

By John Woodcock

Only two men so far decline

By Alan Lee

Was this English c... most desperate c...

... night issued a dramatic ... Union to make a positive ... He said that unless the ... prepared to help to achieve an ... strategic arms limitations, he would ... additional funds of more than ... for new nuclear ...

# ENGLAND'S GLORY DAYS

THE TIMES SATURDAY JUNE 11 1938

CH: A GOOD BEGINNING BY ENGLAND

Sporting News

LAKER'S SUPREME PART IN RETAINING THE ASHES

ALL TEN AUSTRALIAN WICKETS AND 19 IN MATCH

From Our Cricket Correspondent

England won the fourth Test match against Australia at Old ... yesterday by an innings ... retaining the ...

pitch perked up and the ball showed signs of misbehaving.

At luncheon McDonald and Craig were still together. They had then added only 59, but the important thing was that they had each been batting for more than four hours. Ahead of them stretched another four and only 15 minutes of these had ticked away when Laker struck a blow. Craig, still ...

THE TIMES

LOCOMEN'S BAN BOUND TO CAUSE GREATER ... TODAY

HOW THE AUSTRALIANS WERE SKITTLED OUT AT LORD'S

Gaullists may get back with clear majority

Inquiry over bank chief's salary

Police alerted by strike ship

Railways must act alone, Marsh says

13 die in ... rail cra...

dismally surrender Ashes

TEST MATCH

BRADMAN 309 NOT OUT

ALL RECORDS BROKEN

*The Third Test Match between England and Australia was begun at Leeds yesterday. A. P. F. Chapman, for once, lost the toss and Australia went in to bat on a perfect batsman's wicket. By the end of the day they had scored 458 runs for the loss of three wickets and D. G. Bradman ...*

# FIFTH TEST, THE OVAL, 1902

R.H. LYTTELTON

*August 14.* Whatever may be said about the unsatisfactory weather that cricketers have experienced this season, the year has produced two struggles that can never have been surpassed for excitement. England has lost the rubber, but her defeat at Manchester and her victory at the Oval will never be forgotten, and both were much to her credit.

Every batsman on his way to the wicket yesterday felt that on his success or failure depended the fate of the match. In other words, the match was always in a critical position, and every run had to be fought for. The bowling of Mr Trumble could not have been better. Every variety of pitch and break back seemed to be at his command, and he never sent down a ball of bad length. In this he was a very different bowler from Mr Saunders, who bowls a very difficult ball, but many very bad ones – of such bad length that a child could score from them. Mr Trumble bowled from the pavilion end from half-past 11 in the morning until 4 in the afternoon. He was never taken off, nor was his bowling once collared in an innings of 263.

At the end of the second day's play Australia were 255 runs ahead with two wickets in hand. No rain had fallen in the night, but it was generally thought that the wicket would be slow and easy. There was, however, a heavy dew, and the wicket up to luncheon time was very difficult and never became easy all day. Only seven runs were added to the Australians' score. Indeed, the Australians may be said to have lost the match chiefly by their failure in batting on the second day when the wicket was not difficult. As at Manchester, they collapsed in a way that was unworthy of a strong batting side. Lockwood's five wickets cost only 45 runs – a very good performance.

At 11.35 England began the last innings on a wicket that appeared made to suit the Australian attack, and the first three wickets fell for ten runs. The chances were quite four to one on Australia at this stage, and six to one when the fifth wicket fell at 48. The batsmen did not play well, but there was every excuse on such a wicket and against such bowling. But Mr Jackson was still in, and wonderfully free was his play. To him is due, to a very large extent, England's victory. On five occasions in the last five test matches has Mr Jackson had to go in at a critical moment for his side, and only once did he fail. There is no batsman in the world whose nerve is so surely to be relied on. When he was joined by Mr Jessop the great stand that paved the way for victory was made. Up to lunch time the wicket was so difficult that nobody could have felt surprised if either batsman had got out; but they stayed in and brought the score to 87, though Mr Jessop appeared to give a chance of stumping, and was missed by Mr Trumper off a difficult chance in the long field. Runs came far faster after luncheon, Mr Jessop putting in some of his finest work, while Mr Jackson was content to take things steadily. Too much use was made of Mr Saunders, who was now bowling a very bad length and was freely punished by Mr Jessop. Three full pitches and one long hop were bowled consecutively, and 17 runs were scored from one over. Mr Jackson was then caught and bowled by Mr Trumble for 49, after an hour and 40 minutes' first-rate batting. The match appeared to be lost when he left. Hirst came in next, and he, Mr Jessop, and Mr Jackson were the three heroes of this famous innings. It must, however, be confessed that Hirst looked very like being l.-b.-w. to Mr Trumble almost immediately after he went in. Mr Jessop continued his hitting, and sent Mr Trumble twice in an over into the pavilion. Mr Armstrong relieved Mr Saunders, and was vigorously hit by Hirst. But Mr Jessop must have longed for Mr Saunders again. He could not hit Mr Armstrong's leg balls with a little break on in his usual style, and the new bowler got him caught at short leg. Seven wickets were now down for 187, and 76 runs were still wanted. Mr Jessop has accomplished several very wonderful performances in his life, but has frequently, both here and in Australia, failed against the colonial bowling. As long as cricket history lasts will this great performance be remembered. He ran risks, as every man must who makes more than a run a minute, but he only gave two chances, and one of them was very difficult. He completely demoralized Mr Saunders. His wonderful success must have been a great cause of rejoicing to those who, in spite of so many failures, have urged his claim to represent England and all these failures will be forgotten long before this great feat of fierce hitting against first-rate bowling and fielding and on a difficult wicket. Out of 139 runs scored while he was in 104 came from his bat. On several occasions during this innings the prospects of England looked well, but, as so often happens, at a critical moment a wicket fell. Mr Jackson, Mr Jessop, Lockwood, and Lilley all got out just when the chances might have veered round in England's favour. Seventy-four runs were wanting when Lockwood went in, 49 when Lilley succeeded him, and 15 when Rhodes, the last man, came out of the pavilion. All these men played with nerve, but Hirst was the real hero. Nothing seemed to put him out. Indeed, he played with more confidence than in the first innings, and his hits were hard and along the ground. Lockwood stayed while 27 runs were scored, but his share was only two. Lilley got 16 out of 34 by good batting, but was dismissed by a good catch by Mr Darling at mid-off. Rhodes then came in, and it is not likely that he will ever again have to face a more trying ordeal. Nobody could have risen to the occasion better. Hirst went on the even tenor of his way, and Rhodes stopped the straight balls and judiciously left alone, the rising off balls from both Mr Trumble and Mr Noble. And thus the runs were slowly hit off, Rhodes making the winning hit amid a scene of excitement that can never be forgotten. Mr Darling is so experienced a captain that it may seem presumptuous to wonder why he was so unwilling to make use of Mr Noble's bowling, but he undoubtedly was wise to keep on Mr Trumble all the time. In the whole match Mr Trumble bowled 65 overs for 12 wickets at a cost of 14 runs each – a splendid performance.

When all the conditions under which these last two test matches were played are considered, it must be conceded that it was a wonderfully fine feat of England's to lose the first match by only three runs and to win the second by one wicket. Several good judges yesterday said that for England to get 200 runs on the wicket would be a very fine performance, and they got 263. The Australians threw no chances away, and their fielding and throwing were magnificent, Mr Hopkins especially doing grand work. But Englishmen may justly claim for their side superiority in batting on a bowlers' wicket, though, with the exception of Mr Jackson, no batsman shows the skill of Shrewsbury and other great batsmen of former years. Until this season the Colonials have not had much practice on bowlers' wickets, but the blot on their

STATISTICS OF THE FIVE TEST MATCHES.

SUMMARY OF MATCHES.

Played 5—Australia won 2; England won 1; 2 drawn.

May 29, 30, 31, at Birmingham.—England, 376 for nine wickets (innings declared closed); Australia 36 and 46 for two wickets. Drawn.

June 12, 13, 14, at Lord's.—England, 102 for two wickets; Australia did not bat. Owing to rain there was no play on the second and third days. Drawn.

July 3, 4, 5, at Sheffield.—Australia, 194 and 289; England, 145 and 195. Australia won by 143 runs.

July 24, 25, 26, at Manchester.—Australia, 299 and 86; England, 262 and 120. Australia won by 3 runs.

August 11, 12, 13, at Kennington Oval.—Australia, 324 and 121; England, 183 and 263 for nine wickets. England won by one wicket.

AUSTRALIAN BATTING AVERAGES IN THE FIVE TEST MATCHES.

| | Innings. | Runs. | Most in an innings. | Times not out. | Average. |
|---|---|---|---|---|---|
| Mr. C. Hill (S.A.) | 8 | 258 | 119 | 1 | 36·85 |
| Mr. V. Trumper (N.S.W.) | 8 | 247 | 104 | 0 | 30·87 |
| Mr. H. Trumble (V.) | 6 | 107 | 64* | 2 | 26·75 |
| Mr. A. J. Hopkins (N.S.W.) | 7 | 117 | 40* | 1 | 19·50 |
| Mr. M. A. Noble (N.S.W.) | 7 | 129 | 52 | 0 | 18·42 |
| Mr. R. A. Duff (N.S.W.) | 8 | 129 | 54 | 0 | 16·12 |
| Mr. J. Darling (S.A.) | 7 | 109 | 51 | 0 | 15·57 |
| Mr. S. E. Gregory (N.S.W.) | 8 | 100 | 29 | 1 | 14·28 |
| Mr. W. W. Armstrong (V.) | 7 | 97 | 28 | 0 | 13·85 |
| Mr. J. J. Kelly (N.S.W.) | 7 | 48 | 39 | 3 | 11·50 |
| Mr. J. V. Saunders (V.) | 6 | 6 | 3 | 1 | 1·20 |

*Not out.

Mr. W. P. Howell (N.S.W.) (0) and Mr. E. Jones (S.A.) (0) each batted once. Mr. H. Carter (N.S.W.), the reserve wicket-keeper, did not play in any of the five Test matches.

AUSTRALIAN BOWLING AVERAGES IN THE FIVE TEST MATCHES.

| | Overs. | Maidens. | Runs. | Wickets. | Average. |
|---|---|---|---|---|---|
| Mr. H. Trumble (V.) | 172.4 | 55 | 371 | 26 | 14·26 |
| Mr. M. A. Noble (N.S.W.) | 127 | 41 | 307 | 14 | 21·92 |
| Mr. A. J. Hopkins (N.S.W.) | 17 | 5 | 49 | 2 | 24·50 |
| Mr. J. V. Saunders (V.) | 131.1 | 23 | 473 | 18 | 26·27 |
| Mr. E. Jones (S.A.) | 39 | 13 | 107 | 3 | 35·66 |
| Mr. V. Trumper (N.S.W.) | 37 | 11 | 101 | 2 | 50·50 |
| Mr. W. W. Armstrong (V.) | 44 | 10 | 123 | 2 | 61·50 |

Mr. W. P. Howell (N.S.W.) also bowled in the Birmingham match, his figures being 26 8 58 1.

ENGLISH BATTING AVERAGES IN THE FIVE TEST MATCHES.

| | Innings. | Runs. | Most in an innings. | Times not out. | Average. |
|---|---|---|---|---|---|
| Rhodes (Yorkshire) | 7 | 67 | 38* | 6 | 67·00 |
| Hon. F. S. Jackson (Yorkshire) | 8 | 311 | 128 | 1 | 44·42 |
| Hirst (Yorkshire) | 5 | 157 | 58* | 1 | 39·25 |
| Mr. G. L. Jessop (Gloucester) | 5 | 190 | 104 | 0 | 38·00 |
| Tyldesley (Lancashire) | 7 | 245 | 138 | 0 | 35·00 |
| Mr. A. C. MacLaren (Lancashire) | 8 | 193 | 63 | 1 | 23·28 |
| Lockwood (Surrey) | 5 | 86 | 52* | 1 | 21·50 |
| Abel (Surrey) | 4 | 73 | 38 | 0 | 18·25 |
| Braund (Somerset) | 7 | 115 | 65 | 0 | 16·42 |
| Mr. L. C. H. Palairet (Somerset) | 4 | 49 | 20 | 0 | 12·25 |
| Lilley (Warwickshire) | 7 | 46 | 16 | 0 | 6·57 |
| K. S. Ranjitsinhji (Sussex) | 4 | 19 | 13 | 0 | 4·75 |
| Mr. C. B. Fry (Sussex) | 4 | 5 | 4 | 0 | 1·25 |

The following also batted:—Barnes (Lancashire), 7 and 5; Tate (Sussex), 5* and 4; and Hayward (Surrey), 0 and 7.

*Not out.

ENGLISH BOWLING AVERAGES IN THE FIVE TEST MATCHES.

| | Overs. | Maidens. | Runs. | Wkts. | Average. |
|---|---|---|---|---|---|
| Lockwood (Surrey) | 81.1 | 18 | 206 | 17 | 12·11 |
| Barnes (Lancs.) | 32 | 13 | 99 | 7 | 14·14 |
| Rhodes (Yorkshire) | 140.5 | 38 | 336 | 22 | 15·27 |
| Hirst (Yorkshire) | 79 | 18 | 208 | 9 | 23·11 |
| Tate (Sussex) | 16 | 4 | 51 | 2 | 25·50 |
| Braund (Somerset) | 76.5 | 13 | 210 | 7 | 30·00 |
| Hon. F. S. Jackson (Yorkshire) | 61.1 | 12 | 209 | 6 | 34·83 |
| Mr. G. L. Jessop (Gloucester) | 10 | 2 | 28 | 0 | — |

The following scores of over 100 were hit in the test games:—

For Australia—
119, Mr. C. Hill, at Sheffield.
104, Mr. V. Trumper, at Manchester.

For England—
138, Tyldesley, at Birmingham.
128, Hon. F. S. Jackson, at Manchester.
104, Mr. G. L. Jessop, at Kennington Oval.

SUSSEX v. LANCASHIRE.

At Brighton yesterday Lancashire fully maintained the advantage gained on Tuesday and won by seven wickets.

*The statistics of the classic 1902 series were set out in The Times next to the report of England's breathless victory at the Oval*

escutcheon is their collapse in batting on the second day both at Manchester and at the Oval. In both cases the Englishman had the same wicket to play on; perhaps it was a trifle more difficult, but their batting was better. It may be that the fall of Mr Trumper on both these occasions demoralized the side; and this need not be a matter for surprise, for such things are common, and Mr Trumper is the greatest bat in the world.

In this last match Australia had the advantage of occupying the wickets the whole of the first day, the only period when run-getting and batting were easy. Notwithstanding this fact, the English side, who never once in the match had anything but a difficult wicket to bat on, won the match; and this more than redeemed their reputation. The Australians, however, have won the rubber, and hearty congratulations must be to them. They may have had the best of the luck, but this is part of the game, and every true sportsman's will give them the credit of being the better side, taking one wicket with another.

## FOURTH TEST, MELBOURNE, 1911–12

*February 12.* At the close of play on Saturday the M.C.C. had made 370 for the loss of one wicket. As the game stands, therefore, with nine wickets still in hand, they hold a lead of 179 runs on the first innings.

Hobbs and Rhodes, who had made 30 and 23 respectively when stumps were drawn on Friday, were not separated today until 323 runs had been scored. This is easily the best partnership for any wicket in a Test match, and both batsmen played fine cricket, although both gave chances. One of the features of the partnership was the fine judgment displayed in running between the wickets, which showed the thorough understanding that existed between the two players. [...]

The weather was gloriously fine and the pitch had recovered from the recent rain and was in quite good condition when Hobbs and Rhodes continued the Englishman's first innings with the score at 54 for no wicket. Dr Hordern and Mr Cotter were the bowlers, and the former began with two maiden overs. Both batsmen found the 'googlies' very troublesome, and treated them with the utmost respect. Rhodes, when he had scored 27, should have been caught off Dr Hordern's bowling, but Mr Trumper at square-leg, anticipating the stroke, jumped in and thus missed an easy chance. The Yorkshireman scored at a much slower rate than yesterday. A double change in the bowling was soon tried, Mr Armstrong going on for Mr Cotter at 82 and Mr Kelleway for Dr Hordern one run later. Rhodes, when he had made 31, gave a difficult chance at the wicket off Mr Kelleway's bowling, but the ball went to the boundary. Hobbs played in his usual beautiful style; he took the total to 100 with a leg hit for four all run, off a no-ball from Mr Kelleway. Rhodes continued to do very little, and when his score had reached 39 he hit up a ball from Mr Kelleway; the bowler made a great effort to reach the ball but failed. The ground fielding of the Australians was very smart, Mr Trumper and Mr Matthews being really brilliant. There was a burst of cheering when Mr Matthews was put on to bowl for Mr Kelleway at 121. One run later Mr Cotter relieved Mr Armstrong, but neither of these changes met with any success, and the luncheon interval was taken with the total at 137, Hobbs having made 86 and Rhodes 48.

Dr Hordern and Mr Cotter were the bowlers after luncheon. Rhodes was now much more aggressive and there were cheers when he reached his fifty. Soon afterwards Hobbs, with a straight drive off Dr Hordern's bowling for a single, completed his hundred when he had been at the wicket altogether for two hours and twenty-three minutes. He was heartily cheered, all the Australian team joining in the applause. Rhodes's score was then 60, and the total stood at 164. At this point a double change of bowling was again made, Mr Minnett and Mr Matthews being the new pair. Hobbs, with his score still at 100, gave a difficult chance of stumping off Mr Matthews's bowling, and the crowd appeared to be very indignant with Mr Carter. Mr Minnett was sending down some loose balls, and the spectators were disposed to be ironical at the expense of the home eleven. Hobbs, with a drive for a single, made England's score level with the Australian first innings total, amid cheers, and then, with two beautiful square cuts to the boundary off Mr Minnett's bowling, sent up the 200. The batsmen were now giving a masterly display and changes in the bowling made no difference to them. Hobbs gave a difficult chance to Mr Bardsley at square-leg off Mr Kelleway's bowling when he had made 126. Cotter was put on with the total at 220 and completely beat Rhodes twice in one over. Mr Armstrong relieved Mr Kelleway at 243, and Rhodes, with a square cut off the new bowler, completed his hundred, having been batting for three hours and forty minutes. This is Rhodes's first century in a Test match, and he was heartily cheered. At the tea interval the total stood at 249, Hobbs having made 138 and Rhodes 102. The two batsmen were enthusiastically cheered as they returned to the pavilion.

Mr Cotter and Mr Armstrong continued to bowl after tea, but both batsmen scored rapidly and stole runs cleverly. Indeed, the bowlers were quite helpless and runs were scored all round the wicket. Hobbs, when he had made 178, gave an easy chance to Mr Cotter at square-leg off Dr Hordern's bowling; the fieldsman missed the catch, but the mistake was not expensive, for Hobbs was out, caught at the wicket, off the next ball sent down by the 'googlie' bowler. Hobbs played a magnificent innings. Eighty-eight of his runs were scored by boundary strokes; he was batting for four hours and 28 minutes, and he hit splendidly all round the wicket. He met with a fine reception from the crowd. Gunn came out to join Rhodes, who so far had made 132. When the latter had added six to his score he was beaten by a ball from Dr Hordern. The fieldsmen were getting weary, and the batting became rather quieter. Gunn made a characteristically slow start, and when he had scored two gave a hard chance off Mr Kelleway's bowling to Mr Armstrong in the slips, the ball going to the boundary. Soon afterwards Rhodes passed his 150 amid cheering with an on-drive off Dr Hordern's bowling to the boundary. Just before the close of play Rhodes, with his score at 157, gave a chance off Mr Cotter's bowling to Mr Kelleway in the slips.

Stumps were drawn with the total at 370 for one wicket. In spite of many blemishes Rhodes's innings was an admirable one; it was typically solid and steady, but he made several very fine strokes all round the wicket. The Australian ground fielding was good to the end, but their catching was distinctly poor.

*February 14*. England gained an overwhelming victory in the Fourth Test match here today by an innings and 225 runs, and thus also won the rubber in the series of five representative games arranged for the present tour.

The Australians lost the rubber for the simple reason that they were inferior both in batting and bowling. They played at times as if they were dispirited; doubtless the strife between the players and the Board of Control contributed to this. Mr Carter alone of the older players has enhanced his reputation in the present series of Test matches. At the conclusion of the match today the teams assembled in the pavilion and congratulatory speeches were made. Sir John Fuller, the Governor of Victoria, was present. Mr C Hill and others warmly congratulated the Englishmen, and Mr Douglas replying to a toast, paid a tribute to Mr Warner. He said that whenever he was in difficulties he had Mr Warner always at hand to advise him, and on the field he had Mr Foster and the older players to help him. He greatly appreciated the manner in which the Australians had played in the Test matches. There had been no unpleasantness from first to last.

## FIFTH TEST, THE OVAL, 1926

A.C.M. CROOME,
CRICKET CORRESPONDENT

*August 19*. We have won. And after all the lean years we were more than half-pleased. We began to cheer when the Australians' innings was little more than half over, and at the finish we charged, ten thousand of us, across the ground, and massed ourselves in front of the pavilion, where we shouted for the 11 men who had won the game, and for the Chairman of the Committee which selected them. We shouted even more loudly for Mr Collins and the members of his team.

We wanted them to know that we appreciated the high standard of keenness and honourable conduct which they have set up and maintained in this and all their other matches.

This final Test match has been an extraordinarily interesting game. There were grounds for fearing that England had missed a golden opportunity by omitting to make at least 400 on the first day, after Mr Chapman had won the toss on a perfect Oval wicket. But the Australians declined the offered chance. In fact their later batsmen had to extricate the side from a nasty hole. Still it seemed likely that we should have to pay for Saturday's comparative failure in batting. The thunderstorm of Monday night, followed by hot sunshine on the following morning, produced a wicket on which 200 was a remarkably good score against first-rate bowling. Hobbs and Sutcliffe made more than that number between them and raised the aggregate of their combined scores in the last ten Test matches against Australia to something like 2,300. Every moment that has passed since they were parted has emphasized the magnitude of their performance. England's last nine wickets fell at rather frequent intervals and when the Australians went in to make 415, they were put out for 125.

The explanation is simple. We had Rhodes on our side. Larwood, Tate, Geary, and Mr Stevens all bowled well. Larwood, in particular, rendered valuable service by getting rid of Mr Woodfull and Mr Macartney. But these bowlers might possibly have been worn down. From the moment that Rhodes went on the match was over. Rhodes has learnt no new tricks since he used to bowl one end for nearly half the time that England were in the field, and his length is not so regular as it was. Yesterday he sent down a full toss and two long hops to leg, balls which he could not bowl in his palmiest days. The unbowlable ball has had some very distinguished victims in this match. Hobbs, Mr Macartney, Mr Bardsley, and Mr Andrews have all given away their wickets to it. The specimens released by Rhodes were all properly hit for four. Otherwise they found themselves playing forward when they would fain have played back, and he used the spin which his fingers impart to the ball to make it break back sharply, leaving those who will to swerve. On a biting pitch the best batsmen in the world cannot take root against a flighty left-hander who places a man at silly mid-off, another not quite square with the wicket at the point of the bat, and pitches the ball well up to the leg stump, making it break back to hit the top of the off, unless it is stopped by the bat: for there is no second line of defence to this form of attack. Only the two left-handed strikers, Mr Bardsley and Mr Gregory, were even moderately comfortable when facing Rhodes. And he took Mr Bardsley's wicket. In this he was fortunate, for the fatal ball must be included in the category of the unbowlable.

The Australians have been beaten, and even in the moment of defeat, they are generously glad of it. They think that the result will do much good to the game of cricket 'at home'. It will, if English batsmen have learnt the lesson of wise conservatism which Australian example can teach. I do not myself think that the rain which interrupted play between 1.15 and 3 o'clock made the Australians' task more impossible than it already was. At no time yesterday was the pitch so difficult as it had been on Tuesday morning when Hobbs and Sutcliffe were – Hobbs and Sutcliffe. Rhodes needed no rain; the faster bowlers might even have preferred that none should fall. What is not matter of opinion is that Mr Collins may have chanced giving away as many as 20 runs by consenting to resume play so promptly after the shower ceased. But he and his men have come many thousands of miles to play cricket, and have fulfilled their purpose.

The concluding stages of the game were watched by the Prime Minister and an important section of his Cabinet. Some, at least, of them must have been late for their afternoon appointment.

A few spots of rain fell just before noon, but the weather seemed set fair when Rhodes and Geary took guard against Mr Mailey and Mr Gregory, the latter bowling for the first time from the pavilion end with no screen behind his arm. Mr Gregory soon had Geary caught at the wicket and Rhodes played him a trifle diffidently, although he drove an over-pitched ball in great style to the pavilion, and once and again condescended to cut the short one. Tate hit very hard and with discrimination, but Rhodes was out leg-before to Mr Grimmett. who superseded Mr Gregory. The fatal ball kept low. Larwood stayed a while and watched Tate make four extremely ponderous hits to the on boundary. He himself brought off a glorious drive for 4 through Mr Andrews and then was bowled by a googly. Strudwick stayed for nearly two hours while the rain fell and then was caught at silly mid-off.

Mr Collins sent in Mr Ponsford with Mr Woodfull this time, and the bowlers were Larwood and Tate. The heavy roller had been used for the full time allowed, but Larwood at once made the ball fly and might have had Mr Ponsford out if Geary had not been too far forward at third slip. Geary was moved to the left, and in Larwood's next over caught Mr Woodfull, whose stroke was not one of his best. Mr Macartney came in, the man for whom only himself can determine the limits of the possible. He took a couple of minutes to look at the bowling and then set himself to spoil it. He off-drove Tate, forced a fast rising ball from Larwood off his chest to the leg boundary, and cut him splendidly, though he only got a single for the last stroke of the three. But to the intense relief of every Englishman present, from Mr Chapman and the Prime Minister downwards, he shortly afterwards cut an almost similar ball to Geary at third slip. Mr Chapman had a special reason to be elated, for a moment before he had strengthened the field behind the wicket on the off side, for Larwood's bowling. Rhodes was called up to stand in the gully and Geary placed precisely where the decisive chance went. The dismissal of Mr Macartney was of such vital moment that it has caused me to anticipate the order of events. Rhodes had previously been put on in place of Tate, and without another run scored he had Mr Ponsford caught at backward point. A ball of perfect length broke back the breadth of the wicket and reared up sharply. No first-rate batsman's back stroke can be certain to keep that ball down, though the village blacksmith might mow it to square-leg for 6. Larwood actively and intelligently dived forward from backward point and got a hand under it as it fell. Mr Collins and Mr Bardsley were now partnered, but not for long. Mr Collins got something like Mr Ponsford's ball, and snicked it to short slip.

Mr Andrews batted as freely as if the pitch were fast and true. He made some delicious strokes off Rhodes on the off-side, most of which were stopped with apparent ease by Hobbs, and he hit a couple of his loose balls very hard to the on boundary. Since the match was practically won I could with equanimity have watched Mr Andrews play a long innings in the manner of his opening. But it was not to be. He hooked a short ball from Larwood quite well, but not with the driving part of his bat, and Tate at short leg took a nice catch with his right hand. Mr Gregory made some powerful strokes before hitting rather recklessly at Tate and getting himself caught at mid-off. Mr Bardsley dealt with Rhodes better than anybody else, but his efforts at the off balls of the faster bowlers were not convincing. Ultimately Rhodes got his wicket with a long hop which Mr Bardsley skied to short leg.

As in the first innings Mr Oldfield and Mr Grimmett played first-class cricket. Rhodes could deceive neither with his flight and gave way to Mr Stevens, who bowled for this turn medium pace. His first over was expensive, but in his second he made Mr Oldfield play a yorker on to his stumps. Mr Mailey made one slashing cover-drive off Geary, but was clean bowled bv him and, catching Strudwick napping, was able to pocket the ball.

Each of our bowlers got at least one wicket. The fielding was exuberantly keen and Strudwick kept wicket splendidly on a pitch which constrained Mr Oldfield to let 19 byes. It was pleasant to see Mr Chapman captain his side so ably and alone he did it. No doubt he had discussed strategy and tactics in the pavilion with his staff officers, but on the field he relied on his own judgment. The demeanour of his colleagues indicated clearly their absolute approval of his direction.

## FOURTH TEST, BRISBANE, 1932–33

R.B. VINCENT,
CRICKET CORRESPONDENT

*February 17.* England, when they won the Fourth Test match at Brisbane yesterday, regained the Ashes, which they had lost at the Oval in 1930. On that August afternoon there was a feeling that Australia, with a successful team which included many young men, had asserted a superiority which it would take some seasons to shake.

At the beginning of last summer there was still but little indication of the great things to come, but gradually as the team took shape so hope increased. Early in the tour it was evident that England had the making of an excellent side: the Australians, from one cause and another, were faced with difficulties, until at last England's triumph was definitely expected.

That so remarkable a reversal of form should have occurred is due almost entirely to two men, D. R. Jardine and Larwood. The English captain no doubt had in each match a team of reliable and efficient players, each of whom played his part nobly, but in the conditions which prevail in Australia a particular solidity of purpose is demanded, and this virtue Jardine possesses to the fullest degree. His appreciation of the situation was admirable and once he had made up his mind, events followed almost at his dictation. Unreasonable complaints were made from time to time of the dilatoriness of the English batting, but Jardine stuck to his point, hammered away, and now to him fully and ungrudging credit must be given for a splendid victory.

Larwood, for his part, transformed the spirit of Test matches which had become to be considered a batsman's rightful amusement, into being a bowler's affair. He set the tune and controlled the play, for it was he, splendidly supported as he was by G.O. Allen, Voce, Verity, and Hammond, who was the particularly disturbing influence to the Australian batsmen. His record of 28 wickets for 502 runs in these four matches in no measure explains the influence which he brought to bear on the results. As an example of fortitude and stamina alone his performance has been remarkable, for it seems that whenever he was called upon for yet one more desperate effort, even in the most sweltering heat, he responded to the utmost. Comparisons, especially among fast bowlers of different generations, are futile, but he must assuredly be granted a place among the greatest and most willing of his kind.

Jardine's greatest difficulty has been in establishing a satisfactory order of batting, for he was not provided with a suitable partner to Sutcliffe. He sacrificed himself by going in first in this last game, but his proper place is at No.5 where his remarkable power of concentration means everything to a side which shows signs of instability. Sutcliffe has again done splendidly, this time in circumstances which were not controlled by the batting side, but England has a great deal to owe to the courage of batsmen lower in the batting order.

This game at Brisbane will always be thought of as 'Paynter's match'. It was only a game of cricket, but even those least interested in it must have felt that something noble had been achieved at the other end of the world when this sick little Lancastrian came from hospital to the heat and anxiety of a Test match to save his side from the imminent threat of defeat. Certainly had it not been for his brave effort, and the imperturbable Verity, not even Larwood could have prevented England from having yet to fight out the issue at Sydney next week.

## SECOND TEST, LORD'S, 1953

GEOFFREY GREEN,
CRICKET CORRESPONDENT

*July 1.* Out of darkness, through fire into light. Thus did England yesterday rise like some Phoenix from the ashes of apparent defeat to save the second Test match at Lord's and so gain a remarkable draw against Australia with a final score of 282 for seven wickets, just 61 runs behind their original aim for victory.

The age of miracles it proved was not yet past, nor could all the ranks of Tuscany scarce forebear to cheer this most dramatic and most honourable ending to a match already full of the oddest twists. But within the climax there came the longest and most agonizing last half-hour of a match it is possible to imagine, for in that last span Australia stood to snatch back with leg-spin bowling all that three yeomen of England had denied them for nearly the whole of this last gruelling day.

The yeomen, the heroes, stood apart. They were Watson, Bailey, and Compton, and the greatest of them was Watson. The left-handed Yorkshireman, in the centre of the batting order, was the soul and the pulse of England's rearguard action, and he now became the twentieth man in history to score a century on his first appearance in an England v Australia Test match. From six o'clock on Monday evening, when the desperate peril of England was shown in her 12 runs for three wickets, he held the crease until 10 minutes to 6 last evening. A moment before he finally left, mentally and physically exhausted after a personal battle of five hours and three-quarters against all the odds, England stood at 236 for four. Therein lay the measure of his triumph, though mere figures alone can never disclose the heart of his achievement.

But he was not alone. First at his side there stood Compton. Theirs has been a happy association in the past. Three times against South Africa in the summer of 1951 they fashioned century partnerships. But none could now compare with the 61 vital runs that were born of an hour and three-quarters struggle that first turned back the Australian assault. Compton for the second time in this perplexing exciting match batted finely and for the second time it took a really good ball to claim him. It was at 20 minutes to one yesterday that the bounding, left-handed Johnston, loose and long of limb, suddenly had him l.-b.-w. with a ball, a yard quicker through the air, which kept low.

England then were 73 for four and a long, long way yet from any harbour of safety. But already Compton and his partner, footballers both, had achieved something. They had lit a tiny flame of hope. More practically Compton, with three crashing off-drives to the boundary in a single over, seemed to destroy all Benaud's confidence in his own length and leg-spin that lasted far into the day. That was of considerable importance. So with four hours and 50 minutes left Bailey walked down the pavilion steps. Each stride to the crease took him nearer his part in what was to prove an epic achievement of courage, concentration and willpower, not to mention skill. For all but three-quarters of an hour of that wide ocean of time did he and Watson stand firm in the face of all that Hassett and his Australians could hurl at them. Together they fanned that first tiny flame of hope until it spurted up into a sturdy fire. Their fourth-wicket partnership of 163 runs was the greatest of all this great match. And it has been a great match, worth every penny of its world record receipts of over £57,716, a match that day by day took one by the hand down new and unexpected paths.

There were four crises on this last desperate day. The first came at the beginning as Watson and Compton faced Lindwall and Johnston. This crisis at last was passed as Hassett turned to the leg-spin of Ring and Benaud. It was now that Compton set Benaud back with an attack that saw 52 runs arrive in the first hour, three overs costing Benaud 22.

The second critical moment came with Compton's dismissal. This, together with a third anxiety – the arrival of a new ball in the hands of Lindwall and Miller at 3 o'clock with the score 149 for four – was neutralized by the glowing courage and concentration of Watson and Bailey as the bowlers tore at them with pace and lift. Twice indeed at this last point in mid-afternoon Bailey suffered the sharpest of blows on his knuckles from Lindwall that searched out the tendrils of his spirit.

For 40 minutes they scraped together 10 runs and won through. So tea came with England almost miraculously 183, still for four wickets, with Watson 84, Bailey 39 and a 100 partnership already under their pads. The runs had ticked up at a declining rate of 52, 44, 35, and 29 through succeeding hours which showed the intensity of the struggle and the fact that Hassett by now was clearly a worried man. Things had slipped through his fingers slowly, largely because the spin of Ring and Benaud had failed him when most he needed it.

Through all this long span Watson had been passed on the forward stroke once each by Lindwall and Miller and once had snicked Davidson just short of the slips. But mostly he had been firm in his stroke play, turning the ball beautifully off his legs to the on side, whence most of his runs came. Bailey, also beaten once by Miller, again, as he had done before, got his head down well and his bat along the strict line of the ball to present a teasing

THE TI

## Sporting News

### ENGLAND HAVE LAST WORD

#### THREE YEOMEN FOIL AUSTRALIA

#### GREAT STAND BY WATSON AND BAILEY

FROM OUR CRICKET CORRESPONDENT

Out of darkness, through fire into light. Thus did England yesterday rise like some Phoenix from the ashes of apparent defeat to save the second Test match at Lord's and so gain a remarkable draw against Australia with a final score of 282 for

### FIRST WIN FOR ESSEX

#### KENT'S STUBBORN FIGHT

Essex, in winning at Romford by 65 runs, gained their first victory of the season in the county championship but Kent, set to get 363, made them work very hard, keeping them in the field for four hours and 40 minutes.

A Kent collapse appeared likely when, Insole having declared at the Essex overnight total, two wickets fell for 13. Then Ufton, driving and hitting to leg strongly, joined with Woollett in a stand which realized 77 in 85 minutes. Of these runs Ufton obtained 46, including nine boundaries. Woollett, hitting seven 4's, stayed two hours 20 minutes and Mayes batted steadily for an hour and a quarter, but with six batsmen out for 170 the end seemed near.

Once more, however, Ridgway showed excellent form in his new role as No. 7 batsman

### VICTORY AFTER 32 YEARS

#### GLAMORGAN BEAT YORKSHIRE

Glamorgan have been trying for 32 years to beat Yorkshire. They did it yesterday at Cardiff by eight wickets for the first time since they entered the county championship in 1921, and, with the gates thrown open to the public, there was a big crowd to see this history-making event.

The end did not come without some excitement. True, Glamorgan only needed to make 41 to win, but on the worn pitch anything was liable to happen. Brennan realized that there were possibilities in it, if only slight, and, to extract what advantage there was, used his spin bowlers. Barring a miracle their task was almost hopeless, but, even so, Illingworth

*Watson, Bailey and Compton save the day at Lord's in 1953*

barrier, sweeping every now and then any loose ball that was offered and, on one occasion particularly, cutting Johnston beautifully for 4.

The Australian bowling, when faced by this growing problem, seemed strangely out of gear. Its sharp edge of earlier was now surprisingly blunted, though Ring, who occasionally worried Watson, Johnston, and Miller tried everything from both sides of the wicket to various combinations of close fielders outside the leg and off stump.

It was all to no avail until Ring, in a long, last spell after tea, finally began to get some work on the ball down the hill from the Nursery end. But by half-past 5 Watson was past his great hundred, nearly out incidentally at long leg, as he swept Ring for 4 to a mighty cheer; Bailey, too, was beyond his 50. Together they had all but piloted England to safety.

But at 10 minutes to 6 things suddenly began to happen. Watson, almost on his last legs, snicked Ring's googly to slip, to receive a wonderful ovation on his return home; 236-5-109. Then, just short of 6 o'clock, Bailey loosely tried to drive Ring's away spin, pitched well outside the off-stump, and held out at cover-point; 246-6-71. He too, another footballer, received the applause of a hero.

Now came the last fearful half-hour as Australia, suddenly revitalized and on tiptoe, strained every nerve for a dramatic breakthrough. How Brown and Evans at times survived the spin of Ring and Benaud none could truly tell. But Brown at least showed himself a man for this last crisis. With no little sense of discrimination, and some thumping drives, he hit the spin away for four telling boundaries that helped to preserve all that had been built up so patiently through the long hours.

Every ball played was now met by nervous applause as the assembly sensed the tingle of the fading battle. Though Brown, with five minutes left, finally fell to Benaud in the slips, the battle at last was over. The enemy had been deprived of his prey.

## FIFTH TEST, THE OVAL, 1953

GILBERT WOOD

*August 20.* Before Compton's winning hit had reached the boundary yesterday the crowd had started to rush, with a cheer in their throats, across the turf, and the staider spectators, no longer wearing the calm look of a *Wisden* statistician, were uninhibitedly waving their match cards and adding mighty volume to the vocal celebration.

Those who had broken ranks made Edrich and Compton, and then the Australian team, run the gauntlet of hero-worshipping salutes, handshakes, and hearty slaps upon the back. In the tumult of celebration, Davies and Lee, the umpires, were cut off by the crowd. Finally, they were rescued by a posse of police, and continued their dignified course to the pavilion.

Already the cry had been raised for Hutton. As he appeared, a workmanlike cricketing figure in shirt sleeves, on the balcony, the crowd roared out its tribute. Soon both teams were lined up in sight. For Bailey there rose a greeting of special fervour, and the cheering that went up for Hassett and the Australian team surged like the pealing of bells. It was a moment for the Australians to remember when their playing days are done.

In his modest Yorkshire accents Hutton spoke for himself, his team, and the 30,000 or more who listened to him at the Oval. He said that he was happy and thrilled that England should have won the Test series, and especially that it should happen on this ground – 'a happy hunting ground for me.' After commenting that Hassett had had a very hard time this season, he described him as a wonderful opposition captain; and he hoped that Australia would continue to produce cricketers of the quality of Hassett, who had done so much for the game, not only in Australia, but in all parts of the world. 'Thank you,' he ended, 'for a most wonderful reception.'

Then Hassett spoke. 'I would just like to offer my congratulations to Len and the English team, They have earned this victory from the very first ball – of the second to last over, anyway,' he said, amid a roar of laughter from the crowd. 'Len was quite right when he spoke of our difficulties,' he continued, 'especially as I have been suffering from an injured right forearm.' (More laughter.) Hassett then paid a tribute to the Oval crowd for their sporting behaviour throughout the match. 'I feel rather proud of the way the Australian boys played and I think that you also enjoyed the way we played.'

**ENGLAND REGAIN THE ASHES**

**AUSTRALIA BEATEN BY 8 WICKETS**

**MEMORIES OF 1926**

**From Our Cricket Correspondent**

**August 19 at Kennington Oval.** Here was a day and a place to remember, the day English cricket was reborn. After 20 long years in the series against Australia, and 27 years on British soil, England at last won back the Ashes yesterday with a victory of rich flavour by eight wickets in the final Test match. So 1953 turned back to hold hands with 1926, complete the pattern of history in a remarkable way on this same historic ground, and thus consummate this happy

*August 20, 1953: England have regained the Ashes for the first time since the war*

## FOURTH TEST, ADELAIDE, 1954–55

STEWART HARRIS

*February 3.* Many years from now young Cowdrey will point to his broken nose and tell boys yet unborn that he was at Adelaide on February 2, 1955, when England won the Test match and kept the Ashes. And the boys will think him wondrous lucky. A man should dip his pen in blood to write about this day. Let no one talk and write about the wicket and explain away the deeds of heroes in terms more fit for gardening notes. Let no one deal in dull statistics – as if men can be measured!

JOHN WOODCOCK

*January 26, 1995.* Most of all, though, I enjoy reliving the day in 1954–55 when England retained the Ashes on this lovely ground. Being out of writing action after an operation in Hobart, I was commanded by Hutton, the captain, and Geoffrey Howard, the manager of M.C.C., to watch the match from the comfort of the England dressing-room rather than the confines of the press box, in itself a sign of the trust there was, but is no more, between players and correspondents.

I hope I am betraying no confidence when I say what trepidation there was when England, needing only 94 to win, were very soon 18 for three, with Hutton, Bill Edrich and Cowdrey out to a rampaging Keith Miller. The captain couldn't watch for a while after that.

He sat, unseen by the public, with his pads still on, his shirt off and a towel round his neck, just listening and praying. Nobody, I think, cried with emotion when Godfrey Evans hit the winning runs, but it is too easy to be indifferent to the anguish and the pressures that great sportsmen endure.

Sporting News

**HOW ENGLAND KEPT THE ASHES**

**TWO GREAT HEARTS OVERTHROW AUSTRALIA**

England beat Australia by five wickets in the fourth Test match at Adelaide yesterday and so, gaining a lead of three matches to one in the series, have retained the Ashes. In an interview after the match L. Hutton, the England captain, paid a tribute to the younger members of the side. Much of the credit, he thought, should go to J. B. Statham, F. H. Tyson, M. C. Cowdrey and P. B. H. May, together with the wicket-keeper, T. G. Evans.

*Under Len Hutton's leadership in 1954–55, England won a first series victory in Australia since 1932–33*

## SECOND TEST, LORD'S, 1968

JOHN WOODCOCK, CRICKET CORRESPONDENT

*June 25.* By the most effective exploitation of an unpleasant pitch England brought the second Test match against Australia back to life to a dramatic extent. In 33.4 overs they dismissed Australia for 78, their lowest total in this country since they made 65 at the Oval in 1912.

Following on during the afternoon 273 runs behind, Australia, in their second innings, had made 50 for no wicket by close of play. One hour and 40 minutes were lost during the day, and a possible six hours remained. It is asking a lot for England to win; but what they have done once they can do again, there being no reason why things should be a great deal easier today.

What England need if they are to get Australia on the run again is a quick break this morning, and now, of course, they will have to make do without a new ball. Yesterday, when Lawry and Redpath came out for the second time, this was denied them. With resolution, care and courage. these two, between showers, reduced by 100 vital minutes England's time for manoeuvre.

It was, as I say, an awkward pitch, from which the ball moved eagerly on the seam and occasionally lifted waspishly. It was also a raw, damp day, and for some of the time there was a drizzle sweeping across the ground. Conditions, in fact, were alien to batsmen, particularly to Australian batsmen. Seldom at home would they have to grapple with such problems as these.

But this is one of the hazards for a touring side. And England made the very most of their chance. Snow, Brown and Knight all bowled beautifully, until tiredness took the edge off them; and they were brilliantly supported in the field. Unlike the Australians on the first day, when the pitch was lively after rain, England bowled to a full length. Brown was as fast, if not faster, than Snow, and Knight, at a slower pace, gained more movement than either of them.

So between Lord's and Old Trafford we saw the complete contrast. It was Australia now who were harassed and hounded; and before tea the Queen was there to see it. By then England had made up for the time lost last week. And Cowdrey, in the process, had set up a new Test catching record. His three chances in Australia's first innings, all travelling at high speed and held with deceptive ease, took him past W.R. Hammond's bag of 110. On his day, Cowdrey bats and catches them at slip with the same mastery as Hammond, and it is hardly possible to be much better than that.

Australia were in trouble from the opening over, in which Snow, when beating Lawry, hinted at things to come. In Brown's first over Knott, swooping to his right, caught Lawry off a projected glance, a glorious one-handed catch. With Lawry firmly standing his ground, some time passed before umpire Fagg gave his decision. England's fielders made the answer as plain as they decently could.

This was the first of several fine catches. The second came in Brown's next over when Redpath was picked up low down at first slip. Cowdrey held the ball in spite of being momentarily unsighted by Knott, who dived across his line. The score was then 12 for two, and for all Cowper knew it could have been 12 for three, four, five, or six. It had reached 23 when Cowper, driving at Snow, edged him to second slip, where Graveney went down on his knees for the catch, as though in gratitude or prayer.

Walters and Sheahan, sharing a Test match crisis for the first time, doubled the score before being separated. One moment Knight was throwing himself to his right at slip in an unavailing effort to catch Sheahan: the next, before Sheahan had had a chance to add to his score, Knight had him caught at the wicket. In his previous over Knight had undermined Sheahan's confidence by beating him twice, first with a leg cutter, and then with a ball that whipped back from the off.

Propelling himself this time to his left, and now in the gully, Knight took another gem of a catch to get rid of Walters and reduce Australia to 52 for five. At 58 Chappell was leg before to Knight, playing back; and in the last over before luncheon McKenzie lost his off stump to Brown.

Although they had beaten the bat a dozen times or more without anything coming of it, England had no complaints from the morning. When Sheahan was missed, it availed them nothing; and when McKenzie was dropped at mid-on off Knight, he was bowled next ball by Brown. Similarly, when Redpath survived a passionate appeal for leg-before by Brown, he too was out next ball. And when, later on, the drizzle seemed certain to prevent England from finishing off Australia's first innings, it held off.

This was at 3.30. The resumption after luncheon had been delayed by half an hour by rain, and Hawke and Gleeson had stayed together for 20 minutes, with Gleeson making a couple of defiant strokes off Brown. He was out trying for a third, caught at slip by Cowdrey, as Hawke was soon afterwards. In the meantime, poor Jarman had been sent in with his finger broken in two places and left after one ball with it very possibly broken in a third. A ball from Brown lifted off a length and pinned Jarman's finger against the handle of his bat. It was a painful reflection of Australia's plight.

## THIRD TEST, HEADINGLEY, 1981

JOHN WOODCOCK,
CRICKET CORRESPONDENT

*July 22.* England's victory in the third Test match, sponsored by Cornhill, at Headingley yesterday was greeted by the kind of scenes reserved for great sporting occasions. After Australia, needing only 130 to win, had been bowled out for 111, the crowd massed in front of the pavilion, cheering their heroes and waving the Union Jacks they were saving for the Royal wedding.

While at one end of the balcony Brearley and his victorious team were being serenaded, at the other Allan Border, who had not long before been out for nought, was to be seen with his head buried in his hands. It was a moment of disaster as well as of triumph. Kim Hughes, even so, was gracious in defeat, giving credit where it was due and saying that, whereas from tea-time on Monday the luck had gone mostly England's way, before that the Australians had had the greater share of it.

If Botham's unforgettable innings made the recovery possible, it was Willis who crowned it with a marvellous piece of bowling after Australia had got to within only 74 runs of their target with nine wickets standing. When play started yesterday morning the chances seemed to be that Willis was playing in his last Test match. He had bowled below his best in England's first innings and it was not until his second spell now, after he had changed ends, that he caught the wind.

That was where Brearley came in. His return to the England side had not only released Botham to play his game unhampered by the burden of captaincy; it meant that England, with so few runs to play with, were under the command of a supreme tactician. To everyone on the ground, except those who wanted Australia to win, it was a great reassurance to see Brearley handling the situation with calm and understanding.

After England's last wicket had added only another five runs at the start of the day, Brearley opened the bowling with Botham and Dilley, England's third different new ball partnership of the match. His reason for this was partly psychological: Botham and Dilley having shared such a decisive partnership with the bat, it was worth seeing whether they could repeat it with the ball.

In the event Dilley, though he was to hold a great catch later in the innings, was taken off after two unimpressive overs. Although in his second over Botham had Wood caught at the wicket he looked hardly in the mood to move another mountain. That Willis was the man to do this, at the age of 32, and with knees that have often had to be supported by sticks, was a mark of rare courage. He had started with five rather laboured overs from the Football Stand End. At 48 for one, half an hour before lunch, Brearley

# THE TIMES

No 60,996 — MONDAY AUGUST 3 1981 — Price twenty pence

## BA split-up proposal is pressed

A few days before British Airways is expected to report a loss of at least £120m for 1980-81 a group of the airline's managers says that it must be split into at least two financially autonomous operating divisions or should be reduced in size by 40 per cent. The managers say of Sir John King, who was appointed chairman with a brief to pull the airline round: "Either he has been totally fooled by information given to him, or he has sufficient sense to distance himself from events. Certainly his presence is not particularly noticeable." Page 3

## Uncertainty on law of the sea

Another session of the international law of the sea conference opens in Geneva today with many of the 150 nations taking part, particularly those of the Third World, uncertain and pessimistic about the attitude of the United States Government. Final agreement on a convention is not now likely to be reached this year Page 4

## British Rail faces pay talks crisis

Last-ditch pay talks between British Rail and the industry's unions will take place today. Failure to agree on an arbitration award may result in a damaging strike which, union sources indicate, could halt commuter and holiday services as soon as next Monday Page 2

## Talks today on Springbok tour

A last chance attempt to end civil disorders in New Zealand caused by the Springbok rugby tour will be made today at a meeting of the principal parties to the dispute. Mr Muldoon, the Prime Minister, said the law would be enforced Page 5

## BBC accused of political bias

The Labour Party has accused the BBC of political bias over appointing Sir William Rees-Mogg, former editor of *The Times*, as its vice-chairman. The row over E. P. Thompson and the Dimbleby lecture also caused concern Page 3

E. P. Thompson profile, page 10
Letters, page 11

## Thatcher move on pipeline

The Prime Minister will meet ministers today in an attempt to break the deadlock over the financing of the proposed £2,700m North Sea gas pipeline. The Energy Department wants the project to go ahead but the Treasury has its doubts Page 17

## 'Parks' celebrates his life behind the camera

Mr Norman Parkinson, Queen Elizabeth the Queen Mother's favourite photographer, who celebrates 50 years of taking pictures with an exhibition of his work over five decades at the National Portrait Gallery in London. Today a profile of [illegible]

## The risks taken in forming the SDP

The key to the future success of the Social Democratic Party is its electoral alliance with the Liberals. As David Steel confronts the task of persuading Liberal candidates across the country to stand down in favour of an SDP contender, Ian Bradley, in the first extract from *Breaking the Mould*, reveals the influential role played by Steel last year in persuading Roy Jenkins not to join the Liberals but to keep up the pressure on Shirley Williams, Bill Rodgers and David Owen to leave the Labour Party. Page 10

## Intrigue from Ambler

Eric Ambler, a master of the spy thriller since the 1930s, has written another winner — his twentieth novel, *The Care of Time*, from which *The Times* begins publishing a series of extracts today. Page 8


| | | | |
|---|---|---|---|
| Home News | 2, 3 | Lurie cartoon | 5 |
| Overseas | 4, 5 | Obituary | 12 |
| Appts | 12, 18 | Prem Bonds | 24 |
| Archaeology | 3 | Property | 20 |
| Arts | 9 | Religion | 12 |
| Business | 16-19 | Science | 2 |
| Court | 12 | Sport | 13-15 |
| Crossword | 24 | Theatres, etc | 23 |
| Diary | 10 | 25 Years Ago | 12 |
| Features | 7, 10 | TV & Radio | 23 |
| Law report | 20 | Weather | 24 |
| Letters | 11 | Wills | 12 |

University results, page 6
Information service, back page


# Cardinal calls for end to fast as eighth striker dies

From Richard Ford, Belfast

Kieran Doherty, MP for Cavan Monaghan in the Irish Republic, died last night after a 73-day fast at the Maze prison near Belfast.

He is the eighth to die since the hunger strike began five months ago and his death at 7.16 pm came 42 hours after Kevin Lynch died in the prison on the 71st day of his fast.

The man who will replace Mr Lynch on hunger strike is a friend from his schooldays, Liam McCloskey, aged 25, from Dungiven, Co Londonderry, who is serving ten years for conspiracy to disarm security forces and hijacking.

Hours before Mr Doherty died the Primate of All Ireland, Cardinal O'Fiaich, had appealed in Dundalk, for the hunger strikers to end their fast, "not in a spirit of condemnation but in a spirit of compassion with their own suffering and with the grief and suffering of relatives and friends".

The usual brief statement from the Northern Ireland Office said: "Kieran Doherty, a prisoner in HM Prison Maze died today at 7.16 pm. He took his own life by refusing food and medical intervention for 73 days."

If Mr Doherty had lived until tomorrow morning he would have equalled the record set by Terence McSwiney, Lord Mayor of Cork, who died after a 74-day fast in 1922.

As news of the death of Mr Doherty, aged 25, who came from the strongly republican Andersonstown area of west Belfast spread, the familiar banging of dustbin lids, blowing of whistles, stone throwing and rioting began.

Overhead a helicopter equipped with a special camera kept watch on likely trouble spots. Mr Doherty's family had been keeping a vigil at his bedside in the prison hospital at the Maze since the middle of July.

His mother is reported to have told him early last week that she would not ask doctors to save him if he slipped into a coma.

A soldier, aged 21, had both legs amputated below the knee last night and was very seriously ill in hospital after a Soviet-made RPG 7 rocket hit a Saracen armoured car. The attack came only minutes after the announcement of Doherty's death; the armoured car was hit at the junction of the Falls and Beechmounts roads in Belfast.

In rioting which followed Mr Doherty's death a man in his garden in Etna Drive, in the Ardoyne, Belfast, was injured in the chest by shrapnel from an exploding blast bomb. In the Andersonstown area the RUC and Army came under attack from youths throwing stones. Hijacked cars were set on fire and makeshift barricades erected.

Nine children have been left fatherless by an IRA landmine explosion in Co Tyrone in which two policemen were killed. They were named as Mr John Smith, aged 34, who had three children aged between one and five, and Mr Andrew Woods, aged 30, who had six children aged between nine and 20.

Their deaths came as a mother of one of the six men on hunger strike at the Maze pledged that if he became unconscious she would follow the example of another prisoner's mother on Friday and authorize medical attention to try to save his life.

News of Mr Doherty's death reached his constituency while a rally was taking place at Castleblaney and shortly afterwards the sound of bin lids banging could be heard in many towns and villages.

There are fears that it could lead to rioting and violence in the republic. After the death of Kevin Lynch on Saturday, an explosion wrecked an electricity transformer at Monaghan.

With the death of Mr Doherty the IRA has probably gained its most dramatic propaganda coup since Robert Sands, MP for Fermanagh and South Tyrone, died in May.

He had been elected to serve as Deputy in the Dail for a border constituency which has a tradition of republicanism.

During the last few weeks of his life there was surprise at how long Mr Doherty, who was serving a jail sentence for possessing explosives and firearms, had survived after being given the last rites.

But his death could threaten the survival of Dr Garret FitzGerald's Fine Gael-Labour coalition Government in the republic. It has been reported that Paddy Agnew, another Maze prisoner and MP for co Louth, would resign on Mr Doherty's death, causing two by elections in constituencies usually held by Fianna Fail.

The Government has a majority of two over Fianna Fail and the balance is held by independents.

☐ In a statement issued last night from Dublin, Dr FitzGerald said he had learnt with regret of the death (Tim Jones writes from Dublin). He extended his sympathy to the family, members of which he met recently.

Dr FitzGerald said he had also learnt with sorrow of the two RUC constables who had been murdered in the course of their duty.

It is understood that the H-block committee would field candidates in virtually every Irish constituency if by-elections caused by the hunger strike campaign produce a hung parliament.

Propaganda war, page 2
Secularism gains ground, page 12

Victory salutes from man-of-the-match Ian Botham and captain Brearley

## The match winners of Edgbaston

By John Woodcock, Cricket Correspondent

With another thrillingly improbable victory England took a 2—1 lead at Edgbaston yesterday in the summer's series of six Test matches against Australia. They won the fourth Test by 29 runs, although until a few minutes from the finish they had almost always looked like losing it.

As at Headingley in the third Test, which England won by 18 runs, Ian Botham, twice the cricketer under Mike Brearley's leadership than when he is shouldering the burden of captaincy himself, was the man of the match.

Needing only 151 to win, in glorious sunshine and on a pitch which both captains felt was worth many more runs than were scored, Australia looked increasingly likely to make them as Graham Yallop and Allan Border were adding 58 for the fourth wicket. But after these two had fallen to John Emburey, the Middlesex off-spinner, Botham finished off the match with one of his most devastating spells, taking Australia's last five wickets in six overs for two runs.

Whereas at Headingley England caught brilliantly, this time they dropped the one missable chance they had. At times the crowd of 15,000 cheered the home side on as though it was a horse race.

Since Brearley's return after the second Test match to captain England, they have scored two victories after succession of 12 tests which were lost or drawn. Yesterday's play, hard yet good humoured, has left the Australians with more worries than England, which hardly seemed possible a fortnight ago. The fifth Test starts at Old Trafford on Thursday week.

Report, page 13

## Polish unions offer compromise

Warsaw, Monday morning.—Solidarity, the independent trade union organization, indicated early today that it might consent temporarily to the reduced meat ration that went into effect from Saturday.

When its governing board ended an emergency meeting here after midnight, a union source said Solidarity's leaders were willing to accept the reduced ration for the rest of the month, but only if the Government agreed to make up for this with supplementary meat deliveries in September.

The union leaders agreed to start negotiations this morning with Mr Mieczyslaw Rakowski, the Deputy Prime Minister, over the one-fifth cut in the meat ration, which led to large hunger marches in Polish cities.

The union also intends to oppose the big increase in food prices envisaged by the Government, the source disclosed, and to negotiate for self-management and autonomy of state enterprises. Solidarity has often said it would not oppose price increases if they were part of an economic reform based on self-management.

The union meeting came after an announcement that Poland's military commanders had conferred to plan defence strategy and decide how to use the army in a crack-down on speculation.

It was not immediately clear whether the union's decision to talk to the Government would affect plans for a demonstration in Warsaw today, a strike in the region on Wednesday, and protests elsewhere.

The Communist Party's newly elected politburo issued a tough statement condemning the wave of food protests. The Government's decision to use troops as a back-up for civil and police inspectors in the markets, announced by the Polish news agency PAP, pointed to the growing military role in coping with Poland's year-old crisis. Reuter and AFP

☐ Bonn: Leaflets containing a thinly veiled appeal for a Polish-type rebellion in East Germany have been circulating in colleges and scientific institutes in East Berlin, the weekly news magazine, *Der Spiegel*, claimed yesterday (Patricia Clough writes).

Lurie cartoon, page 5

## Deepening Tory rift on economic policy

By Philip Webster, Political Staff

The rift among senior Conservative Party figures over the direction of the Government's economic policy appeared to be deepening last night after Lord Thorneycroft, the party chairman, again challenged the assertion of Sir Geoffrey Howe, the Chancellor, that the recession had ended.

As Mr Michael Foot, the [illegible] vened to claim that the [illegible] don, South, and chairman of the influential Tory backbench finance committee, launched a bitter attack on Lord Thorneycroft and Mr Francis Pym, Leader of the House of Commons, for rejecting the Chancellor's claim and their implied criticism of the Government's handling of the economy.

In a speech on Saturday Mr Pym said that recession was proving deeper and longer than anyone expected. Supporting fresh measures to deal with it, he said: "The British people will not be prepared for very much longer to tolerate the worst effects of recession if there is not a clear sign that the sacrifice will have been worthwhile."

Lord Thorneycroft, in a message to MPs and the party organization yesterday, admitted that the party had its problems and said that the Government should not be approaching its task on the basis of a doctrinaire economic theory, a statement that echoed recent criticisms, by Mr Peter Walker, the Minister of Agriculture, of the Government's rigid monetarist stance.

Lord Thorneycroft contradicted the Chancellor's recent optimism on the economy when he said in a radio interview: "It may be that the recession is not going deeper but it is deep enough for me at the moment. It is deep enough for most industrialists. There are no great signs of it picking up."

Lord Thorneycroft's remarks and Mr Pym's speech have set the scene for a battle in the Cabinet this autumn over public expenditure and are seen as an attempt to outflank Mrs Margaret Thatcher and the Chancellor over their insistence that public borrowing should not be increased.

Lord Thorneycroft's intervention, in particular, was regarded as a reflection of concern in the country; in con- [illegible] yesterday that there were no differences between himself, Mr Pym and Lord Thorneycroft, said: "They are pointing out what Mrs Thatcher and I have been pointing out for some time: that the recovery process when it starts is bound to be long and slow".

He repeated his view that the fall in output was at an end and added, slightly modifying the words he used in the Commons on Thursday, that "in that sense the recession is coming to its end".

In the House he had said: "We are now at the end of the recession".

Asked whether there was any question of a Tory revolt, the Chancellor replied: "By no means". He had had discussions with Mr Pym and Lord Thorneycroft. "There is absolutely no difference between us on the emphasis I have been describing."

In his speech Mr Pym, emphasizing that he was not advocating general reflation, called for more competitive energy prices to be made available to industry, long-term training schemes, a regeneration of the inner cities and a stimulation for the building industry.

Sir William Clark said that the intervention by Lord Thorneycroft and Mr Pym were bound to damage morale. He said that he would raise the matter with Mr Michael Jopling, the Chief Whip, if not Mrs Thatcher herself, because it was essential to present a united front.

Continued on back page, col 1

President Sadat of Egypt acknowledges the greeting he received at Heathrow airport yesterday.

## Sadat starts peace tour

By Our Foreign Staff

President Anwar Sadat of Egypt was given a warm reception at Heathrow Airport yesterday when he arrived in London for the first stage of a three-nation tour.

He was greeted by Sir Ian Gilmour, the Lord Privy Seal, and Lord Cullen of Ashbourne representing the Queen, and by 200 members of Britain's Islamic community singing the Egyptian national anthem.

Mr Sadat is hoping to revive the Palestinian autonomy talks which went into abeyance last year with elections due in the United States and Israel. He will canvass support in London, Washington and Vienna for his peace efforts.

With Mr Menachem Begin likely to be reinstalled soon as Israel's Prime Minister, President Reagan, triumphant over his new economic package, and Britain assuming the presidency of the EEC Council of Ministers, the way is clear for the Egyptian leader to make headway with some of the main parties in the Middle East peace process.

Mr Sadat's talks at Downing Street today with Mrs Thatcher, the Prime Minister, and Lord Carrington, the Foreign Secretary, are expected to explore steps the EEC could take to build confidence between the Israelis and the Palestinians. The EEC's Middle East initiative has been welcomed by President Sadat but has received scant support from the United States as architect of the Camp David agreements.

Mr Sadat is to meet Mr Michael Foot the Opposition leader, Mr James Callaghan, the former Prime Minister, and the Lord Mayor of London and others this afternoon. Tomorrow he has lunch with the Queen.

Leading article, page 11

## Begin offers sabbath flight ban

Tel Aviv, Aug 2.—Mr Menachem Begin, the Israeli Prime Minister, today promised the religious parties he would order the state airline El Al to stop flying on Saturdays and Jewish holidays.

The religious parties have been pressing him to make sabbath observance stricter as [illegible] formation of a new coalition [illegible] that the move would cost El Al $50m (£26m) a year in lost profits. The decision was announced by Mr [illegible], the Finance Minister, who did not say when the flights would cease.

Mr Begin met religious party leaders today, but Government sources said the talks left several differences unresolved. They said Mr Begin told the orthodox leaders he would return his mandate to President Yitzhak Navon if they did not agree by Tuesday to join his government.

A continued Israeli hard line on Middle Eastern issues is signalled in policy guidelines drafted by Mr Begin for the new government, which he is expected to announce on Tuesday.

Mr Aridor said on Israel Radio today that the guidelines had been drafted during the coalition bargaining.—Reuter.

Cabinet plans, page 4

## Labour selects Owen challenger

Devonport Labour Party selected Mr Julian Priestley, aged 31, an Oxford graduate and a moderate, to oppose Dr David Owen (Social Democrats) at the next general election.

Dr Owen, who is 43, held the Devonport seat in May, 1979, as a Labour candidate, but earlier this year left the Labour Party to help to form the new Social Democratic Party.

Labour plan for investment bank

## Private savings to pay for jobs

By Philip Webster, Political Staff

A radical economic industrial and social strategy to transform society involving a huge expansion of the economy by mobilizing private savings, is unveiled today by the Labour Party.

The programme, to be put before the party's annual conference next month by the national executive committee, is based on vastly increased public spending, planning in trade and industry, a wealth tax, EEC withdrawal, abolition of the House of Lords, new public enterprise and renationalization and an attack on poverty.

Under the proposals contained in a lengthy document called *The Socialist Alternative*, a new national investment bank, financed from North Sea oil revenues and the pension funds and life assurance companies would provide funds for long-term investment projects.

The money borrowed would be guaranteed by the government and existing methods of raising savings directly from the public, such as index-linked national savings and government stock, would be extended. The prospect of "orderly" sales of government debt through agreements with the lending institutions is being studied by the party.

The statement is put forward by the NEC as a sweeping programme designed to take Britain through to the end of the century and set the economy on the road to full employment.

Rejecting cautious or piecemeal measures to help the country recover from the crisis caused by "the insanity of monetarism", it commits a Labour government to increasing spending power by spending more itself. The first boost must come not from higher taxation but by borrowing money from people who choose not to spend it, private savers.

### Companies borrow to pay for investment

To say they could not spend more than they earned was nonsense. "Every sensible company will borrow to pay for investment and most families borrow to finance major purchases. If the Government does not mobilize savings to keep up spending and keep resources in use, we will see rising unemployment as goods remain unsold and production falls."

The NEC says its statement stands alongside the document *Economic Issues facing the next Labour government*, published 10 days ago by the TUC-Labour Party liaison committee. It mirrors that document in many crucial respects; but in others it goes much further and develops new ideas.

The abolition of the House of Lords, withdrawal from the EEC, and making the Civil service more accountable are seen as prerequisites for the success of the programme, to prevent it being frustrated by entrenched and undemocratic powers.

Having initiated expansion by increased borrowing, cutting interest rates, undertaking new public sector building projects, directing huge resources into inner cities and social service spending, the NEC stakes its hopes of sustaining it on a powerful new industrial strategy and a policy of trade planning.

To prevent a large balance of payments deficit it proposes a "careful" devaluation of the exchange rate and "import penetration ceilings on an industry-by-industry basis . . . enforced by a range of measures, including tariffs and quotas where necessary" to prevent the growth of imports outstripping the growth of exports.

The objective is not to cut the overall level of imports but to ensure a controlled growth of trade, it says.

To regulate the flow of investment funds overseas the statement foresees the restoration, followed by the strengthening, of the exchange controls which operated until 1979. It suggests a separate exchange rate for current and capital transactions.

### New powers would create jobs

A Labour government would set up a foreign investment unit to monitor the effects on the economy of inward and outward investment, especially by the multinationals.

The industrial strategy would be based on the introduction of new planning machinery to co-ordinate intervention and ensure that the plans of each major public and private company, each industrial sector and each region, fit in with the government's overall expansion plans.

Major companies would be required to enter into planning agreements, to provide the basis on which government support will be given to industry. Through these new powers and new public enterprise the government will steer jobs directly into the regions and create new jobs. Development agencies will be set up for each of the English regions.

Upon election, Labour would act to provide jobs quickly. Extra public spending would be concentrated in areas where new jobs would be created by expanding existing labour-intensive programmes, launching new investment projects and directing public purchasing to firms needing orders.

Labour would establish a public-owned stake in every important industrial sector and take back those sections of public industries hived off by the Tories. A cooperative investment bank would be established to help the formation of workers' cooperatives.

A cooperative investment bank would be established to help the formation of workers' cooperatives.

The statement also proposes longer holidays, earlier voluntary retirement and a 35-hour week.

It pledges Labour to introduce a flexible but comprehensive system of price controls, backed by a new price commission. The party must also strive towards its target retirement pension of one third average gross earnings for a single person and half for a married couple.

Foot wary and excerpt from document, page 2
David Wood and letters, page 11



*In a summer of a royal wedding, economic gloom and inner-city riots, cricket still found its way on to the front page. Here after England's remarkable victory at Edgbaston*

gave him the, breeze, the decision which launched him on his devastating spell.

It was noticeable even in his first over from the Kirkstall Lane End that Willis was bowling faster than in his earlier spell; not only that, he was making the ball lift as well. At 56, he got one to rear almost geometrically at Chappell, who cocked it up for Taylor, running forward, to take the catch. At 58, in the last over before lunch, Hughes and Yallop both went without scoring, Hughes beautifully caught at second slip by Botham, diving to his left, and Yallop also out to a very good catch. Gatting, standing his ground at short leg and reacting quickly to Yallop's desperate attempt to keep down another kicking delivery, threw himself forward for the ball.

Whereas at the start of the day the skies were clear, by now the clouds were rolling in, causing the ball to move about rather more, even to bounce, more steeply. To keep his hands warm for the slip catch that could have gone his way, Brearley was constantly blowing into them.

With Yallop's departure, off the fifth ball of an over, lunch was taken. I harboured a fear that during the interval Willis might stiffen up; but not a bit of it. Brearley had him on again straight away afterwards, bowling as furiously and well as I have ever seen him. When in making a superhuman effort he was occasionally no-balled, Brearley told him not to bother, bowl your fastest, he said, and keep digging it in.

After Old had knocked out Border's leg stump, a vital contribution, Willis did the rest. At 68 he had Dyson caught at the wicket, hooking, as important a wicket as any in view of the skill and resolution with which Dyson had played.

At 74 Marsh, a dangerous customer, hooked him to long leg where Dilley, only a yard in front of the crowd judged to perfection a high and horrible catch. At 75 Lawson gave Taylor his 1,271st first class wicket, or a new wicket-keeping record, though in all the excitement few knew it.

There followed a partnership between Bright and Lillee which rekindled Australia's fading hopes. Taking their lives in their hands, they added 35 in four overs before another fine catch, this time by Gatting, accounted for Lillee. Running in from mid-on, Gatting dived forward for a mis-timed hook. The ball was a long time in the air and Gatting had a lot of ground to cover.

With only 20 needed and Lillee and Bright going as well as they were, Lillee's wicket was a vast relief. There was only Alderman to be dealt with now and to finish things off Brearley brought back Botham in place of Old. Botham would have done it, too, had Old, at third slip, not dropped Alderman twice in the over. As it was in the next over Willis yorked Bright and the match was won.

It was not a good Test pitch. Nor it was at Trent Bridge for the first Test of the series. At Edgbaston next week it should be different. In trying to produce something fast and true, the groundsman at Headingley made, one that was unpredictable and patchy. But at least he tried.

England's choice of four fast bowlers proved, after all, the right one. Had Australia followed suit Lillee, Alderman and Lawson would not have been as tired as they were on Monday evening when Botham played his marvellous innings.

But what does that matter? They shared in a match that was a victory for cricket. To hear them singing *Jerusalem* down below you would think that it had revived a nation, too.

'Ian Botham, they call him Jessop in the paper today. It was the most remarkable innings I've ever seen.' That was Brearley on his young lion.

Botham's 149 not out, as Hughes has said, must be one of the finest innings of all time. Very few could have played it, not only among contemporary cricketers partly because of his enormous strength. He weighs 16 stone, all of which went into the marvellous drives that made up the majority of his 28 boundaries.

Grace, Bradman, Hobbs, Compton, Hutton, Worrell and Sobers, they all had their different ways of playing. Perhaps Botham's resembles most closely among postwar batsmen that of Clyde Walcott, another giant of a man. If Clyde was a better batsman than Ian, not possibly could he have played more magnificently.

## SIXTH TEST, THE OVAL, 1993

ALAN LEE, CRICKET CORRESPONDENT

*August 24.* This was a day which might have come from the yellowed pages of generations-old newsprint, when this improbable cricket ground, hemmed in by gasholders and rumbling commuter traffic, always seemed to produce full houses celebrating famous England wins. Last night, London's evening paper rushed out a special late edition with the simple headline 'We've won it' Was it not always like this?

## FOURTH TEST, ADELAIDE, 1994–95

ALAN LEE, CRICKET CORRESPONDENT

*January 31.* England may not win very often at cricket, but, when they do, they win with a verve and style that takes the breath away. After Barbados last April and the Oval in August, England's first Test victory in Australia since 1986 was achieved here yesterday against apparently insuperable odds and with memorably irresistible cricket.

At the start of the final day of this fourth Test, an England win was comfortably the outsider of three most likely results. Logic suggested a draw, recent history an Australian win. Desperation, however, can be a great leveller. To keep the series alive and avoid the condemnation that would follow an empty tour, England had to win. The imperative inspired great deeds.

The last four England wickets added 108 runs in 18.5 overs, whereupon Australia, setting off confident of making 263 in 67 overs, lost eight wickets inside two hours. Despite gallantry on a grand scale from the ninth-wicket pair, a wonderful match ended with 5.5 overs to spare and the Barmy Army streamed onto the field.

This was the eleventh Test that England have played in this country since retaining the Ashes at Melbourne in December 1986. They have had their chances to win several, but taken none, and that they should end the sorry sequence now, with a team barely recognisable from that which began the tour, beggars belief as much as did the manner of its execution.

The catalyst, just as it had been against South Africa in August, was spectacular batting from the tail, followed by awesomely quick bowling by Devon Malcolm. Phillip DeFreitas, whose partnership with Darren Gough shifted the balance at the Oval, this time went solo. He has never batted so well for so long in a Test, and may never do so again. But a man could die happy after one innings as good as this.

DeFreitas, resuming on 20, added 68 off 57 balls. Exhorted by his captain 'to be positive but selective', he took apart the man who, by common consent, has been the best bowler of the series. Craig McDermott, troubled by recurring stomach and knee problems, may not have been feeling at his best when he began bowling. He felt a good deal worse once DeFreitas had finished with him. His three-over spell with the second new ball cost 41 runs, of which DeFreitas struck 22 in one over, rounded off with a pull over mid-wicket for six.

The tone had been set from the start of a session that recorded Test-best performances from DeFreitas with the bat and Mark Waugh with the ball. John Crawley completed his second half-century in successive Tests and moved so smoothly on to 71 that over-confidence was his downfall, and he fell, like ten other batsmen in this game, to a misjudged pull. He also ricked his neck as his studs snagged when he turned for a second run, and, after his dismissal, took no further part.

A different type of injury topped up DeFreitas's adrenalin. McDermott hit him in the groin, doubling him up for some minutes. His response was controlled aggression of such class that one wonders why it has always been beyond him before now.

Malcolm pumped himself up by hitting Shane Warne out of the ground. When the last wicket fell in the same over, Malcolm sprinted from the field. His eagerness was contagious, though at first impulsive. He chose the wrong end from which to bowl and, after one over labouring into the wind, asked to switch. Atherton agreed and the results were devastating. In the first over after lunch, taken at 16 without loss, Malcolm disturbed Mark Taylor with a well-directed bouncer, taken on the glove in front of his face. Next over, Taylor chased at a wide ball and the reliable hands of Thorpe, at first slip, did the rest. Already, there was something familiar to the plot, and England recognised it. Maybe Australia did, too. David Boon froze against his first ball, which hit an involuntary bat before he had moved, and Fraser removed him through a leg-side catch in the next over.

Malcolm was now in overdrive. Slater, unable to resist the hook, perished to a splendid catch by Tufnell at fine leg, and, to the next ball, Steve Waugh, looking for his customary welcome of a bouncer, was instead beaten for pace and bowled by one of full length.

Malcolm had taken three wickets for four runs in 12 balls. Until Sunday morning, his analysis for this series was a melancholy four for 343; in two bursts, he had now claimed six wickets for 16.

On days such as this, a captain can do no wrong. Mark Waugh was beginning to play with ease when Atherton brought on Tufnell. Waugh turned his first ball firmly off his hip and it hit Mike Gatting, at short leg, on the left boot before popping obligingly into his hands.

Chris Lewis was summoned from the Cathedral End and produced one of his best spells for England. Blewett, Warne and McDermott all fell to him, either side of tea, and if his finger-stabbing gesture to the latter was excessive, it also seemed to signal the end of the game.

Ian Healy, however, had other ideas, and, for the next 112 minutes, he and Fleming stalled the England charge. Only eight overs remained when Lewis removed Fleming leg-before. Malcolm was recalled against the hapless McIntyre, an extraction that required only one ball, and England were left to celebrate a famous victory and regret, once again, that such cricket eludes them when a series is young and impressionable.

## FIRST TEST, CARDIFF, 2009

MIKE ATHERTON,
CHIEF CRICKET CORRESPONDENT

*July 13*. English batsmanship – classic nose-to the-grindstone, down-in-the-trenches, over-my-dead body English batsmanship – finally showed its face on the fifth day in Cardiff. And what a welcome sight, in the ruddy features of Paul Collingwood, it was.

Collingwood, unshaven, sunburnt and mired in sweat and dust, batted for 17 minutes shy of six hours, 245 balls of sheer bloody-mindedness and self-restraint, to take England to the brink of safety. Then, as if the cricketing gods had dreamt up the worst torture imaginable, he had to watch from the balcony, fully padded still and full of remorse after not quite seeing the job through, as Monty Panesar and James Anderson blocked out 69 balls to ensure that England go to Lord's on level terms, the Ashes still there for the taking.

A more unlikely pairing with the bat than Anderson and Panesar you could not imagine. They came together with England trailing by six runs and 11.3 overs remaining. Ricky Ponting turned to Peter Siddle with the second new ball after an erratic spell from Mitchell Johnson and Siddle had justified his captain's faith by inducing a forcing back-foot drive from Collingwood that ended up in the hands of Mike Hussey in the gully at the second attempt. The champagne corks in the Australia dressing room were ready to pop.

Collingwood's 74 runs were vital, but more important was the attitude and example he showed, to the dressing room full of batsmen who had made gifts of their wickets earlier in the day and to Anderson and Panesar, who had to make sure that his good work was not wasted. Certainly, Anderson is better than a rabbit these days, but Panesar is a rabbit of *Watership Down* proportions, the kind of tailender that pros refer to as a ferret – because they go in after the rabbits.

*Before the departure in 1950, the ordeal of the interviews. Denis Compton joins captain Freddie Brown for interrogation at the microphone*

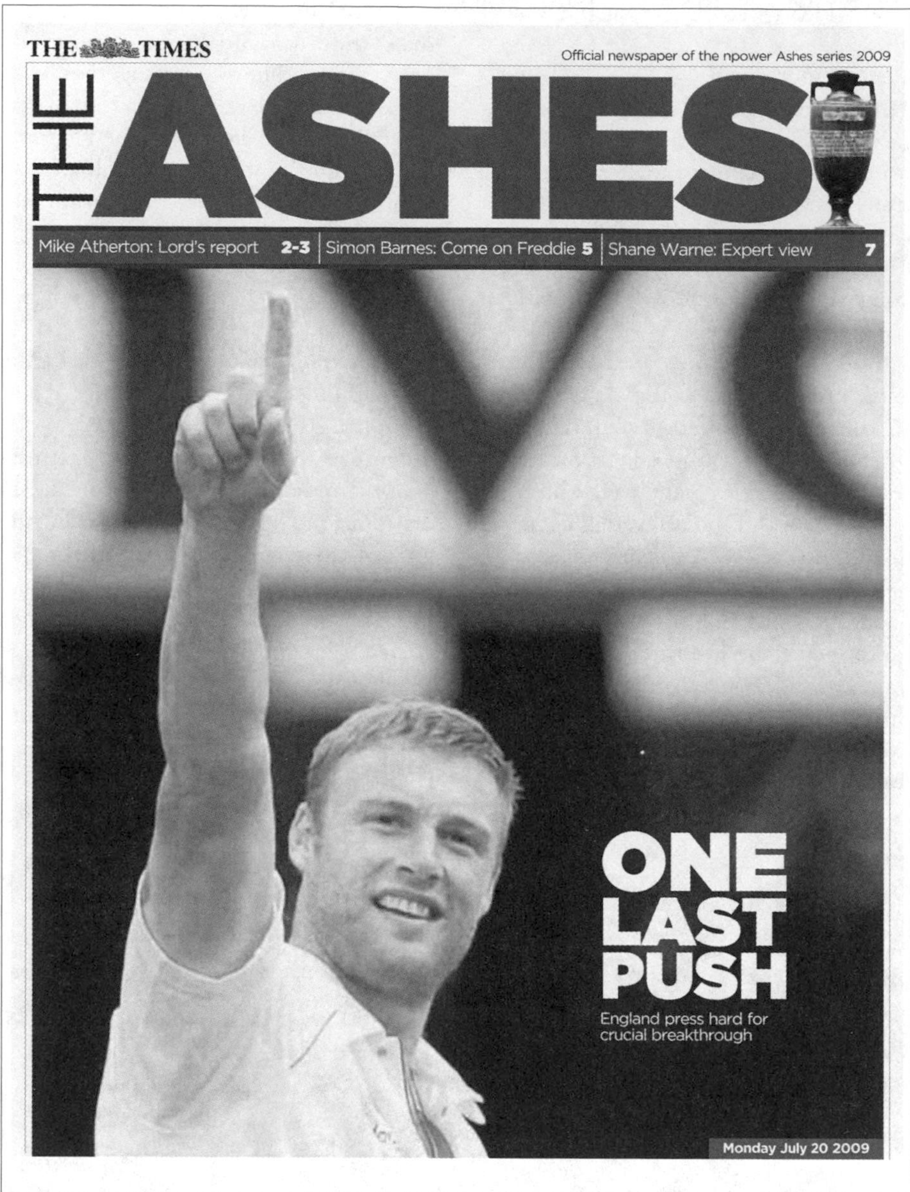

THE TIMES

Official newspaper of the npower Ashes series 2009

THE ASHES

Mike Atherton: Lord's report 2-3 | Simon Barnes: Come on Freddie 5 | Shane Warne: Expert view 7

ONE LAST PUSH

England press hard for crucial breakthrough

Monday July 20 2009

*For the 2009 series,* The Times *produced Monday morning Ashes supplements*

But somehow they repelled everything that was thrown at them. Siddle, fast and loose-tongued, had a newish ball in his hand; Nathan Hauritz, not exactly the spirit of Shane Warne incarnate but still bowling nicely, was teasing from the River Taff End. Anderson lasted for 1hr 12min, facing 53 balls, and Panesar, remarkably, survived 35 balls.

It did not feel so at the time, as fingernails were bitten to the quick, but the two survived without any great alarms, only the odd ball fizzing past the edge as Hauritz's fingers tired after a long day. The biggest danger appeared to be some eccentric running between the wickets.

It was a remarkable end to a Test match that, until the final few hours, had been too one-sided to be considered a classic. But those who were there will not forget the tension as the finish line approached. Each defensive stroke, each run was cheered to the rafters, the first time, surely, that an English team have had such unqualified support in Wales. With 45 balls remaining Anderson squeezed Siddle to the off-side boundary consecutively to take England into the lead and ensure that Australia had to use up two more overs for the change of innings.

Ponting, in desperation, turned to the part-time spin of Marcus North (missing a trick, perhaps, in not trying Michael Clarke's slow left-arm). England, in desperation, began to run down the clock, the twelfth man and the physiotherapist making regular and spurious visits to the middle. The final hour had begun at 5.50pm; so, at 6.39, with ten minutes needed for the change of innings, Anderson settled down to face the final over of the day from Hauritz, with England leading by 12.

At the end of the over Australia, after dominating the game, had run out of time and England, so often in recent times on the receiving end of these agonising draws, had survived. Anderson, Tiger Woods-like, clenched a fist and roared to the gallery.

## FOURTH TEST, MELBOURNE, 2010–11

MIKE ATHERTON,
CHIEF CRICKET CORRESPONDENT

*December 29.* It was six minutes to noon when Tim Bresnan, an honest Yorkshire toiler seemingly transformed over the past two days into a latter-day Frederick Sewards Trueman, produced the wicket that retained the Ashes for England for the first time in 24 years.

More than five sessions and a Test match were remaining in the series, the early destiny of the urn a measure, then, of the visiting team's dominance. It was time to sup.

The moment was regulation: Ben Hilfenhaus pushing half-forward, Matt Prior, the wicketkeeper, accepting a straightforward chance; the celebrations, though, were euphoric, as England's players got together in the tightest of huddles, the massed ranks of the touring side's supporters in the Great Southern Stand saluting them.

Brad Haddin, as flinty an Australian as it is possible to meet, dropped to his haunches, undefeated in a personal sense but also a member of a team that had been overwhelmed. Australia's resistance was risible. Mitchell Johnson fell to the eleventh ball of the morning, Chris Tremlett squeezing one through via bat and pad, and he left the field hurriedly, never a man about whom it could be said that the contest is everything.

Thereafter, and probably for the first time on this tour, England got ahead of themselves, so that there were some sloppy moments, notably when a couple of outside edges off Graeme Swann eluded Paul Collingwood at slip.

Haddin, as proud as his bat was straight, offered some cheer for Australia as he went past fifty, but he could only watch as Peter Siddle skied Swann to long-on before Bresnan mopped up Hilfenhaus, the last man. It is with warriors such as the Australia wicketkeeper that their path must be taken, Haddin one of only two men – Mike Hussey being the other – who have played well enough to make a combined XI selected from both teams.

England's players went first to Australia to shake hands in the time-honoured way, then to their supporters, who have witnessed some horrible moments at this ground in recent years. Four years ago a great Australia team eviscerated inept opponents on the way to a whitewash; four years before that they had to sit through a double century from Justin Langer, now the Australia batting coach, as he powered them to another victory; and eight years before that, on this very day, they had to genuflect before Shane Warne as he celebrated an Ashes hat-trick.

Memories for players and supporters are important because they provide context and give each encounter meaning and significance. Four years ago, on New Year's Eve, it was hard to walk around Sydney without bumping into England supporters who had shelled out their hard-earned and felt shortchanged and badly let down by Andrew Flintoff's team. This time they were rewarded with the kind of memories that last a lifetime. Sport is about losing as much as winning, the experience of the first sweetening that of the second.

For players, great memories reinforce the reasons for playing; sour ones provide the motivation needed to ensure that the contest is continuing, for it is in the dark moments that some kind of rejuvenation must be planned. On the past two occasions in England, Ricky Ponting urged his players to watch England receive the urn at the Oval, the better to motivate them for the next encounter.

But once the handshaking had been done, there were no Australians on the outer this time, although it is in Sydney that the urn will be presented. Ponting, for sure, will not be around for the next series and there are question marks over his participation even in the next game, although he hinted that, fitness permitting, he wants to lead the team there.

But this may be some kind of watershed for Australia, the moment when the realisation hits home that the slide in the world Test rankings is a reflection of reality and not some wheeze dreamt up by a nerdish statistician.

For England, as they shimmied around the MCG to the tune of *We Are the Champions*, it was no time to reflect, rather a time to enjoy. To hell with cold explanations and cool analysis, and even the staid clichés about the match to come, it was time to enjoy and to soak in the kind of experience granted to few. After all, what is all the training, all the practice and all the nervy nights for if not for this?

Only four times since the Second World War have an England team returned with the urn until now, this squad joining those revered names from 1954–55, 1970–71, 1978–79 and 1986–87. Winning in Australia, against any Australian team, is a significant achievement and Andrew Strauss becomes a very significant captain now that he has backed up the triumph of last year with this. That will not be enough for him, though; he will want to become a winning England captain in Australia.

*A happy, united and thoroughly professional England side celebrate a 3–1 series victory in 2010–11*

It will be tempting at this juncture to highlight the weaknesses of the home team: a batting line-up with more holes in it than cellar cheese; an unbalanced, injury-prone bowling attack; and an ageing side. But they would have been good enough to give most England teams of the past 30 years a good game.

It is not that Australia have been very poor, but that England have been exceptionally good. They have looked the best-prepared, best-drilled, most motivated team of my lifetime. The planning was evident in the selection of Tremlett for Perth and Bresnan here.

The attention to detail was evident in two run-outs in the Melbourne Test. The near run-out of Jonathan Trott, who saved himself on 46 with a full-stretch dive, and the run out of Phillip Hughes, who did not dive, the throw from Trott gathered up by Prior in front of the stumps to save a fraction of a second. The fractions count in top-class sport and the fractions throughout this series have gone to England.

A triumph, then, for all members of this squad, from Andy Flower to the lowliest of the backroom staff. But never forget that it is the players who must take the ultimate credit, for it is they who must deal with the nerves, the pressure and the expectation, and they who must deliver.

And what a series they had: only Collingwood struggling for form and looking as though he did not belong, and even then setting new standards in the field.

One who covered himself in glory was Trott, the man of the match in Melbourne, and long after the last of the Barmy Army had left the stadium, the field empty save for two white sheets covering the end pitches and a security guard at each corner, out he came, pushing his baby in a pram. He pushed it out to the middle, stopped at the pitch – no, he did not scrape his mark at the crease – and paused to look around and remember the scene.

It was the kind of day that he will recall to his daughter in years to come, the kind of day that will be talked about for a long time. It was a day when heroes – of the sporting kind, you understand – were made.

## FIRST TEST, TRENT BRIDGE, 2013

MIKE ATHERTON,
CHIEF CRICKET CORRESPONDENT

*July 15.* It was 2005 all over again. Take your pick: either the Edgbaston Test of that series, or Trent Bridge, Old Trafford and the Oval too. All the tension of that unforgettable summer brought back to life over almost three hours on a final day of a dramatic Test that was decided by the finest of margins.

The conclusion was fitting too, given the drama and controversy that had raged over the rights and wrongs of technology and umpiring decisions throughout the game.

**AUSTRALIA** SECOND INNINGS — 296 all out

| | | | |
|---|---|---|---|
| PATTINSON | 25 | Extras | 22 |
| | | Overs | 110.5 |
| Partnership | 65 | Age of ball | 28.5 |
| Current run rate | 2.67 | To Bowl | 50.1 |

Last wicket: Haddin c Prior b Anderson 71

| RADCLIFFE ROAD END | O | M | R | W |
|---|---|---|---|---|
| ●ANDERSON | 31.5 | 11 | 73 | 5 |
| SWANN | 44 | 10 | 105 | 2 |

Fall of wickets: 1 84, 2 111, 3 124, 4 161, 5 161, 6 164, 7 207, 8 211, 9 231, 10 296

| | 1st | 2nd |
|---|---|---|
| ENGLAND | 215 | 375 |
| AUSTRALIA | 280 | 296 |

England won by 14 runs

*The tale of a classic Test: Trent Bridge 2013*

Ten minutes into an afternoon session that had started half an hour late, lunch having been delayed because of prolonged resistance from Australia's last pair, Brad Haddin, playing the innings of his life, drove at an off cutter from James Anderson and stood there, proud and defiant, as England appealed for an inside edge and then reviewed the 'not out' call by Aleem Dar.

And so it was down to Marais Erasmus again, the man in the television umpire's chair, and a man who had angered England, in particular, with his decision against Jonathan Trott in the second innings, and his failure to give out Ashton Agar in the first, when he was six runs into a remarkable debut innings of 98. Erasmus asked for Hot Spot, he asked for the audio and then he asked for both again.

Clear in his own mind that he had seen evidence of the edge and had heard a definite noise, he instructed Dar to overturn his decision.

There, and only there, was the difference between that Test at Edgbaston in 2005 and now; whereas England knew back then, pre-DRS, that they had won the match in the instant that Geraint Jones dived to take the edge from Michael Kasprowicz, now they had to wait and wait, agonisingly so, before Anderson led the charge once Dar had changed his decision.

It was unsatisfactory. England did not mind though; soon enough, Anderson's team-mates engulfed him, in joy and gratitude, too, because without Anderson's heroic bowling, England would not have won the match.

Sporting

# [H]OW ENGLAND KEPT THE ASHES

## [T]WO GREAT HEARTS OVERTHROW AUSTRALIA

England beat Australia by five wickets in the fourth Test match at Adelaide yesterday and so, gaining a lead of three matches to one in the series, have retained the Ashes. In an interview after the match L. Hutton, the England captain, paid a tribute to the younger members of the side. Much of the credit, he thought, should go to J. B. Statham, F. H. Tyson, M. C. Cowdrey and P. B. H. May, together with the wicket-keeper, T. G. Evans.

From Our Special Correspondent

ADELAIDE, FEB. 2

Many years from now young Cowdrey will point to his broken nose and tell boys yet unborn that he was at Adelaide on February 2, 1955, when England won the Test match and kept the Ashes. And the boys will think him wondrous lucky.

the catch. (We asked Hutton afterwards what he thought of Miller's bowling. Hutton thought Miller ought to concentrate much more on batting.) England 10 for 2. In comes the battered Cowdrey. Miller hits him twice running on the pads and appeals, and everybody here who isn't English appeals too. What a man is Miller. He comes in from a shortish run, loose of limb like an African, hair streaming, and as he pulls up the hair goes on and falls about his face.

Meanwhile May has begun driving, and Johnson has gone from mid-off to square-leg. For Cowdrey Miller brings fine-leg up to third slip, and Cowdrey cover drives classically for 4. Miller heaves his shoulders over even faster, and Cowdrey is taken by Archer at first-slip. England 18 for 3. Four Meteor jets fly over at 200ft.; they look and sound quite tame beside this wild man ... His figures now are 3 overs, no ... 2 runs, 3 wickets.

# England all too obliging ... reaches new heights of greatness

One that got away: Gilchrist misses a stumping chance off Warne to give Pietersen an extra life, but it was to make little difference

High five: Warne acknowledges the Melbourne crowd after his haul ripped the heart out of England's fragile batting

# Sporting News

## ENGLAND HAVE LAST WORD

### THREE YEOMEN FOIL AUSTRALIA

### GREAT STAND BY WATSON AND BAILEY

FROM OUR CRICKET CORRESPONDENT

Out of darkness, through fire into light. Thus did England yesterday rise like some Phoenix from the ashes of apparent defeat to save the second Test match at Lord's and so gain a ...

36 TUESDAY AUGUST 1 1989

THE TIMES

# England's abject surrender marks new low in series

By Alan Lee, Cricket Correspondent

## Inglorious procession at Old Trafford

10-1: Curtis c Boon b Alderman 0

25-2: Robinson lbw b Lawson 12

27-3: Smith c Healy b Alderman 1

28-4: Gooch c Alderman b Lawson 13

38-5: Botham lbw b Alderman 4

59-6: Gower c Marsh b Lawson 15

SCOREBOARD FROM OLD TRAFFORD

## Gower unfairly blamed for failings of others

Simon Barnes

## Border rewarded for hard labour

By John Woodcock

## Only two men so far decline

By Alan Lee

# Was this English cricket's most desperate ...

# AUSTRALIA'S GLORY DAYS

THE TIMES SATURDAY JUNE 11 1938

CH: A GOOD BEGINNING BY ENGLAND

4

Sporting News

LAKER'S SUPREME PART IN RETAINING THE ASHES

ALL TEN AUSTRALIAN WICKETS AND 19 IN MATCH

From Our Cricket Correspondent

England won the fourth Test match against Australia at Old T... terday by an innin... retaining the A... achiev...

pitch perked up and the ball showed signs of misbehaving.

At luncheon McDonald and Craig were still together. They had then added only 59, but the important thing was that they had each been batting for more than four hours. Ahead of them stretched another four and only 15 minutes of these had ticked away when Laker stru... blow. Craig, still...

THE TIMES

HOW THE AUSTRALIANS WERE SKITTLED OUT AT LORD'S

LOCOMEN'S BAN BOUND TO CAUSE GREATER ... TODAY

... BETRAYS A NOTE OF REGRET

Gaullists may get back with clear majority

... over bank chief's salary

Police alerted by strike ship

Railways must act alone, Marsh says

13 die in rail cra...

TEST MATCH

BRADMAN 309 NOT OUT

ALL RECORDS BROKEN

*The Third Test Match between England and Australia was begun at Leeds yesterday. A. P. F. Chapman, for once, lost the toss and Australia went in to bat on a perfect batsman's wicket. By the end of the day they had scored 458 runs for the loss of three wickets ...*

... stumped aiming to hit Mallett over the hill, and the end draws nearer.

... dismally surrender Ashes

## FIRST TEST, MELBOURNE, 1877

FROM OUR OWN CORRESPONDENT

*May 14.* You know the result of our great cricket match. Australians will 'blow', to use Mr Trollope's word, about it for some time to come. It was played on the ground of the Melbourne Club, between Lillywhite's eleven and a combined eleven of New South Wales and Victoria. We are told that it is the first match in which an English professional eleven has been beaten out of England. Each side was under a certain disadvantage. Pooley, the English wicketkeeper, had been left in New Zealand, and Allan, the best Victorian bowler, upon whose services the colonial eleven almost entirely depended in his department, suddenly retired, and a substitute had to be found at the last moment. The betting was altogether in favour of the Englishmen before the match began, but the splendid play of Bannerman, from New South Wales, soon altered the odds. He made 165 runs before he retired, not out, with his finger badly cut. The Englishmen declared that they had never seen a finer display of batting, not even by the great Grace. The other Australians brought up the score in the first innings to 245. The Englishmen then went in and made 196. The Australians followed and, with Bannerman disabled, made 104, leaving the Englishmen 155 to make to win, and a most interesting game was brought to a close with the fall of their last wicket for 108 runs, leaving our men the winners by 45 runs. This victory is certainly creditable to Australia. The scores were made against presumably the best English bowlers, among whom were Shaw, Emmett, Ullyett, and Southerton. The fielding of the team was excellent, and, although it is considered relatively weak in batsmen, Jupp, Charlwood, Greenwood, and Selby are said to be strong enough to give, at least, an average efficiency. As may be supposed, the game was watched with intense excitement by enthusiastic crowds, and those who could not get to the ground clustered round the newspaper offices to see the last despatches from the seat of war placarded on the door posts. It began and ended in good temper, and Lillywhite's pecuniary success must have consoled him for his defeat.

## ONLY TEST, THE OVAL, 1882

*August 30.* Our Colonial visitors have added another match to their long roll of victories obtained during the present season, and this, too, the most coveted of them all. Few of the 20,000 spectators on Kennington Oval yesterday were prepared for such a result, even within less than an hour of its accomplishment. In spite of the fact that the rain, which had been falling at intervals during the early morning, had increased to a heavy downpour by 10 o'clock, there was at this hour almost a complete belt of spectators round the field of play, who, protected by umbrellas, macintoshes, &c. maintained their positions throughout all discomfitures. Before 11 there was a break in the clouds, and the rain ceased. It was fortunate for the Australians that they had to go in first, as the wicket played far easier than it otherwise would have done. They did not obtain so many runs, however, as was expected of them. Mr Massie hit vigorously, and his performance was very praiseworthy, in spite of his escape at the hands of usually so reliable a fieldsman as Mr Lucas. Mr Murdoch batted in his usual finished style, and Mr Bannerman hit with great care. Beyond these none of the team did much. Mr Hornby seemed to know the bowling which would most baffle the batsmen, and varied it accordingly, while he altered the disposition of the field with great judgment. Peate's bowling was again excellent. The small total of 85 which England had set them to win caused the match to be regarded by most people as a foregone conclusion for them, and this confidence was increased when the third wicket fell for 51. Thus there remained seven batsmen to be dismissed and only 34 runs to get. The Australians, however, although defeat stared them in the face, played with that thoroughness which we pointed out yesterday as being one of their most admirable characteristics. Two more wickets speedily fell. Yet, with five to go down and only 19 to get, it seemed almost impossible even in the game noted for its surprises that the home team should not be able to get them. Every ball was watched with the keenest interest; but batsman after batsman succumbed with a rapidity that soon caused great anxiety on the part of the onlookers, and at length, after victory appeared to be almost within their grasp, the English Eleven found themselves beaten by seven runs. Mr Spofforth sustained the reputation which secured for him the title of the 'demon' bowler, as in the double innings he claimed 14 wickets for 90 runs. It is needless to say that the excitement was intense, and that

*Bobby Simpson steps on to English soil at the head of his team in 1964*

the winners were warmly congratulated on their success. True, they had the best of the wicket, which played very treacherously during the English innings. Still the gallant manner in which they played an uphill game when there seemed no hope of success will cause their victory to be a subject of lasting admiration.

## THIRD TEST, THE OVAL, 1884

*August 12.* Little was it expected that the Australians against such an eleven as that which they opposed at Kennington Oval yesterday, would make such an extraordinary score. Three of the four batsmen who went in obtained over a hundred runs each, and two of them are still not out. It will be remembered that in May, when the Colonists opposed the Marylebone Club and Ground, Dr Grace, Mr Steel, and Barnes each scored over a hundred in the first innings of Marylebone. Perhaps, since the first appearance of the Australians at the Oval there has rarely been such an assemblage of spectators. No fewer than 14,648 paid for admission, but in the aggregate there were more than 15,000 present. The heat was intense, but the English fielding, with one or two exceptions, was excellent. From first to last the spectators were by no means stinting in their applause both of batting and fielding.

## FIRST TEST, LORD'S, 1888

*July 18.* The turf at Lord's had just sufficiently dried at the time set for resuming this match yesterday to be very difficult. Indeed, the bowlers were completely masters of the situation, and during the two hours and a half's play before the interval 17 wickets were captured. The whole of the cricket only extended over four hours and a quarter, and 27 batsmen were dismissed for an average of less than half-a-dozen runs each. The England total of 53 is the lowest yet made in a representative match against the Australians. Making every allowance for the treacherous wicket bitter disappointment was felt that a carefully chosen England side should twice be disposed of for 115 runs. This was a single below the total in the opening venture of the Australians, who thus practically won by an innings. The Colonial fielding was remarkably fine, and only one extra – a leg-bye – was scored in the double innings. In glancing at the feeble batting of the home team it should be noted that Dr W.G. Grace, although falling short of the great things always expected from him, obtained more runs than any other two batsmen of the Eleven. The company was one of the largest that has ever assembled at Lord's, and at one time mustered about 20,000. This makes the second victory of the Australians against England; the previous occasion was the memorable contest at Kennington Oval six years ago, when they won by seven runs. At the drawing of stumps on Monday evening the Australians had finished an innings for 116, and three England wickets were down for 18.

With strict punctuality the game was continued at half-past 11, when Mr Turner completed his unfinished over of the previous night, Dr Grace being not out, 10. Mr Walter Read went in with the Gloucestershire captain, and Mr Ferris took up the bowling at the nursery wicket. Mr Read having made a single his partner was nearly bowled. Three more runs, including a leg hit for two, were made by Mr Read, who, however, was then out to a splendid piece of stumping by Mr Blackham. Mr O'Brien came next, but from the third ball of the following over Dr Grace was caught at extra mid-off from a ball which he hit with the edge of his bat; Mr Woods just managed to make the catch. The great English batsman had been in an hour for his ten runs. Peel arrived only to see the dismissal of Mr O'Brien, who was altogether beaten by a ball which broke right across the wicket and took the top of the leg stump. Four, five, and six for 22. Gunn and Mr Steel were now associated. Evidently the English captain was bent on hitting, for he at once ran out to meet the ball before it had time to break. After a leg-bye had been recorded Mr Steel obtained three by an off-drive from Mr Ferris. In the next over, however, he ran out to drive, and missing the ball was most easily stumped. Seven for 26. Gunn joined Peel, who obtained four by a leg-hit (run out) and three by a cut, while in the same over the Nottinghamshire batsman secured a couple through the slips. These nine runs made matters look a little brighter for England for there was great possibility of their following on. Two runs were still required to avert this disaster, when Gunn was caught at the wicket, and eight were down for 35. Briggs now joined Peel. Every ball was watched with the greatest excitement. Briggs, however by securing a single from each bowler saved the 'follow', amid general applause a few minutes after noon. Later on Briggs followed up his success by hitting Mr Turner to square leg for four and two, the ball on the first occasion pitching among the spectators near the tennis court. Mr Woods now relieved Mr Ferris, after which eight overs were sent down for half as many runs. Both men seemed likely to get runs, but at 49 Peel had the misfortune to be run out through a misunderstanding with his partner. Nine for 49. Sherwin arrived, but Briggs having cut Mr Woods to the boundary was clean bowled by the next ball, which took the off-stump. Total, 53; time, 12.25. The innings had lasted an hour and 40 minutes.

With the substantial advantage of 63, the Australians went in a second time at 20 minutes to 1. Messrs Bannerman and O'Donnell opened the second innings to the bowling of Peel and Lohmann (pavilion end). Mr O'Donnell obtained a single, but the first ball of Lohmann's second over broke considerably and struck the leg-stump. The downfall of this dangerous batsman caused much cheering among the spectators, and, of course, with an equal amount of dismay among the Australian supporters. The next ball from Peel clean bowled Mr Bannerman, and two wickets were down for a single. Messrs Bonnor and Trott were next together. The former drove Lohmann for four and afterwards cut him for two, but at 13 Mr Trott, who had never seemed at home, had his off-stump bowled down. Three for 13. Mr. Blackham joined Mr Bonnor, who fell to an easy catch at cover-point at 15. Four down. Mr Woods followed in. He made a drive for two and a single from Lohmann after which be skied the ball to Dr Grace at point. Two more wickets fell in succession in Lohmann's next over – Mr Blackham very rashly ran himself out, and Mr Edwards was caught at the wicket, first ball. Thus the fifth, sixth, and seventh batsmen were all out at 18. Mr Ferris now joined Mr Turner. Runs were scored rapidly. Each batsman made a drive for two, while Mr Turner drove Lohmann for four and two, and Mr Ferris secured a couple by a drive. The last-named made seven, and at 42 the first bowling change was tried – Briggs for Peel. Success immediately attended the variation, as

*Ricky Ponting celebrates the return of the urn in double quick time at Perth in 2006-07*

with his second ball the Lancastrian got Mr Turner well caught at point; Dr Grace made a splendid catch, taking the ball high up at the second attempt. Eight for 42. Mr. Worrall stayed while seven runs (including a cut for three by himself) were added, and then had his leg-stump hit out of the ground. Nine for 49. Mr Jarvis joined Mr Ferris, who with a single completed the 50 at 10 minutes to 2. Four runs were scored in the next over, and the English total was passed. A three to leg to each batsman raised the figures to 60, at which score Mr Steel and Peel took up the bowling. With his second ball the latter got Mr Jarvis caught at slip, and the innings terminated at 2 o'clock for 60. This was a far better total than at one time seemed probable.

England had 124 to obtain for victory, which, considering the state of the wicket, was by no means a light task. They began batting at a quarter to 3. Dr W.G. Grace and Abel opened the defence to the bowling of Messrs Turner and Ferris. Abel started the score with a single, and Dr Grace followed with a straight drive for four, and a couple by a similar hit. Each made a single, after which Dr Grace obtained four by a cut and a drive. The batsmen played with great care, but it was almost a matter of impossibility to altogether avoid making bad hits. Thus Dr Grace put the ball close up to Mr Trott at point. Abel appeared very unsettled and frequently started for absurd runs. Twenty were obtained in a quarter of an hour. Three maidens followed, after which Dr Grace drove Mr Ferris for two and four. From the latter of these hits he was nearly caught in the long field by Mr Edwards, who touched the ball with his left hand. A couple of overs later Abel was easily caught at slip, the first wicket falling at 29 – an excellent start. When Peel came in seven overs were sent down for five runs, and then Dr Grace was easily caught at mid-off. He had played a very good innings of 24, which had occupied three-quarters of an hour. Two down. Mr Read came in. Peel scored two singles and Mr Read a couple by a bad hit on the leg side. Peel was then clean bowled, the ball breaking very much and hitting the top of the wicket. Three for 38. Mr O'Brien aided Mr Read, who, having scored a single, was clean bowled. Four for 39. Mr Steel filled the vacancy. His companion registered two by a bad hit in the slips, and 40 went up after an hour's play. Mr Worrall was loudly cheered for stopping a hard drive from Mr O'Brien, who, a few minutes later, had the misfortune to play on. Five for 44. Gunn came in. He secured a single and a couple by drives, while Mr Steel cut Mr Turner for two. Fifty went up amid applause shortly before 4 o'clock. Directly afterwards Gunn made a fine drive for three, good fielding by Mr Edwards at long-off preventing a boundary hit. He was then bowled by a ball which just grazed the of stump and six wickets were lost for 55. The match was now almost over, as 68 runs were still wanted to avert defeat. The Australians fielded with great brilliancy and saved many runs, a single was the only item in the next three overs, and then Briggs had his leg stump struck Seven for 56. When Barnes came in the light had become very bad. Mr Steel might have been stumped had a ball not hit Mr Blackham in the face. In Mr Ferris next over two wickets fell – Barnes was stumped through the ball rebounding off Mr Blackham's pads, and Lohmann was easily dismissed from the first ball sent him. Sherwin, the last man, appeared. Mr Steel hit the ball to square-leg among the people, but his colleague was directly afterwards caught at short-leg, and the innings was over for 62. This was precisely half the number they had required to win. Thus the Australians were victorious by 61 runs. Thousands of the people gathered in front of the pavilion at the close and shouted lustily for the Australians. Mr O'Donnell and other members of the team acknowledged the cheers from the roof of the pavilion. An hour and a half later the threatened storm burst over Lord's and the ground became flooded.

## FIRST TEST, TRENT BRIDGE, 1934

R.B. VINCENT,
CRICKET CORRESPONDENT

*June 13.* Australia beat England in the first of the Test matches at Trent Bridge yesterday, just 10 minutes before time, by 238 runs. Let it be said at once that they thoroughly deserved their victory. They were admirably captained by Woodfull: they played throughout the game with fine spirit and, above all, they must be pleased to know that their young men were a triumphant success. So, too, were their old men, and, if it was anyone's match, I declare it to have been Grimmett's.

The defeat need be no great discouragement, to England, who, perhaps at a date not far distant, may have more fit men available. O'Reilly did the damage in the last innings, but it was Grimmett who continually threatened danger. In any case we have seen a Test match which was a real cricket match, full of good things from beginning to end, and no more could be desired.

When Australia continued their innings yesterday morning with every promise of the sun breaking through to make a beautiful day, though a troublesome one for England, they were 265 runs ahead with seven wickets yet in hand, six and a half hours' play in prospect, and dismal forebodings of cracks in the wicket. Brown, it has been said, had been slow on Monday evening, but as a rule it has been found that one man scoring fast and the other holding his own produces a higher rate of scoring than wild play at each end, and a consequent walking back between wicket and pavilion. Yesterday morning both Brown and McCabe bustled along well – a declaration was almost certain in any event at half- past 12 – and in fact it would have mattered little if two or three batsmen had got out first ball. Walters persisted with Farnes and Geary in his effort to keep down the runs, for nothing really mattered beyond the time when Woodfull would declare the innings closed and the behaviour of Grimmett and the pitch in the fourth innings.

Quite properly the wickets which fell went to Farnes, with the help of Hammond at first slip. McCabe had increased his score from 74 only to 88, having made one lovely stroke to square-leg off Farnes, when he was caught at first slip. It was the kind of stroke he would not have played in his first innings but, none the less, Farnes had deserved his wicket. McCabe had played a fine attacking innings on Monday evening, but one felt that he had served his side even better in the first innings, when wickets were threatening to tumble. Without doubt he was the outstanding Australian batsman. Darling, in the circumstances, was allowed to play a game more natural to himself than had been the case on Friday, and he chased and slashed at the ball outside the off-stump with all the cheer of a left-handed batsman. Brown, when he had made 46, was missed at cover-point off Verity, an escape which mattered very little as there were others to come. Eventually he reached his 50, having been in for three hours and a half, and Geary was brought on again as runs were considered to be coming just too fast.

Farnes in the meantime was bowling from the other end like a hero, and at 219 he had Darling, who was trying to hit the ball to leg, caught at first slip. Chipperfield, who had already gained his spurs and who later in the day, at a most important moment, held a splendid catch at short slip, did not last long, being the third out to the Farnes-Hammond combination. With the score at 244 and the time 10 minutes past 12, Brown was caught at the wicket off Verity. This was surely the occasion for Woodfull to declare his innings closed, but instead there was some pottering along by Grimmett and Oldfield, and it was a quarter to 1 before England went in again.

England accordingly were left 380 runs to make in order to win, and Australia four hours and three-quarters in which to take their wickets. Let us now ignore the runs and concentrate on time, the Australian attack, and the English defence. Woodfull started again with Wall from the City end, Sutcliffe being hit four times on various parts of his body in this first over. That was an indication of how Sutcliffe was facing the situation. Actually more runs were scored off pleasant strokes in the first few overs than the occasion demanded, Walters driving McCabe past cover-point for 4 and twice putting him away to leg.

McCabe was allowed to bowl only while 16 runs were scored before Grimmett came scurrying on in his place, and from that moment, roughly about half an hour before luncheon, until the tea interval and a little afterwards Grimmett was apparently winning the game. His method of attack is not to take wickets one after another in haste with the possibility of a 'hat trick', but at regular intervals of half an hour, with never a bad ball bowled during those intervals. Yesterday afternoon he was truly magnificent, making the most of the wicket and bowling equally well when moved from one end to the other, the limit of rest which his captain in these strained relations could allow him. Luncheon was taken fairly hopefully by England's supporters with the thought to help their digestion that neither Sutcliffe nor Walters was yet out and there was only another four hours for Grimmett to take 10 wickets.

Australian supporters, however – and there were some few of them in Nottingham during these last few days – were still hopeful, and there was a perfectly legitimate roar of pleasure from their enclosure half an hour after the interval when Sutcliffe, the one man whom most they would like to see walk back to the pavilion, was caught in the slips after feeling forward to the kind of ball which hitherto he had played well in the middle of the bat. So long as Sutcliffe had been there the match had seemed to be saved, but the situation thereafter gradually changed. Hammond did his utmost to play a defensive innings, a role which does not come naturally to him, while at the other end Walters was splendid. Hammond took the opportunity twice to drive Grimmett to long-on for 4. For the rest of the time he had to lean forward in order to smother Grimmett's break and to delay for as long as possible the fall of the next wicket. He was lucky once to flick a ball from Wall only just wide of second slip, but at 25 minutes to 4, just when things did look better for England, he was beautifully stumped, playing forward to a break from Grimmett which beat the bat. Ten minutes later Walters was bowled and Australia were quite definitely on top.

The Nawab of Pataudi and Hendren surely could last until the tea interval, but first Pataudi was caught at long-off, hitting the ball to Ponsford of all people, and at 20 minutes past 4 Hendren was caught at short slip. That was five wickets down and an hour and three-quarters to go. After tea, with Grimmett spinning the ball so furiously as to raise spurts of dust and the Australian fieldsmen crowding in on the leg-side, Ames stayed stolidly with Leyland, each being content to push his bat down the wicket. Once again it was agreed that the match was to be left drawn, more especially when the dreadful Grimmett and the equally terrible O'Reilly were taken off for the comparatively innocuous Wall and Chipperfield.

Leyland, the adventurer, was as stolid as could be; calm, with the peak of his cap high in the air, but he lost Ames at a quarter to 6, bowled by a ball from O'Reilly, who had just been put on at the pavilion end. The manner in which Woodfull rested his spin bowlers just so long but no longer than was necessary was the admiration of foes and friends alike. For England there followed another disaster when Geary was caught at short slip, and Chipperfield certainly is as good there as his friends in Australia had said he would be.

Leyland, with his feet firm and still quite imperturbable, played back to O'Reilly's slow or to his fast ball. There was a roar of bewildered excitement when he hit the ball only just short of short-leg, and at 6 o'clock Verity was there, but only just there, to Grimmett, who was bowling with all his great heart. He played another over comfortably enough to O'Reilly, but Leyland, with an appropriate single to the last ball of

Grimmett's next over, spared his partner any more immediate distress. Once he refused to run twice in the next over, only himself to be caught at the wicket. It had been a great innings, but there were still 20 minutes to go and now only two wickets to fall.

Like many another I could hardly stand the strain. There was another roar: Farnes had been caught at the wicket and Mitchell alone stood for England's honour, with a quarter of an hour to go. Someone in front of me said: 'He's out,' someone else said, 'We are going to play out time,' and four runs were rather politely thrown back from long-leg. Then, off the next ball, Mitchell was leg-before-wicket. A better cricket match I shall never see.

## FOURTH TEST, HEADINGLEY, 1948

R.B. VINCENT,
CRICKET CORRESPONDENT

*July 28.* Australia beat England in the fourth Test match of this series at Headingley yesterday by seven wickets. A handsome victory, and in the end plucked from the hands of England's team who at one time had established themselves in what looked to be a possible winning position.

In this respect this Australian team has shown the same quality of its predecessors, that perfect sense of timing of the match, whether it be played over three, four, or five days. The result is what matters to them and they plan and work for that result. Yesterday they were most generously encouraged on their way by England's out cricket. I would be the last to depreciate Australia's victory, but as a spectator I must share in the general opinion that England's bowling and fielding fell far short of what one would hope to see in a Test match.

Bradman, who scored his 19th century against England, and who has perpetuated the legend that runs by right belong to him on the Leeds ground, was yesterday granted four new starts to his innings. Difficult chances they may have been, but this was an over generous allowance to grant such a man. Morris, too, who went on to play an innings of great charm and obvious value was lucky to be excused an error early in the day. Had the chances been taken Australia, with so many fine forcing batsmen to follow, would no doubt have made the runs, for 400 and a few more in a day is nothing to them.

Yardley continued England's innings in the morning, not so much to cramp the Australians for time, but to use the heavy roller with a threat that the pitch might crumble. Two overs only were bowled to Evans and Laker with three runs added to the score when the innings was declared closed. This left Australia 404 runs to make to win in five and three-quarter hours. It had been suggested that there was a worn patch at the pavilion end, but the patch seemed to have become wonderfully darned as Australia's innings advanced. Laker certainly made the ball turn sufficiently to place two slips and a silly mid-off to Morris. Bedser, at the other end, bowled tidily; taken all in, he was the best of England's bowlers in this match, and the first 40 minutes had produced only 30 runs. Hassett, when he had made 13, should have been stumped off Bedser, and Morris once made a false stroke off Laker through the slips. When Laker changed to bowl over the wicket the runs were being kept in check, it it was Compton who first threatened the fall of a wicket when in one over he twice beat Morris.

With the score at 54 Morris was right out of his ground in jumping in to Compton with never a chance of getting back, but Evans did not gather the ball for a heaven-sent opportunity of stumping him. That kind of error is never excused in a Test match against Australia. The first wicket fell when Hassett was caught by Compton wide to the off from his own bowling, and Laker, in the next over, made just one ball pop up to Morris. So still there was some belief in this tale of the broken pitch. Bradman, greeted even more tumultuously than he had been in the first innings, was granted three short legs to Laker's bowling and his first answer was to drive away to the off-side boundary. Yardley then began some experiments in his bowling. Hutton can bowl a googly, so he was given a chance, and a most expensive one, but still, if it had come off, great tribute would have been paid to Yardley's astuteness. Morris struck him for three 4's in one over. Bradman, too, treated himself to two 4's off Hutton before he hit a ball only just a shade short of a fair catch to mid-wicket.

The 100 went up with Bradman giving another sharp chance off Compton in the slips. This was queer cricket, a mixture of peculiar escapes and occasional brilliant strokes by the batsmen. At the luncheon interval the score stood at 121, Bradman then having made 35 and Morris 63. Bradman's first 30 runs had included seven 4's, mostly to the mid-wicket boundary. Morris, for a long time, was the more aggressive of the two, rather kindly treated as he was in the measure of full pitches. Bedser, however, was still bowling well. Bradman, when he had made 39, with a swish of a ball from Laker provided only a tickle past the leg stump and might have been out for all he knew. When he had advanced to 59 he gave a chance to cover-point off Cranston's bowling,

Sporting News (Also on page 4)

**FAMOUS AND THRILLING TEST VICTORY**

**ENGLAND CONFOUNDED BY BENAUD'S LEG SPIN**

**From Our Cricket Correspondent**

Australia made certain of retaining the Ashes at Old Trafford yesterday when they won the fourth Test match against England by 54 runs. It was for them one of their most famous and thrilling victories, made possible at the last by the daring and skill of their captain. For England it was a day that will become a dark and disappointing memory.

At five minutes to four England, needing 256 to win, had reached 150 for one with Dexter in full spate. There were still 105 minutes left. At 4.45 they were 171 for seven, and disaster had come down upon them when they seemed to have the match in hand. It was the second time in the day that they had been stopped in their tracks by an Australian counter-attack imaginative in conception and bril- caught, by O'Neill, placed carefully just behind the square leg umpire.

England's last chance of victory went with the last ball before tea, when Subba Row's long vigil was ended by a yorker from Benaud. In 20 minutes England had plunged to 163 for five, Benaud having taken the four wickets for nine runs in 19 balls. Looking through the glasses at the Australian side, they clearly could hardly believe their fortune. For one who has followed England round the world it was less surprising, and after tea England slipped quietly and ignominiously to defeat.

Murray was quickly caught at slip off Benaud, and Barrington was leg-before to Mackay. Runs were of no importance now, only time, and when Allen was superbly caught by Simpson, left-handed at slip, off Benaud, hope even of survival was all but gone. Trueman lasted for 40 minutes before losing his head, and Flavell

*Richie Benaud spins Australia to victory – and the Ashes – at Old Trafford in 1961*

incidents which must be recorded however much one may admire the eventual effects of his innings.

The 200 went up when Morris twice hit Laker to the on boundary and the partnership not long after had produced 200 runs in 135 minutes. So the pattern of the Australian innings was shaping and the mathematicians then stated that 200 more runs were wanted in three hours, there or thereabout. By this time there was never a gleam of hope that any material amount of wickets, would fall. Bradman reached his century out of 264 runs on the board and Morris, playing now with consummate case, only showed one vestige of a mistake when he was missed at square-leg off Compton. At tea the score was 288 and still there was only one wicket down and 116 runs wanted in 105 minutes.

The rate of scoring at this important time progressed steadily until Morris was caught playing an unexpectedly gentle stroke to mid-off. There entered Miller with the score at 358 and 46 runs to be made in 50 minutes. It was Bradman's hour of hours, and although he lost Miller at a quarter past six, Harvey made the winning stroke with 13 minutes to spare. And so a match which had provided a deal of good cricket, and which during the five days had attracted 158,000 people into the ground, let alone the swarms who were left outside, came to an end.

## FOURTH TEST, OLD TRAFFORD, 1961

JOHN WOODCOCK,
CRICKET CORRESPONDENT

*August 2.* Australia made certain of retaining the Ashes at Old Trafford yesterday when they won the fourth Test match against England by 54 runs. It was for them one of their most famous and thrilling victories, made possible at the last by the daring and skill of their captain. For England it was a day that will become a dark and disappointing memory.

At five minutes to four England, needing 256 to win, had reached 150 for one with Dexter in full spate. There were still 105 minutes left. At 4.45 they were 171 for seven, and disaster had come down upon them when they seemed to have the match in hand. It was the second time in the day that they had been stopped in their tracks by an Australian counter-attack imaginative in conception and brilliant in execution. For some hours earlier, Davidson and McKenzie had added 98 for Australia's last wicket to give the bowlers the ammunition they needed.

England's was a failure of temperament, brought on by their inability to play spin bowling, particularly leg breaks, of the highest class. It may sound cynical, but it is true to say that England's pitiful collapse was true to form. Too often in the past few years they have been found wanting against Benaud, Ramadhin or Tayfield when there has been tension in the air.

For sheer excitement and palpitating changes of fortune the day will never be forgotten. Nor should the crushing anticlimax and England's deplorable batting be allowed to cloud the supreme merit of Australia's achievement. They began by hitting their way out of trouble with the greatest courage and even when England were advancing steadily through the afternoon they kept attacking.

In the 20 minutes before luncheon, England got away to a good start in their effort to score at 67 runs an hour for three hours and 50 minutes. Immediately afterwards, Benaud came on at the Stretford end, where later he was to decide the issue. As his partner he had first Davidson, then Simpson, and then Mackay. Finally, after he had taken six for 70 in 32 overs, and with Statham and Flavell together, he asked Davidson to finish the job.

For a long time the crowd cheered every run as England gathered speed. Pullar and Subba Row added 40 in 42 minutes before Pullar mishooked a long hop gently to midwicket. There followed the splendid phase for England, with Dexter in command. It was the plan that Subba Row should hold down an end and gather what runs he could without taking undue risks. He has a shrewd cricketing brain, as well as a calming influence upon others, and he played just the innings that was wanted from him.

So, too, of course, did Dexter, who came back to form with a resounding bang. Fifty were added in 48 minutes and when McKenzie replaced Davidson, Dexter hit him for 11 in an over. Drinks were taken at 3.15, to quench England's scoring rate as much as the fielders' thirsts. Dexter had been in for an hour before he made the semblance of a mistake, yet nothing would divert Benaud from his determination to attack.

With the runs tumbling forth, he had Simpson bowling at one end and himself at the other. As Simpson was hit for 21 in four overs, most of them scored by Dexter, it must have seemed to some that Benaud was throwing the game away. What really he was doing was chancing all on England's fallibility against flighted spin.

Dexter reached his 50 in 63 minutes with his tenth four, a thundering shot through the covers. Another 50 came in half an hour, and with two hours left England, with nine wickets standing, needed only 132 to win. The equation a quarter of an hour later, immediately before Dexter left, was still more favourable to England, for Dexter by then had driven Mackay like a kicking horse for four, hooked him viciously to the pavilion, and lifted him majestically for six. Hammond, Cowdrey, O'Neill, May, Miller – no one could have batted better than Dexter now, and with a single off Mackay he took England's score to 150 for one.

So there it was. Twenty minutes before tea England were on their way home, the sails billowing. And in shorter time than it takes to tell, they had run upon shoals and rocks and currents. Dexter's magnificent innings ended when he went to hit Benaud off the back foot for four. He had 15 boundaries to his name, every one of them of the purest pedigree. After a brief and smiling discussion with Subba Row, May was sent back second ball by Benaud. From round the wicket he had got this ball to pitch in the footmarks and bowl May behind his legs trying to sweep. Benaud leapt aloft like an astronaut becoming airborne.

Close's innings, which came next, is best talked about in whispers. One of the lessons of Dexter's innings had been the rewards there were for playing straight, a thing Close can do as well as most. As it was, he swung wildly at his first ball and continued to play as if out of his cricketing senses. The one and only time he tried to swing the bat through a true arc, he drove Benaud for a towering six. For the remainder of his innings he thrust his right leg down the pitch and aimed everything to leg. Needless to say, he was eventually caught, by O'Neill, placed carefully just behind the square leg umpire.

England's last chance of victory went with the last ball before tea, when Subba Row's long vigil was ended by a yorker from Benaud. In 20 minutes England had plunged to 163 for five, Benaud having taken the four wickets for nine runs in 19 balls. Looking through the glasses at the Australian side, they clearly could hardly believe their fortune. For one who has followed England round the world it was less surprising, and after tea England slipped quietly and ignominiously to defeat.

Murray was quickly caught at slip off Benaud, and Barrington was leg-before to Mackay. Runs were of no importance now, only time, and when Allen was superbly caught by Simpson, left-handed at slip, off Benaud, hope even of survival was all but gone. Trueman lasted for 40 minutes before losing his head, and Flavell and Statham endured for 10 minutes of the 30 that were left when they were joined together.

Five years ago England were led off the field in this corresponding match by Laker, who looked as though nothing much had happened. It was their turn to have won the Ashes then. Yesterday, at 5.40, Benaud and Harvey walked off arm in arm to open the bottles of champagne. Less than two hours before, Benaud in the match had taken not a single wicket in 52 overs; his last four scores for Australia had been 0, 0, 2 and 1; and his reputation as a captain and a player was in jeopardy. Starting with Dexter's wicket, he then had figures of 6 for 30.

Benaud said afterwards that he knew by the middle of the afternoon that Australia could not save the game but that they might win it. His faith in his own ability, and his tactical appreciation, were wonderfully justified. England for their part had missed Cowdrey with the bat, just as they had missed him on Monday in the slips.

For the first time in this century Australia had come from far behind to beat their oldest enemy. For the first time since 1902 they had won at Old Trafford. They had been watched by record crowds paying record money. Seldom can a match have turned so complete a somersault in so short a time. Seldom can England have had greater cause for self reproach.

It had been from the start no day for the nervous. After 16 minutes, victory, it seemed, was in England's grasp. Allen, after opening with a wide, had Mackay caught at slip off his fourth ball. The first ball of Allen's third over had Benaud leg-before,

*A fashionably attired Ian Chappell with his team, including brother Greg and a young Rod Marsh, outside the Waldorf Hotel in 1972*

playing back after his first movement had been forward. And five balls later Grout hoisted a catch to Statham in the covers.

As the England fielders gathered excitedly together they could hardly have thought to see the Australians rise to their feet again. They might have expected Mackay to be a thorn in their side, or Benaud, or even Grout. But Davidson was looking like an old, old man and the situation would surely be too much for young McKenzie.

But there followed an historic partnership. For the first time on the tour, Davidson rose to his full stature as a batsman. Shrugging off his aches and pains, he played the innings of his life. For its judgment and power and appearance his batting could have been no better. He gave a superb display of clean, crisp hitting, tempered by orthodox defence.

McKenzie played the secondary part like an experienced hand. Before he had scored Statham twice shaved his stumps; once Dexter nearly had him leg-before; and once Trueman made the bails tremble. Yet generally speaking he met whatever came at him with the middle of the bat. The speed with which the picture changed defied belief.

It all began when May asked Close to bowl in place of Statham. Allen, who had taken his three wickets without the concession of a run, was being prevented by Davidson from bowling at McKenzie. May therefore decided, understandably enough, to confront him with spin from the other end, and this as it turned out was just what McKenzie wanted. In two overs Close bowled five full tosses and McKenzie found that even in Test matches they go sweetly off the bat.

After an hour Allen had bowled nine overs for two runs. In his tenth over Davidson suddenly cut loose. There was one flashing stroke off the back foot through the covers, one low straight drive, and two straight hits for six, making 20 in the over. Allen was removed at once and a quarter of an hour later the new ball became available. It was taken at 419 and still the stand continued, eating up the time if now less productive of runs.

McKenzie, when he was 25 and the score was 422, might have been caught by Dexter via bat and pad off Trueman. But even Statham and Trueman with the new ball were repulsed and eventually it was Flavell who ended Australia's innings. Davidson and McKenzie had added 98 in 102 minutes, the first 50 of them in only 39 minutes. It was the third best last-wicket partnership by an Australian pair against England. The other two, in 1903 and 1924, helped to lay the foundations to a stirring finish; now this one had set the stage for one of the most dramatic afternoon's cricket of this or any other age.

## FOURTH TEST, SYDNEY, 1974–75

JOHN WOODCOCK,
CRICKET CORRESPONDENCE

*January 10*. With some more dismal batting England surrendered the Ashes to Australia here today, losing the fourth Test match by 171 runs with only 4.3 of the last 15 overs left. It was four years ago, on this same ground but against a much less good Australian side, that England regained the Ashes after Australia had held them since 1959.

It is sad that the two remaining Test matches of this present series will now be something of an anti-climax. It would have been nice to go to Adelaide in a fortnight's time still with a share of the rubber to play for, as England would be doing had they batted anything like as well as they should have done today.

But Australia are a good side. At times they have looked a very good one. Their success is well deserved. When we left England it seemed that England's chances depended upon how fit Lillee would be. In the event he has made a remarkable recovery and found in Thomson the perfect partner. These two between them have taken 44 wickets. Only four came today, but they still softened England up for Mallett (four for 21) and Walker (two for 46). The series has provided another classic example of a side with two genuinely fast bowlers battering its way to victory.

That England came so close to saving themselves was due in the end to Edrich, who played with a courage and determination unmatched by the other batsmen. This morning his first ball was a short one from Lillee. Ducking into it he was hit a nasty blow in the ribs, bad enough for him to be helped off. When he came back, at three o'clock, England were 156 for six, and there was still an hour and 40 minutes left, as well as the last 15 overs.

No sooner had Edrich returned than he saw Greig get himself out with an entirely unworthy stroke. For an hour Greig had batted as well as he can, which is as well as most people. Then, when Knott was out, he played one reckless stroke after another, until he was stumped trying to hit Mallett on to, or beyond, the Hill. For someone who has worked so hard to keep England alive over the last six weeks it was a ludicrous end. It was as though he had given up the ghost. Edrich, however, had other ideas. He was the captain, too. And he must have been cross at the way England had collapsed, on a pitch that may have been a shade faster today but was still in wonderfully good repair. First with Willis, who batted for 90 minutes and was not out until the third over of the last 15, and then with Arnold, Edrich kept hopes alive.

Lillee's first ball to Arnold was a bumper, there being no love lost between them. The next, according to one of the Australian slips, was Lillee's fastest ball for a long time, but wide of the off stump. Lillee bowled faster here, and better, than at any time in the series. At times, to Thomson, Marsh reckoned he stood back the length of the cricket pitch. To Lillee, in this match, he stood five or six feet closer. For much of the time he resembled a performing dolphin or a goalkeeper at practice.

But with 10 overs of the last 15 gone Arnold was still there. He had already played out an over from Mallett, who, in spite of a new ball, had soon replaced Thomson. Thomson, I gather, was pretty nearly beat, as by now, was Lillee. Thinking, anyway, that Arnold might be more likely to get out to a spinner, Chappell gave Mallett another over and off the fifth ball of it Arnold was caught low down at forward short leg, Greg Chappell's thirteenth catch of the series.

Assuming that Edrich would have played through the two full overs that were sure to be bowled to him, Arnold had to negotiate this one from Mallett and possibly two more, unless Edrich could protect him from the strike, for England to be safe. Maybe England did not deserve to survive, but they were mighty near to doing so.

Amiss and Lloyd had begun the day as though as much interested in winning the match as saving it. In half an hour they made 35 before Lloyd was caught at second slip, slashing at Thomson. Lloyd played nothing like as temperately in this match as in Melbourne, Amiss nothing like as confidently. If Lloyd was beaten once outside his off stump in his second innings he was beaten a dozen times: but he went on flashing away until, predictably, he was caught at slip. It looks to me as though the strain of opening against Lillee and Thomson, when he is not really quite up to it, is beginning to tell on Lloyd.

From 65 for one, when Lloyd was out, England declined within 80 minutes to 103 for four, with Edrich in the doctor's care. Amiss was caught at the wicket off a wicked flier from Thomson. He tried in vain to withdraw. Today, only Amiss, and Greig when he was playing sensibly, caused Chappell to throw back his field.

Edrich, following Amiss, never looked like beating the count after ducking into his first ball from Lillee, and this though he is as hard as a pebble. Although this was not a bouncer to Edrich there was no shortage of those. Lillee bowled five in one over, without anything more than a genial reprimand from umpire Bailhache. Fletcher, too, came under fire from Thomson. It is not possible at the moment to follow the umpires' line of thinking on short-pitched bowling. One day they talk a lot to the bowlers about it, in their rather arbitrary way: the next they turn a blind eye to it. This morning they were far too lenient. Fletcher had three bumpers in the over in which he was out, off the last of which he was neatly caught at cover point. It is hard to imagine a much deadlier ball than this. It followed Fletcher as he tried to sway away from it, hitting the handle of his bat first and then forehead before ricocheting off to cover point. When Thomson pitched one up for a change Fletcher was away from the line, Redpath at third slip taking a very good low catch. By then Cowdrey, after a passive half hour, had been caught at first slip off an indeterminate bat. Even Cowdrey looks to me as though he could be becoming affected by the special pressures of almost ceaseless speed. To be being brainwashed in fact.

He played no positive stroke of any kind today. For three-quarters of an hour this afternoon, while Knott and Greig were together, there was hope. These two could have fought it out. They were on their way to doing so, I thought, when Mallett, coming on for the first time in the innings, had Knott caught at short leg. Knott propped defensively forward, and Redpath threw himself forward to scoop up the catch. Titmus lasted for 35 minutes before swinging wildly at Mallett and being caught at backward square leg. Whereupon Edrich reappeared to a prolonged ovation. When last heard of Edrich had been having difficulty breathing. When Greig had played the stroke that got him out he must have had difficulty containing himself. Greig's and Lloyd's were the poorest strokes of the day.

Australia were a quarter of an hour accounting for Underwood, caught and bowled in the first over of a new spell by Walker. This was 12 minutes before tea: with storms around, none of them near enough for England's good. You can never tell with Willis. Sometimes he throws his wicket away, quite needlessly. Today he knuckled down well, seeing it through until tea and then keeping Edrich company for 75 minutes afterwards. If everyone had played as Willis did, or Edrich, England would have saved it easily. If proof were needed that the sporting public follow a winning side it is provided by the attendance figures. The aggregate of 178,027 spectators is a Sydney record.

# PHOTOGRAPHIC CREDITS

Marc Aspland – 6, 35, 64, 68, 163, 72, 114, 122, 126, 140, 150, 154, 170, 175, 178, 216, 225, 242, 246, 279, 285, 295, 361

Graham Morris – 30, 47, 61, 63, 78, 90, 91, 93, 108, 111, 113, 120, 131, 134, 135, 136, 145, 148, 151, 160, 182, 188, 207, 210, 221, 248, 249, 255, 278, 293, 301, 302, 315, 316, 317, 323, 333, 335, 362, 370

John Cassidy – 259

# ACKNOWLEDGEMENTS

Although only one name appears next to 'editor' in the credits for this book, it was very far from being a solo project. It could not have been completed without the considerable assistance of many others.

Mark Beynon at The History Press was a swift convert to the idea and has been extremely supportive. Thanks are also due to Juanita Hall, the publisher's production supremo, and Jemma Cox, the designer, who has done such a wonderful job.

The esteemed cricket photographer Graham Morris showed great generosity in allowing me access to his formidable archive of images, and *The Times*' chief sports photographer Marc Aspland was a huge help. Without their talents this book would look a great deal greyer. Margaret Clark and Ian Whitbread on the picture desk provided vital technical assistance.

Among the writers, Simon Barnes, Tim de Lisle and Gideon Haigh kindly allowed me to use words that were not copyright of *The Times*.

Nick Mays, *The Times*' archivist, and his assistant, Anne Jensen, were magnificent in rooting out the identities of various anonymous cricket contributors, and I cannot give adequate thanks to Dean Burrows for scouring the paper's photographic library for many of the wonderful older images. Murray Hedgcock and David Frith kindly helped to identify some of the Australians in those pictures.

Various *Times* colleagues also gave inestimable help, especially Tim Rice who read the text so thoroughly and with impressive dedication. He was also the first to suggest that the concept might actually work. Walter Gammie, the world's greatest cricket lover, was helpfully enthusiastic, and gentle encouragement came from Ian Brunskill and Tim Hallissey. Thanks also to my colleagues on the Register.

Christopher Lane at *Wisden* kindly supplied the photographs of Sydney Pardon and thanks are also due to my former colleague Marcus Williams whose book, *Double Century*, provided invaluable information on *Times* cricket correspondents.

But the greatest thanks of all must go to my wife Marion Brinton and son Alex who put up uncomplainingly with my long absences from normal domestic life. I owe them a great debt.

*Richard Whitehead*

# ABOUT THE EDITOR

Richard Whitehead joined *The Times* in 1995 and has held various posts around the paper – on the sports desk, on books, on the Weekend section and in the obituaries department. He is contributing editor of *Wisden Cricketers' Almanack* and a regular contributor to *The Cricketer*.